The Princeton Review®

PrincetonReview.com

THE BEST 167 LAW SCHOOLS

2012 EDITION

**Eric Owens, Esq., John Owens, Esq.,
Jennifer Adams, Adam O. Davis,
Andrea Kornstein, and The Staff
of The Princeton Review**

*Random House, Inc.
New York*

The Princeton Review, Inc.
111 Speen Street, Suite 550
Framingham, MA 01701
E-mail: bookeditor@review.com

ISBN: 978-0-375-42738-1
ISSN: 2161-5764

Senior VP, Publisher: Robert Franek
Production: Deborah A. Silvestrini
Production Editor: Michelle Krapf
Content Manager: David Soto
Editors: Seamus Mullarkey and Laura Braswell

Printed in the United States of America on partially recycled paper.

9 8 7 6 5 4 3 2 1

2012 Edition

ACKNOWLEDGMENTS

Thanks to Laura Braswell for the support and guidance on this book and many others and to Bob Spruill for his LSAT expertise.

In addition, many thanks should go to David Soto, Anne DeWitt, Abe Koogler, and Tyler Alexander for spearheading the law school data collection efforts. Their survey, along with the support and assistance of Adrinda Kelly, allowed for the completion of a totally cohesive stat-packed guide.

A special thanks must go to our production team: Deborah A. Silvestrini and Michelle Krapf. Your commitment, flexibility, and attention to detail are always appreciated in both perfect and crunch times.

—Eric Owens

I'd like to send my thanks:

To Eric Owens, my quasi-cousin, who kept me in mind for this project.

To my editors at The Princeton Review, who trusted me (and the other Eric Owens) enough to give me the chance.

To my family and friends, who support me in the things I do.

To the law students who took the time to complete the law student survey.

—John Owens

ABOUT THE AUTHORS

Eric Owens, Esq., attended Cornell College for his undergraduate degree and Loyola University—Chicago for law school. He is now an American diplomat.

John Owens, Esq., earned his undergraduate degree in accountancy at the University of Illinois, Urbana-Champaign. He then matriculated at Loyola University—Chicago School of Law, where he earned his JD. John works in the tax department of a Chicago law firm. He is currently working on a book, which he hopes to finish up this year. In his spare time, John likes to rock.

Julie Doherty graduated from Stanford University in 1998 with a degree in English. She currently lives in San Miguel de Allende, Mexico, where she works in an art gallery and printmaking studio. She is the co-author of several Princeton Review titles, including *The Best 376 Colleges* and *Planning a Life in Medicine*. She is working on her first novel.

CONTENTS

PREFACE

Welcome to *The Best 167 Law Schools*, The Princeton Review's truly indispensable guide for anyone thinking about entering the law school fray. This is not simply a reprint of the garden-variety fluff in each law school's admissions booklet. We have attempted to provide a significant amount of essential information from a vast array of sources to give you a complete, accurate, and easily digestible snapshot of the best law schools in the country. Here you'll find a wealth of practical advice on admissions, taking and acing the Law School Admissions Test (LSAT), choosing the right school, and doing well once you're there. You'll also find all the information you need on schools' bar exam pass rates, ethnic group and gender breakdown percentages, tuition, average starting salaries of graduates, and much more. For 167 ABA-approved law schools, you'll find descriptive profiles of the student experience based on the opinions of the only true law school experts: current law school students. Indeed, with this handy reference, you should be able to narrow your choices from the few hundred law schools in North America to a handful in no time at all.

Never trust any single source of information too much, though—not even us. Take advantage of all the resources available to you, including friends, family members, the Internet, and your local library. Obviously, the more you explore all the options available to you, the better decision you'll make. We hope you will be happy wherever you end up and that this guide will be helpful in your search to find the best law school for you.

Best of luck!

ALL ABOUT LAW SCHOOL

CHAPTER 1
So You Want to Go to Law School

Congrats! Law school is a tremendous intellectual challenge and an amazing experience. It can be confusing and occasionally traumatic—especially during the crucial first year—but the cryptic ritual of legal education will make you a significantly better thinker, a consummate reader, and a far more mature person over the course of three years.

The application process is rigorous, but it's not impossible. Here's our advice.

WHAT MAKES A COMPETITIVE APPLICANT?

It depends. One of the great things about law schools in the United States is that there are a lot of them, and standards for admission run the gamut from appallingly difficult to not very hard at all.

Let's just say, for example, you have your heart set on Yale Law School, arguably the finest law school in all the land. Let's also say you have stellar academic credentials: a 3.45 GPA and an LSAT score in the 99th percentile of everyone who takes it. With these heady numbers, you've got a whopping two percent chance of getting into Yale, at best. However, with the same 3.45 GPA and LSAT score in the 99th percentile, you are pretty much a lock at legal powerhouses like Duke University School of Law and Boston College Law School. With significantly lower numbers—say, a 3.02 GPA and an LSAT score in the 81st percentile—you stand a mediocre chance of getting into top-flight law schools like Case Western or Indiana. With a little bit of luck, these numbers might land you a spot at George Washington or UCLA.

This is good news. The even better news is that there are several totally respectable law schools out there that will let you in with a 2.5 GPA and an LSAT of 148 (which is about the 36th percentile). If you end up in the top ten percent of your class at one of these schools and have even a shred of interviewing skill, you'll get a job that is just as prestigious and pays just as much money as the jobs garnered by Yale grads. Notice the important catch here, however: You *must* graduate in the top ten percent of your class at so-called "lesser" schools, while almost every Yale Law grad who wants a high-paying job can land one.

> *Fascinating Acronyms*
>
> *LSAC: Law School Admission Council, headquartered in beautiful Newtown, Pennsylvania*
>
> *LSAT: Law School Admissions Test*
>
> *CAS: Credential Assembly Service*
>
> *ABA: American Bar Association*

Ultimately, there's a law school out there for you. If you want to get into a "top-flight" or "pretty good" school, you're in for some fairly stiff competition. Unfortunately, it doesn't help that the law school admissions process is somewhat formulaic; your LSAT score and your GPA are vastly more important to the process than anything else about you. If your application ends up in the "maybe" pile, your recommendations, your major, the reputation of your college alma mater, a well-written and nongeneric essay, and various other factors will play a larger role in determining your fate.

THE ADMISSIONS INDEX

The first thing most law schools will look at when evaluating your application is your "index." It's a number (which varies from school to school) made up of a weighted combination of your undergraduate GPA and LSAT score. In virtually every case, the LSAT is weighted more heavily than the GPA.

While the process differs from school to school, it is generally the case that your index will put you into one of three piles:

(Probably) Accepted. A select few applicants with high LSAT scores and stellar GPAs are admitted pretty much automatically. If your index is very, very strong compared with the school's median or target number, you're as good as in, unless you are a convicted felon or you wrote your personal statement in crayon.

(Probably) Rejected. If your index is very weak compared with the school's median or target number, you are probably going to be rejected without much ado. When Admissions Officers read weaker applications (yes, at almost every school every application is read) they will be looking for something so outstanding or unique that it makes them willing to take a chance. Factors that can help include ethnic background, where you are from, or very impressive work or life experience. That said, don't hold your breath because not many people in this category are going to make the cut.

Well . . . Maybe. The majority of applicants fall in the middle; their index number is right around the median or target index number. People in this category have decent enough LSAT scores and GPAs for the school, but not high enough for automatic admission. Why do most people fall into this category? For the most part, people apply to schools they think they have at least a shot of getting into based on their grades and LSAT scores; Yale doesn't see very many applicants who got a 140 on the LSAT. What will determine the fate of those whose applications hang in the balance? One thing law schools often look at is the competitiveness of your undergraduate program. On the one hand, someone with a 3.3 GPA in an easy major from a school where everybody graduates with a 3.3 or higher will face an uphill battle. On the other hand, someone with the same GPA in a difficult major from a school that has a reputation for being stingy with A's is in better shape. Admissions Officers will also pore over the rest of your application—personal statement, letters of recommendation, resume, etc.—for reasons to admit you, reject you, or put you on their waiting lists.

ARE YOU MORE THAN YOUR LSAT SCORE?

Aside from LSAT scores and GPAs, what do law schools consider when deciding who's in and who's out? It's the eternal question. On the one hand, we should relieve you hidebound cynics of the notion that they care about nothing else. On the other hand, if you harbor fantasies that a stunning application can overcome truly substandard scores and grades, you should realize that such hopes are unrealistic.

Nonquantitative factors are particularly important at law schools that receive applications from thousands of numerically qualified applicants. A "top ten law school" that receives ten or fifteen applications for every spot in its first-year class has no choice but to "look beyond the numbers," as admissions folks are fond of saying. Such a school will almost surely have to turn away hundreds of applicants with near-perfect LSAT scores and college grades, and those applicants who get past the initial cut will be subjected to real scrutiny.

Less competitive schools are just as concerned, in their own way, with "human criteria" as are the Harvards and Stanfords of the world. They are on the lookout for capable people who have relatively unimpressive GPAs and LSAT scores. The importance of the application is greatly magnified for these students, who must demonstrate their probable success in law school in other ways.

CAN PHYSICS MAJORS GO TO LAW SCHOOL?

"What about my major?" is one of the more popular questions we hear when it comes to law school admissions. The conventional answer to this question goes something like, "There is no prescribed, pre-law curriculum, but you should seek a broad and challenging liberal arts education, etc."

Translation: It really doesn't matter what you major in. Obviously, a major in aviation or hotel and restaurant management is not exactly ideal, but please—we beg you!—don't feel restricted to a few majors simply because you want to attend law school. This is especially true if those particular majors do not interest you. Comparative literature? Fine. American studies? Go to town. Physics? No problem whatsoever. You get the idea.

Think about it. Because most would-be law students end up majoring in the *same* few fields (e.g., political science and philosophy), their applications all look the *same* to the folks in law school Admissions Offices. You want to stand out, which is why it is a good idea to major in something *different*. Ultimately, you should major in whatever appeals to you. Of course, if you want to major in political science or philosophy (or you already have), well, that's fine too.

DOES GRAD SCHOOL COUNT?

Your grades in graduate school will not be included in the calculation of your GPA (only the UGPA, the undergraduate grade point average, is reported to the schools) but will be taken into account separately by an Admissions Committee if you make them available. Reporting grad school grades would be to your advantage, particularly if they are better than your college grades. Admissions Committees are likely to take this as a sign of maturation.

ADVICE FOR THE "NONTRADITIONAL" APPLICANT

The term "nontraditional" is, of course, used to describe applicants who are a few years or many years older than run-of-the-mill law school applicants.

In a nutshell, there's no time like the present to start law school. While it's true that most law students are in their early to mid-twenties, if you aren't, don't think for a minute that your age will keep you from getting in and having a great experience. Applicants for full-time and part-time slots at U.S. law schools range in ages from twenty-one to seventy-one and include every age in between. Some of these older applicants always intended to go to law school and simply postponed it to work, travel, or start a family. Other older applicants never seriously considered law school until after they were immersed in other occupations.

Part-time attendance is especially worth checking into if you've been out of college for a few years. Also, dozens of law schools offer evening programs—particularly in urban centers.

MINORITY LAW SCHOOL APPLICANTS

Things are definitely looking up for minority applicants. According to figures published by the American Bar Association's Committee on Legal Education, in 1978 more than 90 percent of the law students in the ABA's 167 schools were white. In recent years, however, the number of non-whites enrolled in law school has nearly doubled, from about 10 percent to more than 20 percent. Taking an even longer view, figures have tripled since 1972, when minority enrollment was only 6.6 percent. These days, the American Bar Association and the legal profession in general seem pretty committed to seeking and admitting applicants who are members of historically underrepresented minority groups.

WOMEN IN LAW SCHOOL

During the past decade, the number of female lawyers has escalated rapidly, and women undeniably have become more visible in the uppermost echelons of the field. According to statistics compiled by the American Bar Association (ABA), more than 17.9 percent of all law firm partners are women, and women make up more than 30 percent of all lawyers.

More and more women are going to law school as well. At a solid majority of the ABA-approved law schools in the United States, the percentage of women in the student population is forty-nine percent, and women make up more than half of the students at a handful of schools.

Gender discrimination certainly lingers here and there, though. You might want to check certain statistics on the law schools you are interested in, such as the percentage of women on Law Review and the percentage of female professors who are tenured or on track to be tenured. (Nationally, thirty-six percent of all full law school professors are women, and twenty-seven percent of tenured faculty are women.) Also, visit each law school and talk with female students and female professors about how women are treated at that particular school. Finally, see if the school has published any gender studies about itself. If it has, you obviously ought to check those out, too.

YOUR CHANCE OF ACCEPTANCE

Who knows how law schools end up with their reputations? Everything else being equal, you really do want to go a to a well-respected school. It will enhance your employment opportunities tremendously. Remember, whoever you are and whatever your background, your best bet is to select a couple of "reach" schools, a couple of schools at which you've got a good shot at being accepted, and a couple of "safety" schools where you are virtually assured acceptance. Remember also that being realistic about your chances will save you from unnecessary emotional letdowns. Getting in mostly boils down to numbers. Look at the acceptance rates and the average LSATs and GPAs of incoming classes at various schools to assess how you stack up.

Waiting Lists

If a law school puts you on its waiting list, it means you may be admitted depending on how many of the applicants they've already admitted decide to go to another school. Most schools rank students on their waiting list; they'll probably tell you where you stand if you give them a call. Also, note that schools routinely admit students from their waiting lists in late August. If you are on a school's waiting list and you really, really want to go there, keep your options at least partially open. You just might be admitted in the middle of first-year orientation.

Engineering and Math Majors Make Great Law Students

A disproportionate number of law students with backgrounds in the so-called "hard sciences" (math, physics, engineering, etc.) make very high grades in law school, probably because they are trained to think methodically and efficiently about isolated problems (which is what law students are supposed to do on exams).

CHAPTER 2
CHOOSING A LAW SCHOOL

There are some key things you should consider before randomly selecting schools from around the country or just submitting your application to somebody else's list of the Top 10 law schools.

LOCATION

It's a big deal. If you were born and raised in the state of New Mexico, care deeply about the "Land of Enchantment," wish to practice law there, and want to be the governor someday, then your best bet is to go to the University of New Mexico. A school's reputation is usually greater on its home turf than anywhere else (except for some of the larger-than-life schools, like Harvard and Yale). Also, most law schools tend to teach law that is specific to the statutes of the states in which they are located. Knowledge of the eccentricities of state law will help you immensely three years down the road when it comes time to pass the bar exam. Even further, the Career Services Office at your school will be strongly connected to the local legal industry. As a purely practical matter, it will be much easier to find a job and get to interviews in Boston, for example, if you live there. Still another reason to consider geographical location is the simple fact that you'll put down professional and social roots and get to know many really great people throughout your law school career. Leaving them won't be any fun. Finally, starting with geographic limitations is the easiest way to reduce your number of potential schools dramatically.

SPECIALIZATION

Word has it that specialization is the trend of the future. General practitioners in law are becoming less common, so it makes sense to let future lawyers begin to specialize in school. At certain schools, you may receive your JD with an official emphasis in, say, taxation. Specialization is a particularly big deal at smaller or newer schools whose graduates cannot simply get by on their school's reputation. Just between us, it's kind of hard to specialize in anything at most law schools because every graduate has to take this huge exam—the bar—that tests about a dozen topics. Most of your course selections will (and should) be geared toward passing the bar, which leaves precious few hours for specialization. You'll almost certainly specialize, but it's not something to worry about until you actually look for a job. All of that said, if you already know what kind of law you want to specialize in, you're in good shape. Many schools offer certain specialties because of their locations. If you are very interested in environmental law, you'd be better off going to Vermont Law School or Lewis and Clark's Northwestern School of Law than to Brooklyn Law School. Similarly, if you want to work with children as an attorney, check out Loyola University Chicago's Child Law Center. So look at what you want to do in addition to where you want to do it.

JOINT-DEGREE PROGRAMS

In addition to offering specialized areas of study, many law schools have instituted formal dual-degree programs. These schools, nearly all of which are directly affiliated with a parent institution, offer students the opportunity to pursue a JD while also working toward some other degree. Although the JD/MBA combination is the most popular joint-degree sought, many universities offer a JD program combined with degrees in everything from public policy to public administration to social work. In today's perpetually competitive legal market, dual degrees may make some students more marketable for certain positions. However, don't sign up for a dual-degree program on a whim—they require a serious amount of work and often a serious amount of tuition.

Dean's List

According to a letter signed by just about every dean of every ABA-approved law school in the country, the following are the factors you should consider when choosing a law school:

- Breadth and support of alumni network
- Breadth of curriculum
- Clinical programs
- Collaborative research opportunities with faculty
- Commitment to innovative technology
- Cost
- Externship options
- Faculty accessibility
- Intensity of writing instruction
- Interdisciplinary programs
- International programming
- Law library strengths and services
- Loan repayment assistance for low-income lawyers
- Location
- Part-time enrollment options
- Public interest programs
- Quality of teaching
- Racial and gender diversity within the faculty and student body
- Religious affiliation
- Size of first-year classes
- Skills instruction
- Specialized areas of faculty expertise

YOUR CHANCE OF ACCEPTANCE

Who knows how law schools end up with their reputations? Everything else being equal, you really do want to go a to a well-respected school. It will enhance your employment opportunities tremendously. Remember, whoever you are and whatever your background, your best bet is to select a couple of "reach" schools, a couple of schools at which you've got a good shot at being accepted, and a couple of "safety" schools where you are virtually assured acceptance. Remember also that being realistic about your chances will save you from unnecessary emotional letdowns. Getting in mostly boils down to numbers. Look at the acceptance rates and the average LSATs and GPAs of incoming classes at various schools to assess how you stack up.

The Dreaded Bar Exam

Once you graduate, most states require you to take a bar exam before you can practice law. Some state bar exams are really, really hard; New York's and California's are examples. If you don't want to take a bar exam, consider a law school in beautiful Wisconsin. Anyone who graduates from a state-certified Wisconsin law school does not need to take the state bar exam to practice law in the Badger State, as long as they are approved by the Board of Bar Examiners.

PERSONAL APPEAL

A student at a prominent law school in the Pacific Northwest once described his law school to us as "a combination wood-grain bomb shelter and Ewok village." Another student at a Northeastern law school told us her law school was fine except for its "ski-slope classrooms" and "East German Functionalist" architecture. While the curricula at various law schools are pretty much the same, the weather, the surrounding neighborhoods, the nightlife, and the character of the student populations are startlingly different. An important part of any graduate program is enjoying those moments in life when you're not studying. If you aren't comfortable in the environment you choose, it's likely to be reflected in the quality of work you do and your attitude. Before you make a $10,000 to $130,000 investment in any law school, you really ought to check it out in person. While you are there, talk to students and faculty. Walk around. Kick the tires. *Then* make a decision.

EMPLOYMENT PROSPECTS

Where do alumni work? How much money do they make? What percentage of graduates is employed within nine months of graduation? How many major law firms interview on campus? These are massively important questions, and you owe it to yourself to look into the answers before choosing a school.

YOUR VALUES

It is important that you be honest about defining your criteria for judging law schools. What do you want out of a law school? Clout? A high salary? A hopping social life? To live in a certain city? To avoid being in debt up to your eyeballs? A non-competitive atmosphere? Think about it.

MAKE A LIST

Using these criteria (and others you find relevant), develop a list of prospective schools. Ideally, you'll find this book useful in creating the list. Assign a level to each new school you add (something like *reach*, *good shot*, and *safety*).

At your *reach* schools, the average LSAT scores and GPAs of incoming students should be higher than yours. These are law schools that will probably not accept you based on your numbers alone. In order to get in, you'll need to wow them with everything else (e.g., personal statement, stellar recommendations, work experience).

Did You Know?

According to the people who take the LSAT, the average applicant applies to four or more law schools.

Your *good shot* schools should be the schools you like that accept students with about the same LSAT scores and GPA as yours. Combined with a strong and *cohesive* application, you've got a decent shot at getting into these schools.

At your *safety* schools, the average LSAT scores and GPAs of current students should be below yours. These schools should accept you pretty painlessly if there are no major blemishes on your application (e.g., a serious run-in with the law).

CHAPTER 3
APPLYING TO LAW SCHOOL

Our advice: Start early. The LSAT alone can easily consume eighty or more hours of prep time, and completing a single application form might take as many as thirty hours if you take great care with the essay questions. Don't sabotage your efforts through last-minute sloppiness or by allowing this already-annoying process to become a gigantic burden.

WHEN TO APPLY

Yale Law School's absolute final due date is February 15, but Loyola University—Chicago's School of Law will accept your application up to April 1. There is no regular pattern. However, the longer you wait to apply to a school, regardless of its deadline, the worse your chances of getting into that school may be. No efficient Admissions Staff is going to wait to receive all the applications before starting to make their selections.

If you're reading this in December and hope to get into a law school for next fall but haven't done anything about it, you're in big trouble. If you've got an LSAT score you are happy with, you're in less trouble. However, your applications will get to the law schools after the optimum time and, let's face it, they may appear a little rushed. The best time to think about applying is early in the year. Methodically take care of one thing at a time, and *finish by December*.

Early Admissions Options. A few schools have Early Admissions options (for instance, New York University's Early Admission deadline is in October), so you may know by December if you've been accepted. Early Admission is a good idea for a few reasons. It can give you an indication of what your chances are at other schools. It can relieve the stress of waiting until April to see where you'll be spending the next three years of your life. Also, it's better to get wait listed in December than in April (or whenever you would be notified for regular admission); if there is a "tie" among applicants on the waiting list, they'll probably admit whoever applied first. Of course, not every school's Early Admission option is the same (and many schools don't even have one), so do your research.

Rolling Admissions. Many law schools evaluate applications and notify applicants of admission decisions continuously over the course of several months (ordinarily from late fall to midsummer). Obviously, if you apply to one of these schools, it is vital that you apply as early as possible because there will be more spots available at the beginning of the process.

Applying Online. Almost all law schools allow applicants to submit applications online. The LSAC online service (LSAC.org) has a searchable database and applications to ABA-approved schools.

LAW SCHOOL ADMISSIONS COUNCIL: THE LAW SCHOOL APPLICATION MAFIA

In addition to single-handedly creating and administering the LSAT, an organization called the Law School Admissions Council (LSAC) maintains the communication between you and virtually every law school in the United States. It runs the Credential Assembly Service (CAS), which provides information (in a standard format) on applicants to the law schools. They—not you—send your grades, your LSAT score, and plenty of other information about you to the schools. You'll send only your actual applications directly to the law schools themselves. Oh, by the way, the fee for this service is $124 of your hard-earned money plus $16 (or more) every time you want CAS to send a report about you to an additional law school.

THE BIG HURDLES IN THE APPLICATION PROCESS: A BRIEF OVERVIEW

Take the LSAT. The Law School Admission Test is a roughly three-and-a-half-hour multiple-choice test used by law schools to help them select candidates. The LSAT is given in February, June, October (or, occasionally, late September), and December of each year. It's divided into five multiple-choice sections and one writing sample. All ABA-approved and most non-ABA-approved law schools in the United States and Canada require an LSAT score from each and every applicant.

Register for CAS. You can register for the Law School Data Assembly Service at the same time you register to take the LSAT; all necessary forms are contained in the *LSAT and CAS Registration Information Book* (hence the name). It can also be done, of course, online.

Get applications from six or seven schools. Why so many? Because it's better to be safe than sorry. As early as July, select a couple of *reach* schools, a couple of schools to which you've got a good shot at being accepted, and a couple of *safety* schools to which you are virtually assured of acceptance. Your safety school—if you were being realistic—will probably accept you pretty quickly. It may take a while to get

CAS Fees

CAS Subscription Fee: $124 (This buys you an CAS "subscription" for 12 months and just one report to one law school.)

CAS Law School Reports: $16

A Legal Education: Priceless

a final decision from the other schools, but you won't be totally panicked because you'll know your safety school is there for you. If, for whatever reason, your grades or LSAT score is extremely low, you should apply to several safety schools. Most schools won't post online applications until mid-September at the earliest. Still, it is a good idea to familiarize yourself with the previous year's applications as soon as possible, as law schools tend not to radically alter components of their applications from one year to the next.

Write your personal statement. With any luck, you'll only have to write one personal statement. Many, many schools will simply ask you the same basic question: "Why do you want to obtain a law degree?" However, just in case you need to write several personal statements and essays, you need to select your schools fairly early.

Obtain two or three recommendations. Some schools will ask for two recommendations, both of which must be academic. Others want more than two recommendations and want at least one to be from someone who knows you outside traditional academic circles. As part of your CAS file, the LSAC will accept up to three letters of recommendation on your behalf, and they will send them to all the schools to which you apply. This is one of the few redeeming qualities of the LSAC. The last thing the writers of your recommendations are going to want to do is sign, package, and send copies of their letters all over the continent.

Fee Waivers

Taking the LSAT, subscribing to CAS, and applying to law schools at $50 to $75 a pop will cost you an arm and a leg (though these costs are but a drop in the bucket compared with the amount of money you are about to spend on your law school education). The LSAC and most law schools offer fee waiver programs. If you are financially strapped and are accepted into the LSAC fee waiver program, you get to take the LSAT and subscribe to CAS free. You also get four CAS law school reports and a complimentary copy of The Official LSAT SuperPrep.

You can download a Fee Waiver form at www.lsac.org, request that one be sent to you at 215-968-1001, or request one in writing at

    Law Services

    Attn: Fee Waiver Packet

    Box 2000

    661 Penn Street

    Newtown, PA 18940-0998

Update/create your resume. Most law school applicants ask that you submit a resume. Make sure yours is up to date and suitable for submission to an academic institution. Put your academic credentials and experience first—no matter what they are. This is just a supplement to the rest of the material; it's probably the simplest part of the application process.

Get your academic transcripts sent to CAS. When you subscribe to CAS, you must request that the Registrar at every undergraduate, graduate, and professional school you ever attended send an official transcript to Law Services. Don't even think about sending your own transcripts anywhere; these people don't trust you any farther than they can throw you. *Make these requests in August.* If you're applying Early Decision, start requesting transcripts as early as May. Law schools require complete files before making their decisions, and CAS won't send your information to the law schools without your transcripts. Undergraduate institutions can and will screw up and delay the transcript process—even when you go there personally and pay them to provide your records. Give yourself some time to fix problems should they arise.

Write any necessary addenda. An addendum is a brief explanatory letter written to explain or support a "deficient" portion of your application. If your personal and academic life has been fairly smooth, you won't need to include any addenda with your application. If, however, you were ever on academic probation, arrested, or if you have a low GPA, you may need to write one. Other legitimate addenda topics are a low/discrepant LSAT score, DUI/DWI suspensions, or any time gap in your academic or professional career.

An addendum is absolutely not the place to go off on a rant about the fundamental unfairness of the LSAT or how that evil campus security officer was only out to get you when you got arrested. If, for example, you have taken the LSAT two or three times and simply did not do very well, even after spending time and money preparing with a test prep company or a private tutor, simply tell the Admissions Committee that you worked diligently to achieve a high score. Say you explored all possibilities to help you achieve that goal. Whatever the case, lay out the facts, but let them draw their own conclusions. Be brief and balanced. Be fair. Do not go into unneccessary detail. Explain the problem and state what you did about it. This is no time to whine.

Send in your seat deposit. Once you are accepted at a particular school, that school will ask you to put at least some money down to hold your place in that year's class. A typical fee runs $200 or more. This amount will be credited to your first-term tuition once you actually register for classes.

Do any other stuff. You may find that there are other steps you must take during the law school application process. You may request a fee waiver, for example. Also make sure to get a copy of the LSAC's *LSAT/CAS Registration and Information Book*, which is unquestionably the most useful tool in applying to law school. It has the forms you'll need, a sample LSAT, admissions information, the current Law Forum schedule, and sample application schedules.

LAW SCHOOL APPLICATION CHECKLIST (suitable for framing)	
January	• **Take a practice LSAT.** Do it at a library or wherever you won't be interrupted. Also, take it all at once.
February	• **Investigate LSAT prep courses.** If you don't take one with The Princeton Review, do *something*. Just as with any test, you'll get a higher score on this one if you prepare for it first.
March	• **Obtain an *LSAT/CAS Registration and Information Book*.** The books are generally published in March of each year. You can get one at any law school, by calling the LSAC at 215-968-1001, or by stopping by The Princeton Review office nearest you. You can also download one in a PDF format at Lsac.org.
April	• **Register for the June LSAT.** • **Begin an LSAT prep course.** At the very, very least, use some books or software.
May	• **Continue your LSAT prep.**
June	• **Take the LSAT.** If you take the test twice, many schools will average them. Your best bet is to take it once, do exceedingly well, and get it out of your hair forever.
July	• **Register for CAS.** • **Research law schools.**
August	• **Obtain law school applications.** You can call or write, but the easiest and cheapest way to get applicationa is via the Internet. This is, of course, only necessary if you plan to send in paper applications. Go to Lsac.org to access and submit online applications. • **Get your undergraduate transcripts sent to LSDAS.** Make sure to contact the registrar at each undergraduate institution you attended.
September	• **Write your personal statements.** Proofread them. Edit them. Edit them again. Have someone else look them over for all the mistakes you missed. • **Update your resume,** or create a resume if you don't have one. • **Get your recommendations in order.** You want your professors to submit recommendations exactly when you send your applications (in October and November).
October	• **Complete and send early decision applications.**
November	• **Complete and send all regular applications.**
December	• **Chill.** • **Buy holiday gifts.** • **Make plans for New Year's.**

CHAPTER 4
The LSAT

As you may know, we at The Princeton Review are pretty skeptical of most of the standardized tests out there. They make us a lot of money, of course, and we like that, but they are hideously poor indicators of anything besides how well you do on that particular standardized test. They are certainly not intelligence tests. The LSAT is no exception. It is designed to keep you out of law school, not facilitate your entrance into it. For no good reason we can think of, this 125-question test is *the single most important factor in all of law school admissions*, and, at least for the foreseeable future, we're all stuck with it.

Unfortunately, with the possible exception of the MCAT (for medical school), the LSAT is the toughest of all the standardized tests. Only 24 to 26 of the 125 questions have a "correct" answer (Logic Games), as opposed to Arguments and Reading Comprehension, for which you must choose the elusive "best" answer. As ridiculous as they are, the GMAT, GRE, SAT, MCAT, and ACT at least have large chunks of math or science on them. There are verifiably correct answers on these tests, and occasionally you even have to know something to get the right answers. *Only the LSAT requires almost no specific knowledge of anything whatsoever, which is precisely what makes it so difficult*. The only infallible way to study for the LSAT is to study the LSAT itself. The good news is that *anybody* can get significantly better at the LSAT by working diligently at it. In fact, your score will increase exponentially directly in proportion to the amount of time and work you put into preparing for it.

HOW IMPORTANT IS THE LSAT?

The LSAT figures very prominently in your law school application, especially if you've been out of school for a few years. Some law schools won't even look at your application unless you achieve a certain score on your LSAT. Most top law schools average multiple LSAT scores, so you should aim to take it only once. By the way, each score you receive is valid for five years after you take the test.

LSAT STRUCTURE

Section Type	Sections	Qustions Per Section	Time Per Section
Logical Reasoning (Arguments)	2	24–26 2 sections, about 25 questions each	35 minute sections
Analytical Reasoning (Games)	1	22–24	35 minutes
Reading Comprehension	1	27–28	35 minutes
Experimental	1	22–28	35 minutes
Writing Sample	1	1	35 minutes

Each test has approximately 99 to 102 questions. Neither the Experimental section nor the Writing Sample counts toward your score. The multiple-choice sections may be given in any order, but the Writing Sample is always administered last. The Experimental section can be any of the three types of multiple-choice sections and is used by the test writers to test out new questions on your time and at your expense.

The Writing Sample is not scored, and unlikely to be read by anyone other than you. However, the law schools to which you apply will receive a copy of your writing sample, so you should definitely do it. A blank page would stand out like a sore thumb, and you wouldn't want the Admissions Office to think you were some kind of revolutionary.

WHAT'S ON THE LSAT, EXACTLY?

We asked the experts in the LSAT Course Division of The Princeton Review for the lowdown on the various sections of the LSAT. Here's what they had to say.

Analytical Reasoning: If you've ever worked logic problems in puzzle books, then you're already somewhat familiar with the Analytical Reasoning section of the LSAT. The situations behind these problems—often called "games" or "logic games"—are common ones: deciding in what order to interview candidates, or assigning employees to teams, or arranging dinner guests around a table. The arrangement of "players" in these games is governed by a set of rules you must follow in answering the questions. Each Analytical Reasoning section is made up of four games, with five to seven questions each. Questions may ask you to find out what *must* be true under the rules or what *could* be true under the rules; they may add a new condition that applies to just that question; or they may ask you to count the number of possible arrangements under the stated conditions. These questions are difficult mostly because of the time constraints under which they must be worked; very few test-takers find themselves able to complete twenty-four questions on this section in the time allotted.

Logical Reasoning: Because there are two scored sections of them, Logical Reasoning questions on the LSAT are the most important to your score. Each Logical Reasoning—sometimes called "arguments"—question is made up of a short paragraph, often written to make a persuasive point. These small arguments are usually written to contain a flaw—some error of reasoning or unwarranted assumption that you must identify to answer the question successfully. Questions may ask you to draw conclusions from the stated information, to weaken or strengthen the argument, to identify its underlying assumptions, or to identify its logical structure or method. There are most often a total of fifty or fifty-one argument questions between the two sections—roughly half of the scored questions on the LSAT.

As of June 2007 a modification, called Comparative Reading, appears as one of the four sets in the LSAT Reading Comprehension section. In general, Comparative Reading questions are similar to traditional Reading Comprehension questions, except that Comparative Reading questions are based on two shorter passages that together are roughly the same length as one Reading Comprehension passage. A few of the questions that follow a Comparative Reading passage pair might concern only one of the two passages, but most questions will be about both passages and how they relate to each other. Also, since June 2007, test-takers no longer are randomly assigned one of two different kinds of writing prompt—decision or argument—for the writing sample. All test-takers will be assigned a decision prompt. The Writing Sample will continue to be unscored.

We strongly recommend that you prep for this test. Although we provide the best prep for the LSAT, you certainly don't have to take The Princeton Review's course (or buy our book, *Cracking the LSAT*, or sign up for our awesome distance learning course), as much as we would obviously like it. There are plenty of books, software products, courses, and tutors out there. The people who make the LSAT will gleefully sell you plenty of practice tests as well. The key is to find the best program for you. Your first step should be taking a free full-length practice LSAT given under realistic testing conditions (we offer them across the country), so you can gauge where you stand and how much you need to improve your LSAT score. Whatever your course of action, however, make sure you remain committed to it, so you can be as prepared as possible when you take the actual test.

WHEN SHOULD YOU TAKE THE LSAT?

Here is a quick summary of test dates along with some factors to consider for each.

JUNE

The June administration is the only time the test is given on a Monday afternoon. If you have trouble functioning at the ordinary 8:00 A.M. start time, June may be a good option. Furthermore, taking the LSAT in June frees up your summer and fall to research schools and complete applications. However, if you are still in college, you'll have to balance LSAT preparation with academic course work and, in some cases, final exams. Check your exam schedules before deciding on a June LSAT test date.

OCTOBER/SEPTEMBER

The October test date (which is sometimes in late September) will allow you to prepare for the LSAT during the summer. This is an attractive option if you are a college student with some free time on your hands. Once you've taken the LSAT, you can spend the remainder of the fall completing your applications.

DECEMBER

December is the last LSAT administration that most competitive law schools will accept. If disaster strikes and you get a flat tire on test day, you may end up waiting another year to begin law school. December test-takers also must balance their time between preparing for the LSAT and completing law school applications. Doing so can make for a hectic fall, especially if you're still in college. You should also remember that, while a law school may accept December LSAT scores, taking the test in December could affect your chances of admission. Many law schools use a rolling admissions system, which means that they begin making admissions decisions as early as mid-October and continue to do so until the application deadline. Applying late in this cycle could mean that fewer spots are available. Check with your potential law schools to find out their specific policies.

FEBRUARY

If you want to begin law school in the following fall, the February LSAT will be too late for most law schools. However, if you don't plan to begin law school until the *next* academic year, you can give yourself a head start on the entire admissions process by taking the LSAT in February, then spending your summer researching schools and your fall completing applications.

UPCOMING LSAT TEST DATES		
TEST DATE	Registration Deadline	Late Registration Ends
October 1, 2011	August 30, 2011	September 9, 2011
December 3, 2011	October 31, 2011	November 11, 2011
February 11, 2012	January 10, 2012	January 20, 2012

HOW IS THE LSAT SCORED?

LSAT scores currently range from 120 to 180. Why that range? We have no idea. The table on page 16 indicates the percentile rating of the corresponding LSAT scores between 141 and 180. This varies slightly from test to test.

Your raw score (the number of questions you answer correctly) doesn't always produce the same scaled score as previous LSATs. What actually happens is that your raw score is compared with that of everyone else who took the test on the same date you did. The LSAC looks at the scales from every other LSAT given in the past three years and "normalizes" the current scale so that it doesn't deviate widely from those scaled scores in the past.

LSAT Score	Percent Below	LSAT Score	Percent Below
180	99.9	160	82.2
179	99.9	159	79.1
178	99.9	158	76.5
177	99.8	157	72.6
176	99.7	156	68.7
175	99.6	155	65.7
174	99.5	154	61.5
173	99.3	153	57.3
172	99.0	152	53.2
171	98.5	151	49.1
170	98.1	150	44.9
169	97.5	149	41.0
168	96.7	148	37.0
167	95.7	147	33.4
166	94.6	146	29.6
165	93.2	145	26.4
164	91.4	144	23.3
163	89.7	143	20.2
162	87.3	142	17.7
161	84.9	141	15.2

A GOOD LSAT SCORE

A good score on the LSAT is the score that gets you into the law school you want to attend. Remember that a large part of the admissions game is the formula of your UGPA (undergraduate grade point average) multiplied by your LSAT score. Chances are, you are at a point in life where your UGPA is pretty much fixed (if you're reading this early in your college career, start getting very good grades pronto), so the only piece of the formula you can have an impact on is your LSAT score. We cannot emphasize enough the notion that you must prepare for this test.

A LITTLE IMPROVEMENT GOES A LONG WAY

A student who scores a 154 is in the 62nd percentile of all LSAT-takers. If that student's score was 161, however, that same student would jump to the 85th percentile. Depending upon your score, a seven-point improvement can increase your ranking by more than twenty-five percentile points.

COMPETITIVE LSAT SCORES AROUND THE UNITED STATES

The range of LSAT scores from the 25th to 75th percentile of incoming full-time students at U.S. law schools is pretty broad. Here is a sampling.

Law School	Score 25 to 75 percentile
Widener University, School of Law, Harrisburg	148–152
Gonzaga University, School of Law	153–157
Rutgers University-Newark, School of Law	155–161
University of Pittsburgh, School of Law	157–161
University of Arizona, College of Law	157–164
Temple University, James E. Beasley School of Law	159–163
University of Florida, Levin College of Law	158–163
University of Tennessee, College of Law	157–161
Case Western Reserve University, School of Law	157–161
University of Alabama, School of Law	159–165
Southern Methodist University, School of Law	157–165
Loyola University Chicago, School of Law	156–161
University of San Diego, School of Law	160–164
Emory University, School of Law	165–167
The College of William & Mary, Law School	161–166
George Washington University, Law School	162–168
University of California-Berkeley, School of Law	165–170
Georgetown University, Law Center	167–172
Stanford University, School of Law	168–172
University of Chicago, Law School	169–173
Yale University, Yale Law School	170–176

PREPARING FOR THE LSAT

No matter who you are—whether you graduated *magna cum laude* from Cornell University or you're on academic probation at Cornell College—the first thing you need to do is order a recent LSAT. One comes free with every *Official LSAT Registration Booklet*. Once you get the test, take it, but not casually over the course of two weeks. Bribe someone to be your proctor. Have them administer the test to you under strict time conditions. Follow the test booklet instructions exactly, and do it right. Your goal is to simulate an actual testing experience as much as possible. When you finish, score the test honestly. Don't give yourself a few extra points because "you'll do better on test day." The score on this practice test will provide a baseline for mapping your test preparation strategy.

If your practice LSAT score is already at a point where you've got a very high-percentage shot of getting accepted to the law school of your choice, chances are you don't need much preparation. Order a half dozen or so of the most recent LSATs from LSAC and work through them over the course of a few months, making sure you understand why you are making specific mistakes. If your college or university offers a free or very cheap prep course, consider taking it to get more tips on the test. Many of these courses are taught by pre-law advisors who will speak very intelligently about the test and are committed to helping you get the best score you can.

If, after you take a practice LSAT, your score is not what you want or need it to be, you are definitely not alone. Many academically strong candidates go into the LSAT cold because they assume that the LSAT is no more difficult than or about the same as their college courses. Frankly, many students are surprised at how poorly they do the first time they take a dry run. Think about it this way: It's better to be surprised sitting at home with a practice test than while taking the test for real.

If you've taken a practice LSAT under exam conditions and it's, say, ten or fifteen points below where you want it to be, you should probably consult an expert. Ask around. Assess your financial situation. Talk to other people who have improved their LSAT scores and duplicate their strategies.

Whatever you decide to do, make sure you are practicing with real LSAT questions and you take full-length practice tests under realistic testing conditions—again and again and again.

SOME ESSENTIAL, DOWN-AND-DIRTY LSAT TIPS

Slow down. Way down. The slower you go, the better you'll do. It's that simple. Any function you perform, from basic motor skills to complex intellectual problems, will be affected by the rate at which you perform that function. This goes for everything from cleaning fish to taking the LSAT. You can get twenty-five questions wrong and still get a scaled score of 160, which is a very good score (it's in the 84th percentile). You can get at least six questions wrong per section or, even better, you can ignore the two or three most convoluted questions per section, *still* get a few more questions wrong, and you'll get an excellent overall score. Your best strategy is to find the particular working speed at which you will get the most questions correct.

There is no penalty for guessing. If you don't have time to finish the exam, it's imperative that you leave yourself at least thirty seconds at the end of each section in which to grab free points by bubbling in some answer to every question before time is called. Pick a letter of the day—like B—don't bubble in randomly. If you guess totally randomly, you might get every single guess right. Of course, you may also get struck by lightning in the middle of the test. The odds are about the same. *You are far more likely to miss every question if you guess without a plan.* However, if you stick with the same letter each time you guess, you will definitely be right once in a while. It's a conservative approach, but it is also your best bet for guaranteed points, which is what you want. By guessing the same letter pretty much every time as time runs out, you can pick up anywhere from two to four raw points per section. Be careful about waiting until the very last second to start filling in randomly, though, because proctors occasionally cheat students out of the last few seconds of a section.

Use process of elimination all the time. This is absolutely huge. On seventy-five percent of the LSAT (all the Logical Reasoning and Reading Comprehension questions), you are *not* looking for the *right* answer, only the *best* answer. It says so right there in the instructions. Eliminating even one answer choice increases your chances of getting the question right by twenty to twenty-five percent. If you can cross off two or three answer choices, you are really in business. Also, very rarely will you find an answer choice that is flawless on the LSAT. Instead, you'll find four answer choices that are definitely wrong and one that is the least of five evils. You should constantly look for reasons to get rid of answer choices so you can eliminate them. This strategy will increase your odds of getting the question right, and you'll be a happier and more successful standardized test-taker. We swear.

Attack! Attack! Attack! Read the test with an antagonistic, critical eye; look for holes and gaps in the reasoning of arguments and in the answer choices. Many LSAT questions revolve around what is wrong with a particular line of reasoning. The more adept you become at identifying what is wrong with a problem before going to the answer choices, the more successful you'll be.

Write all over your test booklet. Actively engage the exam, and put your thoughts on paper. Circle words. *Physically cross out wrong answer choices you have eliminated.* Draw complete and exact diagrams for the logic games. Use the diagrams you draw.

Do the questions in whatever order you wish. Just because a logic game question is first doesn't mean you should do it first. There is *no order of difficulty* on the LSAT—unlike some other standardized tests—so you should hunt down and destroy those questions at which you are personally best. If you are doing a Reading Comprehension question, for example, or tackling an argument, and you don't know what the hell is going on, then cross off whatever you can, guess, and move on. If you have no idea how to solve a particular logic game, don't focus your energy there. Find a game you can do and milk it for points. Your mission is to gain points wherever you can. By the way, if a particular section is really throwing you, it's probably because it is the dastardly Experimental section (which is often kind of sloppy and, thankfully, does not count toward your score).

CHAPTER 5
WRITING A GREAT PERSONAL STATEMENT

There is no way to avoid writing the dreaded personal statement. You'll probably need to write only one personal statement, and it will probably address the most commonly asked question: "Why do you want to obtain a law degree?" This question, in one form or another, appears on virtually every law school application and often represents your only opportunity to string more than two sentences together. Besides your grades and your LSAT score, it is the most important part of your law school application. Your answer should be about two pages long, and it should amount to something significantly more profound than "A six-figure salary really appeals to me," or "I watch *Law & Order* every night."

Unlike your application to undergraduate programs, the personal statement on a law school application is not the time to discuss what your trip to Europe meant to you, describe your wacky chemistry teacher, or try your hand at verse. It's a fine line. While you want to stand out, you definitely don't want to be *overly* creative here. You want to be unique, but you don't want to come across as a weirdo or a loose cannon. You want to present yourself as intelligent, professional, mature, persuasive, and concise because these are the qualities law schools seek in applicants.

THE BASICS
Here are the essentials of writing essays and personal statements.

Find your own unique angle. The admissions people read tons of really boring essays about "how great I am" and how "I think there should be justice for everyone." If you must explain why you want to obtain a law degree, strive to find an angle that is interesting and unique to you. If what you write *isn't* interesting to you, we promise that it won't be remotely interesting to an Admissions Officer. Also, in addition to being more effective, an interesting essay will be far more enjoyable to write.

In general, avoid generalities. Again, Admissions Officers have to read an unbelievable number of boring essays. You will find it harder to be boring if you write about particulars. It's the details that stick in a reader's mind.

Good writing is easily understood. You want to get your point across, not bury it in words. Don't talk in circles. Your prose should be clear and direct. If an Admissions Officer has to struggle to figure out what you are trying to say, you'll be in trouble. Also, legal writing courses make up a significant part of most law school curricula; if you can show that you have good writing skills, you have a serious edge.

Buy and read *The Elements of Style* by William Strunk Jr. and E. B. White. We can't recommend it enough. In fact, we're surprised you don't have it already. This little book is a required investment for any writer (and, believe us, you'll be doing plenty of writing as a law student and a practicing attorney). You will refer to it forever, and if you do what it says, your writing will definitely improve.

Have three or four people read your personal statement and critique it. If your personal statement contains misspellings and grammatical errors, Admissions Officers will conclude not only that you don't know how to write but also that you aren't shrewd enough to get help. What's worse, the more time you spend with a piece of your own writing, the less likely you are to spot any errors. You get tunnel vision. Ask friends, boyfriends, girlfriends, professors, brothers, sisters—somebody—to read your essay and comment on it. Use a computer with a spellchecker. *Be especially careful about punctuation!* Another tip: Read your personal statement aloud to yourself or someone else. You will catch mistakes and awkward phrases that would have gotten past you otherwise because they sounded correct in your head.

Don't repeat information from other parts of your application. It's a waste of time and space.

Stick to the length that is requested. It's only common courtesy.

Maintain the proper tone. Your essay should be memorable, without being outrageous and easy to read, without being too formal or sloppy. When in doubt, err on the formal side.

Being funny is much harder than you think. An applicant who can make an Admissions Officer laugh never gets lost in the shuffle. The clever part of the personal statement is passed around and read aloud. Everyone smiles and the Admissions Staff can't bear to toss your application into the "reject" pile. But beware! Most people think they're funny, but only a few are able to pull it off in this context. Obviously, stay away from one-liners, limericks, and anything remotely off-color.

WHY DO YOU WANT TO GO TO LAW SCHOOL?

Writing about yourself often proves to be surprisingly difficult. It's certainly no cakewalk explaining who you are and why you want to go to law school, and presenting your lifetime of experiences in a mere two pages. On the bright side, the personal statement is the only element of your application over which you have total control. It's a tremendous opportunity to make a great first impression as long as you avoid the urge to communicate your entire genetic blueprint. Your goal should be much more modest.

Websites about Getting into Law School

PrincetonReview.com

You can access tons of information about law school and the LSAT at our site.

Lsac.org

This site is home to the people who bring you the LSAT and the CAS application processing service.

DON'T GET CARRIED AWAY

Although some law schools set no limit on the length of the personal statement, you shouldn't take their bait. You can be certain that your statement will be at least glanced at in its entirety, but Admissions Officers are human, and their massive workload at admissions time has an understandable impact on their attention spans. You should limit yourself to two or three typed, double-spaced pages. Does this make your job any easier? Not at all. In fact, practical constraints on the length of your essay demand a higher degree of efficiency and precision. A two-page limit allows for absolutely no fluff.

MAKE YOURSELF STAND OUT

We know you know this, but you will be competing against thousands of well-qualified applicants for admission to just about any law school. Consequently, your primary task in writing your application is to separate yourself from the crowd. Particularly if you are applying directly from college or if you have been out of school for a very short time, you must do your best to ensure that the Admissions Committee cannot categorize you too broadly. Admissions Committees will see innumerable applications from bright twenty-two-year-olds with good grades. Your essay presents an opportunity to put those grades in context, to define and differentiate yourself.

WHAT MAKES A GOOD PERSONAL STATEMENT?

Like any good writing, your law school application should be clear, concise, and candid. The first two of these attributes, clarity and conciseness, are usually the result of a lot of reading, rereading, and rewriting. Without question, repeated critical revision by yourself and others is the surest way to trim and tune your prose. The third quality, candor, is the product of proper motivation. Honesty cannot be superimposed after the fact; your writing must be candid from the outset.

In writing your personal statement for law school applications, pay particularly close attention to the way your essay is structured and the fundamental message it communicates. Admissions Committees will read your essay two ways: as a product of your handiwork and as a product of your mind. Don't underestimate the importance of either perspective. A well-crafted essay will impress any Admissions Officer, but if it does not illuminate, you will not be remembered. You will not stand out. Conversely, a thoughtful essay that offers true insight will stand out unmistakably, but if it is not readable, it will not receive serious consideration.

THINGS TO AVOID IN YOUR PERSONAL STATEMENT

"MY LSAT SCORE ISN'T GREAT, BUT I'M JUST NOT A GOOD TEST-TAKER."

If you have a low LSAT score, avoid directly discussing it like the plague in your personal statement. Law school is a test-rich environment. In fact, grades in most law-school courses are determined by a single exam at the semester's end, and as a law student, you'll spend your Novembers and Aprils in a study carrel, completely removed from society. Saying that you are not good at tests will do little to convince an Admissions Committee that you've got the ability to succeed in law school once accepted.

Consider also that a low LSAT score speaks for itself—all too eloquently. It doesn't need you to speak for it too. The LSAT may be a flawed test, but don't go arguing the merits of the test to Admissions Officers, because ordinarily it is the primary factor they use to make admissions decisions. We feel for you, but you'd be barking up the wrong tree. The attitude of most law school Admissions Departments is that while the LSAT may be imperfect, it is equally imperfect for all applicants. Apart from extraordinary claims of serious illness on test day, few explanations for poor performance on the LSAT will mean much to the people who read your application.

About the only situation in which a discussion of your LSAT score is necessary is if you have two (or more) LSAT scores and one is significantly better than another. If you did much better in your second sitting than in your first, or vice versa, a brief explanation couldn't hurt. However, your explanation may mean little to the committee, which may have its own hard-and-fast rules for interpreting multiple LSAT scores. Even in this scenario, however, you should avoid bringing up the LSAT in the personal statement. *Save it for an addendum.*

The obvious and preferable alternative to an explicit discussion of a weak LSAT score would be to focus on what you *are* good at. If you really are bad at standardized tests, you must be better at something else, or you wouldn't have gotten as far as you have. If you think you are a marvelous researcher, say so. If you are a wonderful writer, show it. Let your essay implicitly draw attention away from your weak points by focusing on your strengths. There is no way to convince an Admissions Committee that they should overlook your LSAT score. You may, however, present compelling reasons for them to look beyond it.

"MY COLLEGE GRADES WEREN'T THAT HIGH, BUT . . ."

This issue is a bit more complicated than the low LSAT score. Law school Admissions Committees will be more willing to listen to your interpretation of your college performance but only within limits. Keep in mind that law schools require official transcripts for a reason. Members of the Admissions Committee will be aware of your academic credentials before ever getting to your essay. As with low LSAT scores, your safest course of action is to *explain low grades in addendum.*

If your grades are unimpressive, you should offer the Admissions Committee something else by which to judge your abilities. Again, the best argument for looking past your college grades is evidence of achievement in another area, whether in your LSAT score, your extracurricular activities, your overcoming economic hardship as an undergraduate, or your career accomplishments.

"I'VE ALWAYS WANTED TO BE A LAWYER."

Sure you have. Many applicants seem to feel the need to point out that they really, really want to become attorneys. You will do yourself a great service by avoiding such throwaway lines. They'll do nothing for your essay but water it down. Do not convince yourself in a moment of desperation that claiming to have known that the law was your calling since age six (when—let's be honest—you really wanted to be a firefighter) will somehow move your application to the top of the pile. The Admissions Committee is not interested in how much you want to practice law. They want to know *why.*

"I WANT TO BECOME A LAWYER TO FIGHT INJUSTICE."

No matter how deeply you feel about battling social inequity, between us, writing it down makes you sound like a superhero on a soapbox. Moreover, though some people really do want to fight injustice, way down in the cockles of their hearts, most applicants are motivated to attend law school by less altruistic desires. Among the nearly one million practicing lawyers in the United States, there are relatively few who actually earn a living defending the indigent or protecting civil rights. Tremendously dedicated attorneys who work for peanuts and take charity cases are few and far between. We're not saying you don't want to be one of them; we're merely saying that people in law school admissions won't *believe* you want to be one of them. They'll take your professed altruistic ambitions (and those of the hundreds of other personal statements identical to yours) with a (huge) grain of salt.

If you can, in good conscience, say that you are committed to a career in the public interest, show the committee something tangible on your application and in your essay that will allow them to see your statements as more than mere assertions. If however, you cannot show that you are already a veteran in the good fight, don't claim to be. Law school Admissions Committees certainly do not regard the legal profession as a saints versus sinners proposition, and neither should you. Do not be afraid of appearing morally moderate. If the truth is that you want the guarantee of the relatively good jobs a law degree practically ensures, be forthright. Nothing is as impressive to the reader of a personal statement as the ring of truth, and what's wrong with wanting a good job, anyway?

CHAPTER 6

RECOMMENDATIONS

The law schools to which you apply will require two or three letters of recommendation in support of your application. Some schools will allow you to submit as many letters as you like. Others make it clear that any more than the minimum number of letters of recommendation is unwelcome. If you've ever applied to a private school (or perhaps a small public school) then you know the drill.

Unlike the evaluation forms for some colleges and graduate programs, however, law school recommendation forms tend toward absolute minimalism. All but a few recommendation forms for law school applications ask a single, open-ended question. It usually goes something like, "What information about this applicant is relevant that is not to be found in other sources?" The generic quality of the forms from various law schools may be both a blessing and a curse. On the one hand, it makes it possible for those writing your recommendations to write a single letter that will suffice for all the applications you submit. This convenience will make everybody much happier. On the other hand, if a free-form recommendation is to make a positive impression on an Admissions Committee, it must convey real knowledge about you.

WHOM TO ASK

Your letters of recommendation should come from people who know you well enough to offer a truly informed assessment of your abilities. Think carefully before choosing them to do this favor for you, but, as a general rule, pick respectable people whom you've known for a long time. If the writers of your recommendations know you well and understand the broader experience that has brought you to your decision to attend law school, they will be able to write a letter that is specific enough to do you some good. You also want people who can and are willing to contribute to an integrated, cohesive application.

The application materials from most law schools suggest that your letters should come, whenever possible, from people in academic settings. Some schools want at least two recommendations, both of which must be academic. Others explicitly request that the letters come from someone who has known you in a professional setting, especially if you've been out of school for a while.

HELP YOUR RECOMMENDATION WRITERS HELP YOU

Here, in essence, is the simple secret to great recommendations: Make sure the writers of your recommendations know you, your academic and professional goals, and the overall message you are trying to convey in your application. The best recommendations will fit neatly with the picture you present of yourself in your own essay, even when they make no specific reference to the issues your essay addresses. An effective law school application will present to the Admissions Committee a cohesive picture, not a montage. A great way to point your recommendation writers in the right direction and maximize their abilities to contribute to your overall cause is to provide them with copies of your personal statement. Don't be bashful about amiably communicating a few "talking points" that don't appear in your personal statement, as well.

ACADEMIC REFERENCES

Most applicants will (and should) seek recommendations from current or former professors. The academic environment in law school is extremely rigorous. Admissions Committees will be looking for assurance that you will be able not just to survive but to excel. A strong recommendation from a college professor is a valuable corroboration of your ability to succeed in law school.

You want nothing less than stellar academic recommendations. While a perfunctory, lukewarm recommendation is unlikely to damage your overall application, it will obviously do nothing to bolster it. Your best bet is to choose at least one professor from your major field. An enthusiastic endorsement from such a professor will be taken as a sign that you are an excellent student. Second—and we hope that this goes without saying—you should choose professors who do not immediately associate your name with the letter C.

Helpful Websites

findlaw.com

This site is the mother lode of free information about law, law schools, and legal careers.

ilrg.com

Mother lode honorable mention.

hg.org/students.html

Another honorable mention.

jurist.law.pitt.edu

The University of Pittsburgh School of Law's splendid "Legal News and Research" website offers a wealth of useful information.

Specifics are of particular interest to Admissions Officers when they evaluate your recommendations. If a professor can make *specific* reference to a particular project you completed, or at least make substantive reference to your work in a particular course, the recommendation will be strengthened considerably. Make it your responsibility to enable your professors to provide specifics. Drop hints, or just lay it out for them. You might, for example, make available a paper you wrote for them of which you are particularly proud. Or you might just chat with the professor for a while to jog those dormant memories. You might feel uncomfortable tooting your own horn, but it's for the best. Unless your professors are well enough acquainted with you to be able to offer a very personal assessment of your potential, they will greatly appreciate a tangible reminder of your abilities on which to base their recommendation.

ESCAPING THE WOODWORK

If you managed to get through college without any professors noticing you, it's not the end of the world. Professors are quite talented at writing recommendations for students they barely know. Most consider it part of their job. Even seemingly unapproachable academic titans will usually be happy to dash off a quick letter for a mere student. However, these same obliging professors are masters of a sort of opaque prose style that screams to an Admissions Officer, "I really have no idea what to say about this kid who is, in fact, a near-total stranger to me!" Although an Admissions Committee will not outrightly dismiss such a recommendation, it's really not going to help you much.

REELING IN THE YEARS

Obviously, the longer it has been since you graduated, the tougher it is to obtain academic recommendations. However, if you've held on to your old papers, you may still be able to rekindle an old professor's memory of your genius by sending a decent paper or two along with your request for a recommendation (and, of course, a copy of your personal statement). You want to provide specifics in any way you can.

NON-ACADEMIC REFERENCES

Getting the mayor, a senator, or the CEO of your company to write a recommendation helps only if you have a personal and professional connection with that person. Remember, you want the writers of your recommendations to provide specifics about your actual accomplishments. If you're having trouble finding academic recommendations, choose people from your workplace, from the community, or from any other area of your life that is important to you. If at all possible, talk to your boss or a supervisor from a previous job who knows you well (and, of course, likes you).

SEND A THANK-YOU NOTE

Always a good idea. It should be short and handwritten. Use a blue pen so the recipient knows for sure that your note is no cheap copy. As with any good thank-you note and any good recommendation, mention a specific. (Send a thank-you note if you have an interview at a law school, too.)

CHAPTER 7
REAL-LIFE WORK EXPERIENCE
AND COMMUNITY SERVICE

WORK EXPERIENCE IN COLLEGE

Most law school applications will ask you to list any part-time jobs you held while you were in college and how many hours per week you worked. If you had to (or chose to) work your way through your undergraduate years, this should come as good news. A great number of law schools make it clear that they take your work commitments as a college student into consideration when evaluating your undergraduate GPA.

WORK EXPERIENCE IN REAL LIFE

All law school applications will ask you about your work experience beyond college. They will give you three or four lines on which to list such experience. Some schools will invite you to submit a resume. If you have a very good one, you should really milk this opportunity for all it's worth. Even if you don't have a marvelous resume, these few lines on the application and your resume are the only opportunities you'll have to discuss your post-college experience meaningfully—unless you choose to discuss professional experience in your personal statement as well.

The kind of job you've had is not as important as you might think. What interests the Admissions Committee is what you've made of that job and what it has made of you. Whatever your job was or is, you want to offer credible evidence of your competence. For example, mention in your personal statement your job advancement or any increase in your responsibility. Most important, though, remember your overriding goal of cohesive presentation—you want to show off your professional experience within the context of your decision to attend law school. This does not mean that you need to offer geometric proof of how your experience in the workplace has led you inexorably to a career in law. You need only explain truthfully how this experience influenced you and how it fits nicely into your thinking about law school.

COMMUNITY SERVICE

An overwhelming majority of law schools single out community involvement as one of several influential factors in their admissions decisions. Law schools would like to admit applicants who show a long-standing commitment to something other than their own advancement.

It is certainly understandable that law schools would wish to determine the level of such commitment before admitting an applicant, particularly since so few law students go on to practice public interest law. Be forewarned, however, that nothing—*nothing*—is so obviously bogus as an insincere statement of a commitment to public interest issues. It just reeks. Admissions committees are well aware that very few people take the time out of their lives to become involved significantly in their communities. If you aren't one of them, trying to fake it can only hurt you.

CHAPTER 8

INTERVIEWS

The odds are very good that you will never have to sit through an interview in the law school admissions process. Admissions Offices just aren't very keen on them. They do happen occasionally, however, and if you are faced with one, here are a few tips.

BE PREPARED

Interviews do make impressions. Some students are admitted simply because they had great interviews; less often, students are rejected because they bombed. Being prepared is the smartest thing you can do.

Don't ask questions that are answered in the brochures you got in the mail. You have to read those brochures—at breakfast before the interview would be an ideal time.

If there is a popular conception of the school (e.g., Harvard is overly competitive), don't ask about it. Your interviewer will have been through the same song and dance too many times. While you don't want to seem off the wall by asking bizarre questions, you don't want to sound exactly like every other boring applicant before you.

LOOK GOOD, FEEL GOOD

Wear nice clothes. If you aren't sure what to wear, *ask the Admissions Staff*. Get a respectable haircut. Don't chew gum. Clean your fingernails. Brush your teeth. Wash behind your ears. You can go back to being a slob as soon as they admit you.

DON'T WORRY ABOUT TIME

Students sometimes are told that the sign of a good interview is that it lasts longer than the time allowed for it. Forget about this. Don't worry if your interview lasts exactly as long as the assistant said it would. Don't try to stretch out the end of your interview by suddenly becoming long-winded or asking questions you don't care about.

CHAPTER 9
MONEY MATTERS

Law school is a cash cow for colleges and universities everywhere and, especially at a private school, you are going to be gouged for a pretty obscene wad of cash over the next three years. Take American University Washington College of Law, where tuition is about $44,000 a year. If you are planning to eat, live somewhere, buy books, and (maybe) have health insurance, you are looking at about $67,000 per year. Multiply that by three years of law school and you get $201,000. Now faint. Correct for inflation (USC certainly will), add things like computers and other miscellany, and you can easily spend $208,000 to earn a degree. Assume that you have to borrow every penny of that $201,000. Multiply it by eight percent through ten years (a common assumption of law school applicants is that they will be able to pay all their debt back in ten years or less). Your monthly payments will be about $3,015.

On the bright side, while law school is certainly an expensive proposition, the financial rewards of practicing can be immensely lucrative. You won't be forced into bankruptcy if you finance it properly. There are tried-and-true ways to reduce your initial costs, finance the costs on the horizon, and manage the debt with which you'll leave school—all without ever having to ask, "Have you been in a serious accident recently?" in a television commercial.

LAW SCHOOL ON THE CHEAP

Private schools aren't the only law schools, and you don't have to come out of law school saddled with tens of thousands of dollars of debt. Many state schools have reputations that equal or surpass some of the top private ones. It might be worth your while to spend a year establishing residency in a state with one or more good public law schools. Here's an idea: Pack up your belongings and move to a cool place like Minneapolis, Seattle, Berkeley, Austin, or Boulder. Spend a year living there. Wait tables, hang out, listen to music, walk the Earth, write the great American novel, and *then* study law.

COMPARISON SHOPPING

Here are the full-time tuition costs at law schools around the country. The two schools listed for each state are randomly paired schools in the same region (one public and one private) and are provided to help you get a feel of what law school costs are going to run you. Those schools that have the same tuition in both columns are private law schools.

Law School	In-State	Out-of-State
University of Florida, Levin College of Law	$14,301	$14,301
University of Miami, School of Law	$39,918	$39,918
Indiana University—Bloomington, School of Law	$26,000	$42,800
University of Notre Dame, Law School	$42,870	$42,870
University of Tennessee, College of Law	$12,540	$30,984
Vanderbilt University, Law School	$44,900	$44,900
The University of Iowa, Collge of Law	$22,554	$41,322
Drake University, Law School	$31,980	$31,980
Louisiana State University, Law Center	$14,496	$14,496
Tulane University, Law School	$38,500	$38,500
University of California, Hastings College of Law	$36,000	$47,225
University of San Francisco, School of Law	$37,230	$37,230
University of Texas at Austin, School of Law	$29,640	$47,720
Baylor University, School of Law	$36,750	$36,750
University of Illinois, College of Law	$33,000	$40,000
Northwestern University, School of Law	$49,444	$49,444
University of Pittsburgh, School of Law	$25,708	$33,334
University of Oregon, School of Law	$22,770	$28,692
Lewis & Clark College, Northwestern School of Law	$35,048	$35,048

LOAN REPAYMENT ASSISTANCE PROGRAMS

If you are burdened with loans, we've got more bad news. The National Association of Law Placement (NALP) shows that while salaries for law school graduates who land jobs at the big, glamorous firms have skyrocketed in the past few years, salaries of less than $85,000 are more common than salaries of $100,000 to $130,000 for the general run of law school grads. There are, however, a growing number of law schools and other sources willing to pay your loans for you through loan forgiveness programs in return for your commitment to work in public interest law.

The Skinny on Loan Repayment Assistance Programs
For a comprehensive listing of assistance programs and for other loan-forgiveness information, call Equal Justice Works at 202-466-3686, or look them up on the Web at Napil.org.

While doing a tour of duty in public service law will put off dreams of working at a big firm or becoming the next Mark Geragos, the benefits of these programs are undeniable. Here's how just about all of them work. You commit to working for a qualified public service or public interest job. As long as your gross income does not exceed the prevailing public service salary, the programs will pay off a good percentage of your debt. Eligible loans are typically any educational debt financed through your law school, which really excludes only loan sharks and credit-card debts.

MAXIMIZE YOUR AID

A simple but oft-forgotten piece of wisdom: If you don't ask, you usually don't get. Be firm when trying to get merit money from your school. Some schools have reserves of cash that go unused. Try simply asking for more financial aid. The better your grades, of course, the more likely schools are to crack open their safe of financial goodies for you. Unfortunately, grants aren't as prevalent for law students as for undergrads. Scholarships are not nearly as widely available either. To get a general idea of availability of aid at a law school, contact the Financial Aid Office.

PARENTAL CONTRIBUTION?!

If you are operating under the assumption that, as a tax-paying grownup who has been out of school for a number of years, you will be recognized as the self-supporting adult you are, you could be in for a surprise. Veterans of financial aid battles will not be surprised to hear that even law school Financial Aid Offices have a difficult time recognizing when apron strings have legitimately been cut. Schools may try to take into account your parents' income in determining your eligibility for financial aid, regardless of your age or tax status. Policies vary widely. Be sure to ask the schools you are considering exactly what their policies are regarding financial independence for the purposes of financial aid.

BORROWING MONEY

It's an amusingly simple process, and several companies are in the business of lending large chunks of cash specifically to law students. Your law school Financial Aid Office can tell you how to reach them. You should explore more than one option and shop around for the lowest fees and rates.

WHO'S ELIGIBLE?

Anyone with reasonably good credit, regardless of financial need, can borrow enough money to finance law school. If you have financial need, you will probably be eligible for some types of financial aid if you meet the following basic qualifications:

- You are a United States citizen or a permanent U.S. resident.

- You are registered for Selective Service if you are a male, or you have the documentation to prove that you are exempt.

- You are not in default on student loans already.

- You don't have a horrendous credit history.

- You haven't been busted for certain drug-related crimes, including possession.

Let the Law School Pick Up the Tab for Phone Calls Whenever Possible

Many schools have free telephone numbers that they don't like to publish in books like this one. If the number we have listed for a particular law school is not an 800 number, it doesn't necessarily mean that you have to pay every time you call the school. Check out the school's website, or ask for the 800 number when you call the first time.

WHAT TYPES OF LOANS ARE AVAILABLE?

There are three basic types of loans: federal, private, and institutional.

Federal

The federal government funds federal loan programs. Federal loans, particularly the Stafford Loan, are usually the first resort for borrowers. Most federal loans are need-based, but some higher-interest loans are available regardless of financial circumstances.

Private

Private loans are funded by banks, foundations, corporations, and other associations. A number of private loans are targeted to aid particular segments of the population. You may have to do some investigating to identify private loans for which you might qualify. As always, contact your law school's Financial Aid Office to learn more.

Institutional

The amount of loan money available and the method by which it is disbursed vary greatly from one school to another. Private schools, especially those that are older and more established, tend to have larger endowments and can offer more assistance. To find out about the resources available at a particular school, refer to its catalog or contact—you guessed it—the Financial Aid Office.

TABLE OF LOANS

NAME OF LOAN	SOURCE	ELIGIBILITY	MAXIMUM ALLOCATION
Federal Stafford (Subsidized) Student Loan Studentaid.ed.gov/ students/publications/ student_guide/index. html	Federal, administered by participating lender.	Demonstrated financial need.	$8,500/year. The maximum aggregate total for subsidized loans is $65,500. The maximum aggregate total includes any Stafford loans received for undergraduate study.
Federal Stafford (Unsubsidized) Student Loan Studentaid.ed.gov/ students/publications/ student_guide/index. html	Federal, administered by participating lender.	Not need-based.	The total Stafford loan limit is $20,500, including Unsubsidized loans and Subsidized loans not to exceed $8,500. The maximum aggregate total of Stafford loans is $138,500, including Unsubsidized loans and Subsidized loans not to exceed $65,500.*
Health Professions Student Loan/Primary Care Loan (HPSL) Contact school for more information.	Federal, administered by school.	Exceptional financial need; commitment to primary care.	For first- and second-year students, the maximum allocation is the cost of attendance (including tuition, educational expenses, and reasonable living expenses). Third- and fourth-year students may receive allocations beyond this amount.
Perkins Loan (formerly NDSL) Contact school for more information.	Federal, administered by school.	Demonstrated financial need.	$6,000/year, with aggregate of $40,000. Aggregate amount includes undergraduate loans.
Alternative Loan Program (ALP) Aamc.org/students/ financing/	AAMC, administered under MEDLOANS division of AAMC.	Not need-based.	Cost of attendance minus other aid received. Aggregate amount $250,000 (total educational indebtedness from all sources).

*Students pursuing certain health professions and enrolled in programs accredited by the appropriate approved accreditation agency are eligible to receive increased amounts of Unsubsidized Stafford loans. If a student is granted the maximum additional allocation, the maximum aggregate total will be $189,500. This number includes all undergraduate and graduate Subsidized and Unsubsidized Stafford loans. See "Increased Eligibility for Health Professions Students" in the Federal Student Aid Handbook for details and updates.

**Check Studentaid.ed.gov/students/publications/student_guide/index.html.

TABLE OF LOANS (Continued)			
REPAYMENT AND DEFFERAL OPTIONS	**INTEREST RATE**	**PROS**	**CONS**
10–30 years to repay. Begin repayment 6 months after graduation. Forbearance possible for up to 3 years of residency training.	Variable 91-day T-bill plus 2.3%. Capped at 8.25%**.	Most common medical school loan. Interest is paid by the government during school. Once you get a loan, later loans are at the same rate.	None.
10–30 years to repay. Interest begins to accrue from day loan is disbursed; you can pay the interest or have it capitalized (added to principal). Begin repayment 6 months after graduation. Forbearance possible for up to 3 years of residency training.	Variable, 91-day T-bill plus 2.3%. Capped at 8.25%**. (While in school, the rate is variable. 91-day T-bill plus 1.7%. Capped at 8.25%**.)	Not need-based.	Interest is not paid by the government while you're in school.
10 years to repay. Begins 1 year after graduation. Deferrable during residency and under special circumstances.	Fixed, 5%.	Fixed, relatively low interest rate.	Very limited availability.
10 years to repay. Begin repayment 9 months after graduation. Can be deferred for 2 years during residency.	Fixed, 5%	Fixed, relatively low interest rate.	Low maximum allocation.
Standard is 20 years of interest and principal payments. Alternative is 3 years of interest only and 17 years of interest and principal. Repayment generally begins 3 to 4 years after graduation, depending on length of residency.	Prime rate plus 1.25%, variable, adjusted monthly. (While in school, prime rate plus 0%. Variable, adjusted monthly.)	High maximum allocation. Not need-based.	"Loan of last resort." High interest rate.

CHAPTER 10
LAW SCHOOL 101

IS IT REALLY THAT BAD?

The first semester of law school has the well-deserved reputation of being among the greatest challenges to your intellect and stamina that you'll ever face. It requires tons and tons of work and, in many ways, it's an exercise in intellectual survival. Just as the gung-ho army recruit must survive boot camp, so, too, must the bright-eyed law student endure the humbling effects of the first year.

Though complex and difficult, the subject matter in first-year law school courses is probably no more inherently difficult than what is taught in other graduate or professional schools. The particular, private terror that is shared by roughly 40,000 1Ls every year stems more from law school's peculiar *style*. The method of instruction unapologetically punishes students who would prefer to learn passively.

THE FIRST-YEAR CURRICULUM

The first-year curriculum in the law school you attend will almost certainly be composed of a combination of the following courses:

TORTS

The word comes from the Middle French for *injury*. The Latin root of the word means *twisted*. Torts are wrongful acts, excluding breaches of contract, over which you can sue people. They include battery, assault, false imprisonment, and intentional infliction of emotional distress. Torts can range from the predictable to the bizarre, from "Dog Bites Man" to "Man Bites Dog" and everything in between. The study of torts mostly involves reading cases to discern the legal rationale behind decisions pertaining to the extent of, and limits on, the civil liability of one party for harm done to another.

CONTRACTS

They may seem fairly self-explanatory, but contractual relationships are varied and complicated, as two semesters of contracts will teach you. Again, through the study of past court cases, you will follow the largely unwritten law governing the system of conditions and obligations a contract represents, as well as the legal remedies available when contracts are breached.

CIVIL PROCEDURE

Civil procedure is the study of how you get things done in civil (as opposed to criminal) court. "Civ Pro" is the study of the often dizzyingly complex rules that govern not only who can sue whom, but also how, when, and where they can do it. This is not merely a study of legal protocol, for issues of process have a significant indirect effect on the substance of the law. Rules of civil procedure govern the conduct of both the courtroom trial and the steps that might precede it: obtaining information (discovery), making your case (pleading), pre-trial motions, and so on.

PROPERTY

You may never own a piece of land, but your life will inevitably and constantly be affected by property laws. Anyone interested in achieving an understanding of broader policy issues will appreciate the significance of this material. Many property courses will emphasize the transfer of property and, to varying degrees, economic analysis of property law.

CRIMINAL LAW

Even if you become a criminal prosecutor or defender, you will probably never run into most of the crimes to which you will be exposed in this course. Can someone who shoots the dead body of a person he believes to be alive be charged with attempted murder? What if they were both on drugs or had really rough childhoods? Also, you'll love the convoluted exam questions in which someone will invariably go on a nutty crime spree.

CONSTITUTIONAL LAW

"Con Law" is the closest thing to a normal class you will take in your first year. It emphasizes issues of government structure (e.g., federal power versus state power) and individual rights (e.g., personal liberties, freedom of expression, property protection). You'll spend a great deal of time studying the limits on the lawmaking power of Congress as well.

LEGAL METHODS

One of the few twentieth-century improvements on the traditional first-year curriculum that has taken hold nearly everywhere, this course travels under various aliases, such as Legal Research and Writing or Elements of the Law. In recent years, increased recognition of the importance of legal writing skills has led more than half of the U.S. law schools to require or offer a writing course after the first year. This class will be your smallest, and possibly your only, refuge from the Socratic Method. Methods courses are often taught by junior faculty and attorneys in need of extra cash and are designed to help you acquire fundamental skills in legal research, analysis, and writing. The methods course may be the least frightening you face, but it can easily consume an enormous amount of time. This is a common lament, particularly at schools where very few credits are awarded for it.

In addition to these course requirements, many law schools require 1Ls to participate in a moot-court exercise. As part of this exercise, students—sometimes working in pairs or even small groups—must prepare briefs and oral arguments for a mock trial (usually appellate). This requirement is often tied in with the methods course so that those briefs and oral arguments will be well researched—and graded.

Tips for Classroom Success

- Be alert. Review material immediately before class so that it is fresh in your memory. Then review your notes from class later the same day and the week's worth of notes at the end of each week.

- Remember that there are few correct answers. The goal of a law school class is generally to analyze, understand, and attempt to resolve issues or problems.

- Learn to state and explain legal rules and principles with accuracy.

- Don't want to focus on minutiae from cases or class discussions; always try to figure out what the law is.

- Accept the ambiguity in legal analysis and class discussion; classes are intended to be thought provoking, perplexing, and difficult.

- No one class session will make or break you. Keep in mind how each class fits within the course overall.

- Write down the law. Don't write down what other students say. Concentrate your notes on the professor's hypotheticals and emphases in class.

- Review the table of contents in the casebook. This is a simple but effective way of keeping yourself in touch with where the class is at any given time.

- If you don't use a laptop, don't sit next to someone who does. The constant tapping on the keys will drive you crazy, and you may get a sense that they are writing down more than you (which is probably not true).

- Don't record classes. There are better uses of your time than to spend hours listening to the comments of students who were just as confused as you were when you first dealt with the material in class.

THE CASE METHOD

In the majority of your law school courses, and probably in all of your first-year courses, your only texts will be things called casebooks. The case method eschews explanation and encourages exploration. In a course that relies entirely on the casebook, you will never come across a printed list of "laws." Instead, you will learn that in many areas of law there is no such thing as a static set of rules, but only a constantly evolving system of principles. You are expected to understand the principles of law—in all of its layers and ambiguities—through a critical examination of a series of cases that were decided according to such principles. You will often feel utterly lost, groping for answers to unarticulated questions. This is not only normal but also intended.

In practical terms, the case method works like this: For every class meeting, you will be assigned a number of cases to read from your casebook, which is a collection of (extremely edited) written judicial decisions in actual court cases. The names won't even have been changed to protect the innocent. The cases are the written judicial opinions rendered in court cases that were decided at the appeals or Supreme Court level. (Written opinions are not generally rendered in lower courts.)

Your casebook will contain no instructions and little to no explanation. Your assignments will be to simply read the cases and be in a position to answer questions based on them. There will be no written homework assignments, just cases, cases, and more cases.

You will write, for your own benefit, summaries—or briefs—of these cases. Briefs are your attempts to summarize the issues and laws around which a particular case revolves. *By briefing, you figure out what the law is.* The idea is that, over the course of a semester, you will try to integrate the content of your case briefs and your notes from in-class lectures, discussions, or dialogues into some kind of cohesive whole.

THE SOCRATIC METHOD

As unfamiliar as the case method will be to most 1Ls, the real source of anxiety is the way in which the professors present it. Socratic instruction entails directed questioning and limited lecturing. Generally, the Socratic professor invites a student to attempt a cogent summary of a case assigned for that day's class. Hopefully, it won't be you (but someday it will be). Regardless of the accuracy and thoroughness of your initial response, the professor then grills you on details overlooked or issues unresolved. Then, the professor will change the facts of the actual case at hand into a hypothetical case that may or may not have demanded a different decision by the court.

The overall goal of the Socratic Method is to forcibly improve your critical reasoning skills. If you are reasonably well prepared, thinking about all these questions will force you beyond the immediately apparent issues in a given case to consider its broader implications. The dialogue between the effective Socratic instructor and the victim of the moment will also force nonparticipating students to question their underlying assumptions of the case under discussion.

WHAT IS CLINICAL LEGAL EDUCATION?

The latest so-called innovation in legal education is ironic in that it's a return to the old emphasis on practical experience. Hands-on training in the practical skills of lawyering now travels under the name "Clinical Legal Education."

HOW IT WORKS

Generally, a clinical course focuses on developing practical lawyering skills. "Clinic" means exactly what you would expect: a working law office where second- and third-year law students counsel clients and serve human beings. (A very limited number of law schools allow first-year students to participate in legal clinics.)

In states that grant upper-level law students a limited right to represent clients in court, students in a law school's clinic might actually follow cases through to their resolution. Some schools have a single on-site clinic that operates something like a general law practice, dealing with cases ranging from petty crime to landlord-tenant disputes. At schools that have dedicated the most resources to their clinical programs, numerous specialized clinics deal with narrowly defined areas of law, such as employment discrimination. The opportunities to participate in such live-action programs, however, are limited.

> *Watch* **The Paper Chase.** *Twice.*
> This movie is the only one ever produced about law school that comes close to depicting the real thing. Watch it before you go to orientation. Watch it again on Thanksgiving break, and laugh when you can identify prototypes of your classmates.

OTHER OPTIONS

Clinical legal education is much more expensive than traditional instruction, which means that few law schools can accommodate more than a small percentage of their students in clinical programs. If that's the case, check out external clinical placements and simulated clinical courses. In a clinical externship, you might work with a real firm or public agency several hours a week and meet with a faculty advisor only occasionally. Though students who participate in these programs are unpaid, they will ordinarily receive academic credit. Also, placements are chosen quite carefully to ensure that you don't become a gopher.

There are also simulated clinical courses. In one of these, you'll perform all of the duties that a student in a live-action clinic would, but your clients are imaginary.

CHAPTER 11
HOW TO EXCEL AT ANY LAW SCHOOL

Preparation for law school is something you should take very seriously. Law school will be one of the most interesting and rewarding experiences of your life, but it's also an important and costly investment. Your academic performance in law school will influence your career for years to come. Consider the following facts when thinking about how important it is to prepare for law school:

- The average full-time law student spends more than $125,000 to attend law school.

- The average law student graduates with more than $80,000 of debt.

- The median income for law school graduates in both public and private practice is only about $60,000.

Contact Law Preview

Law Preview

10 Cordage Park Circle, Suite 115

Plymouth, MA 02360

Phone: 888-PREP-YOU

E-mail: admin@lawpreview.com

Website: LawPreview.com

As you can see, most law students cannot afford to be mediocre. Money isn't everything, but when you're strapped with close to six figures of debt, money concerns will weigh heavily on your career choices. Even if money is not a concern for you, your academic performance in law school will profoundly affect your employment options after graduation and, ultimately, your legal career. Consider these additional facts

- Students who excel in law school may have opportunities to earn up to $135,000 plus bonuses right out of law school.

- Only law students who excel academically have opportunities to obtain prestigious judicial clerkships, teaching positions, and distinguished government jobs.

As you can see, law students who achieve academic success enjoy better career options and have a greater ability to escape the crushing debt of law school. The point is obvious: Your chances of achieving your goals—no matter what you want to do with your career—are far better if you succeed academically.

Now comes the hard part: How do you achieve academic success? You are going to get plenty of advice about how to excel in law school—much of it unsolicited. You certainly don't need any from us. We strongly advise, however, that you pay close attention to what Don Macaulay, the president of Law Preview, has to say about surviving and thriving as a law student. Macaulay, like all the founders of Law Preview, graduated at the top of his law school class and worked at a top law firm before he began developing and administering Law Preview's law school prep course in 1998.

> All B-pluses put you in the top quarter at most schools and in the top fifth at many.

While there are many resources that claim to provide a recipe for success in law school, Law Preview is the best of the lot. They have retained some of the most talented legal scholars in the country to lecture during their week-long sessions, and they deliver what they promise—a methodology for attacking and conquering the law school experience.

We asked Macaulay a few questions to which we thought prospective law students might like to know the answers:

It is often said that the first year of law school is the most important year. Is this true, and, if so, why?

It is true. Academic success during the first year of law school can advance a successful legal career unlike success in any other year because many of the top legal employers start recruiting so early that your first-year grades are all they will see. Most prestigious law firms hire their permanent attorneys from among the ranks of the firm's "summer associates"—usually second-year law students who work for the firm during the summer between the second and third years of law school. Summer associates are generally hired during the fall semester of the second year, a time when only the first year grades are available. A student who does well during the first year, lands a desirable summer associate position, and then impresses his or her employer, is well on his or her way to a secure legal job regardless of his or her academic performance after the first year.

In addition, first-year grades often bear heavily upon a student's eligibility for law review and other prestigious scholastic activities, including other law journals and moot court. These credentials are considered the most significant signs of law school achievement, often even more than a high grade point average. Many of the top legal employers in the private and the public sectors seek out young lawyers with these credentials, and some employers will not even interview candidates who lack these honors, even after a few years of experience. As a result, a solid performance during the first year of law school can have a serious impact upon your professional opportunities available after graduation.

Websites About Doing Well in Law School

LawPreview.com

Law Preview is an intensive week-long seminar designed to help you conquer law school. Learn why hundreds of students have made Law Preview their first step to Law Review.

LawBooksForLess.com

LawBooksForLess.com is the best place to purchase casebooks and legal study aids, cheap!

How does law school differ from what students experienced as undergraduates?

Many students, especially those who enjoyed academic success in college, presume that law school will be a mere continuation of their undergraduate experience, and that, by implementing those skills that brought them success in college, they will enjoy similar success in law school. This couldn't be further from the truth. Once law school begins, students often find themselves thrown into deep water. They are handed an anchor in the form of a casebook (they are told it's a life preserver), and they are expected to sink or swim. While almost nobody sinks in law school anymore, most spend all of their first year just trying to keep their heads above water. In reality, virtually every student who is admitted into law school possesses the intelligence and work ethic needed to graduate. But in spite of having the tools needed to survive the experience, very few possess the know-how to truly excel and make Law Review at their schools.

What makes the law school experience unique is its method of instruction and its system of grading. Most professors rely on the case method as a means for illustrating legal rules and doctrines encountered in a particular area of the law. With the case method, students are asked to read a particular case or, in some instances, several cases, that the professor will use to lead a classroom discussion illustrating a particular rule of law. The assigned readings come from casebooks, which are compilations of cases for each area of law. The cases are usually edited to illustrate distinct legal rules, often with very little commentary or enlightenment by the casebook editor. The casebooks often lack anything more than a general structure, and law professors often contribute little to the limited structure. Students are asked to read and analyze hundreds of cases in a vacuum. Since each assigned case typically builds upon a legal rule illustrated in a previous case, it isn't until the end of the semester or, for some classes, the end of the year, that students begin to form an understanding of how these rules interrelate.

One of the objectives of Law Preview's law school prep course is to help students to understand the big picture before they begin their classes. We hire some of the most talented law professors from around the country to provide previews of the core first-year law school courses: Civil Procedure, Constitutional Law, Contracts, Criminal Law, Property, and Torts. During their lectures, our professors provide students with a roadmap for each subject by discussing the law's development, legal doctrines, and recurring themes and policies that students will encounter throughout the course. By providing entering law students with a conceptual framework for the material they will study, Law Preview eliminates the frustration that most of them will encounter when reading and analyzing case law in a vacuum.

What is the best way to prepare for law school, and when should you start?

When preparing for law school, students should focus on two interrelated tasks: (1) developing a strategy for academic success, and (2) preparing mentally for the awesome task ahead. The primary objective for most law students is to achieve the highest grades possible, and a well-defined strategy for success will help you direct your efforts most efficiently and effectively toward that goal. You must not begin law school equipped solely with some vague notion of hard work. Success requires a concrete plan that includes developing a reliable routine for classroom preparation, a proficient method of outlining, and a calculated strategy for test-taking. The further you progress in law school without such a plan, the more time and energy you will waste struggling through your immense workload without moving discernibly closer to achieving academic success.

You must also become mentally prepared to handle the rigors of law school. Law school can be extremely discouraging because students receive very little feedback during the school year. Classes are usually graded solely based on final exam scores. Midterm exams and graded papers are uncommon, and classroom participation is often the only way for students to ascertain if they understand the material and are employing effective study methods. As a result, a winning attitude is critical to success in law school. Faith in yourself will help you continue to make the personal sacrifices during the first year that you need to make to succeed in law school, even when the rewards are not immediately apparent.

Incoming law students should begin preparing for law school during the summertime prior to first year, and preparation exercises should be aimed at gaining a general understanding of what law school is all about. A solid understanding of what you are expected to learn during the first year will give you the information you need to develop both your strategy for success and the confidence you need to succeed. There are several books on the market that can help in this regard, but those students who are best prepared often attend Law Preview's one-week intensive preparatory course specifically designed to teach beginning law students the strategies for academic success.

What factors contribute to academic success in law school?

Academic success means one thing in law school—exam success. The grades that you receive, particularly during the first year, will be determined almost exclusively by the scores you receive on your final exams. Occasionally, a professor may add a few points for class participation, but that is rare. In most classes, your final exam will consist of a three- or four-hour written examination at the end of the semester or—if the course is two semesters long—at the end of the year. The amount of material you must master for each final exam will simply dwarf that of any undergraduate exam you have ever taken. The hope that you can "cram" a semester's worth of information into a one-week reading period is pure fantasy and one that will surely lead to disappointing grades. The focus of your efforts from day one should be success on your final exams. Don't get bogged down in class preparation or in perfecting a course outline if it will not result in some discernible improvement in your exam performance. All of your efforts should be directed at improving your exam performance in some way. It's as simple as that.

What skills are typically tested on law school exams?

Law school exams usually test three different skills: (1) the ability to accurately identify legal issues, (2) the ability to recall the relevant law with speed, and (3) the ability to apply the law to the facts efficiently and skillfully. The proper approach for developing these skills differs, depending on the substantive area of law in question and whether your exam is open book or closed book.

Identifying legal issues is commonly known as issue spotting. On most of your exams, you will be given complex, hypothetical fact patterns. From the facts you are given, you must identify the particular legal issues that need to be addressed. This is a difficult skill to perfect and can only be developed through practice. The best way to develop issue-spotting skills is by taking practice exams. For each of your classes, during the first half of the semester, you should collect all of the available exams that were given by your professor in the past. Take all of these exams under simulated exam conditions—find an open classroom, get some blue books, time yourself, and take the exams with friends so that you can review them afterward. It is also helpful for you to practice any legal problems you were given during the semester. Issue spotting is an important skill for all lawyers to develop. Lawyers utilize this skill on a daily basis when they listen to their clients' stories and are asked to point out places where legal issues might arise.

The ability to recall the law with speed is also very important and frequently tested. On all of your exams, you will be given a series of legal problems, and for each problem you will usually be required to provide the relevant substantive law and apply it to the facts of the problem. Your ability to recall the law with speed is critical because, in most classes, you will be under time constraints to answer all of the problems. The faster you recall the law, the more problems you will complete and the more time you will have to spend on demonstrating your analytical skills. For courses with closed-book exams, this means straight memorization or the use of memory recall devices, such as mnemonics. Do not be passive about learning the law—repeatedly reviewing your outline is not enough. You must actively learn the law by studying definitions and using memory-assistance devices like flash cards. When you have become exceedingly familiar with your flash cards, rewrite them so as to test your memory in different words. This is particularly critical for courses such as torts and criminal law where you must learn a series of definitions with multiple elements. For courses with open-book exams, this means developing an index for your outline that will enable you to locate the relevant law quickly. Create a cover page for your outline that lists the page number for each substantive subtopic. This will help you get there without any undue delay.

Books About Doing Well in Law School:

Getting to Maybe: How to Excel on Law School Exams, *Professors Jeremy Paul and Michael Fischl*
This book is excellent! While many books and professors may preach "IRAC"— Issue, Rule, Application, Conclusion— as a way of structuring exam answers, Getting to Maybe rightly points out that such advice does not help students correctly identify legal issues or master the intricacies of legal analysis.

Law School Confidential: A Complete Guide to the Law School Experience (Second Edition), *Robert H. Miller, Esq.*
Robert H. Miller, a former federal judicial clerk, Law Review editor, and graduate of University of Pennsylvania Law School, covers every aspect of the law school experience in thoughtful detail. Whether you are a college student just starting to think about law school, a student in the midst of law school applications, or someone who has already been admitted, Law School Confidential is a book you should not be without. An extensive new chapter is devoted to an exclusive one-on-one interview with Dean of Admissions Richard Geiger of the Cornell Law School, wherein closely guarded secrets of the increasingly competitive admissions process are discussed openly for the first time anywhere. In another chapter, Miller goes one-on-one with the hiring partners of two prestigious U.S. law firms about how to succeed in the hiring process, and what it takes to make it to partnership.

The final skill you need to develop is the ability to apply the law to the facts efficiently and skillfully. On your exams, once you have correctly identified the relevant issue and stated the relevant law, you must engage in a discussion of how the law applies to the facts that have been given. The ability to engage in such a discussion is best developed by taking practice exams. When you are practicing this skill, you should focus on efficiency. Try to focus on the essential facts, and do not engage in irrelevant discussions that will waste your energy and your professor's time.

Any final comments for our audience of aspiring law students?

The study of law is a wonderful and noble pursuit, one that I thoroughly enjoyed. Law school is not easy, however, and proper preparation can give you a firm foundation for success. I invite you to visit our website (LawPreview.com) and contact us with any questions (888-PREP-YOU).

CHAPTER 12
CAREER MATTERS

Okay, it's a long time away, but you really ought to be thinking about your professional career beyond law school from day one, especially if your goal is to practice with a major law firm. What stands between you and a job as an associate, the entry-level position at one of these firms, is a three-stage evaluation: first, a review of your resume, including your grades and work experience; second, an on-campus interview; and last, one or more call-back interviews at the firm's offices. It's a fairly intimidating ordeal, but there are a few ways to reduce the anxiety and enhance your chances of landing a great job.

YOUR RESUME

The first thing recruiters tend to notice after your name is the name of the law school you attend. Tacky, but true. Perhaps the greatest misconception among law students, however, is that hiring decisions are based largely upon your school's prestige. All those rankings perpetuate this myth. To be sure, there are a handful of schools with reputations above all others, and students who excel at these schools are in great demand. But you are equally well situated, if not better off, applying from the top of your class at a strong, less prestigious law school class than from the bottom half of a Top Ten law school class.

FIRST-YEAR GRADES ARE THE WHOLE ENCHILADA

Fair or not, the first year of law school will unduly influence your legal future. It's vital that you hit the ground running because law school grades are *the* critical factor in recruitment. An even harsher reality is that *first-year grades are by far the most critical in the hiring process*. Decisions about who gets which plum summer jobs are generally handed down before students take a single second-year exam. Consequently, you're left with exactly *no* time to adjust to law school life and little chance to improve your transcript if you don't come out on top as a first-year student.

WORK EXPERIENCE

If you're applying to law school right out of college, chances are your most significant work experience has been a summer job. Recruiters don't expect you to have spent these months writing Supreme Court decisions. They are generally satisfied if you show that you have worked diligently and seriously at each opportunity. Students who took a year or more off after college obviously have more opportunities to impress but also more of a burden to demonstrate diligence and seriousness.

Work experience in the legal industry—clerkships and paralegal jobs for instance—can be excellent sources of professional development. They are fairly common positions among job applicants, though, so don't feel you have to pursue one of these routes just to show your commitment to the law. You'll make a better impression by working in an industry in which you would like to specialize (e.g., a prospective securities lawyer summering with an investment bank).

Making Law Review

Every law school has an academic periodical called Law Review, produced and edited by law students. It contains articles about various aspects of law—mostly written by professors. While some schools sponsor more than one Law Review, there is generally one that is more prestigious than all the others. In order to "make" Law Review, you will have to finish the all-important first year at (or very, very near) the top of your class or write an article that will be judged by the existing members of the Law Review. You might have to do both. Making Law Review is probably the easiest way to guarantee yourself a job at a blue-chip firm, working for a judge, or in academia. In all honesty, it is a credential you will proudly carry for the rest of your life.

A Couple Good Books

If you are thinking about law school, here are a few books you might find interesting:

The Princeton Review's Law School Essays That Made a Difference

Check out successful essays written for an assortment of selective schools.

Jeff Deaver, The Complete Law School Companion: How to Excel at America's Most Demanding Post-Graduate Curriculum

This straightforward law school survival guide gives excellent advice on how to brief cases, sample briefs, survive class, and plenty more.

THE INTERVIEWS

There are as many right approaches to an interview as there are interviewers. That observation provides little comfort, of course, especially if you're counting on a good interview to make up for whatever deficiencies there are on your resume. Think about the purpose of the initial thirty-minute interview you are likely to have: it provides a rough sketch of not only your future office personality but also your demeanor under stress. The characteristics you demonstrate and the *impression* you give are more important than anything you say. Composure, confidence, maturity, articulation, and an ability to develop rapport are characteristics recruiters are looking for. Give them what they want.

CHAPTER 13
HOW TO USE THIS BOOK

It's pretty simple.

The first part of this book provides a wealth of indispensable information covering everything you need to know about selecting and getting into the law school of your choice. There is also a great deal about what to expect from law school and how to do well. You name it—taking the LSAT, choosing the best school for you, writing a great personal statement, interviewing, paying for it—it's all in the first part.

The second part is the real meat and potatoes of *The Best 167 Law Schools*. It contains portraits of 167 law schools across the United States and Canada. Each school has one of two possible types of entries. The first type of entry is a two-page descriptive profile. It contains data The Princeton Review has collected directly from law school administrators and textual descriptions of the school we have written based on our surveys of current law students. The second type of entry is a data listing, which includes all the same data that appears in the sidebars of the descriptive profiles but does not have the student survey-driven descriptive paragraphs. For an explanation of why all schools do not appear with descriptive profiles, turn to page 59. As is customary with school guidebooks, all data, with the exception of tuition (which should be for the current year if the school reported it by our deadline), reflects figures for the academic year prior to publication unless otherwise noted on the pages. Since law school demographics vary significantly from one institution to another and some schools report data more thoroughly than others, some entries will not include all the individual data described below.

The third part of the book hosts the "School Says . . ." profiles. The "School Says . . ." profiles give extended descriptions of admissions processes, curricula, internship opportunities, and much more. This is your chance to get even more in-depth information on programs that interest you. These schools have paid us a small fee for the chance to tell you more about themselves, and the editorial responsibility is solely that of the law school. We think you'll find these profiles add lots to your picture of a school.

WHAT'S IN THE PROFILES: DATA

The Heading: The first thing you will see for each profile is (obviously) the school's name. On the facing page, you'll find the school's snail mail address, telephone number, fax number, e-mail address, and website. You can find the name of the Admissions Office contact person in the heading, too.

INSTITUTIONAL INFORMATION

Public/Private: Indicates whether a school is state-supported or funded by private means.

Affiliation: If the school is affiliated with a particular religion, you'll find that information here.

Student/Faculty Ratio: The ratio of law students to full-time faculty.

% Faculty Part-Time: The percentage of faculty who are part-time.

% Faculty Female: The percentage of faculty who are women.

% Faculty Minority: The percentage of people who teach at the law school who are also members of minority groups.

Total Faculty: The total number of faculty members at the law school.

> *Yet Another Good Book:*
>
> *Scott Turow*, One L: The Turbulent True Story of a First Year at Harvard Law School
>
> This law school primer is equal parts illuminating and harrowing.

SURVEY SAYS

The Survey Says list appears in the sidebar of each law school's two-page descriptive profile, and up to three Survey Says items will appear on each list. As the name suggests, these items communicate results of our law student surveys. There are ten possible Survey Says items, each explained below. Of these ten, the three items that appear are those about which student respondents demonstrated the greatest degree of consensus. Survey Says items represent the agreement among students only at *that particular law school* and are not relative to how students at other law schools feel about that particular Survey Says item.

Liberal students: Students report that their fellow law students lean to the left politically.

Conservative students: Students report that their fellow law students lean to the right politically.

Students love Hometown, State: Students are pleased with the location of their law school.

Good social life: Students report a lively social life at the law school.

Students never sleep: Students report a low average number of hours of sleep each night. Little sleep in law school is often an indication of extra-long hours of study on a daily basis.

Heavy use of Socratic Method: Students report that their professors primarily employ the traditional Socratic Method in the classroom.

Beautiful campus: Students report that their law school campus is practical and beautiful.

Great research resources: Students report that the library, computer databases, and other research tools are good.

Great judicial externship/internship/clerkship opportunities: Students rate these opportunities as excellent.

Diverse opinions in classrooms: Students agree that differing points of view are tolerated in the classroom.

STUDENTS

Enrollment of Law School: The total number of students enrolled in the law school.

% Male/Female: The percentage of full-time students with an X and a Y chromosome and the percentage of students with two X chromosomes, respectively.

% Out-of-state: The percentage of full-time students who are out-of-state.

% Full-time: The percentage of students who attend the school on a full-time basis.

% Minority: The percentage of full-time students who represent underrepresented minority groups.

% International: The percentage of students who hail from foreign soil.

# of Countries Represented: The number of different foreign countries from which the current student body hails.

Average Age of Entering Class: On the whole, how old the 1Ls are.

ACADEMICS

Academic Experience Rating: The quality of the learning environment, on a scale of 60 to 99. The rating incorporates the Admissions Selectivity Rating and the average responses of law students at the school to several questions on our law student survey. In addition to the Admissions Selectivity Rating, factors considered include how students rate the quality of teaching and the accessibility of their professors, the school's research resources, the range of available courses, the balance of legal theory and practical lawyering skills stressed in the curriculum, the tolerance for diverse opinions in the classroom, and how intellectually challenging the course work is. This individual rating places each law school on a continuum for purposes of comparing all law schools within this edition only. If a law school receives a "low" Academic Experience Rating, it doesn't mean that the school provides a bad academic experience for its students. It simply means that the school scored lower than other schools in our computations based on

> *Law School Fun Fact*
>
> The least litigated amendment in the Bill of Rights is the Third Amendment, which prohibits the quartering of soldiers in private homes without consent of the owner.

the criteria outlined above. Because this rating incorporates law student opinion data, only those law schools that appear in the section with the descriptive profiles based on student surveys receive an Academic Experience Rating.

Professors Interesting Rating: Based on law student opinion. We asked law students to rate the quality of teaching at their law schools on a scale from 60 to 99. Because this rating incorporates law student opinion data, only those law schools that appear in the section with the descriptive profiles receive a Professors Interesting Rating.

Professors Accessible Rating: Based on law student opinion. We asked law students to rate how accessible the law faculty members at their schools are on a scale from 60 to 99. Because this rating incorporates law student opinion data, only those law schools that appear in the section with the descriptive profiles receive a Professors Accessible Rating.

Hours of Study Per Day: From our student survey. The average number of hours students at the school report studying each day.

Academic Specialties: Different areas of law and academic programs on which the school prides itself.

Advanced Degrees Offered: Degrees available through the law school and the length of the program.

Combined Degrees Offered: Programs at this school involving the law school and some other college or degree program within the larger university, and how long it will take you to complete the joint program.

Grading System: Scoring system used by the law school. (Appears in the data listings section only.)

Academic Requirements: Most law schools require their students to complete some courses and/or programs that go beyond traditional legal theory, whether to broaden their understanding of and experience with the law or to develop important practical lawyering skills.

> **Clinical Program Required?** Indicates whether clinical programs are required to complete the core curriculum.
>
> **Clinical Program Description:** Programs designed to give students hands-on training and experience in the practice of some area of law. (Appears in the data listings section only.)
>
> **Legal Writing Course Requirement?** Tells you whether there is a required course in legal writing.
>
> **Legal Writing Description:** A description of any course work, required or optional, designed specifically to develop legal writing skills vital to the practice of law. (Appears in the data listings section only.)
>
> **Legal Methods Course Requirements?** Indicates whether there is a mandatory curriculum component to cover legal methods.
>
> **Legal Methods Description:** A description of any course work, required or optional, designed specifically to develop the skills vital to legal analysis. (Appears in the data listings section only.)
>
> **Legal Research Course Requirements?** If a school requires course work specifically to develop legal research skills, this field will tell you.
>
> **Legal Research Description:** A description of any course work, required or optional, designed specifically to develop legal research skills vital to the practice of law. (Appears in the data listings section only.)
>
> **Moot Court Requirement?** Indicates whether participation in a moot court program is mandatory.
>
> **Moot Court Description:** This will describe any moot court program, mandatory or optional, designed to develop skills in legal research, writing, and oral argument. (Appears in the data listings section only.)
>
> **Public Interest Law Requirement?** If a school requires participation on a public interest law project, we'll let you know here.
>
> **Public Interest Law Description:** Programs designed to expose students to the public interest law field through clinical work, volunteer opportunities, or specialized course work. (Appears in the data listings section only.)

Academic Journals: This field will list any academic journals offered at the school. (Appears in the data listings section only.)

ADMISSIONS INFORMATION

Admissions Selectivity Rating: How competitive admission is at the law school, on a scale of 60 to 99. Several factors determine this rating, including LSAT scores and the average undergraduate GPA of entering 1L students, the percentage of applicants accepted, and the percentage of accepted applicants who enrolled in the law school. We collect this information through a survey that law school administrators completed for the Fall 2009 entering class. This individual rating places each law school on a continuum for purposes of comparing all law schools within this edition only. All law schools that appear in this edition of the guide, whether in the section with the descriptive profiles based on student surveys or in the section with school-reported statistics only, receive an Admissions Selectivity Rating. If a law school has a relatively low Admissions Selectivity Rating, it doesn't necessarily mean that it's easy to gain admission to the law school. (It's not easy to get into any ABA-approved law schools, really.) It simply means that the school scored lower relative to other schools in our computations based on the criteria outlined in the previous page.

# of Applications Received: The number of people who applied to the law school's full-time JD program.

# of Applicants Accepted: The number of people who were admitted to the school's full-time class.

# of Acceptees Attending: The number of those admitted who chose to attend the school full-time.

Average LSAT/LSAT Range: Indicates the average LSAT score of incoming 1Ls, as reported by the school. The range is the 25th to 75th percentiles of 1Ls.

Average Undergrad GPA: It's usually on a 4.0 scale.

Application Fee: How much it costs to apply to the school.

> **Law School Trivia**
>
> The guarantee that each state must have an equal number of votes in the United States Senate is the only provision in the Constitution of 1787 that cannot be amended.

Regular Application Deadline and "Rolling": Many law schools evaluate applications and notify applicants of admission decisions on a continuous, rolling basis over the course of several months (ordinarily from late fall to midsummer). Obviously, if you apply to one of these schools, you want to apply early because there will be more places available at the beginning of the process.

Regular Notification? The official date by or on which a law school will release a decision for an applicant who applied using the regular admission route.

Early Application Program? Whether the law school has an early application program. If you are accepted to an early decision program, you are obligated to attend that law school. If you are accepted under an early action program, you have no obligation to attend. You just get to know earlier whether you got in.

Early Application Deadline: The official date by which the law school must receive your application if you want to be considered for its early application program.

Early Application Notification: The official date on which a law school will release a decision for an applicant who applied using the early application route.

Transfer Students Accepted? Whether transfer students from other schools are considered for admission.

Evening Division Offered? Whether the school offers an evening program in addition to its full-time regular program. Evening division programs are almost always part-time and require four years of study (instead of three) to complete.

Part-time Accepted? Whether part-time students may enroll in the JD program on a basis other than the standard full-time.

LSDAS Accepted? "Yes" indicates that the school utilizes the Law School Data Assembly Service. *Please note—the organization formerly known as Law School Data Assembly Service is now Credential Assembly Service (CAS).

Applicants Also Look At: The law schools to which applicants to this school also apply. It's important. It's a reliable indicator of the overall academic quality of the applicant pool.

INTERNATIONAL STUDENTS

TOEFL Required/Recommended of International Students? Indicates whether or not international students must take the TOEFL, or Test of English as a Foreign Language, to be admitted to the school.

Minimum TOEFL: Minimum score (paper and computer) an international student must earn on the TOEFL to be admitted.

FINANCIAL FACTS

Annual Tuition (Residents/Nonresidents): What it costs to go to school for an academic year. For state schools, both in-state and out-of-state tuition is listed.

Books and Supplies: Indicates how much students can expect to shell out for textbooks and other assorted supplies during the academic year.

Fees Per Credit (Residents/Nonresidents): That mysterious extra money you are required to pay the law school in addition to tuition and everything else, on a per-credit basis. If in-state and out-of-state students are charged differently, both amounts are listed.

Tuition Per Credit (Residents/Nonresidents): Dollar amount charged per credit hour. For state schools, both in-state and out-of-state amounts are listed when they differ.

Room and Board (On-/Off-campus): This is the school's estimate of what it costs to buy meals and to pay for decent living quarters for the academic year. Where available, on- and off-campus rates are listed.

Financial Aid Application Deadline: The last day on which students can turn in their applications for monetary assistance.

% First-Year Students Receiving Some Sort of Aid: The percentage of new JD students who receive monetary assistance.

% Receiving Some Sort of Aid: The percentage of all the students at the school presently accumulating a staggering debt.

% of Aid That Is Merit-Based: The percentage of aid not based on financial need.

% Receiving Scholarships: The percentage of students at the school who received some sort of "free money" award. This figure can include grants as well.

Average Grant: Average financial aid amount awarded to students that does not have to be paid back. This figure can include scholarships as well.

Average Loan: Average amount of loan dollars accrued by students for the year.

Average Total Aid Package: How much aid each student at the school receives on average for the year.

Average Debt: The amount of debt—or, in legal lingo, arrears—you'll likely be saddled with by the time you graduate.

EMPLOYMENT INFORMATION

Career Rating: How well the law school prepares its students for a successful career in law, on a scale of 60 to 99. The rating incorporates school-reported data and the average responses of law students at the school to a few questions on our law student survey. We ask law schools for the average starting salaries of graduating students, the percentage of graduating students who find employment after graduation, and the percentage of students who pass the bar exam the first time they take it. We ask students about how much the law program encourages practical experience; the opportunities for externships, internships, and clerkships; and how prepared to practice law they will feel after graduating. If a school receives a "low" Career Rating, it doesn't necessarily mean that the career prospects for graduates are bad; it simply means that the school scored lower relative to how other schools scored based on the criteria outlined above. Because this rating incorporates law student opinion data, only those law schools that appear in the section with the descriptive profiles receive a Career Rating.

Rate of Placement (nine months out): Percent of graduates who secured employment within nine months of graduating from law school.

Average Starting Salary: The average amount of money graduates of this law school make the first year out of school.

State for Bar Exam: The state for which most students from the school will take the bar exam.

Pass Rate for First-Time Bar: After three years, the percentage of students who passed the bar exam the first time they took it. It's a crucial statistic. You *don't* want to fail your state's bar.

Employers Who Frequently Hire Grads: Firms where past grads have had success finding jobs.

Prominent Alumni: Those who made it . . . *big*.

Grads Employed by Field: The percentage of students in the most recent graduating class who have obtained jobs in a particular field.

Academia: The percentage of graduates who got jobs at law schools, universities, and think tanks.

Business/Industry: The percentage of graduates who got jobs working in business, corporations, consulting, and so on. These jobs are sometimes law-related and sometimes not.

Government: Uncle Sam needs lawyers like you wouldn't even believe.

Judicial Clerkships: The percentage of graduates who got jobs doing research for judges.

Military: The percentage of lawyers who work to represent the Armed Forces in all kinds of legal matters, like Tom Cruise in *A Few Good Men*.

Private Practice: The percentage of graduates who got jobs in traditional law firms of various sizes or "put out a shingle" for themselves as sole practitioners.

Public Interest: The percentage of (mostly) altruistic graduates who got jobs providing legal assistance to people who couldn't afford it otherwise.

NOTA BENE

If a 60* appears for any of a law school's ratings, it means that the school's administrators did not report by our deadline all of the statistics that rating incorporates.

Please note that we target each law school for resurveying at least every other year, which means we rewrite each law school's descriptive profile at least every other year, too. Student surveys captured via our online survey (http://survey.review.com) are considered current for the purposes of our own rating, rankings, and Survey Says items for two years.

WHAT'S IN THE PROFILES: DESCRIPTIVE TEXT

Academics, Life, and Getting In Sections: The text of the descriptive profiles is broken out into three sections: Academics, Life, and Getting In. The Academics and Life sections of each descriptive profile are driven by the student survey responses collected from current law students at the school, and the quotations sprinkled throughout each of these sections come directly from the written comments students provided us with on their surveys. In the Academics section, we often discuss professors and their teaching methods, the workload, special clinical programs, the efficiency of the administration, and the helpfulness of the library staff. In the Life section, we often discuss how academically competitive the student body is, how (and if) students separate into cliques, clubs, or organizations students often join, and the amenities of the town in which the school is located. We don't follow a cookie-cutter formula when writing these profiles. Instead we rely on students' responses to the open-ended questions on our student survey and analysis of their aggregate responses to our multiple choice questions to determine each profile's major "theme." The information in the Getting In section is based on the data we collect from law school administrators and our own additional research.

DECODING DEGREES

Many law schools offer joint- or combined-degree programs with other departments (or sometimes even with other schools) that you can earn along with your Juris Doctor. You'll find the abbreviations for these degrees in the individual school profiles, but we thought we would give you a little help in figuring out exactly what they are.

AMBA	Accounting Master of Business	MEM	Master of Environmental Management
BCL	Bachelor of Civil Law	MFA	Master of Fine Arts
DJUR	Doctor of Jurisprudence	MHA	Master of Health Administration
DL	Doctor of Law	MHSA	Master of Health Services Administration
EdD	Doctor of Education	MIA	Master of International Affairs
HRIR	Human Resources and Industrial Relations	MIB	Master of International Business
IMBA	International Master of Business Administration	MIP	Master of Intellectual Property
JD	Juris Doctor	MIR	Master of Industrial Relations
JSD	Doctor of Juridical Science	MILR	Master of Industrial and Labor Relations
JSM	Master of the Science of Law	MJ	Master of Jurisprudence
LLB	Bachelor of Law	MJS	Master of Juridical Study (not a JD)
LLCM	Master of Comparative Law (for international students)	MLIR	Master of Labor and Industrial Relations
LLM	Master of Law	MLIS	Master of Library and Information Sciences
MA	Master of Arts	MLS	Master of Library Science
MAcc	Master of Accounting	MMA	Master of Marine Affairs
MALD	Master of Arts in Law and Diplomacy	MOB	Master of Organizational Behavior
MAM	Master of Arts Management	MPA	Master of Public Administration
MM	Master of Management	MPAFF	Master of Public Affairs
MANM	Master of Nonprofit Management	MPH	Master of Public Health
MAPA	Master of Public Administration	MPP	Master of Public Planning or Master of Public Policy
MAUA	Master of Arts in Urban Affairs	MPPA	Master of Public Policy
MBA	Master of Business Administration	MPPS	Master of Public Policy Sciences
MCJ	Master of Criminal Justice	MPS	Master of Professional Studies in Law
MCL	Master of Comparative Law	MRP	Master of Regional Planning
MCP	Master of Community Planning	MS	Master of Science
MCRP	Master of City and Regional Planning	MSEL	Master of Studies in Environmental Law
MDiv	Master of Divinity	MSES	Master of Science in Environmental Science
ME	Master of Engineering or Master of Education	MSF	Master of Science in Finance
MEd	Master of Education	MSFS	Master of Science in Foreign Service
MED	Master of Environmental Design	MSI	Master of Science in Information

MSIA	Master of Science in Industrial Administration
MSIE	Master of Science in International Economics
MSJ	Master of Science in Journalism
MSPH	Master of Science in Public Health
MSW	Master of Social Welfare or Master of Social Work
MT	Master of Taxation
MTS	Master of Theological Studies
MUP	Master of Urban Planning
MUPD	Master of Urban Planning and Development
MURP	Master of Urban and Regional Planning
PharmD	Doctor of Pharmacy
PhD	Doctor of Philosophy
REES	Russian and Eastern European Studies Certificate
SJD	Doctor of Juridical Science
DVM	Doctor of Veterinary Medicine
MALIR	Master of Arts in Labor and Industrial Relations

Law Schools Ranked By Category

ABOUT OUR LAW SCHOOL RANKINGS

On the following few pages, you will find eleven top ten lists of ABA-approved law schools ranked according to various metrics. It must be noted, however, that none of these lists purports to rank the law schools by their overall quality. Nor should any combination of the categories we've chosen be construed as representing the raw ingredients for such a ranking. We have made no attempt to gauge the *prestige* of these schools, and we wonder whether we could accurately do so even if we tried. What we have done, however, is presented a number of lists using information from two very large databases—one of statistical information collected from law schools and another of subjective data gathered via our survey of more than 18,000 law students at 167 ABA-approved law schools. We target each law school's student body for resurveying at least every other year. This means that schools' student opinion data is considered current for the book's rankings and descriptive profiles for two years.

Ten of the ranking lists are based partly or wholly on opinions collected through our law student survey. The only schools that may appear in these lists are the 167 ABA-approved law schools from which we were able to collect a sufficient number of student surveys to accurately represent the student experience in our various ratings and descriptive profiles.

One of the rankings, Toughest to Get Into, incorporates *only* admissions statistics reported to us by the law schools. Therefore, any ABA-approved law school appearing in this edition of the guide, whether we collected student surveys from it or not, may appear on this list.

In the 2010 edition of this book, we introduced the Best Classroom Experience list, based on student assessment of professors' teaching abilities, balance of theory and practical skills in the curricula, tolerance for differing opinions in class discussion, and classroom facilities.

Under the title of each list is an explanation of the criteria on which the ranking is based. For explanations of many of the individual rankings components, go back to page 46–49.

It's worth repeating: There is no one best law school in America, but there is a best law school for you. By using these rankings in conjunction with the descriptive profiles and data listings of the schools in this book, we hope that you will begin to identify the attributes of a law school that are important to you, as well as the law schools that can best help you to achieve your personal and professional goals.

The schools in each category appear in descending order.

TOUGHEST TO GET INTO

BASED ON THE ADMISSIONS SELECTIVITY RATING (SEE PAGE 47 FOR EXPLANATION)

1. Yale University
2. Harvard Law School
3. Stanford University
4. University of Virginia
5. University of California—Berkeley
6. Columbia University
7. University of Pennsylvania
8. University of Chicago
9. Northwestern University
10. New York University

BEST PROFESSORS

BASED ON THE PROFESSORS INTERESTING AND PROFESSORS ACCESSIBLE RATINGS (SEE PAGE 47 FOR EXPLANATIONS)

1. Boston University
2. Duke University
3. University of Chicago
4. Pepperdine University
5. University of Virginia
6. Stanford University
7. Loyola Marymount University
8. University of St. Thomas
9. Wake Forest University
10. Mercer University

MOST COMPETITIVE STUDENTS

BASED ON LAW STUDENT ASSESSMENTS OF: THE NUMBER OF HOURS THEY SPEND STUDYING OUTSIDE OF CLASS EACH DAY, THE NUMBER OF HOURS THEY THINK THEIR FELLOW LAW STUDENTS SPEND STUDYING OUTSIDE OF CLASS EACH DAY, THE DEGREE OF COMPETITIVENESS AMONG LAW STUDENTS AT THEIR SCHOOL, AND THE AVERAGE NUMBER OF HOURS THEY SLEEP EACH NIGHT

1. Baylor University
2. Brigham Young University
3. Thomas M. Cooley Law School
4. Nova Southeastern University
5. Campbell University
6. Regent University
7. Whittier College
8. Roger Williams University
9. Southern University
10. University of California, Hastings

BEST CAREER PROSPECTS

BASED ON THE CAREER RATING (SEE PAGE 49 FOR EXPLANATION)

1. Northwestern University
2. University of Chicago
3. Columbia University
4. University of California—Berkeley
5. Georgetown University
6. University of Pennsylvania
7. Vanderbilt University
8. The George Washington University
9. University of Michigan
10. New York University

BEST CLASSROOM EXPERIENCE

BASED ON STUDENT ASSESSMENT OF PROFESSORS' TEACHING ABILITIES, BALANCE OF THEORY AND PRACTICAL SKILLS IN THE CURRICULA, TOLERANCE FOR DIFFERING OPINIONS IN CLASS DISCUSSION, AND CLASSROOM FACILITIES

1. Stanford University
2. University of Virginia
3. University of Chicago
4. Duke University
5. Northwestern University
6. Boston University
7. University of Michigan
8. University of California—Los Angeles
9. Loyola Marymount University
10. Vanderbilt University

MOST CONSERVATIVE STUDENTS

BASED ON STUDENT ASSESSMENT OF THE POLITICAL BENT OF THE STUDENT BODY AT LARGE

1. Ave Maria School of Law
2. Regent University
3. Brigham Young University
4. George Mason University
5. Samford University
6. Faulkner University
7. University of Notre Dame
8. University of Idaho
9. Baylor University
10. Louisiana State University

MOST LIBERAL STUDENTS

BASED ON STUDENT ASSESSMENT OF THE POLITICAL BENT OF THE STUDENT BODY AT LARGE

1. Northeastern University
2. Vermont Law School
3. New York University
4. University of Oregon
5. American University
6. University of California—Berkeley
7. Lewis & Clark College
8. University of California—Davis
9. Brooklyn Law School
10. University of Wisconsin

BEST ENVIRONMENT FOR MINORITY STUDENTS

BASED ON THE PERCENTAGE OF THE STUDENT BODY THAT IS FROM UNDERREPRESENTED MINORITIES AND STUDENT ASSESSMENT OF WHETHER ALL STUDENTS RECEIVE EQUAL TREATMENT BY FELLOW STUDENTS AND THE FACULTY, REGARDLESS OF ETHNICITY

1. University of Hawaii—Manoa
2. Florida International University
3. Southern University
4. University of the District of Columbia
5. Santa Clara University
6. University of California—Berkeley
7. Loyola Marymount University
8. University of New Mexico
9. St. Thomas University
10. University of Southern California

MOST DIVERSE FACULTY

BASED ON THE PERCENTAGE OF THE LAW SCHOOL FACULTY THAT IS FROM A MINORITY GROUP AND STUDENT ASSESSMENT OF WHETHER THE FACULTY MAKES UP A BROADLY DIVERSE GROUP OF INDIVIDUALS

1. Southern University
2. Florida International University
3. University of the District of Columbia
4. University of Hawaii—Manoa
5. University of New Mexico
6. University of California—Davis
7. Rutgers, The State University of New Jersey—Newark
8. Georgia State University
9. Nova Southeastern University
10. University of California, Hastings

BEST QUALITY OF LIFE

BASED ON STUDENT ASSESSMENT OF: WHETHER THERE IS A STRONG SENSE OF COMMUNITY AT THE SCHOOL, HOW AESTHETICALLY PLEASING THE LAW SCHOOL IS, THE LOCATION OF THE LAW SCHOOL, THE QUALITY OF THE SOCIAL LIFE, CLASSROOM FACILITIES, AND THE LIBRARY STAFF

1. Duke University
2. University of Virginia
3. Chapman University
4. Vanderbilt University
5. Northwestern University
6. University of Colorado
7. University of Memphis
8. Samford University
9. University of Denver
10. Stanford University

MOST CHOSEN BY OLDER STUDENTS

BASED ON THE AVERAGE AGE OF ENTRY OF LAW SCHOOL STUDENTS AND STUDENT REPORTS OF HOW MANY YEARS THEY SPENT OUT OF COLLEGE BEFORE ENROLLING IN LAW SCHOOL

1. University of New Mexico
2. Seattle University
3. Campbell University
4. State University of New York—University at Buffalo
5. University of the District of Columbia
6. The University of South Dakota
7. William Mitchell College of Law
8. University of Maine
9. University of Idaho
10. New England Law | Boston

LAW SCHOOL DESCRIPTIVE PROFILES

In this section you will find the two page descriptive profile of each of the 167 ABA-approved law schools. As there are currently a total of 200 ABA-approved law schools in the country, there are obviously many law schools not appearing in this section; those schools appear in the following section, Law School Data Listings.

In order for a law school to appear in this section, we had to collect the opinions of a sufficient number of current law students at that school to fairly and responsibly represent the general law student experience there. Our descriptive profiles are driven primarily by (1) comments law students provide in response to open-ended questions on our student survey, and (2) our own statistical analysis of student responses to the many multiple-choice questions on the survey. While many law students complete a survey unsolicited by us at http://survey.review.com, in the vast majority of cases we rely on law school administrators to get the word out about our survey to their students. In an ideal scenario, the law school administration e-mails a Princeton Review–authored e-mail to all law students with an embedded link to our survey website (again, http://survey.review.com). If for some reason there are restrictions that prevent the administration from contacting the entire law student body on behalf of an outside party, they often help us find other ways to notify students that we are seeking their opinions, like advertising in law student publications or posting on law student community websites or electronic mailing lists. In almost all cases, when the administration is cooperative, we are able to collect opinions from a sufficient number of students to produce an accurate descriptive profile and ratings of its law school.

There is a group of law school administrators, however, that doesn't agree with the notion that the opinions of current law students presented in descriptive profile and rankings formats are useful to prospective law school students trying to choose the right schools to apply to and attend. Administrators at the twenty-three ABA-approved law schools not appearing in this section are a part of this group. They either ignored our multiple attempts to contact them to request their assistance in notifying their students about our survey, or they simply refused to work with us at all. While we would like to be able to write a descriptive profile on each of these twenty-three schools anyway, we won't do so with minimal law student opinion. So if you are a prospective law school student and would like to read the opinions of current law students about your dream school(s), contact the missing school(s) and communicate this desire to them. (We include contact information in each of the data listings.) If you are a current law student at one of the twenty-three ABA-approved law schools not profiled in this section, please don't send us angry letters; instead, go to http://survey.review.com, complete a survey about your school, and tell all of your fellow students to do the same. If we collect enough current student opinion on your school in the coming year, we'll include a descriptive profile in the next edition of the guide.

SPECIAL NOTE ON THE TEXT OF EACH DESCRIPTIVE PROFILE
The Academics and Life sections of each descriptive profile are driven by the student opinions collected from current law students at the school, and the quotations sprinkled throughout each of these sections comes directly from the written comments with which students provided us on their surveys. The Getting In section is based on the data we collect from law school administrators and our own additional research. Every law school with a descriptive profile has its students resurveyed and its profile rewritten at least every other year.

SPECIAL NOTE ON THE SIDEBAR STATISTICS
Explanations of what each field of data signifies may be found in the How to Use This Book section, which begins on page 45.

ALBANY LAW SCHOOL

Academics

One of the main benefits of going to law school in New York's capital city is "access... to New York government jobs (most importantly, clerkships with federal and state courts)." Albany's geographical advantage adds to the strength of its clinical programs and Government Law Center, and the moot court and journal programs are "well-structured and worth participating in." The school's clinic and placement office is similarly "outstanding," and "can put you in just about any legal environment where you can work, learn, and earn academic credit." Albany students easily branch out to New York City or Boston for summer internships, but "You can't beat the law-student-thrill of begin able to walk up to the highest court in New York, the Court of Appeals, and then walk down two blocks to find yourself at the federal Appellate courthouse."

The school offers many specialties (including health, environmental, and governmental law), as well as an abundance of "practical courses," but students say it "needs to focus on writing skills after first year" and consistency of student skills throughout the years. Many students also claim that some of the course requirements are too restrictive (such as the international law course requirement), and the school could stand a return to form in the focus on bar passage, which "previously was one of their strongest recruiting points," but now has dropped to more average rates. The jury's still out on some of the school's other modifications—the school has recently been experimenting with curriculum mapping, offering differing course loads for the first and second semesters for first-year students, and eliminating the pass/fail option for classes.

Faculty and staff are "the best part of this school," and display "extreme help and openness" with students, particularly during the first year. "There are some incredible, pedigreed professors at this school," says a student, and almost all "are able to take their genius and make it relatable and teachable in the classroom." Adapting to a professor's teaching style, attitude, and methods of grading "are critical to success in law school." "I have had professors that inspire me to learn through their own enjoyment of the field, and I've also had teachers that motivate me to learn through fear of being called on." Overall, the faculty is "approachable," and makes it clear that they "really want you to understand the material and do well in their courses." On the other hand, the executive administration "has illustrated a decided lack of desire to listen to the staff and faculty," though the current administration is expected to change soon. Still, even this hiccup "does not sully the amazing experience students have in every other aspect." Rather, "It brings the students together as an unfortunate reason to bond."

Life

The student body is "competitive but friendly, at Albany and "relations among students are generally very strong." "It's not like people hide books or anything," says a 2L. Listserv usage for "fighting out issues" is also expressly banned, contributing to a general harmony among students. "I would say that the crowd nowadays is more on the conservative side politically, but the liberal side socially," says a 2L.

GAIL BENSEN, DIRECTOR OF ADMISSIONS
80 NEW SCOTLAND AVENUE, ALBANY, NY 12208
TEL: 518-445-2326 FAX: 518-445-2369
E-MAIL: ADMISSIONS@ALBANYLAW.EDU • WEBSITE: WWW.ALBANYLAW.EDU

Speaking of social lives, although students are "very busy," there is ample opportunity for socializing "if you make it a priority." Many claim that Albany Law "is like high school," but few complain about a campus where "smallish cliques are the norm," as the social life is "great" and "people are free to interact with multiple cliques, and those groups often get together to form a whole." There are many student organizations to join if one is inclined, though with many students commuting, they're not as popular as some would like.

Albany, as a city, "is pretty dingy and small," with its fair share of "crime in the city limits." For this reason, many students choose to live outside the city limits and commute (which amounts to only a fifteen-minute drive). Students still often choose to walk around Albany at night, though "There are several colleges and universities [nearby], and so the police chaperone as necessary." Unlike many law schools, parking is not too much of a problem at Albany Law, even for a city campus. "Commuting to internships (even at rush hour) is never problematic," says a student. Overall, the facilities are "well-maintained and look great," and a nice bonus is that the law school is entirely self-contained, with library access in the main classroom building. "It is much appreciated when you need a quiet place to sit with only an hour in between classes and when it's too cold to want to walk outside to get to another building."

Getting In

Admissions officers at Albany Law School consider students' undergraduate GPA, rigor of study, and LSAT scores when evaluating applicants for admission. Students admitted into Albany Law School post an average LSAT score of 155 and average GPA of 3.3. Those students admitted at the 75th percentile have average LSAT scores of 156 and GPAs of 3.56.

Clinical program required	No
Legal writing course requirement	Yes
Legal methods course requirement	Yes
Legal research course requirement	Yes
Moot court requirement	No
Public interest law requirement	No

ADMISSIONS

Selectivity Rating	78
# applications received	2,081
% applicants accepted	41
% acceptees attending	29
Average LSAT	155
LSAT Range	152–158
Average undergrad GPA	3.22
Application fee	$60
Regular application	Rolling, up to 3/15
Early application program	No
Transfer students accepted	Yes
Evening division offered	No
Part-time accepted	No
CAS accepted	Yes

International Students

TOEFL required of international students	

FINANCIAL FACTS

Annual tuition	$32,360
Books and supplies	$900
% first-year students receiving some sort of aid	98
% receiving some sort of aid	90
% of aid that is merit based	89
% receiving scholarships	31
Average grant	$15,337
Average loan	$31,163
Average total aid package	$36,650
Average debt	$80,000

EMPLOYMENT INFORMATION

Career Rating	80	**Grads Employed by Field (%)**
Rate of placement (nine months out)	91	Academic (2)
Average starting salary	$53,276	Business/industry (17)
State for bar exam	NY	Government (15)
Pass rate for first-time bar	78	Judicial clerkship (6)

Employers Who Frequently Hire Grads
Military (1)

Private law firms, government agencies, business and industry, high-tech industry, corporations

Private practice (57)

Public interest (2)

Prominent Alumni
Thomas Vilsack, U.S. Secretary of Agriculture; Richard D. Parsons, Chairman, CitiGroup; Andrew Cuomo, New York Governor; Victoria Graffeo, Associate Justice, New York State Court of Appeals

AMERICAN UNIVERSITY
WASHINGTON COLLEGE OF LAW

INSTITUTIONAL INFORMATION

Public/private	Private
Student/faculty ratio	14:1
% faculty part-time	59
% faculty female	39
% faculty minority	17
Total faculty	214

SURVEY SAYS...

Diverse opinions accepted in classrooms, Abundant externship/ internship/clerkship opportunities, Liberal students

STUDENTS

Enrollment of law school	1,461
% male/female	44/56
% full-time	85
% minority	35
% international	2
# of countries represented	29
Average age of entering class	24

ACADEMICS

Academic Experience Rating	**82**
Profs interesting rating	79
Profs accessible rating	70
Hours of study per day	5.54

Academic Specialties

Commercial, Corporation Securities, Environmental, Government Services, Human Rights, International, Intellectual Property

Advanced Degrees Offered

LLM, International Legal Studies, 12–18 months; LLM, Law and Government, 12 months; SJD, 3–4 years

Combined Degrees Offered

JD/MBA, JD/MA International Affairs, JD/MS Justice, JD/MPA, JD/ MPP, 3.5–4 years; LLM/MBA,LLM/ MPA, LLM/MPP, 2–3 years

Academics

American University's Washington College of Law is an "amazing place" for "public interest law." Students appreciate the "full-tuition scholarship" offered to "ten students every year with a dedicated commitment to social justice work." Adding to the school's civic focus, the issue of international human rights "seems to pervade nearly everything the school does." Also, "The range of courses relating to governmental ideas cannot be matched." "If you have any interest in government, come to this law school," says one student. "An abundance" of "research opportunities," several "excellent study abroad opportunities," and "great clinical programs" are lauded with praise. "The opportunities for internships and externships" in the District of Columbia's courts, government agencies, and nonprofit sector "far exceed those offered by law schools in any other city."

Students note, "Teachers really run the gamut" and "some are very eccentric," but many reports echo the opinion of one student, who says, "Overall I have really liked most of my teachers and feel I have gotten a really good education." An "an amazing open-door policy" permeates WCL. There are many "captivating," "extraordinary teachers" who are "very good at relating their subject matter to social-justice issues." This faculty includes "attorneys on famous cases, a Supreme Court clerk, Ivy League grads, prominent scholars, and even a Jeopardy contestant." Professors here are also "astoundingly liberal." "My professors range between gay-rights-feminist activists and critical-race-theorist-anti-death-penalty activists," comments a 2L.

Though "far from first-rate," WCL's facilities "are more than sufficient." A student explains, "We're starting to outgrow our building, so sometimes space is tight." The "cramped" library is "often crowded and loud." The e-mail program "could be more sophisticated" and "wireless Internet is intermittent, at best." However, "The library and some other offices have received makeovers lately," and the "clean and large" classrooms offer "plenty of space, as well as sufficient electrical outlets to accommodate the many laptops that students have."

All in all, "The school functions fairly smoothly." The administration is "very student-focused" though also "Byzantine" at times. The financial aid staff could stand "to improve communication." The Office of Career Development gets mixed reviews. "Perhaps the top third get interviews" at "mid-size firms" in "the Mid-Atlantic region." "About the top fifteen percent of students have a chance of being selected for on-campus interviews with the major international law firms," says a student. Another notes, "While George Washington is proclaimed to be so much better, every job I've had has been with GW students, so I have no idea what they are doing that we aren't."

Life

WCL is "pretty big." There is "a diverse student body" here "with differing nationalities, opinions, and goals." "There is really every kind of person at WCL, for better or worse," remarks a 2L. "I think generally for the better." Many students "have spent a year or two between law school (or more) doing really fascinating things with their lives." These "extremely intelligent" students "are still idealistic and strive to make the law a better profession and our society a better society." "A lot of students are very politically active." Several "used to work on the Hill." There is "a slight hippy streak," and "Everyone has a cause." Some lament that "The aura of political correctness can be a bit suffocating at times."

AKIRA SHIROMA, ASSISISTANT DEAN OF ADMISSIONS AND FINANCIAL AID
4801 MASSACHUSETTS AVENUE, NW, WASHINGTON, D.C. 20016
TEL: 202-274-4101 FAX: 202-274-4107
E-MAIL: WCLADMIT@WCL.AMERICAN.EDU • WEBSITE: WWW.WCL.AMERICAN.EDU

Academically, though "somewhat of a competitive edge" is "lurking underneath," the atmosphere "isn't hyper-competitive." In fact, WCL is a "very friendly place" full of "genuinely nice people." There is "lots of sharing of notes and outlines." "There is an incredible sense of camaraderie," reports one student. Students are also "incredibly involved with the community." There is an "array" of guest lectures and symposia "every day" and "more academic activities than you could ever attend." "I have had many opportunities to meet students at American through clubs, activities, and community service projects," beams a 3L.

Students think that "it's great that [the school] is in D.C." but say that "for being in D.C.," WCL "has a terrible location." Getting to and from campus can be "difficult" and "time-consuming," meaning at times "It very much feels like a commuter school." In addition, students report, "No taxicabs pass by the school when you're in a pinch." The closest subway station "is slightly over a mile away (though "there is a free shuttle that goes directly to the law school)." Parking remains "an ongoing struggle," especially for 1Ls. (For 2Ls and 3Ls, there is "a garage underneath the building"). On the bright side, "There are a lot of ways to cheat the system" if you drive. "Everyone has all the nooks and crannies figured out."

Getting In

Admitted students at the 25th percentile have LSAT scores of 160 and GPAs of about 3.14. Admitted students at the 75th percentile have LSAT scores of 163 and GPAs of 3.60. WCL says that it considers your highest score if you take the LSAT more than once.

Clinical program required	No
Legal writing course requirement	Yes
Legal methods course requirement	No
Legal research course requirement	Yes
Moot court requirement	No
Public interest law requirement	No

ADMISSIONS

Selectivity Rating	91
# applications received	7,512
% applicants accepted	21
% acceptees attending	24
Average LSAT	162
LSAT Range	160–163
Average undergrad GPA	3.41
Application fee	$70
Regular application	Rolling, up to 3/1
Regular notification	Rolling
Early application program	Yes
Early application deadline	11/13
Early application notification	12/20
Transfer students accepted	Yes
Evening division offered	Yes
Part-time accepted	Yes
CAS accepted	Yes

FINANCIAL FACTS

Annual tuition	$38,652
Books and supplies	$6,569
Fees	$750
Room and board	$13,948
Financial aid application deadline	3/1
% first-year students receiving some sort of aid	84
% receiving some sort of aid	89
% of aid that is merit based	9
% receiving scholarships	25
Average grant	$14,483
Average loan	$42,120
Average total aid package	$50,626
Average debt	$112,276

EMPLOYMENT INFORMATION

Career Rating	89
Rate of placement (nine months out)	95
Average starting salary	$92,000
State for bar exam	MD, NY
Pass rate for first-time bar	83

Employers Who Frequently Hire Grads
Akin Gump Strauss Hauer & Feld LLP; Arent Fox PLLC; Arnold & Porter LLP; Bingham McCutchen LLP; Cadwalader, Wickersham & Taft LLP; Dickstein, Shapiro LLP; Federal Communications Commission; Federal Election Commission; Federal Energy Regulatory Commission; Federal Trade Commission; Finnegan, Henderson, Farabow, Garrett & Dunner, LLP ; Hogan & Hartson LLP; Jones Day; Latham & Watkins LLP; Mayer Brown LLP; Skadden, Arps, Slate, Meagher & Flom LLP & Affiliates; Shearman & Sterling LLP; Sonnenschein Nath & Rosenthal LLP; U.S. Department of Commerce; U.S. Department of Justice; U.S. Securities and Exchange Commission; White & Case LLP

Prominent Alumni
Benjamin R. Jacobs, Managing Partner, The JBG Companies; Peter Sher, Managing Partner, Mayer Brown; Pamela Deese, Partner, Arent Fox; Hon. Gerald Lee, U.S. District Court Judge; Carol Sadler, Senior Vice President, General Counsel, Coach

Grads Employed by Field (%)
Academic (1)
Business/industry (12)
Government (14)
Judicial clerkship (12)
Military (1)
Private practice (50)
Public interest (10)

APPALACHIAN SCHOOL OF LAW

INSTITUTIONAL INFORMATION

Public/private	Private
Student/faculty ratio	20:1
% faculty female	45
% faculty minority	20
Total faculty	20

SURVEY SAYS...

Diverse opinions accepted in classrooms, Great research resources, Great library staff, Students never sleep

STUDENTS

Enrollment of law school	364
% male/female	62/38
% full-time	98
% minority	9

ACADEMICS

Academic Experience Rating	61
Profs interesting rating	61
Profs accessible rating	64

Academic Specialties

Alternate Dispute Resolution

Advanced Degrees Offered

JD, 3 years

Clinical program required	Yes
Legal writing course requirement	Yes
Legal methods course requirement	Yes
Legal research course requirement	Yes
Moot court requirement	Yes

Academics

The Appalachian School of Law is a young, private institution, organized in 1994 and given full accreditation from the American Bar Association in 2006. The traditional-looking campus is very beautiful and the library is "new." Wireless Internet access is available and, in recent years, "The technology aspect of the Law School has shown a significant improvement."

Students report that "trial advocacy training," "moot court programs," and other "practical courses" are "first rate" at ASL. The mock trial team "has trounced big names" in national competitions. "The law school's emphasis on practical legal skills has thoroughly prepared me for everyday situations in the general practice of law," says a 3L. "I will graduate and know what to do in a courtroom besides espouse constitutional theory with opposing counsel at lunch." Appalachian also "distinguishes itself from the majority of other law schools by requiring 150 hours of community service." A summer externship is also "required of all first-year students." "The community-service requirement promotes student involvement in law school organizations, benefits the community, and strengthens the reputations of both ASL and the legal profession in general," explains one student. "The summer externship program provides all rising 2Ls with the opportunity to apply the knowledge they gained from first-year classes to real-life situations." There is also a "mandatory alternative dispute resolution requirement," though the school seems keener on this than the students.

The "knowledgeable" and "very approachable" professors here are "down-to-earth people who have a wide variety of legal experience" and "extensive practical and theoretical knowledge of the subjects they teach." Their dedication means that "they are exceptionally concerned with bar passage" and always "available outside of the classroom." "My experience at the Appalachian School of Law has been nothing short of exceptional," confides one student. "The teachers love interacting with the students and are our greatest cheerleaders, mentors, and leaders." "Faculty turnover" has been a problem, though. The "remote location" is "not the most appealing place" for academics to "hang their hats for the long term." However, "The town and area are progressing."

Students tell us that "the greatest strength" of their law school is its "concern and respect for students as individuals." "The administration, faculty, staff, and students have created a community where you can receive an excellent legal education in the midst of the natural beauty of the Appalachian Mountains," explains one student. However, there is a "communication gap between students and administration," meaning that "it often takes days to cut through whatever hidden red tape or underlying ineptness or unwillingness exists." "The administration is very unpredictable" as well. "I realize every new school needs to work out its quirks, but ASL especially needs to do so," gripes one student. Career Services could stand to be "more active," and there seems to be a revolving door regarding deans. "The school appears to promote diversity among our deans with the tenure running about a dean a year," observes a wry 2L.

NANCY PRUITT, ADMISSIONS COUNSELORS
P.O. BOX 2825, GRUNDY, VA 24614
TEL: 276-935-4349 FAX: 276-935-8261
E-MAIL: ASLINFO@ASL.EDU • WEBSITE: WWW.ASL.EDU

Life

Grundy is a "small community" located near the convergence of Virginia, Kentucky, and West Virginia. "You can't go to the grocery store without seeing another law student." "The remote location of the school" helps to make "studying is [the] number-one priority." One student explains, "There's nothing to do but study in Grundy, so I went from a below-average college student to above average," adds a proud 3L. "I will probably graduate with honors. I'm not so sure that's [because] of the law school itself…[or] the general area."

Town-gown relations are strained. "There is some resentment from locals toward law students and vice versa," most agree. "The rugged, desolate terrain" and "isolation" lead students to say that "Appalachian could benefit from more things to do in Grundy outside of law school activities." Students lament that "there isn't a bar or club in the town" where they could "relieve stress and get a drink." (In fact, there is "no liquor by the drink in the county.") "The three-screen movie theater is the most diversion many will get," says one student. That said, people here take a DIY approach to entertainment and "typically find or make [their] own fun to blow off the steam and stress of law school." "A culture of frugal bacchanalia persists in the form of student-hosted house parties." When cabin fever sets in, students take "sojourns" to the nearest bigger cities, "both of which are over the mountains and about forty-five minutes away."

Not surprisingly, "You definitely develop a sense of family with the law school students and faculty." "The law students are a very tight-knit group," though beware as "gossip flourishes" and "everyone's life is an open book." "With scant few exceptions, the student body is Caucasian." Most students would like to see "diversity promoted" at ALS, feeling that "out in town" "underlying discrimination" exists "based on race, sexual orientation, socioeconomic status, and even geographic origin."

Getting In

Appalachian Law School's admitted students at the 25th percentile have LSAT scores of 146 and GPAs of 2.60. Admitted students at the 75th percentile have LSAT scores of 152 and GPAs of 3.30.

ADMISSIONS

Selectivity Rating	70
# applications received	990
% applicants accepted	46
% acceptees attending	32
Average LSAT	148
LSAT Range	146–152
Average undergrad GPA	2.80
Application fee	$50
Regular application	Rolling
Regular notification	Rolling
Early application program	No
Transfer students accepted	Yes
Evening division offered	No
Part-time accepted	No
CAS accepted	Yes

FINANCIAL FACTS

Annual tuition	$19,900
Books and supplies	$2,500
Room and board	$12,295
% receiving some sort of aid	64
Average grant	$6,468
Average loan	$21,372

EMPLOYMENT INFORMATION

Career Rating	71	**Grads Employed by Field (%)**
Average starting salary	$45,000	Business/industry (11)
State for bar exam	VA, TN, KY, NC, WV	Judicial clerkship (19)
Pass rate for first-time bar	52	Private practice (69)

Arizona State University
Sandra Day O'Connor College of Law

INSTITUTIONAL INFORMATION

Public/private	Public
Student/faculty ratio	9:1
% faculty part-time	29
% faculty female	28
% faculty minority	9
Total faculty	100

SURVEY SAYS...

Diverse opinions accepted in classrooms, Great research resources, Great library staff, Abundant externship/internship/ clerkship opportunities, Students love Tempe, AZ

STUDENTS

Enrollment of law school	614
% male/female	56/44
% from out-of-state	28
% full-time	100
% minority	24
% international	1
# of countries represented	12
Average age of entering class	26

ACADEMICS

Academic Experience Rating	88
Profs interesting rating	83
Profs accessible rating	81
Hours of study per day	4.75

Academic Specialties

International, Legal Philosophy, Intellectual Property; Certificates Indian Law, Environmental, Health Care, Genomics & Biotechnology, Intellectual Property, Law, Pyschology

Advanced Degrees Offered

LLM in biotechnology/genomics, 1–3 years; LLM in tribal policy, law, and government, 1–3 years; LLM in global legal studies, 1–3 years; customized LLM, 1–3 years; MLS, 1–3 years

Combined Degrees Offered

JD/MBA, 4 years; JD/PhD Psychology, approximately 7 years; JD/PhD Justice & Social Inquiry;

Academics

The College of Law at Arizona State University is a smaller law school with smaller classes where "you get a lot of personal attention." At the same time, "The range of courses is extensive." The Indian Legal Program here is one of the finest of its kind in the country. Another point of pride is the Law, Science, and Technology Center, which—not very surprisingly—concentrates on the intersection between law and science. Hands-on opportunities to "get real-world experience in nearly any legal field" are abundant. Seven clinics allow students "to employ lawyer[ing] skills instead of just talking about it or writing legal memos," and virtually every student who wants to participate in a clinic can participate. There are "almost too many opportunities for externships" with judges, legislative offices, and administrative agencies, observes one awed student. The faculty at ASU is "a wide mix of both hardscrabble, old-school courtroom warriors, and young, innovative minds." There are a lot of adjunct faculty members "who enjoy teaching and who bring real practical experience into the classroom" as well. Most professors are "very accessible and happy to help." "They enjoy getting to know students outside of the classroom." Inside the classroom, "professors use the Socratic Method mostly, but not in a scary way." The focus is "more on teaching relevant materials than playing games with students." "Although the material is sometimes as dry as the Arizona desert, the teachers do a great job [of] keeping the class interesting." "I could not have asked for better professors my first semester," beams a 1L. A few students tell us that the administration is "only concerned with raising ASU's ranking" but the overwhelming sentiment is that the top brass is "visionary" and "extremely responsive." The law school staff as a whole is "totally" approachable and "wonderful to work with at every level" (though it's a much different story when you are "forced to deal with the red tape of the general university").

Students here have "amazing access" to the Phoenix legal market and Career Services "will bend over back[ward] for you to help you make contacts in the job market." Students also point out that for better or for worse, they are "bombarded with opportunities to meet with practicing attorneys." Opinions concerning the portability of an ASU degree are decidedly split, though. Some students say it's very easy if you want to work in another state upon graduation. "ASU law degrees actually travel quite well and are respected throughout the United States," boasts a confident 1L. Others disagree. "ASU is well-known in Arizona but needs to gain more national prominence," they say. "If you want to work anywhere out of Arizona, the degree doesn't travel well."

Some of ASU's facilities are "old and outdated." Classrooms are "uncomfortable and downright backwoods when it comes to technological integration." "It would be nice if they took down the paneling from the 1970s," too. The "well-equipped" law library is "pretty nice," though. It's relatively new and it's "state-of-the-art in its technology and environment." In addition to four floors of study space, there's an all-night study room that allows students to come as late or early as they please and stay as long as they want. "I have never had a problem finding a quiet place to study," notes a 1L.

Shelli Soto, Associate Dean for Admissions and Financial Aid
1100 S. McAllister Ave., P.O. Box 877906, Tempe, AZ 85287-7906
Tel: 480-965-1474 Fax: 480-727-7930
E-Mail: law.admissions@asu.edu • Website: www.law.asu.edu

Life

Students describe the academic atmosphere at ASU as "competitive but not overly combative." It's "enough to motivate, but not intolerable." Students are "focused on studies when they need to be," but they "study together, share outlines, and generally help each other." "Courses are tough but the atmosphere is upbeat and actually fun." "The Tempe sunshine makes us friendlier," suggests a 1L. The law school is located on ASU's main campus in a "suburban" part of the fast-growing Phoenix metro area. This "extremely active" law student population is "a mix of students living in Tempe and commuter students." "Students who are married live a little farther away from campus," explains a 3L. "However, most law students only a few years removed from undergrad tend to live very close to campus and are very involved in extracurriculars and other student organizations." Social events are "frequent." "There are opportunities to party, but not the pressure to." "Intramurals are a great way to blow off steam" as well, and if you are an outdoorsy type, "There is always stuff to do" in the vicinity all year round. "Almost always, some club or activity is providing lunch for us," notes a sated 1L. There's "a very stimulating, steady stream of speakers on a variety of legal topics." Also, students can take advantage of all the "opportunities to get involved" on one of the largest public university campuses in the country.

Getting In

The numbers speak for themselves at Arizona State's Sandra Day O'Conner School of Law. Enrolled students at the 25th percentile have an LSAT score of 158 and a GPA of roughly 3.3. Enrolled students at the 75th percentile have an LSAT score of 164 and a GPA of 3.8 or so. If you find yourself somewhere within these two ranges, you've got a fair chance of gaining admission.

JD/MD with Mayo Clinic, approximately 6 years

Clinical program required	No
Legal writing course requirement	Yes
Legal methods course requirement	Yes
Legal research course requirement	Yes
Moot court requirement	Yes
Public interest law requirement	No

ADMISSIONS

Selectivity Rating	89
# applications received	2,457
% applicants accepted	24
% acceptees attending	32
Average LSAT	161
LSAT Range	158–164
Average undergrad GPA	3.54
Application fee	$60
Regular application	Rolling, up to 2/1
Regular notification	Rolling
Early application program	Yes
Early application deadline	11/15
Early application notification	1/31
Transfer students accepted	Yes
Evening division offered	No
Part-time accepted	No
CAS accepted	Yes

International Students

TOEFL required of international students	

FINANCIAL FACTS

Annual tuition (in-state/out-of-state)	$21,259/ $34,808
Books and supplies	$1,850
Fees	$339
Room and board	$11,700
Financial aid application deadline	3/1
% first-year students receiving some sort of aid	92
% receiving some sort of aid	95
% of aid that is merit based	69
% receiving scholarships	50
Average grant	$10,950
Average loan	$34,831
Average total aid package	$37,397
Average debt	$89,038

EMPLOYMENT INFORMATION

Career Rating	89
Rate of placement (nine months out)	99
Average starting salary	$80,850
State for bar exam	AZ
Pass rate for first-time bar	89

Employers Who Frequently Hire Grads

Snell & Wilmer; Perkins Coie; Bryan Cave; Gammage & Birnham; Lewis and Roca; Fennemore Craig; Jennings, Strouss & Salmon; Gallagher & Kennedy; Quarles & Brady Streich Lang; Ryley Carlock & Applewhite; Steptoe Johnson; Mariscal Weeks; Meyer Hendricks; Osborn Maledon; Squires, Sanders & Dempsey; federal, state, and county government

Prominent Alumni

Dan Burk, Oppenheimer Wolff & Donnelly Professor, UMinn Law; Rebecca Berch, Chief Justice, Arizona State Supreme Court; Barry Silverman, U.S. Court of Appeals for the Ninth Circuit; Ed Pastor, U.S. House of Representatives; Joe Sims, Partner, Jones Day, Washington, D.C.

Grads Employed by Field (%)

Academic (4)
Business/industry (11)
Government (11)
Judicial clerkship (7)
Military (3)
Private practice (53)
Public interest (11)

AVE MARIA SCHOOL OF LAW

Academics

ABA-accredited law schools don't often pick up and transport themselves to locations hundreds of miles away. But that's exactly what Ave Maria School of Law did in 2009, relocating from Ann Arbor, Michigan, to Naples, Florida (and not just because of the weather). While the move was not without controversy, students call it "a successful transition." For one thing, the weather is a whole lot warmer and sunnier. Florida's outlook for economic growth appears much brighter, too. Also, southwest Florida is a better fit for Ave Maria's unswerving fidelity to the tenets of the Catholic faith. Ave Maria is "a real Catholic law school" with a "conservative perspective"—"one of the few schools in the nation that could be called right of center." Students call the curriculum "particularly rigorous." In addition to the standard array of first-year course work that you'll find at any law school, 1Ls here must take a course called Moral Foundations of the Law. Students should expect to take a few more ethics-related courses during their second and third years as well. This is because "having morals and great ethics is a top priority here." "Ave Maria does not pull any punches about its Catholic identity," explains a 3L, "and that lends itself particularly well to relevant discussions about contemporary moral and political issues." At the same time, there's a strong focus "on the practical aspect of law." Ave Maria "incorporates the Catholic intellectual tradition in a way that allows students to understand and practically apply such principles into the legal environment."

Students are pretty effusive in their praise of their "knowledgeable, approachable, and fair" faculty. Professors are "delightful to have for class." "They use a balance between the Socratic Method and voluntary student interaction." While "they won't coddle you," they are "dedicated to educating and availing themselves [for] the aid of students." "Our professors know who we are and try to help us overcome our weaknesses and improve on our strengths," gushes a 1L. "It is an amazing environment [in which] to learn very challenging material." Some students call the administration "very open." Others tell us that the top brass is "aloof" and "unreliable at best." One student also gripes that "financial aid is a 'bear' to work with." On the upside, Ave Maria's campus is "beautiful." However, students say it can feel a bit "cramped," and note that there are "very limited facilities." The campus' new location in Naples, Florida, means that virtually all the opportunities to work at law firms in the region belong to Ave Maria students. There's not much competition from other schools because there aren't any other law schools in the immediate vicinity. "I find that many people in this area of southwest Florida have heard of Ave Maria and there is less of a need to 'sell' ourselves to the job world," relates a 3L. Also worth noting is the fact that graduates of Ave Maria have successfully fanned out all over the country.

Life

"Many of the students here are from out of state." Around forty states (and a handful of foreign countries) are represented among these future lawyers, in fact. Catholicism is unmistakably a very big deal at Ave Maria and there are some deeply religious students among the student body. However, students are quick to remind us that there are "tons of non-Catholics" as well. Some students say that "The student body is, as a whole, very conservative." They contend that the milieu tends "to prevent any thorough and fair presentation of opposing opinions or viewpoints." Others maintain "Many students are actually pro-choice, liberal, and apolitical." "There is tolerance for all religions, or no religion." Politics "is not something most are bothered by." "I am not Catholic," relates a

MONIQUE MCCARTHY, ASSISTANT DEAN FOR ADMISSIONS
1025 COMMONS CIRCLE, NAPLES, FL 34119
TEL: 239-687-5300 FAX: 239-352-2890
E-MAIL: INFO@AVEMARIALAW.EDU • WEBSITE: WWW.AVEMARIALAW.EDU

3L, "but I feel my beliefs are accepted and that I can engage in conversations not specifically related to the Catholic position that are well-received. "The academic atmosphere is highly spirited but basically cooperative. "We are very competitive with one another," says a 1L. "However, most of us also want to see our classmates succeed." "One of the greatest strengths of Ave Maria Law is the friendly and helpful atmosphere among its students." Beyond academics, "a large number" of clubs and organizations keep students busy. They also get to live in "the most beautiful city in the world." It's "really like paradise," they say, especially if you like shopping or golf. Another advantage is the fact that the Gulf of Mexico is just minutes away from campus. "Sand always gets in my textbooks when studying on the beach," a satisfied 1L needles.

Getting In

It's not tremendously difficult to get admitted to Ave Maria, as far as law school admissions go. The average GPA of entering students was 3.22 with an average LSAT score of 151. Find yourself within this ballpark, and you've got a pretty good shot.

ADMISSIONS

Selectivity Rating	69
# applications received	1,981
% applicants accepted	47
% acceptees attending	22
Average LSAT	150
LSAT Range	147–153
Average undergrad GPA	3.11
Application fee	$50
Regular application	Rolling, up to 7/1
Regular notification	Rolling
Early application program	No
Transfer students accepted	Yes
Evening division offered	No
Part-time accepted	No
CAS accepted	Yes

International Students

TOEFL required of international students	

FINANCIAL FACTS

Annual tuition	$35,948
Books and supplies	$1,500
Fees	$500
Room and board	$13,131
Financial aid application deadline	6/1
% first-year students receiving some sort of aid	90
% receiving some sort of aid	90
% of aid that is merit based	17
% receiving scholarships	44
Average grant	$16,318
Average loan	$40,810
Average total aid package	$57,447
Average debt	$87,337

EMPLOYMENT INFORMATION

Career Rating	73
Rate of placement (nine months out)	65
State for bar exam	FL, TX, MI, NY, IL

Employers Who Frequently Hire Grads
Federal, state, and trial court judges; United States Military (JAG), the federal government, local public defender and prosecutor's offices, small firms throughout the country, in-house corporate legal departments, nonprofit and legal aid organizations

Grads Employed by Field (%)
Academic (6)
Business/industry (16)
Government (4)
Judicial clerkship (4)
Military (4)
Private practice (29)
Public interest (2)

BAYLOR UNIVERSITY
SCHOOL OF LAW

INSTITUTIONAL INFORMATION

Public/private	Private
Affiliation	Baptist
Total faculty	46

SURVEY SAYS...

Heavy use of Socratic Method,
Great research resources,
Beautiful campus

STUDENTS

Enrollment of law school	465
% male/female	53/47
% from out-of-state	20
% full-time	100
% minority	21
# of countries represented	1
Average age of entering class	23

ACADEMICS

Academic Experience Rating	82
Profs interesting rating	78
Profs accessible rating	80
Hours of study per day	6.61

Academic Specialties

Civil Procedure, Criminal, Intellectual Property, Business Litigation, Business Transactions, Estate Planning, Administrative Practice

Combined Degrees Offered

JD/MBA, JD/M Taxation, JD/MPPA, 3.5–4 years

Clinical program required	Yes
Legal writing	
course requirement	Yes
Legal methods	
course requirement	Yes
Legal research	
course requirement	Yes
Moot court requirement	Yes
Public interest	
law requirement	No

Academics

Baylor University's Sheila & Walter Umphrey Law Center's reputation for being a "tough school" is complemented by its stature as an "excellent school" with "one of the most rigorous [law] courses in the state." Students report that Baylor Law does a good job of preparing them "for the real world by teaching the law, practical lawyering skills, and professionalism." "We learn how to write well, how to research efficiently and effectively, and we most definitely learn how to advocate," says a 1L. "It's the greatest school for future trial lawyers." The "phenomenal" faculty has "a genuine interest in ensuring students know and understand the material," but they "can be tough" and "expect students to be well-prepared for every class." With a reputation as "the Marine Corps of law schools," Baylor students take comfort in the fact that with great effort comes great reward. "Throughout lectures, the professors strike the perfect balance of teaching legal theory and practice," says a 2L. "And this balance must be working as Baylor Law consistently has the highest bar passage rate in the state of Texas and our graduates are ready to practice law the day they graduate." While Baylor's faculty is lauded for its commitment to students, the same can't be said of its administration. Descriptions of the administration range from "disconnected" to "out of touch," with many students reporting that "decisions seem to be made without student input or the students' needs in mind."

Baylor Law places an emphasis on "legal theory and practice" through its "rigorous" Practice Court Program, a course that many feel leaves them "ready to practice law the day they graduate." That said, those uninterested in becoming trial lawyers wouldn't mind seeing it be done away with. "[The school] could end the Practice Court Program as a mandatory requirement and make it optional for only those students who wish to become litigators," says a 2L. A 3L further explains, "You really get a true practical experience from Day One, but it's not for everyone. Practice Court is brutal—eighteen hours a day of studying and class, plus you get humiliated and booted out of class if you are called up and can't recall a holding from one of the fifteen to twenty-five cases you were assigned the night before. The weak of heart need not apply."

Students agree that Baylor Law prepares them "to be lawyers better than almost any school in the country," but they find that "it is very difficult to find jobs." Though the career services office "has improved recently," students want to see the school "reestablish its reputation in Texas as a great law school and try to reach a broader market." "No one outside of Texas has heard of us, and no one respects the hard work we do culminating in the third-year Practice Court unless they've already hired a Baylor grad," says a 2L. Luckily, Baylor's "devoted alumni" can go a long way in helping you secure employment after graduation, provided that "you want to live in Texas."

If there's one word that's used to describe Baylor's campus, it's "beautiful." "[We have] the best building of any law school in Texas (and I would venture to say in the country)," says a 2L. "Students can enjoy looking over the water from the library, student lounge, and the back porch off the student lounge," says a 1L. "Additionally, students enjoy close parking in front of the building." The "state-of-the-art" classrooms and facilities are "stellar," "spacious," and "comfortable."

BECKY BECK-CHOLLETT, ASSISTANT DEAN OF ADMISSIONS
ONE BEAR PLACE #97288, WACO, TX 76798
TEL: 254-710-1911 FAX: 254-710-2316
E-MAIL: BECKY_BECK@BAYLOR.EDU • WEBSITE: LAW.BAYLOR.EDU

Life

With "approximately 420 students," the study body at Baylor Law is "small" and "intelligent." This lends a "close-knit" air to the school, though opinion is divided between the environment being "friendly" and "caring," or "cutthroat." "From Day One, the professors and administration told us that we were all in competition with one another due to the bell curve grading," says a 2L. "It was heavily emphasized, day after day. The competition became extremely cutthroat." Many here find that this pressure "divides" students, with some being "friendly with each other until the first set of grades are released," and others remaining "extremely cooperative" and "down-to-earth." Despite the academic competition, students find "community through suffering." "We all go through the same pain and as a result our bonds with each other are very strong," says a 2L. One point that all students agree on is that "the law school could stand to improve the diversity of its student body and its faculty members."

Perhaps the kindest thing students say about Baylor's location in Waco, Texas, is that the town offers "the perfect place to be engaged in the rigors of law school" (i.e., very few distractions). Students readily admit that despite some "decent bars and things to do" there's "not much going on" in Waco. However, with Dallas and Austin "an hour and a half away," it's "not uncommon for people to quickly flee Waco as soon as a break rolls around." For those who choose to stay on campus, the Student Bar Association "hosts many social and community service opportunities throughout the year, including four intramural sports, Law Prom, four Immunity Days (where students pay money to a designated charity and in return don't get called on in class the next day), an annual blood drive in memory of two alumni, and more."

Getting In

Recently admitted students at Baylor Law at the 25th percentile have LSAT scores of 156 and GPAs in the 3.4 range. Admitted students at the 75th percentile have LSAT scores of 162 and GPAs of roughly 3.8. Minority candidates are strongly encouraged to apply to Baylor Law School and admissions officers may consider minority status as a "plus factor" in the context of the individualized application review.

ADMISSIONS

Selectivity Rating	88
# applications received	2,360
% applicants accepted	32
% acceptees attending	11
Average LSAT	162
LSAT Range	160–164
Average undergrad GPA	3.67
Application fee	$40
Regular application	Rolling
Regular notification	Rolling
Early application program	Yes
Early application deadline	11/1
Early application notification	3/1
Transfer students accepted	Yes
Evening division offered	No
Part-time accepted	No
CAS accepted	Yes

International Students

TOEFL recommended of international students

FINANCIAL FACTS

Annual tuition	$36,750
Books and supplies	$2,007
Fees	$1,658
Room and board (on/off campus)	$9,708/ $9,273
Financial aid application deadline	2/15
% first-year students receiving some sort of aid	99
% receiving some sort of aid	92
% of aid that is merit based	31
% receiving scholarships	70
Average grant	$22,558
Average loan	$33,696
Average total aid package	$45,364
Average debt	$84,683

EMPLOYMENT INFORMATION

Career Rating	91
Rate of placement (nine months out)	95
Average starting salary	$84,931
State for bar exam	TX
Pass rate for first-time bar	98

Employers Who Frequently Hire Grads

Akin Gump; DLA Piper; Thompson & Knight; Haynes & Boone; Bracewell & Giuliani; Jackson Walker; Fulbright & Jaworski; Andrews & Kurth; Winstead; Hunton & Williams; Locke Lord Bissell & Liddell; Patton Boggs; K&L Gates; Jones Day; Vinson & Elkins; district attorneys' offices

Prominent Alumni

Leon Jaworski, Special Prosecutor for the Watergate trials; William Sessions, former FBI Director

Grads Employed by Field (%)

Academic (2)
Business/industry (6)
Government (12)
Judicial clerkship (6)
Military (3)
Private practice (70)
Public interest (1)

BOSTON COLLEGE
LAW SCHOOL

INSTITUTIONAL INFORMATION

Public/private	Private
Affiliation	Roman Catholic
Student/faculty ratio	12:1
% faculty part-time	54
% faculty female	41
% faculty minority	10
Total faculty	114

SURVEY SAYS...

*Great research resources,
Great library staff*

STUDENTS

Enrollment of law school	817
% male/female	50/50
% from out-of-state	70
% full-time	100
% minority	24
% international	2
# of countries represented	4
Average age of entering class	24

ACADEMICS

Academic Experience Rating	89
Profs interesting rating	88
Profs accessible rating	89
Hours of study per day	4.29

Academic Specialties
Civil Procedure, Commercial, Constitutional, Corporation Securities, Criminal, Environmental, Human Rights, International, Labor, Legal History, Legal Philosophy, Property, Taxation, Intellectual Property, Business Law

Advanced Degrees Offered
JD, 3 years; LLM, 1 year

Combined Degrees Offered
JD/MBA, 4 years; JD/MSW, 4 years; JD/MEd, 3 years; JD/MA Philosophy, 3.5 years; JD/MA Environmental law; JD/MD; JD/PhD Philosophy

Academics

Founded in 1929, Boston College Law School is located at the Newton campus location of Boston College, just west of Brookline. The school provides a strong academic curriculum with varied classes and subject matter, in turn "providing its students with an opportunity to grow as individuals and potential lawyers." Some would like a bit more practical experience, saying that "more opportunities for hands-on experience would be beneficial," but BC does have "amazing" and "numerous" clinics with great practical experience. The main reason BC students love their law school lives? The community. "Law school is a tough, stressful place anywhere, but at BC you are never in it alone."

The "charismatic, knowledgeable" professors at BC Law are "very engaging and interested in what they are teaching," and make it a point to "ensure that students are afforded a work/life balance." Though most admit that "there are a few to avoid," all faculty are more than willing to meet with students at any time and to "[help] students find jobs and internships through their personal networks." "Even when faculty [is] researching or writing, there is ample opportunity for student involvement," says a 2L. Everyone here is focused on the students "learning a lot in a relatively stress-free environment," and there are abundant resources for those who are struggling.

Some areas of the administration "seem slightly out of touch with the student body" and "are very difficult to maneuver"—Career Services doesn't have too many fans here—but "most issues can be addressed through [the Student Services] office." The library staff is also "second to none," as they "know everything and are patient and helpful teachers." Upper-level research or writing courses are "so well-taught" (mostly by the law librarians), and "the most useful tool for practicing law." Facilities are well-kept at BC—"everything is pretty much new and gleaming and spotlessly clean"—and though the law school shares a campus with the BC freshman class, there are very few clashes or space issues, particularly in "the large study lounge that stays open all night."

The school's alumni seem to truly love BC and make it a point to "look out for baby eagles." You "definitely have to stand up and ask for assistance," but once you do, there is "an unbelievable network on campus and in the wider world." Alumni at firms seem to still have strong ties to BC and "try to take in 'their own.'" Even in a down economy, students are cheerful about their employment prospects due to their school's "strong brand": "Our students are 'normal' and employers know it."

Living

Though the law school's suburban Newton campus location is hardly around the corner from central Boston, "Most people attending BC have their own vehicles for transportation, which does not make it difficult to access other parts of Boston." After the first week of classes, "It is pretty easy to find rides with friends who have cars," and some people even believe that the mini-isolation helps promote closer relationships. There is also public transportation within Boston and a shuttle that goes to the law school from the main campus. Rent is certainly cheaper here than in Boston proper, but the reason many BC Law students choose to live here is "because they want to be surrounded by people like themselves."

RITA JONES, ASSISTANT DEAN OF ADMISSIONS AND FINANCIAL AID
885 CENTRE STREET, NEWTON, MA 02459
TEL: 617-552-4351 FAX: 617-552-2917
E-MAIL: BCLAWADM@BC.EDU • WEBSITE: WWW.BC.EDU/LAW

"I strongly believe that the school's greatest strength is the type of students that the school attracts," says a 3L of what has come to be known as the "Disneyland of law schools." This "fun and laid-back" group is "very well-rounded and friendly, with diverse interests," forming "an interesting group of people that both attend and work at the school, exposing you to a snapshot of the professional legal world." Most of the students here are in their twenties and thirties, unmarried, and liberal, and "really make it a joy to be on campus every day." There is a "jam-packed list" of getting-to-know-you events for 1Ls once they arrive at BC, including "duck tours, a 1L Bar night, BBQs, a really structured mentor-mentee program, subsidized football games and tailgating, a lunch at the dean's house, and more." Even beyond the first year, people are always willing to pass notes along if you miss a class, and "willing to go out on the weekends for some much needed fun" (at least until finals roll around). Many people see "a group of lifelong friends" in their fellow students.

Getting In

Only about one in five applicants is admitted to BC Law, but the school offers prospective students some nice application options. The admissions process opens in September and runs through March 1. Applicants are admitted on a rolling basis. You may also reactivate an application submitted in the previous year by submitting a new application form, personal statement, LSDAS report, and application fee.

Clinical program required	No
Legal writing course requirement	Yes
Legal methods course requirement	Yes
Legal research course requirement	Yes
Moot court requirement	No
Public interest law requirement	No

ADMISSIONS

Selectivity Rating	**93**
# applications received	6,942
% applicants accepted	20
% acceptees attending	19
LSAT Range	163–167
Application fee	$75
Regular application	Rolling, up to 3/1
Regular notification	Rolling
Early application program	No
Transfer students accepted	Yes
Evening division offered	No
Part-time accepted	No
CAS accepted	Yes

International Students

TOEFL required of international students	

FINANCIAL FACTS

Annual tuition	$40,770
Books and supplies	$1,300
Fees	$340
Room and board	$17,390
Financial aid application deadline	3/15
% first-year students receiving some sort of aid	92
% receiving some sort of aid	83
% of aid that is merit based	28
% receiving scholarships	51
Average grant	$17,166
Average loan	$36,228
Average total aid package	$45,452
Average debt	$103,765

EMPLOYMENT INFORMATION

Career Rating	**96**
Rate of placement (nine months out)	98
Average starting salary	$134,347
State for bar exam	MA
Pass rate for first-time bar	95

Employers Who Frequently Hire Grads

Many of our graduates join private practices initially or after clerkships. The majority of these graduates join large law firms. No one firm hires a majority of our students. The following firms have consistently hired several graduates each of the last few years: Bingham McCutchen; Brown Rudnick; DLA Piper; Foley Hoag; Fried Frank; Goodwin Procter; Goulston & Storrs; Greenberg Traurig; Holland & Knight; McDermott Will & Emery; Milbank Tweed Hadley & McCloy LLP; Mintz Levin; Nutter McClennen & Fish; Paul Hastings; Ropes & Gray; Schulte Roth & Zabel; Shearman & Sterling; Sidley Austin; Skadden Arps; Sullivan & Cromwell; Weil Gotschal & Manges; and WilmerHale. Within the government/public interest sector, our graduates have taken jobs with the federal government, through the Honors Program as well as the Presidential Management Fellowships program, as well as other agencies and federal clerkships; state and local government including positions within state court clerkships; assistant district attorney offices; and public defender offices.

Prominent Alumni

John Kerry, U.S. Senator/Democratic Nominee for President; Debra Yang, former United States Attorney, CA; Scott Brown, U.S. Senator; A. Paul Cellucci, former Ambassador to Canada; Warren Rudman, U.S. Senator; Dannel Malloy, Connecticut Governor

Grads Employed by Field (%)

Academic (5)
Business/industry (7)
Government (4)
Judicial clerkship (8)
Military (1)
Private practice (69)
Public interest (5)

BOSTON UNIVERSITY
SCHOOL OF LAW

INSTITUTIONAL INFORMATION

Public/private	Private
Student/faculty ratio	12:1
% faculty part-time	46
% faculty female	25
% faculty minority	9
Total faculty	106

SURVEY SAYS...
Diverse opinions accepted in classrooms, Great library staff

STUDENTS

Enrollment of law school	822
% male/female	50/50
% full-time	100
% minority	20
% international	3
# of countries represented	18
Average age of entering class	24

ACADEMICS

Academic Experience Rating	98
Profs interesting rating	99
Profs accessible rating	98
Hours of study per day	4.83

Academic Specialties
Corporation Securities, International, Intellectual Property, Health Care, Litigation, Dispute Resolution

Advanced Degrees Offered
LLM Taxation, 1 year full-time, up to 4 years part-time; LLM Banking and Financial Law, 1 year full-time, up to 3 years part-time; LLM American Law, 1 year full-time; LLM Intellectual Property Law, 1 year full-time

Combined Degrees Offered
JD/MA Philosophy, 3 years; JD/MBA, JD/MBA Sector Management, JD/MA International Relations, JD/MS Mass Communication, JD/MA Preservation Studies, JD/MPH Public Health, JD/LLM in Taxation (7 semesters), JD/LLM in Banking and Financial Law (7 semesters), 3.5–4 years; JD/LLM in European

Academics

Boston University School of Law offers a breadth of curricula that is matched by few other schools anywhere in the country. Beyond the first-year curriculum (which includes a mandatory moot court program and a course in legislation), there's a stunning array of courses and seminars. Clinical and externship programs galore "are fabulous and allow for a great deal of hands-on experience." There are six journals, five concentrations, nine dual-degree programs, study abroad opportunities all over the globe, and a host of very cool special programs. Especially noteworthy is the Summer International Internship Program, which connects students with summer internships in other countries. Also, students here can count up to twelve credit hours in other graduate or professional schools at BU toward their law degrees.

The "friendly and open" administration at BU Law is "generally very receptive to students." With the exception of a "few really terrible" professors, the "engaging and committed" faculty is "shockingly good." By virtually all accounts, "the professors are unbelievable" here. "They are talented public speakers, so lectures are rarely boring." "They are available to discuss class issues and career prospects, and they are happy to give general law school or personal advice." "Several of my professors rank as the best teachers I have had at any level," beams a 2L. "There is a strong focus on teaching and cultivating the next generation of lawyers at BU. While intimidating at the outset, there is nothing like feeling yourself grow personally and professionally as you progress in the JD program."

Most students call the Career Development staff "stellar" and promise that they can "find you a summer job overnight if need be." BU students looking for work can also avail themselves of "a close alumni network" locally and their school's "excellent reputation" across the Northeast and all over the country. "BU's reputation carries... throughout the country and has opened a lot of doors."

The facility here is "a big tower" "near downtown" that "provides great views of Boston." "There are outlets at every seat and there is plenty of light in every classroom." "The law library is well-stocked with resources for research." Functionality aside, aesthetics leave much to be desired. Students call it an "imposing concrete monolith" that is "the worst example of 1960s architecture imaginable" and "more on par with a correctional institution than a place of higher learning." The "cramped" classrooms are pretty uncomfortable and "never warm enough or cool enough." "The elevator situation provides daily irritation." While students freely admit that it's not the greatest environment in which to spend three years, they point out that there are many, many other pluses. "I'd rather have a terrible tower and an amazing education than vice versa," observes a 2L.

Life

Students at BU Law describe themselves as "hardworking, smart," and "pretty liberal" politically. A solid majority comes "straight out of undergrad." Some students say the population is "a pretty good reflection of society overall, with a mix of students and not really an abnormal amount of quirky characters." Other students tell us that BU is full of "socially awkward kids who were not popular in college or high school and are hoping that now is their time." Much to the chagrin of many of these future attorneys, there is a grading curve here. It's definitely not the harshest law school curve we've ever seen, but it does "maintain an edge of competitiveness, especially for those who are still massaging their damaged egos from being rejected by Harvard." For the most part, though, "traditional law school competitiveness does not exist." "I think students are ultimately just competing with themselves," proposes a 3L.

Life outside of class at BU is "vibrant, accepting, and wonderful." "There is a student organization for every interest," with some "just having one meeting a semester with free pizza and not amounting to much more, while others are active getting speakers and events." "Many students have tight social circles" and "things can be cliquish," particularly for 1Ls. Nevertheless, students promise "a great social atmosphere," especially if you like "alcohol-centered activities." It's a lot like "college 2.0," really. Bar nights are common, and there are several other big social events on the calendar each year (including a popular 5K race) that "are all well-attended" but don't feature alcohol. When that scene gets old, students here have all the culture and charm of Bean Town at their disposal.

Getting In

BU Law is one of the most prestigious law schools in the country and admission is extraordinarily competitive. Enrolled students at the 25th percentile have LSAT scores of about 164 and GPAs of roughly 3.51. Enrolled students at the 75th percentile have LSAT scores of 167 or so and GPAs in the 3.83 GPA range.

law (with the University of Paris II), 3 years; JD/LLM in Asian Legal Studies (with the National University of Singapore), 3 years

Clinical program required	No
Legal writing course requirement	Yes
Legal methods course requirement	No
Legal research course requirement	Yes
Moot court requirement	Yes
Public interest law requirement	No

ADMISSIONS

Selectivity Rating	93
# applications received	8,515
% applicants accepted	21
% acceptees attending	15
LSAT Range	164–167
Average undergrad GPA	3.52–3.83
Application fee	$75
Regular application	Rolling, up to 3/1
Regular notification	Rolling
Early application program	No
Transfer students accepted	Yes
Evening division offered	No
Part-time accepted	No
CAS accepted	Yes

International Students

TOEFL required of international students	

FINANCIAL FACTS

Annual tuition	$41,780
Books and supplies	$1,374
Fees	$874
Room and board	$12,070
Financial aid application deadline	3/1
% first-year students receiving some sort of aid	91
% receiving some sort of aid	86
% of aid that is merit based	15
% receiving scholarships	67
Average grant	$17,000
Average loan	$37,200
Average total aid package	$48,600
Average debt	$104,000

EMPLOYMENT INFORMATION

Career Rating	**94**
Rate of placement (nine months out)	95
Average starting salary	$126,626
State for bar exam	MA, NY, CA, NJ, IL

Employers Who Frequently Hire Grads
Too many to list

Prominent Alumni
Judd Gregg, U.S. Senator–New Hampshire; William S. Cohen, Former Secretary of Defense; David Kelley, Executive Producer; Gary F. Locke, Secretary of Commerce; Hon. Sandra L. Lynch, Chief Judge, U.S. Court of Appeals, First Circuit

Grads Employed by Field (%)
Academic (20)
Business/industry (8)
Government (7)
Judicial clerkship (8)
Military (1)
Private practice (52)
Public interest (3)

BRIGHAM YOUNG UNIVERSITY

J. REUBEN CLARK LAW SCHOOL

INSTITUTIONAL INFORMATION

Public/private	Private
Affiliation	Church of Jesus Christ of Latter-day Saints
Student/faculty ratio	18:1
% faculty part-time	65
% faculty female	22
% faculty minority	6
Total faculty	76

SURVEY SAYS...

Great research resources, Great library staff, Conservative students

STUDENTS

Enrollment of law school	462
% male/female	64/36
% full-time	100
% minority	17
% international	1
# of countries represented	12
Average age of entering class	26

ACADEMICS

Academic Experience Rating	92
Profs interesting rating	88
Profs accessible rating	88
Hours of study per day	5.37

Advanced Degrees Offered

International comparative law, 1 year

Combined Degrees Offered

JD/MBA, JD/MPA, JD/MAcc, JD/MOB, JD/MEd (education), 4 years; JD/EdD (education), 5 years

Clinical program required	No
Legal writing course requirement	Yes
Legal methods course requirement	No
Legal research course requirement	Yes
Moot court requirement	Yes
Public interest law requirement	No

Academics

Law students at Brigham Young University love the "small class sizes," "superb" academic experience, and the "lowest tuition that you'll find anywhere for a respected law school." Add "great professors" to the mix and you've got the makings of a solid law school experience. "BYU has a great faculty with amazing credentials" (several faculty have moved from top schools and have clerked for the Supreme Court), and "all faculty members are incredibly student-oriented," says a 2L. The school doesn't hedge on the quality of 1L professors either. "The school uses some of its brightest and best faculty to teach first-year classes," explains a 1L. "I have had multiple professors who were previously U.S. Supreme Court clerks as professors in each semester." Professors here are "always open to meeting with students," some going so far as to give out "cell phone numbers in class." "[Professors] take time to attend law school events and make genuine efforts to know students, especially students are willing to get involved and meet professors halfway," says a 2L. Students find the administration "transparent in its policies and responsive to students' needs and concerns." The administration "doesn't please all the students all the time, of course, but my sense is that the school wants to satisfy its students as well as prospective employers and works hard to do so."

Students are quick to point out that for the "minimal tuition price," the "value of the education" at BYU Law "can't be beat." That said, nearly all agree that a "broader range of courses" is needed. In addition to more classes, many note that they could benefit from "a more robust clinical program." "[BYU Law] places a lot of emphasis on externships—and the externship program is pretty awesome—but we could gain a lot more practical experience with on-campus clinical opportunities," says a 2L. Finally, some students would like a school as religious as BYU to be, well, more religious. "I have only had one professor who legitimately integrated gospel aspects into law teaching, and it was only very briefly," says a 2L. "I know many people wonder if BYU Law School is like Sunday School, but I can say it definitely is not."

Most students believe that BYU is "a 'law firm' school" since "that is where most people end up and that is mostly who comes to campus to interview." "I have sought advice on non-firm careers, and have obtained little useful help from BYU thus far," says a 3L. "Both my summer jobs have come from my own work and connections." Regardless, students appreciate the "helpful" Career Services Office, though they "could do a better job marketing the school and its students to the larger, regional firms outside of Utah." The "networking" and "benefits" of "the J. Reuben Clark Law Society and the alumni" are also a plus for BYU Law job hunters.

The school boasts "Internet connection in all the classrooms," "personal study space" (i.e., everyone has their "own individual desk in the library"), and overall "great" facilities. "The law building itself is a bit dated" (circa 1973), but "They're progressively renovating," says a 1L. "The administration is building a state-of-the-art moot court room, and all classrooms, carrels, study rooms, and sitting areas in the library have wireless Internet and computer power jacks." Plenty of students find themselves wishing for a "face-lift" for the building and classrooms, but, as one 2L explains, "When I am paying seventy percent less [in tuition] than my colleagues are at peer schools, I guess I cannot complain."

GAELYNN KUCHAR, DIRECTOR OF ADMISSIONS
340 JRCB, BRIGHAM YOUNG UNIVERSITY LAW SCHOOL, PROVO, UT 84602
TEL: 801-422-4277 FAX: 801-422-0389
E-MAIL: KUCHARG@LAW.BYU.EDU • WEBSITE: WWW.LAW.BYU.EDU

Life

When you've got a student body that's "ninety-nine percent Mormon and sixty-five percent married," the social life is, for lack of better words, "quite unique!" "The reason that the students are so hardworking and competitive is that many of the students are married, or are planning on getting married, so their studies and academic success [mean] more than just mere prestige, or even a high salary," says a 3L. "These students understand that others are depending on them to do well" and are "more willing to take responsibility for their time and efforts." The environment is "competitive, but civil." "I know that everyone else is working very hard, and yet I have never felt that other students were 'out to get me,'" says a 2L. As for diversity, it depends on who you ask. For some students, the lack of diversity can be blamed on BYU Law being "very conservative," which "tends to attract more conservative people." On the other hand, some find that their "colleagues are more diverse" than "expected for a Mormon school in the middle of Utah."

Since a "large percentage" of students are "already married," many find the traditional law school "social dynamic" changed "significantly." "People tend [to] get together for game nights and baby showers instead of parties or clubbing," says a 2L. "It feels less like college and more like real life." Also, as BYU has a strict honor code, don't expect to "find a lot of people here to party with." Conversely, some students wish others adhered a little less to the code in question. "I wish more of my classmates would drink themselves out of the running." "As a completely dry campus nobody does anything but study and the competition is extremely fierce," says a 1L. Indeed, most social life revolves around the library. But when students take a break from the books, Salt Lake City and its more varied social scenery is only "forty-five minutes away."

Getting In

Recently admitted students at BYU Law at the 25th percentile have LSAT scores of 160 and GPAs in the 3.52 range. Admitted students at the 75th percentile have LSAT scores of 166 and GPAs of roughly 3.85.

ADMISSIONS

Selectivity Rating	95
# applications received	790
% applicants accepted	31
% acceptees attending	61
Average LSAT	164
LSAT Range	161–166
Average undergrad GPA	3.63
Application fee	$50
Regular application	Rolling, up to 3/1
Regular notification	Rolling
Early application program	No
Transfer students accepted	Yes
Evening division offered	No
Part-time accepted	No
CAS accepted	Yes

FINANCIAL FACTS

Annual tuition	
(in-state/out-of-state)	$9,240/ $18,480
Books and supplies	$1,760
Room and board	$12,108
% first-year students receiving some sort of aid	86
% receiving some sort of aid	78
% of aid that is merit based	33
% receiving scholarships	50
Average grant	$2,300
Average loan	$13,400
Average debt	$41,000

EMPLOYMENT INFORMATION

Career Rating	93
Rate of placement (nine months out)	99
Average starting salary	$97,386
State for bar exam	UT, CA, NV, AZ, TX
Pass rate for first-time bar	94

Employers Who Frequently Hire Grads

Allen Matkins; Alverson Taylor; Ascione Heideman; Baker & McKenzie; Ballard Spahr; Bryan Cave; Carlsmith Ball; Christensen & Jensen; Covington & Burling; Davis Polk & Wardwell; Dorsey & Whitney; DLA Piper Rudnick Gray Cary; Dorsey & Whitney; Federal and State Courts; Fennemore Craig; Filice Brown; Haynes & boone; Hale Lane; Hill Johnson & Schmutz; Holland & Hart; Holme Roberts & Owen; Jackson White; Jenner & Block; JAGs; Kirkland & Ellis; Kirton & McConkie; Knobbe Martens Olson & Bear; Latham & Watkins; LeBoeuf Lamb Greene & MacRae; Lewis & Roca; Luce Forward Hamilton & Scripps; Milbank Tweed; Morrison & Foerster; Nixon Peabody; O'Melveny & Myers; Parsons Behle & Latimer; Perkins Coie; Pricewaterhouse Coopers; Ray Quinney & Nebeker; Snell & Wilmer; Stoel Rives; Vinson & Elkins; Wiley Rein & Fielding; Workman Nydegger & Seeley

Prominent Alumni

Steve Young, former quarterback, San Francisco 49ers; Dee V. Benson, Senior Judge, Federal District Court, Utah; Chris Cannon, Congressman; Bill Orton, former Congressman

BROOKLYN LAW SCHOOL

INSTITUTIONAL INFORMATION

Public/private	Private
Student/faculty ratio	18:1
% faculty part-time	53
% faculty female	39
% faculty minority	9
Total faculty	161

SURVEY SAYS...

Abundant externship/internship/ clerkship opportunities, Liberal students, Students love Brooklyn, NY

STUDENTS

Enrollment of law school	1,461
% male/female	52/48
% from out-of-state	40
% full-time	89
% minority	26
% international	3
# of countries represented	7
Average age of entering class	24

ACADEMICS

Academic Experience Rating	**83**
Profs interesting rating	81
Profs accessible rating	72
Hours of study per day	4.35

Academic Specialties

Business and Commercial Law, Civil Rights/Human Rights, Criminal Law, Financial/Securities Regulation, Health/Bioethics, Immigration and Refugee Law, Intellectual Property, International Business Law, Law and Psychology, Law and Technology, Legal Ethics/ Professional Responsibility, Products/Liability, Real Estate, Land Use and Development

Advanced Degrees Offered

JD, 3 years full-time, 4 years part-time; LLM for Foreign-Trained Lawyers, 1 year full-time, 1.5–2 years part-time

Academics

Large and private Brooklyn Law School offers a "broad range of classes," "four scholarly journals," five joint-degree programs, and a moot court program that successfully does battle around the country. The legal writing program is reportedly "invaluable" as well. "We do so well at all the competitions because we are taught how to write great briefs and how to advocate well," boasts a 3L. There's "a very strong public interest community." A vast array of clinical programs includes bankruptcy, immigration, securities law, criminal defense, and mediation. There is also a "strong emphasis on" and an "excellent selection of" internships and externships all over New York City. "The practical experience you can get at BLS is amazing."

A nice combination of "young superstars and ancient pillars" comprises the faculty at Brooklyn Law. A few of the pillars are "out of touch" and "appear to not care whether or not they teach the students anything." Most professors, however, are "committed to teaching, enthusiastic," and "very accessible." "They have a unique ability to connect with students, offer valuable insight, and genuinely give the impression that they enjoy doing what they do." Concrete and practical application of the law is big here, too. "All of my professors have tried to incorporate real-world lawyering into the curriculum, rather than sticking solely to the case law," relates a happy 2L. Not everyone is satisfied with the administration but the majority of students call it "competent and efficient." "Everything is run pretty well," most students say. "The financial aid office has been fantastic in helping me navigate the winding path of financing a legal education," notes a 3L.

Some students call the Career Center "hit or miss." "The administration appears too focused on the top of the class, largely pushing clerkships and big law as the best opportunities," complains a 3L. Others think that Career Services should do nothing less and declare that employment prospects for newly minted grads are excellent. They point to a "strong alumni network" that is "always eager to assist Brooklyn students." "Most people who do well have no problem finding competitive jobs," says a 2L. The fact that some of the best firms in the country are "only a subway ride away" certainly doesn't hurt. BLS also provides ample help for students who would rather not work in the private sector. "My expectations of Brooklyn Law School's commitment to assisting students interested in public interest accomplish their dreams have been exceeded," gushes a 3L.

Students are divided in their view of the facilities. "The school's appearance is pretty nice," devotees say. Research facilities are "entirely adequate." "BLS offers several different places for individual as well as group studying on campus." Classrooms are "fairly comfortable." Critics contend that "the classrooms and bathrooms need a serious upgrade." And they hate the chairs. "Whoever chose them must have a great core or an extremely flexible back," speculates a 2L. Detractors also say that the design of the campus is deficient. "The school is comprised of only two buildings yet somehow still manages to be a maze," gripes a frequently lost 1L.

Life

Diversity "in terms of race, ethnicity, and interests" is "thriving" among the "hardworking and intelligent" students here. You'll probably be able to find whatever scene you are after. There's "frat culture spilling out from students who attended straight from undergrad." There's also a strong contingent of slightly older people who have taken some time off and have been living in New York for awhile. A lot of the people here "already have lives and friends" and "have their own things going on." At the same time, "There's a great sense of community," especially for students who live in campus housing.

HENRY W. HAVERSTICK III, DEAN OF ADMISSIONS AND FINANCIAL AID
250 JORALEMON STREET, BROOKLYN, NY 11201
TEL: 718-780-7906 FAX: 718-780-0395
E-MAIL: ADMITQ@BROOKLAW.EDU • WEBSITE: WWW.BROOKLAW.EDU

Academically, BLS is known for having a tough curve "that is a humbling experience for some 1Ls." Nevertheless, students assure us, "There is a spirit of cooperation and unity that creates a very supportive environment." "Students tend to get along and help each other more than compete." Outside the classroom, the school sponsors "tons of" lectures and "student groups are very active." Students call surrounding Brooklyn Heights "a great neighborhood." "You have more courts within two blocks than you could ever visit, much less intern with." "Shops and restaurants dot tree-lined Montague Street on the way to the Brooklyn Heights Promenade (with the best view of Manhattan)," says a 2L. "The rest of the neighborhood consists of well-kept historic brownstones. It's just a great place to wander around." And, of course, the Big Apple offers a never-ending array of activities and nightlife.

Getting In

Admitted students at the 25th percentile have LSAT scores around 159 or so and GPAs of about 3.2. Admitted students at the 75th percentile have LSAT scores of 164 or so and GPAs of around 3.6.

Combined Degrees Offered
JD/MA Political Science, JD/MS City and Regional Planning, JD/MBA, JD/MS Library/Information Science, JD/M Urban Planning, 4–6 years

Clinical program required	No
Legal writing course requirement	Yes
Legal methods course requirement	Yes
Legal research course requirement	Yes
Moot court requirement	Yes
Public interest law requirement	No

ADMISSIONS

Selectivity Rating	88
# applications received	5,984
% applicants accepted	27
% acceptees attending	30
Average LSAT	163
LSAT Range	162–165
Average undergrad GPA	3.43
Application fee	$0
Regular application	Rolling, up to 8/9
Regular notification	Rolling
Early application program	Yes
Early application deadline	12/1
Early application notification	12/31
Transfer students accepted	Yes
Evening division offered	Yes
Part-time accepted	Yes
CAS accepted	Yes

International Students
TOEFL required of international students

FINANCIAL FACTS

Annual tuition	$46,284
Books and supplies	$1,300
Fees	$326
Room and board	$21,950
Financial aid application deadline	4/30
% first-year students receiving some sort of aid	83
% receiving some sort of aid	65
% of aid that is merit based	86
% receiving scholarships	65
Average grant	$24,538
Average loan	$37,172
Average total aid package	$51,141
Average debt	$101,536

EMPLOYMENT INFORMATION

Career Rating	89
Rate of placement (nine months out)	88
Average starting salary	$91,434
State for bar exam	NY
Pass rate for first-time bar	90

Employers Who Frequently Hire Grads
Bronx District Attorney's office; Cadwalader, Wickersham & Taft; Cahill Gordon; Chadbourne & Parke; Cleary Gottlieb; Fried, Frank, Harris, Shriver & Jacobson; Goodwin Proctor; Kings County District Attorney's Office; Milbank Tweed Hadley & McCloy; NYC Law Department; New York County District Attorney's Office; Proskauer Rose; Skadden, Arps, Slate, Meagher & Flom; Simpson Thacher & Bartlett; White & Case; Linklaters LLP

Prominent Alumni
David Dinkins, former Mayor, City of New York; Stephen J. Dannhauser, Chairman, Weil Gotshal & Manges LLP; Barry Salzberg, Deloitte Touche Tohmatsu Limited; Lonn A. Trost, Chief Operating Officerand General Counsel, NY Yankees; Sheldon Silver, Speaker, NY State Assembly

Grads Employed by Field (%)
Academic (1)
Business/industry (18)
Government (20)
Judicial clerkship (7)
Military (4)
Private practice (46)
Public interest (7)

CAMPBELL UNIVERSITY
NORMAN ADRIAN WIGGINS SCHOOL OF LAW

INSTITUTIONAL INFORMATION

Public/private	Private
Affiliation	Baptist
Student/faculty ratio	16:1
% faculty part-time	43
% faculty female	27
% faculty minority	6
Total faculty	49

SURVEY SAYS...

Heavy use of Socratic Method, Diverse opinions accepted in classrooms, Great research resources, Great library staff, Conservative students

STUDENTS

Enrollment of law school	457
% male/female	48/52
% from out-of-state	15
% full-time	100
% minority	12
Average age of entering class	34

ACADEMICS

Academic Experience Rating	73
Profs interesting rating	78
Profs accessible rating	86
Hours of study per day	5.65

Academic Specialties

Tracks in Business/Transactions, Intellectual Property, and Trial & Appellate Advocacy

Advanced Degrees Offered

JD, 3 years, 90 semester hours

Combined Degrees Offered

JD/MBA, Campbell University; JD/MTWM, Campbell University; JD/MBA, North Carolina State; JD/MPA, North Carolina State

Academics

Campbell University School of Law is a small, Baptist-affiliated school in North Carolina that offers a Christian perspective on law and boasts a stellar bar-passage rate. Also, small class sizes prevent you from getting lost in a sea of people. The curriculum is decidedly focused on the actual practice of law "instead of relying on theory." The trial and appellate advocacy programs here are some of the most extensive in the country. "A Campbell lawyer can walk into any courtroom and never feel lost," proclaims a 2L. "Campbell is a hard law school," though. "It over-prepares you," suggests a 1L, "so that when you get out, you are not as surprised as most first-year lawyers." Most professors are dyed-in-the-wool believers in the Socratic Method, so you'll be able to breathe easy only if you've read and actually thought about the assignment for that day. "The pressure lets up after your 1L year," but "Course work is extremely rigorous, and the school is not afraid to fail students who perform poorly." Student complaints generally center on the very limited range of available courses. In short, Campbell needs to "offer more electives." Also, the massive number of required courses is "ridiculous."

Despite their hardcore approach, professors at Campbell are generally beloved by students. The faculty is reportedly "dedicated" and "always happy to answer questions." "Professors are very engaged and take time to get to know students individually." "The accessibility of our professors is one of the greatest strengths of Campbell Law," beams a 1L. "Their open-door policy makes it easy to slip in after class to ask a quick question or stay even longer to discuss legal issues." Critics call the top brass "out of touch with reality," but most students say that the administration is "extremely responsive and attentive." "They really strive to make themselves available to the students."

According to many students, the Career Center is "great for the students who utilize it." They say the staff "does an impressive job" and is "much more efficient and effective than at most law schools." Other students charge that this aspect of Campbell Law "is in need of vast improvement." Whatever the case, this school is located "in the heart of the state capital," "a hop, skip, and a jump away from" a bevy of state courts and government buildings. "Externships and internships (though most are unpaid) can easily be had," and there are "hundreds of attorneys within just a few miles" if you're looking to pad your resume with part-time employment. The "vicious" grading curve is "a hindrance in finding a job," and it's tough "to find jobs outside of North Carolina," but most students seem pretty confident about their career prospects.

Students tell us, "Resources and facilities are fantastic" at Campbell. "There could be additional space for individual study," but the shiny, newer building here is "gorgeous" and technologically "state-of-the-art." Another perk is the fact that "active" state court proceedings "reside at Campbell Law" as well, making Campbell one of the few law schools with a functioning court inside its walls.

DEXTER A. SMITH, MED, JD, ASSISTANT DEAN OF ADMISSIONS AND FINANCIAL AID
POST OFFICE BOX 158, 113 MAIN STREET, BUIES CREEK, NC 27506
TEL: 910-893-1754 FAX: 910-893-1780
E-MAIL: ADMISSIONS@LAW.CAMPBELL.EDU • WEBSITE: WWW.LAW.CAMPBELL.EDU

Life

Students spend a great deal of time together, and the overwhelming sentiment is that there's "a strong community feeling" at Campbell Law. "The size allows you to form close working and personal relationships, not only with your fellow classmates, but also with the professors, deans, and administration," explains a 1L. "You will never be a number at Campbell." "I am able to leave my laptop and purse in the commons area while I attend class," adds a 3L. But some students say there's "no sense of camaraderie at Campbell Law. According to them, many students "go to school, go home, and hang out with a completely unique set of friends."

Opportunities for meaningful participation in extracurricular activities are reportedly plentiful. Social activities are also quite common. Beyond the law school realm, the local area has a lot to offer. In addition to being North Carolina's capital city, Raleigh is the state's second largest city (behind Charlotte). It's also among a rapidly growing city in a geographic region that has burgeoned economically over the past few decades. The metropolitan area here, which encompasses Raleigh, Durham, and Chapel Hill, as well as three huge research universities, offers very adequate amounts of culture and urban energy.

Getting In

Admitted students at the 25th percentile have LSAT scores in the mid 150s and undergraduate grade point averages approaching 3.2. At the 75th percentile, LSAT scores are in the high 150s, and GPAs are close to 3.6.

Clinical program required	No
Legal writing	
course requirement	Yes
Legal methods	
course requirement	Yes
Legal research	
course requirement	Yes
Moot court requirement	Yes
Public interest	
law requirement	No

ADMISSIONS

Selectivity Rating	81
# applications received	1,469
% applicants accepted	31
% acceptees attending	35
Average LSAT	156
LSAT Range	154–158
Average undergrad GPA	3.39
Application fee	$50
Regular application	Rolling
Regular notification	Rolling
Early application program	No
Transfer students accepted	Yes
Evening division offered	No
Part-time accepted	No
CAS accepted	Yes

International Students ·
TOEFL recommended of international students

FINANCIAL FACTS

Annual tuition	$33,400
Books and supplies	$2,300
Fees	$1,510
Room and board	
(on/off campus)	$13,000/
	$13,063
Financial aid application	
deadline	6/15
% receiving some sort of aid	92
% of aid that is merit based	15
% receiving scholarships	37
Average grant	$10,325
Average loan	$43,487
Average total aid package	$58,930
Average debt	$121,648

EMPLOYMENT INFORMATION

Career Rating	73
Rate of placement (nine months out)	84
Average starting salary	$58,000
State for bar exam	NC, SC, VA, MD,
	CO, CT, TN, TX
Pass rate for first-time bar	85

Employers Who Frequently Hire Grads
Small to medium private firms

Prominent Alumni
Elaine Marshall, North Carolina Secretary of State; Donna Stroud, Judge, North Carolina Court of Appeals; Richard Thigpen, General Counsel, Carolina Panthers NFL Franchise; Ann Marie Calabria, Judge, North Carolina Court of Appeals; Laura Bridges, North Carolina District Court Judge

Grads Employed by Field (%)
Business/industry (8)
Government (15)
Judicial clerkship (2)
Private practice (70)
Public interest (1)

CAPITAL UNIVERSITY
LAW SCHOOL

INSTITUTIONAL INFORMATION

Public/private	Private
Affiliation	Lutheran
Student/faculty ratio	17:1
% faculty part-time	41
% faculty female	32
% faculty minority	13
Total faculty	68

SURVEY SAYS...

Diverse opinions accepted in classrooms, Great research resources, Abundant externship/ internship/clerkship opportunities, Students love Columbus, OH

STUDENTS

Enrollment of law school	673
% male/female	56/44
% from out-of-state	5
% full-time	72
% minority	10
% international	1
# of countries represented	4
Average age of entering class	26

ACADEMICS

Academic Experience Rating	**63**
Profs interesting rating	67
Profs accessible rating	71
Hours of study per day	5.50

Academic Specialties

Corporation Securities, Environmental, Government Services, International, Labor, Taxation, Dispute Resolution, Children and Family Law, Environmental

Advanced Degrees Offered

LLM in Taxation, 1–6 years, LLM in Business, 1–6 years, LLM in Business and Taxation, 1–6 years, MT, 1–6 years

Combined Degrees Offered

JD/MBA, 3.5–6 years; JD/MSN, 3.5–6 years; JD/MSA, 3.5–4 years; JD/MTS, 4–6 years

Academics

Capital University Law School "in the heart of downtown" Columbus, Ohio "is a great place to study law," particularly if you seek a balance between "legal theory and actual practice." The "broad range of courses" here emphasizes "practical lawyering skills." "The legal writing program is awesome," says one student. A wealth of externships, internships, and clerkships offers "the best hands-on experience possible." The law school is "only a few short blocks from the Ohio Supreme Court" and is "nestled within two miles" of a bevy of other state and federal courthouses and agencies. Capital has "outstanding" part-time and evening programs and "All of the offices are open longer hours to accommodate this group of students." The "highly reputable" National Center for Adoption Law and Policy "offers a great way to gain expertise" and "get connected with family-law attorneys." Another plus is an Advanced Bar Studies course "designed to prepare 3Ls for taking the bar." It seems to be working. "We are ecstatic about our third-in-the-state passage rate this year," raves a 3L. Employment prospects are also good. Capital is "respected in the Columbus legal community" and has "a strong reputation with local government and private firms for producing students with strong research and writing skills and good practical knowledge." "Many loyal alumni practice locally," so it goes without saying that students find plenty to keep them in Columbus and at Capital.

"With very few exceptions, the teaching faculty is top-notch as communicators and mentors." There is also "an excellent base of adjunct professors who are practitioners by day." Capital's "devoted, highly prepared, [and] usually pretty easygoing" professors "make an effort to stay easily accessible." "So far, minus one pompous and unhelpful professor, my experience with Capital's faculty has been amazing," comments a 1L. "Most professors emphasize the real-world aspects of the curriculum as well as what is required to perform well on the bar exam." Some professors "could make class more interesting," though. Also, be warned: "There is no grade inflation here." Something like "four to eight percent of students in first-year classes" receive an A. The "median grade" is more like a "B-minus." "When someone gets an A at Capital, it should be an unambiguous signal to an employer that the person is highly qualified in the subject matter," explains a student.

The "approachable" administration is "improving every year" and "open to criticisms and suggestions." The "Registrar, Career Services staff, and even the security guards are incredibly friendly and helpful." "Not a lot of people fall through the cracks." Organization can be "very lackluster sometimes," though. There are "small mix-ups (e.g., a classroom for the class not being large enough to accommodate all the students)," and the "terrible" scheduling process is "tiresome."

Capital's "aesthetically boring" facilities are "pretty much completely modern." So "don't be fooled by the gray, outdated exterior." Classrooms are "all equipped with state-of-the-art technology." "The wireless Internet throughout the school is wonderful," claims one student, "The building is a maze." Also, some areas get "a little crowded with everyone's books and laptops."

Life

There is both "a strong sense of camaraderie" and "a somewhat competitive atmosphere" here. Capital is "small" and "very family-oriented." "Everyone is friendly and willing to help out," says one student. Competition for coveted A's can be stiff, though.

Linda J. Mihely, Assistant Dean of Admissions and Financial Aid
303 E. Broad Street, Columbus, OH 43215-3200
Tel: 614-236-6310 Fax: 614-236-6972
E-Mail: admissions@law.capital.edu • Website: www.law.capital.edu

"It is best not to mention grades except among close friends." "There seems to be a sort of divide among students at the law school." "Day and evening students don't interact much at all," and most agree that "the day program is much more competitive." "The evening program is much more relaxed in class" because "Most people have very busy lives outside of school." "Evening students are a different breed," explains one student. "I can honestly report that studying law with people whose resumes are already filled with diverse experience has been very rewarding."

"Students here are generally pretty vocal about issues that matter to them." Ethnically, "Students are mainly white," but "There is a great minority community." You'll find a very high number of "nontraditional law students" here and a "wide range in age" and "professions." "Some spend their days talking about drinking and parties, while other more serious students spend their days studying," observes a 2L. "It is quite obvious which students are fresh out of undergrad."

There are "lots of student organizations" and "ways to get involved." "Community-service projects are everywhere," and "The main law fraternities are very active." Capital sponsors "planned social hours" and "a lot of events and different opportunities for students to get to know each other." "It is very easy to find a group of people with similar interests both in and out of the legal field." Students give the city of Columbus high marks. "It's not San Francisco or Boston," but "There are usually student-group sponsored happy hours at various bars downtown" and "social nights in and around Columbus at other bars." "Often after classes are over on Friday or after a midterm, an impromptu group will just go out somewhere."

Getting In

Admitted students at the 25th percentile here have LSAT scores of about 151 and GPAs hovering just around 3.0. Admitted students at the 75th percentile have LSAT scores of 156 and GPAs of approximately 3.5.

Clinical program required	No
Legal writing course requirement	Yes
Legal methods course requirement	Yes
Legal research course requirement	Yes
Moot court requirement	No
Public interest law requirement	No

ADMISSIONS

Selectivity Rating	76
# applications received	1,269
% applicants accepted	56
% acceptees attending	35
Average LSAT	153
LSAT Range	141–166
Average undergrad GPA	3.31
Application fee	$40
Regular application	Rolling, up to 5/1
Regular notification	Rolling
Early application program	No
Transfer students accepted	Yes
Evening division offered	Yes
Part-time accepted	Yes
CAS accepted	Yes

International Students

TOEFL required of international students	

FINANCIAL FACTS

Annual tuition	$33,180
Books and supplies	$1,501
Room and board	$13,785
Financial aid application deadline	4/1
% first-year students receiving some sort of aid	94
% receiving some sort of aid	93
% of aid that is merit based	40
% receiving scholarships	47
Average grant	$10,000
Average loan	$36,063
Average total aid package	$45,236
Average debt	$103,426

EMPLOYMENT INFORMATION

Career Rating	76	Grads Employed by Field (%)
Rate of placement (nine months out)	85	Academic (3)
Average starting salary	$60,662	Business/industry (21)
State for bar exam	OH	Government (14)
Pass rate for first-time bar	93	Judicial clerkship (3)
Employers Who Frequently Hire Grads		Military (2)
Law firms, Government agencies, Business and corporate employers		Private practice (55)
		Public interest (3)

Prominent Alumni

David Tannenbaum, Partner, Fulbright Jaworski–Patent Law; Deborah Pryce, former U.S. Congress Woman; Paul McNulty, Deputy Attorney General, U.S. Deptartment of Justice; Robert Schottenstein, Chairman, CEO, and President of M/I Homes, Inc.; Thomas Baruch, Founder & Managing Director, CMEA Ventures

Case Western Reserve University

School of Law

Academics

Case Western Reserve University School of Law is "a very supportive, friendly, and welcoming law school community" emphasizing technology and "practical lawyering skills." Numerous cutting-edge academic centers on campus offer instruction in a wide range of unique legal niches, including regulatory law and law and medicine. Case Western Reserve's international law program is "one of the best in the entire country." As one student explains, it's "pretty amazing to have class with international law professors who have helped construct international tribunals—and have them crack jokes with you." Students also say "The CaseArc curriculum with practical lawyer[ing] skills is very good and realistic." Concentration programs include law and technology, litigation, and health law. Dual-degree programs include a JD/MD and a JD/master's in social work. Also, "If you're interested in community-service and public interest work, you have more options than you'd ever have time to pursue."

"Professors are excellent" at Case Western Reserve Law. They are "intelligent, dedicated, and experienced," and "They all seem to love teaching and love the law." Courses are generally "lively and interesting." "Many members of the faculty are younger and they bring energy and enthusiasm to the classroom along with pedagogical methods that keep pace with modern technology." "They have an amazing knack for generating excitement out of mundane material," raves a 2L. "I will enroll in any course that these professors teach, simply because they are so passionate and challenging." The "interesting" adjuncts are "almost always great" as well, "and often come from elite firms." Outside of class, professors are "quite accessible and willing to grab a drink with you." The administration is "amazingly accessible" as well.

On the career front, students are mostly satisfied with the Career Services Office. The school's location in one of the nation's top ten legal markets certainly doesn't hurt. "Case Western Reserve has a strong reputation," and "Students who do exceptionally well academically do not have much of a problem" getting "an incredibly high-paying job" in any number of major cities across the country. Case Western Reserve Law's reputation "does not extend greatly to the coasts," though. "Finding employment outside of the Midwest region has been a problem for some students," and "It can be very difficult" for less-than-stellar students to find work, particularly outside the surrounding area.

Students say the "Case Western Reserve law building is okay, but not great. However, its location is perfect. University Circle is an oasis in Cleveland and I have never lived in a better area." The area is "a pleasure to relax in after the stresses of law school." "The library staff is excellent and always more than happy to help," and there are plenty of "private cubicles with comfortable desks and chairs." The main university library is nearby as well and "open twenty-four hours," which is "a very important plus." "The classrooms are pretty standard," but they are generously outfitted with wireless access and ample power sources for laptops.

Life

"There is a fair amount of race, gender, and social diversity" at Case Western Reserve Law. The majority of students in each class hail from "states other than Ohio," and many "don't plan to stay" after graduation. Some students are competitive, but there are "very few overly competitive students." "Everyone is extremely helpful and people in the same class pass around outlines." "Although students at Case Western Reserve are competitive, there is a real sense of community here. Students help each other and don't try

ELAINE GREAVES, ASSISTANT DEAN FOR ADMISSIONS
11075 EAST BOULEVARD, CLEVELAND, OH 44106
TEL: 800-756-0036 FAX: 216-368-1042
E-MAIL: LAWADMISSIONS@CASE.EDU • WEBSITE: WWW.LAW.CASE.EDU

to undermine their classmates to get ahead." "There is a feeling of community where we all want to be successful and are proud of being Case Western Reserve Law students, and in that sense we compete together against the rest of the legal world."

Socially, "There is a decent sense of community." "You can make your life as social as you want." Students call the "extremely active" Student Bar Association "the best SBA anywhere." Receptions, speakers, and happy hours are frequent. "Every Thursday, you can go to the bars and see people at school on a social level and it's very laid-back," explains a 1L.

Of their environs, students say "the campus is beautiful," located in walking distance from a beautiful orchestra hall, art museum, botanical garden, and planetarium, and only fifteen minutes from the bars, restaurants, and theaters of downtown Cleveland. Much of the rest of the Queen City is "less attractive" but, as one student notes, this feature makes it "a great place to study." "Coming to Case Western Reserve, I was most concerned about living in Cleveland—the 'mistake on the lake'—where even the river caught fire," confides a 3L. "But really, it's not a bad place to spend three years." Another student concurs: "I didn't expect to like Cleveland as much as I did, but I do."

Getting In

With little over 200 spots in Case Western Reserve's entering law school class, competition is high. According to the school's website, "We insist upon diversity in our student body because we believe that the entire law school community benefits from it." The admissions committee evaluates applicants holistically, "looking carefully at the candidate's undergraduate grade point average and LSAT score as well as other, non-quantitative factors, such as level and difficulty of undergraduate course work, writing ability, and work experience."

EMPLOYMENT INFORMATION

Career Rating	82
Rate of placement (nine months out)	92
Average starting salary	$75,420
State for bar exam	OH, NY, IL, CA, PA
Pass rate for first-time bar	86

Employers Who Frequently Hire Grads
Large law firms in major U.S. cities, including Cleveland, New York, Chicago, Los Angeles, Washington DC, and Boston; small- and mid-size law firms throughout the country; corporate legal departments; consulting firms; federal and state government, including the Department of Justice; the federal, state, and local judiciary; and public interest organizations

Prominent Alumni
Barry M. Meyer, Chairman and CEO, Warner Bros. Entertainment; Joseph Hubach, Sr. VP, Secretary and General

Counsel, Texas Instruments; Catherine M. Kilbane, Sr. VP and General Counsel, American Greetings Corp.; Richard North Patterson, Author; Ralph Sargent Tyler, II, Chief Food Counsel, U.S. Food and Drug Administration

Grads Employed by Field (%)

Academic	(1)
Business/industry	(23)
Government	(15)
Judicial clerkship	(5)
Military	(1)
Private practice	(44)
Public interest	(11)

Science, 4 years; JD/CNM Certificate in Nonprofit Management, 3 years; JD/MD Medicine, 7 years

Clinical program required	No
Legal writing	
course requirement	Yes
Legal methods	
course requirement	Yes
Legal research	
course requirement	Yes
Moot court requirement	No
Public interest	
law requirement	No

ADMISSIONS

Selectivity Rating	83
# applications received	2,193
% applicants accepted	38
% acceptees attending	29
LSAT Range	157–162
Average undergrad GPA	3.44
Application fee	$40
Regular application	Rolling, up to 8/15
Regular notification	Rolling
Early application program	Yes
Early application deadline	11/15
Early application notification	12/15
Transfer students accepted	Yes
Evening division offered	No
Part-time accepted	No
CAS accepted	Yes

International Students
TOEFL recommended of international students

FINANCIAL FACTS

Annual tuition	$40,450
Books and supplies	$2,870
Fees	$110
Room and board	$16,785
Financial aid application	
deadline	5/1
% first-year students	
receiving some sort of aid	96
% receiving some sort of aid	82
% of aid that is merit based	100
% receiving scholarships	79
Average grant	$12,000
Average loan	$45,000
Average total aid package	$59,600
Average debt	$94,000

THE CATHOLIC UNIVERSITY OF AMERICA
COLUMBUS SCHOOL OF LAW

INSTITUTIONAL INFORMATION

Public/private	Private
Affiliation	Roman Catholic
Student/faculty ratio	16:1
% faculty part-time	64
% faculty female	27
% faculty minority	16
Total faculty	136

SURVEY SAYS...

Diverse opinions accepted in classrooms, Great research resources, Great library staff, Beautiful campus

STUDENTS

Enrollment of law school	850
% male/female	47/53
% full-time	66
% minority	18
% international	4
Average age of entering class	25

ACADEMICS

Academic Experience Rating	**83**
Profs interesting rating	82
Profs accessible rating	76
Hours of study per day	4.24

Academic Specialties

Corporation Securities, International, Communication; Law and Public Policy

Advanced Degrees Offered

JD, 3 years full-time, 4 years part-time

Combined Degrees Offered

JD/MA programs in accounting, canon law, history, philosophy, psychology, politics, library science, economics, and social work, 3–4 years

Academics

Students who come to Catholic University's Columbus School of Law in Washington, D.C., shouldn't be surprised to learn that Catholic University's religious affiliation is right in the name. The majority of the student body self-identifies as Catholic, and there is a "heavy emphasis on public service and public interest" and there is a university wide Catholic "speaker policy" —"only 'Catholic' speakers are allowed, i.e., no pro-choice and no pro-gay"—but overall, it is" a very diverse group in terms of beliefs and political leanings, which, being in D.C., creates a very stimulating environment."

The law school provides excellent specialization opportunities, including seven institutions and special programs, which allow students who qualify to concentrate in a chosen area of law. Among these are the well-connected (and oldest) Institute for Communications Law Studies and the Securities Law Program, as well as the newest addition, the Intellectual Property Program, and the Institute program is great for those who "have a good idea of what area of law we wish to focus on in practice or are simply interested in and enjoy; the program requirements are rigorous and clearly defined and well suited for focusing on the particular program areas."

Some evening students feel that their program is "poorly administered," especially considering that they "are held to the exact same standards as day students." Many complain about the lack of forethought put into the planning of classes in regard to their needs and the communication skills of the administration, among other things. "We are made aware of school-related obligations and news through a last-minute and piecemeal communication process—more often than not, we have to dig to find out information we need," says a student, though the law school is making efforts to address the communication issue. Many (but not all) full-time students log similar complaints regarding the administration's way of doing things, particularly the incredibly clunky scheduling of classes. There are also grumblings that the school is "not as 'on top of' up-and-coming areas of law as they could be," says another.

Luckily, the faculty "more than compensates for any shortfall" in the administration. Though there are definitely some bad apples, "Most professors are more than willing to help with any request—be it classroom or employment related." "Professors often treat us as colleagues, and there is a mutual respect inside and outside the classroom," says a student. They are "brilliant, accomplished, but also approachable and genuinely care about the students." Another thing the school has going for it is "location, location, location." There are "numerous opportunities to gain practical experience in the legal epicenter that is Washington, D.C.," and that location allows the school to draw professors with "high-powered experience and strong connections." "The stuff happening in town is relevant to what you're studying in class," says a 1L. Facilities here are also "top-notch"—not only are they visually appealing, but "they provide all the required technological advances required by a student in today's world."

SHANI BUTTS, DIRECTOR OF ADMISSIONS
CARDINAL STATION, WASHINGTON, D.C. 20064
TEL: 202-319-5151 FAX: 202-319-6285
E-MAIL: ADMISSIONS@LAW.EDU • WEBSITE: WWW.LAW.EDU

Life

This bunch is a convivial crew who are instilled with the knowledge that "the people in our classes are going to be our colleagues when we are done with school, so everyone is willing to work together if someone needs help." Students here work hard, and "The environment amongst students is about as positive as a system based on pure academic competition can be." Again, there is a split between evening and day students, but as there isn't much overlap, tension is kept at a minimum. The average student here is "smart, conscientious, and fun," and "It seems like there are no 'bad apples'" in this "supportive and positive environment."

As far as student social life goes, there are plenty of opportunities for extracurricular involvement, both social and academic: clubs, organizations, social events/parties, moot court, journal, trial advocacy. "Although I do not have a social life, it is of my own doing as the school provides the opportunity for a vast number of happy hours both on and off campus as well as larger events," confesses a 2L. "The entire law school is self-contained, with "everything from the classrooms, to the library, prof's offices, and cafeteria…all in one gorgeous building made of marble and limestone."

Getting In

Catholic often faces strict competition from Georgetown and GW for students who want to get a law degree in the D.C. area, so typical admissions stats aren't as high. Full-time enrolled students for the most recent class have an LSAT score of 156 at the 25th percentile and a GPA of roughly 3.09. Enrolled students at the 75th percentile have an LSAT score of 160 and a GPA of 3.57. Students in the evening division have slightly lower grades and LSAT scores on average, yet all possess relevant professional experience.

Clinical program required	No
Legal writing course requirement	Yes
Legal methods course requirement	Yes
Legal research course requirement	No
Moot court requirement	No

ADMISSIONS

Selectivity Rating	84
# applications received	3,372
% applicants accepted	34
% acceptees attending	24
Average LSAT	159
LSAT Range	157–161
Average undergrad GPA	3.30
Application fee	$65
Regular application	Rolling, up to 3/11
Regular notification	Rolling
Early application program	Yes
Early application deadline	11/1
Early application notification	12/15
Transfer students accepted	Yes
Evening division offered	Yes
Part-time accepted	Yes
CAS accepted	Yes

International Students

TOEFL required of international students

FINANCIAL FACTS

Annual tuition	$41,830
Books and supplies	$1,800
Fees	$905
Room and board	$17,000
Financial aid application deadline	7/15
% first-year students receiving some sort of aid	87
% receiving some sort of aid	90
% of aid that is merit based	34
% receiving scholarships	31
Average grant	$11,397
Average loan	$39,080
Average total aid package	$43,375
Average debt	$92,000

EMPLOYMENT INFORMATION

		Grads Employed by Field (%)
Career Rating	72	Business/industry (24)
Rate of placement (nine months out)	94	Government (27)
Average starting salary	$64,000	Judicial clerkship (11)
State for bar exam	MD, VA, PA, NY, NJ	Private practice (34)
Employers Who Frequently Hire Grads		Public interest (3)
Akin, Gump, Strauss, Hauer and Feld;		
Clifford Chance; Jones Day; U.S.		
Department of Justice, Securities and		
Exchange Commission		

CHAPMAN UNIVERSITY
SCHOOL OF LAW

INSTITUTIONAL INFORMATION

Public/private	Private
Affiliation	Disciples of Christ
Student/faculty ratio	9:1
% faculty part-time	37
% faculty female	20
% faculty minority	8
Total faculty	99

SURVEY SAYS...

Diverse opinions accepted in classrooms, Great research resources, Beautiful campus, Students love Orange, CA

STUDENTS

Enrollment of law school	555
% male/female	54/46
% full-time	94
% minority	20
% international	1
Average age of entering class	24

ACADEMICS

Academic Experience Rating	**94**
Profs interesting rating	93
Profs accessible rating	93
Hours of study per day	4.60

Academic Specialties

Environmental, International, Property, Taxation, Advocacy and Dispute Resolution, Entertainment Law (with IP courses)

Advanced Degrees Offered

JD, 3 years full-time, 4 years part-time; LLM Tax, 1 year full-time; LLM Prosecutorial Science, 1 year; LLM in Business and Economics; LLM in Entertainment and Media Law; LLM in International and Comparative Law; LLM in Trial Advocacy

Combined Degrees Offered

JD/MBA, 4 years; JD/MFA 4 years

Academics

Chapman University School of Law is located "in the heart of Southern California," "just minutes away from the Orange County courts and only thirty-five miles from downtown" Los Angeles. "The law school itself is beautiful." "The facilities are state-of-the-art," "very modern," "grand yet cozy," and generally "amazing." "Classrooms are a dream." Study space is ample. "The research facilities leave students wanting for nothing." "It is a very nice environment in which to spend large amounts of time." And it's not just all the bells and whistles that make Chapman great—Chapman offers the academic heft to complement its beautiful facilities. The school boasts two law journals and a unique certificate program in entertainment law. Certificates are also available in tax law, international law, environmental law and land use, and dispute resolution. Moot court and other trial competition teams are perennial powerhouses. There are "numerous clinics that provide valuable experience in a broad range of fields," including a family violence clinic and a constitutional jurisprudence clinic. Students seeking international exposure can study abroad in England and Australia. "Chapman also has a very comprehensive bar preparation program that it provides for students at no additional cost" during the spring of their third year. Class sizes tend to be smaller here, which affords "a very intimate feeling, unlike that of a larger school," and students have nothing but praise for their professors. The faculty is brimming with "fun, brilliant" profs who are "challenging but not patronizing." Outside of class, faculty members are reportedly "easily accessible and always open to discussion with students." In class, "they manage to make even subjects like federal income tax exciting." "We have professors that quote popular television shows during class, sing songs about the subject matter, and make witty comments that make us laugh to lighten the mood between the times when they scare us to death with the Socratic method," relates a 1L.

Administratively, "the registrar's office is a nightmare" but complaints are otherwise rare. "It's an ongoing 'love-in' between the administration and the students," explains a 2L. "It's like Woodstock, only without the hallucinogenic substances and endless rain." The top brass reportedly provides "overwhelming and unending support" and "really cares about making the school better." "They have tons of money," adds a 3L, "and they spend it pretty effectively." As a result, high grades are difficult to achieve on a consistent basis here. Students also point out that Chapman's reputation beyond the immediate area "could improve." "The legal community outside of Orange County doesn't know much about the school," laments a 3L, although "the administration is working hard" to change that, starting with the recent hiring of a new high profile dean with connections throughout the state.

Life

"Chapman has a reputation as being a conservative school," explains a 3L, "but I think that reputation is true only when compared to other schools." Students agree, "Chapman has strong diversity of thought." "Regardless of race, ethnicity, sexual orientation, political views, religious preference, or cultural background, the social fabric of the Chapman community is tightly knit, and no one is viewed as an outsider here." "Being a liberal student, I have not felt uncomfortable in any way," declares another 3L. "Quite the opposite, the school has always fostered an environment of healthy discussion and acceptance of all students." Beyond politics, students here are "witty, darn[ed] smart, and pleasant to be around." The Chapman Law population is comprised of "very social" younger students and older students who "seem to spend more time studying and less time hanging out at school, so that when they have free time, they can spend it with their

TRACY SIMMONS, ASSISTANT DEAN OF ADMISSIONS AND FINANCIAL AID, DIVERSITY INITIATIVE
ONE UNIVERSITY DRIVE, ORANGE, CA 92866
TEL: 714-628-2500 FAX: 714-628-2501
E-MAIL: LAWADM@CHAPMAN.EDU • WEBSITE: WWW.CHAPMAN.EDU/LAW

families." The "relaxed but rigorous" academic atmosphere is "very community-oriented." "Everyone is aware that we're being curved against each other, but that doesn't stop us from helping each other succeed," relates a 2L. "Everyone pushes each other to success." "Law students do compete for grades," though, and there are definitely "competitive undertones." When students have the time or just can't bring themselves to brief another case, "There are plenty of opportunities to steal away" from course work. For one thing, "the weather is always perfect." "There is a club for everyone." "The school is also very successful in bringing in high-level speakers, including judges and well-known academics." "A multitude of dialogues, lectures, and panels "presents various legal issues and different perspectives on those issues. "The school is located in an area with a ton of fun restaurants and bars right down the street" as well.

Getting In

Enrolled students at the 75th percentile have LSAT scores of about 160 and GPAs a little lower than 3.68. Enrolled students at the 25th percentile have LSAT scores of approximately 155 and GPAs a little over 3.21. Also worth noting here is the fact that the admissions staff will look at all of your LSAT scores, not just your best one.

Clinical program required	No
Legal writing course requirement	Yes
Legal methods course requirement	Yes
Legal research course requirement	Yes
Moot court requirement	Yes
Public interest law requirement	No

ADMISSIONS

Selectivity Rating	86
# applications received	2,779
% applicants accepted	27
% acceptees attending	14
Average LSAT	159
LSAT Range	155–161
Average undergrad GPA	3.52
Application fee	$75
Regular application	Rolling, up to 4/15
Regular notification	Rolling
Early application program	No
Transfer students accepted	Yes
Evening division offered	No
Part-time accepted	Yes
CAS accepted	Yes

International Students

TOEFL required of international students	

FINANCIAL FACTS

Annual tuition	$41,460
Books and supplies	$1,680
Fees	$403
Room and board	$16,110
Financial aid application deadline	3/2
% first-year students receiving some sort of aid	97
% receiving some sort of aid	96
% of aid that is merit based	23
% receiving scholarships	48
Average grant	$25,623
Average loan	$46,107
Average total aid package	$54,277
Average debt	$115,064

EMPLOYMENT INFORMATION

Career Rating	89
Rate of placement (nine months out)	97
State for bar exam	CA
Pass rate for first-time bar	70

Employers Who Frequently Hire Grads
Dorsey & Whitney, LLP; Payne & Fears, LLP; Gordon & Rees, LLP; O'Melveny & Myers, LLP; Knobbe Martens; Sidley, Austin, Brown & Wood, LLP; Allen Matkins Leck Gamble Mallory; Natsis, LLP; Koeller, Nebeker, Carlson, Haluck, LLP; Walsworth Franklin Bevins & McCall LLP;Collins, Collins, Muir and Stewart LLP; Lane Powell, PC; Tressler LLP; Deloitte; Baker & Hostetler, LLP; Rutan & Tucker; Paul Hastings; Lewis, Brisbois, Bisgaard & Smith LLP; Bonne, Bridges, Mueller, O'Keefe & Nichols; Sedgwick, Detert, Moran & Arnold LLP; Blakely Sokoloff Taylor & Zafman; Jones Day; Nossaman, LLP; Wood, Smith, Henning & Berman LLP; Bremer Whyte Brown and O'Meara LLP; Niagara Bottling, LLC; First American Title Insurance Company; IRS, Office of the Chief Counsel; U.S. Department of Health & Human Services; U.S. Department of Homeland Security; U.S. Secret Service; U.S. Department of Labor;

Department of State, Bureau of Consular Affairs; JAG Corps; State Department of Alcohol Beverage Control, CA; Orange County Superior Court; Orange County Counsel; Orange County District Attorney; Orange County Public Defender; Long Beach City Prosecutor's Office City of Aurora, CO; Anthem Blue Cross; Fireman's Fund Insurance Co.; First American Title; Ayco; PricewaterhouseCoopers; Northop Grumman; Mexicana Airlines; Capitol Records; Rhino Records; Gaylord Sports Management; Riverside County District Attorney; San Bernardino County District Attorney; Los Angeles County Public Defender; San Bernardino County Public Defender

Prominent Alumni
Steve Ruden, Partner, Knobbe Martens; Brian Gadol, Partner, Dorsey & Whitney LLP; Nikole Kingston; Sean Stegmaier; Kelly Wood, Associates, O'Melveny & Myers LLLP; Allison LeMoine-Bui, Brandon Sylvia, Ryan Chavez, Jennifer Farrell, Associates, Rutan& Tucker LLP; Kathryn Casey, Partner, Jackson, DeMarco, Tidus & Peckenpaugh

CHARLESTON SCHOOL OF LAW*

INSTITUTIONAL INFORMATION

Public/private	Private
Student/faculty ratio	19:1
% faculty part-time	41
% faculty female	60
% faculty minority	16
Total faculty	70

SURVEY SAYS...

Diverse opinions accepted in classrooms, Students love Charleston, SC

STUDENTS

Enrollment of law school	743
% male/female	55/45
% from out-of-state	35
% full-time	80
% minority	10
# of countries represented	1
Average age of entering class	24

ACADEMICS

Academic Experience Rating	79
Profs interesting rating	88
Profs accessible rating	89
Hours of study per day	4.74
Clinical program required	No
Legal writing	
course requirement	Yes
Legal methods	
course requirement	No
Legal research	
course requirement	No
Moot court requirement	No
Public interest	
law requirement	Yes

Academics

Charleston School of Law, located in gorgeous Charleston, South Carolina, is so new that it's practically still in the wrapping. Accredited by the ABA in 2006, the school has managed to do a "pretty fantastic job" of creating a supportive and relatively thorough learning environment that doesn't have to answer to centuries-old traditions or any form of "this is how it's always been done." The school was formed with the goal of creating lawyers "who are social engineers," and it works toward this goal by encouraging service through the dozens of pro bono legal opportunities that allow students to get practical experience relating to the substantive material learned in class. "We are not just learning to pass the bar; we are learning to be practitioners of the law," says a 1L. The program's youth also renders the entire school community "highly motivated to be successful."

Faculty here are "beyond outstanding." The school's open-door policy is somewhat of an understatement, as "deans and professors actually bring their 'open doors' to us whenever and wherever you could imagine." "In times of trouble, they are there. In times of joy, they are there. They not only want to be involved in their students' educations; they thrive on it," says another student. "The teaching methods, style, and dedication to academia have amounted to a wonderful experience," says another. The Socratic Method is heavily relied on here, and many professors will call on random students to "stand and deliver" in class. Several professors keep a deck of cards with students' names and pictures, "which they flip through to pick who will be called on."

Professors who go out of their way to make sure that students are comfortable with the material presented are the norm, rather than the exception at Charleston School of Law. "I e-mailed my professor with a question a few days before an exam. She quickly responded by e-mail, but followed up by calling the school, getting my phone number, and calling me to make sure I didn't have any more questions and to provide me with her phone number in case I did," says one first-year student. Staff members are similarly "kind and supportive" and are particularly helpful with letting students know about jobs, externship, and internship opportunities.

Classrooms at the Charleston School of Law are equipped with modern technology and stadium seating and "have proven to be a great place to learn." The library is also top-of-the-line, featuring private study rooms, accessible computers, and a wide variety of print sources. Additionally, the library staff "is passionate about work and always available to help with hard-to-find legal documents." Though students wish there were more elective classes, the school is still in the nascent stage, and the administration is nothing but hands-on in terms of shaping the curriculum and getting involved with student organizations and publications.

Life

The School of Law's location is ideal not just for its beauty and weather conditions, but for the "extraordinary amount of history [that] surrounds us" in the heart of South Carolina. Being situated right down the road from the "Four Corners of Law" means that students "are in a key location to observe many real world legal proceedings." Though Charleston can be an expensive city to live in and "parking is an issue," the school is "split up" among several nearby buildings, making it "nice to get up and move around a bit."

* Provisionally approved by the ABA

P.O. Box 535, Charleston, SC 29402
Tel: 843-329-1000
E-Mail: info@charlestonlaw.edu • Website: www.charlestonlaw.edu

One of the benefits of the school's age is that it "is too young to have an 'old-boy, Southern' feel to it." There's "a great mixture of students" within the student body (though the majority certainly hail from within the state and skew younger), and it's "evident that the student body is changing and diversifying" from its initial population. There's no shortage of social interaction available, but most students "are diligent in working hard first and taking time for social events later." Student organizations go beyond the social realm and "bring in speakers and expose students to new ideas."

Getting In

Having been accredited only since 2006, admission levels aren't yet as strict as they're sure to get once the school finds its reputation and footing. For the moment, around thirty-eight percent of full-time applications get a yes, with the median LSAT and GPA for the class of 2013 hovering around 153 and 3.14, respectively. Solid B students with decent LSAT scores shouldn't have any trouble getting in. About one-half of the school's full-time students are residents of South Carolina.

ADMISSIONS

Selectivity Rating	**80**
# applications received	2,200
% applicants accepted	37
% acceptees attending	23
Average LSAT	155
LSAT Range	153–157
Average undergrad GPA	3.20
Application fee	$50
Regular application	Yes
Regular notification	Yes
Early application program	No
Transfer students accepted	Yes
Evening division offered	Yes
Part-time accepted	Yes
CAS accepted	Yes

FINANCIAL FACTS

Annual tuition	$35,606
Books and supplies	$1,250
Fees	$100
Room and board	$10,800
Financial aid application deadline	4/15
% receiving scholarships	37
Average grant	$7,500
Average loan	$45,512
Average debt	$128,571

EMPLOYMENT INFORMATION

Career Rating	**72**

CITY UNIVERSITY OF NEW YORK
SCHOOL OF LAW

Academics

The incredibly affordable CUNY—Law is "full of school spirit, clinical training, and no page ripping out of library books." Working under the mission "law in the service of human needs," the school is "genuinely committed to the struggle for justice," and tends to attract a different type of law student; unlike a lot of New York law schools, the vast majority of the "dedicated" and "idealistic" students here go on to careers in public interest. This mission creates a law school experience like no other—students are encouraging to one another and help each other to thrive, and everyone involved with the school wishes success on each new class. "Put it this way, I have a number of my professors' cell phone numbers, I call them by their first names, and our janitors come to our graduation because they are proud of us," says a 3L.

The curriculum here provides a well-rounded education of law and case-teaching method, along with policy and legal theory, enabling students to do more progressive work in the legal field. There is no grading curve, classes stress doctrinal work and advocacy, seminars teach practical skills with lawyering, and the research requirements prepare students for internships/careers. Legal clinics offer myriad of practical experience, particularly in the third year. Professors are "diverse, engaged and receptive to students," and many "have amazing histories of advocacy work," with backgrounds in feminist organizing work, gay rights, environmental justice, reproductive rights, and "everything else fun and liberal." There can be a touch of disorganization and bureaucracy in the administration, but it's kept to a minimum, and administrators "can be great if you find them on a good day." The law school building is actually an old middle school in a somewhat remote part of New York City, so the "facilities definitely leave something to be desired," though the law school is moving to a new location in Long Island City, with easy access to public transit and near the Long Island City Courthouse. All classrooms are equipped with at least one computer and a SmartBoard for easy note-taking, and outside of the classroom, discussions are continued "on the course websites that each professor dedicate to maintain."

In the end, it's the complete commitment from faculty, staff, and students to the school's mission that wins students over, and the comfortable, supportive environment created when surrounded by people with similar motives. "No one here is trying to be an ambulance chaser or a barracuda or any of the other stereotypes of lawyers. Everyone here is genuinely interested in being a champion for a cause and the cause is people who genuinely need the law on their side," says a proud student.

Life

Most who attend school here have been out of undergrad for quite awhile and have a wide variety of experience working for nonprofit organizations and activist jobs, so they come to school with a clear idea of the type of public interest law they want to practice. This results in an "incredibly collaborative learning environment" and students want to see each other succeed. In fact, they're downright rabid about the fact that competition does not exist at CUNY: "I had computer problems during midterms and finals my first semester, and people were practically throwing their outlines at me so I would do well!" says a student. Since a lot of people commute and there is no out-of-state housing, it "sometimes feels hard to get everyone together," but "small class sizes make it easier to make 'school friends.'" and people "definitely coalesce around local bars to celebrate midterms, finals and anything in between." There are many student clubs and events, even if students are often too exhausted to take part in them. Though the location in New

Yvonne Cherena-Pacheco, Asst. Dean for Enrollment Mgmt & Dir. of Admiss'ns
65-21 Main Street, Flushing, NY 11367-1358
Tel: 718-340-4210 Fax: 718-340-4435
E-Mail: admissions@mail.law.cuny.edu • Website: www.law.cuny.edu

York City is always a plus and the nearby Flushing cuisine is delicious and authentic, the school itself is a full fifteen-minute bus ride from the closest subway, so the commute can be trying for some students.

Although the school is very liberal in its ideology, when it comes to conversation and debate, "No one is shunned because they aren't of a certain persuasion." This liberalism also translates to action, and "Everything gets heated up, from new listservs, banning Coke products, and scheduling of classes and finals." Still, everyone here gets along really well and is "like a family," but just like in a family, "Any drama is magnified because of the school's small size."

Getting In

CUNY evaluates prospective students based on their demonstrated abilities and intellectual capacity to complete a rigorous legal program, using test scores, previous academic records, and, where applicable, post-college work experience. In addition to these factors, CUNY seeks students who can bring diversity of background and experience to the campus and who express a specific interest in and affinity for the values of the program. Finally, CUNY favors New York residents or students with a particular interest in serving the New York community.

ADMISSIONS

Selectivity Rating	80
# applications received	2,137
% applicants accepted	25
% acceptees attending	31
Average LSAT	154
LSAT Range	152–157
Average undergrad GPA	3.32
Application fee	$60
Regular application	3/15
Regular notification	6/16
Early application program	No
Transfer students accepted	Yes
Evening division offered	No
Part-time accepted	No
CAS accepted	Yes

International Students

TOEFL recommended of international students

FINANCIAL FACTS

Annual tuition	
(in-state/out-of-state)	$10,495/
	$17,445
Books and supplies	$1,712
Fees	$312
Room and board	$16,231
Financial aid application	
deadline	5/3
% first-year students	
receiving some sort of aid	97
% receiving some sort of aid	90
% of aid that is merit based	18
% receiving scholarships	34
Average grant	$7,679
Average loan	$24,680
Average total aid package	$31,965
Average debt	$71,145

EMPLOYMENT INFORMATION

Career Rating	74
Rate of placement (nine months out)	83
Average starting salary	$49,570
State for bar exam	NY
Pass rate for first-time bar	80

Employers Who Frequently Hire Grads
Legal Aid Society; Legal Services Offices; New York Lawyers for the Public Interest; Defenders Office; Public Interest Organizations; Government Services; District Attorney Offices; Public Interest Fellowships

Prominent Alumni
Robert Bank, Executive Vice President, American Jewish World Service; Hon. Diccia T. Pineda-Kirwan, Justice, New York Supreme Court; Kary Moss, Executive Director, American Civil Liberties Union; Hon. Edwina G. Richardson-Mendelson, Administrative Judge, New York Family Court; Hon. Matthew T. Ryan, Mayor, Binghamton, New York; Paula A. Bosco, Director of Compliance, New Mountain Capital, LLC

Grads Employed by Field (%)
Academic (3)
Business/industry (11)
Government (13)
Judicial clerkship (13)
Private practice (19)
Public interest (41)

CLEVELAND STATE UNIVERSITY
CLEVELAND-MARSHALL COLLEGE OF LAW

INSTITUTIONAL INFORMATION

Public/private	Public
Student/faculty ratio	12:1
% faculty part-time	14
% faculty female	46
% faculty minority	16
Total faculty	76

SURVEY SAYS...

Great research resources,
Great library staff

STUDENTS

Enrollment of law school	613
% male/female	59/41
% from out-of-state	20
% full-time	74
% minority	15
% international	1
# of countries represented	8
Average age of entering class	26

ACADEMICS

Academic Experience Rating	**73**
Profs interesting rating	72
Profs accessible rating	68
Hours of study per day	4.44

Academic Specialties
Business Law, Civil Litigation,
Dispute Resolution, Criminal Law,
Employment and Labor Law,
International Comparative Law,
Health Law

Advanced Degrees Offered
LLM, 20–24 credits,1–4 years

Combined Degrees Offered
JD/Master in Public Administration,
JD/Master in Urban Planning,
Design, and Development, JD/
Master of Arts in Environmental
Studies, JD/Master of Science in
Environmental Science, JD/MBA,
4 years full-time

Academics

Students at Cleveland State University's Cleveland-Marshall College of Law call their school "a diamond in the rough." The focus here is squarely on bar preparation and practical training. "The greatest strengths are the opportunities for real-world experience," says a 3L. There are a half dozen clinics and they cover a wide range of legal areas. Externships with judges, government entities, and public interest groups are "readily available" in Cleveland and the greater metropolitan area. The moot court program is strong. The legal writing program thoroughly emphasizes "advocacy skills." If students run into academic difficulties, they can take advantage of Cleveland-Marshall's academic support programs, which provide group training and one-on-one assistance to help students with their course work. Areas of concentration are available in business law, civil litigation and dispute resolution, criminal law, employment law, health law, and international law. There are five dual-degree programs and three journals. Cleveland-Marshall Law is also quite a bargain, particularly if you are an Ohio resident.

"On average, Marshall professors are knowledgeable, passionate, and approachable," relates a 2L. "I have never been taught something as inherently boring as civil procedure in such an invigorating manner," beams a 1L. Professors are also generally accessible outside the classroom. The "excellent" administration is "extremely open to student interaction and answers questions and concerns promptly." However, "Heading to the main campus to get administrative stuff done can be tedious." Students' biggest academic complaint involves the distribution of grades. The curve here, which permits faculty members to give over fifty percent of all 1Ls a grade of C+ or lower, can be pretty rough.

Cleveland-Marshall Law is located in downtown Cleveland on the main campus of the larger university, which means that part-time work at local firms is easy to come by throughout the year. According to some students, "the facilities could be a little fancier." Most say that the layout of the law school is "not only aesthetically pleasing but functional," though. "The library is great." "The new addition is modern and beautiful," relates a 1L. "It's eye-catching from the street and a great place for students to study or relax between classes."

More than seventy-five percent of all newly minted graduates take jobs in either private practice or the corporate world. The overwhelming majority of Cleveland-Marshall's alumni practice in Ohio and the school's reputation is very solid throughout the northeastern part of the state. Students rave about Cleveland-Marshall Law's "connection to the Cleveland legal community" as well as "a supportive, active alumni base that extends opportunities to anyone who seeks them."

Life

The part-time program at Cleveland-Marshall is pretty large and "evening and day students do have very different experiences." As you would expect, full-timers are generally younger while part-timers are older and have "more time in the real world" already under their belts. "In my class, we have architects, engineers, law enforcement officials, researchers, bankers, and people with other varying careers," says a part-time 2L. Some part-time students complain that they are "excluded from a lot of school activities and

CHRISTOPHER LUCAK, ASSISTANT DEAN FOR ADMISSION AND FINANCIAL AID
2121 EUCLID AVENUE, LB 138, CLEVELAND, OH 44115-2214
TEL: 866-687-2304 FAX: 216-687-6881
E-MAIL: ADMISSIONS@LAW.CSUOHIO.EDU • WEBSITE: WWW.LAW.CSUOHIO.EDU

classes." Others assert that "the full- and part-timers are treated equally." "I am a full-time 3L who frequently takes night classes due to my part-time work schedule and I haven't noticed a divide between night and day professors' focus on the students," explains one student. "Some of the best professors I have had in law school teach night classes."

Student opinion concerning the academic atmosphere is mixed. Some students flatly call it "competitive." Others, staking something of a middle ground, say that "people are friendly and willing to help, most of the time." Still others describe "a great sense of camaraderie." "Students here help one another better than at any institution I've ever encountered," declares a 3L. Socially, clubs and extracurricular activities are abundant. "The student bar association plans fun socials at least once a month with free food and drinks for students to unwind." "Everyone seems to fall into whatever groups make them happy and things move right along." "Most of the students know one another," explains a 3L. "We have lockers, prom (Barrister's Ball), socials, drama, and tons of drinking." Beyond the law school orbit, Cleveland isn't generally listed among the greatest cities in the United States but there really are a lot of charming neighborhoods and the cost of living is comparatively low.

Getting In

Enrolled students at the 75th percentile at Cleveland-Marshall have LSAT scores around 157 and grade point averages of 3.66. At the 25th percentile, LSAT scores are 153, and GPAs are 3.09.

Clinical program required	No
Legal writing course requirement	Yes
Legal methods course requirement	No
Legal research course requirement	Yes
Moot court requirement	No
Public interest law requirement	No

ADMISSIONS

Selectivity Rating	82
# applications received	1,851
% applicants accepted	34
% acceptees attending	31
Average LSAT	156
LSAT Range	153–157
Average undergrad GPA	3.45
Regular application	Rolling, up to 5/1
Regular notification	Rolling
Early application program	No
Transfer students accepted	Yes
Evening division offered	Yes
Part-time accepted	Yes
CAS accepted	Yes

International Students

TOEFL required of international students	

FINANCIAL FACTS

Annual tuition (in-state/out-of-state)	$18,200/ $25,000
Books and supplies	$1,400
Fees	$25
Room and board	$11,000
Financial aid application deadline	5/1
% first-year students receiving some sort of aid	90
% receiving some sort of aid	90
% of aid that is merit based	45
% receiving scholarships	40
Average grant	$8,238
Average loan	$24,375
Average total aid package	$37,206
Average debt	$71,477

EMPLOYMENT INFORMATION

Career Rating	75
Rate of placement (nine months out)	88
Average starting salary	$73,815
State for bar exam	OH, NY, IL, FL
Pass rate for first-time bar	84

Employers Who Frequently Hire Grads

Jones Day; Baker & Hostetler; Thompson Hine; Squire, Sanders, & Dempsey; Calfee, Halter, & Griswold; Ernst & Young; Benesch, Friedlander, Coplan, & Arnold; Hahn, Loeser, & Parks, LLP; Fay Sharpe, LLP; Porter, Wright, Morris, & Arthur; Duvin, Cahn, & Hutton; Gallagher Sharpe; Kohrman, Jackson, & Krantz; McDonald Hopkins, LLC; Ulmer & Berne; and Weltman, Weinberg, & Reis are among the many employers who hire our students. A broad range of employers representing small, medium, and large firms, as well as business and government agencies employ our graduates

Prominent Alumni

Hon. Louis Stokes, U.S. House of Representatives, Rtd.; Hon. Maureen O'Connor, Chief Justice, Supreme Court of Ohio; Christopher Vasil, Chief Deputy Clerk, U.S. Supreme Court; Elizabeth Pugh, General Counsel, Library of Congress

Grads Employed by Field (%)

Academic	(1)
Business/industry	(27)
Government	(15)
Judicial clerkship	(5)
Military	(1)
Private practice	(48)
Public interest	(3)

THE COLLEGE OF WILLIAM & MARY
MARSHALL-WYTHE LAW SCHOOL

INSTITUTIONAL INFORMATION

Public/private	Public
Student/faculty ratio	14:1
% faculty part-time	59
% faculty female	33
% faculty minority	12
Total faculty	94

SURVEY SAYS...
Diverse opinions accepted in classrooms, Great research resources, Great library staff

STUDENTS

Enrollment of law school	632
% male/female	51/49
% from out-of-state	62
% full-time	100
% minority	20
% international	1
# of countries represented	11
Average age of entering class	23

ACADEMICS

Academic Experience Rating	89
Profs interesting rating	86
Profs accessible rating	85
Hours of study per day	4.39

Academic Specialties
Civil Procedure, Commercial, Constitutional, Corporation Securities, Criminal, Environmental, Human Rights, International, Labor, Legal History, Property, Taxation, Intellectual Property

Advanced Degrees Offered
JD, 3 years; LLM in the American Legal System, 1 year

Combined Degrees Offered
JD/Master of Public Policy, 4 years; JD/Master of Business Administration, 4 years; JD/Master of Arts in American Studies, 4 years.

Academics

As the oldest law school in the country, the College of William & Mary offers a "helpful and supportive atmosphere" in Williamsburg, Virginia, where the ideal of the "citizen-lawyer" thrives through an emphasis on ethics, both in class and in life. This emphasis, coupled with the school's vaulted honor code—which dates back to the eighteenth century—produces a "competent student body that is...engaged civically and professionally." Even though the school demands a high level of performance and integrity, the "collegial atmosphere" and the sky-high sense of community results in "students willing to cooperate and help each other learn, grow, and succeed." "It's a wonderful place to study law."

The academic experience at William & Mary is one centered on learning and skills, rather than "competition to get the highest grades at the expense of common courtesy." The professors all "really care that we are learning and like to push us to take things farther," and the school also provides all first-year courses with TAs who conduct review sessions several times a term, which everyone finds "*very* helpful when learning to 'think like a law student.'" "I have been invited to dinner at a professor's home at least once each semester," says a student.

Even if the administration doesn't get some things right, it is more than willing to listen to suggestions, and "The dean has town hall meetings where anyone can come raise concerns." This is not to say that there are not a few naysayers who demand more responsiveness for their problems, but overall, "Students, faculty, and administration all freely intermingle and combine to solve problems, innovate, and keep the school moving forward."

Though the price of tuition at the school is "a steal for being well-ranked in the Washington, D.C., market," some do wish there was a broader reach for career opportunities, as many of the current recruitment options are "geographically limited to [Virginia] and D.C." Still, there's bang for your buck, and the law school building has recently been updated, making it "home to the most technologically advanced courtroom in the country," as well as a newly renovated, "state-of-the-art" library that "has lots of study space."

Life

The general consensus is that most here think it would be difficult "to find a law school where people are as collaborative and down-to-earth" as at William & Mary. Everyone is "obviously very serious about...academics," but it "doesn't translate into unnecessary competition or aggression." "No one wants to get ahead by stepping over you," says a student. Humility reigns supreme, and while everyone here is "high-caliber" and intelligent, "people aren't going to strut around telling you about it." The sense of community is one of the main attributes that defines the student body, and people are all supportive of their fellow law schoolers, "even though we are on the same curve." "I could leave my wallet sitting in the middle of the lobby and it will still be there a week later," says a particularly trusting 1L.

FAYE SHEALY, ASSOCIATE DEAN

WILLIAM & MARY LAW SCHOOL, OFFICE OF ADMISSION, P.O. BOX 8795, WILLIAMSBURG, VA 23187-8795

TEL: 757-221-3785 FAX: 757-221-3261

E-MAIL: LAWADM@WM.EDU • WEBSITE: LAW.WM.EDU

Students here all feel that William & Mary "is a really diverse place where minorities aren't concerned about the statistical breakdown." "Our Black Law Students Association is one of the most active groups at the school and won national chapter of the year last year," says a 1L. "Students and professors rely on each other for amusement," and "We are all forced to be friends with each other because there is no one else." As a result, it's a very close-knit group where "very few people just commute in and out." The school does its best to provide amusement, and every Thursday there are bar reviews where students "all go to the same bar that is offering us drink specials," and in the fall, "there is a wine trip and the spring a ski trip." Students are "heavily involved" in activities and clubs, and there are also "a number of unique restaurants, shops, and places to visit within walking distance."

Getting In

Admitted students at the 25th percentile have LSAT scores of 161 and GPAs around 3.4. Admitted students at the 75th percentile have LSAT scores of 166 and GPAs just above 3.6. If you take the LSAT more than once, W&M "will evaluate the LSAT portion of the application by looking to the highest reported score."

Clinical program required	No
Legal writing course requirement	Yes
Legal methods course requirement	Yes
Legal research course requirement	Yes
Moot court requirement	No
Public interest law requirement	No

ADMISSIONS

Selectivity Rating	92
# applications received	6,292
% applicants accepted	19
% acceptees attending	18
Average LSAT	163
LSAT Range	160–166
Average undergrad GPA	3.61
Application fee	$50
Regular application	Rolling, up to 3/1
Regular notification	3/30
Early application program	No
Transfer students accepted	Yes
Evening division offered	No
Part-time accepted	No
CAS accepted	Yes

FINANCIAL FACTS

Annual tuition (in-state/out-of-state)	$19,243/ $28,693
Books and supplies	$1,300
Fees	$4,557
Room and board	$9,114
Financial aid application deadline	2/15
% first-year students receiving some sort of aid	97
% receiving some sort of aid	94
% of aid that is merit based	75
% receiving scholarships	74
Average grant	$10,054
Average loan	$32,670
Average total aid package	$36,523
Average debt	$82,958

EMPLOYMENT INFORMATION

Career Rating	85	Grads Employed by Field (%)
Rate of placement (nine months out)	94	Academic (2)
Average starting salary	$75,082	Business/industry (10)
State for bar exam	VA, PA, NJ, NY, MD	Government (17)
Pass rate for first-time bar	89	Judicial clerkship (20)
		Military (6)
		Private practice (41)
		Public interest (4)

COLUMBIA UNIVERSITY
SCHOOL OF LAW

INSTITUTIONAL INFORMATION

Public/private	Private
Student/faculty ratio	11:1
% faculty part-time	43
% faculty female	32
% faculty minority	15
Total faculty	219

SURVEY SAYS...

Diverse opinions accepted in classrooms, Great research resources, Abundant externship/ internship/clerkship opportunities, Students love New York, NY

STUDENTS

Enrollment of law school	1,229
% male/female	55/45
% full-time	100
% minority	30
% international	7
# of countries represented	44
Average age of entering class	24

ACADEMICS

Academic Experience Rating	92
Profs interesting rating	87
Profs accessible rating	67
Hours of study per day	4.15

Academic Specialties

Civil Procedure, Commercial, Constitutional, Corporation Securities, Criminal, Environmental, Government Services, Human Rights, International, Labor, Legal History, Legal Philosophy, Property, Taxation, Intellectual Property

Advanced Degrees Offered

LLM, 1 year; JSD, 2 semesters in residence and a dissertation

Combined Degrees Offered

JD/PhD, 7 years; JD/MA, 4 years; JD/MBA, 3 or 4 years; JD/MFA (Arts Administration), 4 years; JD/MS Urban Planning, JD/MS Social Work 4 years; JD/MS Journalism, 3 1/2 years; JD/MIA in International Affairs, 4 years; JD/MPA in Public

Academics

Columbia Law School is "a very exciting and dynamic place." The curriculum is very heavy on legal theory "with a dash of practical, just for show," and the "breadth of course offerings" is staggering. There are countless centers and programs specializing in everything from law, media, and the arts to European legal studies to tax policy to gender and sexuality law. "Getting on a journal is remarkably noncompetitive." "Being in New York affords the opportunity to participate in almost any internship you could imagine." Programs in international law and intellectual property law are reportedly excellent. Columbia is also "a corporate lawyer factory" and the "best place in the country for budding transactional lawyers." Public interest law is yet another strong suit here. Students who are involved are "a bit clique-ish" but, if you are in the clique, you'll have access to a wealth of opportunities as well as a tremendously generous loan repayment assistance program.

The "unbelievable," "unmatched" faculty at Columbia is "amazing" "across the board." "Columbia does a good job mixing the young, relatable rising superstars with older, more practiced professors." Virtually all of them "make class interesting," and "they're the number-one reason to come to CLS (besides the prestige, of course)." Professors also "make a huge effort to be approachable" and "are happy to give career-related advice or answer questions." The administration isn't as beloved. Happier students note that there are some "really caring people" on staff. However, the general sentiment seems to be that management is somewhat "disdainful."

When the time comes to find a real job, "employment prospects are unbeatable and the alumni network is extraordinarily strong." Career Services is "very helpful in offering support in a variety of capacities." Columbia boasts a "high placement rate in big law firms" and "the opportunities for working in prestigious government and sought-after public interest positions are unparalleled." "It's Columbia," candidly explains a 2L. "The name buys you a lot." About the only complaint we hear is the contention that "the employment focus is a little too New York–centric."

The facilities here are far from great. "Everything is very modern" and "the building is serviceable and clean, but it is ugly." Classrooms "aren't terribly comfortable," and "They're not as pretty as what you'll find at other Ivy League law schools." "The library is one of the best in the country" as far as the resources on offer are concerned, but its aesthetic "is absolutely hideous," says an appalled 2L.

Life

The population of future lawyers at Columbia is "extremely diverse," generally young, and "quite national." Students describe this place as "a nerd paradise" full of "geniuses" who are "brilliant and accomplished but surprisingly cool." "There are spoiled brats, and awkward types, and public interest people, and friendly people, and inflated egos, and social people," reports a 3L. A few students say there is a "divide between students of different economic and academic" backgrounds. However, many others insist that personal circumstances don't matter at all. "There isn't any sort of conspicuous divide between the student body on socioeconomic or geographic factors until you realize that most of the Ivy kids are terrible at beer pong," quips a 1L.

Academically, "There is an atmosphere of [intensity] here." Students are "constantly assessing how they stack up, which feeds into the collective neurosis." Some students assert that the struggle for top grades is pretty brutal. "People in general are not happy to share notes," claims a 2L. "They are, in fact, very secretive about their notes." "Our reputation for gunning, competitive jerks is unfortunately true for about five percent of the class," laments a 1L. Other students tell us, "People are extremely generous about sharing their outlines and studying together." "If you miss a class," they say, "your neighbors will e-mail you their notes without you even asking."

Columbia's location in a "safe, relatively quiet" neighborhood on Manhattan's Upper West Side provides few distractions when you are trying to study. When students put down their casebooks, though, they can take advantage of a "vibrant student community." "You'll be happy socially here unless you are a complete tool," promises a 2L. "Everyone is fairly involved in all sorts of organizations." "There are multiple lunch events every day, and there's some sort of lecture or panel or firm event with dinner almost every evening." There are "plenty of students who want to party like it's college," too, and "no shortage of happy hours." Living in the Big Apple is also a massive plus. "It's hard to explain the type of magnetic force this place can be unless you've lived here and worked here," reflects a 1L. "New York City means students can do anything they please (with the free hours they have)."

Getting In

Getting into any Ivy League law school is exceedingly difficult and Columbia is certainly no exception. Admitted students at the 25th percentile have LSAT scores of about 170 and undergraduate grade point averages of almost 3.7. At the 75th percentile, LSAT scores are a whopping 175 or so and GPAs are around 3.8.

Administration with Columbia, 4 years; JD/MPA in Public Affairs with Woodrow Wilson School at Princeton, 4 years; JD/MPH in Public Health, 4 years

Clinical program required	No
Legal writing course requirement	Yes
Legal methods course requirement	Yes
Legal research course requirement	Yes
Moot court requirement	Yes
Public interest law requirement	Yes

ADMISSIONS

Selectivity Rating	**98**
# applications received	9,012
% applicants accepted	13
% acceptees attending	34
Average LSAT	171
LSAT Range	170–175
Average undergrad GPA	3.70
Application fee	$80
Regular application	Rolling, up to 2/15
Regular notification	Rolling
Early application program	Yes
Early application deadline	11/15
Early application notification	1/1
Transfer students accepted	Yes
Evening division offered	No
Part-time accepted	No
CAS accepted	Yes

FINANCIAL FACTS

Annual tuition	$48,648
Books and supplies	$1,499
Fees	$1,780
Room and board	$20,200
Financial aid application deadline	3/1
% first-year students receiving some sort of aid	77
% receiving some sort of aid	80
% of aid that is merit based	43
% receiving scholarships	45
Average grant	$16,105
Average loan	$48,100
Average total aid package	$39,105
Average debt	$125,475

EMPLOYMENT INFORMATION

Career Rating	**99**
Rate of placement (nine months out)	99
Average starting salary	$160,000
State for bar exam	NY, CA, NJ, PA, MD
Pass rate for first-time bar	96

Employers Who Frequently Hire Grads
Large international corporate law firms, federal judges, federal government agencies, and public interest organizations

Prominent Alumni
Ruth Bader Ginsburg, Justice/U.S. Supreme Court; George Pataki, Governor/New York State; Franklin D. Roosevelt, former President of U.S.; Paul Robeson, performing artist/civil rights activist; Charles Evans Hughes, former Chief Justice of U. S. Supreme Court

Grads Employed by Field (%)
Academic (1)
Business/industry (2)
Government (2)
Judicial clerkship (8)
Private practice (84)
Public interest (3)

CORNELL UNIVERSITY
LAW SCHOOL

INSTITUTIONAL INFORMATION

Public/private	Private
Student/faculty ratio	10:1
% faculty female	34
Total faculty	97

SURVEY SAYS...

Abundant externship/internship/ clerkship opportunities, Beautiful campus

STUDENTS

Enrollment of law school	605
% male/female	50/50
% from out-of-state	67
% full-time	100
% minority	35
% international	9
Average age of entering class	23

ACADEMICS

Academic Experience Rating	**66**
Profs interesting rating	61
Profs accessible rating	61
Hours of study per day	5.50

Academic Specialties
International

Advanced Degrees Offered
JD, 3 years; LLM, 1 year; JD/LLM in International and Comparative Law, 3 years; JD/Maitrise en Driot French Law degree, 4 years; JSD, 2 years; JD/MLLP Master of German and European Law and Legal Practice, 4 years; JD/ DESS (French degree in Global Business Law), 3 years

Combined Degrees Offered
JD/MBA, 3–4 years, JD/MPA, JD/MA, JD/PhD, JD/MRP, JD/MILR

Academics

Cornell University is a small school with a big name. Thanks to this favorable combination, Cornell students enjoy a world-class education in the context of a personal, student-oriented environment. Across the board, "The professors at Cornell are top scholars in their respective fields" whose "prodigious academic accomplishments" are a significant asset to the classroom experience. What's more, most professors "are witty and make the classes worth getting up early for." Despite their impressive names and backgrounds, Cornell professors invest a lot of time and energy into their roles as teachers and mentors. A 2L insists, "The faculty is focused on teaching, not only publishing, and are clearly the greatest asset at Cornell Law School."

While Cornell boasts the high level of scholarship one would expect to find at a top school, "The close relationship between faculty and students is what sets Cornell apart from its peers." There are few lecture halls at Cornell, and "Small class sizes allow professors to really get to know students." Outside of class, professors are available for academic assistance, mentorship, and advice. "It is an honor to have classes and discussions with my professors. I have never had anyone here meet my questions without enthusiasm or support," gushes one student. Don't mistake kindness for laxness. Cornell is tough, and students caution, "Professors drive us hard." In fact, students are constantly scrambling to keep up with the demands of their educations. A 2L recalls that "Last year, I definitely spent more than nine hours a day studying outside of class."

It is unanimously agreed that "Cornell's strength is in its size," but there's a flip side to that coin, for students point out that Cornell's course offerings are narrower than they would likely be if the school were larger. In addition, since "the faculty is too small, we end up with way too many visiting professors." Still, for many students, "Small seminars with current topics make up for an otherwise small range of classes." In addition, Cornell provides a number of first-rate programs and opportunities within the law school and the greater university. In particular, many students mention the school's excellent international law program: "If you're interested in international law with a European focus, this is the place to be," advises one student. "The school is also adding to its international program by offering new classes in Asian law (e.g., Japanese law)." On top of that, Cornell students say they really benefit from their affiliation with the greater university. For example, "Cornell has a wide range of non-law-school classes" for which law students are able to sign up. "A small community within a large university means that professors and students aren't stretched too thin...we have ample opportunity for a broad curriculum if we try hard enough," is how one student puts it.

When it comes to the administration, students report that "Cornell is run like a well-oiled machine...everything is done quickly and efficiently." Another major benefit to a Cornell education is that the school enjoys "name recognition in NYC," and as a result, "Across the board, Cornell graduates seem to get the very best jobs." Students say, "Cornell's career office is amazing—knowledgeable, accessible, and well connected. I have absolutely no complaints. I just got my dream job for the summer—and most of my classmates will say the same thing." Some students would, however, like to see more connections in public interest firms, as well as outside of New York.

SARAH BUSSE, ASSOCIATE DIRECTOR OF ADMISSIONS
226 MYRON TAYLOR HALL, ITHACA, NY 14853-4901
TEL: 607-255-5141 FAX: 607-255-7193
E-MAIL: LAWADMIT@LAWSCHOOL.CORNELL.EDU • WEBSITE: WWW.LAWSCHOOL.CORNELL.EDU

Life

Cornell attracts ambitious, interesting, and accomplished students who "come from all walks of life and experience." For at least one student, "My classmates are the most uniformly intelligent and ambitious group of which I've ever been a member." Despite their personal accomplishments and drive, "Students are cooperative. Everyone feels they are in this together, and there is no point in trying to knock one another down."

The campus vibe is friendly and social, and "The very active student organizations provide numerous non-academic opportunities." That's good, since "Students here are uniformly amiable and like spending time together" even to the exclusion of other members of the Cornell community; "The majority of law students socialize only with other law students," reports one student.

Consider yourself warned: "People are warm; weather is cold" in Ithaca, New York. Indeed, if there is one resounding complaint among Cornell students, it is that "Ithaca is an isolated college town." Students joke that the best way to improve the atmosphere at Cornell would be to "put the whole school in a bio-dome and turn up the heat and sunshine." However, one student aptly adds, "Everyone knew that before they came here. [There is] not much night life to speak of, but that's not what I am here for." Students make the best of the situation, however, informing us, "Cornell is beautiful [and] it's a great place to study for the lack of distraction."

Getting In

Admissions to Cornell is highly competitive. The Admissions Committee weighs all aspects of an applicant's background, including extracurricular and community activities, graduate work, LSAT scores, letters of recommendation, and undergraduate transcripts. Applicants are also encouraged to submit a separate document that details how their ethnic, cultural, or linguistic background will contribute to the diversity of the school community.

Clinical program required	No
Legal writing course requirement	No
Legal methods course requirement	Yes
Legal research course requirement	No
Moot court requirement	No
Public interest law requirement	No

ADMISSIONS

Selectivity Rating	**93**
# applications received	6,269
Average LSAT	168
LSAT Range	166–169
Average undergrad GPA	3.70
Application fee	$80
Regular application	Rolling, up to 2/1
Regular notification	Rolling
Early application program	Yes
Early application deadline	11/1
Early application notification	12/31
Transfer students accepted	Yes
Evening division offered	No
Part-time accepted	No
CAS accepted	Yes

FINANCIAL FACTS

Annual tuition	$53,150
Books and supplies	$1,100
Room and board	$11,250
Financial aid application deadline	3/15
% first-year students receiving some sort of aid	80
% receiving some sort of aid	75
Average grant	$18,000

EMPLOYMENT INFORMATION

Career Rating	**90**	**Grads Employed by Field (%)**
State for bar exam	NY	Academic (4)
Pass rate for first-time bar	93	Business/industry (3)
		Government (2)
		Judicial clerkship (9)
		Private practice (72)
		Public interest (2)

CREIGHTON UNIVERSITY
SCHOOL OF LAW

INSTITUTIONAL INFORMATION

Public/private	Private
Affiliation	Roman Catholic
Student/faculty ratio	18:1
% faculty part-time	51
% faculty female	32
% faculty minority	6
Total faculty	68

SURVEY SAYS...

Diverse opinions accepted in classrooms, Great research resources, Great library staff

STUDENTS

Enrollment of law school	471
% male/female	59/41
% from out-of-state	65
% full-time	97
% minority	10
% international	1
# of countries represented	3
Average age of entering class	25

ACADEMICS

Academic Experience Rating	81
Profs interesting rating	84
Profs accessible rating	90
Hours of study per day	4.68

Academic Specialties

Commercial, Corporation Securities, Criminal, International, Trial Practice, Dispute Resolution

Combined Degrees Offered

JD/MBA; JD/Master of Arts in International Relations; JD/Master of Science in Government, Organization and Leadership; JD/Master of Science in Information Technology Management; JD/Master of Science in Negotiation and Dispute Resolution. These combined degrees can each be completed in 3 years with summer study.

Academics

Creighton University School of Law in Omaha, Nebraska is a Jesuit-affiliated school with "a strong core curriculum" and an impressive bar-passage rate. The school offers four joint-degree programs and four certificate programs. One of the available certificates is in litigation, and students tell us that this area of the law is where Creighton really shines. "Creighton is the place to go if you want to be a trial lawyer," proclaims a confident 3L. "I feel ultra-prepared for when I go into the real world." Several practice-based courses "allow you to gain confidence and comfort working in a courtroom." Creighton is also home to some of the best trial competition teams in the nation. But it's not all roses here. Some students would like to see "more course offerings" when it comes to electives. Also, while some students call the legal research and writing program "second to none," others gripe that it is "not uniform enough" and "needs substantial improvements." Across the board students say that the top brass and the staff "genuinely care." "It really is like an extended family." Classes are generally "entertaining." "Horrible professors" do exist here but most professors are "stellar." They are "extremely knowledgeable" and "tolerate other points of view." "The faculty is committed to making the students better lawyers and they consistently push each student to really reach their potential." "I'll be the first to admit the Socratic Method is scary, especially the first time your name is called," confesses a 3L, "but the teachers don't punish or ridicule you for wrong answers." Probably the greatest academic perk here is Creighton's "open-door policy." Outside of class, "Professors are all very approachable" and "almost constantly accessible." They spend "an incredible amount" of time at school. "You can walk into their offices any time you have a question." "Teachers know us by name and take pride in that fact," beams a 1L. "The professors at Creighton will talk to you about problems you are having in their class, problems you are having in another class, problems you are having in general with law school, or personal problems you might be having," adds a 2L. "They are also willing to talk to you about the good things going on in your life."

Some students call the Career Development Office "a joke." "It has not been helpful to me in my job search," grumbles a 3L, "and I have never heard anyone say it was particularly helpful to them either." Other students have high praise for Creighton's career development services. "If you want to practice law in Omaha, Nebraska," they tell us, "this is the best way to get into the network." "The ties to the Omaha community are impossible to beat if someone has aspirations in this market." Happy students also point out that Creighton provides "ample opportunities to meet and clerk with lawyers and judges in a variety of legal fields."

The library here is "updated and very nice," and for research purposes, it "has everything under the sun." Also, the library staff is "extremely helpful and passionate about their jobs." However, the rest of the facilities are "sufficient but not outstanding" and many buildings and classrooms are "old" and "need to be renovated." "Laptops are commonplace now [and] Creighton needs more places to plug them in," urges a 3L. More study space "would be nice," too.

ANDREA D. BASHARA, ASSISTANT DEAN
2500 CALIFORNIA PLAZA, OMAHA, NE 68178
TEL: 402-280-2586 FAX: 402-280-3161
E-MAIL: LAWADMIT@CREIGHTON.EDU • WEBSITE: CREIGHTON.EDU/LAW

Life

"The Midwest mentality" is strong at Creighton, and that's a good thing. Students describe themselves as "honest, hardworking," "intelligent," and "down-to-earth." There's "a mix of liberals and conservatives—a few more in the latter category—but the issue does not come up very often." Ethnic diversity at Creighton is pretty much "what you would expect from the Midwest plains." A few students see "high levels of competition." However, most tell us the academic environment is "moderately competitive." "For the most part, people realize it's tough for everyone," explains a 3L, "so why not make each other's lives easier by helping out one another? "Life beyond course work is vibrant. "Creighton is big on bringing in guest speakers"—United States Supreme Court justices, for example. "There are certain students who 'didn't come to make friends' and they don't," and "The school is very clique-y." "There is a very strong sense of community throughout the entire law school," though. "It is very easy to make lifelong friends here." The student bar association is "very active and hosts a variety of activities." Social outings "occur multiple times a week, and participation in intramural sports is very high." "Believe it or not," declares a 2L, "I have had a lot of fun since moving to Omaha." "Obviously, Omaha isn't the sexiest city in the country," adds a 3L. "However, if you are looking for a solid legal education, then Creighton is a great choice."

Getting In

Enrolled students at the 25th percentile at Creighton have LSAT scores around 151 and a GPA slightly above 3.1. At the 75th percentile, LSAT scores are around 156 and GPAs are a little over 3.6. Creighton relies heavily on GPA and LSAT scores to identify the most promising applicants, so if your numbers are on the front end of Creighton's bell curve, chances are gaining admission will be relatively easy.

Clinical program required	No
Legal writing course requirement	Yes
Legal methods course requirement	No
Legal research course requirement	Yes
Moot court requirement	Yes
Public interest law requirement	No

ADMISSIONS

Selectivity Rating	71
# applications received	1,310
% applicants accepted	50
% acceptees attending	21
Average LSAT	155
LSAT Range	151–157
Average undergrad GPA	3.23
Application fee	$50
Regular application	Rolling, up to 5/1
Regular notification	Rolling
Early application program	No
Transfer students accepted	Yes
Evening division offered	No
Part-time accepted	Yes
CAS accepted	Yes

International Students

TOEFL recommended of international students	

FINANCIAL FACTS

Annual tuition	$30,004
Books and supplies	$1,180
Fees	$1,352
Room and board	$13,500
Financial aid application deadline	7/1
% first-year students receiving some sort of aid	89
% receiving some sort of aid	92
% of aid that is merit based	15
% receiving scholarships	50
Average grant	$10,518
Average loan	$39,246
Average total aid package	$41,249
Average debt	$114,030

EMPLOYMENT INFORMATION

Career Rating	79
Rate of placement (nine months out)	87
Average starting salary	$60,651
State for bar exam	NE, IA, AZ, CO, UT
Pass rate for first-time bar	87

Employers Who Frequently Hire Grads
Stinson Morrison Hecker; Husch Blackwell Sanders; Polsinelli Shughart PC; McGrath North Mullin & Kratz; Fraser Stryker; Baird Holm; Koley Jessen; Douglas County Attorney's Office; Lamson Dugan & Murray

Prominent Alumni
Michael O. Johanns, United States Senator; Laura Duffy, U.S. Attorney for the Southern District of California; Bruce Rohde, Former CEO of ConAgra; Walter J.

Smith, Managing Partner, Baker Botts, LLP; Honorable Robert W. Pratt, U.S. District Court, District of Iowa

Grads Employed by Field (%)
Business/industry (13)
Government (10)
Judicial clerkship (8)
Military (2)
Private practice (63)
Public interest (4)

DePaul University

College of Law

INSTITUTIONAL INFORMATION

Public/private	Private
Affiliation	Roman Catholic
Student/faculty ratio	13:1
% faculty part-time	55
% faculty female	41
% faculty minority	12
Total faculty	119

SURVEY SAYS...

Diverse opinions accepted in classrooms, Students love Chicago, IL

STUDENTS

Enrollment of law school	1,056
% male/female	53/47
% from out-of-state	50
% full-time	81
% minority	21
# of countries represented	9
Average age of entering class	24

ACADEMICS

Academic Experience Rating	**77**
Profs interesting rating	76
Profs accessible rating	78
Hours of study per day	5.18

Academic Specialties

Commercial, Corporation Securities, Criminal, Human Rights, International, Labor, Taxation, Intellectual Property, Business Law, Child & Family Law, Health Law, Information Technology Law, Litigation & Practice, Public Interest Law, Real Estate Law

Advanced Degrees Offered

LLM in Health Law, 1–3 years; LLM in Taxation, 1–3 years; LLM in Intellectual Property Law, 1–3 years; LLM in International Law, 1–3 years

Combined Degrees Offered

JD/MBA, 3–4 years; JD/MS in Public Service Management, 4 years; JD/MA in International Studies, 4 years; JD/MA in Computer Science, 4 years; JD/MS in Computer Science, 4 years

Academics

Located in the heart of Chicago near the major courthouses and law offices, DePaul University's College of Law "stresses practical instruction across the board" while enabling its students to get "as much practical experience in the legal community as they can handle while still going to class." "My corporate law, evidence, and tax classes were all centered on learning the law and applying it in future practice," says a grateful 2L. The plethora of practical skills courses that are offered, such as Trial Advocacy and Commercial Arbitration, are also "geared entirely toward teaching students how to employ those skills when they leave the law school." "Through the Field Placement program as well as the legal clinics, I have gained some very useful practical lawyering skills while getting school credit," says a 3L.

With only 240 students in the school's full-time day program, the grading curve can be tough, but this also means that there are "very small classes so each student gets individual attention." "My class only has twelve students and it's very easy to visit office hours for help," says a student. Nearly all of the classes here are also available in the evening. Everyone agrees that the faculty at DePaul is "incredible" and "impressive" in terms of teaching effectiveness and professional experience, with "excellent connections not just in Chicago, but even internationally as well." "I really can't applaud the faculty enough," says a 3L. This "highly approachable, interesting, animated, and even really funny" group of instructors "really care about their classes and the students."

Though some people feel the law school administration is "incredibly receptive," many are on the "very frustrated" side of the fence, feeling that there is "more of an overall student focus" rather than an outreach to individuals. Career services "seems like they always need improvement in helping students—non-law-review students—to get a job." Given the breadth of the school's alumni (which includes three former Chicago mayors), DePaul "definitely opens doors to almost any practice area imaginable" within Chicago, which is "one of the largest legal markets in the country." "Try finding any firm in the greater metropolitan area that doesn't have a DePaul Law grad," challenges a student. Still, Catholic-affiliated DePaul remains a service-oriented school, and for many, "the desire to advocate for the country's less fortunate is stronger than the desire to make money."

Students readily admit that DePaul's classroom facilities are "outdated" and "definitely need to revamp," though "some of the high-tech gadgets do the trick." In addition, the law school is in the middle of a substantial renovation of its facilities, scheduled to wrap up in fall 2011. The library here is more than "complete," with full access to Westlaw and LexisNexis.

MICHAEL S. BURNS, ASSOCIATE DEAN & DIRECTOR OF ADMISSION

25 EAST JACKSON BOULEVARD, CHICAGO, IL 60604

TEL: 312-362-6831 FAX: 312-362-5280

E-MAIL: LAWINFO@DEPAUL.EDU • WEBSITE: WWW.LAW.DEPAUL.EDU

Living

DePaul touts its diversity, which most students feel is up to par with the city that surrounds it. "Everyone has their own background that [they bring] to the experience of school to aid in the workplace after graduation," says a student. The school's small size can lead to some "clique-ish" tendencies, but "anyone who wants an active social life can have one." DePaul's location certainly helps to expand social horizons, as the easy access to non-DePaul activities and people means that "the school is not the normal college bubble." Students "are hard-pressed to not find fun stuff to do, given that we're in a huge city." There is also a "very popular" study abroad program that is given at a substantial discount (per credit hour) to encourage students to attend. Outside of the city's offerings, there are "always events for students to put on and get involved in," and the administration also recently upgraded the registered student organization facilities to allow for the creation of more student organizations.

Though "the school is competitive," there is a real sense of community among students and "a great balance between working very hard during the week and having a social life on the weekends. Everyone is "supportive," though people "are not here to baby you, but help you advance your career in an enjoyable environment." The student body tends to be "extremely liberal politically but very conservative morally."

Getting In

Students admitted for the fall entering class of 2009 at the 25th percentile had an LSAT score of 158 and an average GPA of 3.11, while admitted students at the 75th percentile had an LSAT score of 162 and a GPA of 3.57. Like many law schools, DePaul offers rolling admissions, but first-year students may only be admitted for the fall semester.

Clinical program required	No
Legal writing course requirement	Yes
Legal methods course requirement	No
Legal research course requirement	Yes
Moot court requirement	No
Public interest law requirement	No

ADMISSIONS

Selectivity Rating	81
# applications received	5,109
% applicants accepted	41
% acceptees attending	12
Average LSAT	159.5
LSAT Range	156–161
Average undergrad GPA	3.36
Application fee	$60
Regular application	Rolling, up to 3/1
Regular notification	Rolling
Early application program	No
Transfer students accepted	Yes
Evening division offered	Yes
Part-time accepted	Yes
CAS accepted	Yes

International Students

TOEFL required of international students	

FINANCIAL FACTS

Annual tuition	$38,900
Books and supplies	$1,480
Fees	$462
Room and board	$9,921
% first-year students receiving some sort of aid	94
% receiving some sort of aid	94
% of aid that is merit based	16
% receiving scholarships	47
Average grant	$12,190
Average loan	$40,820
Average total aid package	$44,379
Average debt	$121,324

EMPLOYMENT INFORMATION

Career Rating	81
Rate of placement (nine months out)	88
Average starting salary	$61,213
State for bar exam	IL, CA, NY, IN, WI
Pass rate for first-time bar	90

Employers Who Frequently Hire Grads

City of Chicago Department of Law; Cook County State's Attorney's Office; Deloitte Tax; Katten Muchin Rosenman LLP; Kirkland & Ellis LLP; Sidley Austin LLP; Skadden, Arps, Slate, Meagher & Flom LLP; Winston & Strawn LLP

Prominent Alumni

Richard M. Daley, Mayor, City of Chicago; Mary Dempsey, Commissioner for Chicago Public Library; Frank Clark, President, ComEd; Carla Michelotti, Executive Vice President & General Counsel, Leo Burnett World Wide Inc.; William Bauer, Senior Judge, U.S. Court of Appeals, 7th Circuit

Grads Employed by Field (%)

Academic (5)
Business/industry (20)
Government (15)
Judicial clerkship (2)
Private practice (52)
Public interest (5)

DRAKE UNIVERSITY
LAW SCHOOL

INSTITUTIONAL INFORMATION

Public/private	Private
Student/faculty ratio	14:1
% faculty part-time	48
% faculty female	37
% faculty minority	9
Total faculty	67

SURVEY SAYS...

Great research resources, Great library staff, Abundant externship/ internship/clerkship opportunities

STUDENTS

Enrollment of law school	488
% male/female	54/46
% from out-of-state	42
% full-time	98
% minority	12
% international	1
# of countries represented	3
Average age of entering class	24

ACADEMICS

Academic Experience Rating	83
Profs interesting rating	83
Profs accessible rating	84
Hours of study per day	4.27

Academic Specialties

Constitutional, Human Rights, International, Intellectual Property, Agricultural Law, Children's Rights Law, Health Law, Legislative Practice, Litigation and Dispute Resolution

Advanced Degrees Offered

JD, 3 years; LLM, 1 year

Combined Degrees Offered

JD/MBA, 6 semesters, 2 summers; JD/MPA, 6 semesters, 2 summers; JD/PharmD; JD/MA Political Science, 6 semesters, 1 summer; JD/MS Ag. Econ., 6 semesters, 1 summer; JD/MSW; JD/MPH; JD/MHA

Academics

Students at Drake University Law School are the first to admit that attending "has been the most difficult thing [they've] ever done," but that's not to say the experience has been anything but "positive." As a 2L explains, "My overall experience at Drake far exceeded any of my expectations. The attention to detail the professors provide the students with is unparalleled." The academics place a "premium" on "practical training," which many here feel leaves them "well-equipped to handle the workload of clerking." The "incredible" professors, in particular, are singled out for praise. "If the best professors are the most knowledgeable, and if the only source of knowledge is experience, then Drake Law professors are the best professors," explains a 2L. "Most, if not all, of the professors have practiced law before becoming teachers, and it shows in the classroom." Students also appreciate how "approachable" the faculty is. "You are able to stop and talk to them anytime," says a 1L. Opinions on the administration are a little more hit-or-miss. Depending on who you ask, the administration is "committed to scholarship, committed to the profession, and committed to its students," or "with exception to our new dean, a little out of touch." Ultimately, as a 2L says, the treatment you get is dependent on the treatment you give: "The administration is not rigid if you ask nicely—treat them like humans and they'll work their tail[s] off for you!"

Academically speaking, the "greatest strengths" of Drake Law are "the opportunities for practical experience" (practicum classes, clinics, clerkships, externships, internships, research assistant positions, teaching assistant positions), and "the accessibility of the faculty." The "top-notch" experiential learning opportunities are bolstered by Drake being "located in the state capital," which gives students "the opportunity to clerk at the Iowa Judicial Building, intern in the Iowa House of Representatives or Senate, or work with state lobby groups and other legislative agencies." "By the time I finished my 1L year, I had argued an appellate case in front of the Iowa Court of Appeals, eaten breakfast with the Chief Justice of the Iowa Supreme Court, witnessed a criminal trial from jury selection to final verdict in the law school's legal clinic, and landed a summer clerkship with one of the largest firms in the state," says a 3L. Some would like to see "more diversity in the available classes" and others, while praising the amount of "academic scholarships" offered to "first-year students," warn that only those "in the top thirty-three percent" of the first-year class will hold on to the scholarships in question. "If you perform poorly on the first year exams...you will likely lose your scholarship and have a hard time getting it back," says a 3L.

Thanks to Drake Law's emphasis on using a "hands-on approach" to teach "legal theory," many students feel that they have "an edge on the competition in the legal job market" since they're prepared not just for the "legal analysis required to be an attorney," but also for "the ethical, technical, and [skills-based] parts of the job." According to students, "almost half" of their peers use the Legal Clinic when angling for jobs since it offers "access to the Iowa Legislature through internships," as well as contact with "former [Drake Law] students [who work] in many different capacities there."

Nearly all students agree that from an "aesthetic" point-of-view, Drake Law's facilities could use some "updating," "especially the classrooms" which are "rather plain and sparse." Luckily, renovation is "being presently considered by the administration." On the other hand, the school's "research facilities and resources are outstanding." The library is "beautiful and well-stocked." "If you need something and they don't have it, they will find it."

KARA BLANCHARD, DIRECTOR OF ADMISSIONS AND FINANCIAL AID
2507 UNIVERSITY AVENUE, DES MOINES, IA 50311
TEL: 515-271-2782 FAX: 515-271-1990
E-MAIL: LAWADMIT@DRAKE.EDU • WEBSITE: WWW.LAW.DRAKE.EDU

Life

Despite "a great mix of traditional students and nontraditional students," everyone "seems to get along great" at Drake Law. "The vast majority of our student body is incredibly helpful and willing to offer advice, time, and resources to younger students," says a 1L. "People want to get good grades here and study extremely hard for peak performance on the exam, but there isn't an atmosphere of 'beating' people out of a score." Drake has "a fairly diverse student population, especially with regard to nontraditional students," as many "balance law school with a family." "I'm one of many married students, and there are several students in my section who have children," says a 1L. "The age and experience differences among the students make social interactions more enjoyable for everyone."

When it comes to social life at Drake Law, there is a "large amount of student activities and a majority of the student body [is] involved in at least one student organization." "There are many opportunities for a social life, and the Delts, the law fraternity, make sure that everyone gets away from the books for at least a little bit of socialization," says a 2L. And if you "like alcohol or like hanging out with people consuming alcohol," all while discussing law, look no further than the "weekly" Bar Review "held at different bars in the area." The "great city" of Des Moines has plenty to offer, too. "It's almost like a big-small town in that you have the social life, art, and entertainment of a big city, but with the feeling of living in a small town, which can't be beat," says a 1L. Finally, a word of caution regarding "the Iowa winters." "If prospective students don't like lots of snow, extreme cold, and lack of sun, then this is not the place for you," says a 3L. "But if the prospective student enjoys winter then Drake's facilities, faculty, and location in the capital city are ideal!"

Getting In

Recently admitted students at Drake Law at the 25th percentile have LSAT scores of 153 and GPAs in the 3.1 range. Admitted students at the 75th percentile have LSAT scores of 158 and GPAs of roughly 3.6.

Clinical program required	No
Legal writing course requirement	Yes
Legal methods course requirement	Yes
Legal research course requirement	Yes
Moot court requirement	Yes
Public interest law requirement	No

ADMISSIONS

Selectivity Rating	75
# applications received	1,129
% applicants accepted	49
% acceptees attending	28
Average LSAT	156
LSAT Range	153–158
Average undergrad GPA	3.35
Application fee	$50
Regular application	Rolling
Regular notification	Rolling
Early application program	No
Transfer students accepted	Yes
Evening division offered	No
Part-time accepted	Yes
CAS accepted	Yes

International Students

TOEFL required of international students	

FINANCIAL FACTS

Annual tuition	$31,980
Books and supplies	$1,300
Fees	$534
Room and board	$15,976
Financial aid application deadline	3/1
% first-year students receiving some sort of aid	98
% receiving some sort of aid	91
% of aid that is merit based	17
% receiving scholarships	58
Average grant	$15,593
Average loan	$34,939
Average total aid package	$42,867
Average debt	$91,576

EMPLOYMENT INFORMATION

Career Rating	84
Rate of placement (nine months out)	96
Average starting salary	$55,713
State for bar exam	IA
Pass rate for first-time bar	91

Employers Who Frequently Hire Grads
Davis Brown Law Firm, Des Moines; Nyemaster Law Firm, Des Moines; JAG Corps; Brown Winick; Bradshaw Fowler; Dickinson; Ahlers & Cooney; Gislason & Hunter

Prominent Alumni
Dwight D. Opperman, CEO Publishing Company; Marcia Ternus, Former Chief Justice of Iowa Supreme Court; Robert Ray, Former Governor; Terry Branstad, Governor; Lt. General Russell Davis, Chief of U.S. National Guard 1998–2002

Grads Employed by Field (%)
Academic (1)
Business/industry (23)
Government (15)
Judicial clerkship (4)
Military (2)
Private practice (55)
Public interest (3)

DREXEL UNIVERSITY*
EARLE MACK SCHOOL OF LAW

INSTITUTIONAL INFORMATION

Public/private	Private
Student/faculty ratio	16:1
% faculty part-time	58
% faculty female	40
% faculty minority	16
Total faculty	68

SURVEY SAYS...

Diverse opinions accepted in classrooms, Abundant externship/ internship/clerkship opportunities, Students love Philadelphia, PA

STUDENTS

Enrollment of law school	444
% male/female	56/44
% from out-of-state	47
% full-time	100
% minority	13
% international	1
# of countries represented	3
Average age of entering class	25

ACADEMICS

Academic Experience Rating	79
Profs interesting rating	80
Profs accessible rating	79
Hours of study per day	4.14

Academic Specialties
Intellectual Property, Health Law, Business & Entrepreneurship

Advanced Degrees Offered
JD, 3 years

Combined Degrees Offered
JD/MBA, 4 years; JD/PhD Psychology, 7 years; JD/MPH, 4 years; JD/Master of Science in Public Policy, 4 years

Academics

"The greatest strength of Drexel Law," proclaims a 2L, "is the collaborative experience that students, professors, and faculty bring to the learning process." Indeed, students here find that in everything from "class selection to pro bono opportunities to internship and job selection," they're "given the tools and advice to determine their real strengths and interests, and how to make the most of them." And despite being a "new school," many here are "overwhelmed by the school's reputation and strength across the board." In the words of one 1L, "Drexel Law is a very strong school, and it's only getting stronger." Part of this strength is due to the school's "top-notch" professors who are "truly interested in student success," often "playing a personal and dynamic role in that pursuit." Many here find that this personal touch goes a long way in setting Drexel apart from other law schools. "Drexel Law is different than most law schools," explains a 2L, "because [professors] actually care about each student as an individual. They try to get to know students and help them succeed rather than weed them out." The administration, however, gets a decidedly mixed response. Some students find that the administration "makes things happen" and displays "a willingness to make the school the best it can be." Others admit that "Drexel has had many administration issues and failures because it is a new school," however, they're quick to add that "students have an incredible amount of input and all issues and failures have been learning experiences that are quickly corrected."

"Classes are challenging, but not intimidating; they are inviting in regard to speaking your mind about the material," says a 3L. Students also appreciate the "small class sizes" for 1Ls, which "help us to all get to know each other better." Many note that the "overall academic experience is what you make of it." For most, this statement takes on a very literal sense because "experiential learning is a huge component of the Drexel experience." "Though it isn't required, students have a lot of options to chose from to get their feet wet and see what real-life lawyering is about," says a 2L. A 3L adds, "Part of the reason I chose this school is because it offered more opportunities to have real-world experience in the practice of law. I have had several experiences, through co-ops, internships, and volunteer opportunities to see what we were learning in the classroom practically applied. They teach law students how to be lawyers, not just think like lawyers."

Though law school doesn't come without expense, students find that Drexel Law is "cheap, if you get a scholarship, which is common." That said, the nation's recent economic woes have put a damper on job prospects. "I, like most other graduates of law schools across the country this year, am worried about obtaining employment," explains a 3L, "[but] I don't blame the law school for not trying to give us opportunities to find employment." Impressions of career services are hit-or-miss. Some find that the "career services people here have been wonderful," while others say they "offer rather general, bland advice without many specifics" and "could do a better job of informing and motivating students to do what they need to get ahead at an earlier stage."

* Provisionally approved by the ABA

ISABEL "ISSA" DISCIULLO, ASSISTANT DEAN FOR ADMISSIONS
3320 MARKET STREET, ROOM 102, PHILADELPHIA, PA 19104
TEL: 215-895-1529 FAX: 215-571-4769
E-MAIL: LAWADMISSIONS@DREXEL.EDU • WEBSITE: WWW.EARLEMACKLAW.DREXEL.EDU

Despite being "new," the law school building is "already too small for the expanding student body." "Having to attend classes in a Drexel undergraduate building is unfortunate, but it's encouraging to see the school attracting a growing number of interested students," says a 1L. Others have a less optimistic take. "The classrooms are rather dismal," says a 2L. "You are lucky to get a class in a room with a window." Most readily admit that Drexel Law "could use a few larger classrooms in the law building."

Life

Drexel Law students are "a very diverse bunch." "Everyone comes from a different background and most students have had other life/work experience before coming to law school," explains a 1L. "These experiences make the classroom experience so much more interesting." Many find that students are "not as cutthroat as anticipated" and are "much more likely to help each other than sabotage each other." "The students, and to some extent even the staff and faculty, are all very close," says a 2L. "There is a real 'family' feel to the building and everyone is very supportive of each other." That said, some find this family-like atmosphere constraining. "Law school has been the worst student-to-student interaction in my life," says a 2L. "It's too small of a group and everyone is up in everyone else's business."

Despite the closeness in class, "People don't hang out that much...outside of class." Most agree that this is due to Drexel Law being a "city campus" and that "many people have other lives outside of law school." "Many of the students don't live around the campus because it is in an expensive area," says a 3L. That said, thanks to "dozens of clubs" and "events," there is a "social life" at Drexel. "There are people at all ends of the social spectrum, from bookworms to party animals," explains a 2L. "Most students try to maintain a healthy balance though."

Getting In

Recently admitted students at Drexel Law at the 25th percentile have LSAT scores of 156 and GPAs in the 3.09 range. Admitted students at the 75th percentile have LSAT scores of 163 and GPAs of roughly 3.70.

Clinical program required	No
Legal writing course requirement	Yes
Legal methods course requirement	Yes
Legal research course requirement	Yes
Moot court requirement	No
Public interest law requirement	Yes

ADMISSIONS

Selectivity Rating	**83**
# applications received	2,908
% applicants accepted	36
% acceptees attending	14
Average LSAT	159
LSAT Range	156–162
Average undergrad GPA	3.25
Application fee	$0
Regular application	Rolling, up to 8/1
Regular notification	Rolling
Early application program	No
Transfer students accepted	Yes
Evening division offered	No
Part-time accepted	No
CAS accepted	Yes

International Students

TOEFL required of international students	

FINANCIAL FACTS

Annual tuition	$33,700
Books and supplies	$4,200
Fees	$750
Room and board	$13,950
Financial aid application deadline	5/1
% first-year students receiving some sort of aid	98
% receiving some sort of aid	96
% of aid that is merit based	78
% receiving scholarships	81
Average grant	$15,768
Average loan	$28,823
Average total aid package	$45,567
Average debt	$93,216

EMPLOYMENT INFORMATION

Career Rating	**72**	
Rate of placement (nine months out)	81	
State for bar exam	PA, NJ, NY, FL, CA	
Pass rate for first-time bar	84	

Employers Who Frequently Hire Grads
All of the employers who hired our class of 2010 are listed on our website at http://www.earlemacklaw.drexel.edu/career/statistics/employers/.

Grads Employed by Field (%)
Academic (5)
Business/industry (24)
Government (7)
Judicial clerkship (11)
Military (1)
Private practice (39)
Public interest (8)
Other (5)

DUKE UNIVERSITY
SCHOOL OF LAW

INSTITUTIONAL INFORMATION

Public/private	Private
Student/faculty ratio	10:1
Total faculty	131

SURVEY SAYS...
Great research resources, Beautiful campus

STUDENTS

% male/female	60/40
% full-time	100
% minority	25
Average age of entering class	25

ACADEMICS

Academic Experience Rating	98
Profs interesting rating	98
Profs accessible rating	99
Hours of study per day	3.67

Advanced Degrees Offered

JD, 3 years; LLM, 1 year, for international students only; SJD, 1 year, for international students only

Combined Degrees Offered

JD/LLM in International & Comparative Law, JD/MA in Art History, Cultural Anthropology, East Asian Studies, Economics, Engineering Management, English, Environmental Science and Policy, History, Humanities, Literature, Philosophy, Political Science, Religion, Romance Studies, Sociology, JD/MS in Biomedical Engineering, Electrical and Computer Engineering, Mechanical Engineering, 3.5 years; JD/MBA, JD/MPP, JD/MEM, JD/MTS, 4 years; JD/MD, 6 years; JD/PhD, 7 years

Academics

The School of Law at Duke University is a national powerhouse that boasts "small class sizes," a state-of-the-art facility, a "great collaborative environment," and "accessibility to professors and the administration that is unparalleled." "Professors are the best and brightest in their field." Also, "they are extremely approachable and friendly, which makes law school much more enjoyable." A few students call the administration "often frustrating" but most are exceedingly happy with the deans and the staff. "Everyone's door is always open, and everyone really seems to care," beams a 2L. "Sometimes that caring is manifested in silly ways (like our dean of students reminding us to be careful in a freak snowstorm or suggesting we [adopt] a healthy eating and exercise [regimen] during finals), but it is all out of love."

The resources here are just extraordinary. While the curriculum as a whole tends to be heavy on theory, Duke boasts eight clinics that provide an absolute wealth of opportunities to gain practical experience. Students can delve into claims of wrongful felony convictions made by people who are in jail, or assist low-income clients who are HIV-positive, or work with attorneys who represent military prisoners detained at Guantanamo Bay. There are specialized centers and journals galore, along with several popular dual-degree programs. "Twenty-five percent of Duke Law students are also earning a graduate degree in another school on campus (often in the top of its field as well). Whether it is business (Fuqua), medicine, or the environment (Nicholas School of the Environment), Duke students are prepared to bring diversity of thought into the law classroom and to their future jobs." Other perks include a semester in D.C. and study abroad programs in a throng of cities including—just to name a few places—Buenos Aires, Sydney, Milan, and Hong Kong. Still another cool thing at Duke is the opportunity 3Ls have to create rigorous capstone projects revolving around their own specific interests.

Thanks to "fantastic alumni and networking resources" as well as the illustrious Duke brand name, employment prospects are nothing short of outstanding. Some students complain that the Career Center "should be revamped." Others insist that the staff provides "very personalized attention." Whatever the case, there are thousands of on-campus interviews each year and you don't have to be remotely near the top of the class to participate in them. About three-quarters of all new graduates enter private practice. New York and Washington, D.C., are the most common destinations for new grads, but you can find very high-paying jobs all over the nation and around the world with a diploma from Duke Law. Some ten percent of all alumni practice in a foreign country.

Life

The "fun-loving" and "diverse" student population at Duke comes from all over the country. About half come from either the Northeast or the West. Minority representation is solid. Harmony permeates the academic environment. "Duke Law is an extremely collegial place to study." "The community at Duke is incredibly supportive," says a 1L. "It has all the academic rigor of other big schools but in a kinder, gentler, atmosphere." "Duke is not cutthroat at all," agrees a 2L, "and I think our friendly student body has everything to do with that."

WILLIAM J. HOYE, ASSOCIATE DEAN FOR ADMISSIONS AND STUDENT AFFAIRS
P.O. BOX 90393, DURHAM, NC 27708-0393
TEL: 919-613-7020 FAX: 919-613-7257
E-MAIL: ADMISSIONS@LAW.DUKE.EDU • WEBSITE: ADMISSIONS.LAW.DUKE.EDU

Outside the confines of the classroom, "Everyone knows everybody else" and extra-curricular activity is abundant. "Duke Law has a student-centered culture that facilitates and encourages strong student initiative both in and out of the classroom." There are more than forty clubs and organizations. If you don't like anything already on offer, you can easily start your own. Off campus, Durham certainly isn't New York (or even Kansas City) but the climate is "mild" and it's definitely not an awful place to spend your law school days. "Think about it this way: you will never live in a small town again," suggests a 2L. "Once you stop comparing Durham to a big city, you can really appreciate everything it has to offer." Students assure us that they know how to have a good time and find plenty to do when they aren't briefing cases. In fact, they contend that "Duke is superior to any other top law school" in matters of social life. "Students at Duke study a good deal, but when we're not studying, we're going out," reports another 2L. "If you don't have a robust social life at Duke, it's because you've chosen not to."

Getting In

It's difficult to get admitted to Duke Law. Enrolled students at the 25th percentile have LSAT scores in the high 160s and grade point averages around 3.6. At the 75th percentile, LSAT scores are a little over 170 and GPAs are around 3.8. If you take the LSAT more than once, Duke will consider all available scores as well as the rest of your academic record. An addendum regarding multiple LSAT scores is welcome, particularly if there is a significant difference between them.

Clinical program required	No
Legal writing course requirement	Yes
Legal methods course requirement	Yes
Legal research course requirement	Yes
Moot court requirement	Yes
Public interest law requirement	No

ADMISSIONS

Selectivity Rating	**92**
# applications received	7,905
% applicants accepted	13
% acceptees attending	22
Average LSAT	170
LSAT Range	168–171
Average undergrad GPA	3.80
Application fee	$70
Regular application	Rolling, up to 2/15
Regular notification	Rolling
Early application program	Yes
Transfer students accepted	Yes
Evening division offered	No
Part-time accepted	No
CAS accepted	Yes

International Students

TOEFL required of international students	

FINANCIAL FACTS

Annual tuition	$48,800
Books and supplies	$1,326
Fees	$857
Room and board	$10,890
Financial aid application deadline	3/15

EMPLOYMENT INFORMATION

Career Rating	**90**	**Grads Employed by Field (%)**
Rate of placement (nine months out)	99	Academic (2)
State for bar exam	NY, CA, NC	Business/industry (4)
Pass rate for first-time bar	93	Judicial clerkship (18)
		Private practice (61)
		Public interest (16)

EMORY UNIVERSITY
SCHOOL OF LAW

INSTITUTIONAL INFORMATION

Public/private	Private
Affiliation	Methodist
Student/faculty ratio	11:1
% faculty part-time	36
% faculty female	33
% faculty minority	7
Total faculty	99

SURVEY SAYS...

Diverse opinions accepted in classrooms, Great research resources, Students love Atlanta, GA

STUDENTS

Enrollment of law school	792
% male/female	54/46
% from out-of-state	82
% full-time	100
% minority	31
% international	3
# of countries represented	20
Average age of entering class	24

ACADEMICS

Academic Experience Rating	**88**
Profs interesting rating	89
Profs accessible rating	81
Hours of study per day	4.41

Academic Specialties

Environmental, Human Rights, International, Trial Practice, Law & Religion

Advanced Degrees Offered

LLM, 1 year; SJD

Combined Degrees Offered

JD/MBA, 4 years; JD/MTS, 4 years; JD/MDIV, 5 years; JD/MPH, 3.5 years; JD/REES, 3 years; JD/PhD Religion, 7 years; JD/MA Judaic Studies, 4 years

Academics

Emory University School of Law offers "an extremely strong brand name" that "allows for amazing networking opportunities and instant recognition." "Emory has wonderful connections in the city of Atlanta" and "opportunities to practice law in field placements and other internships" are "diverse." Emory students are "routinely" placed "with the Georgia Supreme Court, the U.S. Attorney's Office, the Eleventh Circuit Court of Appeals," and "major Atlanta-based corporations." A 3L explains, "If you are interested in intellectual property, Emory has a program that works with Georgia Tech to give you real experience." "If you are into criminal justice, Emory works with the Georgia Innocence Projects." The Turner Environmental Clinic and the Barton Child Law and Policy Clinic are "active and renowned." The "joint-degree program with the theology school" is "a very unique and prolific source of scholarship on a range of issues at the nexus of law and religion." Emory's "Feminist and Legal Theory project" garners more raves.

Professors here are described as "world class." "Emory Law's faculty is one of the best kept secrets of any top thirty law school," asserts one student. "They have a great sense of humor and seem to genuinely enjoy teaching." "The professors go the extra mile in terms of helping students network for clerkships and jobs with top firms." This "brilliant," "engaging," and "very dynamic" faculty "includes a couple of the world's foremost human rights scholars (one of whom is the preeminent scholar in Islamic law)." Students are split on Emory's administration. One faction says that the "friendly, approachable, and straightforward" administration is "on the ball" and "willing to listen to student concerns." Others say that those in the administration "take themselves too seriously."

Career prospects for Emory Law grads "abound" in Atlanta and "The Emory degree also carries significant weight outside of Atlanta, especially along the entire East Coast." "The Emory degree has legs," affirms a 2L. "It can take you places. I'm going to Washington, D.C., to work with a great firm. I had offers as far away as Houston, and I'm not near the top ten percent." "I haven't known people to have significant trouble getting jobs in the Northeast or elsewhere," adds another 2L. Nevertheless, "many students complain" that Career Services is Emory's "biggest weakness."

"The library is beautiful, but the classroom building needs a face-lift," says one student. Emory's "stale," "bland," facilities are "uninspiring." "The classrooms are in dire need of some sprucing up," speculates a 2L. "White walls and windowless classrooms give the school an institutional feel." "It seems every year they paint the building, but students are not fooled." "The technology sucks," too, though the "law library is amazingly nice." It's "bright and open with lots of tables and study carrels." An insider's tip: "The trek to the undergraduate library, surprisingly, is worth it if you want quiet study."

Life

Students say "Emory draws an interesting mix of folks from both North and South (though not as many from the West)." "Long Island kids" and "conservative Southerners" create a "strange dichotomy" and an "extremely dynamic student body." There are students fresh out of college and those who "took some time off and are coming in with families or significant others." Politically, there is a "liberal bent," but you will find "various" viewpoints. Emory's "ambitious" students are "impossibly smart" and "focused." Many are "outgoing" and "sociable." Others "stay hidden behind the books the whole semester and you don't even know they are there until they win many of the high-paying

ETHAN ROSENZWEIG, ASSISTANT DEAN FOR ADMISSION
1301 CLIFTON ROAD, ATLANTA, GA 30322-2770
TEL: 404-727-6801 FAX: 404-727-2477
E-MAIL: LAWINFO@LAW.EMORY.EDU • WEBSITE: WWW.LAW.EMORY.EDU

jobs." As good as Emory is, "not everyone is thrilled" to be here. "Some think they should be elsewhere" and "have a chip on their shoulder." But as one student explains, "Overall, the quality of students here is very high, and the reputation of the school will only continue to improve."

"Classes are small, so there is a strong sense of community." Emory can be "moderately competitive," though. "Some students are just downright nasty to each other," claims a 3L. "During first year, it is a very stressful environment." That said, most of the students are "congenial, helpful, and fun to go out with."

Social life at Emory is just swell. There is "an amazing Barrister's Ball" and "The Harvest Moon Ball Halloween party is a howling good time year after year." "We have weekly 'Bar Reviews' around Atlanta," explains one student. "Each Thursday we have a keg in 'Bacardi Plaza' (our atrium)." Atlanta is "an exciting place" and "a great city for twenty-somethings." It's "the economic hub of the South," but at the same time it's "very affordable for students." "Having moved here from New York City, I'm shocked at how much Atlanta has to offer and how easy it is to get off campus and get lost in a genuinely cool city," declares a happy 1L.

Getting In

Emory Law receives more than 4,500 applications. The admitted students at the 25th percentile have LSAT scores of roughly 165 and GPAs of roughly 3.4. Admitted students at the 75th percentile have LSAT scores of about 167 and GPAs of about 3.7. Emory says that it will average scores if you take the LSAT more than once.

Clinical program required	No
Legal writing course requirement	Yes
Legal methods course requirement	Yes
Legal research course requirement	Yes
Moot court requirement	No
Public interest law requirement	No

ADMISSIONS

Selectivity Rating	90
# applications received	4,583
% applicants accepted	27
% acceptees attending	24
Average LSAT	165
LSAT Range	166–167
Average undergrad GPA	3.49
Application fee	$70
Regular application	Rolling, up to 3/1
Regular notification	Rolling
Early application program	No
Transfer students accepted	Yes
Evening division offered	No
Part-time accepted	No
CAS accepted	Yes

International Students

TOEFL required of international students	

FINANCIAL FACTS

Annual tuition	$42,900
Books and supplies	$6,574
Fees	$476
Room and board	$18,836
Financial aid application deadline	3/1
% first-year students receiving some sort of aid	93
% receiving some sort of aid	93
% of aid that is merit based	37
% receiving scholarships	73
Average grant	$23,087
Average loan	$35,362
Average total aid package	$47,263
Average debt	$99,236

EMPLOYMENT INFORMATION

Career Rating	92
Rate of placement (nine months out)	96
Average starting salary	$95,872
State for bar exam	GA
Pass rate for first-time bar	95

Employers Who Frequently Hire Grads

Alston & Bird Arnall Golden Gregory Cadwalader, Wickersham & Taft Chadbourne & Parke Dechert Greenberg Traurig Holland & Knight Jones Day Kilpatrick Stockton King & Spalding Kirkland & Ellis Mayer Brown Rowe & Maw McKenna Long & Aldridge Milbank, Tweed, Hadley & McCloy Morris, Manning & Martin New York City Law Department New York County District Attorney's Office Orrick, Herrington & Sutcliffe Paul, Hastings, Janofsky & Walker Pepper Hamilton Powell Goldstein Schulte Roth & Zabel Smith, Gambrell & Russell Sutherland Asbill & Brennan Troutman Sanders Weil Gotshal & Manges Womble Carlyle Sandridge & Rice

Prominent Alumni

Hon. Sanford Bishop, U.S. Congressman; Hon. Leah Sears, Chief Justice, Georgia Supreme Court; Hon. Sam A. Nunn, U.S. Senator (ret.), CEO Nuclear Threat Initiative; Raymond McDaniel, CEO, Moody's Investor Services; C. Robert Henrikson, President and COO, MetLife, Inc.

Grads Employed by Field (%)

Academic	(2)
Business/industry	(8)
Government	(11)
Judicial clerkship	(11)
Military	(1)
Private practice	(55)
Public interest	(8)

FAULKNER UNIVERSITY
THOMAS GOODE JONES SCHOOL OF LAW

INSTITUTIONAL INFORMATION

Public/private	Private
Student/faculty ratio	10:1
% faculty female	35
% faculty minority	12
Total faculty	26

SURVEY SAYS...

*Heavy use of Socratic Method,
Diverse opinions accepted in
classrooms, Great research
resources, Great library staff*

STUDENTS

Enrollment of law school	304
% male/female	62/38
% full-time	87
% minority	13
Average age of entering class	25

ACADEMICS

Academic Experience Rating	80
Profs interesting rating	88
Profs accessible rating	87
Hours of study per day	4.82

Academic Specialties

Civil Procedure, Commercial,
Constitutional, Corporation
Securities, Criminal, Environmental,
Government Services, Human
Rights, International, Labor, Legal
History, Legal Philosophy, Property,
Taxation, Intellectual Property,
Alternative Dispute Resolution

Academics

Faulkner University's Jones School of Law in Montgomery, Alabama is "a Church of Christ–affiliated school" with "a non-intimidating environment." According to students here, it's "the best-kept secret in Alabama." The "bar-passage rate is very high;" in fact, students report that Faulkner has had "the highest bar-passage rate in the state of Alabama." "The trial advocacy program is top-notch." "The faculty and administration actually care about you as a person" and "make sure you have practical knowledge for the real world." Many appreciate that professors "treat them like a friend and not a subordinate." Some feel that Jones "could benefit from a broader curriculum." While the "small" campus can mean fewer opportunities, many students find that "the resources of the law school are growing everyday."

The many "very knowledgeable" and "distinguished" professors here "truly are a hidden gem." Their ranks include "some of the most experienced legal minds anywhere." They also "possess a great deal of real-world experience" and "give practical lessons about real-life lawyering." The faculty is pretty big on the "Socratic Method." A student explains that his torts professor "writes everyone's name on a playing card. Before class he draws three cards, and the three people have a roundtable discussion presenting the cases that were assigned. It is by far the most memorable first-year experience." "Small class sizes" "allow for greater participation" and "You are able to get to know your professors better." The intimacy "strongly encourages differing viewpoints and class discussion" as well. Professors here "truly care about your success and take an interest in your life outside of the classroom." "The amount of time each professor is willing to dedicate to each student never fails to impress me," agrees another student. "They genuinely want each student to succeed."

The "professional looking" facilities (featuring "marble and mahogany throughout") are "outstanding." There is also "Internet access throughout the school." "Every classroom is equipped with plenty of electrical outlets," notes one student. Nevertheless, an "increase in building size" would be good. Classrooms can "sometimes" get "very hot." "Regulate the temperature in the classrooms," urges a 1L. Most students would also like to see the library "open later hours."

The well-liked administration here is "always available and extremely helpful" It's worth noting that the Jones School of Law was recently granted full ABA approval, becoming the third accredited law school in Alabama. A significant milestone for the school, it basically means that students can take any bar exam in any state when they graduate just like graduates of all ABA-approved law schools.

RACHEL L. RIDDLE, DIRECTOR OF ADMISSIONS
5345 ATLANTA HIGHWAY, MONTGOMERY, AL 36109
TEL: 334-386-7210 FAX: 334-386-7908
E-MAIL: LAW@FAULKNER.EDU • WEBSITE: WWW.FAULKNER.EDU/LAW

Life

"There is a definite sense of community" since "Everyone knows everyone," but students insist that "that's a plus." At the same time, "There is a competitive environment, but that's what the real world is like." "We are all in this struggle together, and we help each other to survive," explains a 3L. "This includes saving someone who is drowning in class when briefing a case or forming study groups for exams." Faulkner University is definitely "Christian oriented," and overall, it's "a very conservative campus." The law school is "extremely conservative" as well, but people who aren't on the political right feel welcome here. "Even though I am very liberal and a bit outside the norm, the faculty and staff do not attempt to curtail my individuality," comments a 3L. "I do not hesitate to be vocal in my opinions and viewpoints (both in and out of class) and have never had any repercussions."

Ethnic diversity "leaves a lot to be desired." However, students do say that their peers "come from all strata of society and bring varying perspectives based upon their personal, professional and educational experiences." "There are people that are directly out of college as well as people that have been out of undergrad for fifteen to twenty years," explains one student.

Outside of class, there are "seminars, speakers," and "even school parties," but students feel "There should be a few more social opportunities, especially on the weekends." Many students are active in church. "I play basketball with friends," says an athletic 2L. "We also play flag football and get together for poker and other events to take our minds off school."

Getting In

Admitted students at the 25th percentile have LSAT scores in the high 140s and GPAs of about 2.79. Admitted students at the 75th percentile have LSAT scores in the low 150s and GPAs of 3.28. If you take the LSAT more than once, Faulkner will use your highest score.

Clinical program required	No
Legal writing course requirement	Yes
Legal methods course requirement	No
Legal research course requirement	Yes
Moot court requirement	Yes
Public interest law requirement	No

ADMISSIONS

Selectivity Rating	66
# applications received	589
% applicants accepted	55
% acceptees attending	39
Average LSAT	150
LSAT Range	147–153
Average undergrad GPA	3.03
Application fee	$30
Regular application	Rolling, up to 6/15
Regular notification	Rolling
Early application program	No
Transfer students accepted	Yes
Evening division offered	No
Part-time accepted	No
CAS accepted	Yes

FINANCIAL FACTS

Annual tuition	$28,000
Books and supplies	$2,400
Fees	$95
Room and board	$12,000
Financial aid application deadline	7/15

EMPLOYMENT INFORMATION

Career Rating		90
Rate of placement (nine months out)		90
State for bar exam		AL, GA, FL, MS, TN
Pass rate for first-time bar		94

Prominent Alumni
Greg Allen, Partner of Beasley, Allen, et al. Patricia Smith, Associate Justice, Alabama Supreme Court; Ernestine Sapp, Partner of Gray, Langford, Sapp, et al. Bobby Bright, U.S. Congressman; Tommy Bryan, Judge, Court of Civil Appeals

Grads Employed by Field (%)
Academic (2)
Business/industry (7)
Government (11)
Judicial clerkship (7)
Private practice (71)
Public interest (2)

Florida International University

College of Law

INSTITUTIONAL INFORMATION

Public/private	Public
% faculty part-time	3
% faculty female	42
% faculty minority	48
Total faculty	35

SURVEY SAYS...

Diverse opinions accepted in classrooms, Great research resources, Great library staff, Beautiful campus

STUDENTS

Enrollment of law school	588
% male/female	66/34
% from out-of-state	4
% full-time	67
% minority	57
# of countries represented	27
Average age of entering class	26

ACADEMICS

Academic Experience Rating	**80**
Profs interesting rating	86
Profs accessible rating	75
Hours of study per day	4.69

Academic Specialties

International, Legal Skills and Values

Combined Degrees Offered

JD/Master of Social Work, 4.5 years; JD/Master of Public Administration, 3.5 years; JD/Master of International Business, 3.5 years; JD/Master of Science in Psychology, 4 years; JD/Master of Latin America and Caribbean Studies, 3.5 years; JD/MBA, 4 years, JD/Master of Science in Criminal Justice, 3.5 years

Clinical program required	No
Legal writing course requirement	Yes
Legal methods course requirement	Yes
Legal research course requirement	Yes

Academics

Florida International University College of Law is a relatively new school. It received its full accreditation from the ABA in 2006. It was created to provide opportunities for underrepresented groups and to serve the immediate community. Students come from all over the globe, and most agree it's a great educational experience for the cost—truly "an affordable gem." One student says, "The school has surpassed all of my expectations." The school offers eight clinical programs, giving students the chance to gain experience in the courtroom by representing real cases. In the human rights and immigration clinic, they represent clients in political asylum, as well as other immigration cases. This real-world experience is "something employers are always looking for" and is a part of the "hands-on" experience many students refer to. At FIU, education is practical. Community service is required, as well as a three-semester legal writing program. Professors spend time teaching how to write memos, petitions, appeals, and oral arguments. Students are prepared for the tangible world of legal practice and claim they measure up well against those of other more established institutions, performing highly in both national and international moot courtroom competitions. "FIU compares to the top law schools of the country," one student boasts. Students attribute this to the faculty, who are some of the "most qualified and brilliant professors in the field." "They care about our success." Another thing that sets this program apart from others is the school's "focus on international education." There's an international law requirement in both the first and last year. Most classes devote some time to global issues, respecting "current legal trends and the importance of globalization." "The curriculum is challenging but fair and offers a good variety of electives in the second and third years." However, some students would prefer a chance to specialize in areas such as tax, business, or criminal law. They hope FIU will confer the LLM degree in the future, as well.

Students love the "familial atmosphere" of FIU, claiming "the deans and administrators know most students by name." The class sizes are small, and students say professors honestly appear happy when they drop by their offices. The professors "provide real-world insight," and even the administrative body is "committed" to its students. The career development office assists students with writing resumes and cover letters, as well as prepping them for mock interviews. "The administration does not just 'operate' the school, but understands itself to be partners of the students in their journey through law school." There are many opportunities for internships within Miami. Another perk is the school's proximity to both state and federal courts. In addition to the many Miami firms, Florida's Third District Court of Appeals is situated right behind the campus. Furthermore, "The dean and the professors do everything that they can to bring the legal world to us." The school hosts visiting lecturers from across the country. Some students argue the school's newness might hamper their vocational opportunities beyond state lines, citing its lack of recognition outside of Florida. "Not many employers conduct on-campus interviews here," but "The administration is working hard at facilitating networking and externship and internship opportunities that could lead to jobs down the road." Most students feel confident that FIU's reputation as a law school will grow, claiming, "It has already made excellent progress in its short history."

ALMA O. MIRÓ, DIRECTOR OF ADMISSIONS AND FINANCIAL AID

FIU COLLEGE OF LAW, OFFICE OF ADMISSIONS AND FINANCIAL AID, RDB 1055, MIAMI, FL 33199

TEL: 305-348-8006 FAX: 305-348-2965

E-MAIL: LAWADMIT@FIU.EDU • WEBSITE: LAW.FIU.EDU

Life

Students at FIU are "very down-to-earth, easily approachable, and thoroughly diverse." They challenge each other in a way better characterized as "Olympic spirit" rather than "academic Darwinism." The student body is comprised of people from more than twenty-seven countries, and "There are student organizations for just about every interest you can imagine."

FIU students enjoy a "beautiful" library, "state-of-the-art facilities," and "courtyards decorated with professional and student art." Students say going to law school in a city is fun for the downtimes when you're not studying. Miami, although admittedly difficult for some transplants, is a true multicultural hub with a population of more than two million people. Students also have access to the Everglades National Park, as well as miles of Florida's beaches.

Getting In

The LSAT and GPA are the most important criteria to the admissions committee, followed by letters of recommendation and personal essay. Admitted students in the 25th percentile have GPAs just under 3.3 and LSAT scores in the low 150s. Admitted students in the 75th percentile have GPAs just under 3.8 and LSAT scores in the high 150s. Transfer students are accepted as long as their current institution is accredited by the ABA and they're in the upper-third tier of their first-year class. A maximum of thirty-one hours can be transferred. Last year, 138 out-of-state applicants were accepted, and the average age of the entering class was twenty-six. Roughly one in five students is admitted.

Moot court requirement	No
Public interest	
- law requirement	Yes

ADMISSIONS

Selectivity Rating	82
# applications received	2,516
% applicants accepted	20
% acceptees attending	32
Average LSAT	155
LSAT Range	152–157
Average undergrad GPA	3.50
Application fee	$20
Regular application	Rolling, up to 5/1
Regular notification	Rolling
Early application program	No
Transfer students accepted	Yes
Evening division offered	Yes
Part-time accepted	Yes
CAS accepted	Yes

International Students

TOEFL required of international students	

FINANCIAL FACTS

Annual tuition (in-state/out-of-state)	$14,203/ $27,988
Books and supplies	$2,836
Fees	$339
Room and board (on/off campus)	$11,440/ $16,978
Financial aid application deadline	3/1
% first-year students receiving some sort of aid	87
% receiving some sort of aid	86
% of aid that is merit based	2
% receiving scholarships	44
Average grant	$5,294
Average loan	$24,784
Average total aid package	$32,924
Average debt	$75,175

EMPLOYMENT INFORMATION

Career Rating	77	**Grads Employed by Field (%)**
Rate of placement (nine months out)	92	Academic (7)
Average starting salary	$48,946	Business/industry (15)
State for bar exam	FL	Government (6)
Pass rate for first-time bar	82	Judicial clerkship (1)

Employers Who Frequently Hire Grads

Military (1)

State Attorney Offices, Public Defender

Private practice (60)

Offices, Law Offices of Berman & Berman,

Public interest (11)

Cole, Scott & Kissane, PA, Astigarraga

Davis, PA

Prominent Alumni

Christopher Kokoruda, Astigarraga Davis, PA; Thomas Juliano, Lydecker Diaz; Ilenia Sanchez-Byson, Legal Services of Greater Miami; Jennifer Remy-Estorino, Kubicki Draper; Michael Hirschkowitz, Hicks, Porter, Ebenfield & Stein, PA

FLORIDA STATE UNIVERSITY
COLLEGE OF LAW

Academics

Florida State University's College of Law "could not be in a better location." It is "literally across the street" from the Capitol and various courts in downtown Tallahassee. This state capitol location—you did know it was the state capitol, didn't you?—is the reason why the school offers "more opportunities for clerkships and judicial externships than any other Florida law school" and "provides a perfect balance between obtaining a legal education while still enjoying your youth." The school (which has a "top-notch" program in environmental law) is currently renovating the courthouse facility formerly occupied by Florida's First District Court of Appeals, which "will give future students an appellate courtroom and even more classroom space." While offering an upgrade in facilities, the new building is right next door to the current law school, maintaining its propitious location. "With state government jobs being a primary area for law school grads to find [employment], what more could you ask for?" asks a student.

Students here are a satisfied bunch, for reasons that start with the affordable in-state tuition, and carry right over to their classmates and faculty. Nearly everyone speaks of the resounding friendliness of the student body; "Everyone is very close, and "competitiveness is healthy and *never* cutthroat." "While we all want to succeed, we are not stepping all over each other to do it," agrees a 2L. Perhaps this travels down from the professors—FSU "has a knack for recruiting talent," apparently—who have a tremendous following amongst the students. The professors here "are extremely knowledgeable [in] their specialty," "have incredible insight," and "are always accessible." The courses on offer from these illustrious professors are "challenging and very helpful for postgraduation" and "make you want to learn from them—even if you weren't particularly interested [in] their topic of instruction at first." Similar kudos go to the "extremely helpful" administrators: "Your problems are their problems, and they work diligently with you to solve them."

In thinking about life beyond the school, FSU also does a solid job of getting people ready. "I am confident that upon my graduation I will be able to face the legal world head-on and embark upon a competitive career!" says a 2L. The moot court team, coached by "engaged alumni and Tallahassee lawyers" is on a winning streak. The school offers "good preparation...for passing the bar exam" and creates a "family bond between all those involved with the school (faculty, administration, students, alumni, etc.)" that carries on past graduation, meaning the "opportunities for networking presented are good." The fact that there are "*tons* of law firms in Tallahassee" doesn't hurt, either. However, a few students do think that the school "needs more name recognition to help with job placement."

JENNIFER L. KESSINGER, DIRECTOR OF ADMISSIONS AND RECORDS
425 WEST JEFFERSON STREET, TALLAHASSEE, FL 32306-1601
TEL: 850-644-3787 FAX: 850-644-7284
E-MAIL: ADMISSIONS@LAW.FSU.EDU • WEBSITE: WWW.LAW.FSU.EDU

Life

Such a friendly and "collegial" group is also a relatively active group: "It's a small enough school where you will get to know at least half of the school." The Student Bar Association does a "fantastic job of helping people to feel comfortable and stay involved," as it "is really good at creating social activities to foster friendships," and "put[s] on the majority of the social functions each year," including weekly socials. "We've got more socials than any other school out there. That's probably why we've received the best SBA award two years running," surmises a student. If you're a partier, "There is definitely a partier segment at the law school." If you're not, "it's fine, too."

Sometimes life at FSU can feel much like a return to high school, and "Things can get a little clique-y." "We call the law school BK Roberts High," says a 2L, referring to the school's hub, and home to most of its classrooms, administrative offices, and student lounge. Though the buildings are admittedly "not the best facilities" and definitely "need improvement," the school is "making improvements slowly," and students know that big things are coming this year "when the massive courthouse across the street becomes part of the law school."

The atmosphere at FSU is "extremely cooperative" and "collegial…but competitive," a healthy mix appreciated by all. "If you have to miss a class for something, you can always find someone to send you notes from class," says a student. People often study and outline together here, and "everyone is friendly and willing and able to help you if you have a problem." "I love it here. I would definitely go here all over again," says a 3L.

Getting In

The actual admissions rate runs about average here, but the freshman profile runs a bit higher than one would expect for a state school. Students admitted had an LSAT score of 162 and an average GPA of 3.52. The school does not offer a part-time or evening program, but it does accept a few highly qualified transfer students from other ABA-accredited law schools, and those students must be in the top third of their class.

Clinical program required	No
Legal writing course requirement	Yes
Legal methods course requirement	Yes
Legal research course requirement	Yes
Moot court requirement	No
Public interest law requirement	Yes

ADMISSIONS

Selectivity Rating	**89**
# applications received	3,621
% applicants accepted	22
% acceptees attending	25
Average LSAT	162
LSAT Range	161–164
Average undergrad GPA	3.52
Application fee	$30
Regular application	Rolling, up to 5/1
Regular notification	Rolling
Early application program	No
Transfer students accepted	Yes
Evening division offered	No
Part-time accepted	No
CAS accepted	Yes

International Students

TOEFL required of international students	

FINANCIAL FACTS

Annual tuition	$14,102
Books and supplies	$1,200
Fees (in-state/out-of-state)	$2,269/ $21,832
Room and board	$10,000
Financial aid application deadline	3/1
% first-year students receiving some sort of aid	85
% receiving some sort of aid	85
% of aid that is merit based	22
% receiving scholarships	38
Average grant	$4,760
Average loan	$27,339
Average total aid package	$24,936
Average debt	$44,442

EMPLOYMENT INFORMATION

Career Rating	**85**
Rate of placement (nine months out)	91
Average starting salary	$58,400
State for bar exam	FL, GA, TX, CA, NY
Pass rate for first-time bar	89

Employers Who Frequently Hire Grads
Akerman Senterfitt; Alston & Bird LLP; Broad & Cassel; Carlton Fields, PA; Foley & Lardner; Gray Robinson; Greenberg Traurig, LLP; Holland & Knight LLP; Hopping, Green & Sams, PA; Stearns, Weaver, Miller, Weissler, Alhadeff & Sitterson, PA; Troutman Sanders; Federal and State Judges; Federal and State Agencies; State Attorney's Offices, Public Defender's Offices; and Legal Aid Organizations

Prominent Alumni
Mark Williamson, Alston & Bird LLP; Justice Rick Polston, Florida Supreme Court; Jeffrey A. Stoops, President of SBA Communications Corp.; Brian D. O'Neill, Dewey & LeBoeuf LLP; Eugene E. Stearns, Esq., Stearns Weaver Miller, et al.

Grads Employed by Field (%)
Academic (4)
Business/industry (11)
Government (27)
Judicial clerkship (3)
Military (2)
Private practice (46)
Public interest (8)

FORDHAM UNIVERSITY
SCHOOL OF LAW

INSTITUTIONAL INFORMATION

Public/private	Private
Affiliation	Roman Catholic
Student/faculty ratio	14:1
% faculty part-time	63
% faculty female	36
% faculty minority	13
Total faculty	237

SURVEY SAYS...

Diverse opinions accepted in classrooms, Abundant externship/ internship/clerkship opportunities, Students love New York, NY

STUDENTS

Enrollment of law school	1,677
% male/female	51/49
% from out-of-state	47
% full-time	83
% minority	21
% international	2
# of countries represented	16
Average age of entering class	24

ACADEMICS

Academic Experience Rating	88
Profs interesting rating	87
Profs accessible rating	79
Hours of study per day	4.37

Academic Specialties

Civil Procedure, Commercial, Constitutional, Corporation Securities, Criminal, Environmental, Government Services, Human Rights, International, Labor, Legal History, Legal Philosophy, Property, Taxation, Intellectual Property

Advanced Degrees Offered

JD, 3 years full-time, 4 years part-time; LLM, 1 year full-time; SJD, 1 year

Combined Degrees Offered

JD/MBA with Fordham Grad School of Business, 4 years full-time; JD/ MSW with Fordham Grad School of Social Work, 4 years full-time

Academics

Fordham University School of Law "in the heart of New York City" takes "a seriously practical approach" to the study of law, and "The breadth of the programs" here is paralleled at few other places. Students laud the excellent and thorough legal writing program. Fordham Law also does a really good job in taking advantage of its location "through courses involving fieldwork," externships, judicial placements, and various extracurricular events. "A large selection of clinics" includes some very unique opportunities in international law, and Fordham "will fund students' trips abroad to engage in human rights work." There are several more meat-and-potatoes offerings, such as family law, federal litigation, and housing rights as well. As befits its Jesuit heritage, Fordham is also very big on public interest law. "A crackerjack team of public interest minds" is willing and able to help students start service projects or find meaningful ways to make the world a better place.

While a few professors are "awful beyond belief," the faculty is mostly filled with "a cross section of bright and charismatic teachers"—"some of the most brilliant minds currently teaching the law." They're "incredibly candid," "witty," and "engaging in the classroom." The faculty interacts with students "out of the classroom," as well. Sadly, dealing with Fordham's bureaucracy is a wholly different story. The "shaky," "disorganized" administration is generally disliked. "Horror stories on registration day" are common. "It works out for those of us who cannot get anything in on time," notes an upbeat 1L. "There is no way they would ever notice."

It's a perennial lament among students here that their school is "extremely underrated" and "would be ranked higher" if only New York University and Columbia weren't each a few subway stops away. Fordham Law boasts a "particularly strong" and loyal alumni network, though, and the school is located in "one of the best locations in Manhattan," within walking distance to several of the world's biggest and most revered white-shoe law firms. Students also tell us that Fordham has a reputation for producing "exceptionally hardworking, occasionally pugilistic (figuratively), and bright" lawyers. Average starting salaries are quite comfortable and employment prospects are pretty good if you can manage a solid class rank. "With good enough grades—at least top third of the class—you can snag a big law job if you want," relates a 2L.

The research facilities are great at Fordham, and the librarians are "incredibly helpful," but students have few other good things to say about the accommodations. The "cramped," "crowded," "decrepit," and generally "inadequate" building "feels more like a 1950s fallout shelter than a law school." Luckily, "Its days are numbered." There's a new building in the works, and "The design is striking." The space concerns and depressing architecture of this drab concrete cinderblock "will no longer be an issue" once the new law school building is completed.

STEPHEN BROWN, ASSISTANT DEAN FOR ENROLLMENT SERVICES
33 WEST 60TH STREET, NINTH FLOOR, NEW YORK, NY 10023
TEL: 212-636-6810 FAX: 212-636-7984
E-MAIL: LAWADMISSIONS@LAW.FORDHAM.EDU • WEBSITE: LAW.FORDHAM.EDU

Life

Many students here "are from the so-called tristate area" (Connecticut, New Jersey, and New York), but there are tons of people from all over the country, as well. Minority enrollment is solid, and the evening program attracts a slew of older students who have professional experience in a variety of fields. The academic environment is "competitive," "but most people work together very well and are friends outside of class." "People still want to get good grades and awesome jobs, but no one is cutting throats to get there," explains a 2L. "There are gunners, of course, but they're lovable gunners."

While many, if not most, students have lives outside of school, "The school has strong esprit de corps." "First-year sections are intimate," and "There is no shortage of interaction and friendship." "Almost every personality type will find a niche here." "It's really a place where you meet lifelong friends and mentors." "Whether you're looking for a new group of close friends, or just nine-to-five friends who will go home to their families and relationships at the end of the day, you'll find people like you at Fordham." "Classy and fun" school-sponsored social activities are plentiful. "There are bar nights every week, kegs in the caf' once a month, and various drinking events throughout the school year." Also, of course, "Fordham's best asset" is its "super nice" (though also super expensive) location in one of the greatest and most exciting cities in the world. There are a million things to do when you take a break from your casebooks.

Getting In

Admitted students at the 25th percentile have LSAT scores in the lower 160s and undergraduate grade point averages just under 3.4. At the 75th percentile, LSAT scores are about 168, and GPAs are a little more than 3.7. If you're a marginal candidate, note that the stats for the evening division are a little lower.

Clinical program required	No
Legal writing course requirement	Yes
Legal methods course requirement	Yes
Legal research course requirement	Yes
Moot court requirement	No
Public interest law requirement	No

ADMISSIONS

Selectivity Rating	94
# applications received	8,883
% applicants accepted	22
% acceptees attending	24
Average LSAT	166
LSAT Range	163–168
Average undergrad GPA	3.62
Application fee	$70
Regular application	Rolling, up to 3/15
Regular notification	Rolling
Early application program	No
Transfer students accepted	Yes
Evening division offered	Yes
Part-time accepted	Yes
CAS accepted	Yes

FINANCIAL FACTS

Annual tuition	$45,850
Books and supplies	$1,664
Fees	$626
Room and board	$18,100
Financial aid application deadline	4/1
% first-year students receiving some sort of aid	74
% receiving some sort of aid	71
% of aid that is merit based	46
% receiving scholarships	36
Average grant	$12,328
Average loan	$45,096
Average debt	$119,120

EMPLOYMENT INFORMATION

Career Rating	93
Rate of placement (nine months out)	92
Average starting salary	$128,017
State for bar exam	NY, CA, NJ, D.C., FL
Pass rate for first-time bar	90

Employers Who Frequently Hire Grads
Firms including Cahill Gordon & Reindel; Cravath, Swaine & Moore; Davis Polk & Wardwell; Dewey & LeBouef; Hughes Hubbard & Reed; Skadden, Arps, Slate, Meagher & Flom; Simpson Thacher & Bartlett; NY Legal Aid; U.S. Federal Courts; U.S. Dept. of Justice; Equal Justice Works Fellowships; Manhattan DA

Prominent Alumni
Christopher Cuomo, Co-anchor, Good Morning America; Geraldine A. Ferraro, first female vice presidential candidate; Patricia M. Hynes, First female named partner at NYC firm; Hon. Joseph McLaughlin, U.S. Court of Appeals for the Second Circuit; Rich Ross, President, Disney Channels Worldwide

Grads Employed by Field (%)
Academic (6)
Business/industry (8)
Government (5)
Judicial clerkship (5)
Private practice (70)
Public interest (5)

GEORGE MASON UNIVERSITY
SCHOOL OF LAW

INSTITUTIONAL INFORMATION

Public/private	Public
Student/faculty ratio	16:1
% faculty part-time	73
% faculty female	25
% faculty minority	7
Total faculty	168

SURVEY SAYS...
Conservative students, Students love Arlington, VA

STUDENTS

Enrollment of law school	751
% male/female	62/38
% full-time	62
% minority	14
% international	2
Average age of entering class	25

ACADEMICS

Academic Experience Rating	**84**
Profs interesting rating	81
Profs accessible rating	64
Hours of study per day	4.53

Academic Specialties
Civil Procedure, Corporation Securities, Criminal, Government Services, International, Legal Philosophy, Taxation, Intellectual Property, Technology Law, Regulatory Law, Law & Economics

Advanced Degrees Offered
LLM, a post-JD degree specializing in (a) Intellectual Property or (b) Law and Economics

Combined Degrees Offered
JD/MA or PhD in Economics; JD/MPP. Details of dual-degree programs may be found on our website: www.law.gmu.edu/academics/llm.html

Academics

George Mason University School of Law has "a very strong reputation in the surrounding area," and "It's got to be one of the best bangs for your buck in the country." A "robust legal clinic program" provides "clinics for almost everything you can imagine." "The school has excellent standing in Washington, D.C. We have lots of interesting speakers and opportunities to work in the nation's capital." A host of specialization programs on offer include intellectual property, technology law, and international business law. Probably the most unique feature here is the ubiquitous emphasis on the nexus between law and economics. "The law and economics approach pervades the curriculum" and "teaches you as much about how the world operates as it does about the law." "It's like getting two degrees for the price of one," says a satisfied 3L. However, "The extent of the econ bent" is the bane of some students. "If you want to focus on something else, you have to pick your classes very carefully," notes a critic. The "arduous," four-semester legal writing program requires an enormous investment of time and is "by far the biggest complaint" among students. Moreover, "The low setting of the mandatory curve doesn't do Mason students any favors in the job market." Fortunately, "apart from the horrors of legal writing…the rest of the experience at George Mason is wonderful."

GMU's "supportive" and "incredibly dedicated faculty" is full of "intelligent, witty," and approachable professors who "coax the best out of their students." "They are always happy to discuss career plans and even send your resume to their friends," beams a 2L. "Some professors are so brilliant that they can't teach," but most "engage the students" and "keep class lively." "Older teachers are more likely to adhere to the Socratic Method, whereas classes with younger teachers are more relaxed and laid-back." "Lots of classes are taught by adjuncts" (including a "large number of judges") who are able to offer "practical, job-related advice." GMU has a reputation as a "right-of-center" law school. For many students, "The collection of so many conservative and libertarian geniuses among the faculty is wondrous and nearly incomparable." Moreover, the "zany libertarian bent…makes class interesting, even if you disagree with them."

"The administration at GMU has an extremely personable approach. From Career Services to Academic Advisors, the administration truly wants to get to know the students, take the student's input, and give each student the best experience possible." Career Services on campus "will go to great lengths to try and assist you in finding a job." "Each year, more and more prestigious law firms and government agencies recruit" at Mason. Also, "Alumni are extremely interested in helping current students meet their career goals." "Mason alums are very active on campus, and love to hire from their alma mater." And the results have been impressive: "My class has graduates heading to top ten firms in the most competitive legal markets," boasts a 3L.

ALISON PRICE, SR. ASSOCIATE DEAN AND DIRECTOR OF ADMISSIONS
3301 FAIRFAX DRIVE, ARLINGTON, VA 22201
TEL: 703-993-8010 FAX: 703-993-8088
E-MAIL: APRICE1@GMU.EDU • WEBSITE: WWW.LAW.GMU.EDU

Life

Many students come to Mason "for the school's conservative reputation." Others "come for the cheap tuition." "The student body is hardly monolithic," and "all kinds of perspectives and political backgrounds are apparent," explains a 3L. "There is a noticeable chasm in social interaction between the straight-out-of-college group and the students who have worked for a few years." Competition for grades is minimal among these "unusually motivated and down-to-earth students." As one student explains, "The law school is actually less competitive and more collegial than I expected. Students compete with each other, but they want everyone else to succeed. Ripping pages out of treatises in the library is a thing of the past." "Except for the total spazzes and the slackers, the majority of us just want to get through it," confesses a 3L.

Some students complain that "There is absolutely no sense of community at Mason, mainly because everyone works at least twenty hours per week and only comes to campus for class." Some say their classmates "seem too busy to enjoy themselves." "Students may try to tell themselves that the social void thing is normal, but it's simply not," says a 2L. Other students perceive that "there's a wealth of school-sponsored social activities" and that GMU's location "in the heart of" suburban Virginia "provides unparalleled social and cultural opportunities." "We have an abundance of student groups with something for everyone—from the GMU Sports Club, to the Jewish Law Student Association, to ACLU, to the Mason Republicans," declares a 1L. "There are hermits and partiers," adds another student, "so you can always find a quiet evening out with friends, or a drunken evening stumbling through the bar-laden streets." "There is a large faction, myself included, who enthusiastically immerse ourselves in the culture and nightlife of D.C. and Northern Virginia," says a fun-loving 2L. "Thursday nights you'll find some of us having dollar beers and tacos at the Mexican restaurant up the road, and you might run into another group of Masonites at two-dollar mug night at Whitlow's in Clarendon."

Getting In

For the fall 2009 entering class, students' median LSAT score was 163, and their average GPA was 3.72. The admissions committee makes decisions on a rolling basis beginning in late December and continuing through July.

EMPLOYMENT INFORMATION

Career Rating 77
Rate of placement (nine months out) 99
Average starting salary $83,871
State for bar exam VA, MD, D.C., CA, NY
Employers Who Frequently Hire Grads
Hunton & Williams; Finnegan, Henderson, Farabow, Garrett & Dunner, LLP; Pillsbury Winthrop Shaw Pittman; Paul, Hastings, Janofsky & Walker, LLP; Wiley Rein LLP; Sterne, Kessler, Goldstein, and Fox; McGuireWoods LLP; Sutherland, Asbill, and Brennan; Foley & Lardner; Reed Smith; Venable; U.S. Dept. of Justice; U.S. Federal Trade Commission

Prominent Alumni
Richard Young, U.S. District Court Judge; Kathleen Casey, Commissioner, Securities and Exchange Commission; Paul Misener, VP of Global Policy for Amazon.com; J. Gregory Bedner, President/CEO Perot Systems Govt Services; William Mercer, Acting U.S. Associate Attorney General
Grads Employed by Field (%)
Academic (3)
Business/industry (14)
Government (22)
Judicial clerkship (12)
Military (3)
Private practice (41)
Public interest (5)

Clinical program required	No
Legal writing course requirement	Yes
Legal methods course requirement	No
Legal research course requirement	Yes
Moot court requirement	Yes
Public interest law requirement	No

ADMISSIONS

Selectivity Rating	**92**
# applications received	5,024
% applicants accepted	20
% acceptees attending	18
Average LSAT	164
LSAT Range	160–166
Average undergrad GPA	3.60
Application fee	$35
Regular application	Rolling, up to 4/1
Regular notification	4/15
Early application program	Yes
Early application deadline	12/15
Early application notification	1/15
Transfer students accepted	Yes
Evening division offered	Yes
Part-time accepted	Yes
CAS accepted	Yes

International Students

TOEFL required of international students	

FINANCIAL FACTS

Annual tuition (in-state/out-of-state)	$15,274/ $26,502
Books and supplies	$1,000
Room and board	$20,228
Financial aid application deadline	3/1
% first-year students receiving some sort of aid	90
% receiving some sort of aid	90
% of aid that is merit based	3
% receiving scholarships	9
Average grant	$8,270
Average loan	$28,424
Average total aid package	$29,084
Average debt	$35,041

THE GEORGE WASHINGTON UNIVERSITY
LAW SCHOOL

INSTITUTIONAL INFORMATION

Public/private	Private
Student/faculty ratio	15:1
% faculty part-time	73
% faculty female	33
% faculty minority	11
Total faculty	394

SURVEY SAYS...

Abundant externship/internship/clerkship opportunities, Students love Washington, D.C.

STUDENTS

Enrollment of law school	1,683
% male/female	56/44
% from out-of-state	96
% full-time	83
% minority	24
% international	1
# of countries represented	17
Average age of entering class	25

ACADEMICS

Academic Experience Rating	86
Profs interesting rating	97
Profs accessible rating	76
Hours of study per day	4.29

Academic Specialties

Civil Procedure, Commercial, Constitutional, Corporation Securities, Criminal, Environmental, Government Services, Human Rights, International, Labor, Legal History, Legal Philosophy, Property, Taxation, Intellectual Property, Government Contracts

Advanced Degrees Offered

JD, 3 years full-time, 4 years part-time; LLM, 1–2 years; SJD, 3 years

Combined Degrees Offered

JD/MBA; JD/MPA; JD/MA International Affairs; JD/MA History; JD/MA Women's Studies; JD/MPH, 4 years with full-time and summer attendance

Academics

The caliber of the "limitless" resources available to a George Washington University law students are outstanding, and the location cannot be beat; its various connections to federal agencies, lobbyists, firms, and judges in the area make it easy to find some area of law that will interest any student, as well as allowing for a wealth of outside placement and internship possibilities. "I have enough room in my schedule to go hear oral arguments at the Supreme Court or the Federal Circuit Court," says a student. "Nearly everyone I know has had the opportunity to intern in the federal or D.C. courts or some federal agency," says another. Even if students aren't happy with the Career Development office (and many outside of the top fifteen percent of the class are not), there's the matter of the upstanding reputation with employers. "People that don't get jobs that attend GW either (1) didn't try hard enough to diversify where they were applying (particularly, geographically—people seem to forget there are jobs outside D.C., NY and the coasts), or (2) aren't trying hard enough period," says a 3L. Add to that stellar academics, and this "close knit, high energy" school is definitely on the move, though the price tag can be steep. The somewhat high enrollment means "at times it feels a bit crowded" at GW, but the law school complex is very big, and the school has done a good job of expanding spaces, having recently developed a café for students and enlarging student conference spaces. In addition to the excellent law library, at one's fingertips on any given day there are lectures, panels, and workshops.

The Student Bar Association is one of the best in the nation, which is a reflection of the close relationship between the students and the administration, who "make a clear effort to engage students on the decisions of the law school." GW Law's Dean is a "terrific fundraiser and cheerleader," and even normally teaches a 1L Criminal Law class. The emphasis placed upon professors' teaching abilities is reflected in the inclusion of a student panel on the Faculty Appointments Committee, where students' views as reflected in their reports to the faculty are "given serious consideration during the appointment process." It shows, too, as the professors at GW are first-rate; there are "so many 'must-takes' here that you are guaranteed a great professor (at least by reputation) for each major doctrinal course." Indeed, GW Law professors are well-known locally and nationally, and "it's not unusual to attend a professor's class, and then later see him or her on the television that evening." These superstars are approachable as well, and "you would be hard-pressed to go to a student function and not find a friendly face from the faculty and staff enjoying time away from the formal school setting and lending their wisdom and wit to the outside student life." Classes mix theory and practice, placing an emphasis on didactic ability, and "There can be a little tough love involved" if needed. Each lecture "is an experience," and while the Socratic Method is used, it is used "very gently, and tends to create more of an open discussion format than a fear-invoking grilling process." However, students would like to see their torts class expanded to two semesters. The student culture and atmosphere at GW Law rounds out the experience, as "people actually like each other and enjoy a good conversation, whether studying or not."

ANNE M. RICHARD, ASSOCIATE DEAN FOR ADMISSIONS & FINANCIAL AID
700 20TH STREET, NW, WASHINGTON, D.C. 20052
TEL: 202-994-7230 FAX: 202-994-3597
E-MAIL: JDADMIT@LAW.GWU.EDU • WEBSITE: WWW.LAW.GWU.EDU

Life

As a large law school, "There is a group (or clique) for everyone," and while "most law students are naturally type-A," the school is not competitive, possibly because most students have a job when graduating. There is a genuine atmosphere of camaraderie, where "students are colleagues not just in the classroom, but in the outside world as well." Only a few blocks from the National Mall and a short walk to Georgetown and Dupont Circle, GW has the perfect location for the social, career, and academic needs of students. It "is expensive to live here," but "The benefits far outweigh the costs." Students are all business for the most part in the classroom, but "relaxed and laid-back outside of it," and most "tend to be social and well-adjusted." The school is a social paradise, with "beautiful people, [a] 200-student ski trip, weekly special events at local bars, formal dances at luxury hotels, intra-class dating, and every other extracurricular activity necessary for keeping your sanity in law school is provided for in healthy amounts." Despite the more visible liberal element at the school, "liberals and conservatives, atheists, Jews, Mormons, the occasional Evangelical, and kids of all different backgrounds and ethnicities get together and enjoy each others' company on a regular basis." Tons of student groups help bring together the already diverse student body, and a huge percentage attend SBA events like the Halloween party and Barrister's Ball.

Getting In

Admission to George Washington is highly competitive. It's not quite as hard to get in as it is at its crosstown rival, Georgetown, but it's close. You should have an LSAT score at or above the 90th percentile and an A-minus average to be seriously considered.

Clinical program required	No
Legal writing course requirement	Yes
Legal methods course requirement	Yes
Legal research course requirement	Yes
Moot court requirement	No
Public interest law requirement	No

ADMISSIONS

Selectivity Rating	95
# applications received	8,225
% applicants accepted	22
% acceptees attending	21
Average LSAT	167
LSAT Range	162–168
Average undergrad GPA	3.75
Application fee	$80
Regular application	Rolling, up to 3/1
Regular notification	Rolling
Early application program	Yes
Early application deadline	12/15
Early application notification	1/15
Transfer students accepted	Yes
Evening division offered	Yes
Part-time accepted	Yes
CAS accepted	Yes

FINANCIAL FACTS

Annual tuition	$40,100
Books and supplies	$1,185
Room and board	$13,600
% first-year students receiving some sort of aid	85
% receiving some sort of aid	87
% of aid that is merit based	48
% receiving scholarships	47
Average grant	$13,000
Average loan	$35,000
Average total aid package	$35,000
Average debt	$107,000

EMPLOYMENT INFORMATION

Career Rating	97	**Grads Employed by Field (%)**
Rate of placement (nine months out)	95	Academic (1)
Average starting salary	$136,643	Business/industry (5)
State for bar exam	NY	Government (12)
Pass rate for first-time bar	94	Judicial clerkship (10)
Employers Who Frequently Hire Grads		Military (1)
Department of Justice; Howrey Simon;		Private practice (65)
Finnegan, Henderson et al.; Akin, Gump,		Public interest (4)
et al.; Shearman & Sterling; Arnold &		
Porter; Wiley, Rein & Fielding; Arent Fox;		
Dickstein, Shapiro, Morin & Oshinsky;		
various government agencies		

GEORGETOWN UNIVERSITY
LAW CENTER

INSTITUTIONAL INFORMATION

Public/private	Private
Affiliation	Roman Catholic-Jesuit
Student/faculty ratio	12:1
% faculty female	27
% faculty minority	11
Total faculty	263

SURVEY SAYS...
Great research resources

STUDENTS

Enrollment of law school	1,960
% male/female	53/47
% full-time	83
% minority	26
% international	2
# of countries represented	31
Average age of entering class	24

ACADEMICS

Academic Experience Rating	**96**
Profs interesting rating	88
Profs accessible rating	77
Hours of study per day	4.39

Academic Specialties
Civil Procedure, Commercial, Constitutional, Corporation Securities, Criminal, Environmental, Government Services, Human Rights, International, Labor, Legal History, Legal Philosophy, Property, Taxation, Intellectual Property, Alternative Dispute Resolution, Clinical Legal Studies, National Security, Global Health

Advanced Degrees Offered
SJD, 2–4 years; LLM taxation, securities and financial regulation, international business and economic law, global health law, individualized, 1 year full-time, 2–3 years part-time; LLM general studies, international legal studies (foreign students only), 1 year; LLM in same substantive areas (foreign students only), 2 years; certificate in employee benefits, 10 credits, 1–3 years part-time only unless part of an LLM; certificate

Academics

The "prestigious," "ridiculously large," and tangentially Jesuitical Georgetown University Law Center is "a choose-your-own-adventure school" in "a prime downtown D.C. location." "The sheer variety of the offerings is stunning," declares a 2L. "If you are looking to do something, odds are there is a club, or a class, or a journal, or some other event on this campus that is targeted at that." The range of courses is "extremely impressive and covers a broad spectrum of subjects." Georgetown is "a particularly great choice for students looking for opportunities in public interest or government." "Its international focus is without par," and there are several study abroad programs offered. In addition to the orthodox first-year curriculum, you can take an alternative set of 1L courses that emphasize the interconnected impact of government regulation and "concentrates on making law school applicable to the legal world." The clinics "cover a breathtaking array of topics." Internships and externships galore on Capitol Hill and all over D.C. during the academic year give students "a leg up on summer internships and future employment." Another fabulous feature here is the Supreme Court Institute's moot court program. Attorneys who are about to appear before the U.S. Supreme Court routinely practice their oral arguments on Georgetown's campus "in front of professors" in "a perfect, scaled-down replica of the actual Supreme Court (right down to the carpeting)." "It's remarkably educational to see an advocate's dry run" and "then, a week later, actually go watch the same argument" for real.

"Classes are very large [during the] first year" but faculty members are "very accessible" and they generally manage to "turn dull information into lively debate." "The professors make all the reading and writing worthwhile," encourage "diverse points of view, and [take] an interest in students' academic, professional, and personal lives," gushes a 3L. Professors are also "extremely accomplished" and they "bring fantastic experience and knowledge to the classroom." Often, though, "the 'big-name' professors are the worst teachers because they just tell war stories that are irrelevant to the exam, albeit interesting." Some students tell us that the top brass is "hardworking" and "surprisingly accessible for a big school." "They definitely make a very conscious effort to make the school seem smaller," opines a 1L. Others students say that "a ton of red tape" plagues Georgetown. "It seems like nothing is ever done on time," they say, and the registrar is "sloppy and inefficient."

Career Services staffers are "far from uber-helpful life coaches," and "There is a general feeling among the student body that Career Services is more interested in statistics (e.g., how many students went to big firms) than in helping students find paths that will make them happy." The Georgetown brand has "an amazing domestic and international presence," though. "A huge range of firms and government agencies" recruits on campus each year. The pool of alumni is colossal. "Georgetown has amazing support for public interest students" as well, including a discrete office tailored to help them "pursue careers and co-curricular options." The biggest chunk of graduates stays in Washington, D.C., or heads to New York City. About seventy-five percent go into private practice.

"The facilities are comfortable and more than adequate" here. Classrooms "are in great condition." The five-story law library is "enjoyable to spend time in and has plenty of nooks and crannies." However, the law school is inconveniently located "away from the main campus."

ANDREW P. CORNBLATT, DEAN OF ADMISSIONS
600 NEW JERSEY AVENUE, NW, ROOM 589, WASHINGTON, D.C. 20001
TEL: 202-662-9010 FAX: 202-662-9439
E-MAIL: ADMIS@LAW.GEORGETOWN.EDU • WEBSITE: WWW.LAW.GEORGETOWN.EDU

Life

Students at Georgetown Law are "very nice and good-natured, but really busy." Minority representation clocks in at about twenty-five percent and people come from all over the planet and all manner of backgrounds. "There is truly a diversity of opinions" as well. "When you put together students from many different walks of life," says a 2L, "you're bound to have an eclectic environment which makes the law school experience more tolerable."

Academically, there are "those few students with an exceptionally competitive attitude" but, for the most part, "students share notes, help each other, and actually want to work together." "I would say the level of competition is moderate," estimates a 1L. Outside of class, "Extracurriculars are very popular." "There are plenty of student organizations and there are always more activities on campus than are possible to attend." "Famous speakers" are ubiquitous. Supreme Court justices "pop by all the time," for example. The swanky, "state-of-the-art" fitness center is a "great escape from studying" and it's exclusively for law students. Amenities include a swimming pool, racquetball courts, a full-size basketball court, and whirlpools. You can also take classes in spinning, yoga, dance, boxing, and much else. "A lot of the student body commutes from a good distance to school," but "There is a buzzing social scene, particularly among 1Ls." On the weekends, "Students tend to go en masse to Dupont Circle and other parts of D.C."

Getting In

Overall, students at the 25th percentile have LSAT scores in the high 160s and GPAs just over 3.4. At the 75th percentile, LSAT scores are in the low 170s and GPAs are approximately 3.8. Part-time students have somewhat less intimidating numbers.

---

in estate planning, 12 credits, 1–3 years part-time only unless part of an LLM

Combined Degrees Offered
JD/MBA, JD/MPH, JD/MPP, JD/MSFS, JD/MSPS, JD/MAAS, JD/MAGES, JD/MALAS, JD/MAREES, JD/MASSP, 4 years; JD/PhD Government, JD/PhD, MA Philosophy, 4+ years; JD/LLM, 3.5 years

Clinical program required	No
Legal writing course requirement	Yes
Legal methods course requirement	Yes
Legal research course requirement	Yes
Moot court requirement	No
Public interest law requirement	No

ADMISSIONS

Selectivity Rating	95
# applications received	12,405
% applicants accepted	21
% acceptees attending	22
Average LSAT	171
LSAT Range	168–172
Average undergrad GPA	3.65
Application fee	$85
Regular application	Rolling, up to 3/1
Regular notification	Rolling
Early application program	Yes
Early application deadline	3/1
Early application notification	Rolling
Transfer students accepted	Yes
Evening division offered	Yes
Part-time accepted	Yes
CAS accepted	Yes

FINANCIAL FACTS

Annual tuition	$45,105
Books and supplies	$1,050
Room and board	$21,845
Financial aid application deadline	3/1
% first-year students receiving some sort of aid	87
% receiving some sort of aid	85
% of aid that is merit based	23
% receiving scholarships	31
Average grant	$17,474
Average loan	$45,298
Average total aid package	$54,577
Average debt	$122,319

EMPLOYMENT INFORMATION

Career Rating	98	**Grads Employed by Field (%)**
Rate of placement (nine months out)	94	Academic (1)
Average starting salary	$160,000	Business/industry (2)
State for bar exam	NY, MD	Government (9)
Pass rate for first-time bar	91	Judicial clerkship (10)
Prominent Alumni		Private practice (67)
The Honorable George J. Mitchell, L'60,		Public interest (11)

U.S. Middle East Envoy; Regina M. Pisa, L'82, Managing Partner, Goodwin Proctor; U.S. Senator Patrick J. Leahy, L'64, Chairman of Senate Judiciary Committee; Marc H. Morial, L'83, President and CEO, National Urban League; Paul C. Saunders, L'66, Cravath, Swaine & Moore

GEORGIA STATE UNIVERSITY
COLLEGE OF LAW

INSTITUTIONAL INFORMATION

Public/private	Public
Student/faculty ratio	14:1
% faculty part-time	26
% faculty female	41
% faculty minority	26
Total faculty	101

SURVEY SAYS...

Diverse opinions accepted in classrooms, Great library staff, Abundant externship/internship/ clerkship opportunities

STUDENTS

Enrollment of law school	679
% male/female	54/46
% from out-of-state	15
% full-time	73
% minority	33
% international	3
# of countries represented	6
Average age of entering class	29

ACADEMICS

Academic Experience Rating	92
Profs interesting rating	90
Profs accessible rating	77
Hours of study per day	4.56

Academic Specialties

Civil Procedure, Commercial, Corporation Securities, Criminal, Environmental, Human Rights, International, Taxation, Intellectual Property

Combined Degrees Offered

JD/MBA, 4 years; JD/MBA/MHA, 4 years; JD/Masters in Public Administration, 4 years; JD/MA Philosophy, 4 years: JD/MCRP, 4 years; JD/MHA, 4 years; JD/MSHA, 4 years; JD/Master of Professional Accounting, 4 years

Academics

According to its students, Georgia State University's College of Law offers "a top-quality law school education without the aggressive environment." Of particular note is the school's "top-notch part-time program full of talented students." "GSU COL offers an incredible value to students—strong academic reputation with a low cost of attendance," says a 2L. "Tuition is unbelievable," adds a 1L. "[With] only about $10,000 a year for a very strong education, you can graduate with minimal debt, enabling you to begin a law career of your choice." The "amazing" professors are "diverse and open-minded." "Impressively, professors believe in the program and voluntarily teach evening classes," says a 2L. "I am challenged every day by brilliant professors who make me think in ways I never thought possible," explains a 1L. Most students find that the administration is "very responsive" and committed to ensuring quality instruction and improving academic instruction." Others students note, "They are always willing to go the extra mile and show concern for the success of their students," while a few outliers grumble, "faculty administrators [do] not seem to care much about student concerns."

Students appreciate GSU COL's "flexible class hours," particularly those involved in the very popular part-time program. Some feel that, due to this program, there is "a weighting toward evening classes" and that those evening classes are "where the best adjuncts teach." That said, others believe the "emphasis on the part-time program is a bit overstated." "It's available and great, but the full-time day classes are on par with any you will find," says a 3L. Regardless of which program students partake in, the "effective" courses offered are roundly praised. "The health law program is dynamic and first-rate," says a 2L. "Charity Scott is a legend in this city and any future health care attorney would be lucky to take a class with her." "The school is not afraid to try new ideas," adds another 2L. "I've taken 'Law and the Internet,' which is all about legal issues and the online community," says one student, and another tells us, "I'm now in a new nontraditional class that combines Wills, Trusts, Estates, and Taxes, in which the students form their own law firms and actually prepare all of the documents as if in the real-world."

By and large, students are very happy with their decision to attend GSU COL. However, when it comes to the school's Career Services Office, opinions range from "they could do a better job" to "an epic fail for students." Despite this, "the access to the Atlanta legal community" that GSU's location offers goes a long way in making up for any career office shortcomings. "I have clerked for a year with a Superior Court judge, worked for a professor as a GRA, competed in a National Moot Court competition, become president of numerous societies, and have a job lined up after graduation," says a 3L.

With a prime spot in downtown Atlanta, GSU's location allows students to "walk to the 11th Circuit, Supreme Court, and Northern District of Georgia courthouses." On campus, the law school's buildings aren't quite as appreciated as the university's metropolitan location. "The technology available in the classrooms and libraries [is] high quality, but the classrooms themselves are not," says a 1L. "The current law school is old, and was never meant to be used for anything aside from administrative purposes." However, plans are in place for a new—and "much more aesthetically pleasing"—building. "We are all looking forward to breaking ground on the new law school in 2012, because a new building will give the professors and students more opportunities to show just how amazing the school really is!" says a 2L.

Dr. Cheryl Jester-George, Director of Admissions
P.O. Box 4049, Atlanta, GA 30302-4049
Tel: 404-413-9200 Fax: 404-413-9203
E-Mail: admissions@gsulaw.gsu.edu • Website: law.gsu.edu

Life

Thanks to GSU COL's robust part-time program, "The school [has] a more diverse student body than most other schools" since "The introduction of older students with more work experience adds a great deal to the classroom experience." While "the part-time (evening) students work well together," among full-time students, "the competition is still severe," though it is "not as cutthroat as it is at other law schools." Students attribute this "to the evening students being older, with full-time jobs," while "the daytime students tend to be right out of undergraduate schools." "The younger students tend to be more social with one another," explains a 2L. "The older students, who come from the working world, are almost entirely focused on school." A 3L gives a more specific breakdown: "First year is difficult and competitive. However, the second and third years are much more cooperative and fun. Students begin to help each other out in terms of outlines, readings, etc." Regardless of whether students are part of the part-time or full-time programs, all agree that their "fellow classmates have been the best thing about law school—they're a great bunch of people."

"On the social side, there is a substantial group of part-time students that get together monthly on an ad-hoc basis, purely for social time, usually with spouses or significant others," says a 2L. "I was pleasantly surprised." Others find that the urban campus has a negative effect on socializing. "So many people are spread out all over the city...that no one stays around to socialize after class" says a 1L. "If you just go to class and go home I think you will miss out on the social life," says a 2L. "If you make an effort to meet people then it is easy to make friends."

Getting In

Recently admitted students at Georgia State University College of Law have median GPAs of 3.3 and LSAT scores of 159. Though ninety percent of GSU COL students are in-state residents, the admissions committee "considers each student's credentials regardless of residence."

Clinical program required	No
Legal writing course requirement	Yes
Legal methods course requirement	No
Legal research course requirement	Yes
Moot court requirement	No
Public interest law requirement	No

ADMISSIONS

Selectivity Rating	91
# applications received	2,555
% applicants accepted	15
% acceptees attending	58
LSAT Range	157–161
Application fee	$50
Regular application	Rolling, up to 3/15
Regular notification	Rolling
Early application program	No
Transfer students accepted	Yes
Evening division offered	Yes
Part-time accepted	Yes
CAS accepted	Yes

International Students

TOEFL recommended of international students

FINANCIAL FACTS

Annual tuition (in-state/out-of-state)	$11,568/ $32,592
Books and supplies	$1,000
Fees	$871
Room and board (on/off campus)	$12,796/ $12,986
Financial aid application deadline	4/1
% first-year students receiving some sort of aid	81
% receiving some sort of aid	78
% of aid that is merit based	12
% receiving scholarships	7
Average grant	$5,051
Average loan	$19,497
Average total aid package	$18,913
Average debt	$39,246

EMPLOYMENT INFORMATION

Career Rating	88
Rate of placement (nine months out)	93
Average starting salary	$88,848
State for bar exam	GA
Pass rate for first-time bar	91

Employers Who Frequently Hire Grads
Alston & Bird; Arnall Golden & Gregory; Drew Eckl; Jones Day; Kilpatrick & Stockton; Holland & Knight; Hunton and Williams; King & Spalding; McKennel Long Aldridge; Paul Hastings, Janofosky and Walker; Powell Goldstein Frazer & Murphy; Troutman & Sanders; Fisher & Phillips

Prominent Alumni
Ronald J. Freeman, Founding Partner at Johnson and Freeman; Honorable Cynthia J. Becker, Judge, Superior Court of Georgia Stone Mountain Judicial Curcuit; Lynne R. O'Brien, Director of Corporate Real Estate, the Coca Cola Company; Scott M. Frank, President, AT&T Intellectual Property; Linda K. DiSantis, General Counsel, C.A.R.E.

Grads Employed by Field (%)
Military (1)

GONZAGA UNIVERSITY
SCHOOL OF LAW

INSTITUTIONAL INFORMATION

Public/private	Private
Affiliation	Roman Catholic
Student/faculty ratio	15:1
% faculty part-time	48
% faculty female	34
% faculty minority	8
Total faculty	65

SURVEY SAYS...

Great research resources, Great library staff, Beautiful campus

STUDENTS

Enrollment of law school	507
% male/female	62/38
% from out-of-state	60
% full-time	99
% minority	11
% international	1
# of countries represented	2
Average age of entering class	26

ACADEMICS

Academic Experience Rating	76
Profs interesting rating	74
Profs accessible rating	83
Hours of study per day	4.60

Academic Specialties

Environmental, Taxation, Business Law, Public Interest Law

Combined Degrees Offered

JD/MBA, JD/MAcc, JD/MSW, 3–4 years

Clinical program required	Yes
Legal writing course requirement	Yes
Legal methods course requirement	Yes
Legal research course requirement	Yes
Moot court requirement	No
Public interest law requirement	Yes

Academics

Relatively small Gonzaga University School of Law has quite a lot to offer. The Jesuit influence is notable in Gonzaga's "great tradition of public service," and the school offers great respect and support to those pursuing a career in public interest (all students must perform thirty documented public service hours to get a diploma). Another perk is the "fabulous legal research and writing program," which "provides an excellent understanding of how to effectively and efficiently explain complex legal issues." "A strong externship program" "provides real-world experience," and the "on-site" University Legal Assistance Clinic gives students "real-life experience while under the supervision of attorneys."

Academically, "It really seems that the professors and administration want you to succeed." The "very driven and dedicated" administration is "open and accessible." "The administration has been very helpful and friendly to even my most idiotic of questions," confides a 1L. The "collegial, approachable, [and] enthusiastic" professors maintain "an open-door policy" and "will find time to meet with you if their office hours don't work." "It is nice to be at a school where the faculty knows you by name and truly cares about your academic success," says a 2L. In class, a few professors are "absolutely horrible," but most are "absolutely incredible." Professors tend to have "unique backgrounds" and "relevant, real-world experience." "While the majority of the faculty is relatively young in comparison to other institutions," Gonzaga's professors "all have very strong backgrounds in their respective subject areas," which gives students "an opportunity to learn what the real practice of law is like."

Gonzaga has "many ties to the local community." "The lawyers in town are practically all from GU and participate in the events here often," notes a 2L. One contingent of students says, "Career Services works very hard to help you find work" and "aggressively" offers assistance with resumes, networking, and job opportunities. "Several times a year, Career Services will bring in attorneys from various fields and give students free pizza while the practitioners talk about their particular area of expertise and how to get into it." The pro–Career Services faction also says that "opportunities to practice in big cities are increasing" for Gonzaga students. "I know plenty of students who are getting into big firms," declares a 2L. However, another group of students says, "Career Services needs a lot of help" because "too many students are worried about finding jobs in desirable locations." "If you want to practice in eastern Washington, Gonzaga is a great school," acknowledges one student.

Gonzaga's "brand-new" facility "sits right next to the Spokane River," affording "beautiful views." The building itself "has limited space for students to gather or study" but it's "almost in the very center of the city," so "commuting every morning is a breeze." "Modern technology" is everywhere and "very reliable" wireless Internet access is available "throughout." The "excellent" library boasts a "helpful staff" and "a large selection of resources." "Only a few" of the classrooms "are less than ideal, and this is only the case when larger classes are held in those particular rooms."

Life

There isn't "very much" ethnic diversity here. "See the handful of minority students in admissions brochures and [the] DVD?" asks a 2L. "They're the only ones." "The Catholic and Mormon students create a fairly conservative atmosphere," but there is more than enough political diversity to go around, with both liberals and conservative abounding.

SUSAN LEE, DIRECTOR OF ADMISSIONS
P.O. BOX 3528, 721 N. CINCINNATI STREET, SPOKANE, WA 99220-3528
TEL: 800-793-1710 FAX: 509-313-3697
E-MAIL: ADMISSIONS@LAWSCHOOL.GONZAGA.EDU • WEBSITE: WWW.LAW.GONZAGA.EDU

ADMISSIONS

Selectivity Rating	78
# applications received	1,924
% applicants accepted	40
% acceptees attending	24
LSAT Range	154–157
Application fee	$50
Regular application	Rolling, up to 4/15
Regular notification	Rolling
Early application program	No
Transfer students accepted	Yes
Evening division offered	No
Part-time accepted	No
CAS accepted	Yes

International Students

TOEFL required of international students	

FINANCIAL FACTS

Annual tuition	$32,640
Books and supplies	$1,000
Fees	$135
Room and board	$8,775
Financial aid application deadline	2/1
% first-year students receiving some sort of aid	100
% receiving some sort of aid	100
% of aid that is merit based	21
% receiving scholarships	76
Average grant	$12,000
Average loan	$36,362
Average total aid package	$47,162
Average debt	$100,092

"The mandatory curve creates a very competitive environment, particularly among first-year students." "Students get especially competitive around finals." "For the most part," though, "fellow students are more than willing to lend a helping hand when you are lost." "It's not nearly as competitive as I expected it to be," emphasizes a 1L. The Student Bar Association routinely "provides review sessions for each first-year class and for each professor." During these sessions, "Students can ask questions in an environment that is less intimidating than the classroom."

"There are tons of opportunities to get involved" in extracurricular activities. Student organizations cover "almost every issue," and "Their participation in the law school community is prominent." "Like any smaller school, Gonzaga has its cliques," but overall, "The sense of community is amazing." "We go to Gonzaga basketball games, run along the Spokane River, or just get together to watch football," says a 2L. "Spokane's small-town nature, the relatively small student body, and the fact that almost all the students are from elsewhere means that there is a tendency for the students to become very close," explains another student. Far and away, the "boring," "blue-collar" town of Spokane is the most griped-about aspect of life here. The cost of living is low, but students end most compliments there. "Spokane is one step above purgatory," reflects one student, "but it is not a very big step." On the bright side, "Glacier National Park, Banff, Seattle, Northern Idaho, and lower British Columbia are all within a few hours' drive." "There are awesome outdoor activities nearby" as well. "There's rock-climbing and mountain biking" as well as "plenty of smooth asphalt for road cyclists." "Tons of great ski areas and golf courses" are nearby and "dirt cheap."

Getting In

Gonzaga's admitted students at the 25th percentile have LSAT scores in the range of 153 and GPAs hovering around 3.0. Admitted students at the 75th percentile have LSAT scores of about 157 and GPAs of about 3.6.

EMPLOYMENT INFORMATION

Career Rating	77
Rate of placement (nine months out)	91
Average starting salary	$60,000
State for bar exam	WA, UT, CA, ID, AZ
Pass rate for first-time bar	70

Employers Who Frequently Hire Grads
Various law firms; various local and state government entities, including military; judges; various corporate entities

Prominent Alumni
Christine Gregoire, Governor, State of Washington; Barbara Madsen, Chief Justice, Washington Supreme Court; Catherine Cortez Masto, Attorney General of State of Nevada; Paul Luvera, Plantiffs Attorney, lead in tobacco litigation; George Nethercutt, U.S. House of Representatives, former

Grads Employed by Field (%)
Academic (3)
Business/industry (17)
Government (5)
Judicial clerkship (15)
Military (3)
Private practice (49)
Public interest (8)

HAMLINE UNIVERSITY
SCHOOL OF LAW

INSTITUTIONAL INFORMATION

Public/private	Private
Student/faculty ratio	15:1
% faculty female	51
% faculty minority	19
Total faculty	43

SURVEY SAYS...

Diverse opinions accepted in classrooms, Great research resources, Great library staff

STUDENTS

Enrollment of law school	650
% male/female	45/55
% from out-of-state	49
% full-time	72
% minority	12
% international	1
# of countries represented	7
Average age of entering class	26

ACADEMICS

Academic Experience Rating	76
Profs interesting rating	81
Profs accessible rating	82
Hours of study per day	4.80

Academic Specialties
Commercial, Criminal, Government Services, International, Labor, Property, Intellectual Property, Health Law, Dispute Resolution

Advanced Degrees Offered
JD, 3 years; LLM for international lawyers, 1 year

Combined Degrees Offered
JD/Masters of Public Administration, 4 years; JD/Masters of Arts in Nonprofit Management, 4 years; JD/Masters Arts in Organizational Leadership, 4 years; JD/MBA, 4 years; JD/Masters of Fine Arts Creative Writing

Academics

In addition to the traditional full-time program, the excellent and "extremely under-rated" Hamline University School of Law in Minnesota's Twin Cities offers a unique part-time, four-year weekend program that "truly creates flexibility for people who want to keep their present job." "Hamline takes a practical approach to legal education that has…a regional reputation for creating graduates who are strong legal writers and are ready to work Day One," explains a 2L. "Hamline graduates end up being the attorneys who like getting their hands dirty and who are probably the most realistic and practical of the law school [graduates] in the area." There are eleven clinics and twelve specialized areas of focus on offer. Hamline does health law "exceptionally well," but the crown jewel is the Dispute Resolution Institute, where students learn the art of the deal. Other perks include an Academic Success Program, which offers structured study groups, workshops, and one-on-one tutoring for free. Study abroad options include programs in Hungary, Israel, and Norway. According to many students, "The writing program is also fantastic." Not everyone loves it, though. "It feels really self-taught," grouses a 1L.

Classes at Hamline are usually conducted in "a semi-Socratic atmosphere." "The majority of professors use the Socratic Method or some sort of system that includes calling on unsuspecting students, but not in a bad way," relates a 3L. Students have very few negative comments about the faculty. "The professors are great." They are "outstanding educators who are passionate about their work," and they "provide a diverse range of expertise and experiences." Once class is over, profs are "highly accessible outside of the classroom" and "individual attention" is plentiful if you seek it out. Some students love the top brass as well. "The administration keeps everything running very smoothly," says a 1L, "such that I don't need to waste any of my time untangling messes." "The administration is strongly focused on the law school experience from start to graduation," emphasizing "bar passage, and career development," adds a 2L. Other students complain that management is "unwilling to respond to student problems with course registration or student complaints."

According to students, "The appearance of the law school building is lackluster." "The interior of the building is comfortable but could be updated." "Some new carpet here and there wouldn't be a bad thing." However, "The classrooms are all up-to-date with the latest technology, including plug-ins for your laptop." Opinions regarding Career Services are decidedly mixed. Critics charge that the staff "hardly does anything worthwhile to help students with their job searches or career issues." Other students counter that Career Services is "incredibly helpful, open, and dedicated to helping students find jobs, internships, and develop skills of professionalism," as well as careers after graduation. A strong alumni network also helps in this regard. "Hamline alumni have been very helpful in connecting me with other attorneys and notifying me when they hear of opportunities that [they] know I am interest[ed] in," notes a 2L.

ROBIN INGLI, DIRECTOR OF ADMISSIONS
1536 HEWITT AVENUE, ST. PAUL, MN 55104-1284
TEL: 800-388-3688 FAX: 651-523-3064
E-MAIL: LAWADM@GW.HAMLINE.EDU • WEBSITE: WWW.HAMLINE.EDU/LAW

Life

A "community atmosphere" is pervasive at Hamline, though the student body is really composed of two very different subgroups. The younger students in the full-time day program here are "competitive but not cutthroat." "Generally, the students are friendly toward each other and are willing to help each other out," relates a 2L. "There are a few zealots, but they tend to identify themselves quickly so you know who to avoid." "I am very comfortable providing my classmates with help and frequently receive assistance in return," adds a 1L. Meanwhile, students in the part-time, weekend program say their program has its own "very special, very communal essence." "The weekend program students have a wealth of experience and are extremely welcoming," explains a 1L. "Law school is merely one important component in our lives."

Socially, "There are cliques and 'in' groups," but "common courtesy" and Midwestern affability is ubiquitous. Intramural sports are pretty popular. There are over two dozen clubs and organizations. The location provides plenty of options for culture and nightlife as well. "The campus is within walking distance of several great ethnic restaurants" and bar review on Thursday nights "at different bars in the Twin Cities area" is pretty well attended.

Getting In

Enrolled full-time students at the 25th percentile have LSAT scores of about 150 and GPAs not much lower than 3.3. Enrolled students at the 75th percentile have LSAT scores close to around 158 and GPAs near 3.1. Stats for the part-time, weekend program are lower, but not by too much.

Clinical program required	No
Legal writing course requirement	Yes
Legal methods course requirement	Yes
Legal research course requirement	Yes
Moot court requirement	No
Public interest law requirement	Yes

ADMISSIONS

Selectivity Rating	75
# applications received	1,331
% applicants accepted	47
% acceptees attending	23
Average LSAT	154
LSAT Range	150–158
Average undergrad GPA	3.42
Application fee	$35
Regular application	Rolling, up to 4/1
Regular notification	Rolling
Early application program	No
Transfer students accepted	Yes
Evening division offered	Yes
Part-time accepted	Yes
CAS accepted	Yes

International Students

TOEFL required of international students

FINANCIAL FACTS

Annual tuition	$31,600
Books and supplies	$2,000
Fees	$414
Room and board (on/off campus)	$12,226/ $15,360
Financial aid application deadline	4/1
% first-year students receiving some sort of aid	98
% receiving some sort of aid	96
% of aid that is merit based	99
% receiving scholarships	53
Average grant	$17,368
Average loan	$30,002
Average total aid package	$47,663
Average debt	$92,794

EMPLOYMENT INFORMATION

Career Rating	78
Rate of placement (nine months out)	95
Average starting salary	$52,000
State for bar exam	MN, WI, IL, NY, WA
Pass rate for first-time bar	92

Grads Employed by Field (%)
Academic (1)
Business/industry (27)
Government (9)
Judicial clerkship (15)
Private practice (41)
Public interest (7)

Harvard University
Harvard Law School

Academics

Harvard Law School—perhaps you've heard of it?—is like the land of Oz for aspiring lawyers, where "anything you want exists." Indeed, the school has plenty of funding for student scholarships, interests, and activities, and the opportunities for "public service, research and publication, faculty mentor relationships, editorial, moot court, or legal aid experience, and international study and service options are endless." The "you name it, it's on the menu" mentality is definitely present for most students, and humility can (understandably) be a bit short in supply. "Harvard is Harvard. This is...simply a reinforcing circle of virtue, i.e., you get brilliant professors, amazing students, interesting courses, great opportunities, attracting brilliant professors and amazing students, etc."

The "abundance of resources" available here lends itself to excellent support for public interest law, including a formidable public interest advising group, who "do a lot to build the community." "Though there's a lot of pressure to take a firm job, the counselors at [the public interest office] do a heck of a job fighting back. They'll chase you down in the hall and tell you it's time to start applying for fellowships, clerkships, and jobs," says a student. "When employers start cutting their recruiting classes, the last place they cut is HLS," says another. Everyone agrees that the economy has taken its toll, though—the ice skating rink closed—and "While the Harvard name will open doors, students still have to put in work and make sure that they are putting their best foot forward."

Though each HLS class is hefty in size, it actually creates an "atmosphere of conversation and collaboration." "Because our class is so big, there is always a critical mass for any interest, activity, or cause students want to pursue," says a 2L. "I was a little concerned entering this school that its size would be intimidating or overwhelming, but in fact I've found that its size is one of its greatest strengths," agrees a 1L.

As expected, the courses offered are top-notch, with "a lot of very random options" to diversify the curriculum, though many students wish there was "more emphasis on practical lawyering skills," not to mention an alternative to the "arcane and mysterious" registration system. Though in recent years, a sizeable portion of the faculty has "fled to Washington, D.C., to work on Change," students are "still terribly spoiled to have as many wonderful professors as we do." According to a student, "O[bama] left us a couple of our best profs," and plenty of "superstar" professors remain at Harvard, and "everyone is extremely accomplished and an expert in his/her field." "Not everyone is a natural teacher," but "Most of them are approachable and have interesting insights into the law (and many other areas)." There are also many research assistant and student writing opportunities offered.

The administration is "very flexible and willing to work with students as circumstances arise," and the school "really strives to please students, even in tough economic times." Classroom buildings are "often ugly, but all are nicely equipped and in good condition," research facilities "could not be better," and the library—the largest law library in the world, by the way—is "huge and lovely, with a staggering quantity of books." In other words, don't come to this corner of Boston if you're looking for the entire package of "sunshine, butterflies and architectural triumphs"—"There are reasons to come here; aesthetic bliss is not one of them."

Josh Rubenstien, Assistant Dean and Chief Admissions Officer
1515 Massachusetts Avenue, Cambridge, MA 02138
Tel: 617-495-3109
E-Mail: jdadmiss@law.harvard.edu • Website: www.law.harvard.edu

Life

There is most definitely "a lot of underlying stress and tension" at HLS, but "It's never about beating your classmates." While Harvard isn't the same cutthroat school of the Paper Chase era, "There are still quite a few gunners"; however, once you hit your second year, "Everyone has relaxed a bit and gotten comfortable with their law school identities."

It's "very easy to find a great group of friends" because people are "generally fun and good-humored (in addition to being extremely smart and accomplished)." There is a Bar Review every week, and "The student government and other organizations host happy hours and other social events." While the size of the school means that students "wouldn't say the school as a whole has a strong general sense of community," it does provide a larger potential pool for friends, and students "are able to find a sense of community by joining various organizations." Be careful—students often "overwhelm themselves with extracurricular activities."

Students tend to be "quite liberal," but "One of the biggest surprises at HLS is how acceptable it is to be a conservative," as students here "tend to be tolerant and accepting of people despite their gender, race, religion, ethnicity, or sexual orientation." "It's very cooperative—there's a definite feeling of 'we're all in this together,'" says a 1L.

Getting In

When students arrive at law school to hear the dean say, "The competition is over. You've won," it's safe to say that getting in wasn't what most would call easy. Admitted students at the 25th percentile have LSAT scores of 171 and GPAs of about 3.78. Admitted students at the 75th percentile have LSAT scores of 176 and GPAs of about 3.96. (Note that Harvard looks at all LSAT scores in their contexts.) The school also aggressively seeks applicants from underrepresented minority groups.

Clinical program required	No
Legal writing course requirement	Yes
Legal methods course requirement	No
Legal research course requirement	Yes
Moot court requirement	Yes
Public interest law requirement	Yes

ADMISSIONS

Selectivity Rating	99
# applications received	7,574
% applicants accepted	11
% acceptees attending	68
LSAT Range	171–176
Application fee	$85
Regular application	Rolling, up to 2/1
Regular notification	Rolling
Early application program	No
Transfer students accepted	Yes
Evening division offered	No
Part-time accepted	No
CAS accepted	Yes

FINANCIAL FACTS

Annual tuition	$45,450
Books and supplies	$1,150
Fees	$2,954
Room and board	$20,546
% first-year students receiving some sort of aid	81
% receiving some sort of aid	83
% receiving scholarships	52
Average grant	$22,813
Average loan	$42,977
Average total aid package	$55,220
Average debt	$114,982

EMPLOYMENT INFORMATION

Career Rating	95
Rate of placement (nine months out)	97
Average starting salary	$120,168
State for bar exam	NY, MA
Pass rate for first-time bar	98

Employers Who Frequently Hire Grads
Major national law firms, federal and state governments, investment banks, consulting firms, law schools

Prominent Alumni
Barack H. Obama, President of the United States

Grads Employed by Field (%)
Academic (1)
Business/industry (3)
Government (4)
Judicial clerkship (22)
Private practice (63)
Public interest (8)

HOFSTRA UNIVERSITY
HOFSTRA UNIVERSITY SCHOOL OF LAW

INSTITUTIONAL INFORMATION

Public/private	Private
Student/faculty ratio	14:1
% faculty part-time	37
% faculty female	29
% faculty minority	14
Total faculty	99

SURVEY SAYS...

Diverse opinions accepted in classrooms

STUDENTS

Enrollment of law school	1,061
% male/female	53/47
% from out-of-state	45
% full-time	89
% minority	27
% international	5
# of countries represented	15
Average age of entering class	24

ACADEMICS

Academic Experience Rating	74
Profs interesting rating	75
Profs accessible rating	65
Hours of study per day	4.84

Academic Specialties

Civil Procedure, Commercial, Constitutional, Corporation Securities, Criminal, Environmental, Government Services, Human Rights, International, Labor, Property, Taxation, Intellectual Property, Family Law, Trial Advocacy, Health Law

Advanced Degrees Offered

JD, 3 years full-time, 4 years part-time; LLM, 1 year full-time, 2 years part-time; in Family Law and American Legal Studies (for foreign lawyers)

Combined Degrees Offered

JD/MBA, 4 years full-time; JD/MA, 4 years full-time

Academics

There is a "professional, collaborative environment" at Hofstra Law School, where the school's students are huge fans of the "outstanding" administration, who, in many cases, "are willing to bend over backwards to accommodate you." "The administration is great because they are very accessible and interested in our success as lawyers and as students," says a 1L. The Career Center here is similarly involved, "not only [in] our futures, but also in helping alumni find new jobs." Right from the first week of class, Hofstra is big on helping students to network with attorneys and alumni and put a realistic perspective on the possibilities out there (Note: The school does rank students within classes.), though a few students do lament the school's rather intense focus on work in the public sector, and far more than a few bemoan the lack of "quality internships." "I've had the opportunity to learn about how much work and how many different areas of law you can practice...now I actually know what I can do with a JD," says a first-year law student. Though not every single person leaves a satisfied customer, the school certainly shows a "desire to improve," and all who go here pretty much all generally agree, "If you are proactive and work hard, Hofstra will work hard for you as well."

Its location close to New York City helps the school to attract "some legendary professors at the top of their fields," most of whom are "readily available outside of class, and...seem to genuinely care about the students' success." "Not a single one stands on ceremony," says a student. Most "do not implement harsh variations of the Socratic Method"; they use "real-world experience that they bring to their lectures" and use "practical methods that help students to try [to] learn, rather than simply memorize the material." Hofstra's focus on practical and legal writing skills "never ceases to pay off during internships/clerkships." "I thought that Hofstra would not offer the same kind of academic experience as those in the top schools. I was very pleasantly surprised," says a student. "They are constantly trying to...help develop the students into lawyers."

Some bigger pictures gripes include that, the school recently "terminated the whole night program," and tuition is not easy on the wallet. "Lower tuition please. I don't have a money tree in my backyard," begs a 1L. Classrooms "are adequate for the purpose they serve"; though the technology is up-to-date (lectures are webcast, Wi-Fi is readily available), the facilities as a whole could use a face-lift. Also, as one weary student puts it, "Not to beat a dead horse, but parking is always an issue."

Life

First-year students have all their classes with the same section, so "there is a sense that we are all getting through together." This instantly creates a nice community for incoming students, who also appreciate their access to 2Ls and 3Ls that "are more than happy to help with information about classes and professors." "There is competition, but that is what keeps us on our toes. It shouldn't be frowned upon," says a student. Students are encouraged to work in study groups (and the overwhelming majority do), and "There is a strong desire to help others understand"; students "get lots of support from...fellow law school brothers and sisters." "We actually like one another!" says a 1L.

John Chalmers, Assistant Dean for Enrollment Management
121 Hofstra University, Hempstead, NY 11549
Tel: 516-463-5916 Fax: 516-463-6264
E-Mail: lawadmissions@Hofstra.edu • Website: law.hofstra.edu

While the school's location on the edge of the somewhat tucked-away neighborhood of Hempstead is far from ideal, "Security on campus is very efficient." Long Island is "a little boring," but "There is ample opportunity for social activities," as the law school itself has many different student organizations, "so it's easy to find a group of people you can relate to and who have interest[s] in common with you." Commuting to and from New York City, for school or for fun, is also an option. Law students here do tend to be a bit "stressed out," but the school as a whole still remains a "very friendly environment that the students really enjoy." It is a "laid-back atmosphere, [where students are] serious about work but not competitive."

Getting In

Hofstra's not the toughest school to get into, but it's not a cakewalk, either. As with almost every school, there's no set minimum score required for admission here, but the entering class of 2010 had LSAT scores of 156 and a GPA of 3.17 at the 25th percentile, and an LSAT score of 160 and GPA of 3.69 at the 75th percentile.

Clinical program required	No
Legal writing course requirement	Yes
Legal methods course requirement	Yes
Legal research course requirement	Yes
Moot court requirement	Yes
Public interest law requirement	No

ADMISSIONS

Selectivity Rating	**83**
# applications received	4,851
% applicants accepted	40
% acceptees attending	18
LSAT Range	156–160
Average undergrad GPA	3.17–3.69
Application fee	$0
Regular application	Rolling, up to 4/15
Regular notification	Rolling
Early application program	Yes
Early application deadline	11/15
Early application notification	12/15
Transfer students accepted	Yes
Evening division offered	No
Part-time accepted	Yes
CAS accepted	Yes

International Students

TOEFL required of international students	

FINANCIAL FACTS

Annual tuition	$43,034
Books and supplies	$1,400
Fees	$626
Room and board (on/off campus)	$23,398/ $22,040
Financial aid application deadline	4/15
% first-year students receiving some sort of aid	90
% receiving some sort of aid	90
% of aid that is merit based	97
% receiving scholarships	49
Average grant	$16,000
Average loan	$37,500
Average total aid package	$44,000
Average debt	$115,705

EMPLOYMENT INFORMATION

Career Rating	**85**
Rate of placement (nine months out)	91
Average starting salary	$90,000
State for bar exam	NY
Pass rate for first-time bar	77

Employers Who Frequently Hire Grads

Dozens of the most prestigious law firms in New York City and Long Island recruit at the law school. In addition, many federal, state and local government agencies and public interest organizations participate in recruiting at the law school

Prominent Alumni

Neil Cole, President & CEO, Iconix Inc.; Hon. Maryanne Trump Barry, Judge, U.S. Ct of Appeals for the Third Circuit; Bradley E. Scheler, Senior Partner and Chairman, Bankruptcy and Restructuring, Fried Frank; Jonathan E. Gradess, Executive Director, NY State Defenders Association; Randy Levine, President, New York Yankees

Grads Employed by Field (%)

Academic (5)
Business/industry (18)
Government (13)
Judicial clerkship (2)
Private practice (52)
Public interest (3)

ILLINOIS INSTITUTE OF TECHNOLOGY
CHICAGO-KENT COLLEGE OF LAW

INSTITUTIONAL INFORMATION

Public/private	Private
Student/faculty ratio	5:1
% faculty part-time	61
% faculty female	29
% faculty minority	8
Total faculty	180

SURVEY SAYS...

Diverse opinions accepted in classrooms, Great library staff, Students love Chicago, IL

STUDENTS

Enrollment of law school	977
% male/female	55/45
% from out-of-state	30
% full-time	82
% minority	21
% international	3
# of countries represented	15
Average age of entering class	25

ACADEMICS

Academic Experience Rating	**78**
Profs interesting rating	76
Profs accessible rating	71
Hours of study per day	4.29

Academic Specialties

Criminal, Environmental, International, Labor, Intellectual Property, Litigation and Alternative Dispute Resolution, Public Interest Law

Advanced Degrees Offered

JD, 3 years full-time, 4 years part-time; LLM, 2–8 semesters

Combined Degrees Offered

JD/MBA, 3.5–5 years; JD/LLM, 4–5 years; JD/MS in Finance, 4–5 years; JD/MPA, 3.5–5 years; JD/MS in Environmental Management & Sustainability, 3.5–5 years; JD/Master of Public Health, 3.5 years

Academics

If you're looking to "feel both challenged and encouraged to learn" rather than "beaten down by the stereotypical combination of sadistic professors and hyper-competitive classmates," then you might want to try the Chicago-Kent College of Law, which works to create a scholarly community under the auspices of a science and engineering heavyweight. Placed "just high enough in the rankings to attract talented students who aren't arrogant, but not too high so that the professors are attracted for research rather than teaching," the school makes it clear up front that the experience "will be competitive," while also stressing "how important it is to not dwell on grades and rank even though they're important."

Known for its "intense" and "well-recognized" legal writing program (one of the few three-year programs in the country), students at Chicago-Kent must endure "several hellish weeks each semester" so they can say, "The memo [I] did in the first three weeks of school is the equivalent of another school's 1L final project." "Every attorney I've worked with in the past three years has commented on the strength of my legal writing skills," boasts one third-year student. Other tough aspects of the school's curriculum include its grading curve, which gives transfer students an unfair advantage "because their GPA is not deflated by the first-year curve" and results in the school awarding more scholarships than students can retain "due to the academic standards that must be maintained." Many also cite the Intellectual Property Program and the variety of in-house clinics (in which students work with actual clients for credit) as strengths.

As one would expect judging from its parent institution, Chicago-Kent's "top-notch" classrooms are "enabled with the best educational technology," including myriad outlets, and the entire campus is blanketed with wireless Internet (some even claim the technology "outranks" the institute itself). The comprehensive library provides plenty of study space, and is run by a "knowledgeable" staff that is "willing to assist you with any issues." Chicago-Kent's location in the West Loop "is crucial to practical experience" and "maximizes chances for great externships," though summer jobs "aren't all that easy to come by with the competition of Northwestern, University of Chicago, U of I, and Michigan so close by."

Despite a large contingent of part-time faculty in the upper-level courses, professors at Chicago-Kent are "passionately engaged in the subject matter" and "totally committed to the students as well as to their research." They "work hard to encourage you and support you outside of the classroom" and are particularly good at "treating the students as adults and expecting them to perform at a higher level," according to a first-year student. Though they're not without complaints, most here say that the administration is "very accommodating [of] students' needs" and "are always quick to reply to questions." The general opinion of the Career Services Office is one of mild discontent, and a large number of students wish the school could "expand its ability to place students in the legal workplace nationwide" having noticed that most of the "prestigious" law firms only hire the top ten percent of Chicago-Kent students. "For some reason, I say we are associated with IIT, and people outside of the legal community think I am going to truck driving school," complains a 3L. After three years at Chicago-Kent, one student can safely say, "Students are happy, teachers want to teach, and learning is fun, yet also difficult."

NICOLE VILCHES, ASSISTANT DEAN FOR ADMISSIONS
565 WEST ADAMS STREET, CHICAGO, IL 60661
TEL: 312-906-5020 FAX: 312-906-5274
E-MAIL: ADMISSIONS@KENTLAW.EDU • WEBSITE: WWW.KENTLAW.EDU

Life

Numerous clubs and organizations "for everything you can imagine" mean that "there is a constant flow of speakers and programs for students to attend that cover all areas of the law." After a hard day of classes and legal writing boot camp, students look forward to the Student Bar Association's monthly "Kent Nights," for which the SBA rents out a different downtown bar for a "really great way to get noses out of books and make the student body relax with each other to have a good time." The student body at Chicago-Kent is a friendly bunch, and while there is a "subtle" competitive streak throughout the program years, most agree, "There is definitely a friendly, helpful attitude that prevails among students here," especially between the different sections of 1Ls. "I love being surrounded by individuals who allow me to have intelligent and insightful discussions about current issues or about what we are discussing in classes," says one student. However, a definite divide exists between day and evening students, with evening students complaining that most of the extracurricular activities are "pretty much unavailable to the evening students due to the timing of special events." While it's true that students live scattered all throughout the Chicago area, preventing some from attending certain events, others see it as a plus: "Most students will spend the better part of their day interacting with each other, instead of simply coming to class and then going home," explains a third-year student.

Getting In

Though admissions are on a rolling basis, Chicago-Kent's binding early decision program is somewhat unique in the field of law school admissions. Recently enrolled students at the 25th percentile had an LSAT score of 155 and a GPA of 3.2, while enrolled students at the 75th percentile had an LSAT score of 163 and a GPA of 3.7.

Clinical program required	No
Legal writing course requirement	Yes
Legal methods course requirement	No
Legal research course requirement	Yes
Moot court requirement	Yes
Public interest law requirement	No

ADMISSIONS

Selectivity Rating	79
# applications received	3,340
% applicants accepted	47
% acceptees attending	16
Average LSAT	159
LSAT Range	155–163
Average undergrad GPA	3.41
Application fee	$0
Regular application	Rolling, up to 7/1
Regular notification	Rolling
Early application program	Yes
Early application deadline	11/1
Early application notification	12/15
Transfer students accepted	Yes
Evening division offered	Yes
Part-time accepted	Yes
CAS accepted	Yes

FINANCIAL FACTS

Annual tuition	$39,690
Books and supplies	$1,262
Fees	$1,190
Room and board	$14,760
Financial aid application deadline	3/15
% first-year students receiving some sort of aid	94
% receiving some sort of aid	92
% of aid that is merit based	26
% receiving scholarships	56
Average grant	$18,693
Average loan	$36,443
Average total aid package	$46,451
Average debt	$99,971

EMPLOYMENT INFORMATION

Career Rating	87
Rate of placement (nine months out)	91
Average starting salary	$78,395
State for bar exam	IL, CA, NY, TX, FL
Pass rate for first-time bar	95

Employers Who Frequently Hire Grads

Historically approximately 55 employers have conducted on-campus interviews. Additional employers request resume collection or direct contact from students, hire students through consortium job fairs (Patent Law Interview Program; Cook County Bar Association; Minnesota Minority Job Fair; EJW Job Fair; AIPLA Job Fair, etc.) and post open job listings with the Career Services Office. 65% of the Class of 2009 graduates reporting employment entered private practice. Of these graduates, where size of firm was known, approximately 57% went to small firms (2–25 attorneys) and 40% to mid-to-large firms (26–500+ attorneys). 3% started their own practices. 16% of the class of 2009 reporting employment were employed in government, public interest, or judicial clerkship positions.

Prominent Alumni

The Honorable Ilana Diamond Rovner, U.S. Court of Appeals for the 7th Circuit; The Honorable Anne Burke, Illinois Supreme Court; Thomas Demetrio, Partner, Corboy & Demetrio; Anita Alvarez, Cook County State's Attorney; Ann M. Cresce, General Counsel Hong Kong Mercantile Exchange

Grads Employed by Field (%)

Academic (7)
Business/industry (21)
Government (9)
Judicial clerkship (3)
Military (1)
Private practice (55)
Public interest (5)

INDIANA UNIVERSITY—BLOOMINGTON
MAURER SCHOOL OF LAW

INSTITUTIONAL INFORMATION

Public/private	Public
Student/faculty ratio	10:1
% faculty part-time	5
% faculty female	34
% faculty minority	13
Total faculty	64

SURVEY SAYS...

Great research resources, Great library staff, Beautiful campus

STUDENTS

Enrollment of law school	646
% male/female	59/41
% from out-of-state	72
% full-time	100
% minority	18
# of countries represented	20
Average age of entering class	24

ACADEMICS

Academic Experience Rating	87
Profs interesting rating	85
Profs accessible rating	74
Hours of study per day	4.55

Academic Specialties

Civil Procedure, Commercial, Constitutional, Corporations Securities, Criminal, Environmental, Government Services, Human Rights, International, Labor, Legal History, Legal Philosophy, Property, Taxation, Intellectual Property, Telecommunications, Trial and Appellate Advocacy

Advanced Degrees Offered

SJD, 1 year in residence, 30 credit hours, completion and defense of doctoral dissertation; LLM Thesis, 2–3 semesters in residence, 24 credit hours, completion and defense of thesis; LLM Practicum, 2 semesters in residence, 24 credit hours plus practicum; MCL, 2 semesters in residence, 20 credit hours; PhD in Law & Social Science, 3 years in residence, 60 credit hours divided between law and collaborating department, 30 hours of dissertation research, final defense of dissertation; PhD in Law & Democracy, 2 years in residence; 69 credit hours divided between courses in law, anthropology, political science, and area studies; 21 credit hours for dissertation research; demonstrated proficiency in the language of the country or countries studied; fieldwork related to the country or countries studied; an internship with the Center for

Academics

Students at the Indiana University Maurer School of Law enjoy "first-rate resources and education" at "an excellent value." The law school boasts no fewer than nineteen clinical programs and projects including a community legal clinic, an entrepreneurship law clinic, and an inmate legal assistance project. Externship programs include the Washington Public Interest Program, which allows 3Ls to earn credit for public interest internships with government agencies and nonprofits in Washington, D.C. Students can study in Paris, Florence, Barcelona, Beijing, Auckland, and a host of other international cities, and they can apply for summer internships in India or Brazil through the school's Center on the Global Legal Profession. An unusual 1L course in the legal profession helps students discover their strengths while they explore career alternatives. Several interesting dual-degree programs, including a three-year JD/MBA and a bevy of specialization programs in taxation, international and comparative law, and intellectual property round out IU's "excellent" academic options.

The "extremely knowledgeable and accessible" faculty at IU "is really impressive." "When you go to class, you get the sense that your professors want to be in the classroom, and that makes engaging yourself in the material much easier," says a 2L. "There's a nice balance between professors who try to scare the pants off of you and the ones who really encourage you to take risks and push yourself, even if you turn out to be wrong." Even "boring" professors "really have a lot of important things to say." Outside the classroom, professors "participate in the law school social events" and "will go to great lengths to help students publish, research, and get placed" in jobs.

IU's administration "is genuinely concerned about students as individuals," and its "helpful and nice" Financial Aid Office "is the best in the country." Though in the past students have noted that "Career Services, while improving, has a long way to go," the Office of Career and Professional Development has since created an alternative career series, lunch-with-a-lawyer programs, and two alumni career service committees as well as expanded off campus interviews, hired new staff and hosted alumni-sponsored welcome-to-the-city events in key cities around the country. Many students tell us that the Office of Career and Professional Development "does all it can to assist students in obtaining jobs." "I think they're great," declares a 1L. "They're not going to get a job for you, but they'll do pretty much everything else." "If you are near the top of the class," "You'll have the Indy firms drooling all over you," and you won't have a problem working at "any of the best firms in Chicago" "or even Washington, D.C."

Everyone here agrees that the campus surrounding the law school is "beautiful." Classrooms once described as "uncomfortable," have been recently renovated. "The entire building has wireless Internet," and "There are electrical outlets at each seat." The gem of IU is the law library, which students claim is "without equal in the world, in part because of its staff." "With large windows that look out on the forest in the middle of campus, it's easy to forget that you're in the middle of a Big Ten school."

Life

IU's Midwestern location helps encourage a collegial attitude that frowns on aggressive competition." Students "simply do not let the abstract, competitive nature of the grading system affect their outward nature or the way they see their classmates." "If there is a more laid-back group of students at any law school in the country, I'd like to see it," challenges a 2L. "Students find their groups and comfort zones relatively quickly." Smaller class sizes "contribute to some minor drama at times," but students "get to know each other better and have a closer relationship with the faculty." "You can learn as much law as well here as at Harvard or Yale," promises a 3L. "But you will pay less, will see people being nicer to each other, and don't have to live in a grungy New England city."

The law school is "settled into a big university" "far away from the real-world" in "one of the greatest college towns in America." "The school is great for young undergraduates who appreciate a small-town environment." "Moving from a city to the boonies is still taking some getting used to," says one urbanite, "but the school offers some phenomenal cultural opportunities." There are "at least thirty ethnically diverse restaurants within a three-minute walk from the law school." Students here "work hard," but "There is great balance between the social life and the academic life." "The fitness and recreation facilities are superb," and "There are law school teams for intramurals." The Law and Drama Society "puts on a play in the school's moot court room." "The annual Women's Law Caucus Auction" is a big hit, as is an annual basketball game in IU's beloved Assembly Hall, which pits students against professors. Mostly, though, "The social environment is aimed at those who like to go out and party." "We're very social, very involved, and very fun," boasts a 2L. "The school is the focal point around which life spins, but there's always something to do, somewhere to go, someone to talk to." "There are after-hours activities sponsored by the school or a student group almost each week, and if there's nothing going on students will always congregate somewhere to have fun."

Getting In

Admitted students at the 25th percentile have LSAT scores of about 156 and GPAs hovering around 3.39. Admitted students at the 75th percentile have LSAT scores of approximately 165 and GPAs of approximately 3.85.

Constitutional Democracy; completion of qualifying examinations; a dissertation and final defense

Combined Degrees Offered

JD/MBA, 3–4 years; JD/MBAA Accounting; JD/MSA Accounting; JD/MSES Environmental Science; JD/MPA Public Affairs; JD/MA Journalism; JD/MA or MS Telecom; JD/MLS Library and Information Science; JD/PHD in Law and Social Science; joint-degree programs are typically 4 years

Clinical program required	No
Legal writing course requirement	Yes
Legal methods course requirement	No
Legal research course requirement	Yes
Moot court requirement	No
Public interest law requirement	No

ADMISSIONS

Selectivity Rating	92
# applications received	3,341
% applicants accepted	25
% acceptees attending	29
Average LSAT	161
LSAT Range	156–164
Average undergrad GPA	3.67
Application fee	$50
Regular application	Rolling, up to 8/1
Regular notification	Rolling
Early application program	Yes
Early application deadline	11/15
Early application notification	12/15
Transfer students accepted	Yes
Evening division offered	No
Part-time accepted	No
CAS accepted	Yes

International Students

TOEFL required of international students

FINANCIAL FACTS

Annual tuition (in-state/out-of-state)	$26,000/ $42,800
Books and supplies	$1,800
Fees	$904
Room and board	$13,396
Financial aid application deadline	3/1
% first-year students receiving some sort of aid	99
% receiving some sort of aid	98
% of aid that is merit based	85
% receiving scholarships	91
Average grant	$17,873
Average loan	$34,885
Average total aid package	$47,984
Average debt	$113,538

EMPLOYMENT INFORMATION

Career Rating	88	**Grads Employed by Field (%)**
Rate of placement (nine months out)	97	Academic (7)
Average starting salary	$78,900	Business/industry (15)
State for bar exam	IN, IL, NY, CA, OH	Government (13)
Pass rate for first-time bar	94	Judicial clerkship (8)

Employers Who Frequently Hire Grads

Baker & Daniels; Ice Miller; Jones Day; Mayer Brown; U.S. Dept. of Justice; U.S. Federal Circuit & District Courts

Military (4)

Private practice (45)

Public interest (8)

Prominent Alumni

Shirley Abrahamson, Chief Justice, Wisconsin Supreme Court; Lee Hamilton, Former Congressman; Robert Long, Partner, Latham & Watkins; Bruce McLean, Managing Partner, Akin Gump Strauss Haver & Fell; Michael Uslan, Executive Producer, Batman

INDIANA UNIVERSITY—INDIANAPOLIS
SCHOOL OF LAW

INSTITUTIONAL INFORMATION

Public/private	Public
Student/faculty ratio	17:1
% faculty part-time	58
% faculty female	49
% faculty minority	10
Total faculty	116

SURVEY SAYS...

Diverse opinions accepted in classrooms, Beautiful campus, Students love Indianapolis, IN

STUDENTS

Enrollment of law school	918
% male/female	54/46
% from out-of-state	16
% full-time	65
% minority	13
% international	4
# of countries represented	17
Average age of entering class	24

ACADEMICS

Academic Experience Rating	**81**
Profs interesting rating	80
Profs accessible rating	71
Hours of study per day	4.21

Academic Specialties

Constitutional, Criminal, Government Services, Human Rights, International, Labor, Taxation, Intellectual Property, Health Law, Litagation

Advanced Degrees Offered

SJD, LLM, 1 year

Combined Degrees Offered

JD/MPA, 4 years; JD/MBA, 4 years; JD/MHA, 4 years; JD/MPH, 4 years; JD/M Phil, 4 years; JD/MLS, 4 years; JD/MSW, 4 years

Clinical program required	No
Legal writing course requirement	Yes
Legal methods course requirement	Yes

Academics

Indiana University—Indianapolis School of Law is a relatively large school on an "urban campus" in "a great downtown location." The "lovely," spacious, and "comfortable" facility here is "a beautiful, high-tech place to learn." "Classrooms are modern and large and sport electric outlets at every seat," and "There are many places, such as the reading room, where students can go to study." Several joint-degree programs are available. There are four law reviews, six clinics, and summer study abroad programs in China and Croatia. Opportunities to specialize include intellectual property law and international law as well as a "particularly strong" health law curriculum.

The faculty as a whole is "excellent" and "engaging." They "do their best to make sure the material is as interesting as possible" and "take a very practical tack in their approach to teaching." "The atmosphere at IU Indy is such that, while the work is intense, I've never felt like not wanting to go to class," beams a 2L. "Ever." Outside of class, "Professors are accessible and students are not afraid to approach them for help on a concept or to share a joke." The two-semester legal writing program (with optional third semester) generally receives high marks. Student opinion concerning the administration is mixed. Defenders of it tell us that the top brass is student-friendly and "does a fairly good job." "The administration always tries its best to help us succeed," says a happy 2L. Detractors complain that "the administration has no idea what's going on." One complaint is that registration can be difficult for 2Ls and 3Ls. "Too many classes clumped at the same time make it difficult" to take all the courses you want (or need). A few professors are "not interested in teaching at all."

IU Indy is the lesser known of the two IU law schools (the other one is in Bloomington), but students say that attending the only law school in Indiana's state capital and commercial hub definitely has its perks. IU—Indianapolis School of Law is close to "all of the large firms" in the city and "within blocks of city, state, and federal government offices, and courthouses." "This enables us to work at some of the state's best and largest firms throughout the school year," explains a 3L. "It also provides us with the opportunity to do externships with all of the state's major courts and organizations." "Being in downtown Indianapolis is excellent for networking opportunities with the legal community," too. Some students applaud the efforts of the "hardworking" staff in the Office of Professional Development to secure career opportunities. Other students are less than thrilled. "They don't help anyone get jobs," gripes a 3L, "and they don't respond to phone calls or e-mails, either." Also, while the school's reputation in the state is very good, "It's an uphill battle to find employment outside of Indiana."

PATRICIA KINNEY, DIRECTOR FOR ADMISSIONS
530 WEST NEW YORK STREET, INDIANAPOLIS, IN 46202-3225
TEL: 317-274-2459 FAX: 317-278-4780
E-MAIL: LAWADMIT@IUPUI.EDU • WEBSITE: INDYLAW.INDIANA.EDU

Life

Students here describe themselves as "quite friendly." "Animosity is pleasantly absent." "Students generally get along quite well with one another and are collegial in the classroom," relates a 1L. While there's "a decent amount of diversity" and IU Indy is "very welcoming environment to students of all backgrounds," a pretty vast chasm exists between the full-time day students and the part-time evening students. A large percentage of the full-timers come "straight out of undergrad" and "chose to attend Indianapolis for its proximity to firm, corporate, and political experiences." The part-time program constitutes about one-third of the student body, and it's mostly "older, nontraditional" students who already have occupations, families, and their own social lives.

IU Indy is located on the campus of Indiana University—Purdue University Indianapolis (where "parking is absolutely atrocious"). "The school's central location is used to its fullest advantage through symposiums, networking functions, alumni activities, and other gatherings where members of the Indianapolis legal community mingle with students," relates a 2L. Life beyond academics gets mixed reviews. By all accounts, Indianapolis is "a great city" with lots to see and do. Some students tell us that the school provides many social outlets. "There are a lot of activities," and you can "relive high school all over again" "with more drinking." Others give the campus "a mediocre rating for social life." "The problem is that it's a commuter school and people are coming from all over the place." "People do their work and go home." "As a result, there is not a whole lot of socializing."

Getting In

Enrolled full-time students at the 25th percentile at IU—Indianapolis School of Law have an average LSAT score of 157 and a GPA of about 3.51. Admissions statistics for part-time students are lower.

Legal research course requirement	Yes
Moot court requirement	No
Public interest law requirement	No

ADMISSIONS

Selectivity Rating	82
# applications received	1,628
% applicants accepted	41
% acceptees attending	42
Average LSAT	157
LSAT Range	153–160
Average undergrad GPA	3.51
Application fee	$50
Regular application	Rolling, up to 3/1
Regular notification	Rolling
Early application program	Yes
Early application deadline	11/15
Early application notification	12/31
Transfer students accepted	Yes
Evening division offered	Yes
Part-time accepted	Yes
CAS accepted	Yes

International Students

TOEFL required of international students	

FINANCIAL FACTS

Annual tuition (in-state/out-of-state)	$19,924/ $43,016
Books and supplies	$1,600
Fees	$630
Room and board	$21,124
Financial aid application deadline	3/10
% first-year students receiving some sort of aid	88
% receiving some sort of aid	83
% of aid that is merit based	9
% receiving scholarships	35
Average grant	$7,567
Average loan	$29,622
Average total aid package	$31,439
Average debt	$83,259

EMPLOYMENT INFORMATION

		Grads Employed by Field (%)	
Career Rating	74	Academic	(4)
Rate of placement (nine months out)	91	Business/industry	(16)
Average starting salary	$72,825	Government	(24)
State for bar exam	IN	Judicial clerkship	(2)
Pass rate for first-time bar	86	Military	(1)

Employers Who Frequently Hire Grads
Private law firms; Baker & Daniels; Barnes & Thornburg; Ice Miller

Prominent Alumni
John Pistole, Deputy Director of the FBI; Ellen Engleman, Chairman of the National Transportation Safety Bd; Mark Roesler, President & CEO, CMG Worldwide, Inc.; Alan Cohen, Chairman, President & CEO, The Finish Line Inc.

Private practice (51)
Public interest (2)

THE JOHN MARSHALL LAW SCHOOL

Academics

The John Marshall Law School is an independent bastion of legal education that offers day and evening programs as well as both fall and spring admission. John Marshall is pretty large as far as law schools go and it "places a huge emphasis on real-world practice." Students report that they are "ready to hit the ground running even as clerks and interns." The "unparalleled" writing program "creates students who can file complaints and briefs immediately, with little or no additional training." The trial advocacy program is "outstanding" as well. "When you graduate from John Marshall, you are ready to work in a courtroom," a 2L says. John Marshall also offers specialized programs and joint JD/LLM programs in a host of areas including employee benefits, information technology and privacy law, international business and trade law, real estate law, intellectual property law, and tax law. "Students are encouraged to find a specific field of interest and are given every opportunity to become experts" in that field.

"The school's faculty is comprised mostly of professors who have accumulated years of experience," a 2L explains. "Their experiences and knowledge give a true and practical look at the actual practice of law." Students boast that John Marshall's "accessible" faculty is comprised of "the best professors, judges, and lawyers in Chicago." It's also worth noting that the hardcore, old-school Socratic Method is very much alive and well at John Marshall. A few professors are "very hard to comprehend" and "not good teachers," though. Opinion concerning the administration is split. One faction of students calls management "extremely helpful." "There seems to be a genuine interest in the needs of the students," they say. Other students aren't so happy. "The deans never get anything done," a 3L says.

About ten percent of each graduating class is able to obtain the really plum jobs at big firms. Most students tell us they are satisfied with their career prospects. "The connections that John Marshall has to the Chicago area are incredible," a 1L says. "It is very easy to connect with other John Marshall alumni, who are very willing to meet with and help you." A 3L adds, "John Marshall has done everything possible to put its graduates in a position of getting a job." Some students aren't as pleased, though. "I have had little help from the staff at the Career Services office," a 2L gripes. "Every time I have asked for assistance, they have merely told me where to look. I really could have figured that out for myself."

John Marshall is located in the middle of Chicago's South Loop "in the heart of the legal community" and "close to all the action." The U.S. District Court of Appeals for the Seventh Circuit is across the street. The Chicago Bar Association is "right next door." As for the actual law school facilities, "The buildings are old Chicago architectural mainstays," and "They've got charm." "The place needs a little sprucing up," though. It "doesn't offer many perks you see on other campuses." "The classrooms that are newer are very good." On the other hand, some classrooms are "a couple decades behind." Students also complain that John Marshall is generally "overcrowded." "Elevators are hard to come by," and "It's slightly hard to get around."

Life

The student population at John Marshall is pretty diverse, ethnically and just about every other way. Some students tell us that the academic atmosphere is cordial. "We help each other, share outlines, and study in groups," a 2L says. However, the prevailing opinion seems to be that John Marshall is home to "a very competitive environment, which rewards achievement." "One thing that sets John Marshall apart is that they give people who would otherwise not get to go to law school a chance," a 2L explains. "That leads to a large number of people failing out the first year." "After first semester things became much more competitive among people in my section," another 2L recalls.

Students here say that it's "very easy to find friends here," and they promise that they are a "very nice, normal bunch." "People are split into those active in school activities, such as trial teams, versus those who choose to work outside of school." "The social aspect really depends on the individual," a 1L says. "Some prefer to get in, do the work, and get out. Others prefer to socialize. There is something for everyone." If you want to get involved, "There are plenty of school-sponsored social events." "We have over fifty student organizations to choose from so that everyone can find their niche," a 3L notes. "Being a joiner at John Marshall is easy and doesn't feel corny like it did in undergrad."

Getting In

Admitted students at the 25th percentile have LSAT scores in the low 150s and GPAs around 3.02. Admitted students at the 75th percentile have LSAT scores in the mid 150s and GPAs in the 3.5 range.

Estate Law, Tax Law, 24 credit hours, approximately 1–3 years

Combined Degrees Offered
JD/MBA, JD/MPA, JD/MA, JD/LLM

Clinical program required	No
Legal writing course requirement	Yes
Legal methods course requirement	Yes
Legal research course requirement	Yes
Moot court requirement	No
Public interest law requirement	No

ADMISSIONS

Selectivity Rating	75
# applications received	3,100
% applicants accepted	43
% acceptees attending	13
Average LSAT	154
LSAT Range	153–159
Average undergrad GPA	3.20
Application fee	$0
Regular application	Rolling, up to 8/1
Regular notification	Rolling
Early application program	No
Transfer students accepted	Yes
Evening division offered	Yes
Part-time accepted	Yes
CAS accepted	Yes

International Students
TOEFL required of international students

FINANCIAL FACTS

Annual tuition	$38,135
Books and supplies	$2,340
Fees	$324
Room and board	$18,680
Financial aid application deadline	Rolling
% first-year students receiving some sort of aid	90
% receiving some sort of aid	85
% of aid that is merit based	95
% receiving scholarships	35
Average grant	$10,000
Average loan	$20,000
Average total aid package	$20,500
Average debt	$126,800

EMPLOYMENT INFORMATION

Career Rating		84
Rate of placement (nine months out)		90
Average starting salary		$72,630
State for bar exam		IL
Pass rate for first-time bar		89

Employers Who Frequently Hire Grads
DLA Piper; Cook County State's Attorneys Office; City of Chicago Law Department; Vedder Price; Jenner & Block; Cassiday Schade

Prominent Alumni
Mark Pedowitz, Chairman, Pine Street Entertainment; Bill Daley, White House Chief of Staff; Leo Melamed, Chair Emeritus, CME Group, Hon. Timothy

Evans, Chief Judge Cook County Circuit Court; Joyce Tucker, VP of Global Diversity & Employee Rights, Boeing

Grads Employed by Field (%)
Academic (7)
Business/industry (22)
Government (15)
Judicial clerkship (2)
Military (1)
Private practice (51)
Public interest (2)

LEWIS & CLARK COLLEGE
LEWIS & CLARK LAW SCHOOL

INSTITUTIONAL INFORMATION

Public/private	Private
Student/faculty ratio	10:1
% faculty part-time	40
% faculty female	39
% faculty minority	19
Total faculty	94

SURVEY SAYS...

Liberal students, Beautiful campus

STUDENTS

Enrollment of law school	744
% male/female	49/51
% from out-of-state	61
% full-time	77
% minority	22
% international	2
# of countries represented	9
Average age of entering class	28

ACADEMICS

Academic Experience Rating	**76**
Profs interesting rating	76
Profs accessible rating	78
Hours of study per day	4.31

Academic Specialties

Commercial, Constitutional, Corporation Securities, Criminal, Environmental, Government Services, International, Labor, Property, Taxation, Intellectual Property, Animal Law

Advanced Degrees Offered

LLM/Environmental & Natural Resources, 12–18 months

Combined Degrees Offered

JD/LLM in Environmental & Natural Resources Law, 3.5 years

Academics

Students who take the legal plunge at Lewis & Clark Law School in beautiful Portland, Oregon, enjoy professors who are "uniformly excellent and approachable for discussion about class topics and other issues striking your fancy." The small size of the law school allows for an extremely personalized educational experience, and students benefit from this cozy setup on multiple levels, "from an academic perspective as well as from a functional perspective." "I have been lucky enough to develop solid mentor relationships with specific professors that were particularly inspirational," says a second-year student. Practically everyone involved in running the school, from the dean to the cafeteria staff, "seem to truly like each other," and the well-regarded faculty is given an "unusual amount of influence in the way that the school is run, and [in the] the school's policies."

Lewis & Clark Law School has a relatively small course load of required classes and offers a night program, bringing a large contingent of older and more experienced students to the classrooms, which "adds a valuable, practical dimension to the learning experience." As one would expect from such an environmentally conscious institution, programs such as environmental and natural resources law and animal law are "unparalleled." No matter what their specialization, the faculty is considered to be "inspirational and knowledgeable enough to stimulate thinking beyond what's required by the curriculum," and the school's size "allows for an ideal student/teacher ratio that goes further to foster a highly effective teaching environment."

Lewis & Clark's National Crime Victim Law Institute is another source of pride for the school, "leading the way in an emerging field of law."

Administrators are friendly, and accessible, "always willing to help out a student," and they keep the law school "running very smoothly." The research librarians are cited for being "very knowledgeable," and the Career Services Department also does its part to make sure students' needs are met, though some would like to see more non-metro area firms on campus. For students who are interested in staying in the area after graduation, there is "heavy support and involvement from the Portland legal community," and for others, "Alumni are distributed all around the world."

Since the school and its student body are known for being nature-friendly, it follows that the buildings on campus are all "green" and "tucked into a forested state park." This is nice, students say, because "when you are facing the gut-wrenching pain of law school, a 'walk in the park' goes a long way." Students are quite pleased with the library and the newer building, Wood Hall, but many are clamoring for an update of the other facilities. Portland is universally beloved as "a great place to live," though students say the parking situation could stand some improvements. A graduating student sums up life at the law school this way: "The professors are passionate about what they teach, and the students actually want to help each other get ahead in school. And where else do you get to study while in an overly large tree house?"

TRACY SULLIVAN, ASSOCIATE DIRECTOR OF ADMISSIONS
LEWIS & CLARK LAW SCHOOL, 10015 SW TERWILLIGER BOULEVARD, PORTLAND, OR 97219
TEL: 503-768-6613 FAX: 503-768-6793
E-MAIL: LAWADMSS@LCLARK.EDU • WEBSITE: WWW.LCLARK.EDU/LAW

Life

No one would argue that "liberal" describes the majority of those enrolled at Lewis & Clark, and as one 3L warns, "If you are conservative, religious, or a meat-eating capitalist, be prepared." Fortunately, the laid-back nature of the majority of the student body means that there is "a complete void of competition"; absolutely "no one participates in the awful game of one-upmanship or cutthroat competition," and "The students are genuinely interested in helping and supporting each other." The day and night students don't often interact outside of class, but this doesn't seem to be a source of much tension. There are plenty of clubs in which they can relate if they so choose, and students here "are spoiled with the number of lunchtime events," including speakers and panels. "Everyone is accepted for who they are," coos a 2L. A second-year student puts it in another way: "Good people go here."

Getting In

The admission rate at Lewis & Clark is thirty-five percent—the majority of applicants are not admitted. The typical student has been in the work force for several years, which plays into the amount of weight placed on various admissions factors. GPA will factor in more heavily for recent grads, and applicants should make sure their letters of recommendation come from the appropriate sources (professors or employers). Recently admitted students at the 25th percentile had an LSAT score of 157 and an average GPA of 3.14, while admitted students at the 75th percentile had an LSAT score of 163 and a GPA of 3.67.

Clinical program required	No
Legal writing course requirement	Yes
Legal methods course requirement	Yes
Legal research course requirement	Yes
Moot court requirement	Yes
Public interest law requirement	No

ADMISSIONS

Selectivity Rating	85
# applications received	3,330
% applicants accepted	36
% acceptees attending	21
LSAT Range	164–157
Application fee	$50
Regular application	Rolling, up to 3/1
Regular notification	Rolling
Early application program	No
Transfer students accepted	Yes
Evening division offered	Yes
Part-time accepted	Yes
CAS accepted	Yes

International Students

TOEFL recommended of international students

FINANCIAL FACTS

Annual tuition	$35,048
Books and supplies	$1,050
Fees	$50
Room and board	$17,100
Financial aid application deadline	3/1
% first-year students receiving some sort of aid	95
% receiving some sort of aid	93
% of aid that is merit based	100
% receiving scholarships	46
Average grant	$10,601
Average loan	$53,198
Average total aid package	$53,198
Average debt	$105,928

EMPLOYMENT INFORMATION

Career Rating	79
Rate of placement (nine months out)	94
Average starting salary	$61,522
State for bar exam	OR
Pass rate for first-time bar	79

Employers Who Frequently Hire Grads

Numerous small and medium-sized firms; State Government (Oregon, Washington, Idaho, Alaska); Multnomah, Washington, and Clackamas Counties; U.S. Government agencies; State & Federal Judiciary; Stoel Rives LLP; Schwabe Williamson & Wyatt; Davis Wright Tremaine LLP; Tonkon Torp LLP; Bullivant Houser Bailey PC

Prominent Alumni

Earl Blumenauer, U.S. Representative; Phil Schrilio, Special Advisor to the President; Honorable Betty Roberts, Former Oregon Supreme Court Justice; Honorable Robert E Jones, U.S. District Court for the District of Oregon; Wayne Perry, CEO Edge Wireless

Grads Employed by Field (%)

Government (14)
Public interest (9)

LOUISIANA STATE UNIVERSITY
PAUL M. HEBERT LAW CENTER

Academics

The "very inexpensive" Louisiana State University Law Center boasts "the highest bar-passage rate in the state" pretty much every year and a unique joint-degree program that provides "exposure to both common and civil law." You'll leave LSU Law with a Juris Doctor as well as a diploma in civil law, which is a mélange of European legal traditions. "The focus on the civil law at LSU is a definite plus because most of us remain in Louisiana to practice," explains a 2L. "It's a much different approach to problems than our common law colleagues use, and the training in the civil law happens early and often." The "first-year curriculum is rich and very demanding." Contracts, torts, civil procedure, constitutional law, and all your standard 1L courses are required. Students must also take course work in Louisiana's codes of torts, civilian property, and much else. After first year, "2Ls and 3Ls [are] more free to specialize and take advantage of the practical law courses available that would be applicable out of state." Some students complain that there aren't nearly enough electives, though. "LSU is small and so the range of courses available isn't very broad, and it's not always clear when a course will be taught." "Some courses offered in the school's course booklet haven't been offered in years," gripes a hardened 3L.

"The classrooms and facilities are phenomenal." Class attendance policies are "relatively stringent." It's a good thing, then, that the academic atmosphere is generally "excellent." "The great thing about LSU Law professors is that many of them have been incredibly influential in the development of Louisiana law," observes a 1L. "In preparing cases for classes, you can't help but notice how often the courts have relied on your professor's doctrinal works in formulating their decisions." "While some are intent on using the Socratic Method at all costs, most use it simply to ensure that you are paying attention and can answer their questions when called upon," relates a 3L. Not all faculty members are fabulous, though. "LSU has some of the best," advises a 2L, "but a couple have to be the worst." Outside of class, most faculty members are "more than willing to talk to students." "They are all accessible if you try a little bit." A few students tell us that the administration "emphasizes bureaucracy," but the overwhelming sentiment here is that top brass "truly works for the students" and is "remarkably responsive to the student body."

LSU Law offers "an abundance of opportunities to be involved" in journals and advocacy programs. There are clinical programs in immigration law, family law, mediation, and juvenile representation. "A well-connected externship program places second- and third-year students with justices and judges in the Louisiana Supreme Court and the U.S. Fifth Circuit Court of Appeals, among others," adds a 3L. A study abroad program in Lyon, France, is also popular. Over 150 employers recruit here each year, but opinion regarding LSU Law's ability to help students find jobs is split. Critics tell us that the Career Services office displays "callous indifference toward students who are not in the top five to ten percent of the class." Other students say that Career Services is "in touch with you from the beginning" and "goes the extra mile to help students and find opportunity for them." "This school does everything it possibly can to ensure that you pass the bar and get a job," beams a confident 1L.

MICHELE FORBES, DIRECTOR OF STUDENT AFFAIRS AND REGISTRAR
202 LAW CENTER, BATON ROUGE, LA 70803
TEL: 225-578-8646 FAX: 225-578-8647
E-MAIL: ADMISSIONS@LAW.LSU.EDU • WEBSITE: WWW.LAW.LSU.EDU

Life

"Students are generally serious and hardworking." "The student body and faculty lean conservative, but all walks of life are welcome" and it's a diverse group, "age-wise and experience-wise." LSU Law "has a collegial feel where there is a place for everyone." "The school is just the right size to allow getting to know everyone," explains a 2L. "No one is just a number. Everyone has the opportunity to be an individual." "We have gunners just like every law school," admits a 1L. For the most part, though, there is only "a mild dose" of competition. "There really isn't a lot of the cutthroat behavior." Students frequently "share outlines and help each other learn the law."

"Social life at LSU Law is great from the library to the tailgate." This school is "in the middle of Cajun country—great food, one of the best football teams in the nation, and good Southern people." "LSU is in the greatest location a student could ask for," gloats a 1L. "Baton Rouge is an amazing city, and the Law Center is located in the heart of one of the most vibrant undergraduate campuses in the nation." "There are many social programs running throughout the semester so that you get to know your classmates personally and you aren't just doing law school 24/7." "There are parties all the time." "There are free drinks nearly every weekend." "Intramural tournaments" are pretty popular, too. "Students strap on pads and play a charity football game once a year," just for instance, complete with tackling.

Getting In

Admitted students at the 25th percentile have LSAT scores around 155 and undergraduate grade point averages not much over 3.0. At the 75th percentile, LSAT scores are about 159 and GPAs are approximately 3.7.

ADMISSIONS

Selectivity Rating	84
# applications received	1,653
% applicants accepted	35
% acceptees attending	38
Average LSAT	158
LSAT Range	155–160
Average undergrad GPA	3.38
Application fee	$50
Regular application	Rolling, up to 5/1
Regular notification	Rolling
Early application program	No
Transfer students accepted	Yes
Evening division offered	No
Part-time accepted	No
CAS accepted	Yes

International Students

TOEFL required of international students

FINANCIAL FACTS

Annual tuition	$14,496
Books and supplies	$2,000
Fees	$1,652
Room and board (on/off campus)	$11,034/ $12,834
Financial aid application deadline	4/20
% first-year students receiving some sort of aid	76
% receiving some sort of aid	88
% of aid that is merit based	7
% receiving scholarships	80
Average grant	$6,945
Average loan	$17,998
Average total aid package	$18,330
Average debt	$59,218

EMPLOYMENT INFORMATION

Career Rating	78
Rate of placement (nine months out)	91
Average starting salary	$60,157
State for bar exam	LA
Pass rate for first-time bar	75

Employers Who Frequently Hire Grads

Adams & Reese; Baker & Hostetler; Breazeale Sachse & Wilson; Phelps Dunbar; McGinchey Stafford; Taylor Porter Brooks & Phillips; Stone Pigman; Vinson & Elkins; Chaffe McCall Phillips Toler & Sarpy; Cook Yancey King & Galloway; Correro Fishman Haygood Phelps Weiss; Courtenay Forstall Hunter & Fontana; Cox & Smith; Crawford & Lewis; Deutsch Kerrigan & Stiles; Fisher & Phillips; Jackson & Walker; Jenkins & Gilchrist; Jones Walker Waechter Poitevent Carrerre; Kantrow Spaht Weaver & Blitzer; Kean Miller Howthorne D'Armond Mcowan; Laborde & Neuner; Lemle & Kelleher; Liskow & Lewis; Milling Benson Woodword; Montgomery Barnett Brown Read Hammond; Onebane Bernard Torian Diaz McNamara & Abell; Orleans Parish District Attorney's Office; Preis & Roy; Thompson & Knight; Voorhies & Labbe'; Baker, Donelson, King & Spalding; Baker Botts; Miami Dade County State Attorney

LOYOLA MARYMOUNT UNIVERSITY
LOYOLA LAW SCHOOL

INSTITUTIONAL INFORMATION

Public/private	Private
% faculty part-time	52
% faculty female	33
% faculty minority	17
Total faculty	138

SURVEY SAYS...

Diverse opinions accepted in classrooms, Great research resources, Great library staff

STUDENTS

Enrollment of law school	1,289
% male/female	47/53
% from out-of-state	21
% full-time	79
% minority	39
% international	1
# of countries represented	7
Average age of entering class	26

ACADEMICS

Academic Experience Rating	97
Profs interesting rating	96
Profs accessible rating	93
Hours of study per day	4.53

Academic Specialties

Civil Procedure, Commercial, Constitutional, Corporation Securities, Criminal, Environmental, Government Services, Human Rights, International, Labor, Legal History, Legal Philosophy, Property, Taxation, Intellectual Property, Entertainment Law, Mediation, Juvenile Justice

Advanced Degrees Offered

LLM in Taxation, full-time 1 year, part-time 3 years; JD/LLM in Taxation, 3 years

Combined Degrees Offered

JD/MBA, 4 years; JD/LLM in Taxation, 3 years

Academics

Loyola Law School (affiliated with Loyola Marymount University, or the "mothership") is "an understated gem" in downtown Los Angeles that "seeks to create top lawyers who use the profession for the betterment of society and [to] give back to [the] legal community." It's a generally happy place that quite simply seeks to make good lawyers, send them out to the world, and repeat; all the people associated with the school, from students to staff, are accordingly pleasant and uncomplicated, if not a little resentful of the relative anonymity as compared to the other law schools in the area. As one 1L puts it, "Masochists would be disappointed at Loyola. For legal torture, look elsewhere in Los Angeles."

Professors are "smart [and] demanding yet understanding of the pressures of a first-year law student." They are of "the highest caliber" and "set the bar high, but [they] give you all of the tools to use at your discretion to meet that bar." Classes are "lively and enjoyable," and teachers keep their doors open for whatever's troubling the masses. "Every professor I have had seems to truly care about the success of their students, both inside and outside the classroom," says a student.

The curriculum itself offers "a strong foundation in legal theory but also the practical skills necessary to excel in the workplace," including a comprehensive legal research and writing program. There are a "broad range of specialists within a variety of fields" to help students narrow down their field of focus, and many "solid opportunities for public interest law," as well as "a tremendous trial advocacy program, moot court, and three law reviews." However, all of this opportunity comes at a private school price, and financial aid is not easy as easy to come by as most students would like. "A break in $40,000 tuition payments would be nice. For a school that boasts itself on public interest, taking out well over $100,000 in tuition loans doesn't exactly amend itself to accepting a $50,000 per year public interest job," says a 3L. Graduates of LLS mainly practice in California and L.A., so the school enjoys a much greater reputation within the state than it does nationally, and for those who do stay nearby (very much the majority), the alumni networking opportunities are strong.

As for the administrators, most here have little to no problems with the administration, which "not only talks the talk, but walks the walk." That is, aside from the Registrar's office, which "is like talking to a brick wall. They need to listen and think about what you are saying before they respond with the scripted answer." The law school has its own "cozy" and completely separate campus from Loyola Marymount, so there are "no undergrads taking up the library study rooms." The school operates a shuttle, which takes students to the financial district and the new L.A. Live entertainment complex every fifteen minutes, which means that "courts, law firms, and our city's phenomenal entertainment are basically our campus."

Life

As expected, happy students make for a happy campus. Competition is at a low here; notes and outlines "are regularly shared," and "There has not been one hint of dirty competition at all." "I can't imagine a better atmosphere considering the pressures of first year. The 2Ls and 3Ls have been amazingly supportive too," says one first-year. Even outside of the classroom, everyone is "peculiarly friendly"—one student was "caught off guard by how helpful everybody was." There is always something new and exciting going on, from "bowling to benefit the public interest law foundation, to lunches with European patent

JANNELL LUNDY ROBERTS, ASSISTANT DEAN OF ADMISSIONS
919 ALBANY STREET, LOS ANGELES, CA 90015
TEL: 213-736-1074 FAX: 213-736-6523
E-MAIL: ADMISSIONS@LLS.EDU • WEBSITE: WWW.LLS.EDU

scholars, to social outings at hot bars and clubs around town." Panel lunches with industry leaders are well-attended at Loyola, and "You could probably go to a meeting and eat for free every day if you wanted."

One of the reasons the lunch hour is so heavily trafficked is the high number of commuters who go to school here, which limits after-class time as an option for socializing and means that "developing a large social network isn't as easy as it might be if everyone lived right next to campus" (where everyone also agrees that it would "be nice if we had a gym"). However, the SBA and student organizations "do a good job of scheduling social activities to bring students closer," and this social bunch obliges for the most part. Downtown L.A. has also undergone a massive revitalization effort, and everyone agrees that it is "incredibly convenient."

Getting In

To be considered for admission to Loyola Law School, students must submit undergraduate transcripts, LSAT scores, and a personal statement. Students also must submit at least one and up to three letters of recommendation, of which at least one should be from an academic source.

Clinical program required	No
Legal writing course requirement	Yes
Legal methods course requirement	Yes
Legal research course requirement	Yes
Moot court requirement	No
Public interest law requirement	Yes

ADMISSIONS

Selectivity Rating	**87**
# applications received	5,303
% applicants accepted	28
% acceptees attending	23
Average LSAT	161
LSAT Range	158–163
Average undergrad GPA	3.49
Application fee	$65
Regular application	Rolling, up to 2/2
Regular notification	Rolling
Early application program	No
Transfer students accepted	Yes
Evening division offered	Yes
Part-time accepted	Yes
CAS accepted	Yes

FINANCIAL FACTS

Annual tuition	$41,270
Books and supplies	$1,050
Fees	$570
Room and board	$16,058
Financial aid application deadline	3/14
Average debt	$132,267

EMPLOYMENT INFORMATION

Career Rating	**88**
Rate of placement (nine months out)	94
Average starting salary	$84,760
State for bar exam	CA
Pass rate for first-time bar	83

Employers Who Frequently Hire Grads
O'Melveny & Myers LLP; Paul, Hastings; Sheppard, Mullin; Jones, Day; Latham & Watkins; Los Angeles County D.A. and Public Defender; Katten Muchin; Allen Matkins

Prominent Alumni
Gloria Allred, Trial Attorney; Harry Sloan, Chairman MGM; Neal Schmale, CEO Sempra Energy; Johnnie Cochran, Trial Attorney; Robert Shapiro, Attorney

Grads Employed by Field (%)
Academic (5)
Business/industry (14)
Government (4)
Judicial clerkship (4)
Military (1)
Private practice (58)
Public interest (14)

Loyola University—Chicago
School of Law

INSTITUTIONAL INFORMATION

Public/private	Private
Affiliation	Roman Catholic
Student/faculty ratio	13:1
% faculty part-time	70
% faculty female	49
% faculty minority	7
Total faculty	162

SURVEY SAYS:...

Diverse opinions accepted in classrooms, Great library staff, Students love Chicago, IL

STUDENTS

Enrollment of law school	851
% male/female	51/49
% full-time	81
% minority	18
% international	1
Average age of entering class	24

ACADEMICS

Academic Experience Rating	82
Profs interesting rating	79
Profs accessible rating	80
Hours of study per day	4.24

Academic Specialties

Corporation Securities, Criminal, International, Labor, Taxation, Intellectual Property; Certificate programs are available in Health Law, Tax Law, Public Interest Law, Advocacy, International Law, Child Law

Advanced Degrees Offered

MJ Health Law, MJ in Child Law, online; MJ Child Law, MJ Business Law, 22 semester hours; LLM Health Law, LLM Child Law, LLM Tax Law, LLM Advocacy, LLM in Business Law, 24 credit hours; LLM in Rule of Law for Development, 27 credit hours, Rome Campus; LLM in Health Law, online; SJD Health Law, DLaw in Health Law, 2 years full-time

Academics

Loyola University—Chicago's School of Law is "a stellar school" that is "well-known in the Midwest" and located "in the most desirable area" of "a world-class city." Perks here include an "unrivaled" sense of community, no fewer than six journals, study abroad programs in, among other places, Rome and Beijing, and eleven individual areas of focus. There are specialty programs and certificates galore, too. "The health law program is one of the best in the country." "Loyola is also extremely well-known for [its] child and family law program." Students say that the way Loyola imparts advocacy skills is another advantage. "Loyola is perhaps the only law school in Chicago which produces trial attorneys as a rule, not as an unexpected happenstance," brags a 3L.

The "very accessible" administration here "is not always the most organized," but it "is composed of smart and kind people" who go "out of their way to help the students." "Honestly, everyone here wants the students to succeed," beams a 2L, "and that feeling is apparent." The full-time faculty is "extraordinarily knowledgeable" and otherwise "really impressive." "The professors are brilliant, but not stuffy," reports a 1L. "They have academic experience and professional experience that meld perfectly." "Professors are friendly and always available," adds a 3L. There's "a strong emphasis on professors having open-door policies and establishing relationships with students," and they "will go out of their way to help students in the classroom and in finding a job." The adjunct professors who teach some specialized elective courses are reportedly "either really great or horribly atrocious, with not much in the way of middle ground."

Some students are critical of the Office of Career Services at Loyola. However, the general sentiment is that the administrative staff is "amazing" and that career prospects are bright. Public service jobs and internships are "easy to find." In the private sector, starting salaries are formidable. "In the greater Chicago legal community, Loyola seemingly carries a hefty reputation for producing good lawyers," relates a 3L. Loyola's "very loyal alumni" are also a tremendous asset when it comes to job searches. "The alumni have a strong connection with the law school," says a 2L. Networking events with alums are common.

The "plush," "state-of-the-art" facility here is relatively new, but "that doesn't seem to deter the administration from constantly updating just about everything." Most classrooms are "spacious and modern." "The new classrooms are really nice" "with plug-ins for your laptop at every space." "The library is really great," comments a 2L. "There are always plenty of tables and study rooms available." "The new courtroom [is] gorgeous." Technology is reportedly "excellent," too. "I can print to the school's printers from my laptop," notes a 1L. "The wireless Internet always seems to be working (knock on wood)."

Life

"There is very little interaction between the day- and evening-section students" but, within those two largely separate groups, "Loyola deliberately fosters an environment of student cooperation." Again and again, students here extol "the administration's ability to create a sense of community within the school" despite the urban location. "Law students at Loyola are genuinely happy and friendly," they tell us. "There is very little competition or animosity." "There is no pettiness." "The atmosphere is productive and encouraging," "even though there is a mandatory grade curve." "People will share notes and have study groups 'til the cows come home."

By all accounts, the quality of life beyond the academic sphere here is high. Loyola's location in Chicago's Gold Coast neighborhood is fabulous. It's "very affluent," which means that "housing around Loyola can be more expensive," but it's very vibrant and very safe. The Magnificent Mile—one of the planet's premier shopping districts—is "just steps away" from campus, which "makes lunchtime errands or emergency business casual clothes purchases for a forgotten networking event very easy." Access to public transit is "ideal" and law offices and federal and state courthouses in the Loop are a reasonable walk away.

"A huge gossip mill" notwithstanding, "Loyola creates a great social scene" and students report that they have "a very good social life." "You would have to try pretty hard to keep from making friends," challenges a 1L. There are over thirty student-run organizations. Rollicking Thursday night bar reviews "create an easy outlet for social interaction and class cohesiveness." If you have the energy and the time, there are "social events every weekend" as well.

Getting In

Admission to the Loyola University Chicago School of Law is competitive. Enrolled students at the 75th percentile have LSAT scores around 161 and GPAs of approximately 3.6. Enrolled students at the 25th percentile have LSAT scores in the higher 150s and GPAs hovering around 3.2.

Combined Degrees Offered
JD/MBA, JD/MSW, JD/MA Political Science, 4 years

Clinical program required	No
Legal writing course requirement	Yes
Legal methods course requirement	No
Legal research course requirement	Yes
Moot court requirement	No
Public interest law requirement	No

ADMISSIONS

Selectivity Rating	86
# applications received	5,538
% applicants accepted	30
% acceptees attending	18
LSAT Range	157–162
Average undergrad GPA	3.03–3.59
Application fee	$50
Regular application	Rolling, up to 3/1
Regular notification	Rolling
Early application program	No
Transfer students accepted	Yes
Evening division offered	Yes
Part-time accepted	Yes
CAS accepted	Yes

International Students
TOEFL required of international students	

FINANCIAL FACTS

Annual tuition	$37,380
Books and supplies	$1,298
Fees	$706
Room and board	$13,200
Financial aid application deadline	3/1
% first-year students receiving some sort of aid	95
% receiving some sort of aid	85
% of aid that is merit based	75
% receiving scholarships	70
Average grant	$12,990
Average loan	$35,700
Average total aid package	$53,000
Average debt	$95,201

EMPLOYMENT INFORMATION

Career Rating	85
Rate of placement (nine months out)	90
Average starting salary	$75,980
State for bar exam	IL
Pass rate for first-time bar	89

Prominent Alumni
Lisa Madigan, Attorney General-IL; Laurel Bellows, President-elect American Bar Association (2012); John Cullerton, Illinois Senate President; Michael Madigan, Speaker of the Illinois House of Rep.; Robert Thomas, Illinois Supreme Court Justice

Grads Employed by Field (%)
Academic (3)
Business/industry (22)
Government (9)
Judicial clerkship (72)
Military (1)
Private practice (51)
Public interest (6)

Loyola University—New Orleans

College of Law

INSTITUTIONAL INFORMATION

Public/private	Private
Affiliation	Roman Catholic
Student/faculty ratio	17:1
% faculty part-time	34
% faculty female	33
% faculty minority	19
Total faculty	79

SURVEY SAYS...

Diverse opinions accepted in classrooms, Students love New Orleans, LA

STUDENTS

Enrollment of law school	847
% male/female	50/50
% from out-of-state	60
% full-time	82
% minority	30
% international	1
# of countries represented	6
Average age of entering class	25

ACADEMICS

Academic Experience Rating	**74**
Profs interesting rating	74
Profs accessible rating	85
Hours of study per day	4.10

Academic Specialties

Environmental, International, Taxation, Public Interest Law

Advanced Degrees Offered

LLM in United States Law for international students, 24 credit hours

Combined Degrees Offered

JD/MBA, JD/Masters of Public Administration, JD/Masters of Urban and Regional Planning. All combined degree programs add an additional year to the JD program.

Academics

Loyola University—New Orleans College of Law is "hands down, the best place to study law" thanks to its "regional reputation, elite professors, great career resources, and guest speakers." Owing to "its location in one of the world's great cultural centers," students here aren't surprised with "the quality and accessibility of the professors," all within an "atmosphere that facilitates learning and making connections." The "top-notch" professors "bring a wealth of practical experience into the classroom" and are "willing to bend over backwards to help students in their career path." It helps that the professors "all have practical experience in their area of law" and "incorporate that [expertise] in the classroom." "It's great to have a professor who helped write the civil code and court opinions teach them to you," says a 3L. Administration can be "very good, very personal, and helpful," and the financial aid department recently acquired new staff, improving the department's efficiency. Those involved in the school's evening program would like to see the administration give them the same "availability of classes and special programs, such as internships or externships," as those in the regular program have. Others appreciate the lack of "long lines" and "red tape." "This law school is completely oriented around the students," says a 1L.

"There are continual opportunities to gain practical legal experience" at Loyola through "constant notices of internships, jobs, volunteer projects, and externships." "Professors share their advice for exam preparation and are very up front with expectations for exams," says a 2L. However, while nearly all students approve of the "moot court and trial advocacy programs," some would like to "have fewer required courses so that students can specialize in a particular area with more ease." Others think that "Loyola needs to do a much better job preparing students to actually practice law." "The odds are severely stacked against a recent graduate arguing anything to an appeals court, as most firms have attorneys with considerably more experience who handle all of the firm's appeals work," explains a 3L. "Therefore, the area in which Loyola could stand to improve the most is offering more trial court advocacy classes and giving those equal, if not greater, focus than moot court."

Opinions on Loyola's career services office range from "fantastic" to "a joke," though which side you'll fall on will likely depend on where you're from. "One area that I think the school could improve on is helping the common law students obtain jobs out of state," says a 3L. "Our career services is terrible if you're not from Louisiana," adds a 2L. That said, most students are happy to stay in New Orleans after graduating. "Loyola's great for people who want to practice in New Orleans," says a 2L. "It offers lots of connections and alumni in the area who like to give back to their own."

"Some of the classrooms, namely the newer ones, are top-notch," says a 1L. Others "are overcrowded and students are relegated to using stand-alone desks along the edges of the classrooms with inadequate surfaces for writing or computer usage." "The facilities could use a drastic update," says a 2L. While the library is "giant" with "many helpful resources," it's in "need of a twenty-first (or even twentieth) century makeover." Students also wouldn't mind having a place where they can "study late at night, segregated from the undergrads," along with "more food options for the law campus."

K. MICHELE ALLISON-DAVIS, DEAN OF ADMISSIONS
7214 SAINT CHARLES AVENUE, BOX 904, NEW ORLEANS, LA 70118
TEL: 504-861-5575 FAX: 504-861-5772
E-MAIL: LADMIT@LOYNO.EDU • WEBSITE: LAW.LOYNO.EDU

Life

Students at Loyola "are generally helpful to each other" and "very friendly regardless of whether they are from the New Orleans area or not." "There is some competitiveness amongst the student body, but I would hesitate to say cutthroat," says a 2L. "Every student seems to view your own personal success as their own," adds a 1L. Though there's a lot of talk about "the rift between Civil and Common Law students," most agree, "It is best explained by the fact that students take largely different courses and study very different material over three years." That said, most admit that they "have never seen an argument or any social outcasting based on a student's choice of study." There's a fair amount of diversity in the student population. "I have never had a group of friends as diverse as what I have found here," says a 2L. "There is not another school that I am aware of that could foster such camaraderie among so diverse a population."

When it comes to social life at Loyola, all students have to do is step outside. Located in "Uptown New Orleans," students can readily hop a streetcar that "provides access to the French Quarter and Central Business District." "New Orleans has the best nightlife in the South," says a 3L. "The city environment is perfect for young professionals." "I would say that most students spend a majority of their social time in Uptown or in the Garden District rather than in the belligerent, tourist-packed French Quarter," says a 2L. "The nightlife in Uptown and the Garden District is much more tailored to the academic crowd." According to a 1L, "This year's 1L class hangs out together in a wide variety of ways, [whether it's] going to the Jay-Z concert as a big group or holding our own Mardi Gras party with the whole class invited to come, grab a drink, and watch the parades." Fundamentally, argues a 2L, "The music, food, and social justice opportunities should encourage anyone to come to law school at Loyola."

Getting In

Recently admitted students at Loyola Law have average undergraduate GPAs of 3.34 and LSAT scores of 154. The admissions office operates a unique Early Admit program that allows those who have completed three-fourths of their undergraduate degree requirements to be admitted. Those who take advantage of this option will be expected to have higher entering credentials than those who will be entering law school with an undergraduate degree.

Clinical program required	No
Legal writing course requirement	Yes
Legal methods course requirement	Yes
Legal research course requirement	Yes
Moot court requirement	Yes
Public interest law requirement	Yes

ADMISSIONS

Selectivity Rating	73
# applications received	1,913
% applicants accepted	45
% acceptees attending	29
Average LSAT	154
LSAT Range	150–157
Average undergrad GPA	3.34
Application fee	$40
Regular application	Rolling, up to 7/15
Regular notification	Rolling
Early application program	No
Transfer students accepted	Yes
Evening division offered	Yes
Part-time accepted	Yes
CAS accepted	Yes

International Students

TOEFL recommended of international students

FINANCIAL FACTS

Annual tuition	$35,160
Books and supplies	$1,500
Fees	$1,036
Room and board	$20,400
% first-year students receiving some sort of aid	70
% receiving some sort of aid	68
% of aid that is merit based	32
% receiving scholarships	46
Average grant	$13,262
Average loan	$37,290
Average total aid package	$50,552
Average debt	$45,350

EMPLOYMENT INFORMATION

Career Rating	74
Rate of placement (nine months out)	91
State for bar exam	LA, TX, FL, GA, MS
Pass rate for first-time bar	73

Employers Who Frequently Hire Grads

Private firms, the judiciary, and government agencies

Prominent Alumni

Pascal Calogero, Chief Justice, Louisiana Supreme Court; Mitch Landrieu, Mayor of New Orleans; Carl Stewart, U.S. Court of Appeals, 5th Circuit; Theodore M. Frois, General Counsel, Exxon Mobil; International; Robert L. Wilkie, Special Assistant to the President, NSA

Grads Employed by Field (%)

Academic (1)
Business/industry (13)
Government (16)
Judicial clerkship (14)
Private practice (54)
Public interest (2)

MARQUETTE UNIVERSITY
LAW SCHOOL

INSTITUTIONAL INFORMATION

Public/private	Private
Affiliation	Roman Catholic
Student/faculty ratio	17:1
% faculty part-time	28
% faculty female	49
% faculty minority	12
Total faculty	42

SURVEY SAYS...

Diverse opinions accepted in classrooms, Great library staff, Abundant externship/internship/ clerkship opportunities

STUDENTS

Enrollment of law school	758
% male/female	57/43
% from out-of-state	40
% full-time	77
% minority	15
% international	1
# of countries represented	7
Average age of entering class	25

ACADEMICS

Academic Experience Rating	**81**
Profs interesting rating	82
Profs accessible rating	86
Hours of study per day	4.60

Academic Specialties

Civil Procedure, Commercial, Constitutional, Corporation Securities, Criminal, Environmental, International, Labor, Legal History, Property, Taxation, Intellectual Property, Sports Law, Dispute Resolution

Combined Degrees Offered

JD/MBA, JD/MBA Sports Business, JD/MA Political Science, JD/MA International Relations, JD/MA Philosophy, JD/MA in History of Philosophy, JD/MA Bioethics, 4 years; JD/Certificate in Dispute Resolution, 3 years

Academics

The Law School at Wisconsin's Marquette University is filled with "students who are interested in each other's success" and "who [make] every day worth going." The school places "a huge emphasis" on the fact that students will be future colleagues and encourages them to begin showing that respect during their schooling. This trickles not only down but up, with "the staff, faculty, and students [having] formed...a cohesive unit." The school's administration is incredibly helpful (and, "oddly enough, entertaining"), and "Even if you're not talking to the right person, they'll get you there."

The school opened a brand-new law building in 2010 that students expect will propel them into the next stratosphere of legal education awesomeness. As a 1L, all of your courses are picked for you (which can be "a scheduling nightmare" but means "there is no trouble getting into required courses"), but beyond the first year, the school "offers courses in a wide variety of specializations," and class sizes are smaller. "Dean Kearney wants to make sure we learn the law, not the latest in pop sociology," says a student.

The legal writing program is "a real superstar in this school. In clerkship after clerkship, the research and writing skills I gained in class have been complimented," says a student. Sports Law is also a program of note at Marquette. The professors are "very knowledgeable, thought-provoking, and engaging," and, to top that off, "unforgettably intelligent and witty." Most come to the school from strong legal careers and top universities, yet "allow students room to debate legal issues in a cordial, professional manner." "It is amazing how a two-second question might turn into an hour discussion outside of class," says a 2L.

The school's "flexible evening program" is "very accommodating to part-time students," offering many night classes that accommodate "full-time work schedules and family lives." The combination of the school's career services center and the location in Milwaukee provides "many opportunities to obtain practical experience through internships and clinic work in the legal community," so that students can get practical experience from day one. As if all of this isn't enough, Marquette keeps making life better even after graduation—the school is also one of two in Wisconsin that offers a state bar exam exemption, meaning students who have graduated from the law school can start practicing law in the state without taking the nationwide test. "My overall experience has blown away the expectations I had when I decided to come here," says a student.

Life

Milwaukee "is all about having fun," which contributes to the communal sense of spirit here, and though the surrounding neighborhoods "are not great," the "campus is good." The school "is not very diverse in faculty or student body," and due to the large part-time program, there is "a broad age range among students" and many people who commute with families, so there's a bit of a divide between these students and the younger ones. Still, everyone is open to meeting new people at Marquette, though "students can be a little clique-y." There are scheduled social events throughout the year, such as the student-faculty basketball game, "Malpractice Ball, Brewers games, Bucks games, and various NCAA Division I sports [games]," and students can play intramural sports or go to the rec center in their free time. Thursday night is Bar Review, "where most students go out to the same bar and blow off steam" and "relax and get ready to study for the weekend."

SEAN REILLY, ASSISTANT DEAN FOR ADMISSIONS
ECKSTEIN HALL, ROOM 132, P.O. BOX 1881, MILWAUKEE, WI 53201-1881
TEL: 414-288-6767 FAX: 414-288-0676
E-MAIL: LAW.ADMISSION@MARQUETTE.EDU • WEBSITE: LAW.MARQUETTE.EDU

Marquette Law students certainly aren't held back by any sort of cutthroat competitive streak. "I feel like I'm in the third round of 'American Idol.' Everyone is watching their own back, and everyone else's," says a student. "I broke my leg and had to miss two days. I had four sets of notes for each class in my e-mail inbox without soliciting them from anybody," says a 2L. The relatively small community can also lead to "a high school-like feeling—everyone knows everyone else, who they are, and likely some detail of their life. Depending on what a person wants, that could be a good or bad thing."

Getting In

The law school employs a modified rolling admissions process, with the admissions committee typically beginning its evaluations in December. As is the case in all rolling admissions systems, there are more spaces available sooner rather than later—especially if you think you may be a borderline candidate quantitatively. An undergraduate GPA of B+ and an LSAT score in the high 150s would make you solidly competitive for admission at Marquette.

Clinical program required	No
Legal writing course requirement	Yes
Legal methods course requirement	No
Legal research course requirement	Yes
Moot court requirement	No
Public interest law requirement	No

ADMISSIONS

Selectivity Rating	79
# applications received	2,282
% applicants accepted	42
% acceptees attending	26
Average LSAT	157
LSAT Range	154–159
Average undergrad GPA	3.46
Application fee	$50
Regular application	Rolling, up to 4/1
Regular notification	Rolling
Early application program	No
Transfer students accepted	Yes
Evening division offered	Yes
Part-time accepted	Yes
CAS accepted	Yes

International Students
TOEFL required of international students

FINANCIAL FACTS

Annual tuition	$37,570
Books and supplies	$1,200
Room and board	$12,950
Financial aid application deadline	3/1
Average grant	$8,000
Average debt	$110,147

EMPLOYMENT INFORMATION

Career Rating	87
Rate of placement (nine months out)	89
Average starting salary	$62,703
State for bar exam	CA, IL, MN, NY, WI
Pass rate for first-time bar	98

Employers Who Frequently Hire Grads
Quarles & Brady; Godfrey & Kahn; Foley & Lardner; Whyte Hirschboeck Dudek; von Briesen & Roper; Reinhart Boerner Van Dueren; Milwaukee County District Attorney's Office; Meissner, Tierney, Fisher & Nichols; Wisconsin State Public Defender; Michael Best & Friedrich

Prominent Alumni
Hon. Diane Sykes, U.S. Court of Appeals Judge; Hon. Terence Evans, U.S. Court of Appeals Judge; Hon. John Coffey, U.S. Court of Appeals Judge; Hon. Janine Geske, Former WI Supreme Court Justice

Grads Employed by Field (%)
Academic (1)
Business/industry (20)
Government (11)
Judicial clerkship (3)
Military (1)
Private practice (59)
Public interest (5)

MERCER UNIVERSITY
WALTER F. GEORGE SCHOOL OF LAW

INSTITUTIONAL INFORMATION

Public/private	Private
Affiliation	Baptist
Student/faculty ratio	13:1
% faculty part-time	34
% faculty female	34
% faculty minority	9
Total faculty	79

SURVEY SAYS...

Great research resources, Great library staff, Beautiful campus

STUDENTS

Enrollment of law school	440
% male/female	56/44
% from out-of-state	27
% full-time	100
% minority	22
% international	1
# of countries represented	4
Average age of entering class	25

ACADEMICS

Academic Experience Rating	**90**
Profs interesting rating	91
Profs accessible rating	97
Hours of study per day	4.72

Academic Specialties

Civil Procedure, Commercial, Constitutional, Corporation Securities, Criminal, Environmental, International, Labor, Legal History, Property, Taxation, Intellectual Property, Legal Research and Writing Certificate Program, Law and Public Service Program, Trial Advocacy, Ethics and Professionalism Program

Advanced Degrees Offered

JD, 3 years

Combined Degrees Offered

JD/MBA, 3–4 years

Clinical program required	No
Legal writing course requirement	Yes
Legal methods course requirement	Yes

Academics

Mercer University School of Law strikes the "perfect balance" between a "familial atmosphere" and one of "healthy competition" thanks to its "smaller size," which "allows for close relationships with other students and productive interaction with professors," and its "emphasis on practical training in the law." "I feel like I'm getting an Ivy League education, but without the higher price tag and without having to move to New England," explains a 1L. "The class sizes are very small compared to other law schools, which encourages thoughtful discussion in class, [and] the professors abide by an open-door policy and are always willing to provide extra help." Most students here agree that the "outstanding" faculty is "interesting," "engaging," and "very welcoming." "The professors that I have had thus far have all been brilliant academics, which can be intimidating at times—especially in the beginning—yet they have the ability to stimulate student thought through engaging discussion and have successfully trained me to 'think like a lawyer,'" says a 2L. The "helpful and friendly" administration gets similarly high marks for being "extremely accessible." "Many of the administrators are helpful, kind, and welcoming of suggestions and questions from the student body," says a 2L.

Students at Mercer Law consider the "outstanding" and "second-to-none" legal writing program—in particular, the Writing Certificate Program—to be one of the school's "greatest strengths." According to a 2L, "As I have seen from moot court competition, higher-ranked schools don't produce better writers than Mercer." A 3L adds, "The substantial emphasis that Mercer Law places on developing superior legal writing skills is an asset that will distinguish all graduates throughout their legal careers." However, students would like to see "more entertainment and [intellectual property] law classes" as well as a more relaxed curriculum. "I haven't dealt with a curriculum this restrictive since I was in high school," explains a 2L. "Not only are there specific courses that you have to take all the way through the first semester of your 3L year, there are certain blocks of courses from which you are required to choose 'electives'...in order to graduate. If one of the block courses interferes with an elective you actually want to take then you are out of luck because most of the elective courses are only offered once a year since the student body is so small."

When it comes to the Career Services Office, student opinion is divided between "terrible" and "wonderful." "Even in a recession, they have managed to produce a large number of opportunities for on-campus interviews, and for other job opportunities as well," says a 3L. However, another 3L would like to see Career Services "reach out to 3Ls who are struggling to find jobs in this terrible economy." "I am in the top five percent of my class and have only managed to land three interviews since last fall. Though the school cannot change the fact that the economy has hurt the legal market, the school could do a better job to assist 3Ls and those who graduated last year."

Though the "facilities probably won't win any beauty contests" due to "sterile" classrooms that could be "mistaken for conference rooms at a Holiday Inn," the "great" law school building itself draws plenty of praise for its "Southern charm." Students also appreciate the "well maintained" library and "renovations" that have provided a "comfortable work environment."

MARILYN E. SUTTON, ASST. DEAN OF ADMISSIONS AND FINANCIAL AID
1021 GEORGIA AVENUE, MACON, GA 31207
TEL: 478-301-2605 FAX: 478-301-2989
E-MAIL: MARTIN_SV@MERCER.EDU • WEBSITE: WWW.LAW.MERCER.EDU

Life

With a "class size of about 150 students," "everybody knows everybody" at Mercer Law. Despite "healthy competition," students are "very friendly and accepting," meaning that Mercer "does not suffer from the same cutthroat, book-stealing plague that runs rampant at the top-tier schools." "It is amazing how open and cooperative the student body here is," says a 1L. "I have yet to encounter any real drama or horror story concerning the cutthroat environment that I had heard about prior to entering law school." Due to Mercer's location in "the heart of the South," students note that "conservative students" will feel "right at home." "It's not unusual for a class discussion with a left-leaning political note to be interrupted by the harrumphs and disapproving commentary from much of the rest of the class," says a 2L. "It's almost enough to make one not want to participate."

Students insist that they're "very social outside of school," but as "it is law school," opportunities to kick back can be slim. Luckily, student clubs and associations "consistently host fun social events, such as charity auctions, dances, and other parties." When it comes to Mercer's location in Macon, students are a little less sunny. "The only problem with Mercer is that it is in Macon, and downtown Macon, though on the verge of improving, is pretty depressed," says a 1L. Macon's lack of excitement can be "a blessing" since it means there are "few, if any, distractions" from academics. However, many students admit that while Macon "isn't exactly the cultural capital of the world," it's "accessible" and "only an hour from Atlanta" if the need for more happening locales arises.

Getting In

Recently admitted students at Mercer Law at the 25th percentile have LSAT scores of 153 and GPAs in the 3.13 range. Admitted students at the 75th percentile have LSAT scores of 158 and GPAs of roughly 3.67.

Legal research course requirement	Yes
Moot court requirement	No
Public interest law requirement	No

ADMISSIONS

Selectivity Rating	**80**
# applications received	1,915
% applicants accepted	32
% acceptees attending	27
LSAT Range	153–158
Application fee	$50
Regular application	Rolling, up to 3/15
Regular notification	Rolling
Early application program	No
Transfer students accepted	Yes
Evening division offered	No
Part-time accepted	No
CAS accepted	Yes

International Students

TOEFL recommended of international students

FINANCIAL FACTS

Annual tuition	$35,495
Books and supplies	$1,380
Fees	$200
Room and board	$14,620
Financial aid application deadline	4/1
% first-year students receiving some sort of aid	93
% receiving some sort of aid	92
% of aid that is merit based	18
% receiving scholarships	32
Average grant	$24,159
Average loan	$39,555
Average total aid package	$45,643
Average debt	$105,585

EMPLOYMENT INFORMATION

Career Rating	**74**
Rate of placement (nine months out)	85
Average starting salary	$58,863
State for bar exam	GA, FL, NC, SC, TN
Pass rate for first-time bar	93

Employers Who Frequently Hire Grads
Atlanta firms King & Spalding; Alston & Bird; Holland & Knight; Troutman Sanders; McKenna, Long, & Aldridge; Bryan Cave; Swift Currie; Moore, Ingram, Johnson, & Steele; Martin Snow, LLP, Macon, GA; James, Bates, Pope, & Spivey, Macon, GA

Prominent Alumni
Griffin Bell, Former Attorney General; Cathy Cox, Former Secretary of State, GA, President of Young Harris College; John Oxendine, Insurance Commissioner, GA; Hugh Thompson, GA Supreme Court; M. Yvette Miller, Chief Judge, Georgia Court of Appeals

Grads Employed by Field (%)
Business/industry (6)
Government (11)
Judicial clerkship (13)
Military (2)
Private practice (61)
Public interest (7)

MICHIGAN STATE UNIVERSITY
COLLEGE OF LAW

Academics

The College of Law at Michigan State University is an East Lansing "hidden gem" that has seen a surge in reputation in recent years. "It feels wonderful to have a part in pushing this school to achieve new things," says a proud student. This success is in no small part due to the ambition of MSU Law's students, coupled with the resources, clinics, and guidance provided by the school. "The tools, facilities, and personnel are there and allow you to fine-tune your legal education into what you want it to be, whether that is an education heavy in academics or practical skills," says a student.

One refreshing thing about the school is the non-cutthroat atmosphere that is contrary to that often found at other institutions, as "there are enough resources to go around for everyone." Though a large state school does mean that students are competitive, it's "not at the expense of being collaborative," and "1L sections have a real family feel to them." The school offers ten focus areas and three certificate programs (including the Geoffrey Fieger Trial Practice Institute program), and it recently approved a new 1L curriculum that took effect in fall 2011.

The College of Law has a well-rounded faculty that engages students with respect, offering them "practical and relevant experience." Professors are "incredibly accessible" and "are solid in their teaching pedagogy," drawing from their prior work/legal research experiences to enhance the students' educational experiences. "They are not only very knowledgeable and experts in their field, but they are also very human," says a 1L. The administration, particularly the new dean, is just as receptive—"Pizza with the dean" is held at least once a month—and most "go above and beyond helping students with issues that arise, from personal problems to academic problems." "They emphasize outside activity, but provide a setting and classes for additional help on the education front."

Facilities are "modern and easy to access." Professors are able to record classes with the push of a button, and the entire first floor of the library is reserved for law student use. Clinical opportunities, journals, and a "plethora of organizations" abound, and the school's reputation among employers is on the rise, as "many firms and lawyers realize this fact and are continually impressed by the product MSU Law produces." Still, many students (particularly those not in the first tier) wish that Career Services brought more employers to campus.

Life

East Lansing is truly a college town, and weekend football games attract hundreds of law students during the regular season. (However, the "availability of parking is brutal.") Luckily, the law school itself "really does offer a great social life, if you have the time to enjoy it." There's an "impressive" amount of inclusiveness in every activity," and "You feel welcomed from day one and get a sense that 'we're all in it together.'" "I feel at home even though I'm so far away from home," says a student from Africa.

There's much diversity in the faculty and student body, and a program or student organization exists "for almost anything you could be interested in, and if it does not exist, the school gives you the tools to create it." While there's a distinct lack of knives between shoulder blades, "There are always gunners, but they are relatively few, and students quickly identify them and learn to keep their distance."

CHARLES ROBOSKI, ASSISTANT DEAN, ADMISSIONS AND FINANCIAL AID
230 LAW COLLEGE BUILDING, EAST LANSING, MI 48824-1300
TEL: (517) 432-0222 FAX: (517) 432-0098
E-MAIL: ADMISS@LAW.MSU.EDU • WEBSITE: WWW.LAW.MSU.EDU

Getting In

The acceptance rate here has varied in recent years, and in the past couple of years, around a third of students have been accepted. Admitted students for the incoming class in fall 2010 at the 25th percentile had an LSAT score of 152 and GPAs in the 3.24 range. Admitted students at the 75th percentile had a LSAT scores around 159 and an approximate GPA of 3.73.

Legal research course requirement	Yes
Moot court requirement	No
Public interest law requirement	No

ADMISSIONS

Selectivity Rating	76
# applications received	2,736
% applicants accepted	46
% acceptees attending	23
Average LSAT	155
LSAT Range	153–159
Average undergrad GPA	3.36
Application fee	$60
Regular application	Rolling, up to 4/30
Regular notification	Rolling
Early application program	No
Transfer students accepted	Yes
Evening division offered	No
Part-time accepted	Yes
CAS accepted	Yes

International Students

TOEFL required of international students	

FINANCIAL FACTS

Annual tuition	$32, 828
Books and supplies	$1,368
Fees	$226
Room and board	$10,886
Financial aid application deadline	4/1
% first-year students receiving some sort of aid	85
% receiving some sort of aid	85
% of aid that is merit based	80
% receiving scholarships	34
Average grant	$20,540
Average loan	$22,590
Average total aid package	$39,811
Average debt	$73,201

EMPLOYMENT INFORMATION

Career Rating	86
Rate of placement (nine months out)	98
Average starting salary	$64,500
State for bar exam	MI, IL, OH, CA, NY
Pass rate for first-time bar	90

Employers Who Frequently Hire Grads
Dykema Gossett Jaffe Raitt Heuer & Weiss Clark Hill Michigan Court of Appeals Honigman Miller Schwartz & Cohn Miller Canfield Paddock & Stone Warner Norcross & Judd Varnum Riddering Schmidt & Howlett Bodman, LLP Foster Swift Collins & Smith City of Chicago Law Department Plunkett & Cooney

Prominent Alumni
Dennis Archer, Leadership; Geoffrey Fieger, Trial Lawyer; Marrianne Battani, U.S. District; Clif Haley, Corporate Law; Bernard Friedman, U.S. District

Grads Employed by Field (%)
Academic (15)
Business/industry (25)
Government (8)
Judicial clerkship (4)
Military (1)
Private practice (41)
Public interest (3)

MISSISSIPPI COLLEGE
SCHOOL OF LAW

Academics

According to students, Mississippi College School of Law is "the best-kept secret in the South" and "an excellent place to start a legal career." Tuition is reasonable as far as private schools go, and you'll pay the same rate you paid as a 1L for the next two years. Also, the school is "generous with scholarships for both entering students and students who excel during the first year." The legal writing and research program is "second to none." MC Law also boasts "one of the very best moot court programs in the United States." Trial teams habitually bag awards in regional and national competitions. There are study abroad programs in South Korea and Mexico. There are law centers that specialize in international and comparative law, children's law, public service, and bioethics and health law. If you want to be an attorney in Louisiana, the four-course program leading to a civil law certificate is another perk. The big curricular criticism is that MC Law needs to "add a wider range of class subjects" and "more courses for specialization."

In MC Law's "wonderful, newly renovated array of classrooms," you'll definitely find an "emphasis on practical lawyering." "Some law schools teach you the law," expounds a 3L. "Mississippi College School of Law teaches you how to be a lawyer." The full-time faculty is full of "very experienced and knowledgeable individuals" who "demand excellence from the very first day." At the same time, professors are "approachable," "helpful," and "always available to students." They "begin [by] intimidating and end by accommodating each and every student the best way they know how." This faculty "remembers who you are and takes an active interest in your life and especially your future." MC Law is also home to a "plethora" of adjunct faculty members who teach in-depth, upper-level courses. They are reportedly "some of the best practitioners and judges in the state." Except for the financial aid staff, which "has no clue," students also have nothing but plaudits for the "very accessible" administration. Management is "a well-oiled machine" that is "dedicated to helping the students at every step of the way." "When the dean of the school gives you a high five on your way to class," explains a 2L, "you can't help but feel at ease."

MC Law is "not well-known outside of the South." However, most students seem pretty happy with their career prospects. Because of the school's location in the middle of Mississippi's capital city, "prestigious law firms" and the capitol building are an easy jaunt from the school. Networking is "ample" and it's easy to "to gain real-life legal experience." "Spectacular opportunities for interaction with Mississippi's bench, bar, and state government" are abundant. Also, an "awesome externship program" "allows any 2L or 3L" to work for a range of nonprofits and government entities. Upon graduation, about seventy-five percent of graduates go into either private practice or work for corporations.

ASSISTANT DEAN PATRICIA H. EVANS, DEAN OF ADMISSIONS
151 EAST GRIFFITH STREET, JACKSON, MS 39201
TEL: 601-925-7152 FAX: 601-925-7166
E-MAIL: HWEAVER@MC.EDU • WEBSITE: WWW.LAW.MC.EDU

Life

MC Law has "somewhat of a homogenous environment" in terms of ethnicity. There's "a great mix of traditional straight-from-college students as well as students who worked prior to law school," though. "There are tons of students from out of state," too. While most students hail from the South, nearly thirty states are represented. "Student camaraderie is a dream." "Outlines are passed. Study groups are plentiful." "I would characterize [MC Law's] student environment as tightly knit," adds a wistful 3L. "I think that in any academic setting there will be factions and competition on some level. However, my experience was that most students were cordial, helpful, and conducted themselves as if they were part of one really big team moving toward one common goal—graduation."

Socially, "The gossip runs rampant" on campus, but there is "a strong sense of community." "Most students, at least in the same class, either know or know of all other students." "The law school often has barbecues in the parking lot where the entire student body, faculty, and administration eat together," relates a 2L, "even the janitors and security staff." MC Law is "full of clubs and organizations," and there are "lots of opportunities to get involved." The Student Bar Association plans "many parties and social events" each year as well. The larger university is Baptist-affiliated, though, so don't expect anything too hardcore. Jackson has "a Southern charm that is not found in most cities," and "The cost of living is extremely low." Some students tell us, "There is a lot to do" here. Others say that Jackson is has "limited options." "A social scene is not the city's highlight," advises a 3L. "Jackson isn't New Orleans, but New Orleans is only two hours away" (if you drive really fast).

Getting In

Admission to Mississippi College School of Law is attainable, if you have the right numbers. Entering students at the 25th percentile have LSAT scores in the high 140s and GPAs a little below 3.0. At the 75th percentile, LSAT scores are around 153 and GPAs are around 3.5

ADMISSIONS	
Selectivity Rating	66
# applications received	1,354
% applicants accepted	54
% acceptees attending	15
Average LSAT	150
LSAT Range	147–154
Average undergrad GPA	3.24
Application fee	$0
Regular application	Rolling, up to 6/1
Regular notification	Rolling
Early application program	No
Transfer students accepted	Yes
Evening division offered	No
Part-time accepted	Yes
CAS accepted	Yes

International Students

TOEFL required of international students	

FINANCIAL FACTS	
Annual tuition	$26,700
Books and supplies	$1,200
Fees	$1,370
Room and board	$12,375
Financial aid application deadline	7/1
% first-year students receiving some sort of aid	85
% receiving some sort of aid	83
% of aid that is merit based	100
% receiving scholarships	32
Average grant	$15,000
Average loan	$33,000
Average total aid package	$35,000
Average debt	$89,000

EMPLOYMENT INFORMATION

		Grads Employed by Field (%)
Career Rating	80	Academic (4)
Rate of placement (nine months out)	93	Business/industry (8)
Average starting salary	$54,542	Government (12)
State for bar exam	MS, AL	Judicial clerkship (11)
Pass rate for first-time bar	80	Military (4)

Employers Who Frequently Hire Grads
Private practice (60)
Public interest (1)

International Law Firms; Multi-state Law Firms; Mississippi Law Firms; State Government; Federal Government; Business; U.S. Military

Prominent Alumni
Sharion Aycock, Federal District Judge; Mike Parker, Federal Magistrate Judge; Linda Anderson, Federal Magistrate Judge; J.P. Compretta, Speaker Pro Tem, MS House of Representatives; Robert Walker, Federal Magistrate Judge

NEW ENGLAND LAW | BOSTON

INSTITUTIONAL INFORMATION

Public/private	Private
Student/faculty ratio	21:1
% faculty part-time	54
% faculty female	27
% faculty minority	14
Total faculty	83

SURVEY SAYS...
Diverse opinions accepted in classrooms, Great library staff, Students love Boston, MA

STUDENTS

Enrollment of law school	1,115
% male/female	44/56
% from out-of-state	63
% full-time	70
% minority	10
% international	2
# of countries represented	8
Average age of entering class	24

ACADEMICS

Academic Experience Rating	78
Profs interesting rating	84
Profs accessible rating	83
Hours of study per day	4.98

Academic Specialties
Criminal, Government Services, Human Rights, International, Taxation, Intellectual Property, Business Law, Public Interest

Advanced Degrees Offered
JD, 3–4 years; LLM, 1 year

Clinical program required	Yes
Legal writing course requirement	Yes
Legal methods course requirement	Yes
Legal research course requirement	Yes
Moot court requirement	Yes
Public interest law requirement	No

Academics

New England Law | Boston is "relatively small" (though classes can sometimes be large), and it's a "stand-alone school," unaffiliated with a larger university. "New England Law is not a flashy school by any means," explains a 2L, "but the education you receive will put you in a position to be successful." Schedules are "incredibly flexible, allowing evening students and part-time students to attend law school while working full-time and having families." "High-level theory" is certainly on offer here, but the approach tends to be more geared toward real life. "Opportunities for practical experience" are plentiful. A great assortment of practicum courses and seminars allows students "to apply their knowledge and really learn how to be a lawyer." A profusion of clinical options varies from pretty mundane to fascinating. An array of study abroad programs and externships involving various international criminal tribunals is another great perk.

Students have nothing but plaudits for New England Law's "passionate" and "extremely knowledgeable" professors. These "amazing human beings" are "absolutely brilliant, but scary as hell" in a good way. Most of them "have deep practical experience" "rather than being pure academics," and they combine "subject-matter mastery with an approach to teaching that is focused on both deep understanding and practical application." Outside the classroom, they're "extremely accessible and helpful." In a nutshell, the faculty is "the reason for going to this school." Like at most law schools, the staff receives more mixed reviews. According to some students, the administration is "very dedicated" and "approachable." "Communication within the school is seamless," one student tells us, and staffers "do a wonderful job." Other students assert that the different management fiefdoms are "unaware of what each is doing." Also, they say, "Registration is a mess."

New England Law's campus consists of four buildings. None of them is "much to write home about." In the main building, things are definitely "a little cramped." "Hundreds of students trying to move in opposite directions down a single hallway" poses annoying logistical difficulties on a daily basis. "The library isn't nearly big enough" either. "There are times when the library and student lounge are completely overcrowded." On the plus side, technology is "really quite good," and "The law librarians are absolute wizards at researching complicated areas of the law."

Nobody is particularly in love with Career Services. As a part of the program, there is a 1L career counseling requirement, a weekly career newsletter, and complementary membership to the Boston Bar Association for graduating students, yet some feel that New England Law "does not provide opportunities similar to other schools." "There is no grade inflation" either, and the tough grading creates problems because students face pretty tough local competition for law jobs. Nevertheless, students say that New England Law enjoys "an excellent reputation around Boston and Massachusetts." An "alumni network that is fiercely loyal" is an additional plus. Also, the location "in the middle of downtown Boston" provides easy access to "all of the downtown firms and government agencies," thus allowing numerous opportunities to gain real-world practice before graduation. "There are a lot of other, more prestigious, law schools in Boston," relates a 2L," but I am never embarrassed to say I am at New England. In fact, I'm always eager to tell people how great I think the school is."

MICHELLE L'ETOILE, DIRECTOR OF ADMISSIONS
154 STUART STREET, BOSTON, MA 02116
TEL: 617-422-7210 FAX: 617-422-7201
E-MAIL: ADMIT@NESL.EDU • WEBSITE: WWW.NESL.EDU

ADMISSIONS

Selectivity Rating	67
# applications received	2,734
% applicants accepted	61
% acceptees attending	23
LSAT Range	151–154
Application fee	$65
Regular application	Rolling, up to 3/15
Regular notification	Rolling
Early application program	No
Transfer students accepted	Yes
Evening division offered	Yes
Part-time accepted	Yes
CAS accepted	Yes

International Students

TOEFL required of
international students

FINANCIAL FACTS

Annual tuition	$39,910
Books and supplies	$1,250
Fees	$80
Room and board	$17,880
Financial aid application deadline	4/7
% first-year students receiving some sort of aid	93
% receiving some sort of aid	92
% of aid that is merit based	89
% receiving scholarships	58
Average grant	$12,901
Average loan	$40,632
Average total aid package	$46,186
Average debt	$108,326

Life

Students here have a "scrappy, going-it-together attitude" and "a strong work ethic." "Frankly, I look forward to entering the legal community and knocking the socks off students from other Boston law schools," announces a 2L, "especially those from stuffy institutions across the river." New England locals comprise the largest segment of the student body, though the school draws students from across the country. Diversity in terms of ethnicity and age is respectable. Politic opinions run the gamut. "Massachusetts tends to be a liberal region, especially Boston," and New England Law reflects that reality. However, "There is a fairly large conservative base at school as well." The academic atmosphere is reportedly "very warm and welcoming." "While there is just enough competition to ensure you excel, there is enough friendly camaraderie to ensure you enjoy your time as well," says a 2L. "The students here support each other and care about the collective success of all classmates."

The social situation is fairly intimate. "After a little while, you recognize everyone in the building and it's a nice familial feeling," reflects a 3L. There's "a rumor about everything." Numerous student organizations "constantly hold fun and interesting events." "Law prom, softball tournaments," and assorted gatherings are commonplace. The food court across the street is loaded with students studying and socializing. The city of Boston also provides plenty of energy and excitement.

Getting In

Admission to New England Law is no great challenge. Entering students at the 25th percentile have LSAT scores of 151 or lower and undergraduate GPAs of 3.02 or lower. At the 75th percentile, LSAT scores are 154 or higher and GPAs are 3.49 or higher.

EMPLOYMENT INFORMATION

Career Rating	80
Rate of placement (nine months out)	84
Average starting salary	$56,917
State for bar exam	MA
Pass rate for first-time bar	94

Employers Who Frequently Hire Grads

A partial list of employers who have hired New England School of Law Graduates can be found on our website http://www.nesl.edu/students/employers_the_facts.cfm.

Prominent Alumni

Leonard P. Zakim, NE Anti-Defamation League, namesake, Boston bridge; The Honorable Susan J. Crawford, Chief Justice, U.S. Court of Appeals for Armed Forces; The Honorable John R. Simpson, Frmr Head of the U.S. Secret Service; The Honorable Karyn F. Scheier, Chief Justice of the MA Land Court; Wendy J. Murphy, Victim Advocacy & Research Group; National TV Commentator

Grads Employed by Field (%)

Academic (3)
Business/industry (29)
Government (10)
Judicial clerkship (2)
Military (2)
Private practice (49)
Public interest (4)

NEW YORK LAW SCHOOL

Academics

Private, "obscenely underrated" New York Law School in lower Manhattan is a hothouse for hands-on preparation that "focuses on training successful lawyers" who are "ready to make an impact on the legal profession" the day they pass the bar exam. The emphasis here is on practical courses, and there are "many opportunities to take part in real lawyering while you are still in law school." "The clinics are exceptional and a great experience." Externships and courses that simulate real legal work abound. With a host of academic centers and more than 250 elective classes available in a ton of different specialized areas of law, it's very easy to tailor pretty much any program you want. Students tell us, "NYLS has the best location in New York City" as well. "Geographic proximity" to courts, government agencies, banks, securities exchanges, and law firms provides hundreds of opportunities to gain experience as a law student.

The NYLS faculty is "very accomplished" and "well-versed." In terms of teaching, there are "a few mediocre professors," but "Most bring a passion about the subject they teach, making class time fly by." "In almost every class, I have been instructed by either a nationally known expert or someone with fantastic real-world legal experience," beams a 2L. "Hardly any of the professors are purely academics." Some students are critical of the administration, calling it "unavailable and hostile to criticism." However, most students are happy with the top brass. Management is "present and very accessible to students," they say, and "very responsive to students' needs." Probably the biggest grievance among students here is the fact that classes are "seriously overcrowded." "There are too many students," protests a 3L. The "awful" writing program also comes in for some derision. Unhappy students call it "arbitrary and too narrowly focused."

Opinions concerning employment prospects are mixed. Some of the future lawyers here say that "career opportunities for students outside the top tier seem to be few and far between." "Getting into prestigious law firms is extremely difficult, and recruitment at NY Law is terrible." Other students have much more positive reviews. "If you're at the top of your class," they say, "it's not difficult to get a big firm job here in NYC." Students also point to the "huge network of practicing alumni" currently practicing around the Big Apple in government, public interest, and firms of all sizes.

Many of the facilities on this tiny campus here are excellent. The gleaming, new building is "an impressive space" that is "aesthetically pleasing" and, by all accounts, "very high tech" and otherwise "state-of-the-art." It's chock full of "brand new classrooms, lounges," and study rooms. There's a new library as well. The older buildings, on the other hand, are "held together in some places literally by duct tape," though by the start of the 2012 school year, more than half of the floors of the main building will have been renovated.

Life

NYLS is home to "a very attractive student body," and the students here don't mind telling you so. The population is laudably diverse as well. Traditionally underrepresented minorities account for about a third of the students. Geographic diversity is abundant. People come here from all over the country and all over the world. Age also varies considerably. Many students are straight out of undergrad or just a year or two removed from college. Many others are significantly older career changers. At the end of the day, though, there are two kinds of students: "those that are from the NYC area [and] those that are not."

WILLIAM D. PEREZ, ASSISTANT DEAN FOR ADMISSIONS & FINANCIAL AID
NEW YORK LAW SCHOOL, 185 WEST BROADWAY, NEW YORK, NY 10013
TEL: 212-431-2888 FAX: 212-966-1522
E-MAIL: ADMISSIONS@NYLS.EDU • WEBSITE: WWW.NYLS.EDU

Some students tell us that the academic atmosphere is "competitive but not brutal." Others maintain that competition doesn't really exist at all. "People are more than willing to share notes, outlines, and briefs," they say. "I was very surprised at how cooperative students are with each other," relates a 1L. Outside of class, "Student groups are plentiful, and there are many leadership opportunities for students." Opinions about the social scene vary widely. Some students see a considerable amount of cohesiveness. "Since New York Law School is not attached to a larger undergraduate institution, we are a more close-knit community," relates a happy 1L, "like a large extended family." "It's a good time," adds a 3L. Others suggest that students are very disjointed. "I would not say that there is a strong New York Law School social scene per se," reflects a 2L. "School spirit, community, and social life at the school should be improved." Either way, no one could doubt that there is plenty for everyone to do. NYLS is located in the hip, trendy (and expensive) neighborhood of Tribeca. The nightlife of Greenwich Village and Soho is right next door, and all of Manhattan is easily accessible by subway.

Getting In

Admitted students at the 25th percentile have LSAT scores in the low 150s and GPAs around 3.0. Admitted students at the 75th percentile have LSAT scores of 157 or so and GPAs of around 3.3.

JD/LLM in Real Estate, JD/LLM in Financial Services Law, 4–5 years; 3+3 Bachelor/JD with Adelphi University, Southern Vermont College, New England College, and Stevens Institute of Technology; guaranteed admission program with Montclair State University

Clinical program required	No
Legal writing course requirement	Yes
Legal methods course requirement	Yes
Legal research course requirement	Yes
Moot court requirement	No
Public interest law requirement	No

ADMISSIONS

Selectivity Rating	73
# applications received	4,520
% applicants accepted	46
% acceptees attending	31
LSAT Range	153–157
Application fee	$0
Regular application	Rolling, up to 4/1
Regular notification	Rolling
Early application program	No
Transfer students accepted	Yes
Evening division offered	Yes
Part-time accepted	Yes
CAS accepted	Yes

International Students
TOEFL recommended of international students

FINANCIAL FACTS

Annual tuition	$44,860
Books and supplies	$1,300
Fees	$1,600
Room and board	$22,765
Financial aid application deadline	4/1
% first-year students receiving some sort of aid	93
% receiving some sort of aid	90
% of aid that is merit based	8
% receiving scholarships	35
Average grant	$15,000
Average loan	$49,000
Average total aid package	$58,000
Average debt	$119,437

EMPLOYMENT INFORMATION

Career Rating	**75**	**Grads Employed by Field (%)**
Rate of placement (nine months out)	91	Academic (4)
State for bar exam	NY, NJ, CT	Business/industry (24)
Pass rate for first-time bar	86	Government (14)
Employers Who Frequently Hire Grads		Judicial clerkship (4)
Private practice; Business & Industry;		Private practice (46)
Government; Public interest		Public interest (7)

Prominent Alumni
John Marshall Harlan, NYLS '24, U.S. Supreme Court Justice 1955–1971; Wallace Stevens, NYLS 1903, Pulitzer Prize–winning poet; David Kelley '86, U.S. Attorney for the Southern District of New York; Robert F. Wagner, NYLS 1900, U.S. Senator, New York 1927–1949; James S. Watson, NYLS '13, first African American admitted to ABA, became a judge

NEW YORK UNIVERSITY
SCHOOL OF LAW

INSTITUTIONAL INFORMATION

Public/private	Private
Student/faculty ratio	9:1
% faculty part-time	31
% faculty female	34
% faculty minority	11
Total faculty	238

SURVEY SAYS...

Great research resources, Students love New York, NY

STUDENTS

Enrollment of law school	1,431
% male/female	57/43
% full-time	100
% minority	25
% international	4
# of countries represented	9
Average age of entering class	23

ACADEMICS

Academic Experience Rating	**87**
Profs interesting rating	90
Profs accessible rating	78
Hours of study per day	4.40

Academic Specialties

Civil Procedure, Clinical Programs, Commercial, Constitutional, Corporate, Criminal, Environmental, Government Services, Human Rights, Innovation, Intellectual Property, Interdisciplinary, International, Labor and Employment, Law and Business, Law and Democracy, Law and Economics, Law and Security, Legal History, Legal Philosophy, Procedure, Property, Public Interest, Securities, Taxation, Trade Regulations

Advanced Degrees Offered

LLM, JSD

Academics

New York University School of Law is a renowned, "rigorous," and "practically focused" legal powerhouse that offers a ridiculous array of courses and a stunning number of programs, colloquia, institutes, and centers. "The academic buildings are wonderful." Resources are world class and "fancy schmancy," including a "huge" library. Students have access to some thirty clinics and over a dozen full-time clinical faculty members. They also have unmatched resources for pursuing public interest opportunities. "The dedication to public interest is unrivaled in the area, and everyone knows it and talks about it," crows a 1L. Students collectively log thousands of volunteer hours, and thanks to "guaranteed" funding, roughly half of each first-year class secures public interest internships for the summer. There's plenty of international flavor here, as well. A few hundred foreign students study law at NYU each year, and there are study abroad opportunities at several of the most distinguished universities in the world.

Class sizes can be pretty large, particularly first year, but they're "not intimidating," and there are "interesting" discussions. Legal theory is part of the deal here, of course, but students also stress the fact that they're exposed to copious amounts of "real law." "The overall quality of the professors is mind-boggling." They're "top-notch academics from a very broad range of legal areas." The faculty is "constantly strengthened by new additions," as well. "NYU has worked tirelessly over the last two decades to amass a faculty that matches or surpasses any other in the country," brags a 1L, "and it has succeeded," largely by "poaching them from places like Harvard and Yale." "I guess money and the opportunity to live in the Village are too much to pass up," muses a 2L. While a few professors are "really inaccessible" "academic researchers" and "less well-regarded as teachers," most offer "real mentorship" and "want to get to know you." "The faculty is deeply committed to student engagement, and they seem to genuinely enjoy it," says a 1L. "The administration is extremely accommodating" as well.

Picky students complain that their degrees are "underappreciated outside of the Northeast," but the employment situation is nothing short of fabulous. There's arguably no law school on the planet that better prepares its graduates for a career in the public sector, and Career Services for those students is "actually as well-resourced as the private-sector employment track." "Anywhere you want to work in public interest law, there will be someone that the Public Interest Law Center can put you in touch with," guarantees a 1L. Students who want to work at big firms are also highly successful. The career and networking opportunities "are fantastic in the New York area." Many NYU Law graduates "with just average grades" have little trouble finding work at top-of-the-market compensation. "If you do well and want to work in a firm, you will," declares a 2L. Other students are a little less cocky, but they're still confident. "If you go to Career Services early enough in the game to fix what you're doing," relates a 2L, "you should be golden."

Life

"It is fantastically expensive to attend NYU, both because of tuition and living in Manhattan," but NYU students enjoy an "epic location" "in the middle of Greenwich Village." Simply put, it's "one of the most desirable locations in the world." Of course, if you're looking for a bucolic, cloistered academic experience, this isn't it. "It's New York City, so there are tons of things to do," explains a 2L. "Bars, movies, the theater—really whatever you want." "Students have a great time enjoying the city," "but it's hard to enjoy when you study so much."

Students at NYU Law describe themselves as "easygoing, yet hardworking." "The people here are accustomed to getting very good grades and have the discipline and focus necessary to achieve them." "There is definitely an air of superiority among some of the students." At the same time, the academic atmosphere is "incredibly cooperative and supportive." "The school has a real sense of community about it." "Classmates are excited to hear of the opportunities others have, and not jealous." "It's not competitive," says a 1L, "and it's the most interesting group of people I've been around." "They're musicians, athletes, playwrights, yoga aficionados, rabbis, musical theater talents, etc." In a nutshell, students at NYU Law are elated to be here. "The professors are great, the students are fantastic, and this is a great place to attend law school."

Getting In

Admission to NYU Law is tremendously competitive. Admitted students at the 25th percentile have LSAT scores approaching 170 and undergraduate GPAs around 3.6. At the 75th percentile, LSAT scores are a whopping 175, and GPAs are pretty close to perfect.

Combined Degrees Offered

JD/LLM, JD/MBA, JD/MPA, JD/MPP, JD/MUP, JD/MSW, JD/MA, JD/PhD, JD/JD (Melbourne), JD/LLB (NUS)

Clinical program required	No
Legal writing course requirement	Yes
Legal methods course requirement	Yes
Legal research course requirement	Yes
Moot court requirement	No
Public interest law requirement	No

ADMISSIONS

Selectivity Rating	97
# applications received	8,461
% applicants accepted	21
% acceptees attending	27
LSAT Range	169–175
Application fee	$75
Regular application	2/1
Regular notification	4/30
Early application program	Yes
Early application deadline	11/15
Early application notification	12/31
Transfer students accepted	Yes
Evening division offered	No
Part-time accepted	No
CAS accepted	Yes

FINANCIAL FACTS

Annual tuition	$46,840
Books and supplies	$1,400
Fees	$1,477
Room and board	$19,877
Financial aid application deadline	4/15
Average grant	$17,000
Average debt	$125,169

EMPLOYMENT INFORMATION

Career Rating	96	
Rate of placement (nine months out)	99	
Average starting salary	$131,139	
State for bar exam	NY	
Pass rate for first-time bar	97	

Employers Who Frequently Hire Grads
Private law firms, public interest organizations, government agencies, corporations, and public accounting firms

Grads Employed by Field (%)
Academic (6)
Business/industry (2)
Government (7)
Judicial clerkship (13)
Military (1)
Private practice (63)
Public interest (14)

NORTH CAROLINA CENTRAL UNIVERSITY
SCHOOL OF LAW

INSTITUTIONAL INFORMATION

Public/private	Public
Student/faculty ratio	13:1
% faculty part-time	31
% faculty female	68
% faculty minority	62
Total faculty	57

SURVEY SAYS...

Diverse opinions accepted in classrooms, Great research resources, Liberal students

STUDENTS

Enrollment of law school	581
% male/female	39/61
% from out-of-state	21
% full-time	82
% minority	62
% international	3
Average age of entering class	27

ACADEMICS

Academic Experience Rating	60*
Profs interesting rating	87
Profs accessible rating	84
Hours of study per day	5.20

Academic Specialties
Constitutional, Taxation, Intellectual Property, Dispute Resolution, Civil Rights

Advanced Degrees Offered
JD Day Program, 6 semesters (3 years); JD Evening Program, 8 semester and 3 summer sessions (4 years)

Combined Degrees Offered
JD/MBA, 4 years; JD/MLS, 4 years

Clinical program required	No
Legal writing course requirement	Yes
Legal methods course requirement	Yes
Legal research course requirement	Yes
Moot court requirement	No
Public interest law requirement	No

Academics

"I rave about my law school," gloats a 3L at the North Carolina Central University School of Law. By all accounts, NCCU is a "great value." It's unquestionably possible to graduate from here with little or no debt. The renovated law school building feels "very new" and it's "always well-kept." The facilities are state-of-the-art and "extremely high-tech." "Practical training is strongly encouraged" and readily available. "NCCU has substantial opportunities for practical legal experience outside the classroom," explains a 1L. "Excellent" clinics, pro bono opportunities, externship programs, and hands-on skills courses provide real world experience galore. "The variety of clinics" (eighteen in all) includes criminal litigation, juvenile law, and a small business clinic—just to name a few. There's also a standard JD/MBA program, a JD/MLS program (for future law librarians), and a unique Biotechnology and Pharmaceutical Law Institute, where you can engross yourself in the labyrinth of prescription drug regulation. It's also worth noting that students here have easy access to the state and federal courts in the nearby state capital, Raleigh.

Inside the classroom, the "passionate, knowledgeable," and "very dedicated" faculty brings plenty of "real-world" know-how. For the most part, professors are also "very clear in explaining concepts." "The teachers are really encouraging, and they want to see each student succeed." "Motivation, guidance, and encouragement" are ample. "Faculty accessibility" is another huge plus. "They are tough but there for you in many ways." Faculty members are "very responsive" and "always available and willing to help" if you stay after class or stop by their offices.

Some students call NCCU "the total package" and wouldn't change a thing. Others, however, see areas that could be better. While some students tell us that management is "organized" and "always helpful," for example, others disagree. Also, despite the fact that a loyal alumni base works "to ensure that you have an opportunity to practice" and a recently reorganized Career Services Office has helped students with job placement, "other support services" could still use "an overhaul." A broader selection of electives would be another improvement. "We could offer a wider variety of classes in more concentrated areas," suggests a 3L.

Life

NCCU began in 1939 as North Carolina's only law school for African Americans. Today, it's quite a diverse bastion of legal education, ethnically and otherwise. "Students come from all over the country and all over the world." Ages run the gamut from students straight out of undergrad to those in their fifties who are training for a second (or third) career. "Different perspectives on life and law" are abundant. "Many schools claim to be diverse and accepting of diversity," observes one 3L. "Yet my school proves it every day. We are a family. It includes the good, the bad, and ugly."

SANDRA BROWN BECHTOLD, DIRECTOR OF ENROLLMENT MANAGEMENT
640 NELSON STREET, DURHAM, NC 27707
TEL: 919-530-5243 FAX: 919-530-7981
E-MAIL: SBROWNB@NCCU.EDU • WEBSITE: WWW.NCCU.EDU/LAW

NCCU's relatively small size lends an intimacy that you just won't find at larger schools. First-year sections are particularly cozy, and the atmosphere for all students is "very friendly." "We are a strong, supportive community," explains a 3L. "We help each other out and truly want each other to succeed." "Upperclassmen are mentors for new law students," and they offer advice "on a daily basis and on a variety of subjects and experiences." Nevertheless, and all of this social comfort notwithstanding, students are often competing for just a few precious A's. "The curve of our grading system can be devastating to a GPA," cautions a 2L," but it does force students to work their hardest to achieve good grades."

Students here are very satisfied with their lives outside of law school. "The campus has some problems with crime," but students stress that safety isn't much of an issue at all. Durham is a growing and revitalizing city that offers a low cost of living, some forty annual festivals, and unbeatable medical facilities. With about 15,000 students in town (at NCCU and at nearby Duke University), there are certainly plenty of lively social options. If you prefer laid-back ones, you can find those, too. An array of outdoorsy activities is available in every direction as well.

Gettin In

Though the acceptance rate at NCCU is low, you don't necessarily need outstanding grades and test scores to get admitted. Admitted students at the 25th percentile have LSAT scores of 142 or so and their undergraduate GPA is right around 3.0. Admitted students at the 75th percentile typically have LSAT scores around 148 and GPAs in B+ to A– territory.

ADMISSIONS

Selectivity Rating	89
# applications received	2,097
% applicants accepted	17
% acceptees attending	48
LSAT Range	142–149
Application fee	$40
Regular application	Rolling, up to 3/31
Regular notification	Rolling
Early application program	No
Transfer students accepted	Yes
Evening division offered	Yes
Part-time accepted	Yes
CAS accepted	Yes

International Students

TOEFL required of international students

FINANCIAL FACTS

Annual tuition	
(in-state/out-of-state)	$7,708/ $21,818
Books and supplies	$2,200
Fees	$2,707
Room and board	
(on/off campus)	$10,172/ $12,850
Financial aid application	
deadline	6/1
% first-year students	
receiving some sort of aid	98
% receiving some sort of aid	98
% of aid that is merit based	22
% receiving scholarships	41
Average grant	$4,000
Average loan	$28,500
Average total aid package	
(in-state/out-of-state)	$31,500/ $41,500
Average debt	$68,000

EMPLOYMENT INFORMATION

Career Rating	74
Rate of placement (nine months out)	88
Average starting salary	$60,000
State for bar exam	NC, VA, GA, NY, NJ
Pass rate for first-time bar	73

Employers Who Frequently Hire Grads
Public Defender and District Attorney Offices NC Department of Justice Legal Aid of NC

Prominent Alumni
Honorable Wanda Bryant, N.C. Court of Appeals; G. K. Butterfield, U.S. House of Rep.; Willie Gary, Private practice; Fred Whitfield, CEO–Charlotte Bobcats

Grads Employed by Field (%)
Academic (2)
Business/industry (10)
Government (18)
Judicial clerkship (4)
Military (2)
Private practice (55)
Public interest (8)

NORTHEASTERN UNIVERSITY
SCHOOL OF LAW

Academics

Northeastern University School of Law in Boston offers an absolute wealth of "practical hands-on learning," a "public interest focus," and "a very strong social-justice vibe." "Hands down," the best thing about this place is the cooperative legal education program. Students take traditional courses and have traditional semesters as 1Ls. Second- and third-year students are on a quarter system and "alternate classes with internships every three months." By the time they graduate, students at Northeastern have had "four full-time, law-related jobs." They are able to "test out different areas of the law" and gain "practical, real-world experience that most law students don't get." "Imagine leaving law school with forty-four weeks of legal experience on your resume," says a 1L. "There are numerous participating employers and students can get a chance to go across the country" and "all over the world." "I have had opportunities and experiences that I never would have had otherwise," gloats a 2L, "including clerking for a judge and working for an international investment bank in New York City." "Switching between co-op and classes every three months makes law school more bearable" as well. "You aren't stuck in school all year long," explains a 2L. "You go to school for eleven weeks, then you go do an awesome job."

Another unique feature at Northeastern is its evaluation system. There is no class rank here and there are no alphabet grades. Instead, students get narrative evaluations from both their professors and their co-op supervisors. Additionally, strong academic 2Ls and 3Ls receive honors and high honors designations. On one hand, "The grading system fosters a cooperative environment that really helps you learn from both the professors and the students you're with." On the other hand, "Excellent grades are indistinguishable from good grades." Regarding employment prospects after graduation, students say, "Northeastern has a great reputation in Boston." It's particularly awesome if you are looking for a public interest career. If you want a job in the private sector, "The school prepares you well for that path," but you "must plan carefully" when selecting courses.

The faculty here is "overwhelmingly on the far left of the political spectrum." There are many "shining stars in their specialties" who "know the material like champs." Most professors are "extremely approachable" as well. There are also "a few egotistical nightmares," though, and "way too many adjuncts." Some students happily attest that "administrators respond immediately to problems which are brought to their attention." Most, however, call management "very bureaucratic" and "borderline incompetent." "They just can't get it right," complains a 3L.

Facilities-wise, "The law campus is a little island in the undergrad campus, with two interconnected buildings of its very own and an underground labyrinth of offices, lockers, and study spaces." "The old building is drafty." The new building is "absolutely beautiful." The library is "sunny and pleasant," and "The library staff is phenomenal." There are "plenty of places to study." Classrooms are "bright and inviting," "with large windows and state-of-the-art equipment, including outlets for laptops at all seats."

Life

Students describe themselves as "welcoming, interesting, and smart." There are many students right out of college and a good percentage that are a little bit older. There's a big gay and lesbian population. Politically, "the student body at Northeastern is incredibly liberal and left-leaning." Some students tell us, "People are very receptive to differing views." Others disagree. A certain segment of the population is "offended by the most inane comments," they say. "If you are not super liberal," counsels a 3L, "do not bother

CARRIE TAUBMAN, ASSISTANT DEAN AND DIRECTOR OF ADMISSIONS
400 HUNTINGTON AVENUE, BOSTON, MA 02115
TEL: 617-373-2395 FAX: 617-373-8865
E-MAIL: LAWADMISSIONS@NEU.EDU • WEBSITE: WWW.NORTHEASTERN.EDU/LAW

applying." Politics notwithstanding, everyone seems to agree that the academic environment is "incredibly collegial." "Collaboration is encouraged." "Students study together, share notes, and help each other out when needed."

Northeastern is "located in an urban area of Boston," and there is plenty to do outside the confines of the law school. "There are great common areas for social gatherings and biweekly bar events around Boston." You definitely don't have to party to have a good time, though. Students here tend to be "less obnoxiously obsessed with drinking than seems to be the law school norm." Social life tends to be "clique-y," primarily because the co-op program is constantly shifting them back and forth from course work to internship work. People leave town for a few months on internships. "There are people who live two blocks away who are hardly ever on campus, and there are people who commute ninety minutes who are always around."

Getting In

Enrolled students at the 25th percentile have LSAT scores of about 155 and GPAs of roughly 3.3. Enrolled students at the 75th percentile have LSAT scores in the 164 range and GPAs a bit over 3.7. Early action applicants who are admitted are not required to attend, as the program is nonbinding.

45 months; JD/MBA/MS in Professional Accounting, 45 months; JD/MS/PhD in LPP with the Graduate School of Arts and Sciences, 45 months

Clinical program required	No
Legal writing course requirement	Yes
Legal methods course requirement	Yes
Legal research course requirement	Yes
Moot court requirement	No
Public interest law requirement	Yes

ADMISSIONS

Selectivity Rating	84
# applications received	4,316
% applicants accepted	32
% acceptees attending	16
Average LSAT	160
LSAT Range	155–164
Average undergrad GPA	3.50
Application fee	$75
Regular application	Rolling, up to 3/1
Regular notification	4/15
Early application program	Yes
Early application deadline	11/15
Early application notification	1/15
Transfer students accepted	Yes
Evening division offered	No
Part-time accepted	No
CAS accepted	Yes

International Students
TOEFL required of international students

FINANCIAL FACTS

Annual tuition	$40,950
Books and supplies	$4,560
Fees	$116
Room and board	$19,500
Financial aid application deadline	2/15
% first-year students receiving some sort of aid	95
% receiving some sort of aid	93
% of aid that is merit based	75
% receiving scholarships	77
Average grant	$9,738
Average loan	$42,045
Average total aid package	$49,160
Average debt	$113,081

EMPLOYMENT INFORMATION

Career Rating	87
Rate of placement (nine months out)	92
Average starting salary	$73,000
State for bar exam	MA
Pass rate for first-time bar	89

Employers Who Frequently Hire Grads
Northeastern University School of Law's cooperative legal education program does more than prepare you for the job market —the experiences students have on co-op often can lead directly to a job offer. On average, almost 40 percent of Northeastern law students accept permanent post-graduate employment offers with a former co-op employer. The following are examples of employers who most frequently hire our graduates: Committee for Public Counsel Services (Public Defender in Massachusetts), Equal Justice Works Fellowships, Suffolk County District Attorney's Offices, Boston, U.S. Department of Labor, U.S. Department of Health and Human Services, Office of Civil Rights, Legal Services Offices in Massachusetts and New York,

Massachusetts Appeals and Supreme Judicial Courts, Health Law Advocates, Bingham McCutchen, U.S. Court of Appeals, Second Circuit Staff Attorney's Office, Ropes & Gray

Prominent Alumni
Mary Bonauto, Civil Rights Project Director, Gay & Lesbian Advocates & Defenders; Harry Daniels, Partner, WilmerHale; Honorable Dana Fabe, Associate Justice (formerly Chief Justice), Alaska Supreme Court; Gordon Fox, Speaker of the Rhode Island House of Representatives; Leocadia Zak, Director, U.S. Trade and Development Agency

Grads Employed by Field (%)
Academic (14)
Business/industry (15)
Government (12)
Judicial clerkship (7)
Private practice (34)
Public interest (18)

NORTHERN ILLINOIS UNIVERSITY
COLLEGE OF LAW

Academics

As the only public school found within the environs of the greater Chicago area, NIUers are released into Illinois' sea of graduating law students equipped with a solid education at a fraction of the price. Known for its commitment to fostering a sense of community and responsibility and pointing its students in the direction of public service jobs, NIU places a high value on pro bono work and makes a number of "public interest stipends" available to its students each summer. The school "has placed a special emphasis on diversity, both amongst its faculty and its student body," and it shows in the number of "divergent viewpoints" that are represented both in and out of the classroom.

Professors are themselves one source of these divergent viewpoints, with many students claiming that "some of the professors are amazing while others clearly enjoy the benefits of tenure." While the vast majority of professors "are well above average" and "do a very good job," offering students a high level of approachability, many students claim to have had a few instructors who were below par. "Simply reciting material straight from the textbook is not teaching," observes a first-year student. For the most part, however, students are happy with the quality of teaching at NIU and say that the school is very good at balancing theory with practice. "A number of the professors go out of their way to expand on topics illustrated in the text and to relate their real-world experiences to the matters at hand. The professors as a group make themselves accessible to students who have issues that need to be discussed," affirms a student. "The faculty and administration practically begs students to come in and talk to them." Other students would like to see a broader spectrum of courses offered.

Although some students have grumbled about "1970s decor," the school recently repainted and refurnished several on-campus buildings, including the law library and the student lounge. One of the greatest resources offered to NIU students, many of whom are older, is the Career Opportunities Office, which "will definitively help you get started toward your career," especially if you're at the top of your class and looking to get into "big law." Though some students speak of the disadvantages facing NIU grads—particularly the distance of the school from Chicago proper—others are reassured by the Career Opportunities Office's strong networking prospects, which complement the school's well-established and reputable clinic and externship programs. "We have a lock on many state attorney and public defenders offices now, and an incredible number of alumni in the judiciary. If you want to be a government trial lawyer in Illinois, this is definitely the school to go to." As an exiting student avers, "The price was right, and if you are willing to do the work you can get a good education."

SARAH E. SCARPELLI, DIRECTOR OF ADMISSIONS & FINANCIAL AID
SWEN PARSON HALL-COLLEGE OF LAW-ROOM 151, DEKALB, IL 60115
TEL: 815-753-8595 FAX: 815-753-5680
E-MAIL: LAWADM@NIU.EDU • WEBSITE: NIU.EDU/LAW

Life

With a strong contingent of older, "second-career" individuals, "a high bar for maturity and professionalism within the student body" tends to be set on campus. Students are friendly enough, but hometown DeKalb can be a "pretty desolate place to kids accustomed to the party life of Champaign-Urbana, Bloomington-Normal, or other major college towns." DeKalb is "without much of the nightlife and amenities that students were accustomed to having from their undergrad experience." There are two fraternities on campus (one is "clearly the party frat, and the other is the academic frat"), and there are a number of student groups that students can join, though "a few struggle to survive" due to lack of participation. As for competition among students, a second-year student assures us, "The shark-eat-shark mentality of other law schools would not be tolerated here." "For one thing, the student body is too small, and we all know each other too well. For another, there's just more a sense of being practical and real-world here; we're 'type-A' people, surely, but we've also mellowed with more life experience than your average law student straight out of undergrad."

Getting In

Northern Illinois encourages students to submit their application early, though they do accept applications after the suggested priority deadline of April 1. Recently admitted students at the 25th percentile had an LSAT score of 150 and an average GPA of 3.27, while students at the 75th percentile had an LSAT score of 155 and a GPA of about 3.55.

ADMISSIONS

Selectivity Rating	76
# applications received	1,227
% applicants accepted	48
% acceptees attending	23
Average LSAT	153
LSAT Range	150–155
Average undergrad GPA	3.27
Application fee	$50
Regular application	Rolling, up to 4/1
Regular notification	Rolling
Early application program	No
Transfer students accepted	Yes
Evening division offered	No
Part-time accepted	Yes
CAS accepted	Yes

International Students

TOEFL required of international students

FINANCIAL FACTS

Annual tuition (in-state/out-of-state)	$14,856/ $29,712
Books and supplies	$1,600
Fees	$3,018
Room and board	$11,210
Financial aid application deadline	3/1
Average grant	$12,513
Average debt	$48,880

EMPLOYMENT INFORMATION

Career Rating	74
Rate of placement (nine months out)	85
Average starting salary	$49,625
State for bar exam	IL
Pass rate for first-time bar	84

Employers Who Frequently Hire Grads
State's Attorneys, Public Defenders, Illinois Appellate Defender, Illinois House of Representatives, Private Firms

Prominent Alumni
Kathleen Zellner, won reversals of 7 murder convictions by DNA; Cheryl Niro, Top 10 Female IL Lawyers & former Pres. of ISBA; Dr. Kenneth Chessick, Firm Specializes in Medical Negligence Litigation; Honorable Patricia Martin-Bishop, Presiding Judge, Cook County Circuit Court

Grads Employed by Field (%)
Academic (5)
Business/industry (21)
Government (10)
Military (3)
Private practice (42)
Public interest (9)

NORTHWESTERN UNIVERSITY
SCHOOL OF LAW

INSTITUTIONAL INFORMATION

Public/private	Private
Student/faculty ratio	9:1
% faculty part-time	52
% faculty female	33
% faculty minority	18
Total faculty	168

SURVEY SAYS...

Students love Chicago, IL

STUDENTS

Enrollment of law school	817
% male/female	54/46
% from out-of-state	15
% full-time	100
% minority	38
% international	9
# of countries represented	25
Average age of entering class	26

ACADEMICS

Academic Experience Rating	98
Profs interesting rating	92
Profs accessible rating	90
Hours of study per day	4.79

Academic Specialties
Corporation Securities, Human Rights, International, Taxation, Business Enterprise, Law and Social Policy, Civil Litigation and Dispute Resolution

Advanced Degrees Offered
JD, 3 years; LLM, 1 year; SJD, 5 years; LLM in taxation, 1 year; LLM in human rights, 1 year; JD for international lawyers, 2 years; Accelerated JD, 2 years

Combined Degrees Offered
JD/MBA, 3 years; JD/PhD, 6 years; JD/MA, 4 years; JD/LLM International Human Rights, 4 years; JD/LLM Tax, 4 years; LLM/certificate in management (Kellogg), 1 year

Academics

Located "in the heart of Chicago," Northwestern University School of Law has a first-rate "national reputation" for "developing practical skills" and offering "world-class" clinics that give students "unbelievable" opportunities to work on "real cases." Many here agree, "It's hard to imagine getting a better mix of academic rigor and practical job training anywhere else." Other highlights at NU include study abroad programs all over the world, a highly touted JD/MBA program, and lots of "self-scheduled exams." One demerit is the "legal writing program" that students wish was "a pass/fail class" due to the "incredible amount of work" it requires.

Northwestern's "brilliant" and "very friendly" faculty is made up of "nationally and internationally renowned scholars" who have "a great sense of humor." Students have "an unparalleled opportunity to learn from the best, starting right at the beginning." "My classes and instruction have ranged from very good to simply outstanding," relates a 2L. "I'd go so far to say that my Constitutional Law class was one of the most intellectually stimulating courses I've encountered." Professors are "accessible" and "seem to really enjoy talking to students outside of class." "It is not uncommon for them to stop me in the hallway and chat about a class topic, my journal comment, or even college football," explains a student. For the most part the administration is "receptive to student concerns" and "always approachable." "Everything goes pretty smoothly," and the atmosphere is "not very bureaucratic," though some note that "change is very slow to come" in regards to "accommodation for disabilities."

Students happily report, "If you do even moderately well in your 1L classes at Northwestern, you're going to have legal employers knocking down your door." "You'd be hard-pressed to find someone coming out of NU to a less-than-excellent job." "Most of us start out at big firms," adds a 1L. "The Chicago firms just love NU students." However, some students complain, "There should be a greater emphasis on public interest career choices," as "not everybody wants to go to a big law firm upon graduation."

The architecture here is "nice, consisting of both old, more traditional buildings, and a newer building." "A quiet atmosphere prevails" and the "gorgeous" library overlooks Lake Michigan. Also, trust us: Lincoln Hall is exactly what a law school classroom should look like. While "good," the classrooms could use some "updating," and "There aren't enough areas to study." Also, "lighting conditions" in the library are "bad," and though "wireless Internet continues to improve," it can still be "insufficient and annoying."

Life

"Northwestern places a huge emphasis on admitting students who have a couple years of work experience after undergrad, and it makes a huge difference," says one student. These future lawyers "come from a variety of backgrounds and offer amazing insights into a range of issues." They "are grounded and have balanced lives." "People have a better sense of the world around them and the realities of life beyond a classroom," observes a 2L. "This keeps the drama to a minimum and also assembles a group of people who've done some pretty interesting things—minor league ball, the military, symphonic bassoon, and so on." "There seems to be the misconception that the students at Northwestern are really old," clarifies another student. "For most students it is only about two years before we come to law school."

Don Rebstock, Associate Dean of Enrollment
375 East Chicago Avenue, Chicago, IL 60611
Tel: 312-503-8465 Fax: 312-503-0178
E-Mail: admissions@law.northwestern.edu • Website: www.law.northwestern.edu

"Class sizes are small" and "The school goes to great lengths to create and foster a sense of community among the students." In this "collegial" atmosphere, students are "intelligent, friendly, [and] laid-back." "There are not too many gunners," reports one student. "We're smart, personable people who mix well socially while doing top-notch legal work," says a 2L. However, some students project an "'I-don't-study-at-all' attitude in the middle of the semester, trying to throw others off base. Then, suddenly, the same person who 'never studies' has a 150-page annotated outline with hyperlinks to all of its sections and subsections."

Outside of class, Northwestern is "a very fun place to attend school." "The school sponsors many events for students every week," and there are "free lunches almost every day," along with "random social events put on by the many, many student organizations." "Lunchtime speakers, panels, and club meetings provide great opportunities to explore different facets of the law school experience and the legal profession without taking up too much time." In addition, "Chicago is a great city" with "a great mix of...hustle and bustle and Midwestern friendliness"—all of which starts right "next door" to campus with "Michigan Avenue's Magnificent Mile."

Getting In

Northwestern claims to be the only law school in the country that strongly encourages all applicants to interview as a part of the admissions process. Knowing this, it behooves you to show up for an interview if you apply. With or without an interview, though, admission is unusually competitive. Admitted students at the 25th percentile have LSAT scores of 166 and GPAs of about 3.4. Admitted students at the 75th percentile have LSAT scores of 171 and GPAs of about 3.9.

Clinical program required	No
Legal writing course requirement	Yes
Legal methods course requirement	No
Legal research course requirement	Yes
Moot court requirement	Yes
Public interest law requirement	No

ADMISSIONS

Selectivity Rating	97
# applications received	4,480
% applicants accepted	18
% acceptees attending	33
Average LSAT	170
LSAT Range	166–171
Average undergrad GPA	3.80
Application fee	$100
Regular application	Rolling, up to 2/15
Regular notification	Rolling
Early application program	Yes
Early application deadline	12/1
Early application notification	12/31
Transfer students accepted	Yes
Evening division offered	No
Part-time accepted	No
CAS accepted	Yes

FINANCIAL FACTS

Annual tuition	$49,444
Books and supplies	$8,828
Fees	$270
Room and board	$12,376
Financial aid application deadline	3/1
% first-year students receiving some sort of aid	85
% receiving some sort of aid	85
% of aid that is merit based	50
% receiving scholarships	31
Average grant	$23,500
Average debt	$127,242

EMPLOYMENT INFORMATION

Career Rating	99
Rate of placement (nine months out)	93
Average starting salary	$130,557
State for bar exam	IL
Pass rate for first-time bar	95

Employers Who Frequently Hire Grads
Kirkland & Ellis; Skadden, Arps, Slate, Meagher & Flom; Sidley Austin; Neal, Gerber & Eisenberg; Latham & Watkins; Winston & Strawn; White & Case; Mayer Brown; Foley & Lardner; Fried, Frank, Harris, Shriver & Jacobson; Ropes & Gray; Cleary, Gottlieb, Steen & Hamilton; Simpson Thacher & Bartlett; DLA Piper; Jones Day; Orrick, Herrington & Sutcliffe

Prominent Alumni
John Paul Stevens, former Supreme Court Justice; Ada Kepley, First American woman to obtain a law degree; Jerry Reinsdorf, Owner, Chicago Bulls and White Sox; Carter Phillips, Managing Partner, Sidley Austin LLP; Matt Ferguson, CEO, Careerbuilder.com

Grads Employed by Field (%)
Academic (4)
Business/industry (11)
Government (4)
Judicial clerkship (11)
Private practice (58)
Public interest (6)

NOVA SOUTHEASTERN UNIVERSITY
SHEPARD BROAD LAW CENTER

INSTITUTIONAL INFORMATION

Public/private	Private
Student/faculty ratio	16:1
% faculty part-time	40
% faculty female	43
% faculty minority	24
Total faculty	114

SURVEY SAYS...

Diverse opinions accepted in classrooms, Students love Fort Lauderdale, FL

STUDENTS

Enrollment of law school	1,087
% male/female	48/52
% from out-of-state	22
% full-time	81
% minority	29
% international	1
# of countries represented	8
Average age of entering class	26

ACADEMICS

Academic Experience Rating	77
Profs interesting rating	76
Profs accessible rating	82
Hours of study per day	5.53

Academic Specialties
Civil Procedure, Commercial, Constitutional, Corporation Securities, Criminal, Environmental, Government Services, Human Rights, International, Labor, Legal History, Property, Taxation, Family Law

Combined Degrees Offered
JD/MBA, JD/MS Dispute Resolution, JD/MS Computer, JD/MURP

Clinical program required	No
Legal writing course requirement	Yes
Legal methods course requirement	No
Legal research course requirement	Yes

Academics

Nova Southeastern University's Law Center is a large law school not too far from Miami that offers "a strong emphasis on legal writing" and a "hands-on approach to legal education." Highfalutin theory definitely isn't the focus at NSU. Here, you "learn how to be a good legal practitioner." NSU's critical skills program coaches students on everything from the basics of briefing cases during first year to bar exam preparation during third year. An "invaluable" clinical program that includes options in seven different areas of law provides a tremendous number of students with "practical experience before becoming an attorney." There are certificate programs in health law and international law. NSU also offers a host of study abroad opportunities. Especially noteworthy are the dual-degree law programs in both Barcelona and Venice that allow students to study civil law systems in addition to American common law. Completion of either one results in two law degrees in two different countries, which is an undeniably impressive set of credentials.

A couple of students say that the administration is "prompt in addressing students' needs," but the overwhelming sentiment seems to be that "it takes forever to get anything done" and that the top brass is "out of touch." "However, the professors are in touch," promises a 1L. "The professors really do care about your success." Some faculty members "have inflated egos" or simply are "not that good." On the whole, though, the "intense, demanding, and entertaining faculty" is "worth every tuition dollar." "I am most pleased with the knowledge, practical experience, and teaching skills possessed by my professors," reflects a 3L. Outside of class, Nova Southeastern's faculty is "extremely approachable." "They are always willing to help outside of the classroom and are very encouraging," promises a 2L. "Almost everyone has an open-door policy." "Some of the professors will sit and talk with you at great length about topics relevant to class and irrelevant," adds a 1L.

The facilities here are mixed. "The campus is absolutely beautiful." "The buildings around the law school are beautiful," too. "The law school building itself is bland," though. It's "fairly industrial and has a built-on-a-budget feel." "The chairs are uncomfortable" in many classrooms. "The library is ugly" and "could definitely use more study rooms." Some students say that Internet connectivity is "great" while others call it "horrible." "The school is very advanced technologically," explains a 3L. "However, half the time the technology is not working."

Some students call the work of the Career Development Office "unparalleled." Others tell us that students are "on their own with regard to finding employment and getting internships." Sentiment regarding job prospects is similarly mixed. One faction of students says that Nova Southeastern is "very reputable locally" while another faction gripes that the school "lacks sufficient connections to major law firms."

BETH HALL, ASSISTANT DEAN FOR ADMISSIONS
3305 COLLEGE AVENUE, FORT LAUDERDALE, FL 33314
TEL: 954-262-6117 FAX: 954-262-3844
E-MAIL: ADMISSION@NSU.LAW.NOVA.EDU • WEBSITE: WWW.NSULAW.NOVA.EDU

Moot court requirement	Yes
Public interest law requirement	No

ADMISSIONS

Selectivity Rating	70
# applications received	2,794
% applicants accepted	40
% acceptees attending	35
Average LSAT	150
LSAT Range	148–153
Average undergrad GPA	3.17
Application fee	$50
Regular application	Rolling, up to 4/1
Regular notification	3/1
Early application program	No
Transfer students accepted	Yes
Evening division offered	Yes
Part-time accepted	Yes
CAS accepted	Yes

International Students

TOEFL required of international students	

FINANCIAL FACTS

Annual tuition	$32,107
Books and supplies	$2,700
Fees	$500
Room and board (on/off campus)	$14,016/ $16,659
Financial aid application deadline	4/15
% first-year students receiving some sort of aid	87
% receiving some sort of aid	86
% of aid that is merit based	21
% receiving scholarships	20
Average grant	$13,263
Average loan	$41,318
Average total aid package	$41,989
Average debt	$121,829

Life

Nova Southeastern is home to "a wide diversity of students" in terms of ethnicity, social class, age, background, and pretty much every other category. Students describe themselves as "bright and "motivated." They are "nice and considerate," too, except possibly when it comes to the delicate subject of class rank. Some students maintain that the academic atmosphere is "generally cooperative" even then. "Fellow students make sure that you know the information and help out as much as possible," promises a 2L. However, many others say that the struggle for precious A's is tense (especially among full-timers) because "overall grades are curved" pretty harshly. "This is a competitive classroom experience," flatly advises a 1L.

"Weekends are nonexistent" for a few die-hard studiers. However, those students who do choose to put away their books "generally get along" and manage to squeeze in a respectable amount of social activity. There are some commuter aspects here, but "it is easy to make friends" if you put forth the effort. "Students regularly hang out together when we aren't studying," reports a 1L. You can choose to become involved in "many organizations" on campus. "The school's location is definitely a big advantage" as well. It's warm and sunny most of the time, of course, and beautiful beaches aren't far away. Downtown Fort Lauderdale is nearby and Miami is not too far south.

Getting In

Nova Southeastern isn't impossible to get into for students with solid grades and test scores. Enrolled students at the 25th percentile have LSAT scores around 147 and GPAs in the 3.0 range. At the 75th percentile, LSAT scores are around 152 and GPAs are about 3.5. Also worth noting is a provisional admission program that allows some applicants who would otherwise be rejected to take two courses at Nova Southeastern in May and June. Those applicants need a cumulative GPA of 2.5 or better in those two courses to get admitted for 1L classes in the fall.

EMPLOYMENT INFORMATION

Career Rating	77
Rate of placement (nine months out)	81
Average starting salary	$61,773
State for bar exam	FL, NY
Pass rate for first-time bar	86

Employers Who Frequently Hire Grads
Private law firms, local and state agencies, state attorney's offices, public defender offices

Prominent Alumni
Melanie G. May, Appeals Court Judge; Rob Brzezinski, VP football operations, Minnesota Vikings; Ellyn Setnor Bogdanoff, FLA House of Representative; Rex Ford, U.S. Immigration Judge

Grads Employed by Field (%)
Academic (2)
Business/industry (19)
Government (8)
Judicial clerkship (1)
Private practice (64)
Public interest (6)

THE OHIO STATE UNIVERSITY
MICHAEL E. MORITZ COLLEGE OF LAW

Academics

The Ohio State University Moritz College of Law is a "kinder, gentler law school," which "supports creativity." "Through career workshops each week, setting students up with legal professionals as private mentors, and a wide breadth of clinics to satisfy each particular taste, OSU invests in its students. And their offerings keep expanding!" The new Entrepreneurial Business Clinic should ease any student fears arising from a perceived lack of focus on corporate law and "fill the one gap Moritz had." OSU advocates pro bono work, and plenty of clinics allow students to gain practical experience in the legal world. Students love this "hands-on" approach. Additionally, there is a strong criminal law program, and "The alternative dispute resolution program is one of the best in the nation." The legal writing program is also outstanding. Students praise the law school's "connection with the university as a whole." The school offers various joint-degree programs, including a master's of public policy that can be completed "for free and in no additional time." Students couldn't be happier with their classroom experience, and professors seem to love what they do. "Almost every professor I've had has been engaging, brilliant, and enthusiastic," says one student. Students agree there's an endless supply of "fantastic educators." Professors are "leaders in their research fields," and "great citizens," who give openly of their time and "have a real passion for instructing." "It's common to see faculty at student events and around the law school." They're "excellent facilitators of class conversation" and create a "friendly environment." "I had no idea how strong the faculty would be," one student proclaims. "I have yet to find a professor, who does not go above and beyond to meet with students and share insight."

The resources at OSU are "focused on student access." The administration doesn't "hesitate to interact with the students to give them advice or even just to have casual conversation." Also, "We are just a hop, skip, and a jump away from downtown Columbus, home of the Ohio Statehouse, Ohio Supreme Court, and many other courts, organizations, and firms." This is very helpful in acquiring externship opportunities and jobs within the community. Although there are "increasing career outreach opportunities through Career Services," some worry that outside the state of Ohio resources might be "limited." There's a strong "network of alumni," and even though some students did stress their concern over finding jobs out of state, one student offers, "Even if you don't plan to stay in Ohio, OSU has great regional ties throughout the Midwest and a strong national reputation." Another student says the alumni and the Columbus legal community believe in the school's mission and will continue to help out when they can. Still students emphasize concern over the lack of east coast firms coming to campus to recruit.

Students mention the "primarily left-leaning" nature of the faculty and student body. While some love this aspect, others disputed it as fact. Whichever way the pendulum might swing, at OSU "a strong current of tolerance pervades." In the classroom and outside it, all views are expressed and accepted. Facilities and technology are a worry at OSU. Both are described as "surprisingly lacking." However, they "just finished remodeling the student union and the main library," and one student admits, "The facilities have gotten much better this year."

JIMMI NICHOLSON, ASSISTANT DIRECTOR
104 DRINKO HALL, 55 WEST 12TH AVENUE, COLUMBUS, OH 43210
TEL: 614-292-8810 FAX: 614-292-1492
E-MAIL: LAWADMIT@OSU.EDU • WEBSITE: MORITZLAW.OSU.EDU

Life

OSU School of Law is referred to as both "supportive" and "surprisingly congenial," and a school in which "people will always share their notes." "While we acknowledge the curve as a fact of life, we have a strong sense of camaraderie." Some students believe competition exists, but that it "does not overshadow a great law school experience." Another student has "never really felt a competitive spirit among the students here." Age at the law school ranges from those just out of undergrad to older students, many of whom "are married and have children."

"The law school is literally right next to the center of campus social life." Most students agree its location is convenient. "Directly across the street is the brand new Ohio Union, twenty restaurants and bars, a concert venue, movie theaters, coffee shops, and more." There are a multitude of places for students to relax and gather before and after class. To further foster a sense of community, "Every weekday at noon, there are no classes and an impressive amount of group and club events, guest speaker presentations, debates, and other special events happen every day."

Getting In

The admissions committee considers LSAT scores, undergraduate GPAs, personal essays, and letters of recommendation all very important in the process of admission. Roughly one in three applicants is accepted. Admitted students in the 25th percentile have undergraduate GPAs around 3.3 and LSAT scores in the high 150s. Admitted students in the 75th percentile have GPAs around 3.8 and LSAT scores in the mid 160s.

Clinical program required	No
Legal writing course requirement	Yes
Legal methods course requirement	No
Legal research course requirement	Yes
Moot court requirement	Yes
Public interest law requirement	No

ADMISSIONS

Selectivity Rating	89
# applications received	2,703
% applicants accepted	36
% acceptees attending	24
Average LSAT	163
LSAT Range	160–164
Average undergrad GPA	3.66
Application fee	$60
Regular application	Rolling, up to 3/15
Regular notification	Rolling
Early application program	Yes
Early application deadline	11/14
Early application notification	12/20
Transfer students accepted	Yes
Evening division offered	No
Part-time accepted	No
CAS accepted	Yes

International Students
TOEFL required of international students

FINANCIAL FACTS

Annual tuition (in-state/out-of-state)	$26,328/ $41,278
Books and supplies	$3,980
Fees	$1,546
Room and board	$17,808
Financial aid application deadline	2/15
% receiving some sort of aid	75
% of aid that is merit based	65
% receiving scholarships	66
Average grant	$8,500
Average loan	$31,546
Average total aid package	$8,860
Average debt	$81,408

EMPLOYMENT INFORMATION

		Grads Employed by Field (%)
Career Rating	86	Academic (7)
Rate of placement (nine months out)	99	Business/industry (17)
Average starting salary	$91,743	Government (14)
State for bar exam	OH, D.C., IL, CA, MI, NY	Judicial clerkship (7)
Pass rate for first-time bar	93	Military (1)

Prominent Alumni
Jack Creighton, Former CEO Weyerhauser Corp. and United Airlines; John Garland, President Central State University; Erin Moriarity, 48 Hours/CBS News Journalist; Karen Sarjeant, Vice President, Legal Services Corp.; George Voinovich, Senator

Grads Employed by Field (%)
Private practice (52)
Public interest (2)

OKLAHOMA CITY UNIVERSITY
SCHOOL OF LAW

Academics

At Oklahoma City University School of Law professors encourage pro bono work, and "The legal research and writing department is excellent." Law students here have the opportunity to work in clinics (Oklahoma City is the state capital), gaining practical field experience under the supervision of a professor. There's an Immigration Law Clinic, Oklahoma Innocence Clinic (Its main function is to identify and exonerate the innocent imprisoned in Oklahoma.), and an American Indian Wills Clinic. OCU is "the top in the state, and one of the leading schools in the country for Native American law." The school also has a good reputation within the state and helpful alumni, whose presence is still felt on campus. "The faculty and administration actually get involved with many of the organizations, as do local alumni. A previous justice for OCU Law's Phi Alpha Delta chapter has played in the school's ABA group's softball tournament since his 1L year." Another student says, "The alumni network is extensive and encouraging." Alumni are found throughout the United States and in several foreign countries. OCU offers services, such as resume assistance, job fairs, and a mentoring program, as well as maintaining employment listings for both current students and recent graduates. "The Career Services department is phenomenal." Students live in close proximity to the bar association, as well as downtown firms and city, county, state, and federal courthouses. The administration helps students determine what particular fields they're interested in and where exactly they want to practice. Furthermore, they're "always very quick to respond to student needs." "The staff is available to address all kinds of concerns from law school issues to personal life issues." Students feel they're treated "like professionals and peers."

Professors at OCU are "awesomely approachable" and "value differing views and non-mainstream discussion." Students almost unanimously agree that the quality of the faculty is the school's greatest strength. "OCU has such a big heart," one student professes. Professors care about the emotional lives of their students, as well as the mandatory integrity necessary to practice law. "Preparing us to be good lawyers is the objective of every class." Although the classroom is a healthy blend of legal theory and practical application, that doesn't mean it's dry as a bone. Tests are created from potential real-world situations, and students are expected to answer as working lawyers might. They get plenty of faculty attention, and "even the 'big' classes have fewer than seventy students." Professors are always "willing to help." Another student claims to have never been "more supported or close with any other group of faculty." They "genuinely care that we understand what we are learning."

When it comes to facilities, students admit maintenance is "lacking." "The historic library loses a lot of function with its current design." While the facilities are "quite outdated, they employ the latest technology and a full-time tech support crew for faculty and students." Also, "The school is proactively looking at expansion possibilities." Students don't feel cheated out of resources by choosing to go to school in Oklahoma. One student "did not expect to have Ivy League–educated professors in Oklahoma." Another is "proud to say that I am a student at OCU."

BERNARD M. JONES, ESQ., ASSOCIATE DEAN FOR ADMISSIONS AND EXTERNAL AFFAIRS
2501 N BLACKWELDER, OKLAHOMA CITY, OK 73106-1493
TEL: 405-208-5354 FAX: 405-208-5814
E-MAIL: LAWQUESTIONS@OKCU.EDU • WEBSITE: WWW.LAW.OKCU.EDU

Life

"OCU is not as cutthroat as some schools can be." Students are more apt to collaborate than compete. One student describes the atmosphere at OCU as "a close-knit community." Another expands on that by saying "the difficulty of the experience binds us together." As far as life outside of the classroom is concerned, "There are social outlets, but we also study very hard." Alternately, "It's not uncommon to see people heading to the bar between or after classes." Yet, on the same topic, another student insists, "Students spend the majority of their time preparing for class."

There are nearly forty student organizations to join, and the law school is comprised of people of all ages, many from outside Oklahoma. Oklahoma City has one of the lowest costs of living in the United States and has been called one of the nation's top ten recession proof cities. More than one million people live in the metropolitan area. A billion dollars has been invested in the downtown in the last decade. OCU abuts a vibrant DIY art scene in the Plaza District. "The neighborhood is revitalizing with more arts emphasis and boutique shopping."

Getting In

The admissions committee places near equal importance on LSAT scores, undergraduate GPAs, letters of recommendation, and personal essays. Extracurricular activities and work experience, although not required, are also valued. Admitted students in the 25th percentile have GPAs just below 3.0 and LSAT scores of 150. Admitted students in the 75th percentile have GPAs just below 3.0 and LSAT scores in the low 150s. The acceptance rate is 45.9 percent.

ADMISSIONS

Selectivity Rating	65
# applications received	1,364
% applicants accepted	45
% acceptees attending	35
Average LSAT	150
LSAT Range	149–153
Average undergrad GPA	3.20
Application fee	$50
Regular application	Rolling, up to 8/1
Regular notification	Rolling
Early application program	No
Transfer students accepted	Yes
Evening division offered	Yes
Part-time accepted	Yes
CAS accepted	Yes

International Students

TOEFL required of international students	

FINANCIAL FACTS

Annual tuition	$31,050
Books and supplies	$1,800
Fees	$2,875
Room and board	$8,760
Financial aid application deadline	3/1
% first-year students receiving some sort of aid	92
% receiving some sort of aid	92
% of aid that is merit based	35
% receiving scholarships	44
Average grant	$14,064
Average loan	$41,297
Average total aid package	$40,244
Average debt	$95,547

EMPLOYMENT INFORMATION

Career Rating	76
Rate of placement (nine months out)	91
Average starting salary	$51,838
State for bar exam	OK, TX, MO, KS, UT
Pass rate for first-time bar	80

Employers Who Frequently Hire Grads
Small to medium law firms, government agencies, corporations

Prominent Alumni
Reta Strubhar, First Woman on Oklahoma Court of Criminal Appeals; Andrew Benton, President, Pepperdine University; Nona Lee, VP and General Counsel, Arizona Diamondbacks; Mickey Edwards, Lecturer, Woodrow Wilson School, Princeton Univers; Marian P. Opala, Justice, Oklahoma Supreme Court; Yvonne Kauger, Justice, Oklahoma Supreme Court

Grads Employed by Field (%)
Academic (3)
Business/industry (20)
Government (11)
Judicial clerkship (1)
Private practice (64)
Public interest (1)

PACE UNIVERSITY
SCHOOL OF LAW

Academics

Pace Law School in the suburbs of New York City offers "a good mix of legal theory and practical lawyering skills." Environmental law and international law are the stand-out programs here. "Pace is the place to go if you want to specialize in environmental law," advises a 2L. Numerous course offerings, a host of externships, and a hands-on environmental litigation clinic provide "unparalleled" opportunities in environmental law and make the program "the heart and strength of this school." The international law program offers an impressive array of internship and study abroad opportunities. You can intern at a war crimes tribunal, for example, or work at a private law firm in some exotic locale. If environmental law and international law don't excite you, Pace also boasts no fewer than fourteen other concentrations and a ton of centers and special programs.

Despite a couple professors "who need to retire" or who "obsess over their scholarship," the faculty on the whole is "very enthusiastic" and "truly excellent." Pace isn't particularly small by law school standards but students tell us that it nevertheless has a very "intimate" feel. "Professors know your name and who you are." "The faculty really puts a lot of effort into being available and helpful," promises a 3L. Professors "are here for the students and that is how they act." They are "always available to answer questions relating to course material or to speak about general concerns or issues" outside of class.

Students can't say enough good things about their "stellar" facilities. The "small and beautiful" campus is "a mix of gothic and modern buildings" and "it's an actual campus, not just a building or two." Classrooms are "pristine, roomy, and bathed in natural sunlight, with auditorium-style seating and comfortable chairs." The library is "very comfortable." Technology is cutting-edge and "the wireless service is excellent."

When it comes to the administration at Pace, students say, "You get everything you need at Pace, most of what you want, and you can get around the things you don't want." Students point out that "the administration does an excellent job of providing out-of-classroom opportunities" and appreciate the fact that "the administration and faculty continually emphasize an 'open-door' policy and truly do adhere to it." Case in point: "If they aren't accessible during their office hours, you can reasonably expect an e-mail within twelve hours or so!" Other students are less enthusiastic, pointing out that though Pace's "well-meaning" administrators "certainly try" to help students, things "could be tightened up." Career prospects are either great or under-leveraged, depending on whom you ask. Satisfied students say that the staff works "very hard to ensure that all students are placed in a variety of practical experiences." They also point out that "there are excellent opportunities for internships and externships in several fields of law." "Pace faculty members...have good connections and...[take] an interest in [students'] education and future careers." Critics contend that the Career Development Center only "caters to the top ten percent of the student body." Further complicating matters is Pace's modest national profile. "The school needs to be more active in selling its programs," urges a 3L. "I think my school is the best kept secret in this geographic area, and that is not a good thing."

Life

"There is no shortage of intelligent, hardworking students at Pace," says a 3L. "Pace is filled with students who are extremely bright, but happened to not have the time to take a million practice LSAT tests because we were working or had other pressing responsibilities." Some students call the academic atmosphere "very cooperative" and say that

CATHY M. ALEXANDER, ASSISTANT DEAN FOR ADMISSIONS
78 NORTH BROADWAY, WHITE PLAINS, NY 10603
TEL: 914-422-4210 FAX: 914-989-8714
E-MAIL: ADMISSIONS@LAW.PACE.EDU • WEBSITE: WWW.LAW.PACE.EDU

students "genuinely want one another to succeed." Others point out that there is "a tougher curve" here. "Pace certainly has a competitive atmosphere and has plenty of cutthroat students," asserts a 2L.

"White Plains is an expensive place to live, but many students commute and the choices for living are unlimited." The proximity to New York City is "socially and occupationally beneficial." Students "have easy access to all the big city's perks without having to live there," explains a happily suburban 2L. On campus, there are "a lot of student groups." "Excellent, high-profile guest speakers" are reportedly common. "Student organizations are very present, vocal, and their events are *very* well-communicated through e-mails [and] campus updates," though "you actually have to read something to know what's going on" one satisfied student wryly points out. On this "close-knit," "supportive" campus, "students take time out of their busy schedule to get involved and support one another." Overall, there is a "very cooperative atmosphere and strong sense of community. Social life is there if you want it, but you're not an outcast if you don't." Most students, however, choose to partake of the campus' many social offerings. "Students from all years tend to mingle and go out together." "Huge groups of students flock to the bars on weekends for happy hours and various social events," relates a 2L.

Getting In

Enrolled students at the 25th percentile have LSAT scores of approximately 152 and GPAs a little less than 3.2. At the 75th percentile, LSAT scores are close to 157 and GPAs are about 3.6. If you are in a hurry to get your JD, Pace has an accelerated program that allows you to start in January and graduate in two and a half years.

Clinical program required	No
Legal writing course requirement	Yes
Legal methods course requirement	Yes
Legal research course requirement	No
Moot court requirement	Yes
Public interest law requirement	No

ADMISSIONS

Selectivity Rating	76
# applications received	2,639
% applicants accepted	40
% acceptees attending	22
LSAT Range	152–156
Application fee	$65
Regular application	Rolling
Regular notification	Rolling
Early application program	No
Transfer students accepted	Yes
Evening division offered	No
Part-time accepted	Yes
CAS accepted	Yes

International Students

TOEFL required of international students	

FINANCIAL FACTS

Annual tuition	$39,546
Books and supplies	$1,120
Fees	$248
Room and board (on/off campus)	$12,620/$19,790
Financial aid application deadline	2/1
% first-year students receiving some sort of aid	90
% receiving some sort of aid	88
% of aid that is merit based	58
% receiving scholarships	40
Average grant	$12,000
Average loan	$26,000
Average total aid package	$36,000
Average debt	$78,000

EMPLOYMENT INFORMATION

Career Rating	88
Rate of placement (nine months out)	92
Average starting salary	$88,693
State for bar exam	NY
Pass rate for first-time bar	85

Employers Who Frequently Hire Grads
Small and medium law firms, corporations, and government employers including District Attorney Offices

Prominent Alumni
John Cahill, Chief of Staff, Former NY Governor George Pataki; Robert F. Kennedy Jr., Co-Director, Pace Environmental Litigation Clinic; Gerry Comizio, Partner, Paul, Hastings, Janofsky & Walker, LLP; Judith Lockhart, Managing Partner, Carter Ledyard & Milburn; Hon. Terry Jane Ruderman, Judge, NY State Supreme Court

PEPPERDINE UNIVERSITY
SCHOOL OF LAW

INSTITUTIONAL INFORMATION

Public/private	Private
Student/faculty ratio	17:1
% faculty part-time	61
% faculty female	25
% faculty minority	16
Total faculty	113

SURVEY SAYS...
Students love Malibu, CA

STUDENTS

Enrollment of law school	633
% male/female	50/50
% from out-of-state	45
% full-time	100
% minority	17
% international	1
# of countries represented	2
Average age of entering class	24

ACADEMICS

Academic Experience Rating	95
Profs interesting rating	95
Profs accessible rating	99
Hours of study per day	4.63

Academic Specialties
Commercial, Corporation Securities, International, Taxation, Intellectual Property, Dispute Resolution, Entrepreneurship

Advanced Degrees Offered
LLM in Dispute Resolution

Combined Degrees Offered
JD/MBA, 4 years; JD/MDR, 3–4 years; JD/MPP, 4 years; JD/MDiv, 5 years

Academics

When your law school can boast "amazing professors," "a challenging academic environment," and a prime location in Malibu, California, there should be little surprise when students report, "Pepperdine Law is truly unlike any other school." "Pepperdine Law's support structure and genuine care for [its] students is unparalleled," says a 2L. "From the administrators to the professors to the employees in the bookstore and cafeteria, Pepperdine creates a very welcoming, family-like environment." For many here, the professors are "the greatest thing" about the school. "In addition to being incredibly knowledgeable, the professors are engaging and keep class interesting," says a 1L. "They make themselves available outside of class for opportunities to get to know them on a social level." A 3L agrees: "Like other schools, class is nerve-wracking, competitive, and difficult, but the professors have a respect for students unlike anything I have seen. They truly want us to learn and to succeed and they have an open-door policy to talk to us about class or even just life, anytime." The administration gets similarly high marks for "making an effort to not only reach out to students," but also for "get[ting] to know students on a personal level." That said, some students wouldn't mind seeing the administration "relax a little more" as it can be "a little intense" with "its announcements" and "required meetings." Being a Christian school, there is the constant debate of whether Pepperdine is too "religious" or "conservative." By and large, students report that "both sides of the political spectrum are represented in class discussions." However, some have found that in the wake of "Prop 8," things got "uncomfortable" for "liberal" students. Despite this, "things are changing and a number of students are trying to facilitate this change."

"It is true that Pepperdine students work very hard," says a 2L. Despite "the competition [being] stiff for grades," students are "very civil and refined." However, expect a challenge as the school "employs a harder curved ranking system than other comparable law schools." "I used to surf almost everyday during my first semester," explains a 1L. "I hardly ever surf any more because I work so hard to keep up with the work ethic of my peers—a great motivator." Students appreciate "the great student mentor program" which assigns "a couple of upperclassmen to the 1Ls" in order to help them "with outlining and law school growing pains." Nearly all students like the "focus on legal research and writing," yet some would also like to see the school "reform [its] first-year curriculum to include a few practical courses that teach lawyering skills outside of the traditional doctrinal classes."

Pepperdine Law's Career Development Office gets something of a backhanded compliment from most students. According to some, they're "particularly nosy" in that they "hold students' hands through every step of law school and the job finding [process]," which can put off "highly independent" people. According to others, they're "extremely helpful" and "very proactive." Though some students have had trouble securing "big firm" jobs after "the economy burst and crumbled," most are heartened by the name and alumni connections a Pepperdine diploma comes with. "I am not applying for a job in the Los Angeles area, and I found that Pepperdine has strong ties to [its] alumni," explains a 3L.

When you think Pepperdine, think Malibu. "There is not a more beautiful campus in the world," says a 2L. "We sit atop a hill, overlooking the beautiful Pacific Ocean." Nevertheless, most students agree that "the facilities could use an upgrade" ("technology" is "very clunky" or "up-to-date" depending on which side of the Mac/PC spectrum you fall) and that "The law school building itself needs to be updated from its 1970s motif." But take heart; "There are plans for remodeling in the next few years."

SHANNON PHILLIPS, EXECUTIVE DIRECTOR, ADMISSIONS
24255 PACIFIC COAST HIGHWAY, MALIBU, CA 90263
TEL: 310-506-4631 FAX: 310-506-7668
E-MAIL: SOLADMIS@PEPPERDINE.EDU • WEBSITE: LAW.PEPPERDINE.EDU

Life

There's no denying that Pepperdine has an 800-pound "conservative" gorilla in the room. However, according to students, the gorilla's more hearsay than fact. "I consider myself to be liberal and was initially concerned about attending a school with a conservative reputation," says a 1L. "Now that I am at Pepperdine, I realize that politics do not find their way into the classroom. Furthermore, there is actually a pretty even distribution among liberal and conservative professors despite the fact that the conservative ones seem to get all the media attention. This would also apply to the students." "By and large, the people at Pepperdine are leaps and bounds more decent than at almost any other law school in the country," explains a 2L. "You can always rely on your fellow students to help you out if you're in a jam." Pepperdine does have "a relatively low amount of ethnic diversity in its student body." However, the school is "very accepting of diverse national and ethnic origins."

There's a "very strong sense of community at Pepperdine" thanks to "many social activities that SBA throws every year for the students, such as the annual Dodgeball Tournament on campus," the "law school prom," and a "poker tournament." For many here, social life revolves around the beach or the bar. "I go to the beach after class and finals—beat that," taunts a 1L. "Social life is like high school again, except alcohol is legally obtained," adds a 1L. "There is less drama though." For something slightly more cerebral, the school is "really good about hosting people to talk at school about current issues." "In the past year, I've seen Supreme Court Justices Scalia, O'Connor, and Thomas speak at my school," says a 3L.

Getting In

Recently admitted students at Pepperdine Law at the 25th percentile have LSAT scores of 160 and GPAs in the 3.43 range. Admitted students at the 75th percentile have LSAT scores of 163 and GPAs of roughly 3.79.

Clinical program required	Yes
Legal writing course requirement	Yes
Legal methods course requirement	No
Legal research course requirement	Yes
Moot court requirement	Yes
Public interest law requirement	No

ADMISSIONS

Selectivity Rating	87
# applications received	2,655
% applicants accepted	32
% acceptees attending	26
Average LSAT	160
LSAT Range	158–162
Average undergrad GPA	3.55
Application fee	$50
Regular application	Rolling, up to 4/1
Regular notification	Rolling
Early application program	No
Transfer students accepted	Yes
Evening division offered	No
Part-time accepted	No
CAS accepted	Yes

FINANCIAL FACTS

Annual tuition	$35,460
Books and supplies	$800
Fees	$60
Room and board	$15,110
% first-year students receiving some sort of aid	87
% receiving some sort of aid	87
% of aid that is merit based	30
% receiving scholarships	75
Average grant	$9,950
Average loan	$35,155
Average total aid package	$45,105
Average debt	$111,163

EMPLOYMENT INFORMATION

Career Rating	79
Rate of placement (nine months out)	97
State for bar exam	CA
Pass rate for first-time bar	74

Employers Who Frequently Hire Grads

Akin, Gump, Strauss, Hauer, & Feld; Best, Best, & Grieger; Bet Tzedek Legal Services; Bingham Mccutchen; Bryan Cave; CA Attorney General, criminal appeals writs and trials; Chapman Glucksman & Dean; Christie Parker & Hale; Deloitte & Touche; Demler Armstrong & Rowland; Disability Rights Legal Center; various DA's offices; Fisher & Phillips; Gibbs Giden Locher & Turner; Gibson Dunn & Crutcher; Harrington Foxx Dubrow & Canter; Howrey; Jones Day; Kaye Scholer, Kirkland & Ellis; Latham & Watkins; Legal Aid Foundation of L.A.; Lork Bissel & Brook; Luce Forward Hamilton & Scripps; Mcdermott Will & Emery; Mckenna Long & Aldridge; Milstein Adelman & Kreger; Mitchell Silberberg & Knupp; Morgan Lewis & Bockius; Musick Peeler & Garrett; Nordman Cormany Hair & Compton; O'melveney & Myers; Paul Hastings Janofsky & Walker; various public defender's offices; Sedgwick Detert Moran & Arnold; Thelen Reid & Priest; U.S. Army & Navy JAG Corps; various U.S. attorney generals; IRS; SEC; White & Case

Prominent Alumni

Pierre Prosper, Ambassador-at-Large for War Crime Issues; Rod Blagojevich; Todd Platts, Congressman, PA; Lisa Stern, International Holocaust Survivor Advocate; Rick Caruso, Real Estate Development

Grads Employed by Field (%)

Academic (3)
Business/industry (20)
Government (13)
Judicial clerkship (1)
Private practice (44).
Public interest (3)

PHOENIX SCHOOL OF LAW

Academics

This brand-spanking new school received accreditation from the ABA in June 2010, making it the only private law school in Arizona with both full- and part-time programs. Though this lack of tradition means that many areas of the school can still be considered "reactive," students claim Phoenix Law is "on the cusp," and its eventual reputation rests on its performance in the next few years. As of now, the rapidly growing (and somewhat expensive) school seems to be aiming to become a "unique, niche law school targeting nontraditional students with practice ready skills." Indeed, "practice readiness" is something the school not only proclaims it focuses on, but also "genuinely centers most of its activities toward."

"Phenomenal" professors are very devoted to their students and "will work with you on any issues and really encourage excellence." The mix of adjunct and full-time teachers "are very accessible, treat us as colleagues, and devote hours to practical, hands-on applications of the law." Phoenix Law has "great teachers and very high expectations" (including a strict attendance policy and a C curve), making the achievement of the elusive A difficult, but there's ample help available from the "knowledgeable, intelligent" professors, and the school even offers intersession classes, which provides even more class availability. "There are many options for class times, if you are willing to take a night class." "The school's administration could not do more to try to help and encourage students to succeed. Every school activity and function is centered toward student success," says a student.

Though the name of the school could certainly use some rooftop screaming, its strong practical focus on experience is highly employable, which bolsters its reputation among those firms that are familiar with Phoenix Law. The externship programs and Center for Professional Development are well-lauded, leading one student to claim that "more than any other school I researched, it really bridges the gap between law school and a law career." The school has also recently begun small-sized review classes, "which are very informative because they discuss how to approach bar questions."

Life

There's a lack of competition at Phoenix Law, due to the friendly, Southwestern nature of the students. "When someone wants notes because they missed class, notes are provided. When someone needs help understanding something, there's always student help nearby. I think the cooperative nature of the student body is a huge asset of this school," says a 3L. Most students are from Phoenix and the sprawling suburbs, and many have come here to embrace a career change. The increased attempt by the administration to gain student opinions is reflected in their recent strides of reaching out to night students to help them to participate in school functions.

4041 N. Central Avenue, Suite 100, Phoenix, AZ 85012
Tel: (602) 682-6800 Fax: (602) 682-6999
E-Mail: admissions@phoenixlaw.edu
Website: www.phoenixlaw.edu

Clinical program required	No
Legal writing course requirement	Yes
Legal methods course requirement	No
Moot court requirement	No

ADMISSIONS

Selectivity Rating	**72**
Early application program	No

Though the school itself doesn't have much of a campus, "It feels like a law school" in its aesthetics. Classes themselves are held in several different, nearby buildings, so the students are spread out throughout the day and night; however, the campus will be changing locations as it grows, with the first move planned for the next six months. The school's busy elevators are a cause of unrest and can often be "crowded and slow" when classes let out, but at least the library is "clean and organized, and the staff is incredibly helpful." Most students have some form of transportation at their disposal (leading to a dearth of parking), but "There is also a light rail and bus system with which people can get anywhere in the city." Social events do exist but typically occur in the city itself. The older average age of students means that many must attend to full-time jobs and families instead of socializing with their fellow classmates.

Getting In

Class sizes have only grown since the school's formation, as has the applicant pool. For the fall 2010, admitted students at the 25th percentile had LSAT scores around 148 and GPAs in the 2.7 range. Admitted students at the 75th percentile had LSAT scores in the mid 150s and GPAs of approximately 3.38.

EMPLOYMENT INFORMATION	
Career Rating	73
Pass rate for first-time bar	97

QUINNIPIAC UNIVERSITY
SCHOOL OF LAW

INSTITUTIONAL INFORMATION

Public/private	Private
Student/faculty ratio	13:1
% faculty part-time	49
% faculty female	30
% faculty minority	6
Total faculty	67

SURVEY SAYS...

Diverse opinions accepted in classrooms, Great research resources, Great library staff

STUDENTS

Enrollment of law school	472
% male/female	51/49
% from out-of-state	52
% full-time	73
% minority	11
% international	1
# of countries represented	8
Average age of entering class	24

ACADEMICS

Academic Experience Rating	72
Profs interesting rating	79
Profs accessible rating	87
Hours of study per day	5.47

Academic Specialties

Criminal, Taxation, Intellectual Property, Health Law, Family Law, Civil Advocacy and Dispute Resolution

Advanced Degrees Offered

JD, 3 years full-time, 4 years part-time; LLM in Health Law

Combined Degrees Offered

JD/MBA, 4 years; JD/MBA in Health Care Management, 4 years

Clinical program required	No
Legal writing course requirement	Yes
Legal methods course requirement	Yes
Legal research course requirement	No

Academics

Quinnipiac University School of Law is "a pretty, quaint, and intimate" "suburban" school with "nice and small" class sizes. At the same time, "The extracurricular opportunities are extraordinary" and students are afforded plenty of opportunities to gain "real-world experience." "It's possible to be a big fish in a small pond here and really amp up your resume," says a 2L. "Nearly every student participates in some sort of practical course, clinic, or externship," adds another 2L. "I've personally been able to do something practical every semester since my first year, and I know other students have had the same experience." There are six areas of concentration including health law, intellectual property, and tax law. "There are also numerous competition teams," and "Dispute resolution is a real strong point." Naturally, smaller schools tend to have fewer courses, and Quinnipiac is no exception. Beyond the concentrations, "There are relatively few courses that are helpful outside of a general practice."

Most students tell us that "the administration here is "receptive" and "visible." "You will never get lost in the mix or stuck on hold for thirty minutes waiting to talk to financial aid." The faculty is largely excellent except for a few "incredibly boring" "bad apples, like anywhere." "Most professors are entertaining," and they're "highly dedicated to helping students achieve success." Faculty members are also "approachable people, which can be hard to come by in law professor types." "They are readily available and willing to help," gushes a 1L. "The professors know you on a personal level and genuinely care about your success." "Many of them have taken a personal interest in my goals for the future," adds a 3L.

Quinnipiac has a steadily growing roster of helpful alums, and the school is nicely situated, close to New Haven and Hartford and not unreasonably far from both Boston and New York. Firms throughout Connecticut participate in on-campus interviews, and the headquarters of several gigantic conglomerates and financial institutions are located nearby, which leads to a lot of corporate positions. "Large firm jobs are hard to come by," however. "Unless you are in the top five percent of the class," advises a 2L, "don't expect to even be considered for a high-paying big firm job for the summer or straight out of school." Job prospects for students who want to work in Connecticut are solid, but the situation for students who want to work elsewhere is "insanely frustrating." "Any job you might be interested in outside of the state, you have to find yourself," though the Career Services office is trying to do more to help these students.

The campus of the larger university here is "beautiful." "Studying on the grass by the lake is the perfect environment in the spring." A state park across the street lends an additional visual appeal. The law school building is newer, and it "takes great advantage of natural lighting." The facilities are "set up very fluidly," and they range from "pretty good" to "state-of-the-art." Classrooms are "modern." The library is "extremely comfortable," and "It's a great place for research." Study carrels abound both in the library and around the building. "The building is breathtaking and a wonderful place to study," says a 2L. "It is extremely accommodating of commuters," at least once they overcome Quinnipiac's "impossible" parking "nightmare."

EDWIN WILKES, EXECUTIVE DEAN OF LAW SCHOOL ADMISSIONS
275 MOUNT CARMEL AVENUE, (LW-ADM), HAMDEN, CT 06518-1908
TEL: 203-582-3400 FAX: 203-582-3339
E-MAIL: LADM@QUINNIPIAC.EDU • WEBSITE: LAW.QUINNIPIAC.EDU

Life

A couple dozen states are represented among the law students at Quinnipiac but the majority of students hail from the Northeast. Students describe themselves as "intelligent," "decent, friendly human beings." There's a "rough" grading curve "that sometimes stinks," but students are mutually respectful and "supportive" in spite of it. "My classmates are extremely helpful and generous with notes and time," relates a 2L. "Our environment is comfortable and relaxed, which makes it easier to not only learn, but make friends."

"The student body is somewhat bifurcated between those who don't realize that they aren't living at a frat anymore and those who are actually serious about law school, though generally the serious students vastly outnumber the party students." If you do come to Quinnipiac seeking ribald fun, however, you're unlikely to find much locally. "Hamden is beautifully boring and therefore the perfect place to go to law school," but it doesn't offer much in the way of interesting activities. "City slickers that need constant action, clubs that stay open 'til 4:00 A.M., or any real nightclubs for that matter will not be satisfied," cautions a 2L. A solid contingent of students frequently heads to nearby New Haven, where fairly lively urban fare is "certainly available." When students need a taste of serious city life, they typically head to New York City or Boston.

Getting In

Admitted students at the 25th percentile have LSAT scores in the mid 150s and under-graduate GPAs around 3.0. At the 75th percentile, LSAT scores are close to 160, and GPAs are approximately 3.6.

Moot court requirement	Yes
Public interest law requirement	No

ADMISSIONS

Selectivity Rating	80
# applications received	2,243
% applicants accepted	45
% acceptees attending	12
Average LSAT	158
LSAT Range	155–160
Average undergrad GPA	3.37
Application fee	$65
Regular application	Rolling, up to 7/1
Regular notification	Rolling
Early application program	No
Transfer students accepted	Yes
Evening division offered	Yes
Part-time accepted	Yes
CAS accepted	Yes

International Students

TOEFL recommended of international students

FINANCIAL FACTS

Annual tuition	$41,960
Books and supplies	$1,200
Fees	$780
Room and board	$15,401
Financial aid application deadline	4/15
% first-year students receiving some sort of aid	98
% receiving some sort of aid	96
% of aid that is merit based	72
% receiving scholarships	72
Average grant	$18,695
Average loan	$37,009
Average total aid package	$47,910
Average debt	$82,780

EMPLOYMENT INFORMATION

Career Rating	77
Rate of placement (nine months out)	90
Average starting salary	$55,249
State for bar exam	CT, NY, NJ, MA, RI
Pass rate for first-time bar	87

Employers Who Frequently Hire Grads
QUSL graduates are hired by law firms, corporations, public defender offices, prosecutor offices, and various govern-ment and public interest organizations.

Grads Employed by Field (%)
Academic (2)
Business/industry (15)
Government (21)
Judicial clerkship (10)
Military (4)
Private practice (38)
Public interest (10)

REGENT UNIVERSITY
SCHOOL OF LAW

INSTITUTIONAL INFORMATION

Public/private	Private
Student/faculty ratio	15:1
% faculty female	28
% faculty minority	17
Total faculty	29

SURVEY SAYS...
Conservative students,
Beautiful campus

STUDENTS

Enrollment of law school	428
% male/female	53/47
% from out-of-state	22
% full-time	96
% minority	4
Average age of entering class	25

ACADEMICS

Academic Experience Rating	86
Profs interesting rating	95
Profs accessible rating	94
Hours of study per day	6.21

Academic Specialties
Advocacy Training, Constitutional Law, Human Rights, International Law

Advanced Degrees Offered
LLM in American Legal Studies, 1 year

Combined Degrees Offered
JD/MBA, 4 years; JD/MA in Management, 4 years; JD/MA in Communication, 4 years; JD/MA in Journalism, 4 years; JD/MA in Counseling, 4 years; JD/MA in Divinity, 4 years; JD/MDiv, 4–5 years; JD/MA in Government, 4 years

Academics

Regent University School of Law in Virginia Beach provides a caring and helpful Christian environment in which "students can earn a law school degree without going through the typically brutal law school experience." Judging from current students, it's possible to get through school here on the sky-high morale of the student body alone, with the "strong sense of community and unity both among the law school administration and student body" serving as huge motivators for success. Regent does a good job of "encouraging all its students to be men and woman of integrity," and even warns students "to only take on as much debt as [they] absolutely need" and to be "aware of the consequences of borrowing money." Despite being a "smallish school," there is no shortage of professional opportunities, including nationally recognized trial advocacy, moot court, negotiation, and mediation teams.

The "incredibly accessible and helpful" faculty is "very intentional about keeping students abreast of new developments in the legal field." Many of the names that stand up at the podiums—former Attorney General John Ashcroft, for example—are "truly proven experts in their respective fields" who are "actively working to prepare you to become an ethical and moral lawyer." "Professors are able to strike a remarkable balance between extremely high expectations and a genuine concern for students' well-being as individuals," says a 1L. Neatly put, "If professors were real estate I would say [their greatest strengths are] accessibility, accessibility, accessibility."

The school's very strong focus on hard skills (oral, research, and written) is an emphasis "which is tremendously beneficial for future attorneys," though quite a few students wish that an emphasis on "more practical skills" were added into the curriculum. Still, "I have no doubt that I have the legal knowledge to compete with anyone," says a student. The Career Services Office gets rave reviews for "[working] hard to provide a variety of programs and opportunities. They are available for reciprocity requests, cover letter and resume drafting, mock interviews, and more." "If you don't have a job or internship, it isn't their fault," says a 2L. A resounding number of students do wish that the school would pay more attention to moving up in the rankings and attracting larger firms for recruitment, and that it would "focus more on students who know they will become transactional lawyers, and support them in that choice," instead of pushing public interest work. One thing that everyone is clear about is that the school is thorough in its training, and demands the best: "If you're not ready and willing to become the best in the field, you will not thrive in this environment."

Classroom facilities here are "second-to-none," with "plenty of space, power outlets, and wireless Internet throughout campus." Though the law school shares classroom space with two other grad schools, no one seems to have any problems. The law library is similarly "amazing."

Life

Life is as beautiful as the campus at this incredibly safe school, where "you can leave your laptop in a public area and it will still be there when you return." "Nothing was ever taken from my study area in the law library," says a 3L nearing graduation. The atmosphere is equally as trusting, with a "mutual encouragement toward excellence" shared by all the students. "Competitive, but not cutthroat," students are very helpful and "will go out of their way to aid each other, whether that means sharing notes, mentoring, or simple

BONNIE CREEF, DIRECTOR OF ADMISSIONS & FINANCIAL AID
1000 REGENT UNIVERSITY DRIVE, ROBERTSON HALL, VIRGINIA BEACH, VA 23464
TEL: 757-352-4584 FAX: 757-352-4139
E-MAIL: LAWSCHOOL@REGENT.EDU • WEBSITE: WWW.REGENT.EDU/LAW

encouragement." "The students are very supportive and happy to help each other, without a hint of the your-loss-is-my-gain mentality that one might expect from the curve," says one.

As a Christian university, Regent has "certain rules...but it's not prison." "We are adults and they expect us to behave as such, especially in the legal profession...but plenty of us have active, if not too active, social lives and find time to go on vacations, go out to restaurants, movies, play intramurals sports or just have a party." Others disagree with the idea of an overflowing extracurricular calendar, claiming that "Most law students are too busy with schoolwork to spend much time socializing outside of class."

One second-year student speculates that "perhaps the expectations are higher than other like-tiered schools because of the desire to refute any negative perceptions of a Christian law school." "Pretty much everyone who comes to visit, even devout atheists or agnostics, are pleasantly surprised, especially with the hospitality," says a 1L. A rising problem here is the lack of on-campus housing, which is "almost intolerable." "You will definitely need a reliable car if you attend here," says a student.

Getting In

The average LSAT score earned by an incoming law student was 153, and the average undergrad GPA was 3.3, but numbers are only part of the story at Regent. As the law school's Admissions Office states, "The admissions committee also attaches significant importance to the applicant's responses to the Regent-specific topics in the personal statement section of the admissions application," which considers, along with academic achievement, the commitment of an individual to "take seriously the critical roles they will assume as counselors, conciliators, and followers of Christ." Application materials should not only reflect a clear desire to practice law, but also a personal and professional dedication to Christian principles.

Clinical program required	No
Legal writing	
course requirement	Yes
Legal methods	
course requirement	Yes
Legal research	
course requirement	Yes
Moot court requirement	Yes
Public interest	
law requirement	No

ADMISSIONS

Selectivity Rating	**75**
# applications received	674
% applicants accepted	48
% acceptees attending	51
Average LSAT	153
LSAT Range	150–156
Average undergrad GPA	3.24
Application fee	$50
Regular application	Rolling, up to 6/1
Regular notification	Rolling
Early application program	No
Transfer students accepted	Yes
Evening division offered	No
Part-time accepted	Yes
CAS accepted	Yes

International Students

TOEFL required of international students	

FINANCIAL FACTS

Annual tuition	$30,750
Books and supplies	$1,480
Fees	$660
Room and board	
(on/off campus)	$10,620/ $9,810
Financial aid application deadline	6/1
% first-year students receiving some sort of aid	98
% receiving some sort of aid	98
% of aid that is merit based	70
% receiving scholarships	86
Average grant	$8,757
Average loan	$34,275
Average total aid package	$43,032
Average debt	$115,734

EMPLOYMENT INFORMATION

Career Rating	**76**
Rate of placement (nine months out)	88
Average starting salary	$50,000
State for bar exam	VA, PA, TX, NY, MD
Pass rate for first-time bar	84

Employers Who Frequently Hire Grads
Virginia Supreme Court; Virginia Court of Appeals; Hirschler, Fleischer, Pender, & Coward; Kaufman & Canoles; Wolcot, Rivers, Gates, Williams, Mullen, Stallings, & Bischoff; Oast & Hook; Keel Group; American Center for Law & Justice; U.S. Air Force JAG Corps; U.S. Army JAG Corps; U.S. Marine JAG Corps; Virginia Beach Public Defender; Norfolk Public Defender; Virginia Beach Commonwealth's Attorney Office; Norfolk Commonwealth's Attorney Office; Winters, King, & Associates, Inc.

Prominent Alumni
Robert F. McDonnell, Governor of Virginia; Scott Dupont, North Carolina Circiut Court Judge; Patrick Yeatts, Lynchburg Circuit Court; Teresa Hammons, Virginia Beach General District Court Judge; Earl Mobley, Portsmouth Commonwealth's Attorney

Grads Employed by Field (%)
Academic (6)
Business/industry (16)
Government (10)
Judicial clerkship (8)
Military (3)
Private practice (54)
Public interest (2)

ROGER WILLIAMS UNIVERSITY
SCHOOL OF LAW

INSTITUTIONAL INFORMATION

Public/private	Private
Student/faculty ratio	16:1
% faculty part-time	16
% faculty female	46
% faculty minority	19
Total faculty	32

SURVEY SAYS...

Diverse opinions accepted in classrooms, Great research resources

STUDENTS

Enrollment of law school	540
% male/female	50/50
% from out-of-state	77
% full-time	100
% minority	11
% international	1
# of countries represented	4
Average age of entering class	24

ACADEMICS

Academic Experience Rating	**72**
Profs interesting rating	89
Profs accessible rating	85
Hours of study per day	5.79

Academic Specialties

Commercial, Constitutional, Corporation Securities, Criminal, Environmental, Human Rights, International, Labor, Property, Intellectual Property, Marine Affairs, Public Interest Law

Advanced Degrees Offered

JD, 3 years full-time

Combined Degrees Offered

JD/MMA Masters Marine Affairs, 3.5 years; JD/MS Masters of Science in Labor Relations & Human Resources, 4 years; JD/MSCJ Masters of Criminal Justice, 3.5 years

Academics

Learning at Roger Williams University School of Law is not only academic, but also experiential. "Through initiatives like the Pro Bono Collaborative, which links law students with area practitioners to work on pro bono projects, the school is always working to integrate itself into the fabric of the RI legal community." The Office of Career Services sets up mock interviews with local attorneys to help students prepare for real interviews. They also regularly run "resume writing events, career fairs, and networking events." "The Feinstein Institute for Legal Service is an integral part of the school. Many students obtain excellent public interest internships and externships through this office." Students have "clerkships with judges," as well as "access to the federal system." The school makes certain that "we not only know the law, but we know how to apply it outside the academic realm." Roger Williams also offers an honors program, comprised of seminars, clinics, and international training for those who qualify. There are summer programs in London, England; Tianjin, China; and Buenos Aires, Argentina and "great human rights–based courses." Other strengths of RW are its public interest and pro bono programs, as well as a full maritime program. There are also criminal defense, immigration, and mediation clinics, which help students by providing "valuable, practical experience."

At RW, most students agree there are "more than a few shining stars" within the faculty, offering "great insight and wisdom." One student says the professors "really have made a difference in my life." This probably arises from the fact that most professors have either practiced law seriously before holding their current positions or are simultaneously working within the Rhode Island legal system. "I have had the excellent opportunity to take classes with five judges in all different levels of the judiciary." Professors have "great practical stories to add to class" and feel they "are also here to mentor." Students who mentioned the dean spoke highly of him, one suggesting he "knows every student personally." Not only are the dean and professors accessible, but so is the entirety of the Rhode Island legal system. The school has "excellent connections with the local bar," and one student boasts, "I've already met both senators, the first circuit court of appeals judges, one congressman, and a RI Supreme Court judge in a semester and a half." Another rhetorically asks, "How many law schools have a U.S. Circuit Court of Appeals hear arguments in your mock court room." The connections between students, faculty, and the real-world of law are many and fortuitous. This may be because Roger Williams is the only law school in the small state of Rhode Island. Those students who wish to practice there after graduation are pleased with these connections, one claiming there's "a plethora of academic, clinical, and law firm opportunities." Some who wish to live and work elsewhere after their time at RW feel differently. Alternately, one student mentions that there's a "wide network of contacts and alumni working all across the nation."

As for the school itself, "Classrooms are always being updated," and "The school feels comfortable, but professional." There are some administrative "hiccups" and scheduling concerns, but overall, the students seem pleased. Students did express concern for the school's ranking; however, one suggested RW was "quietly becoming a great institution."

MICHAEL DONNELLY-BOYLEN, ASSISTANT DEAN OF ADMISSIONS
10 METACOM AVENUE, BRISTOL, RI 02809-5171
TEL: 401-254-4555 FAX: 401-254-4516
E-MAIL: ADMISSIONS@LAW.RWU.EDU • WEBSITE: LAW.RWU.EDU

Life

"While there is a healthy competition among the students, there is also great encouragement and camaraderie." One student described life outside the classroom as "extremely social," while another suggests that same social world has a "huge range." A third says life at Roger Williams is "a perfect balance of work and social activities." "Our fifteen-plus clubs are extremely active and supported by funds and time from the Student Bar Association." Bristol is "serene and beautiful" but can at times feel "remote." "The location is lovely; however, winters can be pretty brisk." What do you expect when your campus sits "directly on the water," "literally ocean front property"? RW is "a walk down the road from a historically zoned Main Street that has nice shops, excellent restaurants, and great views." One student describes Bristol as "gorgeous and wonderful, if not a little quaint and boring." Yet another says its "size is just right." One definite perk is free public transportation for students, and almost everyone can agree, "It's nice to be so close to Providence and Boston."

Getting In

The acceptance rate at Roger Williams is fairly high. The admissions committee considers LSAT scores, undergraduate GPAs, personal essays, and letters of recommendation all very important. Still valued, but not as much, are extracurricular activities and work experience. Admitted students in the 25th percentile have GPAs close to 3.0, and LSAT scores less than 150. Admitted students in the 75th percentile have GPAs of almost 3.5 and LSAT scores in the mid 150s.

Clinical program required	No
Legal writing course requirement	Yes
Legal methods course requirement	Yes
Legal research course requirement	Yes
Moot court requirement	No
Public interest law requirement	Yes

ADMISSIONS

Selectivity Rating	68
# applications received	1,501
% applicants accepted	63
% acceptees attending	21
Average LSAT	152
LSAT Range	149–154
Average undergrad GPA	3.21
Application fee	$60
Regular application	Rolling, up to 3/15
Regular notification	Rolling
Early application program	No
Transfer students accepted	Yes
Evening division offered	No
Part-time accepted	No
CAS accepted	Yes

International Students

TOEFL required of international students	

FINANCIAL FACTS

Annual tuition	$37,350
Books and supplies	$1,820
Fees	$660
Room and board	$10,342
Financial aid application deadline	2/15
% first-year students receiving some sort of aid	95
% receiving some sort of aid	98
% of aid that is merit based	18
% receiving scholarships	50
Average grant	$17,854
Average loan	$47,150
Average total aid package	$60,582
Average debt	$123,338

EMPLOYMENT INFORMATION

Career Rating	80
Rate of placement (nine months out)	83
Average starting salary	$51,000
State for bar exam	MA, RI, NY, CT, NJ
Pass rate for first-time bar	87

Employers Who Frequently Hire Grads
New England judges (state and local) and small New England firms

Prominent Alumni
Eugene Bernardo, Partner, Partridge Snow Hahn, LLP; Peter Kilmartin, Attorney General, Providence, RI; Lucy Holmes Plovnick, Partner, Mitchell Silberberg& Knupp, LLP; Betty Ann Waters, subject of the movie *Conviction;* William Flanagan, Mayor, Fall River, MA

Grads Employed by Field (%)
Academic (2)
Business/industry (15)
Government (8)
Judicial clerkship (16)
Military (2)
Private practice (49)
Public interest (9)

RUTGERS, THE STATE UNIVERSITY OF NEW JERSEY—CAMDEN
SCHOOL OF LAW

INSTITUTIONAL INFORMATION

Public/private	Public
Student/faculty ratio	5:1
% faculty part-time	58
% faculty female	31
% faculty minority	9
Total faculty	116

SURVEY SAYS...

Diverse opinions accepted in classrooms, Great library staff, Abundant externship/internship/ clerkship opportunities

STUDENTS

Enrollment of law school	747
% male/female	58/42
% from out-of-state	29
% full-time	68
% minority	21
# of countries represented	1
Average age of entering class	25

ACADEMICS

Academic Experience Rating	84
Profs interesting rating	89
Profs accessible rating	85

Academic Specialties

Commercial, Constitutional, Corporation Securities, Criminal, Environmental, Human Rights, International, Labor, Taxation, Intellectual Property, Health Law, Family Law/DV, Litigation

Advanced Degrees Offered

JD, 3 year full-time program or 4 year part-time program

Combined Degrees Offered

JD/MBA, 4 years; JD/MPA Public Administration, 4 years; JD/MSW Social Work, 4 years; JD/MS Public Policy, 3.5 years; JD/MCRP City and Regional Planning, 4 years; JD/MD and JD/DO University of Medicine and Dentistry of New Jersey, JD/ MPA Public Administration in Health Care Management and Policy, 4 years

Academics

If going to law school gives you the jitters, your fears will quickly be assuaged at Rutgers, The State University of New Jersey—Camden School of Law. Sure, just like other prestigious JD programs, Rutgers will treat you to a dose of the "Socratic thunderstorm approach," and there is the typical "never-ending workload" throughout the first year. However, Rutgers maintains a remarkably friendly and supportive academic environment. Students insist, "First-year classes don't intimidate you, as there's no fear of speaking your mind in class, and diversity in thinking is highly encouraged." Outside the classroom, Rutgers professors are personable, to say the least: "Every Wednesday afternoon, there's a veritable party in our torts professor's office during his office hours. So many students go to discuss both academic and non-textbook-related topics that there aren't enough chairs and people sit on the floor," recalls one 2L. In fact, "It's common for professors to take students out to lunch, to conferences, and even to show up at student-sponsored pub crawls." The administration draws similar praise from students, who believe it "tries to be very open-door and available for anything we could possibly need." A 1L jokes, "I came to Rutgers expecting to witness students getting 'burned' by professors every day in class. Instead the only burn I got was on the roof of my mouth while eating pizza with the dean."

Students are impressed with the caliber of the Rutgers faculty, describing them as "knowledgeable and passionate about their subjects" and able pedagogues to boot. In the lecture hall, "The faculty is as intelligent as they are witty. Anecdotes from [their] real-world experiences are common in the classroom and make some of the drudgery more interesting." Many also point out the strength of the adjunct staff, who "come from varied fields, providing a unique and practical perspective to current topics." Indeed, a practical approach is emphasized at Rutgers, and classes may even include "spontaneous fieldtrips to the federal courthouse across the street from the campus just so we can view real-world motions to dismiss, jury selection, and final arguments." The school's active alumni network is also called on to contribute to the JD experience, and students tell us that "in many courses, alumni return to give lectures on the practical aspects of the subject, and they have been willing to assist any student [who] has a question."

Among the greatest perks of Rutgers—Camden is its low tuition, offering a "fantastic and highly respected education at a very reasonable price." As a result, students do not experience the financial anxiety common to law students today. "Due to a scholarship and a summer internship at a Philadelphia law firm," reports one 2L, "I will graduate with a top-rate legal education and virtually no debt. That combination is hard to beat, and I expect it will free up my career options considerably."

The school takes advantage of the resources in the surrounding community to instruct students in the playing out of law in the real world. "The federal courthouse is literally around the corner, the county courthouse a couple of blocks [away]," and Rutgers students "have tremendous access to the judges in the area and several teach as adjuncts." Students also praise the fact that "the law school is very involved in the community through its pro bono clinics."

Rutgers is "located close to Philly, Trenton, and New York, so there are plenty of job opportunities." On that note, "Career Services are always on the job helping students get placed for both summer and permanent positions. They also expose students to the different options available to attorneys by having guests come to the law school to provide

ASS. DIRECTOR MAUREEN O'BOYLE, ASSISTANT DIRECTOR OF ADMISSIONS
406 PENN STREET, 3RD FLOOR, CAMDEN, NJ 08102
TEL: 800-466-7561 FAX: 856-225-6537
E-MAIL: ADMISSIONS@CAMLAW.RUTGERS.EDU • WEBSITE: WWW.CAMDEN.RUTGERS.EDU

experiences in different areas." Rutgers is somewhat unique among law schools in that almost half of the graduating class takes judicial clerkship positions, more students than those who take positions in private practice.

Life

Attracting students from all across the nation and the world, the Rutgers student body is "extremely diverse in all aspects, including gender, socioeconomics, age, and interests." On this multicultural campus "There is an organization for just about any interest a person may have, [and] the SBA and other clubs do a great job of providing numerous social functions nearly every week." A 2L explains, "The environment is positive and students are involved with the school. Whether it be moot court, law journals, or politics, students are engaged in society and provide for a very strong sense of community." Off campus, "People are always looking to get together to study or to just go out socially," though most prefer hanging out in Philly to hitting the bars in the surrounding town of Camden. While some describe Camden as "the pit of despair," others tell us that "the waterfront on both sides of the Delaware River is beautiful." In addition, many appreciate the fact that "Philadelphia is exactly a mile away and provides for plenty of social opportunities."

Students warn that there are "a handful of students who are hell-bent on getting a certain GPA." Most, however, value kindness and cooperation over competition. A 3L explains, "My school is both cooperative and competitive. Students here care deeply about being successful, but everyone is quick to lend a hand to bring someone else along for the ride." Indeed, many students praise the fact that "you can always find a good conversation outside after class."

Getting In

Rutgers—Camden recently began an experimental recruitment program, soliciting prospective law students based on their performance on the GRE or GMAT, rather than the LSAT. Therefore, a number of current law students were previously pursuing advanced degrees in other subject areas. For all other prospective students, the admissions process is standard fare: Rutgers admits students who have demonstrated a high level of academic achievement, as well as strong standardized test scores.

Clinical program required	No
Legal writing course requirement	Yes
Legal methods course requirement	Yes
Legal research course requirement	No
Moot court requirement	Yes
Public interest law requirement	No

ADMISSIONS

Selectivity Rating	87
# applications received	2,119
% applicants accepted	32
% acceptees attending	32
Average LSAT	160
LSAT Range	159–162
Average undergrad GPA	3.50
Application fee	$60
Regular application	Rolling, up to 6/7
Regular notification	Rolling
Early application program	No
Transfer students accepted	Yes
Evening division offered	Yes
Part-time accepted	Yes
CAS accepted	Yes

International Students

TOEFL required of international students

FINANCIAL FACTS

Annual tuition (in-state/out-of-state)	$20,860/ $31,054
Books and supplies	$1,000
Fees	$2,262
Room and board (on/off campus)	$7,494/ $12,830
Financial aid application deadline	3/1
% receiving some sort of aid	90
% of aid that is merit based	13
% receiving scholarships	53
Average grant	$3,449
Average loan	$19,213
Average total aid package	$21,001
Average debt	$45,286

EMPLOYMENT INFORMATION

Career Rating	79
Average starting salary	$64,067
State for bar exam	NJ, NY, PA
Pass rate for first-time bar	72

Employers Who Frequently Hire Grads
Federal Judges, New Jersey State Court Judges, Large NJ and NY law firms, Medium NJ firms, NY and NJ Corporations, Legal Services

Prominent Alumni
Robert Menendez, U.S. Senator; Jaynee LaVecchia, NJ State Supreme Court Justice; Ronald Chen, NJ Public Advocate; Virginia Long, NJ State Supreme Court Justice

Grads Employed by Field (%)
Academic (1)
Business/industry (15)
Government (5)
Judicial clerkship (31)
Military (1)
Private practice (43)
Public interest (2)

RUTGERS, THE STATE UNIVERSITY OF NEW JERSEY—NEWARK
SCHOOL OF LAW

INSTITUTIONAL INFORMATION

Public/private	Public
Student/faculty ratio	18:1
% faculty part-time	34
% faculty female	34
% faculty minority	26
Total faculty	62

SURVEY SAYS...
Diverse opinions accepted in classrooms, Great library staff

STUDENTS

Enrollment of law school	818
% male/female	56/44
% from out-of-state	23
% full-time	73
% minority	38
% international	1
# of countries represented	26
Average age of entering class	25

ACADEMICS

Academic Experience Rating	88
Profs interesting rating	89
Profs accessible rating	84
Hours of study per day	4.25

Academic Specialties
Civil Procedure, Commercial, Constitutional, Corporation Securities, Criminal, Environmental, Government Services, Human Rights, International, Labor, Legal History, Legal Philosophy, Property, Taxation, Intellectual Property, International Business; Global Affairs

Combined Degrees Offered
JD/MBA, 4 years; JD/MD, 6 years; JD/PhD (Jurisprudence), 5 years; JD/MA (Criminal Justice), 4 years; JD/MCRP (City, Regional Planning), 4 years; JD/MSW, 4 years

Academics

According to students, Rutgers School of Law—Newark is "truly a gem" "that deserves more respect than it sometimes gets." They also boast that their school offers "definitely the best bang for your buck" among the handful of law schools in or within commuting distance from Manhattan. The academic highlight here is the "very strong," very large, and generally "fantastic" clinical program. Opportunities to gain "incredibly valuable practical experience" while helping real clients with real legal problems are "probably some of the best of any law school in the country" and they are numerous. Nearly two-thirds of the students here participate in a clinic before graduation. Externships are also plentiful. Rutgers—Newark is "located in the same town as a federal court and a state court," and "Many state-sponsored fellowships and internships work specifically with the school." Many students also praise the legal research and writing program for providing "a strong foundation to use in all areas" of the law. Others, however, gripe that the program supplies "very little guidance and very little instruction." Also, "Popular courses are sometimes difficult to get into," and if you are an evening student, "The course selection leaves a lot to be desired."

"Class size is small," and the "diverse" and "really accomplished" faculty brings "a broad range of experiences and expertise to the classroom." As far as teaching, "It's a mixed bag." For the most part, though, professors here "do a great job of employing the Socratic Method, and, above all, have an uncanny ability to communicate and teach these dense and often boring subjects with ease." "They really go above and beyond anything that could be reasonably expected," gushes a 1L. They're also "truly interested in mentoring, teaching, and assisting students." The "very transparent" and "particularly accessible" administration is "on top of everything." Staff members are "the type of people who will stay late hours to help students resolve problems and get answers for their questions." "Every dean is pleasant, capable, and genuinely willing to help students in any way possible," swears a happy 2L.

Rutgers—Newark is located near a great legal market and it has "quite a good reputation among employers." The Office of Career Services is "in touch with students." Rutgers also has "a strong history of public interest" and is "constantly promoting the idea that lawyers have a special opportunity to improve the community." The "focus on public interest tends to alienate those looking for jobs in the private sector somewhat," though. Also, the Career Services staff sometimes works "against the students' interest by weighing them down with bureaucracy and encouraging them to settle on modest goals."

"The facilities are good but not great." "We have everything we need to do what we need to do," explains a 2L. It's a public school, though, and resources are perennially "limited." The big complaint concerns technology. Internet connectivity "leaves very much to be desired" and wireless issues "plague" the otherwise "amazing" library.

ANITA WALTON, ASSISTANT DEAN FOR ADMISSIONS
CENTER FOR LAW AND JUSTICE, 123 WASHINGTON STREET, NEWARK, NJ 07102
TEL: 973-353-5554 FAX: 973-353-3459
E-MAIL: LAWINFO@ANDROMEDA.RUTGERS.EDU • WEBSITE: LAW.NEWARK.RUTGERS.EDU

Life

Diversity of all kinds is "a great strength" here. Students come from "very varied backgrounds" "and are eager to learn." There are plenty of "professional, mid-career individuals"—especially in the evening program—and ethnic minorities make up over a third of the student population. "The administration's dedication to finding students that will not only become great lawyers but great people overall makes this school unique." "If you want to meet intelligent and successful people from an array of backgrounds," declares a 3L, "this is the school for you." Politically, it's "a very liberal school" and a "left-of-center atmosphere" is prevalent both inside and outside the classroom. Students describe the academic environment as generally "cooperative." The struggle for jobs with "with other New York/New Jersey–area schools makes the student body a little anxious" but "there is little to no mean-spirited competition."

A few students tell us there us "no sense of community" here. Many others say there is a "great quality of life." "It is a warm, accepting community and it is very easy to make friends," beams a 2L. "Because the school has students from such diverse backgrounds," submits a 1L, "it makes it easier for anyone to fit in and not feel like an outcast." "There are always lots of talks and events to attend" and "a lot of student organizations" "sponsor mixers and activities." Champions of Newark describe it as "a well-developed commercial city with many large law firms and tons of wonderful places to eat." "Newark simply is not as bad as people think," they insist. Other students call Newark a "dirty city that can be unsafe." "If you could build a wall around the school and never look beyond that wall," suggests a 3L, "the setting would be lovely." Luckily for Newark detractors, New York City is very nearby.

Getting In

Admitted students at the 25th percentile have LSAT in the mid 150s and undergraduate grade-point averages in the 3.1 range. At the 75th percentile, LSAT scores in the low 160s and GPAs are in the 3.6 range.

Clinical program required	No
Legal writing course requirement	Yes
Legal methods course requirement	Yes
Legal research course requirement	Yes
Moot court requirement	Yes
Public interest law requirement	No

ADMISSIONS

Selectivity Rating	86
# applications received	3,519
% applicants accepted	26
% acceptees attending	21
Average LSAT	159
LSAT Range	155–161
Average undergrad GPA	3.34
Application fee	$60
Regular application	Rolling, up to 3/15
Regular notification	Rolling
Early application program	No
Transfer students accepted	Yes
Evening division offered	Yes
Part-time accepted	Yes
CAS accepted	Yes

FINANCIAL FACTS

Annual tuition (in-state/out-of-state)	$17,835/ $26,187
Books and supplies	$4,225
Fees	$1,788
Room and board (on/off campus)	$13,908/ $18,108
Financial aid application deadline	4/1
% first-year students receiving some sort of aid	92
% receiving some sort of aid	92
% of aid that is merit based	25
% receiving scholarships	40
Average grant	$7,000
Average loan	$37,750
Average total aid package	$37,750
Average debt	$113,250

EMPLOYMENT INFORMATION

Career Rating	74
Rate of placement (nine months out)	92
Average starting salary	$81,000
State for bar exam	NJ, NY, PA, CA, TX
Pass rate for first-time bar	81

Employers Who Frequently Hire Grads

All major Philadelphia, New Jersey, and Delaware law firms hire from Rutgers-Camden, as do numerous prestigious firms from New York City, Washington D.C., California, and other major metropolitan areas. Rutgers also ranks second in the country in placing its law graduates in highly desirable judicial clerkships.

Prominent Alumni

Hon. James Florio, former governor, congressman; Hon. Joseph Rodriguez, U.S. federal district judge; Hon. Stephen Orlofsky, U.S. federal district judge; Hon. William Hughes, former ambassador, congressman; Barry Hamerling, CEO/AYCO financial advisor to Fortune 100 executives

Grads Employed by Field (%)

Business/industry (10)
Government (7)
Judicial clerkship (38)
Military (1)
Private practice (38)
Public interest (2)

SAMFORD UNIVERSITY
CUMBERLAND SCHOOL OF LAW

INSTITUTIONAL INFORMATION

Public/private	Private
Affiliation	Southern Baptist
Student/faculty ratio	18:1
% faculty part-time	50
% faculty female	30
% faculty minority	15
Total faculty	46

SURVEY SAYS...
Great research resources,
Great library staff

STUDENTS

Enrollment of law school	491
% male/female	56/44
% from out-of-state	47
% full-time	100
% minority	25
Average age of entering class	24

ACADEMICS

Academic Experience Rating	93
Profs interesting rating	92
Profs accessible rating	93
Hours of study per day	4.92

Academic Specialties
Corporation Securities, Environmental, Taxation, Intellectual Property, Trial Advocacy and Practical Lawyering Skills, Cumberland Community Mediation Center

Advanced Degrees Offered
Master of Comparative Law

Combined Degrees Offered
JD/Master of Accountancy, JD/MBA, JD/Master of Divinity, JD/Master of Public Administration, JD/Master of Public Health, JD/MS in Environmental Management, and JD/Master of Art in Theological Studies, all three and a half to four year programs except the JD/MDivinity which is a 5 year program.

Academics

Students at Samford University's Cumberland School of Law say their school is "a little bit of a hidden gem" and "a great place to become a lawyer." The bar-passage rate is utterly fabulous. There are seven joint-degree programs and a "diverse array" of available courses. "Practical skills are the strength" here, though. The legal writing program is reportedly outstanding. Students have an "incredible amount of opportunity to get experience in trial competition." "As far as trial advocacy goes, you cannot find a better school in the country," vaunts a 3L. "Practicing litigation attorneys train students in specialized trial advocacy programs, and the trial teams consistently win major national tournaments." Externships and a wealth of community service programs also provide "unmatched" opportunities to gain practical experience.

Cumberland is a small school with small class sizes, and it is home to "a diverse faculty with impeccable credentials." The professors are "an amazing group." "There is always going to be that jerk who is a complete know-it-all and thinks he hung the moon in any law school," and Cumberland is no exception. As a rule, though, these professors are "extremely knowledgeable" and "hilarious yet simultaneously intimidating." They "have practice experience, which is helpful in class because it allows for personal experiences to be introduced," and they "emphasize what will actually be useful and necessary" when you are representing clients. "A wonderful open-door policy" is another plus. "Professors are willing to meet with students and discuss the subject matter at any point outside of class," and they "genuinely want to help students in whatever way they can." "I don't even know why they put 'office hours' in their syllabi," adds a happy 2L. Students also rave about their "hands-on," accessible, and "very personable" administration. "They actually know students' names and want to help." And if you want to "shoot the breeze" with the dean, you can.

Facilities-wise, "The campus is beautiful and is extremely convenient to all areas of Birmingham." The "comfortable" and "awesome" library is "a great place to study." "Also, the library resources are exceptional," and the librarians are "wonderful" if you are in a bind. The "outdated" classrooms aren't the greatest. They "can feel a little cramped," and they are "windowless." "In some ways, that is a good thing because it keeps you from getting distracted," explains a 1L. "The technology in the classrooms isn't the best," either.

Students are pretty satisfied with their career prospects, although the "extremely helpful" Career Services Office "could do a better job marketing the school's graduates outside of the Birmingham legal market," laments a 2L. "The alumni network of this school is incredible," beams a 2L. "Cumberland alums are always looking to hire the bright young Cumberland graduates. And if an alum can't help you out, they are always willing to refer you to someone who can."

JENNIFER Y. SIMS, ASSISTANT DEAN FOR ADMISSIONS
800 LAKESHORE DRIVE, BIRMINGHAM, AL 35229
TEL: 205-726-2702 FAX: 205-726-2057
E-MAIL: LAWADM@SAMFORD.EDU • WEBSITE: CUMBERLAND.SAMFORD.EDU

Life

Politically, liberals are seen occasionally, but the overall population leans "pretty far to the right." Academically, there may be "a behind-the-scenes competitiveness," but the atmosphere looks and feels "cooperative and collegial." "Most students are more than willing to help their classmates succeed."

Socially, Cumberland is a decidedly "Southern school." Hospitality is paramount, and "even the slightly awkward students are still warmly received." "There is a real community at Cumberland," relates a 2L. "We study together, hang out together, and have formed a tight bond with each other," adds another 2L. "There is a friendliness and warmth that you just won't find at other schools." "We interact with each other like friendly colleagues; we compete with each other like sibling rivals; and we support each other through the trials of life and death like family," reflects an already wistful 3L. "The school creates a 'work hard' culture but constantly has entertaining social events." Weekly bar reviews around the affordable, growing city of Birmingham are reportedly well attended. In the spring, Cumberland celebrates Rascal Day in honor of its long-deceased canine mascot. There's food and live music, and the dean and the school president lead a march through campus.

Getting In

Enrolled students at the 25th percentile at Cumberland have LSAT scores around 153 and GPAs at just about 3.30. At the 75th percentile, LSAT scores are approximately 157 and GPAs are a little over 3.5. If you want to get started on your law school career a few months early, Cumberland allows admitted students to take two law school electives during the summer before 1L courses begin.

Clinical program required	No
Legal writing course requirement	Yes
Legal methods course requirement	Yes
Legal research course requirement	Yes
Moot court requirement	No
Public interest law requirement	No

ADMISSIONS

Selectivity Rating	**81**
# applications received	1,678
% applicants accepted	33
% acceptees attending	30
Average LSAT	155
LSAT Range	153–158
Average undergrad GPA	3.32
Application fee	$50
Regular application	Rolling, up to 2/28
Regular notification	Rolling
Early application program	No
Transfer students accepted	Yes
Evening division offered	No
Part-time accepted	No
CAS accepted	Yes

International Students

TOEFL required of international students

FINANCIAL FACTS

Annual tuition	$34,528
Books and supplies	$2,000
Fees	$160
Room and board	$13,500
Financial aid application deadline	3/1
% first-year students receiving some sort of aid	86
% receiving some sort of aid	85
% of aid that is merit based	96
% receiving scholarships	36
Average grant	$17,370
Average loan	$43,024
Average total aid package	$44,934
Average debt	$107,850

EMPLOYMENT INFORMATION

Career Rating	**84**
Rate of placement (nine months out)	92
Average starting salary	$65,739
State for bar exam	AL, FL, TN, GA, NC
Pass rate for first-time bar	91

Employers Who Frequently Hire Grads
Burr & Forman; Balch & Bingham; Cabaniss, Johnston, Gardner, Dumas & O'Neal; Sirote & Permutt; Alabama Attorney General's Office; Hand Arendall; Leitner, Williams, Dooley & Neopolitan (Chattanooga, TN); Baker, Donelson, Bearman, Caldwell & Berkowitz (Birmingham and Nashville); Waller, Lansden Dortch & Davis (Nashville); U.S. Senate Judiciary Committee (Washington, D.C.); Emanuel, Sheppard & Condon (Pensacola); Bradley Arant Boult Cummings; Starnes Davis Florie; Haskell Slaughter Young and Rediker

Prominent Alumni
Lee Thuston, Managing Partner at Burr & Forman; the Honorable Joel Dubina, Chief Judge of the U.S. Court of Appeals for the Eleventh Circuit; Charles J. Crist, Jr., 44th Governor of Florida

Grads Employed by Field (%)
Academic (2)
Business/industry (16)
Government (8)
Judicial clerkship (7)
Military (1)
Private practice (63)
Public interest (3)

SANTA CLARA UNIVERSITY
SCHOOL OF LAW

INSTITUTIONAL INFORMATION

Public/private	Private
Affiliation	Roman Catholic
Student/faculty ratio	12:1
% faculty part-time	37
% faculty female	46
% faculty minority	12
Total faculty	67

SURVEY SAYS...

Diverse opinions accepted in classrooms, Students love Santa Clara, CA

STUDENTS

Enrollment of law school	314
% male/female	52/48
% from out-of-state	28
% full-time	75
% minority	45
# of countries represented	14
Average age of entering class	25

ACADEMICS

Academic Experience Rating	76
Profs interesting rating	78
Profs accessible rating	72
Hours of study per day	4.92

Academic Specialties

Constitutional, Criminal, Environmental, Human Rights, International, Labor, Taxation, Intellectual Property. Certificates in Public Interest Law, Intellectual Property Law, International Law

Advanced Degrees Offered

LLM in U.S. Law for Foreign Lawyers, 1 year; LLM in International and Comparative Law, 1 year; LLM in Intellectual Property Law, 1–3 years

Combined Degrees Offered

JD/MBA, 3.5–4 years; JD/MSIS, 3.5–4 years

Academics

Jesuit-affiliated Santa Clara University School of Law "in the heart of Silicon Valley" is a smaller school that manages to offer "a wide range" of courses across a host of legal areas. As you would expect given the location, Santa Clara Law boasts "one of the top-ranking high-tech programs in the nation." The course work in patent and intellectual property law is "tremendous," and students regularly intern with "the vast array" of existing mammoth corporations as well as the next generation of mammoth corporations here "in the venture-capital capital of the country." The international law program is also extensive and "incredible." Study abroad opportunities are mind-blowing. There are a dozen different programs in twenty cities around the globe including—just to cite a few—Istanbul, Budapest, and Shanghai. In addition, there are several unique international judicial externships and international internships available. Still another perk here is the prominent focus on public interest and social justice law. SCU is teeming with institutes, centers, and programs that allow students to do "great things for people."

"Real-world experience" is one of the hallmarks of the professors at Santa Clara Law. "Some are brilliant savants, but you just can't learn from them." On the whole, though, faculty members are "top-notch," "dedicated to teaching," and "obviously committed to their students." Professors are "approachable" as well. They "really engage students" outside of class" "about their past experiences and future hopes." Administratively, lower-level staff can be "somewhat surly," and sometimes the decisions of the top brass "leave much to be desired," but the general consensus is that management is "extremely accommodating" and "very concerned with student feedback." "It would be difficult to find another law school that cares so much about [its] students and actually does something about it," beams a 1L.

Santa Clara's lush, "peaceful" campus is "simply gorgeous and kept very nicely." It's also home to some "great facilities." The law school facilities are pretty mundane, though. "The classrooms are classrooms," says a 3L. The law library is "certainly adequate," but it's "fairly depressing." It's "dark, and the temperature controls suck." On the bright side, the undergrad library "right next door" is "incredibly awesome," and it's a regular haunt for law students.

Santa Clara has a stellar reputation in the Bay Area, and career prospects are solid. More than eighty percent of all newly minted graduates head off to the private sector, where median starting salaries are very impressive. Quite a few students take jobs in Silicon Valley. San Francisco is another common destination. Santa Clara Law's "very accessible, passionate, successful, and helpful alumni network" is a huge advantage when students are looking for work. They are "very willing to give back to the school and provide advice and opportunities to current students." "Sometimes it feels like the entire community of attorneys in the South Bay graduated from Santa Clara," explains a 3L, "especially when it comes to district attorneys, public defenders, and judges." The alumni base and the SCU brand name aren't as strong nationally, though. "Nobody knows about it outside of the San Francisco area," laments another 3L.

Jeanette J. Leach, Assistant Dean for Admissions & Financial Aid
500 El Camino Real, Santa Clara, CA 95053
Tel: 408-554-5048 Fax: 408-554-7897
E-Mail: lawadmissions@scu.edu • Website: law.scu.edu

Life

"The school's location allows it to attract a diverse group of highly educated students." In terms of ethnicity, Santa Clara Law is among the most diverse schools in the country. "Varying ages," radically different life experiences, and a solid geographic distribution also make for "a good mix." Academically, a few students "are jerks and should be quarantined," but "there usually is a positive vibe around the school." "It is a very welcoming environment that engenders very happy students." "We're a social tribe," explains a 1L. "We might be graded on a curve but you'd never know it from how everyone treats each other."

"Student life is collaborative." "There's a club or society for everything under the sun." "Stimulating" speakers including local corporate bigwigs are frequent, and "The school makes a real effort to engage its alumni and host events where students can meet them." "Social activities and opportunities for students to get together" are also commonplace. "We study hard, but we also go out a lot on the weekends and form some close-knit friendships," says a 3L. The cost of living in Silicon Valley is very high, and the city of Santa Clara is "decidedly not a college town." The locale is "green and sunny most of the year," though, and the Bay Area offers quite a bit to do. When students need a break from their casebooks or law school in general, heading up to San Francisco is pretty common.

Getting In

Enrolled full-time students at the 25th percentile have LSAT scores in the high 150s and grade point averages right around 3.1. At the 75th percentile, LSAT scores are in the lower 160s and GPAs are around 3.6. Stats for the part-time program are somewhat lower.

Clinical program required	No
Legal writing course requirement	Yes
Legal methods course requirement	Yes
Legal research course requirement	Yes
Moot court requirement	Yes
Public interest law requirement	No

ADMISSIONS

Selectivity Rating	**80**
# applications received	4,973
% applicants accepted	42
% acceptees attending	15
Average LSAT	158
LSAT Range	158–162
Average undergrad GPA	3.31
Application fee	$75
Regular application	Rolling, up to 5/1
Regular notification	Rolling
Early application program	Yes
Early application deadline	11/1
Early application notification	12/20
Transfer students accepted	Yes
Evening division offered	Yes
Part-time accepted	Yes
CAS accepted	Yes

FINANCIAL FACTS

Annual tuition	$39,360
Books and supplies	$1,218
Room and board	$14,026
Financial aid application deadline	2/1
% first-year students receiving some sort of aid	93
% receiving some sort of aid	90
% of aid that is merit based	78
% receiving scholarships	47
Average grant	$11,312
Average loan	$40,116
Average total aid package	$41,179
Average debt	$106,819

EMPLOYMENT INFORMATION

Career Rating	**81**
Rate of placement (nine months out)	78
Average starting salary	$98,687
State for bar exam	CA, WA, OR, AZ, NY
Pass rate for first-time bar	70

Employers Who Frequently Hire Grads
Bingham McCutchen LLP; Blakely, Sokoloff, Taylor and Zafman LLP; Cisco Systems, Inc.; Cooley Godward LLP; Dewey & LeBoeuf LLP; DLA Piper; Fenwick & West LLP; Intel Corporation; Jones Day; Morgan, Lewis & Bockius LLP; Morrison & Foerster LLP; Orrick Herrington & Sutcliffe LLP; Perkins Coie LLP; Pillsbury Winthrop Shaw Pittman LLP; PricewaterhouseCoopers; Wilson Sonsini Goodrich & Rosati; Cooley LLP

Prominent Alumni
Leon Panetta, Current C.I.A. Director and Former Chief of Staff under President Bill Clinton; Zoe Lofgren, Congresswoman, U.S. House of Representatives; Edward Panelli, Retired California Supreme Court Justice; Rodney Moore, President of the National Bar Association; Robert Durham, Oregon Supreme Court Associate Justice

Grads Employed by Field (%)
Academic (6)
Government (7)
Private practice (43)
Public interest (10)

SEATTLE UNIVERSITY
SCHOOL OF LAW

Academics

"A fairly large school," the Seattle University School of Law offers an "outstanding," "very flexible, evening, part-time program" in addition to full-time day enrollment. "Course options are diverse and offered consistently." No fewer than fourteen specializations include criminal practice, environmental law, and international law. The "tough but very good" legal writing curriculum is far and away the biggest point of pride here. It's "the class that you will despise while you are in it but will be utterly grateful for when you are through." "This school has the best legal writing program and advocacy programs in the country," brags one student. "It is the best and most useful course I've ever taken at a school," adds a 3L. "The legal writing program really does prepare you for the real world and to a level of detail and precision I did not expect." A throng of externships and clerkships gives students the opportunity to "develop practical skills" "in all different areas of law." Seattle U's location, "less than a mile from downtown Seattle businesses and law firms," allows students to walk to many courthouses and downtown law firms. Seattle U Law is also a Jesuit institution, and many students note that many organizations "are devoted to social justice." Other students tell us, "Any mention of the Jesuit influence is off base." "If asked [about] the Jesuit tradition," jokes a 2L, many students would ask, "'Is that a type of mocha latte at Starbucks?'" The biggest gripe among students concerns the need to "reduce the size of the incoming classes" Adding to the challenge, the grading curve has historically been "very tough" at Seattle U, though a new curve went into effect in the fall 2010.

Professors "emphasize the practical side" of law and are "generally extremely capable, intelligent, and knowledgeable." It's the "really hit-and-miss" visiting professors whom "you have to watch out for." Outside of class, some faculty members are "extremely helpful and available." However, other professors are "very hard to access." "I wish that the professors were a bit more accessible," complains a 2L. "They are supposed to have set office hours, but none of the professors are held to that." Thoughts about the administration are similarly mixed. Some students say that the SU administration "is a distant, bureaucratic entity" that manifests "a seeming sense of apathy toward the individual student." Others assert that the deans "work hard to eliminate obstacles so that all you have to worry about is learning."

The Center for Professional Development "makes extraordinary efforts to find job placements for students." Also, "The alumni network is broad and very helpful." "The top ten percent do great and get into private firms with the snap of a finger." Some students complain that SU "should be doing more to market students to regional and national employers." "Seattle University is a regional school," explains a 2L. "It is hard for students to find jobs outside of the Pacific Northwest."

Depending on which students you talk to, the facilities here are either "bordering on beautiful" or "stark and bleak." Whatever the case, the law school is in "a new building with wireless technology" throughout and "very high-tech" gadgetry everywhere. "Superhumanly helpful and friendly research librarians" staff the law library, though "the lack of study space is a serious concern."

Life

"You can always get notes when you need them" at Seattle U Law; "However, there is still a healthy amount of competitiveness among students," who comprise "an interesting mix." "The right-out-of-undergrad students are obviously more competitive, but

CAROL COCHRAN, ASSISTANT DEAN FOR ADMISSION
901 12TH AVENUE, SULLIVAN HALL, P.O. BOX 222000, SEATTLE, WA 98122-1090
TEL: 206-398-4200 FAX: 206-398-4058
E-MAIL: LAWADMIS@SEATTLEU.EDU • WEBSITE: WWW.LAW.SEATTLEU.EDU

much more social too." Older students are "considerably more laid-back and have a completely different attitude." Students (and faculty) tend to lean to the left politically, though "the Federalist Society has a strong presence on campus." Few are particularly religious. "About the most religious this school gets is the Christmas tree and menorah that get put up during the holidays."

"Anyone with minimal social skills can make lifelong friends here," claims one student. "Nobody here is pretentious." "People at the school are tight-knit and supportive of one another." A host of on-campus events "promotes community interaction." However, there isn't much communication between the evening and the day programs. "For the night students who work full-time there aren't many opportunities to socialize with other students. Any socializing is done within the evening section and rarely are any day students involved."

"The school building itself is located just outside of downtown Seattle" in a lively neighborhood called Capitol Hill. "The school is in paradise," brags a 2L. "Seattle really is the greatest city in the world," beams another student. The Emerald City "is a great place to live for a variety of reasons, most notably the climate and the plethora of places to engage in outdoor activities."

Getting In

Admitted students at the 25th percentile have LSAT scores of 155 and GPAs of 3.3. Admitted students at the 75th percentile have LSAT scores of 161 and GPAs of 3.6. If you take the LSAT more than once, Seattle U Law "gives greater weight" to your highest score but also advises you to contextualize the difference in your scores in an addendum.

Clinical program required	No
Legal writing course requirement	Yes
Legal methods course requirement	No
Legal research course requirement	Yes
Moot court requirement	No
Public interest law requirement	No

ADMISSIONS

Selectivity Rating	82
# applications received	2,892
% applicants accepted	35
% acceptees attending	32
Average LSAT	158
LSAT Range	155–160
Average undergrad GPA	3.34
Application fee	$60
Regular application	Rolling, up to 3/1
Regular notification	Rolling
Early application program	No
Transfer students accepted	Yes
Evening division offered	Yes
Part-time accepted	Yes
CAS accepted	Yes

International Students

TOEFL required of international students	

FINANCIAL FACTS

Annual tuition	$38,502
Books and supplies	$903
Fees	$70
Room and board	$11,520
% first-year students receiving some sort of aid	96
% receiving some sort of aid	94
% of aid that is merit based	43
% receiving scholarships	57
Average grant	$5,818
Average loan	$36,229
Average total aid package	$44,252
Average debt	$102,350

EMPLOYMENT INFORMATION

Career Rating	81
Rate of placement (nine months out)	91
Average starting salary	$71,000
State for bar exam	WA, CA, OR, TX, IL
Pass rate for first-time bar	76

Employers Who Frequently Hire Grads

Perkins Coie, K and L Gates, Davis Wright Tremaine, Riddell Williams, Dorsey Whitney, Graham and Dunn and Miller Nash

Prominent Alumni

Mark McLaughlin, President and CEO, Verisign, Inc.; Judge Charles Johnson, Washington State Supreme Court; Sean Parnell, Governor of Alaska; Angela Rye, Executive Director and General Counsel to the Congressional Black Caucus; Lee Lambert, President, Shoreline Community College

Grads Employed by Field (%)

Academic (2)
Business/industry (23)
Government (14)
Judicial clerkship (5)
Private practice (47)
Public interest (8)

SETON HALL UNIVERSITY
SCHOOL OF LAW

INSTITUTIONAL INFORMATION

Public/private	Private
Affiliation	Roman Catholic
Student/faculty ratio	14:1
% faculty part-time	59
% faculty female	41
% faculty minority	14
Total faculty	140

SURVEY SAYS...

Diverse opinions accepted in classrooms, Great research resources, Great library staff, Abundant externship/internship/ clerkship opportunities

STUDENTS

Enrollment of law school	112
% male/female	53/47
% from out-of-state	40
% full-time	63
% minority	18
% international	1
# of countries represented	11
Average age of entering class	24

ACADEMICS

Academic Experience Rating	73
Profs interesting rating	81
Profs accessible rating	75
Hours of study per day	4.76

Academic Specialties

Intellectual Property, Health Law

Advanced Degrees Offered

JD, 3 years full-time, 4 years part-time; LLM, 1 year full-time, 2 years part-time; MSJ, 1 year full-time, 2 years part-time

Combined Degrees Offered

JD/MD, 6 years; MD/MSJ, 5 years; JD/MBA, JD/MADIR International Relations, 4 years; BS/JD, 3+3

Academics

Seton Hall University School of Law is a private, mid-size bastion of legal education, where you'll get an excellent foundation in both the theoretical and the practical aspects of law. Concentrations are available in health law and intellectual property. The Center for Social Justice is "a great resource" that provides "ample opportunities to get hands-on legal experience." It consists of five clinics, and it's among the most comprehensive clinical and pro bono programs in the region, which is quite impressive considering the competition. Opportunities to participate begin during first year. "Very cool study abroad trips" in places such as Cairo, Zanzibar, and Geneva are another nice perk.

The classroom environment at Seton Hall Law is "very conducive to discussion." "There aren't many horrible professors," and "Most rave about their professors." Students say the faculty is full of some of "the wittiest, most passionate, brilliant, best-looking legal minds in the country." "Each of the first-year professors I've had has been really impressive," reports a 1L. "Some of them are pretty idiosyncratic, which provides for some good entertainment outside the classroom, and behind their backs." The faculty is "very accessible," as well. Many students also find the administration "generally helpful." The support staff goes out of its way to accommodate and even anticipate student needs," says a 2L. "It is reliable and makes few mistakes." Other students charge, "The administration at this school is a tsunami of disorganization." We also hear a number of complaints about the legal writing program, which a 3L calls "abhorrent."

"There's very much an on-your-own-feel to finding a job," and some students with middling grades feel "left out in the cold." Nevertheless, most students are pretty satisfied with their job prospects. State and federal court houses "are very close," and "The school has a strong connection to the New Jersey judiciary, so a lot of students get judicial clerkships at graduation." The alumni network is notably loyal, and "Seton Hall Law has a good networking system set in place." "We have the run of New Jersey," boasts a 2L. However, students who want to work in Manhattan have only moderate success. "You can see the city from the library," observes a 1L, "but it seems more like a beautiful dream than a reality for most students." That's not necessarily a drawback, though. "There are plenty of pretty great law firms right here in Newark."

The facilities here are definitely above average. "There can be no debate about that." Not everyone loves "the modern-esque style of the interior," and "The classrooms are more functional than aesthetically pleasing," but upgrades are "constant," and students have few serious grievances. Technology is "particularly smooth." "The library is fantastic," declares a 3L. "It provides especially good electronic resources, even in obscure areas." "I love how everything is in one place," adds a 2L.

Life

The population of future attorneys at Seton Hall Law is reasonably diverse in pretty much every respect except geography. Students report that they have "serious drive, ambition, and talent." While the curve is "severe" and "things get a little competitive during finals time," the academic atmosphere is generally "friendly, fun, and helpful." "Student life at Seton Hall Law delicately balances that line between competition and team work," explains a 1L.

Ms. Gisele Joachim, Asst. Dean of Admissions and Financial Aid
One Newark Center, Newark, NJ 07102
Tel: 888-415-7271 Fax: 973-642-8876
E-Mail: admitme@shu.edu • Website: law.shu.edu

Outside of class, there are frequent seminars and tons of organizations and activities. Attitudes concerning the surrounding city of Newark are seriously mixed. Detractors call it "a notoriously terrible city" that's "lacking in sophistication and charm." "Newark may be the least desirable place to go to law school in the country," reckons a 2L. Other students insist that the Brick City's reputation is unwarranted. "Just because Newark looks crappy doesn't mean it's dangerous," they say. "I feel like a lot of the kids from New Jersey just hate Newark because they bring their prejudices with them," claims a 2L. "Downtown Newark is as safe—if not safer—than any block in NYC. It is a professionally developed area" full of courts and multiple government offices. Whatever the case, the school is "about two blocks from Penn Station, so it's easy enough to commute from a nice area." Despite the commuter ambience, students tell us that there's "a very vibrant social community" at Seton Hall Law. Events sponsored by the student bar association are "pretty awesome," and students "regularly" go out en masse in Hoboken or New York City.

Getting In

Overall, admitted students at the 25th percentile have LSAT scores around 155 and undergraduate GPAs of approximately 3.2. At the 75th percentile, LSAT scores are a little more than 160, and GPAs are around 3.6. Stats for the evening division are somewhat lower across the board.

Clinical program required	No
Legal writing course requirement	Yes
Legal methods course requirement	No
Legal research course requirement	Yes
Moot court requirement	Yes
Public interest law requirement	No

ADMISSIONS

Selectivity Rating	**87**
# applications received	4,169
% applicants accepted	32
% acceptees attending	26
Average LSAT	160
LSAT Range	158–161
Average undergrad GPA	3.48
Application fee	$65
Regular application	Rolling
Regular notification	Rolling
Early application program	No
Transfer students accepted	Yes
Evening division offered	Yes
Part-time accepted	Yes
CAS accepted	Yes

International Students

TOEFL recommended of international students

FINANCIAL FACTS

Annual tuition	$42,200
Books and supplies	$1,200
Fees	$780
Room and board	$13,050
Financial aid application deadline	4/1
% first-year students receiving some sort of aid	89
% receiving some sort of aid	91
% of aid that is merit based	95
% receiving scholarships	53
Average grant	$22,000
Average loan	$40,000
Average total aid package	$64,595
Average debt	$100,371

EMPLOYMENT INFORMATION

Career Rating	**86**
Rate of placement (nine months out)	87
Average starting salary	$91,035
State for bar exam	NJ, NY
Pass rate for first-time bar	91

Employers Who Frequently Hire Grads
Graduates are hired by law firms including the nation's most prestigious firms, federal and state government agencies, public interest organizations, and state and federal judges

Prominent Alumni
Michael Chagares, Judge on Third U.S. Circuit Court of Appeals; Christopher Christie, Governor of the State of New Jersey; Loria B. Yeadon, CEO HIP, Inc., Honeywell International; Peter Larson, Former Chair & CEO of Brunswick Corp.; Amy Park, Skadden, Arps, Slate, Meagher & Flom, LLP

Grads Employed by Field (%)
Academic (1)
Business/industry (11)
Government (6)
Judicial clerkship (34)
Military (1)
Private practice (41)
Public interest (2)

SOUTH TEXAS COLLEGE OF LAW

INSTITUTIONAL INFORMATION

Public/private	Private
Student/faculty ratio	21:1
% faculty part-time	45
% faculty female	35
% faculty minority	15
Total faculty	91

SURVEY SAYS...

Diverse opinions accepted in classrooms, Great research resources, Great library staff, Students love Houston, TX

STUDENTS

Enrollment of law school	1,305
% male/female	53/47
% from out-of-state	10
% full-time	77
% minority	28
# of countries represented	3
Average age of entering class	26

ACADEMICS

Academic Experience Rating	**70**
Profs interesting rating	76
Profs accessible rating	72

Academic Specialties

Advocacy, Transactional Skills, Corporate Compliance, Alternative Dispute Resolution

Combined Degrees Offered

Through a special cooperative program, students in the JD program at South Texas College of Law are eligible to apply for admission to the MBA program at Mays Business School, Texas A&M University. Upon acceptance into the MBA program, students are granted a leave of absence after their second year of law studies to attain their MBA and then return to South Texas to complete their JD degree.

Academics

Centrally located in the heart of downtown Houston, students at South Texas College of Law can take full advantage of the school's proximity to surrounding courtrooms and law firms, not to mention a "very strong network of alumni in practice." Second to none with 100 National Titles, "the pièce de résistance of STCL is its trial advocacy program." Students tell us that STCL "is a great school for practical lawyering skills and is a great choice for those students who wish to practice law in Texas." In addition, South Texas requires four hours of legal research and writing over the first two semesters, and students cannot say enough about the legal research and writing program. According to one 2L, "It is the reason we continually win 'Best Brief' in the moot court competitions, and it will leave you well prepared for your summer clerkships." Another student concludes, "If you want to learn how to practice law instead of just learning theory, South Texas is a great place to be."

"The excellent and accessible faculty makes it a great school, even for part-time students who mainly attend evenings and weekends," says one student. Approachable both in and out of the classroom, the faculty's "love" of teaching, "sense of humor," and support is clearly felt by students who claim that "it is not difficult to excel in class given the great learning environment." Students agree that practical teaching is an aspect of STCL that distinguishes it from other law schools. STCL's professors hail from a variety of backgrounds, and the vast majority of the adjunct faculty are sitting judges or practicing attorneys. According to students, "This gives us a great sense of what is 'really' happening in the legal field versus the theoretical or purely academic focus of other schools." A 3L adds that practical learning, "builds the best practicing lawyers of tomorrow," while another boldly attests, "Our school will teach you how to litigate the day after you pass the bar."

Students note, "The Admissions Office is very professional, knowledgeable, and helpful." Though, in the past students have noted, "The offices of the Registrar, Financial Aid, and Business Office are in three locations and don't seem to communicate well." Fortunately, students report that past headaches surrounding registration have been remedied due to the implementation of a campus-wide integrated database, resulting in a "smoother" process overall. While students admit that the administration has "streamlined many things lately, which goes to show that they listen to students," others argue, "They need to be more responsive to the feedback of their customers—the students."

With regard to facilities at South Texas, students unanimously agree that the "state-of-the-art library is beautiful [and] includes an extensive collection of sources." "It's superior in every respect, and there is never a wait in one of its many computer labs," adds one student. One of its most valued features is the "amazing terrace on the sixth floor," which "provides a relaxing setting in downtown Houston" and can also be utilized for "reading, eating, sunbathing—whatever your pleasure." The only complaint about the library is that it "closes too early!" However, the same enthusiasm doesn't extend to the subject of "deplorable" parking. Due to its downtown location, parking at STCL continues to be the most widely cited grievance.

ALICIA K. CRAMER, ASSISTANT DEAN OF ADMISSIONS
1303 SAN JACINTO STREET, HOUSTON, TX 77002
TEL: 713-646-1810 FAX: 713-646-2906
E-MAIL: ADMISSIONS@STCL.EDU • WEBSITE: WWW.STCL.EDU

Life

"The students in the part-time program are a great mix of experienced and right-out-of-college students, so class discussions are rich and varied," says one student. Diversity is reflected through classes that "explore all sides in a professional manner" and foster "creative and stimulating after class conversations with people that you may never have spoken to without the class discussion."

According to students, "While there is an inevitable degree of competition, [this] is not a cutthroat environment." Most here agree, "Students work together and rely on each other for assistance." While there is no shortage of studying at South Texas, "Students looking for a social atmosphere can definitely find it here." In fact, one student reports, "The students at my school like to party. I have no idea where everyone finds the time, but we do."

In addition, students declare they "have more student interest organizations than you can count—this provides an opportunity to learn about practice areas that aren't covered in the classroom...fantastic!" "Each month, at least one student organization throws a shindig on the terrace of the library," states one student. Usually well-attended, this type of event "breeds camaraderie among the student body. As a result, the law school atmosphere remains upbeat as we all move along the continuum together." Echoing this sentiment, one 2L muses, "I get a big sense of 'we're all in this together.' I only wish this prevailed post-graduation."

Getting In

Students are admitted primarily on the basis of their LSAT score and undergraduate GPA. A segment of each incoming class, however, is selected on the basis of additional factors, including personal accomplishments, recommendation letters, and leadership potential. Admitted students at the 25th percentile have an LSAT score of 150 and a GPA of 3.0. Admitted students at the 75th percentile have an LSAT score of 156 and a GPA of 3.5.

Clinical program required	No
Legal writing	
course requirement	Yes
Legal methods	
course requirement	Yes
Legal research	
course requirement	Yes
Moot court requirement	No
Public interest	
law requirement	No

ADMISSIONS

Selectivity Rating	74
# applications received	2,436
% applicants accepted	45
% acceptees attending	42
Average LSAT	154
LSAT Range	151–156
Average undergrad GPA	3.21
Application fee	$55
Regular notification	5/25
Early application program	No
Transfer students accepted	Yes
Evening division offered	Yes
Part-time accepted	Yes
CAS accepted	Yes

FINANCIAL FACTS

Annual tuition	$25,740
Books and supplies	$3,000
Fees	$600
Room and board	$13,500
Financial aid application	
deadline	5/1
% first-year students	
receiving some sort of aid	88
% receiving some sort of aid	87
% of aid that is merit based	4
% receiving scholarships	74
Average grant	$3,910
Average loan	$32,276
Average total aid package	$29,297
Average debt	$101,354

EMPLOYMENT INFORMATION

Career Rating	**77**	**Grads Employed by Field (%)**
Rate of placement (nine months out)	88	Academic (2)
Average starting salary	$86,047	Business/industry (19)
State for bar exam	TX	Government (12)
Pass rate for first-time bar	87	Judicial clerkship (3)
Employers Who Frequently Hire Grads		Private practice (62)
Large to mid-sized law firms, corporations,		Public interest (1)
and state and federal government entities		

SOUTHERN ILLINOIS UNIVERSITY
SCHOOL OF LAW

INSTITUTIONAL INFORMATION

Public/private	Public
Student/faculty ratio	12:1
% faculty part-time	15
% faculty female	49
% faculty minority	12
Total faculty	41

SURVEY SAYS..:
Diverse opinions accepted in classrooms, Great research resources, Great library staff

STUDENTS

Enrollment of law school	382
% male/female	62/38
% full-time	100
% minority	8
Average age of entering class	26

ACADEMICS

Academic Experience Rating	**78**
Profs interesting rating	77
Profs accessible rating	90
Hours of study per day	3.91

Academic Specialties

Health Law

Advanced Degrees Offered

JD, 3 years; MLS, 2 years; LLM, 2 years

Combined Degrees Offered

JD/MD, 6 years; JD/MBA, 4 years; JD/MPA, 4 years; JD/MAcc, 4 years; JD/MSW, JD/MSEd, JD/MDECE

Clinical program required	No
Legal writing	
course requirement	Yes
Legal methods	
course requirement	Yes
Legal research	
course requirement	Yes
Moot court requirement	No
Public interest	
law requirement	No

Academics

"If you are looking for a great legal education at a reasonable price, then Southern Illinois University School of Law is the place to go." Students across the board are quick to say that "Southern Illinois University School of Law is one of the most under-rated law schools in the nation." A true diamond in the rough, the program here remains a "best kept secret" with "an amazing faculty that truly wants you to succeed," an excellent legal writing and research program, and a practice-based curriculum—all for a price tag that cuts the cost of most legal educations in half. As one student attests, "For the price, I don't think there is a more affordable and solid legal education in the United States Period. Law school is outrageously expensive as it is, and it is refreshing to know you can still earn a quality education at the fraction of the price. Paying $60,000 for law school versus $120-plus makes a hell of a difference."

Affordability does not equal inferior legal training at SIU. In fact, students tell us, "The instruction is comparable to any Tier One school." The professors are "top-notch" and "very specialized in their respective fields." In addition, instructors "are extremely accessible with an open-door policy." "Each professor seems to really care and will take the time to develop a relationship with the student, if the student is willing to seek guidance." Though, as at any program, professors vary in talent and enthusiasm, students at SIU say "the brilliant faculty far outweigh the incompetent."

The greatest strength of the Southern Illinois University School of Law is "its focus on practical application of legal skills." In addition, "the legal writing and research program is magnificent" and offers "excellent legal writing and research training in the first year." In essence, "The faculty and administration understands that SIU Law is preparing graduates to be good practitioners, and the curriculum and instruction is organized accordingly."

The administration at SIU "runs the school at the peak of efficiency." "They are in constant contact with the students making sure that all of our needs are fulfilled. The Deans are easy to talk to so a student won't feel afraid to go to one of them with a problem." And the resources "are amazing!" "From the library, to career services, to opportunities for externships/internships/clerkships, everything is very helpful and a sure way to further your education." When it comes to the top brass student say, "the only office that lacks the school's welcoming and friendly demeanor is the law school's Registrar's Office," which students qualify as "not helpful."

Facilities may not be fancy, but students say it hardly matters given the low cost of tuition. "Honestly, I am sure that other schools have better aesthetics, but SIU has all of the necessary resources to learn the law." High on their wish lists? A "reputation" with more national cache.

Life

Hometown Carbondale "is a tight-knit community." "There is generally no escaping the smallness of it all, but the law school, as well as the larger university, provides many opportunities to 'play' so to speak, as a community." Students here "have a competitive bent, but they're willing to help each other on everything." "Although GPA is important, it isn't so important that we ruin relationships with fellow students or purposely hide information and techniques." In fact students here tend "to get along great." "We all have the mindset that we are in it together, while still remaining competitive. We are an amazingly diverse group of students with different backgrounds and interests, yet we all get along."

AKAMI MARIK, DIRECTOR OF ADMISSIONS & FINANCIAL AID
SIU SCHOOL OF LAW WELCOME CENTER, 1209 W. CHAUTAUQUA, MAILCODE 6811,
CARBONDALE, IL 62901
TEL: 618-453-8858 FAX: 618-453-8921
E-MAIL: LAWADMIT@SIU.EDU • WEBSITE: WWW.LAW.SIU.EDU

Others concur, "I was very pleased to find that the majority of the students here were happy to work together, share ideas, and help others understand. It is not at all the stereotypical law school cutthroat environment." "Everyone knows your name, which can be both a good and bad thing. It is sort of like high school, with quickly spreading rumors and a popular crowd."

Situated in Carbondale, a city of 26,000 tucked among the hills of the Illinois' southern corridor, SIU "is located in the most beautiful area of Illinois at the heart of wine country with numerous forests and lakes in the area." "The law school is within driving distance of outdoor recreation areas." One student captures the atmosphere as such: "An undergrad professor once said that living in Carbondale was like someone took Berkeley and dropped it in Arkansas. It's a great place to be a law student. Rent and food and entertainment are all very affordable. The town has a very outdoors[-y] and relaxed environment. It also tends to be a fairly liberal environment politically." "We are surrounded with bluegrass music, wineries, and country roads for miles." On the downside, students say the smallness of the town can become a bit pressing for some by the start of second year; "Cabin fever hits at the end of the first year. For those who work locally, the second year can feel like forever. No good shopping, and the nearest metropolitan area is St. Louis, about an hour and a half away!"

Getting In

Admitted candidates in 2010 had an average GPA of 3.3 and an average LSAT of 153. Though scores are important, personal statement, letters of recommendation, and resume are also considered.

ADMISSIONS

Selectivity Rating	76
# applications received	658
% applicants accepted	55
% acceptees attending	40
Average LSAT	153
LSAT Range	151–157
Average undergrad GPA	3.24
Application fee	$50
Regular application	Rolling, up to 4/1
Regular notification	Rolling
Early application program	No
Transfer students accepted	Yes
Evening division offered	No
Part-time accepted	No
CAS accepted	Yes

International Students
TOEFL required of international students

FINANCIAL FACTS

Annual tuition	
(in-state/out-of-state)	$11,574/ $29,925
Books and supplies	$1,150
Fees	$3,127
Room and board	$10,724
Financial aid application deadline	4/1
Average grant	$6,827
Average loan	$25,847
Average total aid package	$29,240
Average debt	$63,517

EMPLOYMENT INFORMATION

Career Rating	78
Rate of placement (nine months out)	82
Average starting salary	$45,000
State for bar exam	IL
Pass rate for first-time bar	91

Employers Who Frequently Hire Grads
Various Illinois state's attorney's offices, large and small law firms, public interest organizations

Prominent Alumni
William Enyart, State Adjutant General, IL Dept. of Military Affai; Karen Kendall, Partner, Heyl, Royster, Voelker & Allen; Hon. William E. Holdridge, Illinois Appellate Court, 3rd District; Hon. Leslie J. Gerbracht, District Court Judge, Las Animas County Court, Colorado; Hon. David R. Herndon, U.S. District Court Chief Judge, So. Dist. of IL

Grads Employed by Field (%)
Academic (4)
Business/industry (10)
Government (18)
Judicial clerkship (6)
Private practice (59)
Public interest (4)

SOUTHERN METHODIST UNIVERSITY
DEDMAN SCHOOL OF LAW

INSTITUTIONAL INFORMATION

Public/private	Private
Affiliation	Methodist
Student/faculty ratio	16:1
% faculty part-time	56
% faculty female	27
% faculty minority	10
Total faculty	159

SURVEY SAYS...
Beautiful campus, Students love Dallas, TX, Good social life

STUDENTS

% male/female	53/47
% from out-of-state	17
% full-time	67
% minority	23
# of countries represented	17
Average age of entering class	24

ACADEMICS

Academic Experience Rating	74
Profs interesting rating	75
Profs accessible rating	61
Hours of study per day	4.51

Advanced Degrees Offered
LLM (Taxation), 1 year; LLM (General), 1 year; LLM (for Foreign Law School Graduates), 1 year; SJD

Combined Degrees Offered
JD/MBA, 4 years; JD/MA (Economics), 4 years

Clinical program required	No
Legal writing course requirement	Yes
Legal methods course requirement	No
Legal research course requirement	Yes
Moot court requirement	Yes
Public interest law requirement	Yes

Academics

Boasting "a great program...great size...in a city with great opportunity," the Dedman School of Law at Southern Methodist University has it all. "The local legal community draws heavily from the law school, and with a little initiative, a law student can easily network with numerous lawyers and judges in the area and beyond." "Diverse course offerings" in "everything from the philosophical to the tediously practical" define the curriculum here, and "The legal clinics are absolutely amazing." Externships and scholarly journals are abundant. Students say there are plenty of opportunities to get involved: "We have consistently won national moot court and mock trial competitions over the past two years, and the school has a great Trial Advocacy program co-taught by practitioners and judges." A unique JD/MA program allows students to study economics as well as law, and students have the opportunity to study abroad in Oxford each summer.

Academic complaints often revolve around the legal writing program, which "needs a massive overhaul" and, "while informational, [can] feel more like fifth grade English in the way [it is] approached." Fortunately, the "very distinguished" yet "easily approachable" professors "are very receptive to students and concerned with [their] learning" and "make an effort to be available." They are "demanding of their students," but "interesting and entertaining in the classroom."

Professors "make the classroom experience fun," gushes one student. "My civil procedure exam was one of the funniest things I have ever read, with witty undercurrents and subtle political satire." Opinions of the administration vary considerably. Some students say the deans seem "distant at times, but whenever you need them, they're available and helpful." Others tell us that the administration "does not care about the students" and gripe about "bureaucratic inefficiencies."

Job prospects are very promising for SMU grads. Career Services is "actually concerned with helping you find a job." "Dallas is a wonderful market that pays salaries on par with New York, but the quality of life is so much better," according to students. "If you want to stay and practice in Dallas, you could not go to a better school." SMU's "exceptionally strong relationship with the Dallas legal market" provides an "extensive network of attorneys" "in every field imaginable." "The alums are very supportive and willing to help out." "A lot of doors are opened by attending the SMU Dedman School of Law, regardless of your class rank." "I was able to secure a six-figure job without being on law review or moot court," says a 3L. "There is definitely a huge hurdle" for students to face who do not want to practice in Texas, though.

The "gorgeous" campus is full of "very pretty, collegiate-looking brick buildings" and "nestled in one of the nicest, most affluent neighborhoods in the Dallas area." "The law school itself is further cloistered away from the rest of the university and, once inside, it is easy to forget you are sitting in the middle of a bustling metropolis." "Large oak trees provide shady walkways, and outdoor study places are ample." "The majority of classrooms are "very comfortable and accommodating," and the "nearly flawless" wireless signal is "strong in every corner of the law school." The library is "amazing," "both with regard to holdings and ease of use."

JILL NIKIRK, DIRECTOR OF ADMISSIONS
P.O. BOX 750110, DALLAS, TX 75275-0110
TEL: 214-768-2550 FAX: 214-768-2549
E-MAIL: LAWADMIT@SMU.EDU • WEBSITE: WWW.LAW.SMU.EDU

Life

"Students in the full-time day program tend to be younger—either directly out of their undergraduate program or with only a year or two of work experience. Nevertheless, there are still many full-time students in their thirties or older." Most are "Texas natives," and all are "fun, attractive, and smart." Some students are "cooperative, collegial, and very supportive of one another." Others are "very competitive." "There are definitely a few trust fund kids, but a lot of us are living off student loans as well," says one student. "The parking garage does boast an unusual concentration of BMWs and Hummers," agrees a 2L. "But as a non-Texan who shares a beat-up Honda with my wife, I've never felt out of place." "Political views run the gamut, but the large majority of students are tolerant of opposing views." SMU is also "remarkably GLBT-friendly."

Regarding social events on campus, students say "There's a club for everyone, whether you're a gun-toting Second Amendment crusader or a die-hard liberal." "The students put together a lot of fun activities," ranging from happy hours to baseball games to tailgating events. "The highlight of everyone's week is Bar Review where the Student Bar Association gets drink specials at a different local bar every Friday." There's also "a picnic/sports spectacular every semester." SMU's ritzy location is "great" in terms of safety but "can make finding student housing right next to school virtually impossible." Beyond the neighborhood surrounding campus, "Big D" is one of the liveliest cities in the South and "a fun place to live." "You get a great all-around legal education and have the resources of the Dallas–Fort Worth Metroplex right at your doorstep."

Getting In

For the fall 2009 entering class the median LSAT score among applicants to the full-time program was 164 and the median GPA was 3.76. Applicants to the part-time evening program posted slightly lower numbers: the median GPA was 3.62 and the median LSAT score was 159.

ADMISSIONS

Selectivity Rating	96
# applications received	2,790
% applicants accepted	22
% acceptees attending	38
Median LSAT	164
LSAT Range	157–166
Median GPA	3.76
Application fee	$75
Regular application	Rolling, up to 4/1
Regular notification	5/15
Early application program	Yes
Early application deadline	11/1
Early application notification	1/31
Transfer students accepted	Yes
Evening division offered	Yes
Part-time accepted	Yes
CAS accepted	Yes

FINANCIAL FACTS

Annual tuition	$35,745
Books and supplies	$1,800
Fees	$4,441
Room and board	$14,500
Financial aid application deadline	6/1
% first-year students receiving some sort of aid	50
% of aid that is merit based	100
Average loan	$28,508

EMPLOYMENT INFORMATION

Career Rating	89
Rate of placement (nine months out)	95
Average starting salary	$92,775
State for bar exam	TX
Pass rate for first-time bar	83

Employers Who Frequently Hire Grads
Akin, Gump, Strauss, Hauer, & Feld; Baker, Botts, Fulbright, & Jaworski; Haynes & Boone; Jones, Day, Reavis, & Pogue; Vinson & Elkins; Locke, Liddell, Thompson, & Knight; Dallas County district attorney's office; TX Supreme Court

Prominent Alumni
Michael Boone, founding partner, Haynes & Boone; Bill Hutchison, President, Hutchison Oil & Gas; Angela Braley, CEO, WellPoint; Edward B. Rust Jr., Chairman & CEO, State Farm Insurance; David B. Dillon, CEO and Chairman, The Kroger Company

Grads Employed by Field (%)
Academic (1)
Business/industry (21)
Government (6)
Judicial clerkship (5)
Private practice (66)
Public interest (2)

SOUTHERN UNIVERSITY
LAW CENTER

INSTITUTIONAL INFORMATION

Public/private	Public
Student/faculty ratio	14:1
% faculty part-time	4
% faculty female	37
% faculty minority	61
Total faculty	41

SURVEY SAYS...

Diverse opinions accepted in classrooms, Great research resources, Great library staff, Good social life

STUDENTS

Enrollment of law school	480
% male/female	45/55
% from out-of-state	15
% full-time	86
% minority	60
# of countries represented	3
Average age of entering class	27

ACADEMICS

Academic Experience Rating	**71**
Profs interesting rating	71
Profs accessible rating	61
Hours of study per day	4.75

Academic Specialties
Civil Procedure, Commercial, Criminal, Environmental, Government Services, Taxation, Intellectual Property

Combined Degrees Offered
JD/MPA, 4 years

Clinical program required	No
Legal writing	
course requirement	Yes
Legal methods	
course requirement	No
Legal research	
course requirement	Yes
Moot court requirement	No
Public interest	
law requirement	No

Academics

With roughly 600 full-time and part-time students, Southern University Law Center is "small and personable." "I don't feel like just another number at my school," says a 1L. "You feel that the people around you want you to be successful." SULC is also "ridiculously affordable." "While others will be coming out of law school hundred of thousands of dollars in debt, Southern grads will have debt that is approximately one fifth of the cost." Additional perks here include a decently broad selection of courses and six clinics that provide hands-on experience with the realities of practicing law for a very good percentage of students. If you want to pursue both a JD and MPA, the school offers a joint-degree program in cooperation with Southern's Nelson Mandela School of Public Policy and Urban Affairs. There's also a study abroad program in London, in which students take courses in international law.

Louisiana is a civil law jurisdiction (in the tradition of France and Continental Europe), while law in every other state is based on the common law tradition (of England). While SULC students learn both, the required curriculum focuses on civil law both substantively and procedurally. If you plan to practice in the Pelican State, Southern is a great choice. The "wealth of alums" doesn't hurt when it comes to finding a job, either. However, if you want to practice in another state, learning Louisiana's unique system of law and trying to apply it to another state's bar exam won't be the easiest thing in the world.

"Some profs can be very intimidating," but the full-time faculty is full of "sincere, challenging, intelligent people" who are "downright awesome." The faculty is notoriously approachable as well. Most professors are "always willing to help." "I have a great amount of respect for ninety percent of my professors," explains a 2L. "I feel that all of them have been knowledgeable in the subject matter." The "generally excellent" part-time program tends to have more adjunct professors. They're more of a mixed bag. "Some of the evening professors are practicing attorneys during the day and are not as accessible or as devoted as the full-time day professors." Students offer considerable praise for the "very professional" administration. Deans are "approachable and available," and they "work diligently in their efforts to help the students succeed" and to "know who their students are." Some students tell us that the financial aid process can be a "nightmare," though. The legal writing program is another complaint. Students say that it "could use a lot of improvement." SULC's "somewhat new facilities" are "very poorly maintained." Otherwise, they are "really good" and "very hospitable." Classrooms have wireless Internet and plenty of electrical outlets. The library is "stocked with great resource materials."

Life

"This school is probably the most diverse school in the country in terms of the student body," gushes a 2L. SULC is a historically black institution, and some sixty percent of the students are African American. Students come here "from all over the country," and they "have very interesting backgrounds." The range of ages is vast as well.

VELMA E. WILKERSON, COORDINATOR OF ADMISSION
A.A. LENOIR HALL, P.O. BOX 9294, 2 ROOSEVELT STEPTOE STREET, BATON ROUGE, LA 70813
TEL: 225-771-4976 FAX: 225-771-2121
E-MAIL: ADMISSION@SULC.EDU • WEBSITE: WWW.SULC.EDU

"Southern charm is alive and well at SULC." A "kind and friendly" "family atmosphere" reigns supreme, and "a strong sense of camaraderie and support is evident in every aspect." "Some people are competitive," says a 1L, "but I don't get that extremely competitive vibe from Southern." "It's a smaller law school," explains a 2L, "which allows students to work more cooperatively, instead of against each other as at most law schools." Most everyone "goes out of their way to help." The biggest social divide is probably between the day program, which is generally composed of younger students, and the evening program, which is "mostly older professionals."

During the school day, "the school regularly has speakers and attorneys come in during the noon hour to give practical advice on the practice of law." Students are split when it comes to life beyond the confines of campus. Some tell us that Baton Rouge—the state capital and the second largest city in Louisiana—is a student's Shangri-la, especially if you like music and food. Baton Rouge is home to unique art and culture, tons of festivals, and mouthwatering cuisine of every kind. When students take a break from hitting the books, a good number of bars and clubs and a raging live music scene keep life interesting. Other students aren't feeling the cultural love, though. "The main chances for socialization seem to be at a bar or a church," suggests a 2L. "What if you don't drink or believe?"

Getting In

Admitted students at the 25th percentile have LSAT scores around 143 and GPAs in the 2.6 range. Admitted students at the 75th percentile have LSAT scores of 149 or so and GPAs of around 3.2.

ADMISSIONS

Selectivity Rating	**84**
# applications received	994
% applicants accepted	31
% acceptees attending	58
Average LSAT	147
LSAT Range	144–151
Average undergrad GPA	2.84
Application fee	$25
Regular notification	Rolling
Early application program	No
Transfer students accepted	Yes
Evening division offered	Yes
Part-time accepted	Yes
CAS accepted	Yes

International Students
TOEFL recommended of international students

FINANCIAL FACTS

Annual tuition	
(in-state/out-of-state)	$6,676/
	$11,276
Books and supplies	$5,581
Room and board	$8,727
Financial aid application	
deadline	4/15
% first-year students	
receiving some sort of aid	86
% of aid that is merit based	20
% receiving scholarships	20
Average grant	$7,000
Average total aid package	$18,500

EMPLOYMENT INFORMATION

Career Rating	72	**Grads Employed by Field (%)**
State for bar exam	LA, FL, GA, IL, TX	Academic (1)
Pass rate for first-time bar	61	Business/industry (5)
		Government (15)
		Judicial clerkship (6)
		Private practice (37)
		Public interest (7)

SOUTHWESTERN LAW SCHOOL

INSTITUTIONAL INFORMATION

Public/private	Private
Student/faculty ratio	14:1
% faculty part-time	29
% faculty female	40
% faculty minority	22
Total faculty	95

SURVEY SAYS...

Diverse opinions accepted in classrooms, Great research resources, Great library staff, Beautiful campus

STUDENTS

Enrollment of law school	1,146
% male/female	46/54
% from out-of-state	15
% full-time	68
% minority	34
% international	1
# of countries represented	10
Average age of entering class	26

ACADEMICS

Academic Experience Rating	78
Profs interesting rating	74
Profs accessible rating	71
Hours of study per day	4.42

Academic Specialties

Civil Procedure, Commercial, Constitutional, Corporation Securities, Criminal, Environmental, Government Services, Human Rights, International, Labor, Legal History, Legal Philosophy, Property, Intellectual Property, Entertainment & Media Law

Advanced Degrees Offered

In addition to the JD, Southwestern offers the first LLM in Entertainment and Media Law and an individualized LLM program, 1 year full-time, 2 years part-time

Combined Degrees Offered

JD/MBA, JD/Master of Arts in Management, JD/MA in Conflict Resolution, Negotiation, and Peace

Academics

Large, private, and independent Southwestern Law School boasts an "emphasis on practical skills" and an impressive array of bells and whistles. In addition to your standard full-time day and part-time evening programs, there's a very intensive two-year program that features small classes and integrates plenty of real-world training. There's also a part-time day program that helps nontraditional students juggle the demands of work, family, and school. A "broad" and "ever-increasing" range of courses includes summer law programs in Argentina, Canada, England, and Mexico. Clinics are available in immigration law, street law, and children's rights. "The externships are amazing and very available to all class ranks." There's a JD/MBA program allied with the Drucker Graduate School of Management. If you are interested in entertainment and media law, Southwestern is home to a huge contingent of professors who specialize in that area, and the school maintains impressive connections "within the entertainment industry." Another perk is Southwestern's unique "three-track approach" to legal writing. As a 1L, you can choose from specialized writing programs in trial practice, negotiation, or appellate advocacy. While Southwestern sort of exists in the shadow of other law schools in the local area with national reputations, students tell us that they are happy with their employment prospects. Career Services has "tons of resources," they say, and Southwestern has a "huge alumni network," "especially in the Los Angeles area."

The faculty is composed of "an array of ages, ethnicities, and eccentricities." There are "some really outstanding teachers" here "who could not be more dedicated to their craft," and the faculty as a whole is "helpful and accommodating." They "genuinely care about your success in law school." "They are engaging and really care about what each student takes away from their class," explains a 3L. "The school is attempting to teach us to be good lawyers," explains a 1L, "with less emphasis on maintaining the 'hide-the-ball' pedagogy of the Socratic Method." There's the stray "incompetent" prof here, though, and some of the older ones are "standard fare." "Most professors are available to students on a regular basis" once class ends. "I was surprised by the support from teachers and access to them outside of the classroom," reports a 1L. "This institution is committed to a student-first ideology." Some students say that the administration "treats everyone like an individual, not just another customer." Others say that there is "too much bureaucracy, in all aspects."

The facilities at Southwestern are within easy commuting distance to the downtown district of Los Angeles. Students say they are "world-class." The crown jewel is a legendary, enormous, and very distinctive Art Deco building. It used to be a fancy department store and now it is listed on the National Register of Historic Places. "The administration clearly takes pride in the campus upkeep." "Everything is new and high-tech." Classrooms are "really nice." "The library is beautiful and basically kicks the ass out of the other law school libraries in Los Angeles," pronounces a 1L. There are also ample study areas, terraces with sweeping city views, and a gigantic fitness center for student use.

LISA GEAR, ASSISTANT DEAN FOR ADMISSIONS
3050 WILSHIRE BOULEVARD, LOS ANGELES, CA 90010-1106
TEL: 213-738-6717 FAX: 213-383-1688
E-MAIL: ADMISSIONS@SWLAW.EDU • WEBSITE: WWW.SWLAW.EDU

Life

By all accounts, diversity is "great" at Southwestern in every way. Students come here from pretty much every state and all walks of life. Ethnic minorities constitute about a third of the population. Roughly two-thirds of the students have either previous work experience or some kind of advanced degree already. The academic atmosphere is "very professional and collegiate." "It's very cooperatively competitive," explains a 3L. "Everyone wants to do better than the next person but is always willing to help the next person out." "There's a lot of mentoring that goes on at Southwestern" between 1Ls and upper-division students as well.

Southwestern's campus is "an oasis in seedy Koreatown." Some students contend that social life is pretty dismal. "There is a social disconnect at the school," laments a 1L. "Clubs are not really active and there is a commuter atmosphere." Other students strongly disagree. According to them, Southwestern is "very social." "Everyone is friendly with each other, which has made for a pleasant experience," declares a 3L. "I've created some bonds with certain students that I will cherish forever." Whatever the case, the inexhaustible sprawl of the metropolitan Los Angeles area offers something for every taste and predilection imaginable.

Getting In

Enrolled full-time students at the 25th percentile have LSAT scores in the low 150s and GPAs around 3.2. Enrolled students at the 75th percentile have LSAT scores around 158 and GPAs a little over 3.5. If you enroll in the two-year program, classes start in mid-summer.

Building, 4–4.5 years (longer if part-time). Dual-degree programs are offered in collaboration with The Drucker Graduate School of Management and California State University Dominguez Hills.

Clinical program required	No
Legal writing course requirement	Yes
Legal methods course requirement	Yes
Legal research course requirement	Yes
Moot court requirement	Yes
Public interest law requirement	No

ADMISSIONS

Selectivity Rating	80
# applications received	3,383
% applicants accepted	29
% acceptees attending	30
Average LSAT	156
LSAT Range	153–158
Average undergrad GPA	3.43
Application fee	$60
Regular application	Rolling, up to 6/30
Regular notification	Rolling
Early application program	No
Transfer students accepted	Yes
Evening division offered	Yes
Part-time accepted	Yes
CAS accepted	Yes

FINANCIAL FACTS

Annual tuition	$42,000
Part-time tuition	$28,000
Books and supplies	$1,250
Fees	$200
Room and board	$19,620
Financial aid application deadline	6/1
% first-year students receiving some sort of aid	88
% receiving some sort of aid	92
% of aid that is merit based	22
% receiving scholarships	38
Average grant	$11,647
Average loan	$48,056
Average total aid package	$53,182
Average debt	$136,000

EMPLOYMENT INFORMATION

Career Rating	83
Rate of placement (nine months out)	94
Average starting salary	$75,000
State for bar exam	CA, NY, NV, OR, AZ
Pass rate for first-time bar	71

Employers Who Frequently Hire Grads

Gibson, Dunn, & Crutcher; Lewis Brisbois; O'Melveny & Meyers; Sedgwick Detert; Bonne Bridges; Gilbert Kelly; Lynberg & Watkins; IRS; Los Angeles public defender's office; Los Angeles district attorney's office

Prominent Alumni

Tom Bradley, L.A. mayor for 20 years; Stanley Mosk, longest serving CA Supreme Court justice; Hon. Vaino Spencer, first American American female judge in CA, third in U.S.; Gordon Smith, former senator; Daniel Petrocelli, won O.J. Simpson civil trial

Grads Employed by Field (%)

Academic (2)
Business/industry (27)
Government (8)
Judicial clerkship (1)
Military (1)
Private practice (56)
Public interest (5)

ST. JOHN'S UNIVERSITY
SCHOOL OF LAW

INSTITUTIONAL INFORMATION
Public/private	Private
Affiliation	Roman Catholic
Student/faculty ratio	15:1

SURVEY SAYS...
Diverse opinions accepted in classrooms, Great research resources, Great library staff, Abundant externship/internship/clerkship opportunities

STUDENTS
Enrollment of law school	341
% male/female	59/41
% full-time	78
% minority	26
Average age of entering class	23

ACADEMICS
Academic Experience Rating	73
Profs interesting rating	76
Profs accessible rating	66
Hours of study per day	4.67

Advanced Degrees Offered
JD, 3 years full-time day, 4 years part-time evening; LLM in Bankruptcy, 1 year full-time, 2–3 years part-time; LLM in U.S. Legal Studies for Foreign Lawyers, 1 year full-time, 2–4 years part-time

Combined Degrees Offered
JD/MBA; JD/MA(MS); BA(BS)/JD; JD/LLM

Clinical program required	No
Legal writing course requirement	Yes
Legal methods course requirement	Yes
Legal research course requirement	Yes
Moot court requirement	Yes
Public interest law requirement	No

Academics

St. John's University School of Law "places an emphasis on how to actually become a lawyer, not an academic" and boasts a bar-passage rate that's consistently higher than the Empire State's overall percentage. St. John's also comes equipped with an impressive array of academic bells and whistles. "There are very strong programs in bankruptcy and labor and employment law." The host of clinics is "a big draw." Highlights include securities arbitration, and a couple interesting programs involving immigration rights. There's also "a wide range of courses," "numerous journals and organizations," and an "outstanding" speaker series.

"There are some really incredible professors and some really miserable professors" at St. John's Law. "There's no in-between." Students say that most fall in the incredible category, though. They "do an outstanding job of mixing the Socratic Method while making clear the purpose of each class." "Our professors make the law real," declares a 1L. "They make sure we know the legal theories, but they also make sure we know why the theories matter and how we'll use those theories in practice to advocate for our clients." Full-time professors are "always around and accessible." "They eat breakfast and lunch in the cafe and sit with students to chat with them." Adjuncts are often a very different story. "Meeting with adjunct professors without an office on campus can be so difficult to arrange, it's headache-inducing," grumbles a 2L. Some students say that the top brass takes "an active, positive role in students' lives." "The dean makes an effort to know the name of every student in the school," they say. Other students contend that bureaucracy is "nightmarish," particularly if you're unlucky enough to face anyone outside the law school. "I dread having to deal with the general university's administrators," notes a 2L.

Without question, St. John's has a "broad" and "engaged" alumni network, which is "invaluable, especially for students looking to practice in the New York area." "The alumni provide you with positions or connections in any way they can," beams a 1L. "Alumni give their time to a significant number of the school's activities, such as panels and mock interview programs." "Career Services could be better," though and students seeking to work in big firms face grimly stiff competition from the gaggle of big-name schools in the region. Networking with loyal alums is paramount because "few St. John's students" land plum jobs through traditional on-campus interviews.

The larger university is quiet by New York City standards. Although "the building is pretty run down," there's ample space and the facilities are "very modern." "The library is fantastic." "Classrooms are comfortable," but occasionally crowded. Climate control can be a problem. "The environmental control system cannot regulate the temperature properly," explains a 3L, "so you need to come dressed prepared for anything as each room has the potential to range from Arctic to Sahara."

ROBERT M. HARRISON, ASSISTANT DEAN FOR ADMISSIONS
8000 UTOPIA PARKWAY, QUEENS, NY 11439
TEL: 718-990-6474 FAX: 718-990-2526
E-MAIL: LAWINFO@STJOHNS.EDU • WEBSITE: WWW.LAW.STJOHNS.EDU

Life

Most students are from New York, or at least from the Northeast, and ethnic diversity is laudable. Students at St. John's Law describe themselves as "type-A personalities with something to prove." They have "a sense that they will only get ahead through hard work and actually learning how to practice the law." Nevertheless, they're "very pleasant to be around." "The student body is respectful of one another and welcoming to everyone," promises a 1L. "There are only a few people in every year who are competitive," adds a 2L, "and they are usually ridiculed." Note, however, that the grading curve here is on the unforgiving side, "so your average grades will be lower than that at other law schools."

The location "in the middle of nowhere Queens" hinders the social scene somewhat. The bright lights of Manhattan are a very reasonable train ride away, but "It can sometimes be inconvenient to get to the city from here." "The Queens campus is a crappy location if you don't have a car," flatly advises a 1L. Socially unhappy commuters say, "Most clubs are little more than resume boosters, and few of them hold more than one or two meetings per semester." "Sometimes the student body does not have the same sense of family that other law schools possess." However, a large number of students live on campus or in the "affordable surrounding neighborhoods," and they report a much higher level of "social life and school spirit." "There are some good restaurants within walking distance," and it's common for students to "meet at the bars for a drink after studying." "The school's community is what you make of it," reflects a 3L. "Opportunities abound, but you have to make an effort to find them."

Getting In

Admitted students at the 25th percentile have LSAT scores in the mid 150s and undergraduate GPAs close to 3.2. At the 75th percentile, LSAT scores are a little more than 160, and GPAs are around 3.7.

ADMISSIONS

Selectivity Rating	86
# applications received	4,510
% applicants accepted	35
% acceptees attending	21
Average LSAT	161
LSAT Range	156–162
Average undergrad GPA	3.55
Application fee	$60
Regular application	Rolling
Regular notification	Rolling
Early application program	No
Transfer students accepted	Yes
Evening division offered	Yes
Part-time accepted	Yes
CAS accepted	Yes

FINANCIAL FACTS

Annual tuition	$44,280
Books and supplies	$1,000
Room and board	$16,900
Financial aid application deadline	2/1
% first-year students receiving some sort of aid	93
% receiving some sort of aid	91
% of aid that is merit based	25
% receiving scholarships	46
Average grant	$28,030
Average loan	$45,422
Average total aid package	$52,935
Average debt	$112,365

EMPLOYMENT INFORMATION

Career Rating	83	**Employers Who Frequently Hire Grads**
Rate of placement (nine months out)	89	Many private law firms, corporations, gov-
Average starting salary	$108,225	ernmental agencies and judges hire St.
State for bar exam	NY	John's graduates
Pass rate for first-time bar	87	

ST. THOMAS UNIVERSITY
SCHOOL OF LAW

INSTITUTIONAL INFORMATION

Public/private	Private
Affiliation	Roman Catholic
Student/faculty ratio	18:1
% faculty part-time	46
% faculty female	45
% faculty minority	20
Total faculty	40

SURVEY SAYS...
*Great research resources,
Beautiful campus*

STUDENTS

Enrollment of law school	665
% male/female	53/47
% from out-of-state	20
% full-time	100
% minority	44
% international	2
# of countries represented	9
Average age of entering class	25

ACADEMICS

Academic Experience Rating	**79**
Profs interesting rating	82
Profs accessible rating	89
Hours of study per day	5.18

Academic Specialties
Human Rights

Advanced Degrees Offered
LLM in Intercultural Human Rights, 1 year; JSD in Intercultural Human Rights, 2–5 years

Combined Degrees Offered
JD/MS in Marriage & Family Counseling, 3 years; JD/MS in Sports Administration, 3 years; JD/MBA in Sports Administration, 3 years; JD/MBA in Accounting, 3 years; JD/MBA in International Business, 3 years; JD/BA, 3+3, 6 years; JD/BS in Environmental Justice, 3 years

Academics

The Catholic-affiliated, "cozy, and community-oriented" St. Thomas University School of Law in Miami is a "smaller law school" offering a "personal touch," lots of "attention," and a "practice-driven approach." The curriculum is very heavy on lawyering skills and hands-on training. "There is a practicum component in almost every class, where they make you do real-life work—writing motions, memos, letters, interviewing fake clients, etc.," explains a 1L. Every course also includes an ethics element. A wide variety of clinical courses and externships placements allow students to gain practical experience in bankruptcy law, criminal law, appellate litigation, immigration law, and much else. Interns who land spots in the prestigious Pax Romana Clinic get to follow major policy issues at the United Nations in New York City. The requirement that all students must complete forty hours of pro bono work during their 2L and 3L years also enhances practical skills. Other highlights here include two law reviews, a notable tax law program, and joint-degrees in sports administration, business, and marriage and family counseling. There's also a "great" summer program in Spain with a curriculum focused primarily on international law.

"Professors, for the most part, are very helpful and friendly." "Classes are interactive and fun," reports a 1L. "You really do learn a lot." Outside of class, professors are "dedicated to helping the students," and faculty approachability is reportedly "phenomenal." "You are not just a number." You'll frequently see faculty members "hanging out at school with the students." "The total access I have to professors is second to none," gushes a 2L. "You can talk to all the professors for as long as you need, and as many times as you need." The "visible," "magnificent" administration is "always available and willing to assist with any issue you may have" as well. Students do have complaints about the financial aid staff, though. To address this issue, St. Thomas Law has now hired a full time financial aid advisor, starting in fall 2011. "Getting financial aid is a mission every semester," advises a 3L. Also, "classrooms are cold and bare with very little personality." The library is a little on the small side, too. On the upside, "the research facilities are excellent," and "the librarians are extreme knowledgeable."

Despite the relative newness of STU Law (it was established in 1984), students tell us that the alumni base is loyal and "very strong." The school isn't really well-known beyond South Florida, though, and some students complain that "The school needs more focus on...career placement." The vast majority of recent grads stay in the immediate area or at least in the Sunshine State. About three-quarters of all graduates enter private practice or find jobs in the corporate world upon graduation.

Life

"This law school is very diverse." In fact, it's one of the most ethnically diverse bastions of legal education in the country. There is a very high Latino student enrollment. There's also "a substantial number of second-career types as well as attorneys from Latin American and other countries who are revalidating their degrees" in the United States. "About half of the student body came to St. Thomas via the 'traditional' student method," estimates a 1L, "and the other half is a little older and brings a wide range of practical understandings. This dichotomy leads to some truly enlightening classroom discussions." Some students tell us, "There is a good deal of competition" academically. Others say that students "join forces" and share notes regularly and copiously at exam time.

STU Law is situated on the main campus of the larger university in a suburb between Fort Lauderdale and Miami. Some students tell us that the location is "not so good." The cost of living in these parts isn't the cheapest, either. On the plus side, the weather in South Florida is "very relaxing" virtually year-round, and the Floridian campus boasts palm trees, ponds, and tennis courts. The area also offers tons of activities and nightlife. Bars, restaurants, shopping, and cuisine are all world-class and, of course, "you always have the beaches." Socially, there are "enough student organizations to find something you like." This law school is a pretty tight-knit place, too. "Close relationships" are easily formed, and students know pretty much everyone in their class year. Also, "The school design invites socialization." "There is a breezeway always full of students talking and hanging out, sharing thoughts, and talking about the professors and classes."

Getting In

Enrolled students at the 25th percentile have LSAT scores in the high 140s and grade point averages in the 2.9 range. At the 75th percentile, LSAT scores are in the low 150s and GPAs are a little under 3.4.

Clinical program required	Yes
Legal writing course requirement	Yes
Legal methods course requirement	Yes
Legal research course requirement	Yes
Moot court requirement	Yes
Public interest law requirement	Yes

ADMISSIONS

Selectivity Rating	68
# applications received	2,628
% applicants accepted	40
% acceptees attending	22
Average LSAT	149
LSAT Range	147–151
Average undergrad GPA	3.08
Application fee	$60
Regular application	Rolling, up to 6/1
Regular notification	Rolling
Early application program	No
Transfer students accepted	Yes
Evening division offered	No
Part-time accepted	No
CAS accepted	Yes

International Students

TOEFL recommended of international students	

FINANCIAL FACTS

Annual tuition	$25,340
Books and supplies	$1,000
Fees	$1,240
Room and board (on/off campus)	$10,341/ $10,575
Financial aid application deadline	4/1
% first-year students receiving some sort of aid	95
% receiving some sort of aid	98
% of aid that is merit based	30
% receiving scholarships	39
Average grant	$14,000
Average loan	$20,500
Average total aid package	$31,250
Average debt	$82,000

EMPLOYMENT INFORMATION

Career Rating	76
Rate of placement (nine months out)	71
Average starting salary	$54,292
State for bar exam	FL, NY, GA, CA
Pass rate for first-time bar	73

Employers Who Frequently Hire Grads

Private law firms of all sizes; government agencies, including the U.S. Department of Justice, Florida State Attorney's Office, Prosecutors and Public Defender's Offices, public interest organizations and corporations

Prominent Alumni

Brett Barfield, Partner, Holland & Knight; Mark Romance, Partner, Richman Greer; Representative J.C. Planas, Florida House of Representatives; The Honorable Margaret T. Courtney, 13th Judicial Circuit, FL; The Honorable Pedro Dijols, 17th Judicial Circuit, FL

Grads Employed by Field (%)

Academic (2)
Business/industry (15)
Government (17)
Judicial clerkship (3)
Private practice (53)
Public interest (10)

STANFORD UNIVERSITY
SCHOOL OF LAW

INSTITUTIONAL INFORMATION

Public/private	Private
Student/faculty ratio	8:1
% faculty female	33
% faculty minority	15
Total faculty	52

SURVEY SAYS...

Great research resources,
Great library staff

STUDENTS

Enrollment of law school	571
% male/female	55/45
% full-time	100
% minority	35
Average age of entering class	25

ACADEMICS

Academic Experience Rating	99
Profs interesting rating	99
Profs accessible rating	93
Hours of study per day	4.06

Academic Specialties

Civil Procedure, Commercial, Constitutional, Corporation Securities, Criminal, Environmental, Government Services, Human Rights, International, Labor, Legal History, Legal Philosophy, Property, Taxation, Intellectual Property. We offer courses on the above topics, but no specializations/ concentrations.

Advanced Degrees Offered

MLS, 1 year; JSM, 1 year; LLM, 1 year; JSD, 4 years

Combined Degrees Offered

JD/MBA, 3.3–4 years; JD/MA, 3 years; JD/PhD, 6 years

Academics

"People are happy" at Stanford Law School, and why wouldn't they be? There are "tons of programs," an array of specialized centers, and a couple dozen joint-degree options. The ten clinics here include a Supreme Court litigation clinic and a cyber law clinic, just to list a couple. "The resources available to us at Stanford are fantastic, and sometimes unbelievable," gushes a 2L. The "amazingly brilliant" and "diverse" faculty is "a great mix of practically minded and experienced—professors and wild-minded theorists." Professors are "incredible lecturers and easy to approach outside of the classroom." "I have yet to meet a professor who is not only doing something amazing but is completely approachable and dying to help us get jobs and do research," gloats a 2L. Moreover, Stanford is "so small that everything is very easy to do." "All of my seminars have had fewer than ten people," gloats a 2L. "The university as a whole has a lot of red tape," but the law school's administration is "very receptive" and accessible at almost every level. "It's the opposite of the 'factory' feeling at large professional schools," explains a 3L. "If you want to do something new or nontraditional, just ask. Usually you can work something out."

The Stanford campus is "sprawling" and "beautiful," with "acres of rolling green hills for hiking, and palm trees everywhere." "The law school is hideous from the outside but, inside, it's quite nice." The library is a world-class research facility "and all law students have twenty-four-hour access to study there." "I can't study in any other university library," admits a comfortable 1L, "because I have become too accustomed to the law school's Aeron chairs."

A few students call Career Services "underwhelming," but "Pretty much everyone can get a firm job if they want one." They can get that job anywhere in the country, too. Less than fifty percent of all newly minted Stanford Law grads take jobs in California. Stanford is also "seriously committed to public interest law," and the "great loan repayment program" here is arguably the best in the country. Also worth noting is the impressive historical fact that well more than 100 Stanford law graduates have clerked for one of the Supreme Court Justices.

Of course, nothing is perfect, even at Stanford. Some students love the pass/fail grading system while others say it provides little incentive to work hard. Despite these complaints, though, students call Stanford "the best law school west of the Appalachians," and they "have a hard time seeing why anyone would choose to go to law school anywhere else."

Life

"Small size makes for a more personal experience" at Stanford. Here, "You really get to know your classmates, and there is consequently no competitive behavior." The academic atmosphere is "very collaborative." There are "study groups galore." Students describe themselves as "ridiculously smart people" who are "highly ambitious" and "work extremely hard." "It easy to feel like you must have been admitted by mistake," confesses an awed 1L. There is "lots of diversity" in terms of age, background, ethnicity, and pretty much every attribute. Some students call the political environment "overwhelmingly liberal." Other students say "there's a critical mass of right-of-center students," and they point out that you definitely won't see too many protests among law students. "Perhaps that's because everyone harbors secret Supreme Court ambitions and wouldn't want to pigeonhole their position on an issue somewhere the Senate Confirmation Committee could find it," suggests a 1L.

OFFICE OF ADMISSIONS
559 NATHAN ABBOTT WAY, STANFORD, CA 94305-8610
TEL: 650-723-4985 FAX: 650-723-0838
E-MAIL: ADMISSIONS@LAW.STANFORD.EDU • WEBSITE: WWW.LAW.STANFORD.EDU

Certainly, "you won't have to contend with snow or gloomy weather" at this school. "The weather is perfect ninety percent of the time." Some students call Palo Alto "a cultural wonderland" that has everything you need including "incredibly nice" graduate student housing located right next to the law school. Other students gripe, "Living in Palo Alto is like living in a suburb, which to anyone who is coming from an urban area will be a shock." "A big percentage of Stanford students are married, or commute from San Francisco, so they have their own lives away from the school." Extracurricular activity is constant for everyone, though. "Having the law school right in the middle of Silicon Valley allows for many practitioners, general counsels, venture capitalists," and the like to drop by. Student organizations are profuse. "Everyone at Stanford is president of a club, editor of a journal, director of a pro bono, and a board member of a society," claims a 2L. "Social events are plentiful," and they are "always a hoot." There is something of a fraternity-like culture if that's what you are looking for, but it's "not [an] overwhelming scene," and we aren't talking about people doing multiple keg stands. "You have to remember that everyone had to be pretty studious and dorky in order to get in here," says a 1L.

Getting In

Admission to Stanford Law is very competitive. Enrolled students at the 25th percentile have LSAT scores of about 167 and GPAs of roughly 3.74. Enrolled students at the 75th percentile have LSAT scores above 170 and GPAs pretty close to 4.0.

Clinical program required	No
Legal writing course requirement	Yes
Legal methods course requirement	No
Legal research course requirement	Yes
Moot court requirement	No
Public interest law requirement	No

ADMISSIONS

Selectivity Rating	99
# applications received	4,248
% applicants accepted	9
% acceptees attending	47
Average LSAT	170
LSAT Range	168–172
Average undergrad GPA	3.83
Application fee	$75
Regular application	Rolling, up to 2/1
Regular notification	4/30
Early application program	No
Transfer students accepted	Yes
Evening division offered	No
Part-time accepted	No
CAS accepted	Yes

FINANCIAL FACTS

Annual tuition	$44,880
Books and supplies	$1,863
Fees	$1,200
Room and board (on/off campus)	$17,955/ $19,248
Financial aid application deadline	3/15
% first-year students receiving some sort of aid	87
% receiving some sort of aid	80
% receiving scholarships	57
Average grant	$25,009
Average loan	$38,235
Average total aid package	$54,773
Average debt	$104,425

EMPLOYMENT INFORMATION

		Grads Employed by Field (%)	
Career Rating	95	Academic	(2)
Rate of placement (nine months out)	99	Business/industry	(2)
State for bar exam	CA, NY, MD, NJ, PA	Government	(5)
Pass rate for first-time bar	99	Judicial clerkship	(29)

Prominent Alumni

Private practice (59)

Sandra Day O'Connor, First female
Supreme Court Justice (1981–2006);
Anthony Romero, Executive Director of
ACLU (2001–Present); Max Baucus,
U.S. Senator (1979 to Present);
Ron Noble, Secretary General of Interpol
and law professor

Public interest (3)

STATE UNIVERSITY OF NEW YORK—UNIVERSITY AT BUFFALO
LAW SCHOOL

Academics

Students are all agreed on the single best aspect of the University at Buffalo Law School: "Cost, cost, and...oh...cost! There is no better bargain for the quality of education." This public law program is one of the most affordable options in New York State. Educationally, Buffalo emphasizes a comprehensive approach to the study of law, and the "dedicated, competent, and personable administrators" have developed a well-balanced curriculum to this end. There's also a once-every-semester town hall meeting and regular potlucks, which help to facilitate interaction with the administration, professors, and students. "Student concerns are taken seriously, and our concerns are well received. I've seen many of our suggestions implemented," says one.

Throughout the curriculum, you'll have access to "some of the top scholars in their fields," and in the classroom, "Creative legal thinking is highly encouraged." The JD kicks off with a full course load in traditional legal subjects like contracts, torts, and civil procedure. In the second year, students may begin taking elective courses, while further tailoring their academic experience through extracurricular activities and research centers. Buffalo's curriculum has been redesigned to emphasize practical skill development. Aside from the numerous clinic programs offered, the school is part of a very involved legal community, and students "are able to clerk, or intern at local firms, courts, or public service organizations during the regular semester and summer." The school also has various study abroad programs. The city's legal talent is also used to augment the academic staff: "I've had several classes where members of the local legal community come in to lecture or to facilitate," says a 3L, and many of the classes (such as evidence, criminal procedure, etc.) are taught by members of the bench and bar.

Perhaps University at Buffalo's most distinctive characteristic is its incredibly supportive, noncompetitive atmosphere. Instructors sit behind open doors and "are wonderfully smart, challenging, and generally fair." Mutual respect is clearly an effective approach, as Buffalo professors "expect the best from their students," but they "build an environment of constructive learning versus intimidation and scare tactics." At the same time, they're "open to differing opinions," and if you need a little extra instruction outside the lecture hall, professors "are always available to meet with you." Many classes demand group work and discussion outside of the classroom, and "professors, as well as students, are encouraged to hold events together." "We've even had picnics and potlucks together," exclaims a 1L. "We all work together while competing with ourselves," says another. Perhaps this is due to the shared light at the end of the tunnel: "When you're stuck in the snow for six months a year, you have ample time to tone your brain."

In the past, students lamented the hours spent in "unsightly lecture halls with hideous brick-patterned walls." Renovations have been completed at the Law School and include a new student space in the Law Library and technological enhancements to several classrooms. The study areas have been redecorated and "even come with baskets of snacks (the best part) during finals." Fortunately, even today, the library is excellent, and the school's research librarian "is amazing, always willing to help, and excited about whatever endeavor you are on."

After graduation, job prospects look good for Buffalo's well-trained young lawyers. In particular, many appreciate the low-stress decision making they enjoy thanks to minimal educational debt. A first-year student shares, "I'm not sure exactly what type of legal job I'll be looking for, but with the low cost of tuition and minimal loans, I'll have the option to take a job that I'm passionate about—not just the one that pays the most." For those

LILLIE V. WILEY-UPSHAW, VICE DEAN FOR ADMISSIONS AND FINANCIAL AID
309 O'BRIAN HALL, BUFFALO, NY 14260
TEL: 716-645-2907 FAX: 716-645-6676
E-MAIL: LAW-ADMISSIONS@BUFFALO.EDU • WEBSITE: WWW.LAW.BUFFALO.EDU

looking to work outside of the region, the Career Services office has seen improvement in recent years, following the addition of a new dean.

Life

The school's stimulating academic atmosphere is no doubt due to its sparkling student body, which encompasses "lots of diversity in age, ethnicity, gender, and background in general." Everyone gets along fabulously, and "Students are encouraged to play fair and help each other out." The camaraderie easily spills out of the classroom. "The social life at UB is tops," one student explains. "There is always something to do, and the 1Ls, particularly in each section, are very close." You don't have to wait until Friday to have some fun, as "most Thursday nights during the semester, one group or another sponsors a bar night, and many of the students attend with relative regularity to socialize."

The university grounds, facilities, and resources are excellent, boasting "at least three libraries, easily more than twenty places to eat (both dining services and chains), any number of different student services (including free massages at the Wellness Center), a CVS, and a speaker on most any topic at some point every week." Students warn us, however, that unless you were born and raised in upstate New York, "You've never experienced weather like this! An average winter day is twenty degrees with a thirty-mile-per-hour wind."

Getting In

UB enrolls about 220 new students each year, evaluating applicants based on both qualitative and quantitative factors. In particular, the admissions committee seeks students whose academic backgrounds suggest a high probability for scholastic achievement in law school, who have demonstrated excellence in work or community activities, or who display potential for substantial contribution to the law after graduation. Students of the class of 2013 at the 75th percentile had a GPA of 3.69 and LSAT scores of 160, and those at the 25th percentile had a GPA of 3.18 and an LSAT of 155.

Clinical program required	No
Legal writing	
course requirement	Yes
Legal methods	
course requirement	No
Legal research	
course requirement	Yes
Moot court requirement	No
Public interest	
law requirement	No

ADMISSIONS

Selectivity Rating	**84**
# applications received	1,894
% applicants accepted	38
% acceptees attending	31
Average LSAT	158
LSAT Range	155–160
Average undergrad GPA	3.48
Application fee	$75
Regular application	Rolling, up to 3/1
Regular notification	Rolling
Early application program	No
Transfer students accepted	Yes
Evening division offered	No
Part-time accepted	No
CAS accepted	Yes

International Students

TOEFL required of international students

FINANCIAL FACTS

Annual tuition	
(in-state/out-of-state)	$17,450/ $29,110
Books and supplies	$1,161
Fees	$1,662
Room and board	$12,612
Financial aid application	
deadline	3/1
% first-year students	
receiving some sort of aid	94
% receiving some sort of aid	75
% of aid that is merit based	55
% receiving scholarships	84
Average grant	$5,188
Average loan	$20,500
Average total aid package	$22,900
Average debt	$56,394

EMPLOYMENT INFORMATION

Career Rating	**87**
Rate of placement (nine months out)	98
Average starting salary	$78,110
State for bar exam	NY, NJ, MA, FL, TX
Pass rate for first-time bar	83

Employers Who Frequently Hire Grads
Ropes & Gray; Hodgson Russ; Phillips Lytle; NYS Court of Appeals; NYS App. Div. 4th Dept.; Dewey & LeBoeuf; DLA Piper; Nixon Peabody; New York County District Attorney; Kings County District Attorney; Erie County District Attorney; White & Case; Bond, Schoeneck & King; Schulte Roth & Zabel; Jones, Day; Sullivan & Cromwell; Weil, Gotschal & Manges; Harter Secrest; Damon & Morey; Jaeckle, Fleischmann & Mugel; Nassau County District Attorney; New York State Attorney General; Presidential Management Fellows Program; U.S Department of Justice; Wilson Elser Moskowitz Edelman & Dicker; U.S. Army, Air Force and Navy JAG Corps

Prominent Alumni
Hon. Julio Fuentes, U.S. Court of Appeals for the 3rd Circuit; Nicole Lee, Executive Director, TransAfrica; Kenneth Forrest, Partner, Wachtell Lipton Rosen & Katz; Virginia Seitz, Nominee for Assistant Attorney General heading the Office of Legal Counsel in the Department of Justice; Denise O'Donnell, Nominee to head the Justice Department's Bureau of Justice Assistance

Grads Employed by Field (%)
Government (10)

STETSON UNIVERSITY COLLEGE OF LAW

Academics

Stetson University College of Law in Florida offers "a good mix of practicality and theory." Points of pride here include a serious first-year emphasis on research and writing. "The pace and the intensity of it are not matched by other schools," declares a 1L. There's a "wide variety of" "excellent" internships and clinics as well, and pro bono opportunities abound." While three certificate programs are available (in advocacy, elder law, and international law), advocacy is far and away the principal focus here. Students gloat that Stetson is home to "the best trial advocacy school in the country." "Every week, a different trial team is out competing and winning something." "For a litigator who wants to practice in Florida, or an appellate practitioner who wants access to judicial internships in the area," counsels a 2L, "Stetson is ideal." "You will know your way around a courtroom long before graduating." However, some students say that this school overemphasizes litigation. Course offerings in some other areas are slim pickings, even in areas that are on the bar exam. Students also note that Stetson isn't cheap. "I had considered transferring just to save money," admits a 3L, "but I had such a great environment at Stetson. I couldn't leave."

There are quite a few adjunct professors, and some full-time professors "can make a semester seem unbearable," but by and large, the faculty at Stetson Law is "caring," "very dedicated," "and eager to make your learning experience successful." Professors are "knowledgeable in both their areas of expertise and general law and life." They're also "available and approachable." Students brag that Stetson has "one the most accessible faculties imaginable." "Despite their busy schedules, they always make time for students and are happy to do so," relates a 3L. Some members of the administration "go to great lengths to get to know students on a personal basis." Others are "arrogant [and] incompetent" and "seem to manage to screw over their students on biweekly basis."

On the employment front, "One of the biggest assets is that Stetson is the only law school in the Tampa Bay Area." Students tell us that Stetson has an excellent reputation locally. "Judges rave about Stetson's professionalism," asserts a 3L. The name carries some weight throughout the Sunshine State as well. Outside of Florida, however, "Very few people know where or what Stetson is," and "There just are not too many firms that are recruiting" on campus. Views concerning Career Services are conflicting. Some students call the staff "outstanding." Others gripe that Career Services "has little connection with practicing alumni in the area and is not very organized overall."

The facilities here are generally impressive. "The campus is exclusively a law school," and the hacienda-style architecture creates a kind of "old resort" vibe, which "takes away some of the sting of having to go to class." "The school has plenty of room, with large classrooms that are modern and comfortable and several gorgeous, usable courtrooms on campus." Library resources are "very impressive," and "the librarians are the best around." A 2L likens them to "fairy godmothers of legal research." Technology is a bit of sore spot, though. The server "seems to be down once a week," and "There are constant problems" with various gadgetry. Also, bring a sweater because "the air-conditioning is freezing cold."

LAURA ZUPPO, EXECUTIVE DIRECTOR OF ADMISSIONS & STUDENT FINANCIAL PLANNING
1401 61ST STREET SOUTH, GULFPORT, FL 33707
TEL: 727-562-7802 FAX: 727-343-0136
E-MAIL: LAWADMIT@LAW.STETSON.EDU • WEBSITE: WWW.LAW.STETSON.EDU

Life

Students tell us that there's "a family-like atmosphere" here. "Stetson is very open," relates a 1L. "There is a great sense of community between the students, faculty, and staff." The academic atmosphere is amicable. "Students are generally very helpful to each other, and the environment is friendly and noncompetitive for the most part. Competition is healthy rather than cutthroat or underhanded."

When students aren't hitting the books, it's easy "to get involved in organizations," and everyone here is pretty social. Students also say that they're situated in an ideal place to learn the law. "You cannot beat the location," wagers a 1L. Obviously, this is a "year-round warm place," which has numerous advantages. Stetson's "affordable, tranquil" suburban environs make for an ideal atmosphere to work, study, and play. World class beaches are a short drive away. The reasonably lively city of St. Petersburg is also close, and the broader Tampa Bay Area is a growing, bustling region of close to three million people.

Getting In

Admitted students at the 25th percentile have LSAT scores in the mid 150s and undergraduate GPAs close to 3.2. At the 75th percentile, LSAT scores approach 160, and GPAs are close to 3.7.

Clinical program required	No
Legal writing course requirement	Yes
Legal methods course requirement	Yes
Legal research court requirement	Yes
Moot court requirement	Yes
Public interest law requirement	Yes

ADMISSIONS

Selectivity Rating	77
# applications received	2,663
% applicants accepted	38
% acceptees attending	29
Average LSAT	157
LSAT Range	154–159
Average undergrad GPA	3.37
Application fee	$55
Regular application	Rolling, up to 3/15
Regular notification	Rolling
Early application program	No
Transfer students accepted	Yes
Evening division offered	Yes
Part-time accepted	No
LSDAS accepted	Yes

International Students

TOEFL required of international students	

FINANCIAL FACTS

Annual tuition	$33,000
Books and supplies	$1,800
Room and board	$11,664
% first-year students receiving some sort of aid	89
% receiving some sort of aid	91
% of aid that is merit based	58
% receiving scholarships	25
Average grant	$17,025
Average loan	$42,542
Average total aid package	$47,904
Average debt	$122,289

EMPLOYMENT INFORMATION

Career Rating	73
Rate of placement (nine months out)	82
Average starting salary	$56,124
State for bar exam	FL
Pass rate for first-time bar	81

Employers Who Frequently Hire Grads

Small, medium, and large firms in the greater Tampa Bay area, state attorney's offices, public defender's offices

Prominent Alumni

Chief Justice Carol Hunstein, Supreme Court of Georgia; Hon. Elizabeth Kovachevich, USDC Middle District Florida; Rich McKay, President, Atlanta Falcons; Bruce Jacob, Dean Emeritus and Professor of Law, Argued Gideon v. Wainwright, 372 U.S. 335 (1963); Rhea F. Law, CEO and Chair, Board of Directors, Fowler White Boggs PA

Grads Employed by Field (%)

Academic (2)
Business/industry (10)
Government (12)
Judicial clerkship (4)
Military (2)
Private practice (62)
Public interest (8)

SUFFOLK UNIVERSITY
LAW SCHOOL

INSTITUTIONAL INFORMATION

Public/private	Private
% faculty part-time	42
% faculty female	38
% faculty minority	14
Total faculty	98

SURVEY SAYS...

Great research resources, Beautiful campus, Students love Boston, MA

STUDENTS

Enrollment of law school	1,681
% male/female	52/48
% from out-of-state	45
% full-time	65
% minority	17
% international	2
# of countries represented	24
Average age of entering class	25

ACADEMICS

Academic Experience Rating	**78**
Profs interesting rating	79
Profs accessible rating	72
Hours of study per day	4.32

Academic Specialties
International, Intellectual Property, Health and Biomedical Law, Business Law and Financial Services, Civil Litigation

Advanced Degrees Offered
JD, 3 years full-time, 4 years part-time; LLM in Global Technology, 1 year full-time, 3 years part-time; LLM in U.S. Law for International Business Lawyers, 3 years in Budapest, Hungary; SJD, 1–3 years

Combined Degrees Offered
JD/MBA, JD/MPA, JD/MS in International Economics, JD/MS in Finance, JD/MS in Criminal Justice, 4 years full-time, 5 years part-time; JD/MBA, 3 years

Academics

A very strong evening program, "high level of pro bono participation," and a fantastic bar passage rate (the third highest in the state) are just a few of the many attributes that make Suffolk Law students love their school. Students say the peer-mentoring program, Academic Support Services, and specialized tutoring, as well as the school's top clinic programs, many journals, and student organizations "make for a rich law school experience." "I participated in the Juvenile Defenders Clinic, and...have been able to appear in court nearly a dozen times on behalf of my clients," says a 3L. "The practical experience you can acquire, should you desire such experience, is unparalleled." Because of the school's connection with the legal community of greater Boston, Suffolk "has a large number of current and former judges on its faculty, which provides for an excellent learning experience."

The school offers a "vast array" of different courses in all specialty areas of the law (as well as a thorough legal writing program), and the "tough but understanding" professors are "consummate professionals and experts in their field." "I have found that respectful dissenting opinions, even radical ones, are met with enthusiasm and serious consideration," says a student. These teachers are the "best part" of Suffolk, "come from all walks of life," and "are not using their positions to launch their career somewhere else." "I even had a tax law professor (a subject I dreaded) who made tax interesting and, dare I say, exciting," says a 3L.

The administration here receives similar kudos for its "fair" treatment of student concerns, particularly the Registrar's Office. "Everyone is willing to work with you [administration, registrar, faculty], but no one is going to work for you," sums up a student. Academic support and bar prep are both "excellent," though Career Services "needs to do better about reaching out to students and professionals in the field to actually place students while in law school," by "building alumni connections within private employers in the city."

Another perk of Suffolk Law is the strong alumni network, which, "in a city with so many law schools...is very important." "Anywhere you go, anywhere you work, there will be a Suffolk grad," says a 1L. A 2L puts it a little less delicately: "I think we're all aware that we're probably not getting by on the name of the school like other Boston schools, so everybody is really focus[ed] on building their networks and learning the skills they need."

The facilities here are brand-new and "outstanding." "I feel like I am part of a grand tradition of lawyers, yet have access to state-of-the-art classrooms," says a 3L. Still, many students wish the school's reputation had more of a "national presence," as the name "doesn't immediately curry the same sort of respect as a more highly ranked school." "Something is holding the school back from being respected as a top law school. It is not the faculty and it is not the students," says one of many puzzled students.

Life

The "fairly large student body" is divided into 1L sections upon entrance to the school, which does a lot "to create close friendships and collaborative relationships between new students." The school is pretty much composed of "nice, young people, mostly from the Boston area," which makes for "a cohesive bunch—none of that *Paper Chase* nonsense." "I am so happy to be at a school where I feel challenged by my classmates, but not threatened," says a student. A surprising number of students refer to the "professionalism" of

GAIL ELLIS, DEAN OF ADMISSIONS
120 TREMONT STREET, BOSTON, MA 02108-4977
TEL: 617-573-8144 FAX: 617-523-1367
E-MAIL: LAWADM@SUFFOLK.EDU • WEBSITE: WWW.LAW.SUFFOLK.EDU

their classmates, possibly due to the frequent intermingling of day and evening students in evening classes, which "is of benefit to both, with the evening students bringing a lot of real-world experience to class discussions." On the flip side, "It's hard to get involved in the social side of life at Suffolk when you're in the evening program."

The central Boston location "couldn't be better," and lends to the school the quality of a "social paradise, with frequent events at school and local bars." "You're [a] ten-minute walk from the Prudential Center, a five-minute walk from Faneuil Hall, a two-minute walk from Pemberton Square, ten minutes from the BMC, and thirty seconds from the Boston Common or the State House." Most first-year students "gather at the local watering hole on Friday afternoon to let off steam and talk trash about the other sections" in a good-natured way. There are also "consistent events throughout the academic year" involving clubs, job opportunities, networking seminars, political groups, and more.

Getting In

Suffolk's Admissions Committee seeks candidates who are poised to contribute to the life of the campus community as well as to the future of the legal profession. Prospective students can demonstrate their potential in these areas by getting involved in community service, extracurricular undergraduate organizations, and pre-professional societies and are also evaluated on the growth and maturity exhibited by work experience since graduation. The 2010 incoming class scored a mean score of 157 on the LSAT and boasted a 3.3 undergraduate GPA, on average.

Clinical program required	No
Legal writing course requirement	Yes
Legal methods course requirement	Yes
Legal research course requirement	Yes
Moot court requirement	Yes
Public interest law requirement	No

ADMISSIONS

Selectivity Rating	76
# applications received	2,726
% applicants accepted	54
% acceptees attending	22
Average LSAT	157
LSAT Range	155–159
Average undergrad GPA	3.30
Application fee	$60
Regular application	Rolling, up to 3/1
Regular notification	Rolling
Early application program	No
Transfer students accepted	Yes
Evening division offered	Yes
Part-time accepted	Yes
CAS accepted	Yes

International Students

TOEFL required of international students	

FINANCIAL FACTS

Annual tuition	$42,540
Books and supplies	$1,000
Fees	$120
Room and board	$18,890
Financial aid application deadline	3/1
% first-year students receiving some sort of aid	86
% receiving some sort of aid	85
% of aid that is merit based	49
% receiving scholarships	40
Average grant	$14,769
Average loan	$40,260
Average total aid package	$48,424
Average debt	$112,668

EMPLOYMENT INFORMATION

Career Rating	**83**	
Rate of placement (nine months out)	84	
Average starting salary	$74,202	
State for bar exam	MA, NY, FL	
Pass rate for first-time bar	93	

Employers Who Frequently Hire Grads
Suffolk alumni practice in numerous large, medium and small law firms in Boston. Many practice in the Public Sector, work in all levels of Government Service, and serve on the Judiciary

Prominent Alumni
John Joseph Moakley, U.S. Congressman; James Bamford, Author; Kristen Kuliga, Principal, K Sports and Entertainment; Patrick Lynch, Rhode Island Attorney General; Nina Wells, New Jersey Secretary of State

Grads Employed by Field (%)
Academic (6)
Business/industry (24)
Government (13)
Judicial clerkship (3)
Military (1)
Private practice (49)
Public interest (3)

SYRACUSE UNIVERSITY
COLLEGE OF LAW

INSTITUTIONAL INFORMATION

Public/private	Private
Student/faculty ratio	11:1
% faculty female	42
% faculty minority	17
Total faculty	65

SURVEY SAYS...

Diverse opinions accepted in classrooms, Great library staff, Abundant externship/internship/clerkship opportunities, Good social life

STUDENTS

Enrollment of law school	638
% male/female	60/40
% full-time	100
% minority	20
% international	2
# of countries represented	25
Average age of entering class	24

ACADEMICS

Academic Experience Rating	75
Profs interesting rating	74
Profs accessible rating	70
Hours of study per day	5.58

Academic Specialties

Constitutional, Corporation Securities, Criminal, Environmental, Government Services, Human Rights, International, Labor, Legal History, Property, Taxation, Intellectual Property, Joint Degrees (MPA, MBA, MS), National Security Law, Technology Commercialization Law, Politics and Media Law, Family Law

Combined Degrees Offered

JD/MPA, JD/MS in Accounting, Library Science, Communication, Newspaper/Magazine Media, JD/MBA, JD/MA in Economics, History, International Relations, JD/MS in Education, Disability Studies, JD/MS in Forensic Science, JD/MSW, JD/MS, JD/PhD in Environmental Studies, JD/MS Engineering, Computer Science,

Academics

In 1895, the College of Law was born at Syracuse University. Today, it has seven clinical programs, multiple certificate programs, several specialized institutes, and a multitude of externships opportunities and student organizations. Clinics grant students "the invaluable opportunity to work on real cases and begin to understand how the process of law really works." Even more, "The programs are well-organized and very well-liked among students." The office of student life "provides endless academic support through lecture series, exam-taking strategies, and tutors." They assist students in getting internships and externships ("learning through experience is the best way"), although some students complain that the offices "are not particularly helpful unless you are a top student" and that the administration can be "very out of touch" at times. The school fosters openness, and experimentation is encouraged as students are told to "run with new ideas."

Currently, twelve percent of upper-class students are pursuing joint degrees, using the other graduate programs within the university system. There are a wide variety of possibilities in this respect, including the following disciplines: environmental science, international relations, education, engineering, and philosophy, just to name a few. Most students make the decision for a joint degree in their second semester, so there's no need to worry if you don't know exactly what you want when applying. Syracuse also offers the chance for students to specialize. Fields such as National Security and Counterterrorism Law are popular. Also, students say the legal writing and advocacy programs are "second to none." However, more than a few students worry about career options after graduation, feeling they're on their own when it comes to finding work. Another student says, "The office of Professional Development and Student Affairs are constantly putting on workshops and reaching out through interactive activities to the student body." Yet another opinion is that "there is a huge divide between the caliber of professor at our school (which is for the most part exceptional) and the administrative staff."

Students are consistently impressed by the track records of their professors. According to one student, "We have a faculty member who is employed by the president, another who is often called upon by Congress to testify or CNN for interviews, and another who was a United States attorney." Another says, "Two of my first-semester professors were Fulbright scholars, and all went to Ivy League schools." Within the classroom itself the experience is primarily a Socratic one. Still, the "incredible" professors "honestly care" about their students. One student says the greatest part of SUCOL is "the accessibility of faculty and the relationships that are built between faculty and students." Another student refers to the faculty as "exceptional" and truly having "the students' best interests at heart." However, some worry that 1L professors don't quite measure up and that emphasis might be weighing too heavily on passing the bar, as the past year's class didn't have a very high success rate. Other students attribute success or failure at the test to individual studying practices, not a lack of courses that focus on it.

Overall, students are quite pleased with their librarians. "Each student is given their own library research guide, who is one of the librarians, to help with research skills and preparation." Most say this is a huge help. They also agree better facilities are needed, "but we have already begun the groundbreaking procedures for a brand-new law school to remedy this problem."

NIKKI S. LAUBENSTEIN, DIRECTOR OF ADMISSIONS
OFFICE OF ADMISSIONS; SUITE 340, SYRACUSE, NY 13244
TEL: 315-443-1962 FAX: 315-443-9568
E-MAIL: ADMISSIONS@LAW.SYR.EDU • WEBSITE: WWW.LAW.SYR.EDU

Life

Students agree, "There is no pervasive feeling of competition at Syracuse," and students are "generous and helpful to others." Another went so far as to say, "It feels like a family." And yet another agreed that students are supported by not only the faculty, but also each other. For older students who might have children or separate lives, the school attempts to foster "a sense of community" by organizing "monthly get-togethers." Whether you attend is up to you, and essentially, "The experience is what you make of it." There are also organized weekly social nights, as well as a seasonal flag football league. Another way students socialize is through the student-run Syracuse Law Review. There are a multitude of law journals for them to join as well as moot court competitions. Students admit Syracuse can be "trying in the winter," and the inclement weather might prevent weekend socializing; however, another student reminds, "Don't forget to mention the world-class salmon and steelhead fly fishing thirty minutes away!" Upstate New York is famous for its hiking, biking, and skiing. Cost of living is inexpensive in Syracuse, as well.

Getting In

When considering applicants for admission, the committee weighs each of the following equally: LSAT scores, GPAs, and personal essays. Admitted students in the 25th percentile have LSAT scores in the low 150s, and GPAs just higher than 3.1. Admitted students in the 75th percentile have LSAT scores in the high 150s, and GPAs close to 3.6.

JD/MA in Political Science, English, Philosophy, 3–3.5 years; JD/MBA, 4 years

Clinical program required	No
Legal writing course requirement	Yes
Legal methods course requirement	Yes
Legal research course requirement	Yes
Moot court requirement	No
Public interest law requirement	No

ADMISSIONS

Selectivity Rating	79
# applications received	2,335
% applicants accepted	41
% acceptees attending	26
Average LSAT	155
LSAT Range	153–157
Average undergrad GPA	3.32
Application fee	$75
Regular application	Rolling, up to 4/1
Regular notification	Rolling
Early application program	No
Transfer students accepted	Yes
Evening division offered	No
Part-time accepted	No
CAS accepted	Yes

International Students

TOEFL required of international students

FINANCIAL FACTS

Annual tuition	$43,500
Books and supplies	$1,340
Fees	$1,626
Room and board	$12,230
Financial aid application deadline	2/15
% first-year students receiving some sort of aid	93
% receiving some sort of aid	89
% of aid that is merit based	58
% receiving scholarships	74
Average grant	$14,980
Average loan	$42,064
Average total aid package	$52,445
Average debt	$119,769

EMPLOYMENT INFORMATION

Career Rating	81
Rate of placement (nine months out)	92
Average starting salary	$67,400
State for bar exam	NY, NJ, CA, PA, MA
Pass rate for first-time bar	73

Employers Who Frequently Hire Grads

Medium and small law firms, and local government

Prominent Alumni

Joseph R. Biden, Jr., Vice President of the United States; Theodore A. McKee, Federal Appeals Court Judge; David Gordon, Managing Partner, Latham & Watkins; Melanie Gray, Ptr & Lit Co-Chair, Weil, Gotshal & Manges LLP; James E. Graves, Jr., Federal Appeals Court Judge

Grads Employed by Field (%)

Academic (6)
Business/industry (27)
Government (12)
Judicial clerkship (6)
Military (1)
Private practice (38)
Public interest (10)

TEMPLE UNIVERSITY
JAMES E. BEASLEY SCHOOL OF LAW

INSTITUTIONAL INFORMATION

Public/private	Public
% faculty female	44
% faculty minority	24
Total faculty	68

SURVEY SAYS...

Diverse opinions accepted in classrooms, Great research resources, Liberal students

STUDENTS

Enrollment of law school	976
% male/female	53/47
% from out-of-state	36
% full-time	80
% minority	23
% international	1
# of countries represented	9
Average age of entering class	25

ACADEMICS

Academic Experience Rating	83
Profs interesting rating	85
Profs accessible rating	82
Hours of study per day	4.77

Academic Specialties

Commercial, Constitutional, Corporation Securities, Criminal, Environmental, Government Services, Human Rights, International, Taxation, Intellectual Property, Trial Advocacy, Public Interest

Advanced Degrees Offered

JD, 3 years full-time, 4 years part-time; LLM in Trial Advocacy, 1 year; LLM in Taxation, 1 semester–1 year; LLM in Transnational Law, 1 semester–1 year; Graduate Teaching Fellowships, 2 years; LLM for graduates of foreign law schools, 1 year; SJD

Combined Degrees Offered

JD/MBA, 3–4 years; JD/LLM in Taxation and Transnational Law, 3.5 years; JD with individually designed joint-degrees

Academics

Temple University School of Law is "a public school in Philadelphia" that "prepares students to become real practicing attorneys." Without question, "Temple's greatest strength is its focus on the practical." There are five areas of specialization here. "The public interest program offers a broad range of opportunities." "International programs are fabulous." The diversity and sheer number of clinics is ridiculous. However, students assert that the year-long and very intensive trial advocacy program here is Temple's most awesome feature. "The trial advocacy program is top-notch, making the best litigators in the nation," vaunts a 2L. Under the guidance of judges and practicing trial attorneys, students in the program spend many hours conducting depositions, arguing motions, and honing "real-world lawyering" skills. Other perks here include five law journals and a flexible evening program that is "well-suited for students with personal and professional commitments." A vast range of course offerings is yet another plus. "There are a lot of different directions you can take your law school experience." "For Pennsylvania residents," says a 1L, "you can't beat the value and experience that Temple can provide."

Temple's "very dedicated" professors receive high marks. "Temple Law is not composed of a faculty of faces," beams a 1L, "but instead it is comprised of personalities, teachers, and mentors." Faculty members are usually "engaging, whether they use the Socratic Method or not," and they "spend a considerable amount of time emphasizing the practical aspects of their area of law." "For the most part, professors are very accessible outside of class" as well. Some students are very happy with the top brass. They say that the deans "make sure that every type of support you need to succeed" is available. "The administration knows and cares about me," adds a 3L.

Most students say that career prospects are good, particularly if you plan on staying in the City of Brotherly Love after graduation. Temple has an "amazingly strong network" locally. Basically, "Temple Law lawyers run the city," and the school "has a wonderful reputation in the greater Philadelphia area for turning out capable lawyers" in the private, public, and government sectors.

The facility here is a "big concrete block" that really is pretty hard to like. "You could literally spend a whole day in the school without looking out a window," submits a 2L. The school's location is "really convenient" and defenders of the neighborhood say that it "has a true Philadelphia feel to it." "The campus itself is very well maintained, lit well at night, and is very safe with a police force larger than some cities'." Some students tell us that "inside, the law school is very nice." Others describe the interior as "kind of gritty." The library is "adequate," but it "sounds like a bowling alley" and it's "not a very good study environment," though administrators are in the process of adding more group study areas. Technology isn't the worst but students say it's not the best, either. Fortunately, plans are in place to upgrade all the computers in the library and all the computers in the computer lab were recently updated and replaced.

JOHANNE L. JOHNSTON, ASSISTANT DEAN FOR ADMISSIONS & FINANCIAL AID
1719 NORTH BROAD STREET, PHILADELPHIA, PA 19122
TEL: 800-560-1428 FAX: 215-204-9319
E-MAIL: LAWADMIS@TEMPLE.EDU • WEBSITE: WWW.LAW.TEMPLE.EDU

Life

Across the board, students here appreciate that their peers and are "generally very friendly and intelligent" as well. Day students are typically twenty-something, "from upper-middle-class backgrounds." The evening program is a lot more diverse in every way and the people enrolled in it say it's "like a brotherhood." Though the formerly tough curve made students more competitive, today some students say "competitiveness is not extremely high" at Temple, and among first-years there is "a lot of section pride."

Outside the confines of the classroom, "students get along very well." According to one view, "Temple is primarily a commuter school, so there is not a great sense of community." Other students describe the social environment as "pretty collegial and tight-knit." "There's an excellent sense of community," they contend, and there are "plenty of opportunities to socialize." Certainly, "there are a ton of organizations to get involved with to meet people with similar interests." "Guest speakers that come to Temple are amazing" as well. Students who enjoy the social and extracurricular scene also report that "there is always something happening on the weekends somewhere," and they point out that "Philadelphia in general is quite fun."

Getting In

At Temple, enrolled students at the 25th percentile have LSAT scores of 160 or so and GPAs in the 3.2 range. At the 75th percentile, LSAT scores are in the mid 160s and GPAs are about 3.7. Be warned, however: Temple's highly competitive admission process is designed to look at the whole person. Your personal statement and recommendation letters will be carefully considered by the admissions committee.

Clinical program required	No
Legal writing course requirement	Yes
Legal methods course requirement	No
Legal research course requirement	Yes
Moot court requirement	No
Public interest law requirement	No

ADMISSIONS

Selectivity Rating	83
# applications received	4,651
% applicants accepted	40
% acceptees attending	16
Average LSAT	162
LSAT Range	159–164
Average undergrad GPA	3.39
Application fee	$60
Regular application	Rolling, up to 3/1
Regular notification	Rolling
Early application program	No
Transfer students accepted	Yes
Evening division offered	Yes
Part-time accepted	Yes
CAS accepted	Yes

International Students

TOEFL recommended of international students

FINANCIAL FACTS

Annual tuition (in-state/out-of-state)	$17,566/ $30,580
Books and supplies	$1,500
Fees	$640
Room and board	$11,416
Financial aid application deadline	3/1
% receiving some sort of aid	86
% of aid that is merit based	95
% receiving scholarships	46
Average grant	$9,472
Average loan	$26,638
Average total aid package	$31,157
Average debt	$78,502

EMPLOYMENT INFORMATION

		Grads Employed by Field (%)
Career Rating	88	Academic (5)
Rate of placement (nine months out)	88	Business/industry (11)
Average starting salary	$82,276	Government (8)
State for bar exam	PA	Judicial clerkship (13)
Pass rate for first-time bar	96	Military (1)
Employers Who Frequently Hire Grads		Private practice (41)
District Attorney, Public Defender, national		Public interest (7)
law firms, state and federal judges, non-		
profit legal organizations		

TEXAS TECH UNIVERSITY
SCHOOL OF LAW

Academics

Students dole out praises for Texas Tech's rigorous and practical JD program, which really "teaches you what you need to know to be a good lawyer." From day one, real-world principles are incorporated into the learning experience, and throughout the program "the instruction [features] a good balance of the Socratic Method with practical advice." During the 1L curriculum, "emphasis is put on legal writing and research so that we are able to go straight into practice during the summer of our first year." 1Ls have a "year-long legal practice requirement," which "gives you a fantastic foundation before you step your foot in the real world." In addition to curricular offerings, the school offers an incredible breadth of "opportunities to gain practical experience through procedure classes, barrister competitions, clinics, and national competitions."

While the JD curriculum is "rigorous and demanding," it would be very difficult to slip through the cracks at Texas Tech. When they start the program, students are grouped into sections that serve as a support network during 1L, and "all of the first-year classes have upper-level students as tutors to supplement your classroom hours." The teaching staff is also committed to student success, and maintains consistent office hours so that students "can stop by and talk to professors at any time." A totally user-friendly experience, "the resources provided by the school are top-notch and they've designed everything to revolve around the student and their schedule." To top it all off, the school has completed the construction of the Lanier Professional Development Center building, which added 34,000 square feet to the law school building. The school is already equipped with a first-rate library, and "the library staff is amazing and always available."

When it's time to start looking for a job or clerkship, Texas Tech maintains "a great reputation in the Texas legal markets as producing hard-working, effective lawyers." Students choose Tech precisely for this reputation and are proud of the results. A third-year student asserts, "I've been told on several occasions that a firm would rather pick up a Tech Law graduate who knows what to do when he steps foot in the office than some Ivy League grad who knows more about theory and less about how to get the job done." While career placement is highly successful in Texas, many students feel that the school could improve its national reputation and help "out-of-state students find jobs in their home states." In general, students would like their top school to take a more leading role in the national legal community, urging the administration to "spend more money to attract more nationally known, rather than regionally known, guest speakers and employers."

Life

The surprisingly friendly and open atmosphere at Texas Tech is all due to students who aren't afraid to "help one another, encourage one another, and be kind to one another." No need for first-year jitters. You'll quickly feel at home at Texas Tech, thanks to a "tremendous student-run mentoring program for incoming students." Within the law school, there are a number of students clubs and organizations—plus many more in the larger university—and if you're married, there are "resources and social networking opportunities for students with spouses and their families." Conservative politics predominate, but students reassure us that "you can survive as a liberal." In fact, "the Tech democrats are more active than the republicans," and everyone listens to and respects different opinions.

STEPHEN M. PEREZ, ASSISTANT DEAN FOR ADMISSIONS & RECRUITMENT
TEXAS TECH UNIVERSITY SCHOOL OF LAW 1802 HARTFORD AVENUE, LUBBOCK, TX 79409
TEL: 806-742-3990 FAX: 806-742-4617
E-MAIL: ADMISSIONS.LAW@TTU.EDU • WEBSITE: WWW.LAW.TTU.EDU

If you've never been to West Texas, a student dryly describes it for us as "a vast, treeless, invariably flat expanse of dirt…They even have tumbleweeds here—like out of a John Wayne movie or *Looney Tunes*." Although it sounds a bit inhospitable, students say the advantage to Lubbock's small city environment and arid landscape is that there are fewer distractions, which makes it easier to focus on your homework. More importantly, "Lubbock is a great environment for law students to partner with local lawyers and learn the ropes." "The Lubbock legal community is extremely strong and polite, and the relationship is emphasized over the case," one student says.

If you are looking for nightlife and social outlets, "Lubbock is not the most exciting town on the universe." However, students guarantee us that the lively campus community can make life surprisingly entertaining. For sports fans, "There is a very good football team on the field," and the basketball team isn't too shabby either. On top of that, the law school's friendly students "have managed to carve out a pretty decent social life. The bars here are okay, but the law students will sponsor various events and they are typically very fun."

Getting In

Texas Tech evaluates students based on their previous academic performance, LSAT scores, letters of recommendation, and personal statements. While no specific pre-law curriculum is required, the admissions committee favors students who have reading and writing skills, an understanding of public institutions and government, and the ability to think both creatively and critically.

Clinical program required	No
Legal writing course requirement	Yes
Legal methods course requirement	Yes
Legal research course requirement	Yes
Moot court requirement	No
Public interest law requirement	No

ADMISSIONS

Selectivity Rating	**81**
# applications received	1,407
% applicants accepted	40
% acceptees attending	44
Average LSAT	156
LSAT Range	153–158
Average undergrad GPA	3.43
Application fee	$50
Regular application	Rolling, up to 2/1
Regular notification	Rolling
Early application program	Yes
Early application deadline	11/1
Early application notification	1/15
Transfer students accepted	Yes
Evening division offered	No
Part-time accepted	No
CAS accepted	Yes

International Students

TOEFL required of international students	

FINANCIAL FACTS

Annual tuition (in-state/out-of-state)	$14,220/ $22,620
Books and supplies	$1,000
Fees	$3,535
Room and board	$8,404
Financial aid application deadline	3/1
% first-year students receiving some sort of aid	83
% receiving some sort of aid	91
% of aid that is merit based	17
% receiving scholarships	52
Average grant	$6,790
Average loan	$23,328
Average total aid package	$24,500
Average debt	$60,124

EMPLOYMENT INFORMATION

Career Rating	**82**
Rate of placement (nine months out)	93
Average starting salary	$65,165
State for bar exam	TX, NM, UT, AZ, FL
Pass rate for first-time bar	92

Employers Who Frequently Hire Grads
Allen, Shepherd, Lewis, Syra & Chapman; Baker & McKenzie; Brown & Fortunato; Carrington Coleman; Cox Smith; Decker Jones; Fulbright & Jaworski; Haynes and Boone; Kelly Hart & Hallman; Lloyd Gosselink; Mullin, Hoard & Brown; Passman & Jones; Scherr & Legate; Thompson Coe; Wilson Elser

Prominent Alumni
Karen Tandy, Senior Vice President, Motorola, Inc.; Brian Quinn, Chief Justice, 7th Court of Appeals for Texas; Philip Johnson, Texas Supreme Court Justice; Mark Lanier, Litigator in Houston, Texas; Rob Junell, Federal Judge

Grads Employed by Field (%)
Academic (1)
Business/industry (18)
Government (18)
Judicial clerkship (6)
Private practice (54)
Public interest (3)

THOMAS M. COOLEY LAW SCHOOL

Academics

The Thomas M. Cooley Law School in Michigan is the "the largest law school" in the United States in terms of enrollment. There are four campuses—one in the state capital of Lansing, one in the northern suburbs of Detroit, one in Grand Rapids and its newest location in Ann Arbor. Cooley prides itself on "flexible" and "accommodating" scheduling. There are "daytime, nighttime, and weekend" classes. There are "three terms year-round" as well, and you can start in January, May, or September. Some students complain that "the cost is very high." Others tell us the price tag is "very affordable." Either way, Cooley offers "a lot of financial aid and scholarship opportunities." Technology is also "cutting-edge," and the law library is one of the most extensive in the country.

Students here describe Cooley as an "underrated" "lawyer-making machine." It's not the place for you if you want to imbibe legal theory, though. "The school promotes practical application so you are ready to jump into your career" immediately upon graduation. Real legal experience "is required." Every student must complete a clinic, internship, externship, or otherwise demonstrate the equivalent in work experience. "Lectures are practical and grounded instead of theoretical." Course selection is broad and specializations are available but the number of mandatory courses is "a little ridiculous," and it "may prevent you from taking many electives and delving deeply into a particular area of interest." Basically, "Cooley's thinking is that if it is tested on the bar, it should be a required class." "This law school prepares you for the bar exam." Period.

Some students love the "hard-working" administration. Others say that the top brass is "frigid." Far and away, the biggest administrative complaint is that Cooley takes its sweet time posting grades. Like, "forever." The faculty is "interesting, entertaining, and knowledgeable," and it's full of professors who have "actually practiced law." There are also "many adjunct professors." They're typically judges, partners at big law firms, or general counsel for major corporations. Outside of class, faculty members are very approachable. "The accessibility of the professors is second to none," beams a 3L.

The "rigorous" academic atmosphere here is "not for the faint hearted." "Class sizes tend to be quite large." Professors generally "employ the Socratic Method and are always seeking to test your knowledge of the material." "The majority of students get C's." "Exams are tough, and an A is well earned." "Cooley lowers the bar for admissions, but after that you are on your own to sink or swim," warns a 1L. "Cooley is very hard to stay in." "Few students here have above a 3.0." Although the school has a fully staffed academic support resouce center, students uniformly promise that "you will struggle to survive through all three of your years here." "You better know the law," they say. "If you slack off, you'll fail out."

Life

Cooley "accepts just about anyone and everyone." The student population is "a mixture of students who didn't get in any place else and students who are on full scholarships because their LSAT and GPA were so high." An overwhelming majority of students is enrolled part time. Diversity of all kinds is a fabulous strength. Well more than half the future attorneys here come from some state other than Michigan. More than one third represent an ethnic minority. There are "nontraditional students from many different professions." "Age, background, and socioeconomic status" really run the gamut. "Cooley is

STEPHANIE GREGG, ASSISTANT DEAN OF ADMISSIONS
P.O. BOX 13038, 300 SOUTH CAPITOL AVENUE, LANSING, MI 48901
TEL: 517-371-5140 FAX: 517-334-5718
E-MAIL: ADMISSIONS@COOLEY.EDU • WEBSITE: WWW.COOLEY.EDU

so diverse that one could not even attempt to discriminate without confusing himself," declares a 3L. On the one hand, the vast assortment of students "makes for excellent class discussions." On the other hand, "people divide into cliques easily" outside the classroom.

The three campuses each have their own identity. In Lansing, students have a "beautiful" building downtown "by the capitol." However, the surrounding area is largely "bleak" and "depressing." The Grand Rapids campus is similarly located in "a refurbished old building in the heart of downtown," and it's not in the greatest neighborhood, either. The decidedly suburban Auburn Hills campus is a nice and new facility "tucked away in a wooded compound" that feels like "a generic corporate headquarters."

Social life can be hit or miss. Cooley is home to a tremendous number of student organizations," and "most students are nice people." However, there isn't much of a community. "A lot of people come to class and then leave immediately after," explains a 1L. "Building a social life takes effort." The fact that "grades are impossible during the first few terms" certainly doesn't help. "Those who are social butterflies mostly ended up failing out after one or two semesters," cautions a 2L. "People get along, but it's best to focus on studying."

Getting In

Cooley is one of the easiest law schools to get admitted to in the country. The acceptance rate hovers at about sixty percent annually. Admitted students at the 25th percentile have LSAT scores around 145 and GPAs of roughly 2.75. Admitted students at the 75th percentile have LSAT scores of 152 or so and their undergraduate GPA is about 3.3. Be warned, though: Cooley also has an extremely high attrition rate. The philosophy here is to give students with lesser credentials a chance but throw them out if they can't cut the demanding academics.

Clinical program required	Yes
Legal writing course requirement	Yes
Legal methods course requirement	Yes
Legal research course requirement	Yes
Moot court requirement	No
Public interest law requirement	No

ADMISSIONS
Selectivity Rating	65
# applications received	5,718
% applicants accepted	66
% acceptees attending	44
Average LSAT	146
LSAT Range	144–149
Average undergrad GPA	3.05
Application fee	$0
Regular application	Rolling, up to 9/1
Regular notification	Rolling
Early application program	No
Transfer students accepted	Yes
Evening division offered	Yes
Part-time accepted	Yes
CAS accepted	Yes

International Students
TOEFL recommended of international students

FINANCIAL FACTS
Annual tuition	$24,220
Books and supplies	$800
Fees	$40
Room and board	$6,860
Financial aid application deadline	9/6
% first-year students receiving some sort of aid	88
% receiving some sort of aid	87
% receiving scholarships	57
Average grant	$7,507
Average total aid package	$18,500
Average debt	$93,067

EMPLOYMENT INFORMATION

Career Rating	71
Rate of placement (nine months out)	82
Average starting salary	$47,500
State for bar exam	MI, NY, NJ, FL, IN
Pass rate for first-time bar	63

Employers Who Frequently Hire Grads
Michigan Court of Appeals Prosecutors Legal Services programs Michigan law firms

Prominent Alumni
John Engler, Former Governor; Bart R. Stupak, U.S. Representative; Jane Markey, Michigan Court of Appeals; Chris Chocola, U.S. Representative

Grads Employed by Field (%)
Academic (2)
Business/industry (20)
Government (13)
Judicial clerkship (7)
Military (4)
Private practice (46)
Public interest (6)

TOURO COLLEGE
JACOB D. FUCHSBERG LAW CENTER

Academics

Located on suburban Long Island, Touro Law Center boasts "many clinics on site." Six in-house clinics give full-time and part-time students the opportunity to serve real clients in civil rights litigation, elder law, family law, mortgage foreclosure and bankruptcy, and veterans and servicemembers' rights clinic, and not-for-profit corporation law. Off-campus clinics include business, technology law, civil practice, judicial clerkship, and criminal law. The school also offers an intensive, twenty-hour-a-week rotation program with the U.S. attorney's office. Touro's "focus on internships and externships" and its unique location, "only a five-iron shot" from federal and state courthouses, draws many students to the school. "Being located next to district, family, supreme, and federal courthouses gives Touro students a unique real-life look at what attorneys do while in court," explains one student. "I've randomly visited the court in the morning and observed attorneys conduct direct and cross-examinations in a $150 million court case." "We have a court [observation] program for the 1Ls, which is the first of its kind in law school academia," describes a 1L. "This program allows us access to more than just viewing a proceeding. With the hard work of the school staff, we have been given extra privileges at the court house including visits to chambers, personal audiences with both prosecutors, defense counsel, and all levels of court officers." "The direct contact with judges and attorneys and their input helps to [provide] insight into different areas of law." Also, "Having a better perspective on the various areas of law helps with deciding which area of law one may want to practice."

The course work at Touro "emphasizes legal writing and analysis." "Class sizes are pretty small, so it's not so intimidating to speak in front of everyone." The "smart, friendly, and approachable" professors are "excited to educate" (though there are a few "pretty boring ones"). "Plenty of judges and practitioners also teach classes." Accessibility is not a problem. "There is a high level of morale, and the daily interaction between student and professor is priceless." Faculty members are "always willing to meet with and talk to the students outside the classroom," "no matter how long—or how many times—they have to go over a given concept." "Professors can be seen dining with students in the school's cafeteria while casually discussing the law," adds a 1L.

Some students call the Career Services Office "exceptional." "They will do their absolute best to make sure you are prepared for interviews and aware of upcoming opportunities," says one happy customer. Other students gripe that Career Services is "not at all helpful." Also, though Touro offers very flexible full-time and part-time programs, course scheduling is a huge problem. "There is not a lot of flexibility with regard to course selection," and "There are too many required courses after the first year." The administration, though "very accessible," seems "out of touch with the student body," "and they never seem to know what is going on."

The facilities here are "brand-new," and students love them. Touro has a "state-of-the-art building" in which "Everything is high-tech and top-of-the-line." The "layout of the classrooms is odd," and "There are some problems with acoustics," but the "roomy" library has ample study space. There is a ton of free parking as well. The Law Center "follows a Jewish calendar," and one student notes that Touro "could improve by staying open on Saturday."

SUSAN THOMPSON, DIRECTOR OF ENROLLMENT
225 EASTVIEW DRIVE, CENTRAL ISLIP, NY 11722
TEL: 631-761-7010 FAX: 631-761-7019
E-MAIL: ADMISSIONS@TOUROLAW.EDU • WEBSITE: WWW.TOUROLAW.EDU

Life

"Generally people get along very well" at Touro. "There is a good mix of both young and older, more experienced students." "The greatest strength of my law school is the sense of community that begins from the moment you enter the school," waxes a 3L. "In the full-time program you spend a full year with your incoming section and then half your classes the second year," adds a 2L. "This enables you to form strong bonds for study groups and lifelong friendships. Also, even though everyone studies a lot during the week, students find time to be social on Thursday or Friday nights."

"The location of the school is perfect from an educational standpoint because of the proximity to the courthouse." There's "an on-campus lecture-luncheon series with state and federal judges." The downside to life here is the "almost nonexistent social atmosphere." "The majority of the students commute from great distances, which doesn't facilitate social opportunities." "People try to get involved and sponsor extracurricular social activities" and there are "plenty of opportunities to party and have fun," but you have to seek them out. "We need more social activities that cater to more students and bring us together as a community," suggests a 2L. The inescapable fact that "Central Islip is not exactly the party capital of the world" doesn't help. Fortunately, the culture and nightlife of New York City is only about an hour away.

Getting In

At Touro Law Center, recently admitted students at the 25th percentile have LSAT scores of approximately 150 and GPAs of approximately 2.8. Admitted students at the 75th percentile have LSAT scores of 153 and GPAs of roughly 3.4.

Clinical program required	No
Legal writing course requirement	Yes
Legal methods course requirement	Yes
Legal research course requirement	Yes
Moot court requirement	No
Public interest law requirement	Yes

ADMISSIONS

Selectivity Rating	**76**
# applications received	2,018
% applicants accepted	43
% acceptees attending	32
LSAT Range	149–153
Application fee	$60
Regular application	Rolling, up to 8/1
Regular notification	Rolling
Early application program	No
Transfer students accepted	Yes
Evening division offered	Yes
Part-time accepted	Yes
CAS accepted	Yes

International Students

TOEFL recommended of international students	

FINANCIAL FACTS

Annual tuition	$40,950
Books and supplies	$4,869
Fees	$120
Room and board	$19,140
Financial aid application deadline	5/1
% first-year students receiving some sort of aid	89
% receiving some sort of aid	89
% of aid that is merit based	68
% receiving scholarships	61
Average grant	$6,000
Average loan	$40,000
Average total aid package	$42,000
Average debt	$125,481

EMPLOYMENT INFORMATION

Career Rating	**74**
Rate of placement (nine months out)	76
Average starting salary	$69,585
State for bar exam	NY
Pass rate for first-time bar	76

Employers Who Frequently Hire Grads
Mid-size and small law firms; D.A. Offices, Legal Aid Offices and County Attorney Offices in Suffolk County, Nassau County and the five NYC Boroughs (Bronx, Brooklyn, Queens, NYC and Staten Island)

Prominent Alumni
Lewis Lubell, Justice, NYS Supreme Court; Kathleen Rice, Nassau County District Attorney; Seymour Liebman, Corporate Counsel, Canon USA; Kenneth LaValle, NYS Senate; Jothy Narendran, Partner, Jaspan Schlesinger LLP

Grads Employed by Field (%)
Academic (2)
Business/industry (14)
Government (14)
Judicial clerkship (4)
Private practice (62)
Public interest (7)

TULANE UNIVERSITY
LAW SCHOOL

INSTITUTIONAL INFORMATION

Public/private	Private
Student/faculty ratio	14:1
% faculty female	24
% faculty minority	12
Total faculty	42

SURVEY SAYS...

*Students love New Orleans, LA,
Good social life*

STUDENTS

Enrollment of law school	770
% male/female	55/45
% from out-of-state	85
% full-time	100
% minority	18
% international	3
# of countries represented	20
Average age of entering class	24

ACADEMICS

Academic Experience Rating	88
Profs interesting rating	86
Profs accessible rating	81
Hours of study per day	4.68

Academic Specialties

Environmental, International, Intellectual Property, Admiralty & Maritime Law, Sports Law, Civil Law, Public Interest Law, European Legal Studies

Advanced Degrees Offered

SJD, 2–3 years depending on time to complete dissertation; Master of Laws in Admiralty, Energy and Environment, 1 year full-time, 2 years part-time; Master of Laws, General LLM, Master of Laws in Admiralty, Energy and Environment, International and Comparative Law, American Law, American Business Law, 1 year full-time

Combined Degrees Offered

JD/MBA, JD/MHA, JD/MPH, JD/MSW, JD/MACCT, JD/MS International Development, 4 years

Academics

Tulane University Law School is "extremely enjoyable because it provides you with the same resources as all the top law schools, with a more laid-back atmosphere." "The quality of teaching is superb." The "world-renowned faculty" here is full of "experts and kick-ass attorneys" who are "funny, extremely smart, and extremely approachable." "They are highly qualified and accomplished but remain accessible and down-to-earth." Some students call the administration "ridiculously awesome," too. The deans are "nice and helpful," they say, "and most of them teach a 1L or 2L class, which gives you the opportunity to be exposed to them early on in your career." More critical students call the management merely "vaguely competent."

Tulane is home to "quite a few unique programs and strengths." In addition to "exceptional clinical opportunities" and a host of dual-degree programs, students edit no fewer than eight journals. Tulane also offers certificates in international and comparative law, admiralty law, environmental law, sports law, and civil law. Also, Louisiana is a civil law state (whereas every other state is a common law state), so students are exposed to two very different legal systems. "The ability to follow a common law or civil law track not only opens up opportunities in Louisiana, but it also makes an international law career more feasible." The big academic complaint here is the research and writing program. "I am not sure whoever designed it has ever heard the term 'best practices,'" speculates a 1L. "If you came as a strong technical writer, you will leave with no new skills. If you did not, you are on your own."

Students note that the academic program is competitive and challenging, and it is important to maintain strong performance if you want to gain the interest of local employers. Tulane is "extremely active in helping everyone secure summer employment and beyond." Students also note that their school's brand name is often a real advantage on a resume. "We're the best law school in Louisiana, and the firms know it," brags a 2L. "We are not all competing for the same thirty spots at the top law firm in our city because our goals are incredibly diverse," adds a 2L.

Facilities wise, Tulane has "a wonderful library." Some students say that "classrooms are nice." Others disagree. "The actual building and classrooms are forgettable," they tell us. "The horrid ergonomics of it all!" bemoans a 2L. "To plug in your laptop can take two minutes and can set the stage for an awkward encounter with the person sitting next to you while you fumble around under the table like a teenager on a first date."

Life

New Orleans is definitely located in "the American South, and many students come from the South." Geographic diversity is pretty abundant, though. Some eighty-five percent of the students come from a state other than Louisiana. About twenty percent of the students represent an ethnic minority. There's a "wide range of international students" and plenty of "diversity of opinion and background." Some students insist that "there's no cutthroat competition here." They say that the typical student is as "friendly, cooperative, and as laid-back as a stressed law student could possibly be." Others tell us that competition exists "but it's not as prevalent until exam time."

Outside of class, Tulane students are an "extremely social," "fun-loving bunch." There are "plenty of cliques, largely organized according to special interests areas of law, ethnicity, and age." At the same time, the environment is "very collegial." "The community atmosphere is a definite plus." Quite a few students "enjoy a good party." There are "a lot

ADAM KANCHER, ASSISTANT DIRECTOR
WEINMANN HALL, 6329 FRERET STREET, NEW ORLEANS, LA 70118
TEL: 504-865-5930 FAX: 504-865-6710
E-MAIL: ADMISSIONS@LAW.TULANE.EDU • WEBSITE: WWW.LAW.TULANE.EDU

of the smart kids who had fun in undergrad" here, and their good times continue unabated in law school. "Socializing is in overdrive at TLS," cautions a 2L, "which can be a distraction from your studies if you let it." "Most people go out at least once or twice a week." "Whether it's a run-of-the-mill bar review or renting out a restaurant on the Mardi Gras parade route, there's always a social event on the horizon."

Off campus, the Big Easy is reportedly "the most relaxed city in the USA" and "a perfect place to unwind on weekends or after finals." Students love the food, the nightlife, and the "warm winter weather." There's the debauchery of Bourbon Street, of course, but there's also an array of "incredible" streets and neighborhoods. "The sidewalk bistros and beautiful, lush scenery add significant character to your day-to-day experience as a law student." Beyond the city of New Orleans, "there are lots of good places for weekend trips in the area" as well.

Getting In

Tulane has a fabulous regional reputation and a very good national reputation. Admitted students at the 25th percentile have LSAT scores around 160 and GPAs not much less than 3.4. Admitted students at the 75th percentile have LSAT scores of 164 or so and GPAs around 3.7.

Clinical program required	No
Legal writing course requirement	Yes
Legal methods course requirement	No
Legal research course requirement	Yes
Moot court requirement	Yes
Public interest law requirement	Yes

ADMISSIONS

Selectivity Rating	88
# applications received	2,828
% applicants accepted	31
% acceptees attending	30
Average LSAT	162
LSAT Range	160–164
Average undergrad GPA	3.50
Application fee	$60
Regular application	Rolling, up to 6/1
Regular notification	Rolling
Early application program	No
Transfer students accepted	Yes
Evening division offered	No
Part-time accepted	No
CAS accepted	Yes

International Students

TOEFL recommended for international JD students; TOEFL required for LLM

FINANCIAL FACTS

Annual tuition	$38,500
Books and supplies	$7,386
Fees	$3,644
Room and board	$12,320
% first-year students receiving some sort of aid	87
% receiving some sort of aid	87
% of aid that is merit based	95
% receiving scholarships	60
Average grant	$20,000
Average loan	$40,000
Average total aid package	$60,000
Average debt	$122,000

EMPLOYMENT INFORMATION

Career Rating	83
Rate of placement (nine months out)	81
Average starting salary	$80,900
State for bar exam	NY, LA, TX, FL, D.C.
Pass rate for first-time bar	90

Employers Who Frequently Hire Grads
Adams & Reese; Alston & Bird; Barrasso Usdin Kupperman Freeman & Sarver; Cadwalader Wickersham & Taft; Chadbourne & Park; Cleary Gottlieb; Exxon Mobil Corporation; Fragomen Del Roy Bernsen & Loewy; Jones Day; Jones Walker; Krebs Farley & Pelleteri; Liskow & Lewis; National Labor Relations Board; Orleans Parish District Attorney's Office; Proskauer Rose; Ropes & Gray; Shulte Roth & Zabel; U.S. Army; U.S. District Court Eastern District of Louisiana; Vinson & Elkins

Prominent Alumni
Gail Agrawal, Dean; University of Iowa College of Law; Winston Chang, former president, Soochow University, Taiwan; Edith Clement, U.S. Court of Appeals 5th Circuit Judge; Randall Ebner, Chief Attorney, Exxon Mobil Corporation; Angela Ellard, Chief Trade Counsel, U.S. House Committee on Ways & Means; Marc Firestone, General Counsel, Kraft Foods; Ian Forrester, Partner and Head of Global Pro Bono Practice, White & Case, Brussels, Belgium; Paul Friedman, Senior Vice President, Sony Pictures Entertainment; Timothy Griffin, Congress, AR; Jonathan Hensleigh, Screenwriter; Liane Hinrichs, Senior Vice President, General Counsel, Corporate Secretary, McDermott International, Inc.; Madeleine Johnson, General Counsel of Southwest Airlines; Victoria Reggie Kennedy,

President, Common Sense About Kids and Guns, Board Member, Brady Center to Prevent Gun Violence; James Letten, U.S. Attorney, Eastern District of LA; Dean Lombardi, President and General Manager, L.A. Kings; Anne Segrest McCulloch, Senior Vice President and Deputy General, Fannie Mae; L. Richard McMillan, Senior Vice President and General Counsel, Freeport-McMoRan; Kenneth McClintock, Lt. Governor of Puerto Rico; Vicky Neumeyer, Vice President and General Counsel, New Orleans Saints; Terry O'Neill, President, National Organization for Women; William Pryor, U.S. Court of Appeals 11th Circuit Judge; Sang-hyun Song, President, International Criminal Court; Luther Strange, Attorney General, AL; William K. Suter, Clerk, U.S. Supreme Court; Michael Tannenbaum, General Manager, New York Jets; Rod West, President and CEO, Entergy; John G. Weinmann, former U.S. Ambassador to Finland and U.S. Chief of Protocol; Jacques L. Weiner, U.S. Court of Appeals 5th Circuit Judge; John Clint Williamson, Special Expert to the Secretary General of the UN, former Ambassador-at-Large for War Crimes Issues; John Minor Wisdom, U.S. Court of Appeals 5th Circuit and champion of civil rights

Grads Employed by Field (%)
Academic (3)
Business/industry (16)
Government (13)
Judicial clerkship (7)
Military (2)
Private practice (52)
Public interest (6)

THE UNIVERSITY OF AKRON
SCHOOL OF LAW

INSTITUTIONAL INFORMATION

Public/private	Public
Student/faculty ratio	13:1
% faculty female	40
% faculty minority	8
Total faculty	35

SURVEY SAYS...

Diverse opinions accepted in classrooms, Great research resources, Great library staff

STUDENTS

Enrollment of law school	506
% male/female	56/44
% from out-of-state	30
% full-time	59
% minority	14
# of countries represented	2
Average age of entering class	26

ACADEMICS

Academic Experience Rating	76
Profs interesting rating	78
Profs accessible rating	74
Hours of study per day	4.58

Academic Specialties

Corporation Securities, Criminal, International, Labor, Taxation, Intellectual Property, Litigation, General/Bar

Advanced Degrees Offered

LLM in Intellectual Property, 1 year full-time, 2–3 years part-time

Combined Degrees Offered

JD/MBA, JD/Master in Taxation, JD/MPA, JD/Master in Applied Politics, 1 additional semester with summer hours

Clinical program required	No
Legal writing course requirement	Yes
Legal methods course requirement	Yes
Legal research course requirement	Yes

Academics

The University of Akron School of Law is an "undervalued," "regional law school" that offers a lot of perks. "The tuition is very reasonable," especially if you can claim residency in Ohio. The bar-passage rate is solid. Course load options are "extremely flexible." It's very easy to switch between the full-time and part-time programs. The four specialized centers here "are very well-known." The "high-powered" certificate program in intellectual property is particularly notable. There's also a certificate in litigation and areas of concentration galore. Akron Law also boasts five joint-degree programs, a couple of "pretty freaking amazing" journals, and the chance to study abroad in Geneva, Switzerland. The curriculum here focuses primarily on the hard-boiled application of law. "If you want a legal education that emphasizes practical skills needed in the real-world," declares a 1L, "Akron Law is for you." The trial advocacy program is "outstanding" and the trial team is "one of the best" in the nation, routinely bagging trophies at national tournaments. Clinics are "very strong" and reportedly a cinch to get into. One of the clinics is the Clemency Project, which aids low-income people who have been convicted of crimes in securing pardons from the state governor. Another is the new business legal clinic, which helps people start businesses in the Akron area. As far as academic complaints, some students call the legal writing program "poor." Also, "Internships and externships placements are not readily available," and grading can be "pretty harsh."

Students heap praise on both the faculty and the administration. "The professors at Akron are the crown jewel of the school," beams a 1L. "They make even esoteric, archaic concepts like the rule against perpetuities interesting and understandable." "It is evident that they are passionate about teaching." "Many could probably make double or triple their salary by working in a big-city law firm." Faculty accessibility outside of class is "great," too. Professors here are "really interested in helping you find your way as a lawyer." They are "constantly walking the halls and willing to chit-chat." "Every professor I have had in class knows my name," reflects a 3L. The "ultra-helpful" and "very flexible" administration is "also very accessible and interested in the students" and "willing to work with" them.

While you can find Akron Law graduates all over the country, the great mass of alumni ends up practicing in northeast Ohio. While critics charge that the Office of Career Planning "does not do a great job at placing students," most students seem pretty happy with their post-law school employment prospects. The school has a "good reputation in the region." "The local bar association has a very close relationship with Akron Law," and "The school provides countless opportunities for" mentoring and networking.

Students tell us, "Akron is in the process of building a brand-new law school." In the meantime, the current facility "isn't grotesque-looking" but it's "less than stellar" and it just "doesn't feel like a law school." "The physical plant is a mess," explains a 3L. "The law school is actually two buildings that were combined in the cheapest way possible." "Areas of the building can seem cramped." "The heating and cooling system is consistently broken." On the plus side, classrooms are adequate. "They are all equipped for wireless Internet access and have plug-ins for every student laptop." Also, the location is excellent. City, county, state, and federal courts "are all steps from the door of the school."

LAURI S. THORPE, ASST. DEAN OF ADMISSION, FIN. AID, STUDENT SVCS.
THE UNIVERSITY OF AKRON SCHOOL OF LAW, 302 BUCHTEL COMMON, AKRON, OH 44325-2901
TEL: 800-425-7668 FAX: 330-258-2343
E-MAIL: LAWADMISSIONS@UAKRON.EDU • WEBSITE: WWW.UAKRON.EDU/LAW

Life

The vast majority of students at Akron Law are residents of Ohio. They describe themselves as "pretty outgoing and friendly." "The biggest surprise about law school is the fact that the other students are normal," relates a 1L. "I was expecting snobs and nerds but I have found people that I look forward to seeing every day." Student opinion concerning the academic atmosphere is decidedly split. Some students perceive "healthy amounts of competition." Others don't. "You see your fellow classmates as colleagues," says a 1L. "Students here aren't that competitive," adds a 3L. "I have helped several students and others have helped me study for exams."

Beyond the confines of the classroom, a respectable number of speakers come to campus and the student bar association is "very active." Socially, "There is quite a divide between day and evening students" and "there are a lot of cliques." The city of Akron is "a small, insular community." It's not the worst place in the world, but it's certainly not a world-class city, either. "Downtown Akron is not, shall we say, appealing in many ways," explains a 2L. "Some areas are nice, but some areas abutting campus are sketchy."

Getting In

Admitted full-time students at the 25th percentile have LSAT scores in the low 150s and undergraduate grade point averages a little under 3.2. At the 75th percentile, LSAT scores are close to 160 and GPAs are in the 3.7 range. Stats for admitted part-time students are somewhat lower.

Moot court requirement	No
Public interest law requirement	Yes

ADMISSIONS

Selectivity Rating	77
# applications received	2,003
% applicants accepted	39
% acceptees attending	23
Average LSAT	155
LSAT Range	152–158
Average undergrad GPA	3.35
Application fee	$0
Regular application	Rolling, up to 8/1
Regular notification	Rolling
Early application program	No
Transfer students accepted	Yes
Evening division offered	Yes
Part-time accepted	Yes
CAS accepted	Yes

International Students

TOEFL required of international students	

FINANCIAL FACTS

Annual tuition (in-state/out-of-state)	$17,816/ $29,773
Books and supplies	$900
Fees	$3,635
Room and board	$11,134
Financial aid application deadline	3/1
% first-year students receiving some sort of aid	90
% receiving some sort of aid	92
% of aid that is merit based	98
% receiving scholarships	46
Average grant	$11,546
Average loan	$24,148
Average total aid package	$27,758
Average debt	$60,149

EMPLOYMENT INFORMATION

Career Rating	68
State for bar exam	OH
Pass rate for first-time bar	94

Employers Who Frequently Hire Grads

Buckingham, Doolittle, & Burroughs; Brouse & McDowell; Roetzel & Andress; Vorys, Sater, Seymour and Pease; Squire, Sanders & Dempsey; Sughrue Mion; Jones Day; 9th District Court of Appeals; U.S. Army JAG Corps; City of Akron Law Dept; Hahn, Loeser; Brennan, Manna & Diamond; Benesch, Friedlander, Coplan & Aronoff; Black, McCuskey, Souers & Arbaugh; Krugliak, Wilkins, Griffiths & Dougherty; Harrington, Hoppe & Mitchell

Prominent Alumni

Deborah Cook, Judge, U.S. Court of Appeals-Sixth Circuit; Rochelle Seide, Partner, Schwegman Lundberg Woessner; John Vasuta, VP, Gen. Counsel & Sec., Bridgestone Firestone; Alice Batchelder, Judge, U.S. Court of Appeals-Sixth Circuit; Alex Shumate, Managing Partner-Squire, Sanders, Dempsey

THE UNIVERSITY OF ALABAMA—TUSCALOOSA

SCHOOL OF LAW

INSTITUTIONAL INFORMATION

Public/private	Public
Student/faculty ratio	10:1

SURVEY SAYS...

Great research resources, Great library staff, Abundant externship/internship/clerkship opportunities

STUDENTS

% full-time	100

ACADEMICS

Academic Experience Rating	74
Profs interesting rating	84
Profs accessible rating	92
Hours of study per day	4.07

Advanced Degrees Offered

LLM in Taxation, 2 years part-time; LLM for international graduates, 1 year full-time

Combined Degrees Offered

JD/MBA, 3–4 years; dual enrollment with various university graduate programs

Clinical program required	No
Legal writing course requirement	Yes
Legal methods course requirement	No
Legal research course requirement	Yes
Moot court requirement	Yes
Public interest law requirement	No

Academics

Students seeking a very good and very affordable legal education might want to check out the University of Alabama School of Law. "It is unlikely that you will receive a better legal education for the amount of tuition anywhere in the country," ventures a 3L.

"The bang for the buck can't be beat." "A robust trial ad competition program, extensive clinical opportunities, and the judicial externship program all provide great opportunities to see the courtroom—both in front of and behind the bench—and to hone practical skills." "Great study abroad and exchange programs" send students to Switzerland, India, Israel, and Australia. In a word, the "overall academic experience is excellent."

"The administration and faculty are friendly and seem to genuinely care about the students." "Alabama professors integrate theory with real-world practicality." "The faculty's mission is not to turn out legal academics, but rather to prepare capable attorneys for real-world situations." In terms of teaching, professors are either "excellent in the classroom" or "deplorable." "There aren't a whole lot of middle-of-the-road professors," explains one student. "I've had the best professors in my life at this school—and the worst." Outside of class, "Professors get to know their students" and "welcome the opportunity to help students in a variety of endeavors." "Although the student body is probably overwhelmingly conservative, classroom discussions are well-balanced and professors do a good job of presenting both sides." Students sing the administration's praises. "Our administration cares about students and is actively involved." They are "responsive to any student concerns and constantly seeks self-improvement. A single student concern is always addressed and is appropriately responded to." "

Career Services is "still a work in progress, but it is improving." "Because the school is so inexpensive," "Alabama is a no-brainer" for students who are interested in public interest careers. For students interested in private-sector work, UA's reputation is "still regional." Students are "confident" that their degrees "will open doors" throughout the Southeast, but they admit that Career Services tends to "focus on the big regional firms and because of that, most of the attention goes to the students at the very top of the class." "Attracting more out-of-state firms to on-campus recruiting" would be a big improvement.

The facilities here are mostly excellent. The library "screams 1970s," but "has more than sufficient resources."

Life

"The average student is young and direct from college," and "usually" from Alabama "or from a neighboring state." Students describe themselves as "very smart" and "down-to-earth." Politically, it's a pretty conservative atmosphere, and "expressing a more liberal viewpoint can sometimes be intimidating.'" The UA law student population is "not very diverse." But, "In recent years, racial and geographic diversity has been a priority of the law school. The average age of the law students has increased as well."

Academically, some students are "very grade-oriented" ("bordering on obsession") but, overall, "The competition appears healthy." "Civility among students is paramount," and "The atmosphere at Alabama is extremely collegial." Students enjoy "the perfect balance of friendly competition" among "an obviously motivated group of students, but never any cutthroat antics." That is, until you get to the best of the best. "People at the top are very competitive with each other. But there is also a sort of

Ms. Claude Reeves Arrington, Associate Dean
Box 870382, Tuscaloosa, AL 35487
Tel: 205-348-5440 Fax: 205-348-5439
E-Mail: admissions@law.ua.edu • Website: www.law.ua.edu

community with those people as well." "We don't have too many gunners or too many of the socially inept," says one student. "It's friendly competition, because we know we'll all be working together throughout our careers." "Students share course outlines freely." At UA, "you can get a law degree without selling your soul."

Socially, UA is "really a great place to study the law." "Students are overwhelmingly friendly and very cooperative." "It has been very easy for me to make several good friends among very diverse individuals with differing interests," says a 2L. "While we study a great deal, we also find time to hit up the bars in large groups." "The Student Bar Association throws parties every other week, and the students all socialize together." Tuscaloosa offers "great weather" and it's "a great college town." If you're not "super-interested" in football, though, "That's sacrilegious down here." Alabama's social scene generally "revolves around sports," and "Football is a near-religious experience." Devotion to the Crimson Tide definitely extends to the law school. Students have their own cheering section, "right there with the fraternities." "We schedule our work so that we can attend Crimson Tide ball games," says a 1L. If you "don't like football, you'll probably have a harder time finding your niche." "However, it is possible to escape that and do your own thing." "Birmingham is an awesome city a mere forty-five minutes away from Tuscaloosa and it offers everything an urbanite could need," including "fantastic shopping, excellent restaurants, lots of young singles, a sense of community, and even a little bit of the hipster scene (somewhat of a rarity in Alabama)."

Getting In

Applicants' LSAT and undergraduate GPA are the two significant factors considered in the admissions process at the University of Alabama School of Law. The median LSAT for the class enrolling in fall 2010 was 165. The admissions committee "also carefully considers the essay that you include with your application and your letters of recommendation."

ADMISSIONS

Selectivity Rating	**90**
# applications received	2,384
% applicants accepted	23
% acceptees attending	30
LSAT Range	159–167
Application fee	$40
Regular application	Rolling
Regular notification	Rolling
Early application program	No
Transfer students accepted	Yes
Evening division offered	No
Part-time accepted	No
CAS accepted	Yes

International Students

TOEFL required of
international students

FINANCIAL FACTS

Annual tuition	
(in-state/out-of-state)	$15,760/
	$28,070
Books and supplies	$1,400
Room and board	$10,400

EMPLOYMENT INFORMATION

Career Rating	**89**	Lightfoot, Franklin & White, LLC; Kilpatrick
Rate of placement (nine months out)	97	Stockton LLP; Alston & Bird LLP; Sirote &
State for bar exam	AL, GA, FL, TX, VA	Permutt, PC; Baker, Donelson, Bearman,
Pass rate for first-time bar	95	Caldwell & Berkowitz, PC; Adams and
Employers Who Frequently Hire Grads		Reese LLP; Cabaniss, Johnston, Gardner,
Bradley Arant Boult Cummings LLP;		Dumas & O'Neal LLP; Hand Arendall, LLC;
Maynard Cooper & Gale, PC; Balch &		Lanier, Ford, Shaver & Payne, PC
Bingham LLP; Burr & Forman LLP;		

UNIVERSITY OF ARIZONA
JAMES E. ROGERS COLLEGE OF LAW

INSTITUTIONAL INFORMATION

Public/private	Public
Student/faculty ratio	11:1
% faculty part-time	56
% faculty female	40
% faculty minority	12
Total faculty	106

SURVEY SAYS...

Great research resources,
Beautiful campus

STUDENTS

Enrollment of law school	460
% male/female	50/50
% from out-of-state	40
% full-time	100
% minority	25
% international	1
# of countries represented	3
Average age of entering class	25

ACADEMICS

Academic Experience Rating	**84**
Profs interesting rating	75
Profs accessible rating	91
Hours of study per day	4.12

Academic Specialties

Business (Certificate), Commercial, Constitutional, Corporation Securities, Criminal (Certificate), Environmental, Human Rights, International and Business (Certificate), Legal History, Legal Philosophy, Property, Taxation, Intellectual Property, Indian Law, Indigenous Peoples Rights and Policy (Certificate), International Trade Law

Advanced Degrees Offered

JD, 85 units, 3 years; LLM in International Trade Law, 24 units, 1 year; LLM in Indigenous Peoples Law and Policy, 24 units, 1 year; SJD, 3 years; JD with advanced standing, 2 years

Combined Degrees Offered

JD/PhD in Philosophy, Psychology, Economics, 6 years; JD/MBA,

Academics

The University of Arizona James E. Rogers College of Law offers "small class sizes"; "a very friendly, welcoming environment"; and "a price tag that lets students pursue careers in public service and nonprofit organizations" without racking up a gargantuan debt. Opportunities to gain practical experience are plentiful. The "strong" judicial externship program "can accommodate students interested in everything from bankruptcy court to superior court to district court." Clinics offer "hands-on experience" in eight areas including immigration, child advocacy, and indigenous peoples' law.

"This school is the most student-focused academic institution I have ever attended," says a happy 3L. Faculty members "truly care about their students" and "are available constantly." In the classroom, professors "make every effort to make the classes interesting and enjoyable," and "The small-section format during first year allows students to build a relationship with at least one professor." "They encourage discussion before and after class and are more than willing to provide letters of recommendation and reference." "They are approachable, friendly, and most even greet you by name as they pass you in the lobby or going to and from class." "Most are around campus all day and not just available during their office hours." "I e-mailed my property professor on a Sunday at roughly 10:30 P.M., with a pretty lengthy question," describes a 2L. "The question was answered at length by 10:45 P.M." "The administration is great too," enthuses a 1L. "Everyone is very helpful and interested in you getting a good education." "The quality of instruction is outstanding, and the responsiveness of the faculty and staff are remarkable. I am so very happy that I ended up at the U of A," sums up one pleased student.

Some students tell us that the "very helpful" Career and Professional Development Office at the U of A is "active in helping students connect with amazing internship and job opportunities in both the public sector and in law firms" in Arizona, California, and other Western states. If a student "is clear about where she wants to live or what she wants to do, the Career Office will give that student personal attention to strategize a plan to get there," although some complain that "they don't care what job you get, as long as you get one somewhere."

Facilities on campus are impressive. "The new building is gorgeous, especially the library. Tons of technology and connectivity. Little things like plugs at every desk and the latest projectors for classrooms make a big difference." Another student concurs, "The classrooms are brand-new and state-of-the-art—in my Family Law Class last semester we were able to video conference with a teacher in Canada to talk about divorce law without any extraneous equipment. Everything we needed to videochat was in the classroom!"

Life

There is a "relaxed Arizonan attitude" among the "amazingly friendly, smart" students at the U of A. "There is definitely competition here, as is unavoidable, but the school has a very laid-back atmosphere that allows you to keep things in perspective." "The second- and third-year students are very active in assisting the first-years adapt to law school through tutorials for all first-year classes," and teaching assistants "help with briefing and outlining." "Despite the curve, grades are not a big issue among students, and we tend to be excited for others' successes," declares a 1L. "This place is the opposite of cutthroat." Small sections for first-year students "are really conducive to forming lasting friendships." "I became very close with the other twenty-six students in my small section and continue to be good friends with several of them," says a 2L. "There is an overriding sense

JAMES E. ROGERS, ASSISTANT DEAN FOR ADMISSION AND FINANCIAL AID
P.O. BOX 210176, COLLEGE OF LAW, UNIVERSITY OF ARIZONA, TUCSON, AZ 85721-0176
TEL: 520-621-3477 FAX: 520-626-3436
E-MAIL: ADMISSIONS@LAW.ARIZONA.EDU • WEBSITE: WWW.LAW.ARIZONA.EDU

that everyone, from faculty to administration to students, really wants to be at the school and wants to see the school succeed."

The social atmosphere is "very vibrant." "There are thirty-plus student organizations that cover different religious, political, social and ethnic categories." That translates into lots of events. " "I have had so much fun in law school," gushes a 1L. "Almost every day, there are informative and thought-provoking guest speakers, panel discussions, or film screenings, especially during the lunch hour." Intramural sports are also popular. Social life tends to be "polarized between younger people coming straight out of college and older students with families." "The crowd divides into three groups," elaborates a 3L, "the married/serious relationship/older crowd, the nerds who rarely go out, and those who are trying to extend their undergraduate experience by going to law school." Without question, if you are "interested in partying, you cannot beat the University of Arizona bar scene."

The U of A campus itself is "beautiful, complete with palm trees and a gigantic, ideal student union." "The weather is ideal." The low cost of living is "fabulous, especially from a student's perspective." If you like outdoor activity, there are "myriad" activities within minutes of campus, including hiking, biking, swimming, and rock climbing.

Getting In

Admitted students at the 25th percentile have LSAT scores in the range of about 158 and GPAs in the range of 3.3 or so. Admitted students at the 75th percentile have LSAT scores of about 164 and GPAs approaching 3.8.

JD/MPA, JD/MA in American Indian Studies, Economics, Women's Studies, Latin American Studies, 4 years; JD/MMF Management Finance	
Clinical program required	No
Legal writing course requirement	Yes
Legal methods course requirement	No
Legal research course requirement	Yes
Moot court requirement	No
Public interest law requirement	No

ADMISSIONS

Selectivity Rating	**87**
# applications received	2,000
% applicants accepted	25
% acceptees attending	30
Average LSAT	162
LSAT Range	150–177
Average undergrad GPA	3.50
Application fee	$65
Regular application	Rolling, up to 2/15
Regular notification	Rolling
Early application program	No
Transfer students accepted	Yes
Evening division offered	No
Part-time accepted	No
CAS accepted	Yes

International Students

TOEFL required of international students	

FINANCIAL FACTS

Annual tuition (in-state/out-of-state)	$25,154/ $40,116
Books and supplies	$1,000
Fees	$920
Room and board	$11,840
Financial aid application deadline	3/1
% first-year students receiving some sort of aid	80
% receiving some sort of aid	82
% of aid that is merit based	50
% receiving scholarships	75
Average grant	$15,000
Average loan	$20,500
Average total aid package	$30,000
Average debt	$80,000

EMPLOYMENT INFORMATION

Career Rating	**86**
Rate of placement (nine months out)	95
Average starting salary	$70,000
State for bar exam	AZ, CA, WA, NV, D.C.
Pass rate for first-time bar	93

Employers Who Frequently Hire Grads

Snell & Wilmer; Perkins Coie; Lewis & Roca; Kirkland & Ellis; Quarles & Brady; Bryan Cave; Greenberg Traurig; Squire Sanders; Gibson Dunn; Osborn Maledon; Jennings Strouss & Salmon; Latham & Watkins; Fennemore Craig; Gallagher & Kennedy; Beus Gilbert; Cohen Kennedy; Ballard Spahr; Steptoe & Johnson; Polsinelli Shughart; Golder Silver; AZ Supreme Court; AZ Court of Appeals; U.S. Dist. Courts; U.S. Circuit Courts; Dept. of Justice; State Attorney General's Office; Pima Co. and Maricopa Co. prosecutor and public defender; county and city attorneys offices in AZ, CA, NV; legal services offices in AZ and CA; Deloitte; Raytheon; OGE Energy Corporation; Starbucks

Prominent Alumni

Morris K. Udall, Former Congressman; Stewart Udall, Former Congressman & Secretary of Interior; Dennis DeConcini, Former Senator; Stanley Feldman, AZ Supreme Court Justice; John Kyl, U.S. Senator

Grads Employed by Field (%)

Academic	(6)
Business/industry	(10)
Government	(18)
Judicial clerkship	(20)
Military	(2)
Private practice	(40)
Public interest	(5)

UNIVERSITY OF ARKANSAS—FAYETTEVILLE

SCHOOL OF LAW

INSTITUTIONAL INFORMATION

Public/private	Public
Student/faculty ratio	11:1
% faculty part-time	36
% faculty female	41
% faculty minority	8
Total faculty	59

SURVEY SAYS...

Diverse opinions accepted in classrooms, Great research resources, Students love Fayetteville, AR

STUDENTS

Enrollment of law school	390
% male/female	56/44
% from out-of-state	35
% full-time	100
% minority	17
Average age of entering class	25

ACADEMICS

Academic Experience Rating	86
Profs interesting rating	84
Profs accessible rating	86
Hours of study per day	4.39

Advanced Degrees Offered

LLM in Agricultural Law, 1 year

Combined Degrees Offered

JD/MBA, 3/1.5 years; JD/MPA, 3/1 years; LLM/MS, 1/1.5 years

Clinical program required	No
Legal writing	
course requirement	Yes
Legal methods	
course requirement	No
Legal research	
course requirement	No
Moot court requirement	No
Public interest	
law requirement	No

Academics

The University of Arkansas School of Law in Fayetteville is "a smaller school" that offers a "five-star, New York restaurant quality education for a McDonald's price." "In choosing a school that has very low in-state tuition, I gained an extremely valuable education at a fraction of the cost I would have paid at other institutions," brags a miserly 3L. "It's a pretty unbelievable education for the cost." "Various trial and counseling competitions are a few of the greatest strengths" here. Clinical courses and certified skills courses offer "excellent opportunities to get hands-on experience with the actual practice of law." In addition to traditional judicial externships, there are legislative externships and corporate counsel externships. A "strong legal writing program" is another plus. "You'll hear the students whining about it around the time appellate briefs are due," promises a 3L, "but we finish the program with excellent practical writing skills."

"The faculty is comprised of both older professors using more traditional teaching styles such as the Socratic Method, and younger professors that bring helpful insight[s] into today's practice of law into the classroom," explains a 2L. While a few professors here "would be better suited to write articles all day long and not get anywhere near the classroom, "the quality of the instruction is fantastic" overall. "Most of the professors are really energetic and relevant," says a 1L, "and they encourage lively discussion." This faculty is also "devoted" and "almost always accessible" outside of class. The "very accessible and accommodating" administration is "always putting the students first" and "committed to raising the school's profile." "I have never had a problem too big or too small for them to address," reminisces a 3L. "It has been great." The big academic complaint at the University of Arkansas is the dearth of specialized courses. "The law school needs to add more electives," flatly asserts a 3L. "In a given semester there are not more than ten electives, several which are offered at the same time of day, substantially narrowing the choices."

Career Services isn't perfect but the staff is generally "wonderful" and employment prospects are reportedly excellent. Starting salaries are lower than what you'll find in more populous places. Arkansas is very inexpensive, though, and it's one of those states where everybody seems to know everybody else. Consequently, "the networking abilities within the city and state" are definitely a strength. Also, with Wal-Mart and gargantuan food conglomerate Tyson "just down the road," Northwest Arkansas is a relatively booming area of the country that "provides many unique opportunities for employment with both law firms and major corporations." "We have some students who go 'big law' in the major cities; we have some students who set up shop in rural Arkansas; we have some who go in-house; and we have a lot of government employees, too," says a 3L.

"The facilities are old in some areas but brand-new in others," and there are "lots of small nooks to study in." The old classrooms that are still used for nearly all of the first-year classes are "okay" at best. "The wood paneling is dark and depressing and reminiscent of an old station wagon," describes a 2L. A newer wing has "ergonomic and aesthetically pleasing" classrooms that are "technology-friendly." "The research facilities are great" in the "comprehensive" library. There's an onsite coffee shop, too, "which is great for study breaks when you need to recaffeinate."

James K. Miller, Associate Dean for Students
University of Arkansas School of Law, Fayetteville, AR 72701
Tel: 479-575-3102 Fax: 479-575-3937
E-Mail: jkmiller@uark.edu • Website: law.uark.edu

Life

Some students describe the academic atmosphere as "very competitive." It's "cut-throat" during the first year, they allege. Other students dispute that characterization. "Students here are pretty laid-back," rejoins a 1L. "We work hard but it's not a cutthroat environment where people are trying to claw their way to the top of the class no matter what."

According to one view, social life can be hard for transplants because a lot of students come preequipped with their own cliques. "People who went to undergraduate school here seem to hang out with each other," says a 3L. "Many of the groups do not appear to be very inclusive of other students not in their normal social circle." Other students describe the environment as "very communal." "You get to know your fellow students and professors very well," says a 2L. Socially satisfied students also point to the "wide availability" of clubs and organizations and the fact that the student bar association is "active in providing events outside of the law school to…[help] get your mind off of classes." Campus sporting events are another big draw—especially football—and the surrounding Ozarks provide plenty of options for adventure activity. Fayetteville is very much a college town with "a unique feel that allows for people of many different cultures and backgrounds to feel at home." Dickson Street, the hub of Fayetteville nightlife, adjoins the campus, so you can revel with party-hardy undergrads any time you want to blow off your cases.

Getting In

Admitted students at the 25th percentile have LSAT scores in the low 150s and undergraduate grade point averages not too much over 3.0. At the 75th percentile, LSAT scores approach 160 and GPAs are 3.7 or so.

ADMISSIONS

Selectivity Rating	83
# applications received	1,514
% applicants accepted	27
% acceptees attending	34
Average LSAT	157
LSAT Range	153–160
Average undergrad GPA	3.49
Application fee	$0
Regular application	Rolling, up to 4/1
Regular notification	Rolling
Early application program	No
Transfer students accepted	Yes
Evening division offered	No
Part-time accepted	No
CAS accepted	Yes

International Students

TOEFL required of international students

FINANCIAL FACTS

Annual tuition (in-state/out-of-state)	$9,686/ $20,820
Books and supplies	$1,162
Fees	$1,681
Financial aid application deadline	4/1
% first-year students receiving some sort of aid	87
% receiving some sort of aid	87
% of aid that is merit based	65
% receiving scholarships	39
Average grant	$6,000
Average loan	$19,345
Average debt	$56,358

EMPLOYMENT INFORMATION

Career Rating	74
Rate of placement (nine months out)	91
Average starting salary	$53,505
State for bar exam	AR, GA, MO, OK, TX

Employers Who Frequently Hire Grads
Wright, Lindsey & Jennings LLP; Friday, Eldredge & Clark LLP; Mitchell Williams; Kutak Rock LLP

Prominent Alumni
George W. Haley, Former Ambassador to Gambia; Mark Pryor, U.S. Senator from Arkansas; Mike Beebe, Governor of Arkansas; Rodney Slater, Former U.S. Secretary of Transportation; Thomas A. Mars, Exec. VP, Chief Administrative Officer, Wal-Mart, Inc.

Grads Employed by Field (%)
Academic (2)
Business/industry (17)
Government (15)
Judicial clerkship (3)
Private practice (62)
Public interest (1)

University of Arkansas—Little Rock

William H. Bowen School of Law

Academics

The "perfectly sized" University of Arkansas—Little Rock School of Law is located "right in the heart of downtown Little Rock"—"the economic and government center of the state"—and it is thoroughly "tied into the local community through its connections with legislators, judges, government agencies, and private firms." Clerkships and externships are "bountiful." Access to part-time jobs at law firms is "second to none." Other perks at UALR include three clinical programs, five dual-degree programs, and "a bargain-basement price." There are around twenty different areas of concentration here and some students tell us that "the overall breadth of course choices makes it possible to study almost any topic you find particularly interesting." Others grumble that course selection is actually pretty limited. "Students here get a strong, basic legal education," says a 2L. "However, if you want more variety in more subject-specific courses, you won't really find them at this school."

Professors "expect you to come to class prepared." The faculty is "highly qualified, and there is a great mix of" adjuncts who teach specialized courses. Not every professor is great but most are "dedicated" teachers "who really want to see their students learn." "They make sure we understand," says a 1L, "and if we don't, they go back over it." Students also laud the legal writing program and say that the "writing instructors epitomize true excellence in their fields." Outside of class, faculty members are reportedly "very approachable." "The student body is small enough that you can have ample one-on-one time with the profs after hours," reports a 3L, "if you're brave enough." Student opinion concerning the administration is drastically split. Some students call management "incompetent." "The school is run like a low-budget movie set," charges a 2L. Other students contend that UALR is "very well-run." "The administration is very helpful and accessible," they contend, and the deans make "an effort to hear student comments and feedback, and implement changes accordingly."

The law school itself is "ugly-looking from the outside" and it's "in a rough section of town." The facility is "very pretty" on the inside, though, "with great marble stairs" and "nice views" from the upper levels. Incidentally, we think the "haunted floors" are just a legend. "Classrooms are top-notch" "with plenty of outlets" for laptops. "This law school is one of the only schools in the nation with state-of-the-art video lecture capture in nearly every room," beams a 3L. "Missed something in class? Watch it again, including any slides or videos that were shown." The building is also "fully equipped for Wi-Fi access and remote printing." There's a fabulous student lounge, too. Even "parking is awesome," which is something law students at many schools complain about to high heaven. "Overall, our school works to provide us with a comfortable environment," says a 2L. The spacious library is "the law library for the state of Arkansas, so it is excellent," too. The staff is "phenomenal." It's a public library, though, and "There are definitely some pro se misfits who can be distracting."

Life

Some students call UALR "a diverse school." Others argue, "There is not much diversity," beyond a solid contingent of nontraditional, older students. Views of the academic atmosphere also vary. "There are some students who are very competitive," relates a 3L, "and there are others like me who do the best that I can regardless of what others do." Other students say, "There is no rivalry" when it come to grades. "There is a definite sense that we are all in this together," says a 1L, "and most everyone is willing to help out a fellow student if that students asks."

AARON N. TAYLOR, ASSISTANT DEAN FOR ADMISSIONS
1201 MCMATH AVENUE, LITTLE ROCK, AR 72202-5142
TEL: 501-324-9903 FAX: 501-324-9433
E-MAIL: LAWADM@UALR.EDU • WEBSITE: WWW.LAW.UALR.EDU

Socially, it's "a very congenial atmosphere." "There are plenty of student organizations." In addition, there are "wonderful lunch meetings and seminars, as well as dinner programs on a regular basis that accommodate both part-time and full-time students." "The school is intimate and definitely allows for getting acquainted with people," reports a 2L, though "if you're not from Arkansas it is a lot harder to find a social niche." Also, "there does seem to be a line" between the students who find it "hard turning down the temptation of going out" and those who would rather crack the books all day, every day. Beyond the confines of the law school, Little Rock is "the largest city in Arkansas," but it's "still a small town" that approximates "a suburb" when compared to a lot of bigger cities. "There is not a whole lot to do in Little Rock outside of school," explains a 2L. "There is a downtown area with bars and shops, but nothing huge."

Getting In

For admitted students at the 25th percentile, LSAT scores hover a little over 150 and undergraduate grade point averages are in the 3.0 range. At the 75th percentile, LSAT scores are around 157 and GPAs are a little under 3.6.

Clinical program required	No
Legal writing course requirement	Yes
Legal methods course requirement	Yes
Legal research course requirement	Yes
Moot court requirement	No
Public interest law requirement	No

ADMISSIONS

Selectivity Rating	81
# applications received	1,514
% applicants accepted	27
% acceptees attending	38
LSAT Range	151–157
Application fee	$0
Regular application	Rolling, up to 8/15
Regular notification	Rolling
Early application program	No
Transfer students accepted	Yes
Evening division offered	Yes
Part-time accepted	Yes
CAS accepted	Yes

International Students

TOEFL recommended of international students

FINANCIAL FACTS

Annual tuition (in-state/out-of-state)	$10,062/ $22,058
Books and supplies	$1,250
Fees	$1,395
Room and board	$8,000
Financial aid application deadline	7/1
% receiving scholarships	36
Average grant	$5,090
Average loan	$19,500
Average total aid package	$19,500
Average debt	$26,000

EMPLOYMENT INFORMATION

Career Rating	73
Rate of placement (nine months out)	82
Average starting salary	$50,000
State for bar exam	AR, TN, TX, GA, FL
Pass rate for first-time bar	86

Employers Who Frequently Hire Grads
Wright, Lindsey & Jennings Law Firm; Friday, Eldredge & Clark Law Firm; Prosecuting Attorney; Mitchell, Williams, Selig, Gates & Woodyard; State Supreme Court; State Court of Appeals, State Attorney General's Office

Prominent Alumni
Vic Snyder, Member, U.S. Congress; Annabelle Imber Tuck, State Supreme Court; Colette Honorable, State Public Service Commission; H.E. 'Bud' Cummins, U.S. Attorney; Charles W. 'Bill' Burton, Attorney, Jones Day, Houston, TX

Grads Employed by Field (%)
Academic (2)
Business/industry (23)
Government (18)
Judicial clerkship (5)
Private practice (49)
Public interest (3)

UNIVERSITY OF CALIFORNIA
HASTINGS COLLEGE OF THE LAW

Academics

University of California Hastings College of the Law, "in the heart of San Francisco," has "a great reputation in the Bay Area" and students love its "worthwhile focus on practical" training. "The emphasis on concrete lawyering skills over abstract theory and the Socratic teaching method makes Hastings a very desirable place to be," brags a 3L. "Hastings is well-known for creating lawyers capable of hitting the ground running from the moment they graduate." "All Hastings students learn how to be successful oral advocates," vaunts a 2L. "This school will turn the softest young student into a tough lawyer." "The diversity of curriculum is unparalleled" as well. There are seven concentration areas. There are nine journals. There are fourteen study abroad programs. Clinics galore run the gamut from mediation to legislation to human rights to environmental law. The "great" moot court program is among the finest in the nation and UC Hastings competition teams bag a host of awards annually. The extensive externship program "is one of a kind." Hastings is located "in a hub of legal activity for California," "near courts at nearly every state and federal level." As a result, over 100 students work for judges each year.

"The faculty is very eclectic and cultured" and, for the most part, "extremely accessible." "Many professors are well-known in their respected field." Even better, most are "compelling," "fun-loving, and immensely talented" in the classroom. They "do a nice job of mixing legal theory with practical knowledge." "However, there are a few who are just bad. They simply don't know how to teach and just babble." Also, class sizes "can be large." "The number of students is really too large for the facilities and the number of professors." The administration here is probably a little better than what you would expect from a state school in California. "They respond to e-mail quickly," though there's "very little handholding."

Career-wise, "This school is heavily weighted toward public interest law." It's a big feeder for district attorney and public defender offices. Some students would like to see "more of an emphasis on private-sector and corporate placement." Complaints are minimal, though. The "career services office is pretty good." There's a "large alumni network" that likes to help the latest batch of graduates. Employers conduct a few thousand on-campus interviews with Hastings students each year. Average starting salaries are considerable.

Life

"Hastings is so diverse it makes Berkeley look like BYU," boasts a 3L. Students (and professors) here tend to be very, very politically liberal but they are quite a diverse group otherwise. Many come straight from college. "However, an equal or greater number of students have been many years out of undergrad." Some of the future attorneys here tell us that the academic culture is "competitive and a little annoying." "I have generally found the students to be closed to outsiders, competitive, and suspicious of others," advises a 3L. "It is a little intimidating." Others assure us that any cutthroat behavior is "isolated to relatively few students and does not infect the entire atmosphere." "I had heard a lot about the hyper-competitive reputation of Hastings before matriculating, but have actually found almost all the students to be very pleasant," says a 2L. "No one will help the slacker but we will all help a friend and fellow classmate who pulls their weight," adds a 1L.

GREG CANADA, ASSISTANT DEAN OF ADMISSIONS
200 MCALLISTER STREET, SAN FRANCISCO, CA 94102
TEL: 415-565-4623 FAX: 415-581-8946
E-MAIL: ADMISS@UCHASTINGS.EDU • WEBSITE: WWW.UCHASTINGS.EDU

There is a solid contingent of people who "kind of do the school thing and go home" but "the social life at Hastings is very lively" if you want it to be. There are tons of student organizations, "and the school helps students fund and run their organizations." "There are campus-wide events all the time." There's something for everyone, from students fresh out of undergrad who "need to play some beer pong and have a jam-packed social life to students with families and other commitments who prefer to treat law school as a nine-to-five job." "If you can't find social events to attend then you're not looking," admonishes a 2L. Students also love to explore all of the Bay Area in their precious downtime. Certainly, though, they don't love the "pretty horrible" neighborhood that immediately surrounds Hastings, an area "teeming with homeless people and drug addicts." Some students don't see what the fuss is, though. "The Tenderloin is a low-income community," counters a 2L, "but it's not that dangerous or even ugly. Even the worst places in the Tenderloin at the worst times of night are better than Oakland."

Getting In

Admitted students at the 25th percentile have LSAT scores around 160 and undergraduate grade point averages in the 3.4 range. At the 75th percentile, LSAT scores are about 165 and GPAs are 3.7 or so. Hastings has a special admissions program for students who come from seriously difficult backgrounds. The median LSAT score among students admitted through this program is in the high 150s and median GPA is approximately 3.5.

Clinical program required	No
Legal writing course requirement	Yes
Legal methods course requirement	No
Legal research course requirement	Yes
Moot court requirement	Yes
Public interest law requirement	No

ADMISSIONS

Selectivity Rating	92
# applications received	5,881
% applicants accepted	23
% acceptees attending	29
Average LSAT	164
LSAT Range	160–165
Average undergrad GPA	3.60
Application fee	$75
Regular application	Rolling, up to 3/1
Regular notification	5/30
Early application program	Yes
Early application deadline	11/15
Early application notification	12/15
Transfer students accepted	Yes
Evening division offered	No
Part-time accepted	No
CAS accepted	Yes

FINANCIAL FACTS

Annual tuition (in-state/out-of-state)	$36,000/ $47,225
Books and supplies	$1,150
Fees	$2,906
Room and board	$14,040
Financial aid application deadline	3/1
% first-year students receiving some sort of aid	90
% receiving some sort of aid	91
% of aid that is merit based	1
% receiving scholarships	80
Average grant	$9,682
Average loan	$35,090
Average total aid package	$42,801
Average debt	$92,327

EMPLOYMENT INFORMATION

Career Rating	**95**	**Grads Employed by Field (%)**
Rate of placement (nine months out)	92	Academic (9)
Average starting salary	$122,378	Business/industry (9)
State for bar exam	CA, NY	Government (11)
Pass rate for first-time bar	82	Judicial clerkship (4)
Employers Who Frequently Hire Grads		Private practice (60)
Major San Francisco and Los Angeles large and medium-size law firms		Public interest (6)

Prominent Alumni
Marvin Baxter, Associate Justice, CA Supreme Court; Willie Brown, Former Mayor, San Francisco; Carol Corrigan, Associate Justice, CA Supreme Court; Joseph Cotchett, Founding Partner, Cotchett Pitre & Simon; Ann M. Veneman, Executive Director, UNICEF

UNIVERSITY OF CALIFORNIA—BERKELEY
BERKELEY LAW

INSTITUTIONAL INFORMATION

Public/private	Public
% faculty female	36
% faculty minority	20
Total faculty	144

SURVEY SAYS...

Great library staff, Liberal students, Students love Berkeley, CA

STUDENTS

Enrollment of law school	916
% male/female	47/53
% from out-of-state	44
% full-time	100
% minority	47
Average age of entering class	25

ACADEMICS

Academic Experience Rating	85
Profs interesting rating	87
Profs accessible rating	81
Hours of study per day	4.29

Academic Specialties

Corporation Securities, Environmental, International, Intellectual Property, Law & Technology, Comparative Legal Studies, Business Law & Economics, Social Justice

Advanced Degrees Offered

LLM, 1 year; JSD, varies; PhD in Jurisprudence and Social Policy, approximately 6 years

Combined Degrees Offered

Students sometimes pursue joint-degrees: JD/MBA, JD/MA, JD/MA Asian Studies, International Area Studies, JD/MCP City and Regional Planning, JD/MJ Journalism, JD/MPP Public Policy, JD/MSW, JD/MS Energy and Resources Group. Students can arrange other joint-degrees on an individual basis, subject to approval from each institution. JD/MA or MS, 4 years; JD/PhD, varies

Academics

UC Berkeley School of Law is indisputably one the nation's most celebrated citadels of legal education. The curriculum includes a great mix of legal theory and practical courses, and the breadth of specialized courses is dazzling. "Students have the opportunity to pursue virtually any sub-genre of the law and receive credit for it," says a satisfied 3L. "There are extensive externship opportunities at nonprofit organizations and governmental agencies." There are nearly a dozen journals. Unlike at most law schools, all of them (except for the Law Review) are open membership, and students are allowed to participate immediately. Students tell us that the immense clinical opportunities "are the absolute highlight of Boalt," though. "We get to start clinical opportunities, just like journals, from day one," gloats a 1L. "There are a number of 1L clinics in employment, education, immigration and asylum, tenant rights, homeless aid—you name it."

The "illustrious" faculty at Berkeley Law is crammed with "almost frighteningly brilliant" professors who are "some of the most well-known and well-respected scholars in the field." The "quality of instruction can vary widely" "from the poor to the most excellent," but it's always worth showing up to lectures for the dynamic classroom interaction. "Boalt's intellectual rigor is most evident in class discussions," reports a 2L, "where students' learnedness, insightfulness, and curiosity come shining through." Outside of class, professors are "incredibly devoted," "always approachable," and "want to develop relationships." Sipping coffee with faculty members is practically customary, and it's not uncommon to go to a professor's house "for sushi and great wine, while discussing the Uniform Commercial Code." Some students are "disgruntled" with the top brass, especially in light of ever-increasing tuition. However, even the harshest critics admit that management "runs things fairly smoothly." "The administration is always ready to help," declares a 1L, "whether it's dealing with the crashing of a laptop during a final or hearing and considering an idea for school improvement."

Like every other law school, Berkeley Law is engaged in "a constant arms race to be better positioned for firm hiring." The difference is that Berkeley usually wins. The "name has street cred," and the Career Development Office "can and will help you find a job." Job opportunities are beyond plum, and the school's prestigious reputation helps students land summer associate jobs and extravagantly salaried full-time positions at prestigious firms around the country. Also, the loan repayment assistance program for students who choose to go work in the public interest is one of the best in the nation.

"No one picks Boalt for its facilities," and "Boalt's exterior will never be much to write home about." However, the interior of the school is "generally quite up-to-date," if not "freaking gorgeous." "Classrooms are pretty standard, not really good or bad," but they're "modern and laptop friendly." The newly renovated library boasts a pretty striking reading room and, as you would expect, world-class resources.

Life

Students at Berkeley Law are "weird" and "wildly intelligent, but not wildly egotistical." "Diversity is wonderful." "Every student at Berkeley is passionate about something, and it is just incredible to hear their experiences," gushes a 2L. Views of the political landscape are conflicting. Some students find it "overly politically correct." "The liberal Bezerkeley mania occasionally—not as often as you'd expect—takes over the student body and affects the tenor of class discussions," says a 1L. However, liberalism isn't unconditionally pervasive. "I am very conservative and haven't even noticed which side of the political scale most people fall on," relates a 1L, "because no one really shoves

EDWARD TOM, ASSISTANT DEAN OF ADMISSIONS
2850 TELEGRAPH AVENUE, SUITE 500, BERKELEY, CA 94705-7220
TEL: 510-642-2274 FAX: 510-643-6222
E-MAIL: ADMISSIONS@LAW.BERKELEY.EDU • WEBSITE: WWW.LAW.BERKELEY.EDU

it in your face, especially the professors." "There are weirdoes from the right and the left here," adds a wizened 3L, "who all come together to learn and grow."

Academically, "The culture is fantastic." It's "an atmosphere that's as noncompetitive as you can hope for with a building full of law students." "Even the gunners are relaxed." The relatively tolerant grading scale (which is sort of an all-or-nothing curve) relieves a lot of pressure. Still, "No matter how smart you are, you have to try hard." Beyond the confines of the classroom, a multitude of clubs and organizations forms the backbone of student life. "Boalt is a collegial place," reports a 2L. "Students have fun studying together, partying together, and just hanging out." "Berkeley quirkiness," "great weather" at all times of the year, and the fact that "you get to live and work in the Bay Area" are also fabulous perks. "If you have to spend three years studying law," counsels a happy 2L, "there's no better place than Berkeley to do it."

Getting In

It's extremely difficult to get admitted to Berkeley Law. Admitted students at the 25th percentile have LSAT scores around 163 and undergraduate GPAs just higher than 3.6. At the 75th percentile, LSAT scores are approximately 170, and GPAs are pretty close to 3.9.

Clinical program required	No
Legal writing course requirement	Yes
Legal methods course requirement	Yes
Legal research course requirement	Yes
Moot court requirement	Yes
Public interest law requirement	No

ADMISSIONS

Selectivity Rating	**98**
# applications received	8,297
% applicants accepted	10
% acceptees attending	34
LSAT Range	162–170
Application fee	$75
Regular application	Rolling, up to 2/1
Regular notification	4/1
Early application program	No
Transfer students accepted	Yes
Evening division offered	No
Part-time accepted	No
CAS accepted	Yes

International Students

TOEFL required of international students	

FINANCIAL FACTS

Annual tuition (in-state/out-of-state)	$45,300/ $49,507
Books and supplies	$1,495
Fees	$3,796
Room and board	$17,524
Financial aid application deadline	3/2
% first-year students receiving some sort of aid	89
% receiving some sort of aid	88
% of aid that is merit based	5
% receiving scholarships	60
Average grant	$16,437
Average loan	$35,082
Average total aid package	$43,749
Average debt	$91,277

EMPLOYMENT INFORMATION

Career Rating	**98**	**Grads Employed by Field (%)**
Rate of placement (nine months out)	96	Academic (1)
Average starting salary	$160,000	Business/industry (1)
State for bar exam	CA	Government (7)
Pass rate for first-time bar	92	Judicial clerkship (11)
Employers Who Frequently Hire Grads		Private practice (69)
Roughly 450 employers recruit at Boalt		Public interest (11)
Hall each fall including national firms,		
multinational corporations, public interest		
groups, and governmental agencies		

UNIVERSITY OF CALIFORNIA—DAVIS
SCHOOL OF LAW

INSTITUTIONAL INFORMATION

Public/private	Public
Student/faculty ratio	11:1
% faculty part-time	26
% faculty female	47
% faculty minority	33
Total faculty	70

SURVEY SAYS...

Diverse opinions accepted in classrooms, Great library staff, Liberal students

STUDENTS

Enrollment of law school	618
% male/female	51/49
% full-time	100
% international	1
# of countries represented	12
Average age of entering class	24

ACADEMICS

Academic Experience Rating	91
Profs interesting rating	90
Profs accessible rating	91
Hours of study per day	4.53

Academic Specialties

Criminal, Environmental, Human Rights, International, Taxation, Intellectual Property, Business, Social Justice

Advanced Degrees Offered

LLM, 1 year

Combined Degrees Offered

JD/MBA, 4 years; JD/MA, JD/MS, 4 years

Clinical program required	No
Legal writing course requirement	Yes
Legal methods course requirement	Yes
Legal research course requirement	Yes
Moot court requirement	No
Public interest law requirement	No

Academics

The "cozy" University of California—Davis, School of Law is "one of the smallest law schools in California." The "dynamic" professors here "know what they're talking about" and are "passionate about teaching." Sure, some teachers are less student-oriented but overall, "The faculty is the best part of King Hall." "Most use some form or other of the Socratic Method." "My professors have at least added humor to my life, ranging from role play (like arresting people in class) and poking fun at our being stumped over relatively simple questions just because it's sometimes terrifying to be called on," relates a 2L. These "incredibly approachable" professors are also "willing to help in anyway they can to enhance your education or career goals." Tutors in the highly praised teaching assistant program "hold office hours and review sessions to solidify big-picture concepts" for 1Ls. The UCD administration is good at "seeking student involvement in decision-making."

The whopping eleven clinics at UCD "are a great way to really understand how to practice law." The prison law clinic in particular "has enjoyed a great deal of success and acclaim." There are certificate programs in public service law and environmental law, and students say they are "truly are committed to public interest work." "We take the fact that we are named after Martin Luther King Jr. very seriously," asserts a 2L. "It's great to be in an environment where people truly care about cause lawyering." However, many students pine for more of a course selection. "About one-fourth of a class has the opportunity to take Pre-Trial Skills, but there are so many classes like Latinos and the Law and Disability Rights with classrooms that sit half empty."

As for employment, alumni are "supportive," and with San Francisco and Sacramento nearby, "Davis is conveniently connected to two powerful cities that are full of federal, state, and local agencies as well as important judicial offices." The school has responded to students' complaints that Career Services "needs to get its act together" by hiring new staff, including a new Assistant Dean. "'Big-law' possibilities are fairly good," and "approximately twenty-five percent of the student body will work in a large law firm after graduation." There is "an awesome loan forgiveness program" for graduates who pursue public interest careers.

The King Law building recently underwent a massive expansion and renovation, which included the construction of new classrooms and offices, as well as a new appellate courtroom. The library is an "exceptional" research facility, but it's "grungy," "with a little bit of a 1960s industrial feel." "Fortunately the school is about to undergo a dramatic facelift." "Future classes should have newer and more spacious facilities."

Life

Student diversity is comparatively strong on campus, with a visible "Asian and Pacific Islander" presence and a "decent" Hispanic student population. "There are active Jewish, Muslim, and Catholic student groups in the law school, as well as a feminist forum, a pro-choice group, a GLBT group, and a Federalist society." Politically, "Students are often very liberal or very conservative," and "Moderates aren't very vocal."

SHARON L. PINKNEY, DIRECTOR OF ADMISSION
SCHOOL OF LAW-KING HALL, 400 MRAK HALL DRIVE, DAVIS, CA 95616-5201
TEL: 530-752-6477
E-MAIL: ADMISSIONS@LAW.UCDAVIS.EDU • WEBSITE: WWW.LAW.UCDAVIS.EDU

"There is certainly competition" among students, but "the King Hall Spirit" "keeps it from getting dirty or uncomfortable." "A laid-back atmosphere" permeates. "People loan notes and books without a qualm." "Not that we all hold hands in the hallway and sing Kumbaya," elaborates a 3L, "but everybody is very respectful and has a good time together." Socially, "Most people find a niche," and events and parties occur "pretty much every weekend." "There are a large number of traditions at King Hall that students really get into" as well, including "softball and bowling leagues, the law school talent show, and a law school prom." "While these may seem lame and tacky, they are actually really fun, and the large majority of students get involved," explains a 3L. There's also "a co-op nursery, so students with children can drop their kids off while in class."

"The city of Davis is a delightful college town." "You don't have to fight traffic, and people are just downright friendly." "Armies of students ride bicycles to classes, and the fun downtown area is a short walk from campus." There is a "dearth of interesting restaurants," but "The weather is nice." "You can focus," notes a 3L, because "It's quiet." "Davis is a fantastic place to spend three years of graduate school," adds another 3L.

"Sacramento is fifteen minutes away and the Bay Area is only an hour [away]." "Great skiing" and "wine country" are not far. Davis is also "a town where hippies settle down after...making high salaries." As a result, apartments aren't cheap. "The housing crunch cannot be overstated enough," warns a 2L. "Students considering Davis should immediately check Craigslist and do everything in their power to get housing secured as soon as they accept."

Getting In

Admitted students at the 25th percentile have LSAT scores of 161 and GPAs of nearly 3.5. Admitted students at the 75th percentile have LSAT scores of 166 and GPAs of 3.8. UC Davis will consider all LSAT scores and asks that applicants add an addendum explaining increases of 5 points or more for multiple LSAT scores.

ADMISSIONS

Selectivity Rating	90
# applications received	4,020
% applicants accepted	23
% acceptees attending	21
Average LSAT	162
LSAT Range	160–165
Average undergrad GPA	3.63
Application fee	$75
Regular application	Rolling, up to 2/1
Regular notification	Rolling
Early application program	No
Transfer students accepted	Yes
Evening division offered	No
Part-time accepted	No
CAS accepted	Yes

International Students

TOEFL required of international students	

FINANCIAL FACTS

Annual tuition	$12,245
Books and supplies	$1,014
Fees	$41,763
Room and board	$11,862
Financial aid application deadline	3/2
% first-year students receiving some sort of aid	87
% receiving some sort of aid	90
% of aid that is merit based	26
% receiving scholarships	84
Average grant	$12,579
Average loan	$32,921
Average total aid package	$45,500
Average debt	$98,179

EMPLOYMENT INFORMATION

Career Rating	93
Rate of placement (nine months out)	99
Average starting salary	$105,086
State for bar exam	CA
Pass rate for first-time bar	81

Employers Who Frequently Hire Grads
State of California, private law firms, district attorneys, public defenders, public interest entities. Contact Career Services Office for list of firms.

Prominent Alumni
Tani Cantil-Sakauye, Chief Justice, California Supreme Court; Darrell Steinberg, President Pro Tem, California State Senate; George Miller, Member, U.S. House of Representatives, CA 7th district

Grads Employed by Field (%)
Academic (9)
Business/industry (6)
Government (10)
Judicial clerkship (5)
Military (1)
Private practice (44)
Public interest (10)

UNIVERSITY OF CALIFORNIA—LOS ANGELES
SCHOOL OF LAW

INSTITUTIONAL INFORMATION

Public/private	Public
Student/faculty ratio	12:1
% faculty part-time	36
% faculty female	36
% faculty minority	14
Total faculty	169

SURVEY SAYS...
Great research resources,
Great library staff, Students love
Los Angeles, CA

STUDENTS

Enrollment of law school	999
% male/female	52/48
% from out-of-state	31
% full-time	100
% minority	15
% international	2
# of countries represented	13
Average age of entering class	25

ACADEMICS

Academic Experience Rating	97
Profs interesting rating	89
Profs accessible rating	86
Hours of study per day	4.07

Academic Specialties
Constitutional, Corporation Securities, Criminal, Environmental, Human Rights, International, Labor, Legal Philosophy, Property, Taxation, Intellectual Property, Public Interest Law and Policy, Business Law and Policy Program, Critical Race Studies, Entertainment and Media Law and Policy Program, Law and Philosophy Program

Advanced Degrees Offered
In addition to the JD degree, we offer a 1-year LLM for domestic and foreign students seeking a year of advanced legal studies, with specializations in Entertainment and Media Law and Policy, International and Comparative Law, and 4 business-related fields. With the Graduate Studies Committee's approval, students may design specializations. Our SJD is a highly selective program open to applicants who possess a distinguished prior academic record in law, show promise of outstanding scholarship, and demonstrate a high potential for completing a scholarly dissertation of required quality. Applicants must hold a JD or foreign equivalent and an LLM (or be enrolled in a program leading to an LLM).

Academics

"If you are looking for professors who encourage you, want you to do well, and want to interact with you outside of school, UCLA School of Law is ideal," proclaims a satisfied 1L. Though in the past students have noted that class sizes "are probably larger than they are at most schools," the first-year curriculum has been changed. Students have three small sections of forty students or less. "UCLA has a very positive academic atmosphere." "The resources are boundless," and students brag that they are receiving "a world-class legal education in a beautiful city." "Superstar professors" regularly teach 1L courses and the faculty as a whole is full of "amazing and dedicated teachers" who are "quite witty and entertaining." They "will cold-call students, but if you're not able to answer the question, saying 'I don't know' is fine, and they'll leave you alone." The administration is hit-or-miss. Some administrators are "amazingly accessible." "One particular time I went in to get an extension on an independent study paper and wound up playing Barrel of Monkeys for twenty minutes with the Dean of Students," relates a 3L. "I won and she wants a rematch." Students admit that the school's bureaucracy can often be "horribly inefficient and a pain to wade through," though the law school recently hired a new Director of Financial Aid to help streamline financial processes and paperwork. "I don't know how much of that is the law school's fault as opposed to the UC system's," offers a 1L.

"The grading curve is not particularly brutal." "About sixty percent get B's," estimates one student. The curriculum stresses theory as well as practical skills (though one student calls the legal writing curriculum "completely impractical"). The "incredibly valuable" clinical program "is truly the institution's crown jewel." "Trial advocacy is the best class that I have taken at any level," attests a 3L, and the "incredible" public interest program "can turn out lawyers who want to make the world better." Still, many wish that there was less focus placed upon gearing students toward corporate law.

Graduates don't have much of a problem finding jobs. "It is completely standard to leave here and earn $130,000" in your first year as an attorney. UCLA has an "excellent reputation among the big firms in Los Angeles" and is "highly regarded nationally." "Many students also go to work in New York and Washington, D.C." "Those who, for some absurd reason, want to leave behind the fantastically high quality of life offered here and instead earn the same money but for more hours in Manhattan seem to have no problem doing so," notes a 1L.

The UCLA campus as a whole is "stunning." "The school is located on the most beautiful part of the generally gorgeous UCLA campus, in one of the most upscale parts of Los Angeles." "The law school building looks great on the outside, but is outdated on the inside." The "cramped" classrooms "are equipped for laptops," but "need some aesthetic upgrading." On the upside, the "luxurious and modern law library" has "big windows," making it "a pleasing place to study."

Life

Students describe themselves as "very smart." A lot of students complain about the lack of ethnic diversity on campus; "It bears no resemblance to the demographics of the population of the United States, much less that of California." Whatever the case, students "interact well with each other." "Different backgrounds and opinions are not merely tolerated, they are encouraged and respected." "UCLA has a large and active

KARMAN HSU, DIRECTOR OF ADMISSIONS
71 DODD HALL, BOX 951445, LOS ANGELES, CA 90095-1445
TEL: 310-825-2080 FAX: 310-206-7227
E-MAIL: ADMISSIONS@LAW.UCLA.EDU • WEBSITE: WWW.LAW.UCLA.EDU

GLBT community, with a think tank and an academic journal both housed at the law school dedicated to sexual orientation law and policy." Politically, "students seem predominantly liberal but there are definitely conservatives too."

"People get quite stressed and preoccupied with grades and jobs," and "There is a serious spirit of competition" at UCLA. It's "not personal," though. "Students generally root for each other, rooting for themselves just a bit more." Also, you can easily "find your own space away from the gunners." At the end of the day, it's hard to be stressed out "when you study so close to the beach" (in "shorts and flip-flops"), and "It's eighty degrees in January." "The sunny weather compromises students' ability to stay indoors and study," admits a 1L.

"Lunch in the courtyard is probably the best part of being at UCLA." "People are always outside, reading or eating lunch, with the sun beaming down and the giant red-woods providing shade." "People study hard" but social activities are very prevalent (particularly early in each semester). There is "no shortage of people going out on a random Thursday night." "Rent is fairly expensive" in the surrounding area, but "UCLA offers pretty good, convenient housing to many law students." "If you can deal with a commute, there are many cheaper areas to live that are not too far" as well. Overall, UCLA students are among the more satisfied groups of law students in the country. "After my brother asked me how law school was going, he listened patiently to my answer and then told me that it sounded like Club Med with some required reading," says a 3L. "I couldn't be happier with my experience."

Getting In

Recently admitted students at UCLA at the 25th percentile have LSAT scores of 165 and GPAs in the 3.56 range. Admitted students at the 75th percentile have LSAT scores of 170 and GPAs of 3.87.

Combined Degrees Offered

JD/MA in African American Studies, American Indian Studies, Public Policy, Urban Planning; JD/MBA; JD/PhD in Philosophy; JD/MPH; JD/MSW. Students may create a tailored program by under-taking work from multiple disciplines within UCLA and applying to the JD program; students may design a joint-degree program with another school with administrative approval.

Clinical program required	No
Legal writing course requirement	Yes
Legal methods course requirement	Yes
Legal research course requirement	Yes
Moot court requirement	No
Public interest law requirement	No

ADMISSIONS

Selectivity Rating	97
# applications received	8,748
% applicants accepted	16
% acceptees attending	22
Average LSAT	166.8
LSAT Range	165–170
Average undergrad GPA	3.70
Application fee	$75
Regular application	Rolling, up to 2/1
Regular notification	Rolling
Early application program	Yes
Early application deadline	11/15
Early application notification	12/31
Transfer students accepted	Yes
Evening division offered	No
Part-time accepted	No
CAS accepted	Yes

FINANCIAL FACTS

Annual tuition (in-state/out-of-state)	$40,616/ $50,638
Books and supplies	$1,953
Room and board	$14,295
Financial aid application deadline	3/2
% first-year students receiving some sort of aid	91
% receiving some sort of aid	88
% receiving scholarships	64
Average grant	$14,877
Average loan	$40,335
Average total aid package	$48,493
Average debt	$103,956

EMPLOYMENT INFORMATION

Career Rating	94
Rate of placement (nine months out)	93
Average starting salary	$116,969
State for bar exam	CA
Pass rate for first-time bar	83

Employers Who Frequently Hire Grads
Leading employers from law firms, corporations, government agencies, and public interest organizations visit the School of Law annually and recruit for their offices in Southern California, New York, San Francisco, Washington, D.C., Chicago, Seattle, Boston and other major national and international legal centers

Prominent Alumni
Hon. Kirsten Gillibrand '91, United States Senator for New York; Howard Berman '65, U.S. House of Representatives (28th District); Hon. Henry Waxman '64, U.S. House of Representatives (30th District); Stewart Resnick '62, President and CEO, Roll International Corporation; Nelson Rising '67, Chairman, Rising Realty Partners, LLC

Grads Employed by Field (%)
Academic (6)
Business/industry (9)
Government (10)
Judicial clerkship (8)
Military (1)
Private practice (58)
Public interest (9)

THE UNIVERSITY OF CHICAGO
THE LAW SCHOOL

INSTITUTIONAL INFORMATION

Public/private	Private
Student/faculty ratio	10:1
% faculty part-time	54
% faculty female	23
% faculty minority	10
Total faculty	120

SURVEY SAYS...

Heavy use of Socratic Method, Diverse opinions accepted in classrooms, Great research resources, Great library staff, Abundant externship/internship/clerkship opportunities

STUDENTS

Enrollment of law school	634
% male/female	56/44
% full-time	100
% minority	28
% international	2
Average age of entering class	24

ACADEMICS

Academic Experience Rating	**99**
Profs interesting rating	98
Profs accessible rating	90
Hours of study per day	4.87

Academic Specialties

Civil Procedure, Commercial, Constitutional, Corporation Securities, Criminal, Environmental, Government Services, Human Rights, International, Labor, Legal History, Legal Philosophy, Property, Taxation, Intellectual Property

Advanced Degrees Offered

JD, 3 years; LLM, 1 year; JSD, depends on dissertation (up to 5 years)

Combined Degrees Offered

JD/MBA, 4 years; JD/PhD in conjunction with Graduate School of Business, depends on dissertation; JD/AM Public Policy, 4 years; JD/AM International Relations, 4 years

Academics

The rigorous and ultra-prestigious Law School at The University of Chicago offers "an incredibly dynamic educational environment full of quirky but brilliant professors and an eclectic mix of students." "Expectations are high" and a unique trimester system means "There is little rest for the weary." Even so, students report, "There is no other place like The University of Chicago when it comes to intellectual curiosity." Course work is cerebral and highly analytical. Classes "have a strong theoretical bent" and are "geared to those who like thinking about the law." Chicago is virtually synonymous with the interdisciplinary combination of law and economics. The humanities, the social sciences, and the natural sciences are all integrated into the curriculum as well.

Students swear that their school has, "without a doubt, the best faculty in the country." The professors are "unquestionably the greatest part of this school." Somehow "they manage to produce brilliant work" while maintaining "a real emphasis on teaching" and making students "feel like top priority." "It's incredible to take classes from...Richard Epstein, and numerous others as a 1L, and to find out how accessible they are," beams one satisfied student. These "rock stars of legal academia" "treat students with respect," "are often in the common areas, and readily have lunch with students." "I have been amazed by the accessibility of my professors, particularly considering who they are," says a 3L. "They are always available for office hours." "The professors can help you get amazing jobs, can impart unparalleled wisdom, and are the people who write the books you use," explains another student. "I don't know where they find the time."

The administration "makes the experience seamless" and is quite popular with most students. "I would call the administration extremely overqualified if it weren't for the negative implications of that label," says a 1L. "I can't imagine a more enthusiastic and at-your-service administration." "The law school tries harder than any other school I've heard of to make its students happy," declares another student. Career Services does a good job too. There are "no worries about jobs." "Over 400 employers compete for only 190 students in each class," so "everyone will get a great job (public or private) making top dollar." There are some complaints, though. "The grading system is a little bizarre. It's tough on the ego because nearly everyone gets the same grade." Students must "lottery" into many seminars and clinical programs. Once in, however, students say the law school's ten clinics are "great" for real-world experience. Though the recent introduction of a summer public interest program has guaranteed funding for public interest jobs, the majority of students become corporate lawyers.

"The facilities are state of the art" at the U of C, though the "boringly modern" architecture won't exactly elevate your soul—unless, of course, a floating-cube-of-glass design is your idea of beautiful. Inside the law school, "The 1L classrooms are gorgeous but cramped." The library has undergone extensive renovation recently and boasts "a great number of resources and a willing and helpful staff."

Life

Chicago is "small" and home to "an intense intellectual environment." "It's quite an experience to know that some of my friends will clerk for the Supreme Court and work at the highest level in the field," relates one student. Debates are "constant and vibrant." "Our faculty and student body has many liberals, libertarians, moderates, and conservatives," explains a 2L. "The political views...range from ultra-liberal to ultra-conservative, but all

ANN PERRY, ASSISTANT DEAN FOR ADMISSIONS
1111 EAST 60TH STREET, CHICAGO, IL 60637
TEL: 773-702-9484 FAX: 773-834-0942
E-MAIL: ADMISSIONS@LAW.UCHICAGO.EDU • WEBSITE: WWW.LAW.UCHICAGO.EDU

viewpoints are respected. Great weight is placed on academic inquiry and discussion, as opposed to vacuous politicking." "People are very interested in learning and maturing as legal thinkers."

Many students tell us that the academic environment is "easygoing" and "mostly non-competitive." "It is an extremely friendly school with a low degree of competition," they say, where "2L and 3L students frequently offer their assistance to the 1L class." However, other students tell us "The competition is tough." "Students are definitely not laid-back about getting jobs," observes a 3L. "Even though everyone ends up with plenty of great job offers, students are intense and cutthroat."

Socially, there is "community atmosphere" and "a great attitude on campus." People are "interesting and cool" and "genuinely excited to be a part of the law school." "Lots of people…participate in social events." Because many people hail from outside the Midwest, everyone arrives looking for friends. "The 1L class bonds quickly." "The small class size is a phenomenal advantage because I feel as if I get to know everyone," comments a 1L. Also, "weekly events such as Wine Mess and Coffee Mess" are perennial social institutions where students mingle with classmates and professors. "Nearly every day there is free food for some political or legal guest speaker," which is great if you like "sandwiches, pizza, or Thai food." The biggest complaint about life here appears to be the law school's affordable but "inconvenient" Hyde Park location. When students need to get away for work or any other reason though, downtown Chicago is "easy enough to live in and get to school" by car, bike, or public transportation.

Getting In

If you can get admitted here, you can get admitted to virtually any law school in the country. Admitted students at 25th percentile have LSAT scores of about 169 and GPAs of about 3.6. Admitted students at 75th percentile have LSAT scores of 173 and GPAs over 3.8. If you take the LSAT a second time, Chicago will consider your higher score.

Clinical program required	No
Legal writing course requirement	Yes
Legal methods course requirement	Yes
Legal research course requirement	Yes
Moot court requirement	Yes
Public interest law requirement	No

ADMISSIONS

Selectivity Rating	**98**
# applications received	5,579
% applicants accepted	15
% acceptees attending	24
Average LSAT	171
LSAT Range	168–172
Average undergrad GPA	3.78
Application fee	$75
Regular application	Rolling, up to 2/1
Regular notification	Rolling
Early application program	Yes
Early application deadline	12/1
Early application notification	12/31
Transfer students accepted	Yes
Evening division offered	No
Part-time accepted	No
CAS accepted	Yes

International Students

TOEFL required of international students	

FINANCIAL FACTS

Annual tuition	$45,405
Books and supplies	$1,650
Fees	$825
Room and board	$13,455
Financial aid application deadline	2/1
% first-year students receiving some sort of aid	90
% receiving some sort of aid	84
% of aid that is merit based	75
% receiving scholarships	65
Average grant	$11,723
Average loan	$55,000
Average total aid package	$60,000
Average debt	$127,997

EMPLOYMENT INFORMATION

Career Rating	**99**	**Grads Employed by Field (%)**
Rate of placement (nine months out)	99	Academic (4)
Average starting salary	$160,000	Business/industry (2)
State for bar exam	IL, NY	Government (3)
Pass rate for first-time bar	98	Judicial clerkship (13)
Employers Who Frequently Hire Grads		Private practice (70)
Cravath Swain & Moore, Latham & Watkins, Gibson Dunn & Crutcher, Sidley & Austin, Kirkland & Ellis, Skadden Arps Slate Meagher & Flom		Public interest (8)

UNIVERSITY OF CINCINNATI
COLLEGE OF LAW

Academics

Students at the University of Cincinnati get the "small class sizes" and "intimate environment" typical of a private college while paying the comfortable, low tuition you would expect from a public institution. With roughly 125 students in each entering class, the school strikes an "excellent" balance with "its affordability, reputation, small class size, and excellent faculty. Students agree that UC professors are an "amazing and diverse group of people who care just as much for teaching and students as they do about publishing their own work." UC is particularly noted for its focus on "public interest" and "international" law; however, "There is no shortage of brilliant legal minds in a broad range of subjects—that goes for students as well as the professors." In addition to the accomplished tenured faculty, students rave about the school's recent acquisition of "exceptional young faculty members that have great teaching skills to match their great scholarship." A 2L sums it up, "As one of the smallest public law schools in the country, I feel my educational experience has been fantastic, and yet, at very little cost. Because our class consists of only 128 people, all of my professors know my name."

University of Cincinnati runs several "amazing" legal institutes and research centers focused on unique topics such as domestic violence, law and psychiatry, and corporate law. Through these centers, students can earn credit hours while doing fulfilling and useful work in the community. Many students make particular note of the Ohio Innocence Project, an institute at the University of Cincinnati through which students conduct substantive work to impact legislative reform, and work on real criminal cases. The institute also brings notable speakers to campus. Students also have the opportunity to research and write for the school's renowned publications, including the Human Rights Quarterly, Law Review, and Freedom Central Journal. While students at other schools might scramble for spots on the school's law review or clinic programs, "Since the school is small, each student can participate in and get involved in a number of organizations."

Thanks to an "ambitious but not overly competitive student body," the learning environment is charged, but not cutthroat, at University of Cincinnati. A 3L attests, "While academic achievement is always a numbers game in law school, the atmosphere at UC is nonpretentious and noncontentious." When it comes to the job and internship placements, University of Cincinnati maintains a "deep and well-regarded history as a legal educational institution" both locally and nationally. As a result, most students say the school "is a great place for students with all different kinds of career aspirations, and especially has a public interest/human rights orientation that I think is unparalleled in the Midwest." In fact, "Public interest students can actually obtain funding for their summer jobs through the school's Public Interest Group." Most UC grads stay in the Cincinnati area and meet with good results while those looking outside the region must do a little extra legwork to find a good placement. "While plenty of our grads go on to excellent careers in major firms, federal clerkships, and other government positions, I don't feel like our school does enough PR work to get out-of-town employers interested in our students," says one student.

Life

For starving students/aspiring lawyers, Cincinnati is an excellent home base offering the unbeatable combination of "small town prices (housing, dining, entertainment) with big city amenities." For both professional and recreational pursuits, the UC campus is pleasantly located "close to downtown so it's easy to get to work, ballgames, and

AL WATSON, ASSISTANT DEAN AND DIRECTOR OF ADMISSION AND FINANCIAL AID
P.O. BOX 210040, CINCINNATI, OH 45221
TEL: 513-556-6805 FAX: 513-556-2391
E-MAIL: ADMISSIONS@LAW.UC.EDU • WEBSITE: WWW.LAW.UC.EDU

entertainment." While Cincinnati has its charms, students complain that the law school could use "more outlets and better lighting." "Windows would be nice," adds another. However, students are optimistic that the school will consider remodeling the law school along with other campus projects. The good news is that "the new parking garage has been built, and there are brand-new (and attractive) living units pretty much right across the street." Not to mention that a few "ice cream shops have opened within a short walk from school."

Despite the rigors of the academic curriculum, "The students that are here create a suitable balance between academic and social life. There are plenty of opportunities to go out and have fun and not be completely overwhelmed with school." On and off campus, "There are frequently SBA social events for students, such as happy hours at local bars." In fact, the SBA is very active and "most of the students are friends and spend time together outside of the law school." On the other hand, students remind us that Cincinnati also attracts "a large contingent of commuter students who spend little if no time involved in the school outside of actual class."

Getting In

To apply to the University of Cincinnati College of Law, students must submit LSAT scores and register with the Law School Data Assembly Service Report. If the LSAT was taken more than once, the highest score will be considered by the Admissions Committee. More than 1,800 hopefuls applied for 135 spots in the JD program. Students in the 25th percentile had LSAT scores of 157 and GPAs of 3.31, while those in the 75th percentile had LSAT scores of 162 and GPAs of 3.80.

Clinical program required	No
Legal writing course requirement	Yes
Legal methods course requirement	No
Legal research course requirement	Yes
Moot court requirement	No
Public interest law requirement	No

ADMISSIONS

Selectivity Rating	82
# applications received	1,823
% applicants accepted	43
% acceptees attending	19
Average LSAT	161
LSAT Range	157–162
Average undergrad GPA	3.56
Application fee	$35
Regular application	Rolling, up to 3/1
Regular notification	Rolling
Early application program	Yes
Early application deadline	12/1
Early application notification	1/15
Transfer students accepted	Yes
Evening division offered	No
Part-time accepted	No
CAS accepted	Yes

International Students

TOEFL required of international students	

FINANCIAL FACTS

Annual tuition (in-state/out-of-state)	$20,946/ $36,526
Books and supplies	$1,308
Room and board	$10,596
Financial aid application deadline	3/1
% receiving some sort of aid	84
% receiving scholarships	67
Average grant	$7,741
Average debt	$58,455

EMPLOYMENT INFORMATION

Career Rating	74	**Grads Employed by Field (%)**
Rate of placement (nine months out)	87	Academic (15)
Average starting salary	$62,918	Business/industry (15)
State for bar exam	OH, KY, NY, IN, IL	Government (10)
Pass rate for first-time bar	91	Judicial clerkship (7)

Employers Who Frequently Hire Grads
All major law firms in Cincinnati and other Ohio cities as well as other Midwestern cities

Military (5)
Private practice (28)
Public interest (6)

Prominent Alumni
Stan Chesley, Class Action; Cris Collinsworth, Journalist; Billy Martin, Washington, D.C. based high-profile case attorney; Andrew Savage, IP Guru; Survivor Contestant; William Howard Taft, President & Supreme Court Justice

UNIVERSITY OF COLORADO
LAW SCHOOL

INSTITUTIONAL INFORMATION

Public/private	Public
Student/faculty ratio	11:1
% faculty part-time	29
% faculty female	36
% faculty minority	18
Total faculty	66

SURVEY SAYS...
*Great research resources,
Beautiful campus*

STUDENTS

Enrollment of law school	546
% male/female	53/47
% from out-of-state	60
% full-time	100
% minority	22
% international	1
# of countries represented	2
Average age of entering class	24

ACADEMICS

Academic Experience Rating	**87**
Profs interesting rating	85
Profs accessible rating	83
Hours of study per day	4.76

Academic Specialties
Environmental, Taxation, American Indian Law, Juvenile and Family Law, Telecommunications Law

Advanced Degrees Offered
JD, 3 years

Combined Degrees Offered
JD/MBA, 4 years; JD/MPA, 4 years; JD/Master of Science and Telecommunications, 4 yrs; JD/Master of Environmental Science, 4 yrs; JD/MD; JD/MURP

Clinical program required	No
Legal writing course requirement	Yes
Legal methods course requirement	Yes
Legal research course requirement	Yes

Academics

"Much like Boulder itself, the University of Colorado Law School provides a small, laid-back and friendly community" where "it is easy to interact with everyone." However, despite the relaxed atmosphere on campus, the academics at CU "are superb" and the professors "are top-notch and, for the most part, extremely interesting people, from all walks of life." CU boasts "phenomenal environmental and natural resources law programs with a huge range of course offerings," as well as "the best American Indian Law program" in the country. To top it off, cutting-edge classes are delivered in the new state of the art Wolf Law Building, which is "entirely green" and "probably the most intuitive and modern law school building in the country."

Students at CU say that when it comes to the study of law, they have the best of all worlds; "We have an Ivy League faculty without the Ivy League smog, the Ivy League vindictiveness, or the Ivy League flatlands." The school mixes "scholarly integrity and relaxed informali[ty]." In addition to the strength of its environmental and natural resources programs, "The entrepreneurial/IP law program is top-notch and well-connected to the MBA program and local business scene." The "technology/business law courses (including the Silicon Flatirons program, the Entrepreneurial Law Clinic, and the Journal on Telecommunications and High Technology Law)," are other strengths.

Academically, "This school is very sound." Students say the curriculum offers "a good mix of theory and practical [instruction]," in a "positive atmosphere" with "moderate class size." However, some feel that "not enough value is placed on learning how to practice law; too much value is placed on abstract academic exercises."

The faculty at CU "create[s] an interest in the material through a positive and dynamic presentation rather than through fear of being made to look foolish through an unforgiving Socratic style." Students say top-notch faculty are continually drawn to the school for its ideal weather and location; "I am really challenged and taught by very talented professors. In fact, I find most of their backgrounds to be quite intimidating. Yet, all of the professors are highly accessible and friendly. Ultimately, they want everyone to succeed." Others lightheartedly joke, "Faculty range from jeans and cowboy boots–wearing, Western-focused, law wizards to small, nerdy-looking, East Coast types. Watching them interact is a treat and a learning experience in itself."

When it comes to areas where they would like to see improvement, students say it comes down to three simple words: "Employment, employment, employment." Luckily, the Career Development Office is currently being reorganized to add counseling services and more placement/networking efforts. However, when it comes to the top brass, "The law school administration is next to perfect." "Everyone is surprisingly approachable, from the dean to the library research staff."

Life

Students at the University of Colorado Law School say they "couldn't imagine attending school in a more beautiful place." "The law school is nestled at the bottom of the famous Boulder Flatirons and is only a few blocks from Chautauqua Park, Boulder's contribution to the Chautauqua Movement." The quality of life in Boulder "is second-to-none; finding something exhilarating to do outside law school is never, ever a problem."

Moot court requirement	No
Public interest law requirement	No

ADMISSIONS

Selectivity Rating	**89**
# applications received	2,906
% applicants accepted	27
% acceptees attending	23
Average LSAT	163
LSAT Range	161–166
Average undergrad GPA	3.54
Application fee	$65
Regular application	Rolling, up to 3/15
Regular notification	Rolling
Early application program	Yes
Early application deadline	11/15
Early application notification	12/23
Transfer students accepted	Yes
Evening division offered	No
Part-time accepted	No
CAS accepted	Yes

International Students

TOEFL required of international students	

FINANCIAL FACTS

Annual tuition (in-state/out-of-state)	$27,072/ $33,930
Books and supplies	$1,749
Fees	$1,843
Room and board (on/off campus)	$17,236/ $14,919
Financial aid application deadline	4/1
% first-year students receiving some sort of aid	94
% receiving some sort of aid	86
% of aid that is merit based	18
% receiving scholarships	53
Average grant	$9,450
Average loan	$34,220
Average total aid package	$36,796
Average debt	$63,193

And whereas some schools focus on a cutthroat academic experience, the University of Colorado encourages a collaborative atmosphere where students feel like family."

Most students at CU "have a strong appreciation of life outside of law school that mitigates the workaholic tendencies of law students in general." The school hosts social gatherings once a week (sponsored by different student organizations) "making it a great place for a social life." In addition, "there are lots of great student organizations, one of which runs a mentorship program for incoming 1Ls which really helps incomers get adjusted to law school life and meet people." CU's new, environmentally friendly, LEED-certified building "is gorgeous, and the view from the library is the foothills of the Rockies—if you have to spend all day studying—it doesn't get much better!"

Boulder is often touted as "a bohemian paradise." But city-folk be warned. Boulder-lovers joke, "Those coming from and who are used to metropolitan/urban life…won't find it here. Denver is only twenty minutes away, but it seems like a world away most of the time. If you like fun people, beer, snowboarding/skiing, and living the nostalgia of college life, you'll love it out here."

Getting In

The average GPA for the fall entering class of 2010 was 3.54 with an average LSAT of 163.

EMPLOYMENT INFORMATION

Career Rating	**78**
Rate of placement (nine months out)	74
Average starting salary	$69,498
State for bar exam	CO
Pass rate for first-time bar	95

Employers Who Frequently Hire Grads
Ballard Spahr Andrews & Ingersoll; Brownstein Hyatt Farber Schreck; Gibson Dunn & Crutcher; Hogan & Hartson; Patton Boggs; Arnold & Porter; Davis Graham & Stubbs; Faegre & Benson; Holland & Hart; Holme Roberts & Owen; Kutak Rock; Otten Johnson; Rothgerber Johnson & Lyons; Sherman & Howard; numerous small local firms; U.S. District Court for the District of Colorado; Tenth Circuit Court of Appeals; Colorado Supreme Court; Colorado Court of Appeals; Colorado State District Courts; various District Attorney offices; various Public Defender offices; and additional government offices

Prominent Alumni
Wiley B. Rutledge, Former Associate Justice, U.S. Supreme Court; Bill Ritter, Jr., former Governor of Colorado; Roy Romer, former Governor of Colorado; Glenn R. Jones, Chairman & CEO, Jones International, Ltc.; Hank Brown, former U.S. Senator from Colorado

Grads Employed by Field (%)
Academic (1)
Business/industry (10)
Government (12)
Judicial clerkship (11)
Private practice (34)
Public interest (4)
Other (1)

UNIVERSITY OF CONNECTICUT
SCHOOL OF LAW

Academics

The University of Connecticut School of Law in Hartford offers "the resources of a large, public institution with the feel of a small, private school." There's no doubt that the school is great for current and future Connecticut residents, as the low in-state tuition and "strong relationship with pretty much every firm/agency/government office in the state" are a built-in benefit of a degree from UConn Law. However, for those looking to leave the state after graduation, the resounding complaint is that Career Services tends to be "Connecticut-oriented," meaning the opportunities for those who want to work elsewhere "are quite limited." "Most of the recruitment is self-selecting/self-motivating," says a 3L. As for the school's administration, the opportunities for interaction are plentiful, which allows students to see that they are "excellent, very accessible, and very responsive to student needs and concerns."

The "approachable" professors here "are for the most part great," but many admit, "There are a few duds that teach required courses, so there is no way around them," particularly in the first year. One 1L observes, "A great professor will create a great educational and academic experience, and I did have several great professors." Many of the higher-level courses are taught by practitioners in the field, whose practice-oriented instruction allows you to "hit the ground running" and give classes "a more practical feel as opposed to the strictly academic aim of many classes." "I really get the sense that no one wants me to fail," says a 1L. Some students wish for a wider availability of classes for evening students and "more classes" overall. One believes the opportunities for specialization are the school's "greatest strength"; another thinks that that lies with "the ability to conduct your own research project, as well as [to] compete in trial and appellate competitions across the country and conferences around the world." Clinics are especially well received at UConn Law: "Students are given cases and work with clients; it is very exciting to do real legal work."

Now that the renovation of the library has reached completion, everyone is thrilled with the results, which only add to the effect of the "gorgeous" campus and its "castle-like buildings." The modernized facilities come equipped with "state-of-the-art research capabilities and plenty of private study areas with full Internet access at every desk," which sometimes border on space age. "In my last seminar class, the flat screen television started ringing and we began a satellite conference call with someone in England," says a student.

Life

Despite being a public school, UConn Law's small size "really fosters a sense of community among students." Everyone "gets along great and really supports each other," and "There is very little competition among students, which makes for a great learning environment." "In all UConn law school classes, you learn as much from your peers as you do the professors," says a member of the student body, noting that it "leans way to the left." People here help each other out, and "There is never a problem borrowing notes, getting outlines from upper-classmen or seeing old exams from the professors."

Hartford represents the best and the worst of Connecticut. Home to UConn and Trinity College, the city's academic culture is robust. Nevertheless, the city itself can be "shady" and is "not a particularly nice place," though the school has taken steps to increase safety

KAREN DeMEOLA, ASSISTANT DEAN FOR ADMISSIONS AND STUDENT FINANCE
45 ELIZABETH STREET, HARTFORD, CT 06105
TEL: 860-570-5100 FAX: 860-570-5153
E-MAIL: ADMISSIONS@LAW.UCONN.EDU • WEBSITE: WWW.LAW.UCONN.EDU

on and around the campus. There is "a lot of social interaction if you want it," but many students are commuters and/or older; still, there seems to be "many activities, both structured and informal, in which the younger, full-time students make time to participate." UConn Law is also "very welcoming to LGBT students," offering a diversity in sexual and gender orientation "both among the students and the staff," which "makes for very lively and interesting discussions."

Getting In

Students are admitted to UConn School of Law once annually, for entry in the fall semester. No numeric index is used to rank applicants to UConn School of Law (though the LSAT is required) and each applicant is considered individually; the school is also veteran-friendly. Connecticut residents receive special consideration in an admissions decision, though no absolute preference is given. Of the 135 1Ls accepted for the entering class of 2010, the mean undergraduate GPA was 3.43 and the mean LSAT score was 162.

Clinical program required	No
Legal writing	
course requirement	Yes
Legal methods	
course requirement	Yes
Legal research	
course requirement	Yes
Moot court requirement	Yes
Public interest	
law requirement	No

ADMISSIONS

Selectivity Rating	89
# applications received	2,257
% applicants accepted	23
% acceptees attending	26
Average LSAT	162
LSAT Range	160–164
Average undergrad GPA	3.43
Application fee	$60
Regular application	Rolling, up to 3/15
Regular notification	Rolling
Early application program	No
Transfer students accepted	Yes
Evening division offered	Yes
Part-time accepted	Yes
CAS accepted	Yes

International Students
TOEFL required of
international students

FINANCIAL FACTS

Annual tuition	
(in-state/out-of-state)	$20,712/ $43,632
Books and supplies	$1,350
Fees	$876
Room and board	$11,800
Financial aid application	
deadline	3/15
% first-year students	
receiving some sort of aid	93
% receiving some sort of aid	84
% of aid that is merit based	5
% receiving scholarships	63
Average grant	$14,040
Average loan	$29,824
Average total aid package	$38,489
Average debt	$66,457

EMPLOYMENT INFORMATION

Career Rating	87
Rate of placement (nine months out)	86
Average starting salary	$86,055
State for bar exam	CT, NY, MA
Pass rate for first-time bar	90

Employers Who Frequently Hire Grads
District of Columbia Office of the Attorney General; State of Connecticut Judicial Branch; State of Maryland Office of the Public Defender; Sterne, Kessler, Goldstein & Fox PLLC; Sullivan & Worcester, LLP; Sulloway & Hollis PLLC; The Guardian Life Insurance Company of America; The Nature Conservancy; U.S. Air Force; U.S. Army Judge Advocate General Corps; U.S. Coast Guard; U.S. Court of Appeals for the Second Circuit; U.S. Green Building Council; U.S. Marshals Service; U.S. Navy Judge Advocate General's Corps

Prominent Alumni
Kathleen A. Murphy, CEO, ING U.S. Wealth Management, named to Fortune Magazine's 50 Most Powerful Women in Business List; Pedro E. Segarra, City of Hartford Mayor; Michael Callahan, Executive Vice President, Yahoo!; Randall Pinkston, CBS News; Edward Kennedy, Jr.; Joe Courtney, Congressman; Chris Murphy, Congressman; Richard N. Palmer, Lubbie Harper, Jr., Dennis G. Eveleigh, Justices CT Supreme Court; Christine S. Vertefeuille, Senior Justice CT Supreme Court

Grads Employed by Field (%)
Academic (3)
Business/industry (20)
Government (13)
Judicial clerkship (10)
Military (1)
Private practice (48)
Public interest (5)

UNIVERSITY OF DAYTON
SCHOOL OF LAW

INSTITUTIONAL INFORMATION

Public/private	Private
Student/faculty ratio	16:1
% faculty part-time	50
% faculty female	37
% faculty minority	11
Total faculty	49

SURVEY SAYS...

Diverse opinions accepted in classrooms, Great research resources, Great library staff, Beautiful campus

STUDENTS

Enrollment of law school	524
% male/female	61/39
% from out-of-state	51
% full-time	100
% minority	12
% international	1
# of countries represented	1
Average age of entering class	25

ACADEMICS

Academic Experience Rating	73
Profs interesting rating	75
Profs accessible rating	77
Hours of study per day	5.47

Academic Specialties

Civil Procedure, Criminal, Property, Intellectual Property, Computer/Cyberspace Law, Advocacy and Dispute Resolution, Personal and Transactional Law

Advanced Degrees Offered

MSL or LLM in Law and Technology

Combined Degrees Offered

JD/MBA, 4 years

Academics

Students at the University of Dayton School of Law call their school "a diamond in the rough." "The number of elective classes is extremely limited," but class sizes are smaller. There's a notable program in intellectual property law and a "very strong legal writing program." There's an "extremely helpful" bar prep course available for credit, too. You can enroll in either May or August. Probably the most unique thing here is the accelerated program. "UDSL allows summer starters and fall starters but also allows students to graduate in five semesters." If you are really gung-ho, you can squeeze a JD into two years here (and still get a summer off). The facilities are still another perk. By all accounts, the "clean, modern, comfortable," "absolutely beautiful," and "totally brand-new" building is "a joy." "The classrooms and the courtroom are equipped with the latest technology." Students also laud the "big, comprehensive" library.

Students tell us that they love the "emphasis on applicable skills" throughout the curriculum. Among other things, "UDSL encourages students to learn practical lawyering skills by requiring students take either a clinic or a capstone." Clinical opportunities allow students to work with real, live clients, "preparing all aspects of a case, from the initial client interview to preparing for trial and possibly even participating in a trial." Capstone courses are lot like simulated clinics. Externships, which allow students to work, just for example, at a government agency, or for a judge, or in a law firm, are another big hit. "The externship program is world-class," gloats 2L. "It gives students real-world experience that is invaluable." However, "The externship classroom portion is comprised of a bunch of busy work and touchy-feely exercises that do not belong in a law school."

"There are a few professors that are difficult to deal with," but students say that, for the most part, faculty members "make classes very enjoyable." "The professors are wonderful," reflects a 3L. "Choosing a favorite would be an impossible task, because it would be a fifteen-way tie." Outside of class, the faculty is reportedly "open-door all the way." "Professors are approachable before class, after class, and almost anytime a student needs." The "professional and cordial" administration is almost universally beloved as well—rare for a law school, we might add, or any kind of school. The dean "knows students by name," and the top brass on the whole is "extremely accommodating." "They really get to know the students and will do whatever they can to help." "They are constantly in communication with us," adds a 1L, "and I like that."

Students are divided when it comes to career prospects. Many say that the school has a "terrific reputation in Ohio." "The school is very connected within the Dayton community and Ohio for jobs, references, and resources," promises a 2L. Other students disagree. "Career Services could be bolstered," counters another 2L. "More lobbying for what UDSL students can provide would be helpful."

JANET L. HEIN, ASST. DEAN, DIR. OF ADMISSIONS AND FINANCIAL AID
UNIVERSITY OF DAYTON SCHOOL OF LAW, 300 COLLEGE PARK, 112 KELLER HALL,
DAYTON, OH 45469-2760 • TEL: 937-229-3555 FAX: 937-229-4194
E-MAIL: LAWINFO@NOTES.UDAYTON.EDU • WEBSITE: WWW.UDAYTON.EDU/LAW

Life

The population of soon-to-be attorneys here hails "mainly from the Midwest." They're "generally very welcoming, sincere, and enthusiastic." Academically, "things are competitive." "Many people spend a great deal more time studying than they let on," speculates a 3L. However, students are quick to point out that "the community feel of UDSL is evident from the moment one steps through the doors." "There is a sense of togetherness within each class." "There are jerks, but they are few and far between."

Socially, life can be "very dramatic" at times because of the school's small size. "Like anywhere, there are cliques." Overall, though, it's "a very pleasant environment." "Most students are involved in student organizations." "There are always school and non-school gatherings to attend." "We have organized parties," adds a 1L, "and I don't just mean drinking at a bar, but actual social adult functions that are classy." If you "still have that college mentality in terms of partying," don't worry. You can find a good deal of that here, too. The medium-sized metropolis that surrounds the school has its advantages and disadvantages. On one hand, Dayton is a good place to go to law school because there aren't many distractions. On the other hand, at least according to a 2L here, it's "one of America's top ten dying cities."

Getting In

The acceptance rate here isn't crazy high, but it's pretty high. Admitted students at the 25th percentile have LSAT scores that hover around 150 and GPAs a little under 3.0. Admitted students at the 75th percentile have LSAT scores of 154 or so and GPAs a little over 3.4.

Clinical program required	Yes
Legal writing course requirement	Yes
Legal methods course requirement	Yes
Legal research course requirement	Yes
Moot court requirement	No
Public interest law requirement	No

ADMISSIONS

Selectivity Rating	66
# applications received	2,147
% applicants accepted	55
% acceptees attending	17
Average LSAT	153
LSAT Range	150–154
Average undergrad GPA	3.11
Application fee	$50
Regular application	Rolling, up to 5/1
Regular notification	Rolling
Early application program	No
Transfer students accepted	Yes
Evening division offered	No
Part-time accepted	No
CAS accepted	Yes

International Students

TOEFL recommended of international students	

FINANCIAL FACTS

Annual tuition	$33,330
Books and supplies	$1,500
Fees	$350
Room and board	$14,000
Financial aid application deadline	5/1
% first-year students receiving some sort of aid	91
% receiving some sort of aid	91
% of aid that is merit based	12
% receiving scholarships	51
Average grant	$9,207
Average total aid package	$39,418
Average debt	$67,856

EMPLOYMENT INFORMATION

Career Rating		77
Rate of placement (nine months out)		86
Average starting salary		$56,841
State for bar exam		OH, NY, IL, KY, IN
Pass rate for first-time bar		75

Employers Who Frequently Hire Grads
Proctor & Gamble, Ohio Attorney General, Thompson Hine, Frost Brown Todd, LexisNexis, Jackson Kelly PLLC, Dinsmore & Shohl LLP

Prominent Alumni
Barbara Gorman, Judge, Common Pleas Court; Ron Brown, CEO, Milacron Inc.; Honorable Mary Donovan, Justice of 2nd District Court of Appeals; Susan Harty, Partner, Vorys, Sater, Seymour and Pease LLP; Michael Coleman, Mayor, Columbus, Ohio

Grads Employed by Field (%)
Academic (3)
Business/industry (21)
Government (10)
Judicial clerkship (6)
Military (2)
Private practice (58)
Public interest (1)

UNIVERSITY OF DENVER
STURM COLLEGE OF LAW

INSTITUTIONAL
INFORMATION

Public/private	Private
Student/faculty ratio	12:1
% faculty female	47
% faculty minority	8
Total faculty	79

SURVEY SAYS...

Great research resources, Beautiful campus, Students love Denver, CO

STUDENTS

Enrollment of law school	908
% male/female	51/49
% full-time	82
% minority	17
# of countries represented	2
Average age of entering class	24

ACADEMICS

Academic Experience Rating	86
Profs interesting rating	82
Profs accessible rating	78
Hours of study per day	4.75

Academic Specialties

Commercial, Constitutional, Corporation Securities, Environmental, International, Labor, Taxation

Advanced Degrees Offered

LLM Taxation, 1 year; LLM Natural Resources, 1 year

Combined Degrees Offered

Business, International Management, International Studies, Legal Administration, Professional Psychology, Psychology, Social Work

Clinical program required	No
Legal writing course requirement	Yes
Legal methods course requirement	Yes
Legal research course requirement	Yes
Moot court requirement	No
Public interest law requirement	Yes

Academics

The luxury liner of law schools, the University of Denver Sturm College of Law boasts "amazing" facilities, "several" journals and clinical experiences, an "increasing" endowment, and a "strong" alumni network in the Denver metropolitan area. This large private school is "great" for its public interest and environmental law programs, though a wider range of interests, such as a Lawyering in Spanish program and "numerous opportunities for those of us that want to work for a corporate law firm" also garner praise. Diverse as the courses they teach, DU's "kind, brilliant, tough, and challenging" faculty is comprised of a "mixture of tenure-track professors and practicing attorneys." Despite the variety, students find that "the scheduling and availability of classes could be a little more diverse," especially when it comes to "basics" and "bar classes."

A practical perspective is paramount to the academic experience at University of Denver. For those interested, Career Services hosts frequent—almost daily—sessions (many offering free lunch) on "topics in international law, human rights, politics, practical career advice, debates on current issues, etc." Students say that these daily extra talks allow them to gain a better grasp of "life out of law school and after law school, which is a huge help." Through the mentorship program, "All students have regular opportunities to get career advice and direction from lawyers in the Denver community." To top it off, the school operates a large number of clinic programs, five law journals, and, from day one, "1Ls are invited and encouraged to participate in almost every moot court competition, so students develop exceptional trial advocacy skills early on."

Students explain, "As with any large law school, there are some administrative problems"; however, one student sums it up this way: "Right now DU is like a teenager whose metaphysical development is just a little behind his or her physical growth. Make no mistake, all indications are that DU's going to be a stunner; however, on occasion administrative clumsiness leads to collective student body headaches." That said, students dole out praise for the new and spacious facilities, housed in an environmentally friendly (aka "green") building. One student explains, "The building is beautiful and well designed. There are lots of commons areas, and it would be nearly impossible to make it through a day without interacting with other people."

Students get a jump start on their career through the school's "outstanding" externship program that offers externships "with sole practitioners, large firms, and judges in legal fields ranging from water law to criminal law to administrative law." Come graduation, satisfied students praise the school's "incredible alumni network in the community and its incredible reputation in Denver and Colorado." Job-seekers are given an additional edge due to the fact that "DU is the only law school in Denver, and one of only two law schools in the state of Colorado, which creates numerous opportunities for DU graduates to find jobs." Plus, the Career Development Center does an "excellent" job introducing students to the local legal community. A current student elaborates, "between guest speakers, networking events, on-campus interviews, resume and writing sample coaching, and weekly e-mails announcing new job/internship opportunities, if you don't have a job or at least some leads when you graduate, it's because you didn't want it."

SUSAN ERLENBORN, ASSISTANT DIRECTOR OF ADMISSIONS
2255 E. EVANS AVENUE, DENVER, CO 80208
TEL: 303-871-6135 FAX: 303-871-6992
E-MAIL: ADMISSIONS@LAW.DU.EDU • WEBSITE: WWW.LAW.DU.EDU

Life

While DU is a large school, the program is structured in a way that creates a more intimate atmosphere. One student says, "Day students are divided into one of three sections comprised of eighty students. I see the same people day in and day out for every class." Many find this "very helpful for forming close friendships" since it allows students to get "to know and become comfortable" with each other while "forming study groups." No matter what your background, you're likely to find a friend or two amongst the large student body. "There's a wide range of social groups, from 'high school' gossiping, partying groups, to academic and career-centered groups," explains one student. In addition, "There's a club for every interest you could think of, which is great."

Not surprisingly, many law students admit that they are "too busy studying to go out and have a social life." However, if you are looking for a good time, "The straight-out-of-college crew is probably the most social, or at least the ones that seem to go out and hang out the most," and "There are lots of informally organized nights at the local restaurant or bar that are open to all." Students agree, "Denver is a great city" with "so much to do." And being only "an hour from the mountains," winter sport fans find that "you can be in court in the morning and on the slopes by afternoon."

Getting In

Applicants to the University of Denver Sturm College of Law must have a bachelor's degree from an accredited college and current LSAT scores. Competition is steep as for the entering class, the school received just more than 3,000 applications for its full-time division and enrolled 238 full-time and 63 part-time students. The median LSAT score for matriculated students was 159 with a median GPA of 3.5.

ADMISSIONS

Selectivity Rating	86
# applications received	2,820
% applicants accepted	33
% acceptees attending	25
Average LSAT	160
LSAT Range	158–162
Average undergrad GPA	3.46
Application fee	$60
Regular application	Rolling, up to 5/30
Regular notification	Rolling
Early application program	No
Transfer students accepted	Yes
Evening division offered	Yes
Part-time accepted	Yes
CAS accepted	Yes

International Students

TOEFL required of international students

FINANCIAL FACTS

Annual tuition	$36,480
Books and supplies	$1,698
Fees	$672
Room and board	$9,765
Financial aid application deadline	3/30
% first-year students receiving some sort of aid	97
% receiving some sort of aid	94
% of aid that is merit based	17
% receiving scholarships	39
Average grant	$18,220
Average loan	$34,492
Average total aid package	$42,014
Average debt	$111,459

EMPLOYMENT INFORMATION

Career Rating	83
Rate of placement (nine months out)	91
Average starting salary	$67,484
State for bar exam	CO
Pass rate for first-time bar	89

Employers Who Frequently Hire Grads
Small, medium, and large law firms, government agencies (DA's office, PD's office, etc.), corporations, nonprofit organizations, courts

Grads Employed by Field (%)
Business/industry (16)
Government (25)
Judicial clerkship (3)
Military (2)
Private practice (40)
Public interest (11)

UNIVERSITY OF THE DISTRICT OF COLUMBIA
DAVID A. CLARKE SCHOOL OF LAW

Academics

The David A. Clarke School of Law at the University of the District of Columbia is founded on an "enthusiasm for equality and justice." It's a small school, one of only a few ABA-accredited law schools at Historically Black Colleges and Universities. The school offers training to those underrepresented at the bar. Its mission is "to serve the public and equip lawyers who will promote social justice." Students don't just study law, but "Learn how to make the legal system work for the most vulnerable populations in our society." UDC is "on the cutting-edge of clinical practice." There's a required 700 hours of clinical experience, within which are a "great variety" of fields to choose from. In clinic, students are responsible for their own cases and clients and "have a chance to hone their research and writing skills." Unique to UDC School of Law is a "complete public interest focus and a commitment to serving the impoverished." The school operates by the credo, "Tolerance, service, and commitment to ensuring equal access to justice." After graduation, students say they feel confident taking on their own cases due to the heavy clinical requirement.

"Our professors are committed to educating the next generation of public interest lawyers." "They are by far the best thing going for the institution. Their experience and expertise is priceless." Professors choose to teach at UDC School of Law because they believe in its mission. They're "truly passionate" and try to prepare students for the "issues most of us will face as public interest attorneys." "I had the opportunity to learn from a D.C. Superior Court Judge, a nationally renowned civil rights attorney whose record and experience comprise nearly fifty years of service to the profession and to society, and an Ivy League–educated criminal defense superstar from D.C.'s Public Defender Service." These professors represent the "spirit of tolerance, dedication, and advocacy." The curriculum is "designed to equip each graduate with not merely an intellectual grasp of the law, but also the skills required to make practice of the law a reality." Students feel prepared for the real world of law outside the doors of UDC and also praise the professors' "compassion for humanity."

Students are divided on the usefulness of the administration. One says they're both "helpful" and "attentive," and another claims they do a good job "making the school feel like a community." However, others feel quite the opposite. "The school's administration often leaves students very frustrated," and "UDC Law is sometimes crippled by bureaucracy." Most of the complaints come from part-time students who wish the administration kept better hours. They would also like more opportunities to fulfill the clinical requirement and participate in student organizations. Yet another claims, "The administration here knows individuals by name, and it is not uncommon for an administrator to e-mail an important deadline reminder to a forgetful student."

Students agree, "It would be nice if the law school had a bit more room." The law school is growing, and if it "were in its own stand-alone building, this would be best." One student says there are "constant maintenance and temperature issues." On the bright side, "I've never had an instance where I was unable to find a research tool I needed." One student claims the library is a "second home," and another says, "The school is undergoing renovations to add space and modernization." "The law school will probably move into a bigger space closer to downtown D.C. within a few years."

VIVIAN CANTY, ASSISTANT DEAN OF ADMISSION
4200 CONNECTICUT AVENUE, NW, BUILDING 38, WASHINGTON, D.C. 20008
TEL: 202-274-7336 FAX: 202-274-5583
E-MAIL: VCANTY@UDC.EDU • WEBSITE: WWW.LAW.UDC.EDU

Life

Students "come in all shades, ages, income levels, and backgrounds." UDC law is left-leaning, and no matter what your ethnicity or sexual orientation may be, you'll fit in well, as diversity is the school's "greatest strength." The atmosphere is "noncompetitive" and, "UDC-DCSL doesn't keep class ranks, because, well, everyone is encouraged to succeed." Students say it's an "extremely positive environment." Fellow classmates "help each other succeed" and, even more, are "invested" in that success. "I never feel isolated," another student adds.

The majority of students are recent graduates of their undergraduate institutions. Students love D.C. for the location! The school is "minutes from the historic streets and monuments of downtown D.C. The location is great for available transportation, travel to the many other D.C. law schools and colleges, and all types of recreation and entertainment for singles, couples, families, and the young at heart."

Getting In

The admissions committee focuses on work experience, extracurricular activities, letters of recommendation, and the personal essay. Roughly one in four candidates is accepted. Admitted students in the 25th percentile had GPAs around 2.8 and LSAT scores just below 150. Admitted students in the 75th percentile had GPAs just beneath 3.4 and LSAT scores at 155.

ADMISSIONS

Selectivity Rating	**80**
# applications received	1,742
% applicants accepted	24
% acceptees attending	32
LSAT Range	149–155
Application fee	$35
Regular application	Rolling, up to 3/15
Regular notification	Rolling
Early application program	No
Transfer students accepted	Yes
Evening division offered	Yes
Part-time accepted	Yes
CAS accepted	Yes

International Students

TOEFL required of international students

FINANCIAL FACTS

Annual tuition (in-state/out-of-state)	$7,350/ $14,700
Books and supplies	$2,000
Fees	$630
Room and board	$30,440
Financial aid application deadline	3/31
% first-year students receiving some sort of aid	92
% receiving some sort of aid	89
% of aid that is merit based	65
% receiving scholarships	60
Average grant	$5,594
Average total aid package	$4,500
Average debt	$24,889

EMPLOYMENT INFORMATION

Career Rating	73	**Grads Employed by Field (%)**
Rate of placement (nine months out)	67	Academic (2)
State for bar exam	MD, D.C., VA, CA, NY	Business/industry (19)
Pass rate for first-time bar	62	Government (19)
Employers Who Frequently Hire Grads		Judicial clerkship (7)
Local and federal government agencies,		Private practice (35)
legal service providers and public interest		Public interest (19)
advocacy groups, small law firms, judicial		
clerkships, business and industry		

UNIVERSITY OF FLORIDA
LEVIN COLLEGE OF LAW

INSTITUTIONAL INFORMATION

Public/private	Public
Student/faculty ratio	15:1
% faculty female	37
% faculty minority	22
Total faculty	51

SURVEY SAYS...

Diverse opinions accepted in classrooms, Great research resources, Good social life

STUDENTS

Enrollment of law school	1,044
% from out-of-state	13
% full-time	100
% minority	23
% international	3
Average age of entering class	23

ACADEMICS

Academic Experience Rating	**76**
Profs interesting rating	83
Profs accessible rating	71
Hours of study per day	4.90

Academic Specialties

Environmental, International, Taxation, Intellectual Property, Family Law, Estates & Trusts Practice

Advanced Degrees Offered

LLM in Taxation, LLM in International Taxation, LLM in Comparative Law, LLM in Environmental Law, 1 year; SJD in Taxation, multiyear

Combined Degrees Offered

More than 30 joint degree programs (JD/Masters & PhD); length of program varies

Clinical program required	No
Legal writing course requirement	Yes
Legal methods course requirement	No
Legal research course requirement	Yes

Academics

The University of Florida Levin College of Law is a large school that offers the "resources of a large research university" and a "very good value for the price," particularly if you have or can wrangle residency in the Sunshine State. "The greatest strength is how cheap it is, at least relative to other law schools, for the top law school in Florida," proclaims a 3L. "There are several certificate programs" available, including intellectual property, family law, international and comparative law, and environmental and land use law. Joint-degree programs are extensive. "Clinics and trial practice classes are very hands-on." You can also study abroad in a host of far-flung places, including South Africa, Poland, and Costa Rica.

Most students call the faculty "outstanding." Professors are "enthusiastic about both research and teaching," they say, and you'll find a broad range of teaching styles and personal viewpoints. "The overall experience is memorable." "I love my professors," gushes a 2L. "I find myself interested in types of law that I never thought I would enjoy simply because the professors are excited about the material and show that the law doesn't have to be boring." According to other students, though, "Professors vary widely." "I've had good professors," reflects a 3L, "but I have also had professors that made me dread going to class." Critics also say, "Professor accessibility is minimal," and first-year classes are "too large for good interaction and discussion." It's possible to feel "totally lost in the shuffle." For a law school that's attached to a gargantuan state university, the administration is definitely "decent," and staffers "totally cater to student needs." Nevertheless, expect to be "victimized by some significant red tape" at some point in your law school career here.

Employment prospects are solid. Throughout the state of Florida, "UF Law has a great reputation with the law community" and "prestige," not to mention respectable pull with big firms and government agencies. The alumni base is substantial and "strong." If you do well here, you stand a very good chance at landing a plum job at "the best firms." The name is somewhat transferable beyond the state line, as well. "The school's location allows students an opportunity to network throughout the entire Southeastern United States, not just Florida." "Outside the state borders, UF has less influence," though, and some students complain that the staff of the Center for Career Development is "unable or unwilling to help students find jobs." "They do not have the resources to help enough students find the jobs they should be finding for the top law school in the state," gripes a disgruntled 3L. Fortunately, UF is working on improving their offerings, currently concluding a national search for a new director of the Center for Career Development.

The shiny building here is "relatively new, and everything within it works." "Classrooms are mostly well-equipped," and technology ranges from solid to excellent. "The library is first-rate" and very conducive to long study sessions. In fact, UF Law's library may be too good. The undergraduates "come in droves," and "Their infiltration has damaged its quiet reputation."

Life

The overwhelming majority of students here are Florida residents. Otherwise, though, "UF Law is unique in its ability to achieve a diverse incoming class." Ethnic minorities make up a pretty considerable contingent, and all kinds of students enroll here. "The best part of law school is conversing with people of different backgrounds and history," says a thrilled 2L. "It's fascinating." Some students "can be cutthroat," but for the most part, the law student population is "intelligent and harmonious," and "There is a nice sense of community." "You will be able to find a friend or two to study with regularly and many friends to interact with socially," promises a 1L. Students do tend to stick to their sections first year, but "There's a lot of cross-section interaction starting in second year."

Despite a "problematic" parking situation, "Gainesville is nice." Certainly, if you're into big-time college sports, the University of Florida is hard to beat. The "sunny weather" is spectacular, provided that you enjoy heat and a constant dose of humidity. Gainesville is also indisputably among the best college towns in the country, in both its ideal size and its smorgasbord of restaurants, performing arts, culture, and rowdy bars. Sadly, though, getting to any of those things isn't easy because the law school is nestled in a very remote corner of the larger campus. It's "not within walking distance of any dining options, and the on-campus options are paltry." In the event that you become bored with the Gainesville scene, several good-sized cities, such as Jacksonville, Orlando, and Tampa, are within reasonable driving distance.

Getting In

Admitted students at the 25th percentile have LSAT scores of 160 and below and undergraduate GPAs of about 3.4. At the 75th percentile, LSAT scores are 164 and above, and GPAs are about 3.8.

Moot court requirement	No
Public interest law requirement	No

ADMISSIONS

Selectivity Rating	92
# applications received	3,357
% applicants accepted	24
% acceptees attending	38
Average LSAT	162
LSAT Range	160–164
Average undergrad GPA	3.60
Application fee	$30
Regular notification	4/30
Early application program	No
Transfer students accepted	Yes
Evening division offered	No
Part-time accepted	No
CAS accepted	Yes

FINANCIAL FACTS

Annual tuition	$14,301
Books and supplies	$1,910
Fees	$2,086
Room and board (on/off campus)	$8,980/$10,110
Financial aid application deadline	4/7
% first-year students receiving some sort of aid	88
% receiving some sort of aid	87
% of aid that is merit based	3
% receiving scholarships	22
Average grant	$6,542
Average loan	$24,434
Average total aid package	$24,697
Average debt	$62,432

EMPLOYMENT INFORMATION

Career Rating	87
Rate of placement (nine months out)	100
Average starting salary	$80,246
State for bar exam	FL, GA, NY, CA, NJ
Pass rate for first-time bar	86

Employers Who Frequently Hire Grads

Foley & Lardner; Proskauer Rose; Holland & Knight; White & Case; Greenberg Traurig; Hunton & Williams; Bryan Cave; Shook Hardy; Baker Hostetler; Hogan Lovells; Weil; Gunster; Kilpatrick Stockton; O'Melveny & Myers; Akerman Senterfitt; Gray-Robinson; Federal and state judges; government

Prominent Alumni

Martha Barnett, Holland & Knight LLP; ABA President 2000; W. Reece Smith Jr., Carlton, Fields; ABA President 1980; Stephen Zack, Boies, Schiller & Flexner; ABA President, 2010; Lawton M. Chiles Jr., Florida Governor 1991–1998; Honorable Susan Black, U.S. 11th Circuit Judge

Grads Employed by Field (%)

Academic (9)
Business/industry (9)
Government (16)
Judicial clerkship (5)
Military (4)
Private practice (51)
Public interest (6)

UNIVERSITY OF GEORGIA
SCHOOL OF LAW

INSTITUTIONAL INFORMATION

Public/private	Public
Student/faculty ratio	12:1
% faculty part-time	19
% faculty female	36
% faculty minority	9
Total faculty	70

SURVEY SAYS...

Diverse opinions accepted in classrooms, Great research resources, Great library staff

STUDENTS

Enrollment of law school	710
% male/female	60/40
% from out-of-state	31
% full-time	100
% minority	20
# of countries represented	4
Average age of entering class	24

ACADEMICS

Academic Experience Rating	95
Profs interesting rating	96
Profs accessible rating	86
Hours of study per day	4.64

Academic Specialties

Civil Procedure, Commercial, Constitutional, Corporation Securities, Criminal, Environmental, Government Services, Human Rights, International, Labor, Legal History, Legal Philosophy, Property, Taxation, Intellectual Property

Advanced Degrees Offered

LLM, 1 year

Combined Degrees Offered

JD/MBA, JD/Master of Historic Preservation, JD/MPA, JD/MSW, JD/Master of Education in Sports Studies, 4 years; JD/MA, JD/PhD, various fields, varies

Academics

At the University of Georgia Law, students rave about the education they receive for a "bargain price." Everyone gets in-state rates after the first year, and many out-of-state residents receive scholarships for their first year. That's not to mention the school's "great academic reputation" and position as a "feeder to the most prominent city in the South." "It is really nice to be able to afford a JD from a reputable school and not be faced with the 'golden handcuffs,'" says a student not looking to work at a firm. All in all, "The professors, the people, the curriculum, and the facilities contribute to an overall competitive and comprehensive program that still embodies southern hospitality."

The "stellar" teachers at Georgia Law are "compassionate, while still demanding excellence," and it's "very easy to meet with professors and discuss things unrelated to class," as well as many student groups that allow for diverse ideas and discussions among students. "They genuinely care about us as individuals and have never been too busy to assist," says a student. Though students "are definitely left to figure things out on our own in many respects" ("Communication about how to get grades, apply for residency, etc., are somewhat lacking."), the school "provides a wide range of clinical opportunities for its students," as well as its nationally recognized moot court and mock trial programs and three major journals. It also offers study and work abroad programs to help reinforce its focus on global issues, and concurrent enrollment with the university's other programs is an option.

There's a wide variety of courses from which students can choose their electives, and the school has a unique approach to grading in the "intense" first year. Students don't receive grades for the first semester (with the exception of criminal law), and at the end of 1L, fall semester performance counts toward the final grade, but it's weighted significantly less than spring exam scores. The school wants students to focus on their studies and discourages 1Ls from taking jobs during the first year of law school.

Georgia Law has one of the largest law libraries in the nation—students love its "huge, picturesque windows and accommodating seating and tables"—and it's embarking on a renovation and expansion that will only improve the quality of life. Classroom facilities are "also great," and the school produces an enthusiastic alumni base that helps during interview season. Still, many students do wish that more job opportunities outside of Georgia found their way to the UGA Law campus.

Life

Students say that the "small Southern town" of Athens, with its coffee shops and music scene, is the "quintessential college town," but one that can be "somewhat limiting for older students." Though the school is just a couple of blocks from downtown, "Housing options are pretty limited around the law school and most students live two to three miles away," and often must drive to school as "the Athens bus service is not great." Atlanta is about an hour-and-a-half away, so students who must frequently travel for their internships have a bit of a hike, but it's still close enough that its myriad entertainment options can be enjoyed without much trouble. "The camaraderie of the students, an awesome social scene, and proximity to Atlanta make a good educational experience that much better," says a student.

PAUL ROLLINS, DIRECTOR OF LAW ADMISSIONS
225 HERTY DRIVE, ATHENS, GA 30602-6012
TEL: 706-542-7060 FAX: 706-542-5556
E-MAIL: UGAJD@UGA.EDU • WEBSITE: WWW.LAW.UGA.EDU

UGA Law offers a "great balance between traditional legal education and strong social environment." Small class sizes mean, "Everyone is very independently driven," providing at most a "friendly competition," instead of a cutthroat one, but "Grabbing a beer with friends after a long Friday full of classes makes law school really bearable." "No one is hiding books; no one is refusing to help. We are all in this together and at the end of the day, the person next to you is a future referral and professional colleague," says a 2L. "One thing that Dean White reminds all incoming 1Ls at orientation is that our classmates are our colleagues, not our competition, and students really take this to heart," says another student.

Getting In

Admission to the University of Georgia is selective, and the school prides itself on the diverse backgrounds that its students bring. Members of the class of 2013 include a professional baseball player in Israel, the lead singer of a band, a published author, an intern for the SEC, and a former Miss Georgia. The school has received record numbers of applications in recent years. There was a thirty-nine percent increase for the class of 2012 from the previous year. The class of 2013 had a median LSAT of 164 and a median undergraduate GPA of 3.7.

Clinical program required	No
Legal writing course requirement	Yes
Legal methods course requirement	No
Legal research course requirement	Yes
Moot court requirement	No
Public interest law requirement	No

ADMISSIONS

Selectivity Rating	94
# applications received	4,220
% applicants accepted	23
% acceptees attending	26
Average LSAT	164
LSAT Range	162–166
Average undergrad GPA	3.70
Application fee	$50
Regular application	Rolling, up to 3/1
Regular notification	Rolling
Early application program	No
Transfer students accepted	Yes
Evening division offered	No
Part-time accepted	No
CAS accepted	Yes

FINANCIAL FACTS

Annual tuition (in-state/out-of-state)	$15,434/ $32,542
Books and supplies	$1,500
Fees	$2,190
Room and board	$14,478
Financial aid application deadline	7/1
% first-year students receiving some sort of aid	90
% receiving some sort of aid	90
% of aid that is merit based	88
% receiving scholarships	50
Average grant	$11,000
Average loan	$27,030
Average total aid package	$20,415
Average debt	$53,126

EMPLOYMENT INFORMATION

Career Rating	**94**	**Grads Employed by Field (%)**
Rate of placement (nine months out)	96	Academic (1)
Average starting salary	$85,000	Business/industry (8)
State for bar exam	GA	Government (19)
Pass rate for first-time bar	95	Judicial clerkship (15)
Employers Who Frequently Hire Grads		Private practice (56)
Alston & Bird, King & Spalding, Troutman		Public interest (2)
Sanders, Jones Day, Greenberg Traurig,		
U.S. Department of Justice, public defend-		
ers and prosecutors, Federal District and		
Circuit Court Judges, JAG Corp		

UNIVERSITY OF HAWAII—MANOA
WILLIAM S. RICHARDSON SCHOOL OF LAW

INSTITUTIONAL INFORMATION

Public/private	Public
Student/faculty ratio	8:1
% faculty part-time	45
% faculty female	43
% faculty minority	42
Total faculty	84

SURVEY SAYS...
Diverse opinions accepted in classrooms, Students love Honolulu, HI

STUDENTS

Enrollment of law school	353
% male/female	41/59
% from out-of-state	23
% full-time	84
% minority	70
% international	3
# of countries represented	6
Average age of entering class	26

ACADEMICS

Academic Experience Rating	86
Profs interesting rating	85
Profs accessible rating	83
Hours of study per day	4.52

Academic Specialties
Environmental, International, Native Hawaiian Law

Advanced Degrees Offered
JD, 3 years; LLM, 1 year

Combined Degrees Offered
JD/Environmental Law, JD/Pacific-Asian Legal Studies, 3 years; JD/Graduate Ocean Policy, JD/MA, JD/MBA, JD/MS, JD/MSW, JD/PhD, varies

Clinical program required	Yes
Legal writing course requirement	Yes
Legal methods course requirement	Yes
Legal research course requirement	Yes

Academics

Nestled at the "crossroads of the Pacific," the University of Hawaii—Manoa William S. Richardson School of Law offers local, national, and international students an equal opportunity to get a law degree while enjoying a little piece of heaven on earth. Don't be fooled by the laid-back nature of the students and faculty—academics here are plenty "rigorous," particularly in the school's strong Pacific Island law and environmental law programs. Fortunately, it's easy to wind down from a long day of hitting the books when you're surrounded by beaches and happy fellow students. As a second-year student eloquently observes: "Just the right mix of *aloha* and Socratic thrashing yields capable, happy lawyers."

Richardson's "first-rate" faculty has a reputation for being "very accessible and easy to work with," and it's obvious to students that "they take pride in teaching." Even the handful of students who aren't raving about their instructors can only offer up the mildest criticism, as one second-year demonstrates: "A few I've encountered are just okay." Abiding by an open-door policy and demonstrating an openness "to discussing topics at most anytime," Richardson professors take the time to make sure that everyone understands the concepts, while at the same time being "very supportive of independent research." "I generally feel that I am able to explore my intellectual pursuits as I deem fit, with guidance and support from the faculty," states a 2L.

The "very friendly" administration is certainly accessible; the Richardson School of Law is "the kind of school where the dean is seen in the halls everyday and says hello to you by name," and administrators are often spotted participating in school activities. In return, they ask for student input on many school matters, such as the hiring of professors, expansion of the school library, and improving student services. Richardson students speak very highly of the regard shown by the entire campus community for the well-being of first-year students, from the "truly concerned" deans to "supportive" upperclassmen. The island is a magnet for a great deal of "very impressive" adjunct faculty and visiting lecturers. "Professors from top law schools are always looking for an excuse to spend a semester or a year in paradise," surmises a 2L. "[During] my 1L year, I had two visiting professors from Georgetown and one from Duke, in addition to the excellent professors tenured at UH." Networking opportunities are "exceptional if you're staying in Hawaii," although some students seeking employment in the continental United States wish they had more assistance in their job search.

Both the facilities and the library are "useful" and sufficient for the typical student's needs, and include "access to up-to-date online sources, as well some print materials." Unsurprisingly, students prefer to congregate outside whenever possible, and a "courtyard where students can relax or talk" is usually where you'll find them. Even so, students clamor for more study and meeting rooms, and complain about the state of the library and the "very cold" air conditioning levels in classrooms. Luckily, the law school facilities are up for renovation within the next few years.

Life

A good mix of students fresh out of undergrad and those with more life experience bring diversity to Richardson' student population. Some students say that the school is "trying too hard to get diversity," which results in the enrollment of "lots of mainland people who will get their degree and bolt back." "Diversity of opinion and views is important, but not at the expense of the community at large," says a student. Still, there's not many downsides to life at Richardson. As one can imagine, "It's a very tightly knit community." Most students agree that competition at this "small, intimate" school is present and "healthy," but it takes a back seat to "learning how to be both a zealous advocate for clients and a responsible officer of the court." Classmates definitely "don't claw each other to get to the top of the class." It's hard to imagine all that much back-stabbing going on when "The culture and values of Hawaii permeate the school and administration," and the general happiness of students contributes to a "communal atmosphere" in which students "build ties and form lifelong bonds." "You become *ohana* (family) when you attend the Richardson School of Law," says one student. Still, there's a bit of "Hawaiian/not Hawaiian, *haole*/not *haole* tension" present on the island, but "in general, it's civil." The options of things to do in your downtime are unrivaled. "How many schools have a Surf Club?" asks a first-year. There are a "wide variety" of student clubs and organizations on campus (it's also easy to start one), and these groups do "a nice job" of promoting events such as guest speakers and symposiums.

Getting In

As the only ABA-accredited law school in the Pacific Asia region, the University of Hawaii—Manoa Richardson School of Law can afford to be selective. They've got a lock on the local talent and anyone looking to practice within the area will be competing for a limited number of seats. The school is very strict about its deadlines, and all applications must be received by February 1.

Moot court requirement	No
Public interest law requirement	Yes

ADMISSIONS

Selectivity Rating	86
# applications received	1,093
% applicants accepted	19
% acceptees attending	42
Average LSAT	158
LSAT Range	153–159
Average undergrad GPA	3.45
Application fee	$60
Regular notification	4/1
Early application program	No
Transfer students accepted	Yes
Evening division offered	Yes
Part-time accepted	Yes
CAS accepted	Yes

International Students

TOEFL required of international students

FINANCIAL FACTS

Annual tuition (in-state/out-of-state)	$15,960/$30,024
Books and supplies	$1,146
Fees	$511
Room and board (on/off campus)	$9,410/$12,536
Financial aid application deadline	3/1
% first-year students receiving some sort of aid	73
% receiving some sort of aid	73
% of aid that is merit based	20
% receiving scholarships	47
Average grant	$6,502
Average loan	$21,943
Average total aid package	$21,976
Average debt	$58,609

EMPLOYMENT INFORMATION

Career Rating 77
Rate of placement (nine months out) 83
Average starting salary $57,510
State for bar exam HI
Pass rate for first-time bar 80

Employers Who Frequently Hire Grads
Hawaii State Judiciary; Office of the Prosecuting Attorney; Public Defenders Office; Ashford & Wriston; Bays Lung et al.; Case Lombardi & Petit; Cades Schutte; Carlsmith Ball; Goodsill Anderson Quinn & Stifel; McCorriston Miller et al.; Starn O'Toole Marcus & Fisher

Prominent Alumni
John Waihee, former Governor of Hawaii; Sabrina McKenna, Hawaii Supreme Court;

Alexa Fujise, Lisa Ginoza, Katherine Leonard, Associate Judges, Hawaii Intermediate Court of Appeals; James Duke Aiona, former Lieutenant Governor, State of Hawaii; Junichi Yanagihara, Managing Director & Producer, Sprite Animation Studios

Grads Employed by Field (%)
Academic (2)
Business/industry (2)
Government (12)
Judicial clerkship (27)
Military (9)
Private practice (30)
Public interest (15)

UNIVERSITY OF HOUSTON
LAW CENTER

INSTITUTIONAL INFORMATION

Public/private	Public
Student/faculty ratio	10:1
% faculty part-time	77
% faculty female	17
% faculty minority	9
Total faculty	207

SURVEY SAYS...

Diverse opinions accepted in classrooms, Great library staff, Abundant externship/internship/ clerkship opportunities

STUDENTS

Enrollment of law school	995
% male/female	56/44
% from out-of-state	10
% full-time	78
% minority	35
% international	4
# of countries represented	11
Average age of entering class	25

ACADEMICS

Academic Experience Rating	82
Profs interesting rating	81
Profs accessible rating	73
Hours of study per day	4.33

Academic Specialties

Commercial, Criminal, Environmental, Immigration, International, Labor, Taxation, Intellectual Property, Health, Energy, Consumer Law, Clinical Programs, Trial Advocacy, Higher Education

Advanced Degrees Offered

LLM in Health, Intellectual Property, Tax, Energy & Natural Resources, International Law, Foreign Scholars (for foreign attorneys), 24 credit hours

Combined Degrees Offered

JD/MBA, JD/MPH, JD/MA History, JD/MSW, 4 years; JD/PhD in Medical Humanities, JD/MD, 6 years

Academics

As large and lively as the state of Texas, the University of Houston Law Center enrolls fewer than 900 students in its diverse and challenging JD, LLM, and joint-degree programs. Drawing top names from the Houston legal community, professors are "either extremely accomplished attorneys or nationally renowned experts in a particular field of law." Though they represent the top of their field, "There are no 'bigger than Texas' egos with any of the faculty." In fact, "The entire faculty is very accessible and willing to help students learn in any way they can." Students agree that their professors are "not only available during office hours, many professors host lunches or parties in their homes to learn more about their students."

In the classroom, the professors are "very much focused on teaching us to think creatively" and throughout the JD program the "Practical aspects of lawyering are stressed." Things here begin with a bang as "All first-year students are required to take part in a moot court competition, and it's a great experience for everyone." In addition, "There are six different law journals in which a student may participate, including the Houston Law Review, which consistently ranks in the top fifty of all Law Reviews in the country." What's more, the school operates a number of clinics and research institutes that augment classroom experiences with hands-on experience. "I have spent three semesters working at the Immigration and Civil Clinic and will always remember this time as the most exciting and rewarding aspect of my law school experience," explains one clinic participant. "We are given enormous responsibility for our clients and the experience has given me an invaluable opportunity to learn actual lawyering skills."

Those looking for great value relative to cost in their education will be extremely satisfied with U of H. Students love that they get a "high-value education for a low cost in a great legal market." If you can manage a "scholarship" or are "a Texas resident" it only sweetens the proverbial deal. Even so, students admit there are some sacrifices associated with a U of H education, particularly with regard to the school's facilities which most agree "need improvement." There are no ivy-lined walls at U of H; instead, think "East German bunker school of architecture." However, most students take the environs in stride. "Students who enter with high expectations of facilities will be disappointed," says one student. "But you learn at this school in an environment conducive to learning." On that note, U of H "fosters a community and not a rivalry among students. Fellow students are always willing to answer a question, share notes, and form study groups."

Outside the classroom, "There are lots of opportunities to work with major law firms and other community organizations during the summer and during the school year," and the "Office of Career Services is particularly helpful for summer job opportunities." After graduation, Houston is a well-suited environment for future attorneys, boasting its reputation as one of the "largest legal markets in the country." A current student insists, "If you want to succeed, you can, and you can get a great job when you graduate too—with all the top firms in Texas including all the elite New York satellite offices."

Life

Students say the school is a great place to work on your powers of persuasion as there's lots of debate on the U of H campus. A student explains, "Because the student body is fairly conservative, but, at the same time, lawyers generally exhibit liberal thinking (at least in the social realm), you get a nice balance of liberal and conservative, often leading to lively debate absent from more liberal institutions." Even so, don't expect

JAMIE WEST DILLON, ASSISTANT DEAN FOR ADMISSIONS
100 LAW CENTER, HOUSTON, TX 77204-6060
TEL: 713-743-2280 FAX: 713-743-2194
E-MAIL: LAWADMISSIONS@UH.EDU • WEBSITE: WWW.LAW.UH.EDU

"any cutthroat type of competitive environment" here since students agree that "even if they have polar opposite views in the classroom, afterwards they hang out."

On campus, the prevailing atmosphere is "friendly" with "an awesome SBA that is very active in helping make UHLC a better place." Students tend to form strong friendships in their first-year sections, and when the weekend arrives "Plenty of people…go out on a regular basis." Night students are generally less involved in the campus community, admitting that there is something of a "social divide between part-time and full-time students"; many complain that events and activities take place during the day (while they are working) and that "most of the social events are geared toward single people or those without children."

Unfortunately, the campus isn't much of a social hub because "It is in a part of Houston that nobody really cares to live in, so most people come in for class and then head home." However, the cosmopolitan city of Houston is a great place to live, offering "a standing symphony, opera, and ballet, NFL, NBA, MLB, and MLS sports teams (and minor league ice hockey) a great zoo and museums, and a multitude of golfing opportunities."

Getting In

There is no set minimum LSAT score or undergraduate GPA required for acceptance to the University of Houston Law Center; all applicants are reviewed individually. In 2010, the lowest LSAT score accepted was in the upper 140s, while the median score for accepted applicants was 163. The median GPA was 3.49. Non-Texans comprise approximately eleven percent of the student population and the acceptance rate is equally competitive for out-of-state and in-state residents.

Clinical program required	No
Legal writing course requirement	Yes
Legal methods course requirement	Yes
Legal research course requirement	Yes
Moot court requirement	Yes
Public interest law requirement	No

ADMISSIONS

Selectivity Rating	88
# applications received	3,942
% applicants accepted	24
% acceptees attending	27
Average LSAT	162
LSAT Range	159–164
Average undergrad GPA	3.41
Application fee	$70
Regular application	Rolling, up to 2/15
Regular notification	5/15
Early application program	Yes
Early application deadline	11/15
Early application notification	2/28
Transfer students accepted	Yes
Evening division offered	Yes
Part-time accepted	Yes
CAS accepted	Yes

International Students

TOEFL required of international students

FINANCIAL FACTS

Annual tuition (in-state/out-of-state)	$22,404/ $35,576
Books and supplies	$1,200
Fees	$4,328
Room and board (on/off campus)	$7,538/ $9,234
Financial aid application deadline	4/1
% receiving some sort of aid	82
% of aid that is merit based	33
% receiving scholarships	33
Average grant	$2,556
Average loan	$24,990
Average total aid package	$27,500
Average debt	$65,802

EMPLOYMENT INFORMATION

Career Rating	91
Rate of placement (nine months out)	92
Average starting salary	$90,933
State for bar exam	TX
Pass rate for first-time bar	90

Employers Who Frequently Hire Grads
Baker & Botts; Fulbright & Jaworski; Vinson & Elkins; Bracewell & Giuliani; Harris County D.A.; Weil Gotshal & Manges; Locke Lord Bissell & Liddell; Hanes & Boone; Jones Day; King & Spaulding; Exxon Mobil Corporation; Texas Attorney General's Office

Prominent Alumni
Richard Haynes, Litigation; Charles Matthews, former Vice President and General Counsel, Exxon Mobil; Philip Zelikow, Executive Director of the 9/11 Commission; Gene Green, U.S. Congressman; Ted Poe, U.S. Congressman

Grads Employed by Field (%)
Academic (2)
Business/industry (23)
Government (10)
Judicial clerkship (4)
Private practice (57)
Public interest (4)

UNIVERSITY OF IDAHO
COLLEGE OF LAW

Academics

"Handwritten on my letter of acceptance were the words 'We would love to have you in the Idaho family,'" beams a 1L at the University of Idaho College of Law. "I didn't think anything of it at the time, but it really does have that kind of feel here." "The low tuition is a bargain," and "The administration is kind, fair, and involved." Plus, "The dean rocks." "There are a few profs here and there who obviously just want to do their research, and teaching is a bit of a dead weight for them, but they are definitely in the minority." Most "dedicated" professors at this "small public law school" are "unbelievably friendly and accessible" and "genuinely care about the students." The faculty "knows students by name by the end of their first year, even if you do not have a class with them." "I've never seen anything like it, quite frankly," says an impressed 1L. "Sure, one moment they're using the Socratic Method to grill you in class," says a 2L, "but after class they take the time to discuss any topic with you."

Some students complain that "practical legal skills, other than writing, seem to get short shrift." Others contend that there are "ample opportunities for pro bono work" and "other ways to allow students to get some practical experience before they graduate." "Many of these programs are student run, which I think is great," notes a 1L. "The externship, internship, clinic, and semester-in-practice programs are wonderful."

U of I is the only law school in Idaho, "and its graduates are extremely well-respected throughout the state and throughout the geographic region in general." "Because Idaho is a small state with a relatively small legal community, alumni are very actively involved at the law school." "During orientation, a group of us were eating lunch on the lawn outside the law school," explains a 1L. "A man approached us and asked to join us. Only after five minutes of casual conversation did he mention that he was the Attorney General for the state of Idaho." "There are quite a few job opportunities in the area surrounding Moscow," but "It is hard to get good placements" for jobs, internships, and externships because of the school's relatively remote location. "You pretty much have to live in Spokane or Boise for the summer to get a really well-paid job with valuable experience."

The "somewhat old" and "small" law school facilities are "functional," but "could be more aesthetically pleasing." The administration is "working to improve aesthetics," and major renovations have just been completed. The study areas are "roomy and nice," and classrooms are "comfortable" and "very large." "There is a beautiful courtroom where the Idaho Supreme Court and Court of Appeals come twice a year and provide the students an opportunity to observe actual proceedings." The library is "pretty good for a small school."

Life

The administration "is striving to increase diversity," but it's not easy because U of I is "somewhat isolated by its location and lack of diversity in the general population." Students do run the gamut in terms of age. "I am enjoying my experience of returning to school as an older student," says a 2L. Also, "There is a sizeable Mormon population." Politically, the student population is "divided between extreme conservatives and extreme liberals," which "creates tension" occasionally.

"This is a tremendously friendly law school." Students describe themselves as "cooperative and accepting." "The 1Ls, though competitive," demonstrate a "strong camaraderie." Cliques do tend to form, though, and gossip runs "rampant." Outside of class, there is "a lot of student involvement." "Because of the limited number of students

JENIFER FINNEY, JD, DIRECTOR OF ADMISSIONS
6TH & RAYBURN, MOSCOW, ID 83844-2321
TEL: 208-885-2300 FAX: 208-885-5709
E-MAIL: LAWADMIT@UIDAHO.EDU • WEBSITE: WWW.LAW.UIDAHO.EDU

[at the law school], there are countless opportunities for involvement in extracurricular activities, legal aid clinics, positions in student groups, and for membership on administration committees." "About half of the students socialize on a regular basis," and there are "some pretty hard partiers."

Moscow is "a fairly remote," "beautiful," rural hamlet "in northern Idaho," "closer to Seattle than Boise," and "two hours from a city of any size (Spokane, Washington)." Idaho boasts "many recreational opportunities." "If you love hiking, biking, skiing, and the outdoors, then it is heaven," counsels a 2L. "If you need constant activity and entertainment, U of I is not for you, but if you're serious about getting a good-quality, inexpensive education, you'll get both here." "The cost of living is affordable," and "There is a large food co-op" and "an impressive farmer's market." There are "great parks" and "many festivals" as well. It's "easy to walk anywhere." "There isn't an apartment in town that isn't five minutes from the school."

Getting In

Enrolled students at the 25th percentile have LSAT scores of 151 and GPAs a little over 3.1. Admitted students at the 75th percentile have LSAT scores of 157 and GPAs of nearly 3.6. If you take the LSAT more than once, the U of I "may put more weight on the most recent score, especially when there is several years between scores."

Clinical program required	No
Legal writing course requirement	Yes
Legal methods course requirement	No
Legal research course requirement	Yes
Moot court requirement	Yes
Public interest law requirement	Yes

ADMISSIONS

Selectivity Rating	**76**
# applications received	862
% applicants accepted	44
% acceptees attending	35
LSAT Range	151–157
Application fee	$50
Regular application	Rolling, up to 7/1
Regular notification	4/15
Early application program	No
Transfer students accepted	Yes
Evening division offered	No
Part-time accepted	No
CAS accepted	Yes

International Students

TOEFL required of international students	

FINANCIAL FACTS

Annual tuition (in-state/out-of-state)	$12,940/ $24,532
Books and supplies	$1,474
Room and board	$9,318
Financial aid application deadline	2/15
% first-year students receiving some sort of aid	100
% receiving some sort of aid	100
% of aid that is merit based	100
% receiving scholarships	22
Average grant	$5,910
Average loan	$30,518
Average total aid package	$31,593
Average debt	$78,013

EMPLOYMENT INFORMATION

Career Rating	**72**
Rate of placement (nine months out)	78
State for bar exam	ID, WA, UT, OR, CA

Employers Who Frequently Hire Grads
Employers and agencies with offices in Idaho, Washington, Oregon, Utah, Nevada, Montana

Prominent Alumni
Linda Copple Trout, Justice & past Chief Justice, Idaho Supreme Court; Frank A. Shrontz, Former CEO Boeing Co.; Dennis E. Wheeler, President, Coeur: The Precious Metals Co.; James A. McClure, Former United States Senator; Nancy Morris, Secretary of the Securities & Exchange Commission

University of Illinois
College of Law

INSTITUTIONAL INFORMATION

Public/private	Public
Student/faculty ratio	14:1
% faculty part-time	35
% faculty female	28
% faculty minority	11
Total faculty	71

SURVEY SAYS...

Diverse opinions accepted in classrooms, Great research resources, Great library staff

STUDENTS

Enrollment of law school	640
% male/female	59/41
% from out-of-state	45
% full-time	100
% minority	25
% international	1
# of countries represented	11
Average age of entering class	24

ACADEMICS

Academic Experience Rating	87
Profs interesting rating	85
Profs accessible rating	89
Hours of study per day	1.50

Academic Specialties

Civil Procedure, Commercial, Constitutional, Corporation Securities, Criminal, Environmental, Government Services, Human Rights, International, Labor, Legal History, Legal Philosophy, Property, Taxation, Intellectual Property

Advanced Degrees Offered

JD, 3 years; LLM, 1 year

Combined Degrees Offered

JD/MBA, JD/Masters of Urban Planning, 4 years; JD/PhD Ed, JD/ DVM, JD/MD, 6 years; JD/Masters of Human Resources and Industrial Relations, JD/MEd, JD/MS of Chemistry, JD/MS of Journalism, JD/MS of Natural Resources & Environmental Sciences, 3.5 years; JD/MS Computer Science, 3 years

Academics

"You'll definitely get the bang for your buck" at the University of Illinois College of Law, "a jewel amid the cornfields [that boasts] the best mix of academic excellence, social interaction, and human decency for the best price available." Tuition is especially afford-able for in-state students. The "tireless [administration] is also very accessible" and extraordinarily popular among students. "The new dean is extremely supportive of the students and does a wonderful job of building community."

Students at the U of I tell us emphatically that "the faculty is the school's greatest strength." The "tough but not unreasonable" professors are "prolific writers [who are] clearly brilliant and accomplished." Students say the professors "are, for the most part fantastic, both in and out of the classroom [and] always able to clarify concepts that are confusing. More significant, they are completely available [and] genuinely interested in teaching and working with students." The professors make an effort to be reached in that they "have open-door policies and are available for discussions with students about class, a job, or just life in general." Students also note that the school "employs a nice mix of tenured and adjunct faculty, which makes for a perfect balance of legal theory and real-world experience. The primary complaint that students have with regard to the faculty is "keeping the good professors around. "One student explains, "There's not much reason for them to stay in central Illinois. The school really needs to make an effort to not let the good ones get away."

Graduates enjoy "a great employment rate" thanks to an aggressive Career Services Office. As one transfer student attests, "I'm in a unique position in that I've seen how two different law schools operate. I was blown away by the quality of the Career Services Department at the University of Illinois. The administration goes to great lengths to make sure that not only do all University of Illinois College of Law graduates get jobs, but that they get the jobs they want." "If you do well here, nothing in Chicago will be off limits." However, students complain that the college "needs to broaden its resources [and] expand beyond the Midwestern market." Until that happens, "It is difficult to get much traction" on either coast "when searching for jobs in Champaign."

The facilities at the U of I "are good" in that large chunks "are wired," and the research resources of the library are as abundant as you'll find anywhere. Overall, though, the "rather Spartan [College of Law] could use some serious help." Suffice it to say, the "incredibly ugly and cheap-looking [building] does not give anyone goose bumps for the grand study of the law." One student writes, "There are no windows in any of the rooms." It's like going to school in a casino." Students note, "Sometimes seats are scarce [in the] crowded" classrooms, as well as in the "cramped" library, though now that the school has reduced the size of the incoming class, this should help to alleviate the prob-lem. Also, wear layers because "There also seems to be a bit of a temperature control problem" no matter what the season.

Life

If they do say so themselves, the students at the U of I are "very amiable, noncom-petitive, [and] very intellectually minded, yet not stuck on themselves." These are the "brightest [and] most fun" people—"all the cool, smart kids." Students at the U of I are also "a bit neurotic [and] love to hear their own voices." The student population "has a wonderful mix of student ethnicities, religions, sexual orientation, and gender." There is

PAUL D. PLESS, ASSISTANT DEAN FOR ADMISSIONS AND FINANCIAL AID
504 EAST PENNSYLVANIA AVENUE, ROOM 201, MC-594, CHAMPAIGN, IL 61820
TEL: 217-244-6415 FAX: 217-244-1478
E-MAIL: ADMISSIONS@LAW.UIUC.EDU • WEBSITE: WWW.LAW.UIUC.EDU

also a laid-back atmosphere on campus. "Everybody really cares about you. They want you to succeed, and it's almost difficult not to."

"The school truly is a community because of its manageable size. Lunches with the dean" are common, and there are "endless other ways to connect with the other students and, more important, the faculty." One content student writes, "The cafeteria has good food and, best of all, they carry Starbucks coffee." Students also say, "Although U of I is located in the corn fields of Illinois, it is impossible to feel isolated" because the administration "is constantly bringing in lecturers, symposiums, and guest speakers." In addition, the College of Law sponsors "a weekly happy hour, [at which] professors and administrators act as the celebrity bartenders."

Life outside the classroom has many positive aspects. Students are very "sports-oriented" and say "It is great to be on a Big Ten campus and be able to devote yourself to the study of law full-time," and surprising though it seems, "There is actually a lot to do in Urbana-Champaign." There are "great bars, coffee houses, [and] centers for the arts." There is also "a progressive music scene." Some students gripe that "social life can seem dominated by a frat/sorority type atmosphere," even at the law school level. "The town is basically designed for college students, so it gets a little dullsville at times." Many students would "prefer to be in a larger city," with Chicago being the example of choice. "Socially, we do the best we can with the town we're in," asserts one student. "That means we drink a lot [and] go en masse to football and basketball games."

Getting In

The average LSAT score for admitted students is 166. The median GPA is 3.5. Those numbers are serious but not forbidding. Note also that, while it's substantially cheaper for Illinois residents to attend the college, residency in the Land of Lincoln will not get you one iota of special treatment from the admissions office.

Clinical program required	No
Legal writing course requirement	Yes
Legal methods course requirement	No
Legal research course requirement	Yes
Moot court requirement	No
Public interest law requirement	No

ADMISSIONS

Selectivity Rating	95
# applications received	4,833
% applicants accepted	20
% acceptees attending	23
Average LSAT	167
LSAT Range	163–168
Average undergrad GPA	3.80
Application fee	$0
Regular application	Rolling, up to 3/1
Regular notification	Rolling
Early application program	Yes
Early application deadline	10/31
Early application notification	12/15
Transfer students accepted	Yes
Evening division offered	No
Part-time accepted	No
CAS accepted	Yes

International Students

TOEFL required of international students	

FINANCIAL FACTS

Annual tuition (in-state/out-of-state)	$33,000/ $40,000
Books and supplies	$4,028
Fees	$3,420
Room and board	$12,058
Financial aid application deadline	3/15
% first-year students receiving some sort of aid	99
% receiving some sort of aid	99
% of aid that is merit based	95
% receiving scholarships	83
Average grant	$12,500
Average loan	$37,500
Average total aid package	$50,000
Average debt	$80,005

EMPLOYMENT INFORMATION

Career Rating	79
Rate of placement (nine months out)	100
Average starting salary	$100,000
State for bar exam	IL, CA, D.C., NY, MO
Pass rate for first-time bar	97

Employers Who Frequently Hire Grads
Baker & McKenzie; Brinks Hofer Gilson & Lione; Bell Boyd & Lloyd; Foley & Lardner; Sidley Austin Brown & Wood, McGuire & Woods, McAndrews Held & Malloy; Deloitte Touche; Gardner Carton & Douglas; Husch & Eppenberger; Jenner & Block; Jones Day; Kirkland & Ellis; KMZ Rosenman; Latham & Watkins; Littler & Mendelson; Lord Bissell & Brook; Mayer Brown Rowe & Maw; McAndrews Held & Malloy; Neal Gerber & Eisenberg; Office of the State Appellate Defender; Piper Rudnick; Seyfarth Shaw; Sidley Austin Brown & Wood; Skadden Arps Slate Meagher & Flom; Sonnenschein Nath & Rosenthal; Thompson Coburn; U.S. DOJ; U.S. Securities and Exchange Commission; and Winston & Strawn

Grads Employed by Field (%)
Academic (4)
Business/industry (12)
Government (5)
Judicial clerkship (7)
Military (1)
Private practice (67)
Public interest (7)

THE UNIVERSITY OF IOWA
COLLEGE OF LAW

INSTITUTIONAL INFORMATION

Public/private	Public
Student/faculty ratio	11:1
% faculty part-time	28
% faculty female	37
% faculty minority	10
Total faculty	67

SURVEY SAYS...

Diverse opinions accepted in classrooms, Great research resources, Great library staff

STUDENTS

Enrollment of law school	580
% male/female	55/45
% from out-of-state	52
% full-time	100
% minority	16
% international	3
# of countries represented	11
Average age of entering class	24

ACADEMICS

Academic Experience Rating	84
Profs interesting rating	89
Profs accessible rating	82

Academic Specialties

Commercial, Constitutional, Corporation Securities, International, Property, Intellectual Property

Advanced Degrees Offered

LLM in International and Comparative Law, 24 credit hours and a thesis, 1 year

Combined Degrees Offered

JD/MBA, JD/MA, JD/MHA, JD/MSW, JD/MPH, JD/MS, 4 years; JD/MD, 6 years

Clinical program required	No
Legal writing course requirement	Yes
Legal methods course requirement	Yes
Legal research course requirement	Yes

Academics

Students at the affordable University of Iowa College of Law are unanimous on one point: Iowa is "the most underrated school in the country." "If you want to learn from the best without giving an arm and a leg for tuition," they say, "come to this school." The "sympathetic" faculty at Iowa is "very concerned with providing the best academic experience." "Professors are demanding in a way that I know will make me a better lawyer," relates 2L. "They are brilliant yet not egomaniacs." "Some scare the crap out of you, and some create a warm classroom environment." Outside of class, "The professors are, for the most part, interesting and cool people," and interaction between students and professors is exceedingly common. Sure, they are "awkward socially," but "Even the most distinguished professors welcome you into their offices, and it's not uncommon to go out to dinner with your professor and a few classmates."

Classes here "tend toward the theoretical." "Iowa presents kind of a contradiction," proffers a 2L. "It is a theory-driven program that produces mostly practicing attorneys." Iowa's ten practice clinics are "very strong," "and there are plenty of slots available" (though you do have to lottery into them). "The Iowa City/Cedar Rapids area has opportunities to practice while in law school, but those opportunities are somewhat limited." The legal writing program garners mixed reviews. "We are learning to write legal briefs and memos from the best," contends a satisfied 1L. Others feel "cheated." "We could use a lot more hands-on training with writing and research," says one student. Pretty much everyone who mentions the moot court program is unhappy with it. "The faculty can't be bothered to provide meaningful coaching or instruction," laments one student.

The Career Services staff here "is a group of all-stars" that provides "all of the assistance you need." "The top twenty-five to thirty percent of students don't seem to have any trouble finding work in cities across the country, including New York, San Francisco, Los Angeles, and Boston." By and large, though, students end up practicing in one of "several large markets" throughout the Midwest. Some students complain that "Iowa could do better in attracting and encouraging employers outside of the Midwest." "If you want to work in the Midwest, this school is considered good, and employers are eager to interview you," advises a 2L. "If you want to work anywhere else, go to law school in that region."

The "really space-constrained" law school building is "functional, though it looks pretty awful." "It was built in the early '80s, and I think at that time people thought it was cool and futuristic," adds a 2L, "but now it just looks like something out of *Star Trek IV*." "Classrooms are pretty typical," though students "appreciate the plentiful outlets and wireless Internet." "There is no shortage of PCs available in the computer labs," and "The school also has very friendly tech gurus." The "extensive" law library is "a little bubble of greatness." It's "open late" and "always staffed by friendly librarians who know more about the law than anyone ever should."

Life

Students are "mostly white and from Iowa or Illinois," but there is also "a surprisingly large number of kids from the coasts." "I was actually surprised by how many non-Midwestern students are currently at the school," admits a 1L. Overall, it's "a good mix of people from all walks of life." There are "some very conservative points of view" but "young crazy liberals" predominate. There are "a lot of do-gooders who are very socially conscious and commit a tremendous amount of time to community and national issues." "U of I law students and most of the professors have a definite liberal slant," says a 2L. "If you're conservative and not articulate and able to defend your opinions, you'll never survive classroom discussion."

"Students at Iowa are competitive, certainly." "I was surprised by how many gunners there actually are," relates a 3L. It's "friendly" gunning, though. Iowa students are "a group of people who have their priorities in order, who are willing to lend a hand, and who are remarkably grounded in reality." "There's an earnestness and commitment to integrity and excellence that Iowa students, faculty, and staff all share," enthuses a 3L. "It makes Iowa a unique place, and it makes me hopeful for the legal profession as a whole. As a jaded California native and East Coast private college graduate, I never cease to be surprised by the quality and professionalism I've found here in the heartland."

Socially, though "People tend to buckle down when it is demanded," "You can be sure to find friends out at a bar" on virtually any given weekend night. "Everyone is very good friends with each other," and Iowa City is "a fun town." Coffee shops, libraries, bookstores, and great restaurants abound. There are "weekly Law Nights held at a local drinking establishment." "There's no such thing as a grad student bar in Iowa City," and there is "a pretty big divide between people who took time off and people who came straight from undergrad."

Getting In

Admitted students at the 25th percentile have LSAT scores of 158 and GPAs in the range of 3.3. Admitted students at the 75th percentile have LSAT scores of 163 and GPAs of around 3.8.

Moot court requirement	Yes
Public interest law requirement	No

ADMISSIONS

Selectivity Rating	86
# applications received	1,757
% applicants accepted	39
% acceptees attending	29
Average LSAT	161
LSAT Range	158–164
Average undergrad GPA	3.56
Application fee	$60
Regular application	Rolling, up to 3/1
Regular notification	Rolling
Early application program	No
Transfer students accepted	Yes
Evening division offered	No
Part-time accepted	No
CAS accepted	Yes

International Students

TOEFL required of international students	

FINANCIAL FACTS

Annual tuition (in-state/out-of-state)	$22,554/ $41,322
Books and supplies	$2,300
Fees	$1,600
Room and board	$9,900
% first-year students receiving some sort of aid	90
% receiving some sort of aid	90
% of aid that is merit based	11
% receiving scholarships	34
Average grant	$22,554
Average loan	$31,833
Average total aid package	$41,153
Average debt	$87,891

EMPLOYMENT INFORMATION

Career Rating	78
Rate of placement (nine months out)	97
Average starting salary	$89,409
State for bar exam	IA, IL, MN, MO, CA
Pass rate for first-time bar	94

Employers Who Frequently Hire Grads
Business/industry, national law firms, government agencies, state and federal judges

Prominent Alumni
Kimberly Teehee, Senior Policy Advisor for Native American Affairs, Washington, D.C.; Victor Alvarez, Partner, White & Case, Miami; John J. Bouma, Chairman, Snell & Wilmer, Phoenix; Kelly Hnatt, Partner, Willkie, Farr and Gallagher, New York; The

Honorable Susan Bolton, U.S. District Court Judge, District of Arizona, Phoenix

Grads Employed by Field (%)
Academic (5)
Business/industry (14)
Government (10)
Judicial clerkship (8)
Private practice (55)
Public interest (8)

UNIVERSITY OF KANSAS
SCHOOL OF LAW

INSTITUTIONAL INFORMATION

Public/private	Public
Student/faculty ratio	13:1
% faculty part-time	33
% faculty female	39
% faculty minority	10
Total faculty	61

SURVEY SAYS...
Great research resources

STUDENTS

Enrollment of law school	497
% male/female	61/39
% from out-of-state	28
% full-time	100
% minority	19
% international	4
# of countries represented	14
Average age of entering class	24

ACADEMICS

Academic Experience Rating	75
Profs interesting rating	75
Profs accessible rating	90

Academic Specialties
Commercial, Constitutional, Corporation Securities, Criminal, Environmental, International, Property, Taxation, Intellectual Property, Elder Law, Media Law and Policy, Native American Law

Advanced Degrees Offered
LLM Program in Elder Law, 1 year; SJD, 3 years

Combined Degrees Offered
JD/MBA, JD/ Master of East Asian Languages and Cultures, JD/MA in Economics, Global Indigenous Nations Studies, Russian, East European and Eurasian Studies, Philosophy, Political Science, JD/ Master of Health Services Administration, JD/MS in Journalism, JD/MPA, JD/MSW, JD/ Master of Urban Planning, 4 years

Academics

The "extremely affordable" University of Kansas School of Law "produces good attorneys and loyal alumni." "If you like the Midwest, you can't get better than KU," declares a 1L. "If you don't like the Midwest but ended up here anyway, you really can't get any better than KU." There are "a lot of different kinds of clinical opportunities available" for students looking to gain practical experience. Certificate programs at KU include elder law, environmental law, media law, tax law, tribal law, advocacy law, and business and commercial law. There is also a program in international trade and finance. Another nifty feature here is a Summer Start program, which allows first-year students to enroll in 1L courses during the summer before the traditional first semester begins. It was "a big help in getting plugged in to the social aspect of law school," reports a student. Career Services "does an excellent job of bringing potential employers from all over the country for on-campus interviews." However, students do note that the legal research and writing program could use some "improvement."

KU's "sharp" and "funny" professors are "highly qualified, both academically and professionally." "The faculty seems genuinely interested in seeing the students happy and successful at the end of the day," explains a student. "We have a good balance between the more 'scholarly' professors—the ones who do lots of research and writing and are known in their field for these activities but maybe only practiced a few years— and professors who have lots of real-world experience," says a 2L. The Socratic Method, though "scary at first," "really helps students to learn." Outside of class, KU professors are notoriously "approachable" and "friendly." "I feel comfortable walking into any professor's office, whether I'm currently taking a class from them or not," claims a 3L.

Many students tell us that KU's "very student-oriented" administration maintains "an open-door policy" and is "available to help students in a variety of ways." "You can tell the administration is truly concerned about student satisfaction and preparation," gushes a 1L. Other students see room for improvement, citing the "outdated" law building.

KU Law is located on "one of the prettiest campuses in the country." Though "there have recently been renovations" to the law building, students complain that the facilities are "far too small" and could use "an interior designer." That said, the "state-of-the-art classrooms" are "laptop friendly," and Internet access is "anywhere and everywhere." However, the library "needs more printers and computers." "The long and ridiculous lines at the restrooms are a serious consideration" as well. On the bright side, common areas are "aesthetically pleasing" and offer "a comfortable place to spend the time between classes."

Life

KU is "generally a young school, so if you are coming just out of undergrad you will be pretty happy," says one student. The "dynamic student body" also includes students "who have worked for a few years" and "those who have lived and worked throughout their lives and are now returning in their 1940s and 1950s." Students here come primarily from Kansas and its neighboring states and exhibit plenty of "Midwestern charm." Though students would like to see KU "encouraging diversity," members of ethnic minorities feel quite at home. "Everyone knows me and treats me with respect," says one minority student. Politics are "rarely discussed in classes," though that isn't to say that people don't "have opinions and vote." Ultimately, "There are just as many conservative students as there are liberal." "I wouldn't say that students are obnoxious in their liberality, it is just part of the package at a university like KU," explains a 2L.

Wendy Rohleder-Sook, Associate Dean for Student Affairs
1535 W. 15th Street, Lawrence, KS 66045-7577
Tel: 785-864-4378 Fax: 785-864-5054
E-Mail: admitlaw@ku.edu • Website: www.law.ku.edu

Students report that "there is some competition," but this is mostly a "cooperative and friendly" group. By and large, KU Law has a "very collegial" and "laid-back" atmosphere. "Students tend to get along pretty well" and, "as a whole, do not tolerate rudeness." "There are some cliques," says one student, but, by and large, "camaraderie and good will" are the rule. "We regularly trade outlines, discuss cases, and help each other out," says a happy 1L.

"The social life is pretty great at KU," and "Most students find a good balance between school and personal life." Student-organized activities are popular. "If you attend student organization meetings, you can enjoy several free pizza lunches each week and learn more about different areas of law," explains a student. "The student body has numerous pub crawls and other events" as well. The surrounding college town of Lawrence provides for off-campus fun, and when students want to escape to the plains, Kansas City is only a short drive away.

Getting In

Admitted students at the 25th percentile have LSAT scores of roughly 155 and GPAs of roughly 3.2. Admitted students at the 75th percentile have LSAT scores of about 160 and GPAs of just under 3.7. If you are coming to KU from another state, note that it is very tough to become recognized as a resident of Kansas for tuition purposes if you aren't one already.

Clinical program required	No
Legal writing course requirement	Yes
Legal methods course requirement	Yes
Legal research course requirement	Yes
Moot court requirement	No
Public interest law requirement	No

ADMISSIONS

Selectivity Rating	85
# applications received	1,120
% applicants accepted	37
% acceptees attending	40
Average LSAT	158
LSAT Range	155–160
Average undergrad GPA	3.43
Application fee	$55
Regular application	Rolling, up to 3/15
Regular notification	Rolling
Early application program	No
Transfer students accepted	Yes
Evening division offered	No
Part-time accepted	No
CAS accepted	Yes

International Students

TOEFL required of international students

FINANCIAL FACTS

Annual tuition (in-state/out-of-state)	$14,703/ $26,180
Books and supplies	$1,100
Fees	$858
Room and board	$10,318
Financial aid application deadline	3/1
% first-year students receiving some sort of aid	90
% receiving some sort of aid	89
% of aid that is merit based	7
% receiving scholarships	70
Average grant	$2,117
Average loan	$23,620
Average total aid package	$24,399
Average debt	$45,662

EMPLOYMENT INFORMATION

Career Rating	76
Rate of placement (nine months out)	89
Average starting salary	$61,510
State for bar exam	KS, MO, CA, CO, TX
Pass rate for first-time bar	90

Employers Who Frequently Hire Grads
Baker Sterchi Cowden & Rice, Husch Blackwell Sanders, Bryan Cave, Fleeson Gooing, Foulston Siefkin, Hinkle Elkouri, Lathrop & Gage, Lewis Rice & Fingersh, Martin Pringle, Polsinelli Shughart, Shook Hardy & Bacon, Snell & Wilmer, Spencer Fane Britt & Browne, Stinson Morrison Hecker, Thompson & Knight, Kansas Legal Services, Legal Aid of Missouri, U.S. Attorney's Office, trial and appellate courts in Kansas and Missouri, federal courts in Kansas and Missouri

Prominent Alumni
Sheila Bair, Chair, FDIC; Sam Brownback, State of Kansas Governor; Mary Beck Briscoe, 10th Circuit Judge; Jerry Moran, United States Senate

Grads Employed by Field (%)
Academic (3)
Business/industry (10)
Government (14)
Judicial clerkship (2)
Military (4)
Private practice (59)
Public interest (8)

UNIVERSITY OF KENTUCKY
COLLEGE OF LAW

INSTITUTIONAL INFORMATION

Public/private	Public
Student/faculty ratio	15:1
% faculty female	29
% faculty minority	13
Total faculty	31

SURVEY SAYS...

*Heavy use of Socratic Method,
Diverse opinions accepted in
classrooms, Students love
Lexington, KY*

STUDENTS

Enrollment of law school	415
% male/female	55/45
% from out-of-state	22
% full-time	100
% minority	15
# of countries represented	6
Average age of entering class	23

ACADEMICS

Academic Experience Rating	**72**
Profs interesting rating	74
Profs accessible rating	72
Hours of study per day	3.84

Advanced Degrees Offered
JD only; No LLM or Masters of Law
programs offered

Combined Degrees Offered
JD/MPA, JD/MBA, JD/Masters in
Diplomacy and International
Commerce, 4 years

Clinical program required	No
Legal writing	
course requirement	Yes
Legal methods	
course requirement	No
Legal research	
course requirement	Yes
Moot court requirement	Yes
Public interest	
law requirement	No

Academics

At the University of Kentucky College of Law, located in Lexington, the "greatest strength...is its small size." The low cost of attendance at this public school, coupled with the great "student atmosphere" and much beloved faculty, provide for a "very pleasant and academic environment." "I feel that I received an excellent legal education at a price that...is less than comparable schools," says a graduating 3L.

The professors at UK Law "are what make it"—"definitely the high point of the university." Faculty here "are always willing to talk and help in any way they can," and they "really want to teach and help you learn." "They make themselves available to you whenever you need help. I can walk into my professor's office and sit and talk with him about any concepts I was having trouble with or curious about," says a happy student. Some will even help "with matters outside the classroom." There's a diverse array of classes offered (with first-year classes relying strongly on the Socratic Method), as well as a "large number of externships," adding to the school's strong reputation within the state. Still, many wish the curriculum were more focused on clinical experience and practical skills (such as "more emphasis on legal drafting" and improved researching courses).

Students are vocal about improvements that need to be made when it comes to the administration, which they say could use "drastic improvement." Students say administrators can often get caught up in red tape and bureaucracy, not to mention routine errors. "They are always good for at least two 'Sorry, I forgot to attach—insert document name—per semester'," says one student. However, the school hopes that the recent addition of an assistant dean will help to further improve turnaround time and efficiency in handling student requests. The course selection process is also "completely antiquated and incomprehensible," and more bar preparation is needed.

The law school building itself is pretty old (more than fifty years), but aside from "having its issues, it gets the job done." "Some people compare the law school [building] unfavorably to a high school, with its mosaic tile floors and locker wells, but I find it charming and cozy." Unfortunately, "Plans to build the new law school have been postponed over and over." On the upside, "The information technology department (IT) guys are the unsung heroes of UK Law. No one is more afraid than a law student when a laptop bites the dust, but they are very handy."

Life

This fun-loving law school provides "many opportunities to participate in social events without sacrificing grades," though a fair number "are centered around...drinking." There are also many Student Bar Association–sanctioned events, as well as "frequent weekly or biweekly social outings for dinner or lunch put together by students...[with] open invitations made to many of the classes for these events." As for the "low-key, family-friendly movement," some say, "The people interested in that sort of lifestyle seem to keep to themselves," but "everyone gets along pretty well and it works out nicely."

While the law school "does a great job of creating a sense of family," the close proximity of students and the size of the classes means the school can get somewhat "cliquey." "Everyone is very close, but sometimes too close," says a 2L. Of course, it also "gives the students a great sense of community and ownership in the law school." "I believe it is the least competitive law school out there because our legal community in Kentucky [is] so tight knit—you realize quickly you will be practicing with these people for the rest of

DRUSILLA V. BAKERT, ASSOCIATE DEAN
209 LAW BUILDING, LEXINGTON, KY 40506-0048
TEL: 859-257-6770 FAX: 859-323-1061
E-MAIL: DBAKERT@EMAIL.UKY.EDU • WEBSITE: WWW.UKY.EDU/LAW

your life so it is better to make friends early on," says a wise 2L. "With the exception of the 'gunners' most people are quite willing to work together and help each other out." "The week before finals I saw many students explaining concepts that escaped their fellow classmates, instead of simply studying what they needed to know," says another student.

Getting In

The University of Kentucky starts with a prospective student's LSAT scores and GPA when making an admissions decision. However, all applications are reviewed in full and other academic factors (such as writing ability, grade trends, and letters of recommendation) are also considered. Last year, the school extended just 433 offers of admission to more than 1,100 candidates, the majority of which were not residents of Kentucky. The median LSAT score for the entering class was 160 and their median GPA was 3.55.

ADMISSIONS

Selectivity Rating	88
# applications received	1,191
% applicants accepted	36
% acceptees attending	32
Average LSAT	160
LSAT Range	157–162
Average undergrad GPA	3.55
Application fee	$50
Regular application	Rolling, up to 3/1
Regular notification	Rolling
Early application program	No
Transfer students accepted	Yes
Evening division offered	No
Part-time accepted	No
CAS accepted	Yes

International Students

TOEFL required of international students

FINANCIAL FACTS

Annual tuition (in-state/out-of-state)	$17,300/ $30,710
Books and supplies	$900
Fees	$1,006
Room and board	$11,460
Financial aid application deadline	3/15
% first-year students receiving some sort of aid	85
% receiving some sort of aid	75
% receiving scholarships	65
Average grant	$6,000
Average loan	$20,500
Average total aid package	$26,500
Average debt	$50,000

EMPLOYMENT INFORMATION

Career Rating	81
Rate of placement (nine months out)	99
Median starting salary	$45,000
State for bar exam	KY
Pass rate for first-time bar	86

Employers Who Frequently Hire Grads

All KY legal employers; major firms in Cincinnati, Nashville, West Virginia, and Atlanta. Through job fairs students also have access to employers nationwide, with most popular locations being Washington, D.C., NYC, Chicago, Atlanta, and Nashville.

Prominent Alumni

Mitch McConnell, U.S. Senator; Hal Rogers, U.S. Representative; Ben Chandler, U.S. Representative; Steve Bright, National Public interest Attorney; Jennifer Coffman, Federal Judge; James Wollery, J.P. Morgan; James E. Rogers, CEO of Duke Energy

Grads Employed by Field (%)

Academic (2)
Business/industry (8)
Government (9)
Judicial clerkship (18)
Private practice (52)
Public interest (10)

UNIVERSITY OF MAINE
SCHOOL OF LAW

INSTITUTIONAL INFORMATION
Public/private	Public
% faculty part-time	45
% faculty female	35
% faculty minority	3
Total faculty	29

SURVEY SAYS...
Diverse opinions accepted in classrooms, Great library staff, Students love Portland, ME

STUDENTS
Enrollment of law school	264
% male/female	58/42
% from out-of-state	23
% full-time	99
% minority	9
# of countries represented	1
Average age of entering class	27

ACADEMICS
Academic Experience Rating	72
Profs interesting rating	85
Profs accessible rating	77
Hours of study per day	4.64

Combined Degrees Offered
JD/MA Public Policy & Management, JD/MCP Community Planning & Management, JD/MS Health Policy and Management, JD/MBA, 4 years

Clinical program required	No
Legal writing course requirement	Yes
Legal methods course requirement	No
Legal research course requirement	Yes
Moot court requirement	No
Public interest law requirement	No

Academics

The University of Maine School of Law is "a small school with many opportunities to develop personal, professional relationships." Students tell us there's a nice balance of academic legal subjects and practical lawyering skills. In addition to the standard tenets of legal theory, there's a pretty good selection of clinics. Internships and externships are ample, as well. There's also a patent law program and a notable marine law institute. While "the cost of tuition is not low for out-of-state students," it's worth noting that Maine Law accepts a limited number of students from New England states (except Connecticut) at a reduced tuition rate.

Students tell us, "The very small class size—as compared to other law schools—is a great advantage." Small class sizes let students "become familiar with the entire student body and the faculty" and "encourage class participation, which in turn encourages thoughtful interaction with the subject matter of the class." By virtually all reports, the faculty is "absolutely amazing." Professors are "very interactive and caring." "The professors are as talented as they are accessible and make students feel like they are names instead of numbers," says a 1L. Outside of class, faculty members are "easily accessible." The "lovely" administration "likewise is very approachable." There's some red tape, though. Sometimes, students have "no idea what is going on, which is not a good thing for such a small school." Registration can be problematic, as well. "There are way too many lottery classes," vents a 2L. "Students are sometimes stuck with taking classes they are not truly interested in taking."

Maine Law is "the only law school in Maine," and if you're looking to hang out your shingle or otherwise find legal work in the Pine Tree State, there's really no question that this school is the place for you. Students enjoy "unparalleled access to externships and jobs in public interest law, private practice, the judiciary, and governmental agencies." "You will make connections and network with your Maine peers in a way that just wouldn't be possible at an out-of-state school," promises a 2L. Career Services is reportedly "very kind, warm, and helpful," as well. You can "ask a question without needing an appointment or waiting in a line."

Despite "significant improvements," the overall state of the accommodations here remains "pretty terrible." "Don't come to Maine expecting top-notch facilities," warns a 2L. "The school itself is a physically strange building." We have to agree with the 3L, who calls it a "concrete toilet-paper roll." Technology is merely adequate, and there's a "lack of community space to chat with students and professors between classes or hold study groups." On the plus side, "Library resources are as good as you'll find anywhere."

Life

The student population isn't very ethnically diverse, but "There are individuals from all walks of life and many differing ages and opinions" at Maine Law. Nontraditional students "with families and children and prior careers" are fairly common. "Weirdoes abound." The political spectrum runs the gamut. "There is a nice mix at the school," relates a 1L, "conservatives and liberals, environmentalists and capitalists." "Most anybody would feel welcome to engage in a friendly debate here, regardless of their leanings."

The "low-competition" academic atmosphere is "warm and inviting." All first-year students "take almost all of their classes together and get to know each other." "There is a real sense of community," and "Nothing about the school is cutthroat." "Maine Law is as small as it gets, so it naturally engenders a close-knit community," explains a 1L. "How people present themselves during their three years at Maine Law will very likely carry forward into their future legal careers. There's a good chance that most Maine Law students will practice law in Maine, and the legal community in Maine is small, too. Our classmates of today will be our professional peers of the future."

The social scene at Maine Law is generally solid. Student events are widely attended and opportunities to gather at various bars are common. Portland is the largest city in Maine, but that's not saying much. Portland does have great oceanfront scenery and kind of an old New England feel, and it's a fantastic little city for living and working. The bright lights of Boston are within reasonable driving distance. A handful of ski resorts and a multitude of outdoor activities are also nearby.

Getting In

The admissions profile at Maine Law is slightly more competitive than your average public law school in a sparsely populated state. Admitted students at the 25th percentile have LSAT scores about 153, and undergraduate GPAs average just less than 3.2. At the 75th percentile, LSAT scores approach 160, and GPAs are about 3.6.

ADMISSIONS

Selectivity Rating	77
# applications received	702
% applicants accepted	49
% acceptees attending	26
Average LSAT	154
LSAT Range	152–158
Average undergrad GPA	3.33
Application fee	$50
Regular application	Rolling, up to 3/1
Regular notification	Rolling
Early application program	Yes
Early application deadline	11/15
Early application notification	12/31
Transfer students accepted	Yes
Evening division offered	No
Part-time accepted	Yes
CAS accepted	Yes

International Students

TOEFL recommended of international students

FINANCIAL FACTS

Annual tuition (in-state/out-of-state)	$19,470/ $29,970
Books and supplies	$1,500
Fees	$1,180
Room and board	$14,867
Financial aid application deadline	2/15

EMPLOYMENT INFORMATION

Career Rating	78
Rate of placement (nine months out)	86
Average starting salary	$60,795
State for bar exam	ME, MA, NY, NJ, NH
Pass rate for first-time bar	84

Employers Who Frequently Hire Grads

Maine law firms and businesses, state and local government, Maine courts (judicial clerkships), local public interest, legal service

Prominent Alumni

Hon. John A. Woodcock, Chief District Judge, United States District Court of Maine; Hon. Leigh I. Saufley, Chief Justice of the Maine Supreme Judicial Court; Janet Mills, Attorney General of Maine; Peter Carlisle, Agent to athletes, such as Michael Phelps; Paula D. Silsby, U.S. Attorney, District of Maine

Grads Employed by Field (%)

Academic (3)
Business/industry (23)
Government (10)
Judicial clerkship (7)
Military (3)
Private practice (45)
Public interest (10)

UNIVERSITY OF MARYLAND
SCHOOL OF LAW

INSTITUTIONAL INFORMATION

Public/private	Public
Student/faculty ratio	12:1
% faculty part-time	39
% faculty female	47
% faculty minority	15
Total faculty	128

SURVEY SAYS...

Diverse opinions accepted in classrooms, Great research resources, Beautiful campus

STUDENTS

Enrollment of law school	953
% male/female	48/52
% from out-of-state	39
% full-time	75
% minority	32
% international	2
# of countries represented	6
Average age of entering class	23

ACADEMICS

Academic Experience Rating	**83**
Profs interesting rating	75
Profs accessible rating	72
Hours of study per day	4.95

Academic Specialties

Commercial, Constitutional, Corporation Securities, Criminal, Environmental, Human Rights, International, Labor, Taxation, Intellectual Property, Health Care Law, Public Interest/Policy, Clinical Law, Litigation/Advocacy

Advanced Degrees Offered

JD, 3 years full-time day, 4 years evening, LLM

Combined Degrees Offered

JD/PhD Public Policy, JD/PharmD, 7 years; JD/MA Public Policy, JD/MBA, JD/MA Public Management, JD/MA Liberal Arts, JD/MA Community Planning, JD/MPH, JD/MS Risk Assessment & Environmental Law, JD/MS Nursing, 4 years; JD/MA Criminal Justice, JD/MSW, 3.5–4 years

Academics

With "great opportunities for hands-on lawyering," and low in-state tuition for residents, the University of Maryland School of Law is "very well-connected to the Baltimore/Maryland legal community," with a "strong commitment to public service and social justice," and recognized legal specialties in health, environmental law, clinical law, and trial advocacy. The school "has tremendous relationships with organizations in Washington, D.C., the Maryland legislature, and many congressional offices," which makes it "extremely easy" to gain the kind of practical experience legal employers will be looking for come hiring season. The clinical offerings here are both required and "hard to beat": "Not only was I able to argue before a state appellate court during my second year, but I have also received credit for doing to externships during my third year," says a 3L.

Seven professional schools all share the same campus in Baltimore, which can overburden some of the administrative offices; students cite the financial aid office's lag time, and a career development office that "generally lacks important contacts in the work field." Still, the school boasts an active recruiting program and a high job placement rate, while the main head honchos at the school are very accessible, and "many of the deans also teach classes and are available to all students, even if you don't have them as a professor." The school's great strength is "teaching you how to be a smart and effective lawyer," through a few students say there is relatively little class time devoted to "cutting-edge legal scholarship and critical theory," and complain that "the popular courses are filled so quickly."

Maryland professors are "top-notch," being both "incredibly smart legal thinkers and, more importantly, fantastic teachers in the classroom." Nearly all of the professors "have practiced law for a decade or more before coming to the law school," which not only contributes to their legal experience, but to their sympathy for the demands of the profession. Professors and staff are all "very accommodating" to students trying to get through law school while working—night classes are made available to students in their second and third years—and faculty are "very helpful in advising students on how to mitigate stress and handle the competing interests of law school." "I have had a number of brilliant and committed adjunct professors who understand the burdens associated with working and going to school full-time," says a student. "Even if you are not in their class, they help you with course-related questions, study skills, and exam strategies," says another.

Life

As a whole, there is a presiding "positive attitude" among the "friendly" student body, which is "smart and capable." Cliques do tend to form within sections (as with many law schools), and "day students are way more social than the evening students," but there is definitely a sense of "we're all in it together." The student body is also quite diverse, and people "don't have the sense that cultural groups self-segregate here."

While the law school itself is "beautiful," and "new and gorgeous with all the technical bells and whistles," the location of the law school is "truly the worst...although that is not really the school's fault." "Baltimore is an impressive city in many respects, but the campus is not located in one of the city's many pleasant neighborhoods," says a student of the surrounding area, where "things around school shut down as soon as it is dark." There is

CONNIE BEALS, EXECUTIVE DIRECTOR OF ADMISSIONS & STUDENT RECRUIT
500 WEST BALTIMORE STREET, BALTIMORE, MD 21201
TEL: 410-706-3492 FAX: 410-706-1793
E-MAIL: ADMISSIONS@LAW.UMARYLAND.EDU • WEBSITE: WWW.LAW.UMARYLAND.EDU

"no need to go out and buy a Kevlar vest or anything," but "just be sure to do your research, and if you have a chance to, come look around before signing a lease—I would advise that." Students who live on campus are often disappointed with restaurant and nightlife options, and some students feel that finding entertainment "is difficult if you don't own a car," as the social life at the school struggles "because many students commute…and this damages the sense of community." On-campus activities tend to be based on legal issues and career-building, rather than pure socialization, though law students can take advantage of the gym, pool, and student lounge at the brand new campus center.

The law school curve does incite a bit of competition among students, which is more "collaborative" than cutthroat, but it still creates an atmosphere "with enough competition to encourage a race to the top." "Although we all compete against each other, I do not think that anyone at this law school would sabotage another student in anyway," says one, and everyone seems to agree.

Getting In

The school prides itself on a "holistic review" of each applicant's file, which takes into account the background and experiences that students might bring to help diversify classroom discussions. Students may also transfer to the school after completing a year of law school elsewhere. Admitted students for the entering class of 2009 at the 25th percentile have LSAT scores of approximately 159 and GPAs around 3.2. Admitted students at the 75th percentile have LSAT scores of 166 and GPAs in the 3.7 range.

Clinical program required	Yes
Legal writing course requirement	Yes
Legal methods course requirement	Yes
Legal research course requirement	Yes
Moot court requirement	Yes
Public interest law requirement	Yes

ADMISSIONS

Selectivity Rating	**95**
# applications received	3,073
% applicants accepted	19
% acceptees attending	38
Average LSAT	160
LSAT Range	157–163
Average undergrad GPA	3.50
Application fee	$70
Regular application	Rolling, up to 3/15
Regular notification	Rolling
Early application program	No
Transfer students accepted	Yes
Evening division offered	Yes
Part-time accepted	Yes
CAS accepted	Yes

International Students

TOEFL required of international students	

FINANCIAL FACTS

Annual tuition (in-state/out-of-state)	$23,744/ $35,023
Books and supplies	$1,725
Fees	$1,606
Room and board (on/off campus)	$22,086/ $27,756
Financial aid application deadline	3/1
% first-year students receiving some sort of aid	43
% receiving some sort of aid	67
% of aid that is merit based	30
% receiving scholarships	53
Average grant	$10,426
Average loan	$35,228
Average total aid package	$55,971
Average debt	$72,990

EMPLOYMENT INFORMATION

Career Rating	**86**
Rate of placement (nine months out)	94
Average starting salary	$76,290
State for bar exam	MD
Pass rate for first-time bar	87

Employers Who Frequently Hire Grads
Skadden, Arps, et al.; DLA Piper; Arnold & Porter; Venable; Covington & Burling; Hogan Lovells U.S.; Dickstein, Shapiro; Finnegan, Henderson; U.S. Department of Justice; U.S. Department of Health & Human Services; Securities Exchange Commission; Environmental Protection Agency; NYC Law Department; U.S. Courts; MD Judiciary; MD Office of the State's Attorney; MD Office of the Public Defender

Prominent Alumni
Christine A. Edwards, Partner, Winston & Strawn; Benjamin R. Civiletti, former U.S. Attorney General; Partner, Venable; Francis B. Burch, Jr., Joint Chief Executive Officer, DLA Piper; Benjamin L. Cardin, U.S. Senator for MD; Elijah Cummings, U.S. Representative, 7th Congressional District

Grads Employed by Field (%)
Academic (10)
Business/industry (17)
Government (13)
Judicial clerkship (15)
Military (1)
Private practice (40)
Public interest (4)

UNIVERSITY OF MEMPHIS
CECIL C. HUMPHREYS SCHOOL OF LAW

INSTITUTIONAL INFORMATION

Public/private	Public
Student/faculty ratio	18:1
% faculty part-time	58
% faculty female	33
% faculty minority	15
Total faculty	48

SURVEY SAYS...

Beautiful campus, Students love Memphis, TN

STUDENTS

Enrollment of law school	432
% male/female	59/41
% from out-of-state	3
% full-time	94
% minority	10
Average age of entering class	25

ACADEMICS

Academic Experience Rating	84
Profs interesting rating	77
Profs accessible rating	84
Hours of study per day	4.49

Academic Specialties

Civil Procedure, Commercial, Constitutional, Criminal, International, Labor, Property, Taxation, Intellectual Property, Corporate Law, Domestic Relations, Estate Planning and Probate

Advanced Degrees Offered

JD, 6 semesters

Combined Degrees Offered

JD/MBA, 105 credit hours; JD/MA Political Science, 107 credit hours

Clinical program required	No
Legal writing course requirement	No
Legal methods course requirement	Yes
Legal research course requirement	Yes
Moot court requirement	No
Public interest law requirement	No

Academics

The University of Memphis provides "an excellent legal education in a beautiful setting." Affordable, practically minded, and unfailingly diverse, students say the Cecil C. Humphreys School of Law "is an academic underdog on a real mission," with its sights set on "becoming one of the top law schools in the nation." Much optimism is underfoot after the law school's recent relocation. The school is now housed in "the historic Customs House on the Mighty Mississippi." Student joke, "The building may be historic, but our technology is state-of-the-art." Around every corner "is a glorious room waiting for you to marvel at." Others agree, "The new facility has changed the nature of the study of law in Memphis," as "it has seemingly reinvigorated those within it. Students seem more eager to learn and, as a result, the professors seem more eager to teach." In addition, "This move has allowed the downtown legal community to be so much more involved in the law school's day to day activities especially moot court and mock trial competitions."

Academically, the University of Memphis's program is "well-balanced." True to its practical roots, the school boasts "the highest bar-passage rate in the state." Overall, professors "are excellent and are not only entertaining but really care about their students." "Every professor is accessible and willing to help." The core curriculum consists of first-year courses that are two semesters each. Students say this provides "an excellent starting foundation in the law." In class, the "use of the Socratic Method, waning at other schools, is still fairly prevalent." However, students say this "encourages students to be more engaged and industrious in their studies." Students concur that U of M offers a "solid educational experience and very high standards for students." All students and faculty "have a lot of integrity." However, those seeking more classes outside the box would like to see U of M invest in "expanding the courses related to specialty areas such as environmental law, regulatory compliance, etc."

When it comes to career placement and finding jobs, students note, "The Career Services Department needs work." "There are not enough firms interested in doing on-campus interviews and getting a job has been pretty difficult even for the most successful students." Though the school enjoys a great reputation in the Memphis area and a long arm into the Tennessee legal community at large, practicing outside the state can be a bit of a challenge. Students add, "The law school should work to promote itself better on a national level." Particularly given its new state-of-the-art facilities, "It is certainly deserving of such attention!" In a move to address these concerns, the university hired a new Assistant Dean of Career Services in August 2010."

The administration at U of M "is incredibly accessible." The dean "does his best to maintain an 'open-door' policy for students to discuss matters like career options and school improvements." As one satisfied U of M law student notes, "If you're planning on practicing law, there's nothing more to think about. Well, to be fair, cost should be of some consideration; [fortunately,] the University of Memphis is very reasonably priced as well."

Life

Since moving to downtown Memphis, the University of Memphis Cecil C. Humphreys School "has gained a huge advantage over other schools around the country." A "$42 million renovation to the historic riverfront Customs House transformed the University of Memphis law school" into a state-of-the-art campus with the most up-to-date resources and technology. One U of M student describes the move with the following anecdote: "A

DR. SUE ANN MCCLELLAN, ASSISTANT DEAN FOR LAW ADMISSIONS
1 N. FRONT STREET, MEMPHIS, TN 38103-2189
TEL: 901-678-5403 FAX: 901-678-0741
E-MAIL: LAWADMISSIONS@MEMPHIS.EDU • WEBSITE: WWW.MEMPHIS.EDU/LAW

fellow classmate said moving to the new law building was like going from coach to owning your own jet—I don't think his statement gives it justice."

However, despite the fancy new locale and equipment, the tight-knit atmosphere at U of M hasn't changed. Students at the University of Memphis have always "created a warm community." "Even the most competitive and bright students are willing to help others." The school provides "a very diverse student body coming from many different backgrounds (urban/rural, ethnic, income, political spectrum), yet retains a positive balance of competition and cohesion." While there "is healthy competition at our school," students "have an energizing camaraderie among them. We are all willing to help one another succeed."

The law school environment may be "very competitive," but there is "a family aspect as well." Many students "have formed close bonds with each other and spend a lot of time outside of class." In addition, "There are endless eating and social venues within walking distance of the law school." Also, "The students get together every Thursday night." Being in downtown Memphis "is awesome; we have so many places to go to lunch and hang out and we are intermingling with the rest of the legal community…Also the social scene in Memphis is really cool if you ever get time to play."

Getting In

In 2010, the entering class had a median GPA of 3.28 and a median LSAT score of 155. In addition to regular admission, The University of Memphis also offers the Tennessee Institute for Pre-Law (TIP), an alternative admission summer program for applicants from underrepresented groups in Tennessee.

ADMISSIONS

Selectivity Rating	84
# applications received	964
% applicants accepted	33
% acceptees attending	50
Average LSAT	156
LSAT Range	153–157
Average undergrad GPA	3.28
Application fee	$25
Regular application	Rolling, up to 3/1
Regular notification	4/15
Early application program	No
Transfer students accepted	Yes
Evening division offered	No
Part-time accepted	Yes
CAS accepted	Yes

International Students

TOEFL required of international students

FINANCIAL FACTS

Annual tuition (in-state/out-of-state)	$12,560/ $34,432
Books and supplies	$1,800
Fees	$1,738
Room and board (on/off campus)	$8,731/ $8,906
Financial aid application deadline	2/15
% first-year students receiving some sort of aid	76
% receiving some sort of aid	79
% of aid that is merit based	9
% receiving scholarships	29
Average grant	$8,891
Average loan	$23,398
Average total aid package	$24,815
Average debt	$67,074

EMPLOYMENT INFORMATION

Career Rating	78
Rate of placement (nine months out)	86
Average starting salary	$58,990
State for bar exam	TN, AR, MS, CA, NY
Pass rate for first-time bar	90

Employers Who Frequently Hire Grads
Major area and regional law firms, Tennessee attorney general, public defenders office, TN Supreme Court and Court of Appeals, major area corporate legal departments, city and county government

Prominent Alumni
Honorable Bernice Donald, U.S. District Court, Western District of TN; Steve Cohen, U.S. Congressman, TN 9th District; Caroline Hunter, Commissioner, Federal Election Commission; Karen Clark, VP & General Counsel, Procter & Gamble Corporation, Global Health Care & Global Beauty Care; Bill Sanderson, Actor

Grads Employed by Field (%)
Academic (6)
Business/industry (6)
Government (12)
Judicial clerkship (11)
Military (1)
Private practice (61)
Public interest (3)

UNIVERSITY OF MIAMI
SCHOOL OF LAW

Academics

Set in one of the "most unique cities in the U.S.," students flock to the University of Miami School of Law for its "incredibly diverse" student body, "accomplished, approachable" professors and the incredible "weather." UM Law provides all of the advantages of being on the doorstep of a vibrant legal and business community while also offering a location on the university's beautiful main campus in Coral Gables. Corporate, international, and intellectual property law are among the school's strengths. In addition to pursuing a typical JD degree, UM Law offers five LLM programs including International Law, Ocean and Coastal Law, Real Estate Law, Estate Planning, and Tax Law. Students also have the opportunity to pursue joint degree programs, combining their JD/LLM degrees and JD/master's degrees in Business Administration, Music Business and Entertainment Industries, Marine Affairs, Communications, and Public Health.

The student body at UM is "incredibly diverse in terms of work and life experience." Some say, "The student body is too large for comfort," but at least the crowd is impressive. Students say their peers are "highly intelligent, driven people."

Students say they are "quite impressed with professors and their accomplishments." "Beyond office hours, they are available to their students." Given the large class sizes, "Professors expect students to be prepared for class and to work hard." In return, "They take an active interest in the students' learning, and generally treat students as younger colleagues." When it comes to professorial accolades, students say that, for the most part, there are plenty of opportunities to learn from the best: "Miami is a flashy city with lots to do, and the accolades of the faculty speak to that big-city, flashy, sleek, Miami feel especially well."

The administration is "very diverse, intelligent, and engaging." "We gain access to a variety of famous speakers and experts in the legal community." Due to Miami's reputation of being an international hub, "particularly with South America we receive great visiting professors from that area in the fields of international transactions and arbitration/mediation." Despite the beauty of the law school's campus, the facilities themselves "are aging," and the classrooms are "too small," and are "not up-to-date in terms of technology." Fortunately, "New facilities are in the works." As it stands, "The law library and undergrad library are outstanding. Although it lacks computers, everyone has laptops complete with wireless network accessibility." The librarians "continually provide training in both Lexis and Westlaw which [is] quite helpful." Others note, "The new administration has started to overhaul how the school is run." "I am very optimistic about the direction the law school is taking under Dean Patricia White. She has already done wonderful things in [a] short time at the law school. Her accomplishments range from grand (a new building scheduled to be completed in two years in addition to a complete overhaul of our writing program) to subtle (more clinical space, no increase in tuition, and greater accessibility to the students than the prior administration)." In recent years, "UM [has] made significant increases in clinical opportunities. There are so many clinical opportunities now that picking between them is a tough choice."

Beyond the occasional griping about the facilities, students' only major complaint is the limited resources for students planning on practicing outside the Florida area. However, for those looking to put down their legal roots in Florida, "as the only premier law school in the South Florida–area...students [here] have a tremendous advantage in

THERESE LAMBERT, DIRECTOR OF STUDENT RECRUITMENT
1311 MILLER DR, ROOM F203, CORAL GABLES, FL 33124-8087
TEL: 305-284-6746 FAX: 305-284-4400
E-MAIL: ADMISSIONS@LAW.MIAMI.EDU • WEBSITE: WWW.LAW.MIAMI.EDU

the local (Miami, Fort Lauderdale, etc.) job markets. Local employers love Miami Law students, and it makes networking very easy." The school also recently created the Legal Corp program, a postgraduate fellowship that places recent law graduates in public sector organizations nationwide.

Life

The University of Miami campus, as a whole, "is a beautiful tropical oasis, with a large lake, fountains, and tropical landscaping everywhere." "The campus is beautiful; it looks like a country club," which provides "a very peaceful and pleasant environment." However, students note, the law school facilities "are getting a little rundown, but rumor has it that a new facility is in the works for sometime in the next year or two."

The student body at UM "is relatively easygoing and likes to work hard and play hard." Those drawn to study here are a mirror of the city itself, "elite in intelligence and social skills compared to most law schools." Others add, "It's Miami, enough said. Beautiful campus, beautiful people, perfect weather. We wear shorts to class almost every day." When it comes to socializing, nightlife in the city is spectacular. On campus, "There are many ways to get involved in students org[anization]s and meet people." "Football games are a blast, the student bar association provides a tailgate for law students where games are played and food and beer are provided."

Getting In

UM reigns supreme in the legal community of South Florida. If you want to practice in this region, you can't do much better than this school. The average undergraduate GPA for the fall 2010 entering class was 3.4 with an average LSAT of 158.

Taxation, 3.5 years; JD/MA in Communication; JD/MM in Music Business and Entertainment Industries; JD/LLM/MBA Triple Degree Program

Clinical program required	No
Legal writing course requirement	Yes
Legal methods course requirement	Yes
Legal research course requirement	Yes
Moot court requirement	No
Public interest law requirement	No

ADMISSIONS

Selectivity Rating	**77**
# applications received	4,972
% applicants accepted	46
% acceptees attending	22
Average LSAT	158
LSAT Range	156–160
Average undergrad GPA	3.40
Application fee	$60
Regular application	Rolling, up to 7/31
Regular notification	Rolling
Early application program	No
Transfer students accepted	Yes
Evening division offered	No
Part-time accepted	No
CAS accepted	Yes

International Students

TOEFL required of international students	

FINANCIAL FACTS

Annual tuition	$39,918
Books and supplies	$1,200
Fees	$930
Room and board	$13,734
Financial aid application deadline	3/1
% first-year students receiving some sort of aid	86
% receiving some sort of aid	86
% of aid that is merit based	31
% receiving scholarships	31
Average grant	$15,232
Average loan	$38,475
Average total aid package	$43,916
Average debt	$98,986

EMPLOYMENT INFORMATION

Career Rating	**88**
Rate of placement (nine months out)	92
Average starting salary	$78,132
State for bar exam	FL, NY, IL, GA, CA
Pass rate for first-time bar	86

Employers Who Frequently Hire Grads
Holland & Knight; Greenberg Traurig; Hunton & Williams; White & Case; Weil, Gotshal & Manges; Morgan Lewis & Bockius; Carlton, Fields; Hogan & Lovells; Shutts & Bowen; Gunster; McDermott, Will & Emery; Stearns Weaver; Shook Hardy & Bacon; Kenny Nachwalter; U.S. Department of Justice; Miami Dade County State Attorney; Miami Dade County Public Defender; Broward County State Attorney; Broward County Public Defender; State of Florida Attorney General; Legal Aid; Legal Services; Florida Immigrant Advocacy Center; PricewaterhouseCoopers; Sidley Austin; Akerman Senterfitt; Bilzin

Sumberg; United States Social Security Administration

Prominent Alumni
Hon. Fred Lewis, Chief Justice, Florida Supreme Court; Roy Black, Prominent Criminal Defense Attorney, Legal Expert; Deborah Enix-Ross, U.S. Counsel, International Business; Dennis Curran, Sr. VP/Gen. Counsel, NFL Management Council; Marco Rubio, United States Senate; Carolyn Lamm, White & Case

Grads Employed by Field (%)
Academic (12)
Business/industry (11)
Government (12)
Judicial clerkship (6)
Military (2)
Private practice (57)
Public interest (11)

UNIVERSITY OF MICHIGAN
LAW SCHOOL

INSTITUTIONAL INFORMATION

Public/private	Public
Student/faculty ratio	11:1
% faculty part-time	24
% faculty female	32
% faculty minority	14
Total faculty	127

SURVEY SAYS...
Great research resources,
Beautiful campus

STUDENTS

Enrollment of law school	1,134
% male/female	55/45
% from out-of-state	78
% full-time	100
% minority	24
% international	2
# of countries represented	30
Average age of entering class	24

ACADEMICS

Academic Experience Rating	97
Profs interesting rating	89
Profs accessible rating	86
Hours of study per day	4.38

Academic Specialties
Civil Procedure, Commercial, Constitutional, Corporation Securities, Criminal, Environmental, Government Services, Human Rights, International, Labor, Legal History, Legal Philosophy, Property, Taxation, Intellectual Property, Asylum and Refugee Law

Advanced Degrees Offered
LLM Master of Laws, International Tax LLM, MCL Master of Comparative Law, and SJD Doctor of the Science of Law

Combined Degrees Offered
JD/MBA, JD/Master of Public Policy, JD/Master of Science in Natural Resources, JD/Master of Health Services Administration, JD/MSW, JD/MPH, 4 years; JD/PhD Economics, 5 years; JD/AM in Modern Middle Eastern and North

Academics

Students are drawn to the University of Michigan Law School for its "collegial atmosphere," "engaged and approachable" faculty and "challenging" curriculum. Students say an appropriate slogan here is: "Ivy league brains, Midwest heart." As one first-year attests, "Unlike other law schools I applied to, Michigan places a very strong emphasis not just on producing a top ten legal education, but on producing the very best lawyers." The spirit of critical collaboration trickles down from the top. "Dean Baum, Dean of Students, is one big 'yes.'" Others concur, "The administration at Michigan Law School truly loves the school and wants every student to enjoy their time here, at least as much as one can enjoy law school." "The spunky, generally delightful letters from Dean Zearfoss set the tone even before I came here."

Michigan's Legal Practice curriculum is "practical and challenging." Michigan breeds "a uniquely competitive yet collegial environment, and it maintains it by selecting only people who would excel in this environment." In fact, students say the best thing about the study at Michigan is the student body itself. Eager legal eagles hail "from all over the country and, upon graduation, spread out all over the country. Our broad alumni base helps us get plugged in to the legal community literally anywhere in the world, and the diverse backgrounds of the students make for an interesting classroom experience." The collegial relationship between fellow classmates "is so wholly expected that you forget that most law schools are considered cutthroat."

Professors at Michigan "are amazingly brilliant and frequently lead you to understand the law in ways you never would have seen on your own." Universally touted as "geniuses, and leaders in their field," "many of them literally wrote the book they are teaching," however, unlike some legal researchers, "They seem to be able to teach as well." This "all-star" teaching roster contains "both established giants of their fields... and lawyers blazing today's new legal trails." The administration follows suit and is "very easy to deal with." In addition, the top brass "takes seriously its commitment to public service through the loan repayment program, well-staffed Public Interest Office, and funding for non-profit summer work."

The Career Services Department is "also excellent." They "not only help you find a job, but also listen to and empathize with your personal career goals and any bad interview stories you need to get off your chest." However, class registration remains "a Byzantine process, but it's made up for by the fact that many professors will let a waitlisted student into a class if he pleads his case in person."

When it comes to resources, the library's "collection is second to none." However, the classrooms "are rather old and outdated (the heat seems centrally controlled and any changes to the level takes about three days to take effect)." However, "The facilities are currently in the process of being upgraded, so it's difficult to comment before seeing the final product." If everything goes according to plan, construction will be completed by fall 2011.

SARAH C. ZEARFOSS, ASSISTANT DEAN AND DIRECTOR OF ADMISSIONS
625 SOUTH STATE STREET, ANN ARBOR, MI 48109-1215
TEL: 734-764-0537 FAX: 734-647-3218
E-MAIL: LAW.JD.ADMISSIONS@UMICH.EDU • WEBSITE: WWW.LAW.UMICH.EDU

Life

Students universally exclaim, the greatest strength of Michigan Law "is the student community." "My fellow students are absolutely incredible." The camaraderie "is second to none. We eat together, drink together, study together, and one day we will all be there for each other." In class and out, the environment "is very collegial and collaborative." "Students all strive to do their best, but do not seek to do so at the expense of others." "The 1L horror stories of fiercely competitive classmates and pages being ripped out of library books do not exist here."

There is definitely the opportunity "to have a healthy social life at Michigan." Due to the diversity of the student body, "There are a range of people who attend Michigan; whether you are a work hard/play hard type, enjoy bumming around, or prefer to spend your time in the library over the weekend, you shouldn't have any trouble finding your own niche." As a 1L, "Living in the Lawyers Club is a great way to meet people." In addition, with "about half of the 1L class live[s] in the same dorm," so "you can't help but get to know your classmates." (Unfortunately, the Lawyers Club will be closed for renovation during the 2012–2013 school year.) In fact some warn, "Law school can start to feel a lot like high school (for better or worse)." Overall, "Students are quite friendly and open to sharing notes and helping out other students"; however, that's "not to say there isn't competition or that students aren't hardworking."

Ann Arbor "is great." True to its college atmosphere, "It's a beer town and it's pretty low-key." "You'll find micro breweries, diners open all night, dive bars, nice bars with organic food—but there is only one wine bar in the whole town and the 'clubs' are filled with undergrads. It's definitely not a city but it's the best college town I've ever seen." However, despite the warmth of the cozy small town feel, bring your woolens for the weather. Those who crave the sun warn, "Michigan weather is like…winter all year-round."

Getting In

Michigan Law is a tough nut to crack. The average undergraduate GPA on a 4.0 scale for the fall 2010 entering class was 3.73, with an average LSAT of 169. If you take the LSAT multiple times, Michigan will give the most weight to the highest score but will consider the lowest score as well.

African Studies, JD/MA Japanese Studies, JD/Masters Chinese Studies, 3.5–4 years; JD/AM in Russian and East European Studies, JD/AM in World Politics, 3.5 years; JD/Master of Science in Information, JD/Master of Urban Planning, 8 terms

Clinical program required	No
Legal writing course requirement	Yes
Legal methods course requirement	Yes
Legal research course requirement	Yes
Moot court requirement	No
Public interest law requirement	No

ADMISSIONS

Selectivity Rating	97
# applications received	6,312
% applicants accepted	19
% acceptees attending	32
Average LSAT	169
LSAT Range	167–171
Average undergrad GPA	3.73
Application fee	$75
Regular application	Rolling, up to 2/15
Regular notification	Rolling
Early application program	Yes
Early application deadline	11/15
Early application notification	12/15
Transfer students accepted	Yes
Evening division offered	No
Part-time accepted	No
CAS accepted	Yes

FINANCIAL FACTS

Annual tuition (in-state/out-of-state)	$44,360/ $47,360
Books and supplies	$6,164
Fees	$240
Room and board	$11,586
% first-year students receiving some sort of aid	92
% receiving some sort of aid	91
% of aid that is merit based	83
% receiving scholarships	15
Average grant	$12,430
Average loan	$42,189
Average total aid package	$47,967
Average debt	$103,963

EMPLOYMENT INFORMATION

Career Rating	97	Grads Employed by Field (%)	
Rate of placement (nine months out)	97	Business/industry (3)	
Average starting salary	$134,921	Government (3)	
State for bar exam	NY, IL, CA, MI, MA	Judicial clerkship (14)	
Pass rate for first-time bar	93	Private practice (73)	
		Public interest (8)	

UNIVERSITY OF MINNESOTA
LAW SCHOOL

INSTITUTIONAL INFORMATION

Public/private	Public
Student/faculty ratio	10:1
% faculty female	38
% faculty minority	8
Total faculty	65

SURVEY SAYS...

Great research resources, Liberal students, Students love Minneapolis, MN

STUDENTS

Enrollment of law school	752
% male/female	58/42
% from out-of-state	53
% full-time	100
% minority	18
% international	3
# of countries represented	11
Average age of entering class	25

ACADEMICS

Academic Experience Rating	84
Profs interesting rating	80
Profs accessible rating	64
Hours of study per day	4.68

Academic Specialties

Business Law, Criminal Justice, Health Law and Bioethics, Human Rights, International and Comparative Law, Labor

Advanced Degrees Offered

JD; LLM for foreign lawyers, 1 year

Combined Degrees Offered

JD/MBA, 4 years; JD/MPA, 4 years; JD/MA; JD/MD; JD/MPP, 4 years; JD/MURP, 4 years; JD/MS, 4 years; JD/PhD; JD/MBT; JD/MBS; JD/MPH

Clinical program required	No
Legal writing	
course requirement	Yes
Legal methods	
course requirement	No
Legal research	
course requirement	Yes

Academics

Located in the heart of Minnesota's Twin Cities, University of Minnesota Law School offers students an amazing "cost to ranking ratio: it's relatively quite cheap for how highly ranked a school it is." Students especially appreciate the fact that the school provides "balance across academic fields—you can leave Minnesota practicing employment, environmental, transactional, international, immigration, etc. and be very competent in your field. You aren't pigeonholed into a certain area by any means." Additionally, "the University of Minnesota Law School has all the resources of a top-quality public university available to it. Interested students can get a dual degree in business, public policy, medicine, health care administration or any other field."

Of course, as one would expect from any esteemed institution, one of the "greatest strengths of our law school is the quality of the instructors." A content third year shares, "We are lucky to have top notch tenured faculty as well as talented lecturers from venerable institutions such as the Federal Reserve Bank." Indeed, many students describe their professors as "supportive, encouraging, available, and brilliant." Another student excitedly states, "We have some of the smartest people in the nation teaching us what they know, and on the whole, they actually seem to enjoy it. Sometimes I feel awed to be in the same place as my professors." And a satisfied second-year adds, "Not only are they always accessible, but they take a genuine interest in you and help you in your law school career. I once had a job I was considering applying for and had the employer call me up personally before I sent in any notification of interest because a professor I talked to about the job called on my behalf."

However, one aspect of University of Minnesota that does leave students wanting is the school's actual facilities. As one chagrined third-year puts it, "The classrooms are underground and windowless. It feels like you're in a dungeon." A fellow third-year continues, "The building is ugly and outdated, the printers and internet connection are unreliable, and the classrooms are poorly designed and filled with old equipment." Many students also feel that "the school could benefit from better lighting." Fortunately, "There are several lounges on various floors that are friendly and sunny."

Additionally, the "administration is generally effective and communicates well with the students." They are "very approachable and flexible" and "work to accommodate [students] to the fullest extent possible." Perhaps it's best to sum up student sentiment using the words of an ecstatic first-year student, "Minnesota is the Midwest at its best. Being in a place with four distinct seasons is amazing, and the people here are so nice, you can't help but feel welcomed right away. If you can manage to put up with the cold winters, Minneapolis is an extraordinary place to be. The city is large enough to afford its residents plenty of employment and entertainment opportunities, while at the same time still having the quick and easy accessibility of a smaller city."

Life

Students at University of Minnesota are generally quite content with life at the law school. Most respondents define their peers as "friendly and easygoing" and "willing to share notes and help each other with assignments." Though some do warn that "students [can be] extremely competitive with each other for grades and jobs."

Additionally, there are some grumblings from students who generally fall on the right of the political spectrum. As one second-year shares, "As a conservative libertarian, the political bent of the university's faculty, administration and student body is sometimes very frustrating and challenging. From time to time my viewpoints have been, shall we say, less than welcome in class discussions and more importantly, outside of the classroom."

Fortunately, once you get outside of the classroom, "social life is pretty solid." Students can participate in a number of activities such as "Bar Review Weekly, Legal Bowling, and Theatre of the Relatively Talentless," which "provide some opportunity for students to be real with each other." And as a supremely satisfied third-year reveals, "The great thing about Minnesotans is that they love to drink. So do lawyers. This is a fantastic combination. Also, beer in Minneapolis can be as cheap as a dollar a pint...It's worth putting up with the bad weather to party with UMN law kids!"

Getting In

Admission to University of Minnesota Law School is competitive, and interested candidates will need a stellar undergraduate record along with strong LSAT scores. Applicants will need to demonstrate that they can handle rigorous course work and that they've acquired solid communication skills. The admissions committee will also consider other factors such as previous work experience, public service, other graduate work and ethnic background. Admission is granted on a rolling basis, so the earlier an applicant applies the better.

Moot court requirement	No
Public interest law requirement	No

ADMISSIONS

Selectivity Rating	**90**
# applications received	3,866
% applicants accepted	27
% acceptees attending	25
Median LSAT	167
LSAT Range	160–168
Median undergrad GPA	3.71
Application fee	$75
Regular application	Rolling, up to 4/1
Regular notification	4/1
Early application program	Yes
Early application deadline	11/15
Early application notification	12/1
Transfer students accepted	Yes
Evening division offered	No
Part-time accepted	No
CAS accepted	Yes

International Students

TOEFL required of international students	

FINANCIAL FACTS

Annual tuition (in-state/out-of-state)	$28,824/ $37,330
Books and supplies	$1,666
Fees	$3,058
Room and board	$14,262
Financial aid application deadline	5/1
% first-year students receiving some sort of aid	88
% receiving some sort of aid	88
% receiving scholarships	61
Average grant	$12,020
Average loan	$35,106
Average total aid package	$34,870
Average debt	$91,314

EMPLOYMENT INFORMATION

Career Rating	**91**
Rate of placement (nine months out)	99
Average starting salary	$87,059
State for bar exam	MN, IL
Pass rate for first-time bar	97

Employers Who Frequently Hire Grads
Dorsey & Whitney, Faegre & Benson, Fried Frank, Gibson Dunn, Hogan & Hartson, Kirkland & Ellis, Legal Ais Society of Minneapolis, Mayer Brown, Skadden Arps, Sidley & Austin, Snell & Wilmer, Minnesota Supreme Court, Minnesota Court of Appeals, U.S. Department of Justice, U.S. District Courts

Prominent Alumni
Walter F. Mondale, Former Vice President of The United States; Keith Ellison, U.S. Representative; Jean E. Hanson, Partner Fried, Frank, Harris, Shriver, & Jacobson; Arne M. Sorenson, President and Chief Operating Officer of MarriottMarriott International, Inc.; Jim Blanchard, Partner at DLA Piper & former state Gov. & former U.S. Ambassador

Grads Employed by Field (%)
Business/industry (12)
Government (8)
Judicial clerkship (11)
Military (2)
Private practice (47)
Public interest (12)

UNIVERSITY OF MISSISSIPPI
SCHOOL OF LAW

INSTITUTIONAL INFORMATION

Public/private	Public
% faculty part-time	30
% faculty female	31
% faculty minority	13
Total faculty	52

SURVEY SAYS...

Diverse opinions accepted in classrooms, Great library staff, Students love University, MS

STUDENTS

Enrollment of law school	495
% male/female	57/43
% from out-of-state	13
% full-time	100
% minority	15
Average age of entering class	24

ACADEMICS

Academic Experience Rating	**84**
Profs interesting rating	84
Profs accessible rating	83
Hours of study per day	3.83

Academic Specialties

Commercial, Corporation Securities, Criminal, Environmental, International, Taxation. Remote Sensing, Aviation, Space Law

Combined Degrees Offered

JD/MBA, JD/MA Tax, JD/MA Accounting, 4 years

Clinical program required	No
Legal writing course requirement	Yes
Legal methods course requirement	Yes
Legal research course requirement	Yes
Moot court requirement	No
Public interest law requirement	No

Academics

Students at Ole Miss love the combination of "a down-home, small-town atmosphere where everyone knows your name" and a law degree that is "given much credit within the state." Though "academically strenuous," the school's "laid-back atmosphere" prevails, and students praise the "easily accessible" staff, the "large student mall with plenty of couches and chairs for discussions between classes," and the "professors with awesome senses of humor." By all accounts, Ole Miss is not a school that "makes you feel like they are trying to weed you out." As one student explains, "I love the dynamics of the classes and the size of the student body. It is nice to be friends with 2Ls and 3Ls and not feel like a freshman again." "Everyone in the administration is incredibly friendly and helpful," a classmate adds. "If you have any question, even if it has nothing to do with their particular job, they will do everything they can to get you the right answer." Professors here hail from "a broad diversity of backgrounds" and "are all extremely knowledgeable and very experienced." Not only do they "present the material in an entertaining way," they "take a special interest" in students, "which can help build up [students'] confidence and help them to excel."

The professors at Ole Miss are a major reason why its students say the school is a "great value." "It is not nearly as expensive to go to school here as the other schools to which I applied or was accepted," says one student. "I can still get pretty much any job I want coming out of Ole Miss, yet I have zero debt." Other students, however, temper such expectations, noting that while Ole Miss' "Career Services Office is always there to help with a resume or to provide Tylenol during exams," securing a job outside of Mississippi can be an uphill battle. That said, this situation seems to be on the upswing thanks to the school's "great relationship with alumni" and also in that "Ole Miss changed their grading curve [a few years ago] and that has significantly helped those who are looking to get a job out of state."

Students consistently report that the faculty is one of the school's "greatest strengths." "They take away the mundane, stereotypical experience of law school and present the material in an entertaining way without compromising the integrity of the institution," says one student. Many feel that "there is a lot of potential in the legal writing and research classes"; however, they are damaged by "the lack of communication between...departments." Others would like "more classes to choose from," particularly in the area of entertainment law. Students are divided on the school's aesthetics, finding that the "great library" is "extremely up to date with the latest technology" while the building itself is "not very pretty" and "somewhat outdated." A 1L provides some perspective, explaining that "the law school building would be aesthetically pleasing at most major schools, but when compared to the columned architecture and tree-lined walkways of the rest of the campus, you can immediately tell it is a relic of the early 1970s...Instead of being 'postmodern,' it simply looks out of place." However, "a new state-of-the-art building" "will soon be under construction."

Life

Ole Miss students emphasize that theirs is a "relaxed learning environment," one that "promotes collaboration between students instead of the cutthroat competition that you hear about at other law schools." The school divides 1Ls into sections of "about sixty

BARBARA VINSON, DIRECTOR OF ADMISSIONS
OFFICE OF ADMISSIONS, P.O. BOX 1848, LAMAR LAW CENTER, UNIVERSITY, MS 38677
TEL: 662-915-6910 FAX: 662-915-1289
E-MAIL: LAWMISS@OLEMISS.EDU • WEBSITE: WWW.LAW.OLEMISS.EDU

students." While this can be "good for making friends" and forming "study groups and TV nights," it can at times seem "like high school all over again with the distinct social circles." "In true Southern form," law students at Ole Miss "like to work hard and play hard," and "There is a huge effort to make sure that students do more than study." "There is a great Law School Social Board that throws parties, organizes intra-mural teams, and puts together community-service projects so that students have a way to get to know each other and put the books down for a few hours," a 1L reports. When they do take a break, Ole Miss students find themselves in a pleasant location. The university's campus is "beautiful," and hometown Oxford is "a unique place" with "a healthy social scene." Though most will tell you that "drinking is a big part of social life" here, popular opinion states that "you can absolutely have a good time without drinking." "There are two great new movie theaters, and there are plans to open a 'New Square,'" says one student. "Oxford is constantly growing, and hopefully there will be a lot more for students to do soon." One thing that students agree could be improved a more "diverse student body."

Getting In

The early bird gets the worm at Ole Miss since admitted first-year students can begin their studies during the summer. Certain factors, such as "residency, undergraduate institution, difficulty of major, job experience, social, personal or economic circumstances, non-academic achievement, letters of recommendation and grade patterns and progression," can impact your application favorably, according to the school. Admitted students at the 25th percentile have an LSAT score of 152 and a GPA of 3.25. Admitted students at the 75th percentile have an LSAT score of 158 and a GPA of 3.76.

ADMISSIONS

Selectivity Rating	79
# applications received	1,380
% applicants accepted	34
% acceptees attending	37
Average LSAT	154
LSAT Range	151–157
Average undergrad GPA	3.49
Application fee	$40
Regular application	Rolling, up to 3/1
Regular notification	4/15
Early application program	No
Transfer students accepted	Yes
Evening division offered	No
Part-time accepted	No
CAS accepted	Yes

International Students

TOEFL required of international students

FINANCIAL FACTS

Annual tuition (in-state/out-of-state)	$9,350/ $19,620
Books and supplies	$1,300
Room and board	$18,832
% of aid that is merit based	90
Average grant	$5,788
Average loan	$15,334
Average debt	$41,632

EMPLOYMENT INFORMATION

Career Rating	83	
Rate of placement (nine months out)	96	
Average starting salary	$64,025	
State for bar exam	MS, TN, GA, FL, TX	
Pass rate for first-time bar	90	

Employers Who Frequently Hire Grads
Top regional employers from across the South and Southeast

Prominent Alumni
C. Trent Lott, Former U.S. Senator; Thad Cochran, U.S. Senator; John Grisham, Author; Robert C. Khayat, Chancellor, The University of Mississippi

Grads Employed by Field (%)
Private practice (50)

UNIVERSITY OF MISSOURI
SCHOOL OF LAW

INSTITUTIONAL INFORMATION

Public/private	Public
Student/faculty ratio	14:1
% faculty part-time	15
% faculty female	33
% faculty minority	10
Total faculty	53

SURVEY SAYS...
Diverse opinions accepted in classrooms, Great research resources, Great library staff

STUDENTS

Enrollment of law school	446
% male/female	62/38
% from out-of-state	16
% full-time	99
% minority	14
% international	1
# of countries represented	2
Average age of entering class	23

ACADEMICS

Academic Experience Rating	74
Profs interesting rating	78
Profs accessible rating	78
Hours of study per day	3.50

Academic Specialties
Criminal, Government Services, Alternative Dispute Resolution

Advanced Degrees Offered
LLM in Dispute Resolution Began Fall 1999. This is a 1 year program.

Combined Degrees Offered
JD/MBA, JD/MPA, JD/MA (Economics), JD/MS (Human Development and Family Studies), JD/MA (Educational Leadership & Policy Analysis), JD/MA (Journalism), JD/MLS (Library and Information Science), JD/MHA (Health Administration), JD/MA (Certified Financial Planning), JD/MS (Personal Financial Planning); JD/PhD (Journalism), 6 years

Academics

The University of Missouri School of Law, "provides a high-quality legal education at an affordable price." Its small size, collegial atmosphere and "absolutely outstanding" faculty make Mizzou a "place where you can find all the challenge you want in a law school, without unnecessary stress on top of it." In the words of one student, "If you want to practice in the state of Missouri, there's no better place. Our law school consistently produces the future leaders of Missouri."

Students offer nothing but the utmost praise for their faculty. "The professors are intelligent yet not intimidating; they really care about the students." They "are leading scholars in their field yet available outside the classroom." "Although the Socratic Method is used throughout the first year, and often in other classes, it is used effectively, to help teach students to think like lawyers, but not to embarrass them." Of particular note, one student expresses pleasure in discovering that "classes integrate well with each other, in that professors seem aware of the other classes students are taking, and they draw connections between various fields of the law, thus helping students see how the law comes together." In the words of one particularly enthusiastic student, "The university is the reason I chose MU School of Law, but the faculty is why I would recommend it to any future students. Go Tigers!"

Similar feelings resonate over the administration. One student shares, "The dean of the law school teaches one of my classes. That's probably one of the coolest things about the law school—everyone is so attainable. The administration knows me, and probably every other student in the school, and they genuinely do have our best interests in sight." An older student returning to school after having a family, remarks, "The administration and professors are willing to work with students when those pesky issues of life come along and interfere with the school schedule." Another fan declares, "Law school is hard, MU made it easier."

Academically, students are challenged "within the comfort of a community." Students appreciate "the rigor and intensity of the curriculum" and especially call attention to Mizzou's noteworthy program in alternative dispute resolution. However, of greatest frustration to students are course offerings that conflict with scheduling. One student explains, "Although the course catalog offers a nice variety, students sometimes will have only one opportunity to take a particular class during their student careers, since some 2L/3L classes are offered only every other year." Unfortunately, the wait for in-demand classes can range from a semester to a year, depending on availability.

Career services receive mixed reviews. One student feels that "Career Services does an excellent job with the top twenty-five percent of the class, but the other three-fourths could use more attention, in my opinion." Another agrees, remarking that "the career development services are probably the most deserving of attention." Specifically, some feel that "the Career Office could do a better job attracting employers from more geographical areas." Fortunately, it appears that Career Services is addressing some of these issues; as one student reports, due to recent changes, "Career Services has done a much better job at providing job and internship opportunities for the students."

Lisa E. Key, Assistant Dean
103 Hulston Hall, Columbia, MO 65211
Tel: 573-882-6042 Fax: 573-882-9625
Email: umclawadmissions@missouri.edu • Website: www.law.missouri.edu

While instructional technology is current, the facilities have some shortcomings. "The classrooms do not have electrical outlets, which makes it difficult to take notes on a computer when you have class for four hours straight." As a result, "Students are commonly seen lugging around extension cords" with them on campus. Additionally, students feel that "physical facilities are starting to show their age and need to be remodeled."

Life

"Mizzou is a great place for law school, the vast majority of people get along well with everyone else, and we all socialize together as well." "As [for] social life—you can get exactly what you want out of it. If you want to be involved, you got it. If you want to be a hermit and just come in for class," go ahead. "It is an environment that allows people to be flexible with their time, but it is also demanding in a sense that it has the proper time constraints to get people motivated." "Furthermore, Columbia is a great city, and the law school is right in the heart of campus with easy access to the recreation center as well as all of the amenities of downtown."

The degree of competition varies depending on who you ask. One student notes, "The thing I like best about this school is that very few individuals are worried about hiding books from each other in the library in order to get that cutthroat best grade." Another explains, "Students are friendly, but not shy about competition. We are here to learn how to be good lawyers, not to tear each other up." "MU is not a love fest though; people are here because they want to succeed."

Getting In

While application decisions are made on a rolling basis as long as the entering class has openings (class size is 150), the school recommends early application, preferably in the fall of the year prior to enrollment. Admitted students at the 25th percentile have an LSAT score of 156 and a GPA of 3.2. Admitted students at the 75th percentile have an LSAT score of 160 and a GPA of 3.7.

Clinical program required	No
Legal writing course requirement	Yes
Legal methods course requirement	Yes
Legal research course requirement	Yes
Moot court requirement	Yes
Public interest law requirement	No

ADMISSIONS

Selectivity Rating	81
# applications received	1,025
% applicants accepted	38
% acceptees attending	38
Average LSAT	159
LSAT Range	157–161
Average undergrad GPA	3.43
Application fee	$55
Regular application	Rolling, up to 3/1
Regular notification	Rolling
Early application program	Yes
Early application deadline	11/15
Early application notification	12/31
Transfer students accepted	Yes
Evening division offered	No
Part-time accepted	Yes
CAS accepted	Yes

International Students

TOEFL required of international students	

FINANCIAL FACTS

Annual tuition (in-state/out-of-state)	$15,291/ $30,191
Books and supplies	$1,550
Fees	$1,132
Room and board	$8,590
Financial aid application deadline	3/1
% first-year students receiving some sort of aid	90
% receiving some sort of aid	90
% of aid that is merit based	22
% receiving scholarships	52
Average grant	$4,000
Average loan	$16,500
Average total aid package	$18,500
Average debt	$57,889

EMPLOYMENT INFORMATION

Career Rating	75
Rate of placement (nine months out)	78
Average starting salary	$62,303
State for bar exam	MO, IL, TX, CA, NY
Pass rate for first-time bar	95

Employers Who Frequently Hire Grads
Missouri law firms of all sizes; Missouri, federal and governmental agencies; business, accounting and insurance industries; and federal and state judges, both inside and outside the state of Missouri

Prominent Alumni
Claire McCaskill, U.S. Senator; Jay Nixon, Governor of Missouri; Ted Kulongowski, former Governor of Oregon; John R. Gibson, U.S. Court of Appeals, 8th Circuit

Grads Employed by Field (%)
Academic (1)
Business/industry (7)
Government (16)
Judicial clerkship (10)
Private practice (64)
Public interest (2)

UNIVERSITY OF MISSOURI—KANSAS CITY
SCHOOL OF LAW

INSTITUTIONAL INFORMATION

Public/private	Public
% faculty part-time	25
% faculty female	36
% faculty minority	7
Total faculty	56

SURVEY SAYS...

Diverse opinions accepted in classrooms, Students love Kansas City, MO

STUDENTS

Enrollment of law school	515
% male/female	60/40
% from out-of-state	24
% full-time	95
% minority	11
% international	1
# of countries represented	6
Average age of entering class	25

ACADEMICS

Academic Experience Rating	**72**
Profs interesting rating	80
Profs accessible rating	84
Hours of study per day	4.54

Academic Specialties

International, Taxation, Intellectual Property, Business & Entrepreneurial Law, Urban, Land Use & Environmental Law, Litigation, Child & Family Law

Advanced Degrees Offered

LLM, 1–3 years

Combined Degrees Offered

JD/MBA, JD/MPA, 3–4 years; JD/LLM, 3.5–4 years

Clinical program required	No
Legal writing course requirement	Yes
Legal methods course requirement	No
Legal research course requirement	Yes
Moot court requirement	Yes
Public interest law requirement	No

Academics

The University of Missouri-Kansas City School of Law offers "relatively low" tuition and "really focuses on" "nuts-and-bolts legal skills." Five emphasis areas include litigation, business and entrepreneurial law, and land use and environmental law. There are also three dual-degree options. The clinical programs here include a tax clinic and the Midwestern Innocence Project, which provides pro bono legal and investigative services to wrongfully convicted prisoners. Also, opportunities to spend the summer abroad are spectacular. They include a program that takes students on a whirlwind tour of Ireland (with a stop in Wales) and an "outstanding" Beijing program "at China's premier university," which offers lectures in the mornings and cultural field trips in the afternoons. The legal writing program at UMKC is "very intensive," but "needs a little work."

"The professors here genuinely care about the well-being and success of their students," and they make "even the most mundane topics intriguing." "Some teachers use humor to get points across and to enhance memorization, while others will use scare tactics and examples of bar complaints or malpractice suits to teach a lesson," relates a 3L. "Overall, when the semester has ended, one way or another, the knowledge is retained." Faculty members are also "very accessible and willing to help students." "The open-door policy of every professor is incredibly beneficial," observes a 2L. Depending on the students you talk to, the administration is "always on the ball" and "never seems too far away" or "seems to be a bit flustered at times."

Students who are fond of Career Services say that the staff places "a very big emphasis on helping its students obtain internships, externships, and jobs during school" and "has a lot of information and connections to attorneys in the area." Students who don't like Career Services charge that the staff is "notably absent" and "wonder what they are doing sometimes." Most students agree that the career outlook is largely positive, though. "UMKC alums dominate" the legal scene throughout Kansas City, and "Connections to the local market" are a big draw. "The school is geographically located very close to the action in downtown Kansas City," adds a 1L. "Many UMKC Law grads are very active and do a lot to support students." Also, the school's unique mentorship program, which is called the Inns Program, provides students with valuable opportunities to build relationships with the local practitioners.

The biggest source of dissatisfaction among students concerns the "admittedly dated" and "borderline embarrassing" law school building at UMKC. "It needs a face-lift without question," laments a 1L. "The furniture looks and feels like it was donated in the 1970s," gripes a 3L. "The bathrooms put some bus stop facilities to shame." Parking is another perennial source of frustration. "Unless you arrive early in the morning, you probably get to enjoy a nice walk." Generally, though, "The problems are largely cosmetic," and this place is "not a dump by any stretch of the imagination." Many classrooms are "modern and comfortable." "The library is accommodating, and the research resources are pretty comprehensive." Technology is "up-to-date." "Another huge asset is the computer technician dedicated to fixing law students' computers free of charge," says a 1L. "My computer has crashed twice on me since school began, and each time, the computer technician has rebuilt the device and had it back in my possession within a week's time."

DEBBIE BROOKS, ASSISTANT DEAN
UMKC SCHOOL OF LAW, 5100 ROCKHILL ROAD, KANSAS CITY, MO 64110
TEL: 816-235-1644 FAX: 816-235-5276
E-MAIL: LAW@UMKC.EDU • WEBSITE: WWW.LAW.UMKC.EDU

Life

The UMKC School of Law is home to an impressive variety of people. "The diversity of age, work experience, and background of the students is very interesting and enriches the learning environment," declares a 1L. While many students come to UMKC right out of college, there's also a large number of students "commuting in each day" who have been out of school for any years. Opinions concerning the academic atmosphere are mixed. According to some students, the vibe is "generally friendly and helpful with little trace of competition." Other students tell us that tough grading policies produce "quite a competitive atmosphere."

Students report that there are plenty of ways to fill up your free time here. "Awesome" clubs and organizations "are always putting on events for law school students to lessen the turbulence and stress." Also, UMKC is not far from "all the coolest hangouts in Kansas City." Some of the greatest barbecue in the world is also available if you're into that sort of thing. "The social life here is very, very active," promises a 1L. "UMKC students love to" have a good time.

Getting In

Admitted students at the 25th percentile have LSAT scores in the low 150s, and undergraduate GPAs of about 3.0. At the 75th percentile, LSAT scores are around 157 and GPAs are very close to 3.6. Part-time stats are typically a little lower.

ADMISSIONS

Selectivity Rating	76
# applications received	950
% applicants accepted	47
% acceptees attending	36
Average LSAT	154
LSAT Range	152–157
Average undergrad GPA	3.28
Application fee	$50
Regular application	Rolling
Regular notification	Rolling
Early application program	No
Transfer students accepted	Yes
Evening division offered	No
Part-time accepted	Yes
CAS accepted	Yes

International Students

TOEFL required of international students

FINANCIAL FACTS

Annual tuition (in-state/out-of-state)	$14,316/ $28,266
Books and supplies	$4,474
Fees	$904
Room and board (on/off campus)	$10,467/ $8,443
Financial aid application deadline	3/1
% first-year students receiving some sort of aid	91
% receiving some sort of aid	84
% of aid that is merit based	13
% receiving scholarships	31
Average grant	$8,322
Average loan	$29,738
Average total aid package	$31,242
Average debt	$75,093

EMPLOYMENT INFORMATION

Career Rating	76
Rate of placement (nine months out)	91
Average starting salary	$55,492
State for bar exam	MO, KS
Pass rate for first-time bar	95

Employers Who Frequently Hire Grads
Bryan Cave LLP; Husch Blackwell Sanders, LLP; Jackson County Circuit Court; Lathrop & Gage LC; Legal Aid of Western Missouri; Lewis Rice & Fingersh, LC; McAnany, Van Cleave & Phillips, PA; McDowell, Rice, Smith & Buchanan, PC; Missouri Attorney General's Office; Missouri Court of Appeals, Western District; Missouri Public Defender; Polsinelli Shughart, PC; Seigfreid Bingham Levy Selzer & Gee, PC; Shook Hardy & Bacon LLP; Sonnenschein Nath & Rosenthal, LLP; Spencer Fane Britt & Browne, LLP; Stinson Morrison Hecker LLP; U.S. Army JAG; U.S. Air Force JAG; Wallace, Saunders Austin, Brown & Enochs, Chtd

Prominent Alumni
Harry S Truman, President of the United States; Charles E. Whittaker, U.S. Supreme Court Justice; Clarence Kelley, FBI Director; Lyda Conley, First Native American Woman Lawyer; H. Roe Bartle, Mayor of Kansas City

UNIVERSITY OF NEBRASKA—LINCOLN
COLLEGE OF LAW

INSTITUTIONAL INFORMATION

Public/private	Public
Student/faculty ratio	14:1
% faculty part-time	38
% faculty female	32
% faculty minority	3
Total faculty	59

SURVEY SAYS...

Great research resources, Great library staff, Beautiful campus

STUDENTS

Enrollment of law school	436
% male/female	64/36
% from out-of-state	28
% full-time	99
% minority	6
Average age of entering class	24

ACADEMICS

Academic Experience Rating	80
Profs interesting rating	77
Profs accessible rating	88
Hours of study per day	4.03

Academic Specialties

Commercial, Corporate Law, Cyber and Telecommunications Law, Environmental, Intellectual Property, International, Labor, Litigation, Space, Taxation

Advanced Degrees Offered

JD, 3 years; MLS, 1 year; LLM, 1 year

Combined Degrees Offered

JD/PhD Psychology, 6 years; JD/MA Economics, JD/MBA, JD/MPA, JD/MA Political Science, JD/Community of Regional Planning, JD/MA; JD/PhD Education Administration, 5 years; Journalism, 4 years

Academics

The University of Nebraska College of Law offers a high-quality education at an unbeatable price. With costs and tuition totaling far less than comparable schools, one student incredulously declares, "Where else can you get a top-rate legal education for that cheap?" Students say that Nebraska offers a first-rate education with a "brilliant and very approachable" faculty and staff. "Not only are the professors walking through the library, talking to the students and answering questions, but the staff throughout the college is amazing."

The administration, faculty, and research staff undoubtedly serve as the law school's greatest assets. One student remarks, "Honestly, I don't think that one could find a better school administration or research librarians. They always meet you with a helpful smile," and are willing to do all that they can to assist students. Another notes, "The faculty and staff at Nebraska Law care about the success of each student," and help "student[s] find their place within the law." According to many, professors are "extremely engaging" and "are able to connect the subject matter to practical experience and real-life cases, which makes class more interesting."

Students warn, "The first year is extremely demanding, especially spring semester [since] our classes are a year long and most of the tests in the spring are cumulative," though the curriculum is under review and this could change in the future. While April and May in the first year might be "almost unbearable," one seasoned 3L reassures us, "During my three years at UNL, most of my classes have been very interesting. Some of them have changed my life and outlook on the world." Students rave about Nebraska's prosecutorial clinic, as it is one of the few of its kind amongst an array of defense clinics. One student emphatically declares it "the best class that I took at UNL. Another student is of the opinion that though "there are a lot of classes in varying subjects, [the law school] is lacking in public interest/pro bono–type classes or topics for students wanting a different type of experience," though the school's Pro Bono Initiative has helped ameliorate matters.

Students are divided when it comes to the subject of employment after graduation. One student expresses an appreciation for "how UNL is trying to branch out and help students land jobs outside of Nebraska." Another argues that while "The school is great for finding jobs for students with higher grades that want to stay in Nebraska," "There is not enough emphasis on employment after law school if a student wants to work in public interest." One 3L would like "employers more involved in recruiting for clerkships," but in the same breath concedes that "most [students] were able to get clerkships if they wanted them as a 2L."

"The renovation of the school is almost complete," students gladly report. "It's great having brand new classrooms and facilities, as well as complete access to technology anywhere in the building." The almost fully renovated classrooms are "extremely comfortable" and "all have wireless access and plugs for laptops." Overall, students seem content with the refurbished facilities and as one satisfied 1L affirms, "After six years on the East Coast, the beautiful library and outstanding professors made returning to the Midwest an easy decision."

KIRK KLUVER, ASSISTANT DEAN FOR ADMISSIONS
P.O. BOX 830902, LINCOLN, NE 68583-0902
TEL: 402-472-2161 FAX: 402-472-5185
E-MAIL: LAWADM@UNL.EDU • WEBSITE: LAW.UNL.EDU

Life

"UNL recruits some very intelligent and exceptionally talented students," and students agree, "The law school does a really good job of creating community among the students." Specifically, the small class size creates a "close-knit group mentality" and particularly helpful is the practice of scheduling first years "so they have at least one class with most of the students" in their cohort. One reassured student remarks from experience, "I know that if I need any help, albeit from a librarian, administrator, faculty member, or fellow law student, that I will receive it."

There is no shortage of social opportunities at Nebraska. "People take the initiative to organize mixers and activities to help people get to know one another and to keep law school stress at bay as much as possible." The SBA, Women's Law Caucus and American Constitution Society and the law fraternities routinely host speakers, discussion panels and philanthropic events. Academic groups like Moot Court and Client Counseling also bring students together in social-academic environments that don't revolve around the bar scene. The bottom line remains clear as expressed in one student's words, "students aren't just classmates—we're friends."

Getting In

LSAT scores and undergraduate GPA are the main factors that the Admissions Committee considers when evaluating applications. Admitted students at the 25th percentile have an LSAT score of 152 and a GPA of 3.35. Admitted students at the 75th percentile have an LSAT score of 160 and a GPA of 3.84. The law school tries hard to create a class that is diverse.

Clinical program required	No
Legal writing course requirement	Yes
Legal methods course requirement	No
Legal research course requirement	Yes
Moot court requirement	No
Public interest law requirement	No

ADMISSIONS

Selectivity Rating	82
# applications received	678
% applicants accepted	53
% acceptees attending	40
Average LSAT	156
LSAT Range	147–169
Average undergrad GPA	3.60
Application fee	$50
Regular application	Rolling
Regular notification	Rolling
Early application program	No
Transfer students accepted	Yes
Evening division offered	No
Part-time accepted	No
CAS accepted	Yes

International Students

TOEFL required of international students

FINANCIAL FACTS

Annual tuition (in-state/out-of-state)	$10,271/ $25,583
Books and supplies	$1,375
Fees	$3,066
Room and board (on/off campus)	$9,248/ $8,796
Financial aid application deadline	5/1
% first-year students receiving some sort of aid	82
% receiving some sort of aid	82
% of aid that is merit based	40
% receiving scholarships	42
Average grant	$11,300
Average loan	$21,368
Average total aid package	$25,762
Average debt	$53,636

EMPLOYMENT INFORMATION

Career Rating	79
Rate of placement (nine months out)	89
Average starting salary	$58,816
State for bar exam	NE, IA, CO, TX, AZ
Pass rate for first-time bar	90

Employers Who Frequently Hire Grads
Private practice, business, government

Prominent Alumni
Ted Sorensen, Special Counsel to President John F. Kennedy; Harvey Perlman, Chancellor, University of Nebraska—Lincoln; Ben Nelson, U.S. Senator and former Governor of Nebraska; Lee Rankin, Former Solicitor General of the United States; John Hendry, Former Chief Justice of the Nebraska Supreme Court

Grads Employed by Field (%)
Academic (3)
Business/industry (17)
Government (16)
Judicial clerkship (7)
Private practice (53)
Public interest (2)

UNIVERSITY OF NEVADA—LAS VEGAS
WILLIAM S. BOYD SCHOOL OF LAW

INSTITUTIONAL INFORMATION

Public/private	Public
% faculty part-time	5
% faculty female	41
% faculty minority	19
Total faculty	58

SURVEY SAYS...
Diverse opinions accepted in classrooms, Great research resources

STUDENTS

Enrollment of law school	157
% male/female	56/44
% from out-of-state	29
% full-time	70
% minority	35
Average age of entering class	25

ACADEMICS

Academic Experience Rating	81
Profs interesting rating	80
Profs accessible rating	88

Combined Degrees Offered
JD/MBA, JD/MSW, JD/PhD in Education, 4 years

Clinical program required	No
Legal writing course requirement	Yes
Legal methods course requirement	Yes
Legal research course requirement	Yes
Moot court requirement	No
Public interest law requirement	Yes

Academics

ABA-accredited in 2003, many students feel, "The greatest strength of Boyd is its newness," which lends a sense of optimism, excitement, and challenge to the campus. Because it's not "steeped in tradition, there's an entrepreneurial spirit here. Everyone senses we're building something special." With a quality teaching staff, top-notch facilities, a talented student body, and reasonable tuition costs, students are confident that their school will continue to climb in the ranks. In fact, this sense of excitement extends throughout the city and state. Boyd is the only law school in Nevada; students report, "The legal community and the community in general are excited to have us here and the whole city [and state] is invested in all of us succeeding."

Professors boast impressive educational and professional backgrounds and are known to be both "intelligent and well-respected in their fields." More important, they are "stimulating individuals who are skilled teachers." Students are "consistently amazed by the ease with which the faculty so effectively employs the Socratic Method, such that the student body...is able to break down even the most complex legal scenarios and digest them as fully understandable rules and concepts." Outside the classroom, "Professors are extremely approachable, even for a shy student."

The administration is generally regarded as "accessible and very pro-student." A 2L affirms, "The administrators I deal with on any sort of regular basis are fantastic. Not only do they know their stuff; they are anxious to help and are just all-around fabulous people." Students particularly applaud the efforts the administration has made to help new students make the transition into law school, citing the "optional thirty-minute classes once a week where we are taught exam skills, note-taking, and outlining tips."

Classrooms at Boyd are "new and clean" and very high-tech. The "top quality facilities" include "wireless Internet and cable Internet hook-ups throughout the building," as well as "a state-of-the-art library." Off campus, students say, "Being the only law school in Nevada, in the middle of one of the fastest-growing economies in the United States, opportunities abound." For example, UNLV students "have opportunities for something close to eighty-five judicial externships each year (out of a class of 150)" and additionally "have extraordinary access to the local, regional, and state governments." When it comes to landing a job after graduation, UNLV is extremely well located. In the city of Las Vegas, "The local law firms are eager to hire graduates, and the private sector opportunities in gaming, hospitality, real estate, corporate, entertainment, and litigation are abundant and highly lucrative."

ELIZABETH KARL, ADMISSIONS & RECORDS ASSISTANT
4505 MARYLAND PARKWAY, BOX 451003, LAS VEGAS, NV 89154-1003
TEL: (702) 895-2440 FAX: (702) 895-2414
E-MAIL: REQUEST@LAW.UNLV.EDU • WEBSITE: WWW.LAW.UNLV.EDU

Life

While located in the heart of Las Vegas, "Most of the students commute into campus… and that can put a strain on the nearby social scene." In lieu of a hopping campus life, "Student organizations are great and have become central to social events at the school." Students have no trouble making friends among their interesting and talented classmates since "The people make the school." One student writes, "I love coming to school because I've made really great friends and don't mind seeing them everyday."

Commuter student or not, "Being in the center of Las Vegas, there is always something to do and somewhere new to go." You may be surprised to learn, however, that law school in Sin City is actually quite serious. Some students feel the competitiveness is a product of the high caliber of the student body. A 1L explains particularly in the school's early years many "of the students in the entering class are in their forties, and several of them are doctors and dentists, so the bar is set quite high." Though the level of commitment remains the same, the profile of the average entrant may have changed over time as the school's applicant pool has widened in terms of age and experience. In addition to their diligence, UNLV students are a fairly homogenous and quite conservative group. One student points out that some of "the faculty is comprised of very liberal individuals from a diverse background, whereas a majority of the students are very conservative and tend to have similar life experiences."

Getting In

When selecting applicants, the Admissions Committee looks for students with demonstrated academic capability, including depth and breadth of undergraduate course work, grades, concurrent work experience, and extracurricular activities. The school also considers non-academic factors, such as community service and work experience. Older students should feel particularly welcomed at Boyd.

ADMISSIONS

Selectivity Rating	89
# applications received	1,755
% applicants accepted	23
% acceptees attending	39
Average LSAT	158
LSAT Range	155–160
Average undergrad GPA	3.44
Application fee	$50
Regular notification	4/30
Early application program	No
Transfer students accepted	Yes
Evening division offered	Yes
Part-time accepted	Yes
CAS accepted	Yes

FINANCIAL FACTS

Annual tuition	
(in-state/out-of-state)	$18,000/
	$30,000
Books and supplies	$1,080
Fees	$500
Room and board	$8,370
Financial aid application	
deadline	2/1
% first-year students	
receiving some sort of aid	88
% receiving some sort of aid	86
% of aid that is merit based	90
% receiving scholarships	33
Average grant	$7,400
Average loan	$26,200
Average total aid package	$28,000
Average debt	$55,700

EMPLOYMENT INFORMATION

Career Rating	74	**Grads Employed by Field (%)**
Rate of placement (nine months out)	94	Private practice (55)
Average starting salary	$75,532	
State for bar exam	NV, AZ, UT, CA	
Pass rate for first-time bar	75	

Employers Who Frequently Hire Grads
State, regional, and national private firms
local and state governmental agencies
state and federal judiciary

UNIVERSITY OF NEW MEXICO
SCHOOL OF LAW

INSTITUTIONAL INFORMATION

Public/private	Public
Student/faculty ratio	12:1
% faculty female	59
% faculty minority	45
Total faculty	34

SURVEY SAYS...

Great library staff, Abundant externship/internship/clerkship opportunities, Students love Albuquerque, NM

STUDENTS

Enrollment of law school	351
% male/female	47/53
% from out-of-state	13
% full-time	100
% minority	49
# of countries represented	3
Average age of entering class	28

ACADEMICS

Academic Experience Rating	85
Profs interesting rating	79
Profs accessible rating	90
Hours of study per day	3.87

Academic Specialties

Environmental, Indian Law

Advanced Degrees Offered

JD, 3 years full-time. A limited number of students may elect to participate in the Flexible Time Legal Education Program and take 9 credit hours per semester during the first year of law school and as few as 8 credit hours per semester in the second and later years of law school. Students taking part in the Flexible Time program must complete the JD degree in no more than 5 years, including summers.

Combined Degrees Offered

JD/MBA, JD/MA in Latin American Studies, JD/MA in Public Administration, JD/MS, JD/MA, JD/PhD

Academics

"The essence of the University of New Mexico School of Law is community," sums up one student. Community "demonstrated through our professors' and administrators' ease in accessibility to students, alumni involvement, and peer[s'] competitive yet supportive spirit." In addition, students are drawn here for "the required clinic program, the small class sizes, the diversity of faculty, staff, and students, and the laid-back atmosphere." The Family Law and Criminal Law curricula are popular, and certificates are available in Natural Resources Law and in the legendary Native American Law program. Dual-degree programs include a JD/MA in Latin American Studies, a JD/MPA in Public Administration, and a JD/MBA. The school also boasts study abroad programs in Mexico, Tasmania, and Canada.

Due to the small class sizes, UNMSOL "creates a unique opportunity to connect with your professors, administrators, and classmates providing for further personal and professional development." This tight-knit atmosphere also "fosters a less competitive learning environment unlike other law schools." When it comes to instructors, by and large the professors here "are an extremely diverse and prestigious group." "It's incredible to learn about Con Law from someone who has argued in front of the Supreme Court and written countless appellate briefs for them." Others warn it can be a bit of a mixed bag, "I have had some excellent professors and some [that are just] okay."

The highlight of the program here is the mandatory clinic experience, which is universally lauded as an "outlet where students learn how their legal classes apply to actual practice." In addition, "UNMSOL collaborates with the New Mexico Court of Appeals so that students can take classes with the judges, have them for moot court coaches, and participate in summer externships." One student elaborates, "One of the highlights of my law school experience at UNMSOL was arguing before three of our state's Supreme Court justices and two of our state's appellate court judges in preparation for a moot court competition. Our state's legal community, at every level, is exceptionally generous with its budding lawyers. The strength and depth of this partnership between the legal community and the law school is one of the unique advantages of a law school experience at UNMSOL." In addition to the exceptional clinical opportunities, there is also "ample opportunity to compete for a position on one of the school's three academic journals: the Natural Resources Journal, the New Mexico Law Review, and the Tribal Law Journal."

When it comes to gastronomical concerns, students are left to grovel among "poor food offerings in the building." They also offer a word to the wise about post-law school placement; "This can be a boon if you plan to practice here, or in the Southwest. However, [career opportunities] are lacking in a more broad, federal sense."

Susan Mitchell, Assistant Dean for Admissions & Financial Aid
MSC 11-6070, 1 University of New Mexico, Albuquerque, NM 87131-0001
Tel: 505-277-0958 Fax: 505-277-9958
E-Mail: admissions@law.unm.edu • Website: lawschool.unm.edu

Life

Relations among students at UNMSOL "are great." It is "a very cooperative learning environment." "Everyone is treated the same by both their peers and the professors with no regard for ethnicity, sex, or any other personal background." In addition to "a large percentage of minority and female students," "there is a substantial diversity in age background at UNM." This leads to a "feisty group." "We all have strong opinions, but still help each other out." On the whole, students here tend to be "extremely liberal"; however, "The school is very supportive of diversity, allowing for a broad range of ethnic and political backgrounds." In fact, students say, "The greatest strength in the law school is the community atmosphere." UNM has "a strong collaborative environment where all are intent on making sure that everyone comes through together." The "cutthroat competition that one hears so much about at many law schools is nonexistent here" which "makes for a much better learning environment." The "only issue as far as community goes" is "the general lack of immediate housing directly next to campus. This creates a little bit a of a 'commuter school' issue with people living all over the city."

The surrounding city of Albuquerque is an "extremely affordable place to live." The warm, temperate climate makes New Mexico a haven for outdoorsy types. Summers are relatively hot during the day with cool dry evenings. During the winter, there is skiing in the nearby mountains.

Getting In

The admissions committee at University of New Mexico School of Law "gives a decided preference to New Mexico residents." In addition, "the committee recognizes that special prelaw programs for underrepresented and disadvantaged applicants provide valuable information about an applicant's ability to succeed in law school, and participation in such programs is taken into account." The average undergraduate GPA for the fall 2010 entering class was 3.32. The average LSAT scores for the fall 2010 entering class was 156.

Clinical program required	Yes
Legal writing course requirement	Yes
Legal methods course requirement	Yes
Legal research course requirement	Yes
Moot court requirement	No
Public interest law requirement	No

ADMISSIONS

Selectivity Rating	**83**
# applications received	1,200
% applicants accepted	21
% acceptees attending	47
Average LSAT	156
LSAT Range	153–159
Average undergrad GPA	3.34
Application fee	$50
Regular application	Rolling, up to 2/15
Regular notification	Rolling
Early application program	No
Transfer students accepted	Yes
Evening division offered	No
Part-time accepted	No
CAS accepted	Yes

International Students

TOEFL required of international students

FINANCIAL FACTS

Annual tuition (in-state/out-of-state)	$13,660/ $30,654
Books and supplies	$1,110
Room and board	$8,392
Financial aid application deadline	3/1
Average total aid package	$54,122

EMPLOYMENT INFORMATION

Career Rating	**83**
Rate of placement (nine months out)	91
Average starting salary	$54,755
State for bar exam	NM, CA, PA, TX
Pass rate for first-time bar	89

Employers Who Frequently Hire Grads
Private firms, government agencies, federal and state judges and public interest organizations

Prominent Alumni
Honorable Charles W. Daniels, Chief Justice New Mexico Supreme Court; The Honorable Tom Udall, United States Senate; Gary King, New Mexico Attorney General; Marty Esquivel, Albuquerque Public School Board Member; The Honorable C. Leroy Hansen, Senior United States District Judge

Grads Employed by Field (%)
Academic (5)
Business/industry (2)
Government (19)
Judicial clerkship (14)
Private practice (50)
Public interest (10)

THE UNIVERSITY OF NORTH CAROLINA AT CHAPEL HILL
SCHOOL OF LAW

Academics

The School of Law at The University of North Carolina at Chapel Hill is, according to students, "one of the best public law schools in the country." Many claim that "the faculty here couldn't be more down to earth and accessible." They have "a literal 'my-door-is-open-all-the-time policy' and never hesitate to "[take] the time to talk to every single student before class." Still, some students feel that "there is a strong liberal bias at the school" and that professors sometimes "bring their political views with them into the classroom." To correct this, they are calling for the law school to "improve on fostering a more diverse political atmosphere." UNC Law's "excellent" and "accessible" administration is "unparalleled" in its efforts to promote a "positive and supportive environment for the study of law." Everyone here seems to practice "the 'We're all family at UNC' motto to a fault."

Most UNC survey respondents are pleased about their employment prospects. One student credits the Career Services Office as being "the greatest strength of UNC. Even when they are too busy for a brief meeting about resumes or cover letters, you can just leave your stuff under the door, and someone will get it back to you by the next day with recommendations about what you should fix." However, some feel that it could "stand to improve, particularly with communicating jobs to 1Ls." However, jobs in North Carolina and neighboring states are fairly abundant, though, in large part because the law school maintains "strong connections" with in-state employers.

Student organizations and learning opportunities are aplenty. According to one student, "There are lots of organizations to get involved in, and the pro bono program is one of the best." About sixty percent of all students do some kind of pro bono work—many during the summer or during winter or spring breaks. Students who have performed more than seventy-five hours of pro bono service receive certificates of acknowledgment from the state bar association, and those who perform more than 100 hours of pro bono service get special shout-outs at graduation. Other notables include UNC's clinical programs, in which students handle more than 350 civil and criminal cases every year and "really get a lot of hands-on experience" along with "solid academic[s]" in the process. Joint-degree programs include the standard JD/MBA as well as master's of public policy science and a handful of others. UNC also offers a summer program down under in Sydney, Australia, that concentrates on Pacific Rim issues and semester-long programs in Europe and Mexico.

The general consensus is that facilities at UNC are middling, but in terms of the availability of information, "The resources are outstanding." Also, "The school is improving the technology of each classroom every year." In the meantime, a cry of "more parking!" can be heard throughout campus.

MICHAEL J. STATES, JD, ASSISTANT DEAN FOR ADMISSIONS
CB# 3380, VAN HECKE-WETTACH HALL, UNC SCHOOL OF LAW—ADMISSIONS,
CHAPEL HILL, NC 27599-3380
TEL: 919-962-5109 FAX: 919-843-7939
E-MAIL: LAW_ADMISSIONS@UNC.EDU • WEBSITE: WWW.LAW.UNC.EDU

Life

"Carolina offers a healthy balance between academic and student life." UNC is home to "diverse, interesting, charming, and intelligent people." One student exclaims, "I am constantly amazed by how interesting my classmates are." Most agree that "everyone gets along" in this "very friendly" and "very cooperative" academic atmosphere. "It is competitive but not necessarily with each other. It seems we all want to see everyone do well," explains one student.

Students insist that "there is no better college town in the United States than Chapel Hill," a Southern hamlet of about 54,000 souls that offers a good supply of part-time jobs, affordable housing, and a mild climate. These fine qualities have not gone unnoticed: *Money* magazine has before named the Raleigh-Durham-Chapel Hill area the "Best Place to Live in the South," in 2000, and *Sports Illustrated* named Chapel Hill "the Best College Town in America" a few years earlier. "It's a great place to live," says one student. "The people are amazing" and the "campus and city are breathtaking." As one student puts it, "While you don't go to law school for the social life, it makes a big difference to have something to do when you actually do find free time."

"Social life is good" at Chapel Hill because "on the whole, students are very social outside of class." There are always a multitude of "school-sponsored social events in town" and "parties being thrown by law students to celebrate a wide array of milestones" (for instance, there is a "we just took our second practice exam" party). However, some students lament that there is little to do "for someone who does not drink."

Getting In

While perhaps easier than you might think, admissions here is no cakewalk. Admitted students at the 25th percentile have an LSAT score of 158 and a GPA of 3.4. Admitted students at the 75th percentile have an LSAT score of 164 and a GPA of 3.8. If applying as a non-resident, keep in mind that you'll want to be ready to dazzle with your academic prowess as around seventy percent of each admitted year at Chapel Hill are residents of North Carolina, and competition for the remaining slots in the class is stiff.

Clinical program required	No
Legal writing course requirement	Yes
Legal methods course requirement	No
Legal research course requirement	Yes
Moot court requirement	Yes
Public interest law requirement	No

ADMISSIONS

Selectivity Rating	96
# applications received	2,905
% applicants accepted	15
% acceptees attending	61
Average LSAT	162
LSAT Range	157–164
Average undergrad GPA	3.60
Application fee	$70
Regular application	Rolling, up to 3/1
Regular notification	Rolling
Early application program	No
Transfer students accepted	Yes
Evening division offered	No
Part-time accepted	No
CAS accepted	Yes

International Students

TOEFL required of international students	

FINANCIAL FACTS

Annual tuition (in-state/out-of-state)	$16,334/ $30,664
Books and supplies	$1,028
Room and board	$14,714
Financial aid application deadline	3/1
% first-year students receiving some sort of aid	86
% receiving some sort of aid	78
% of aid that is merit based	30
% receiving scholarships	53
Average grant	$4,000
Average total aid package	$22,803
Average debt	$59,329

EMPLOYMENT INFORMATION

Career Rating	94	**Grads Employed by Field (%)**
Rate of placement (nine months out)	93	Academic (2)
Average starting salary	$105,916	Business/industry (11)
State for bar exam	NC, NY, FL, GA, VA	Government (6)
Pass rate for first-time bar	93	Judicial clerkship (9)
Prominent Alumni		Military (3)
Jim Delany, Big 10 Conference		Private practice (55)
Commissioner; Julius Chambers, Civil		Public interest (14)
Rights Attorney; Sarah Parker, Chief		
Justice NC Sct; Henry Frye, Chief Justice		
NC Sct		

University of North Dakota
School of Law

Academics

At the University of North Dakota School of Law, there's "the feeling that when you first set foot in the door, you have come home and you are family." Students describe the experience as "incredibly worthwhile," "enlightening," and "surprisingly rigorous." UND "embodies a small-town atmosphere," and more than one student describes the experience as "the best three years of my life." Students are convinced they're "getting a superb legal education at a fraction of the cost of other law schools." Class sizes are small, and professors practice an "open-door policy." The "stellar" clinical education refers to a law firm housed in the basement. "There are a variety of externships, clinics, moot court and trial teams, law review, and multiple student groups. Because the school is small, it is easy to get involved in one or many of these opportunities." Also, UND is the only law school in the state, which greatly benefits the students. "Judicial externships and clerkships are easier to obtain," and "The North Dakota Supreme Court is available for lectures." North Dakota alone has its benefits. "While other areas of the country are experiencing an overabundance of lawyers, in North Dakota, there are jobs." Students have access to these jobs through the "great alumni network and influence."

Professors do their part by "notifying students of job opportunities," providing "meaningful" letters of recommendation, and helping with resume rewrites. "The accessibility of the faculty is unmatched." "A broad range of interests are represented, and there really isn't a bad teacher in the bunch." They "work hard to teach in various styles, so that all students are engaged," "diving deep into legal issues to break down complex matters in a digestible fashion." In the classroom, professors draw on their field experiences. "It's really helpful to learn contracts from someone who has a written a multitude of million dollar contracts." Professors are genuinely interested in students' lives, initially calling them into meetings just to get to know them. Students receive "regular one-on-one contact with their professors." One student was "blown away" by her professor's "kindness." Another described a standing ovation given by students for a professor's final lecture of the semester. No one "feels uncomfortable asking a professor to clarify an idea." But even more than that, UND faculty can "teach the pants off more famous professors."

"We are experiencing growing pains," one student says in reference to the law school's need for expansion. "There are only really four classrooms, two courtrooms, the library, and the clinic." Of those few classrooms, some "lack adequate technology." However, UND is "in the process of getting renovation funding," and the "new" classrooms that do exist "are wonderful." The law clinic could use a makeover, as well. It is described as "cramped and outdated." However, students view growth as a positive thing, even if for the moment, there's no container to hold it. UND does, however, have the biggest law library in the state, and "The library staff is excellent." Students are given free access to WestLaw, LexisNexis, CALI, and Audio Case Files. There's also a section of the library dedicated to study aides and treatises. Students voice concerns about the larger institution they're forced to contend with from time to time, preferring the confines of the law school, which inevitably "contributes to the closeness of the student body."

BEN HOFFMAN, DIRECTOR OF ADMISSIONS & RECORDS
CENTENNIAL DRIVE, P.O. BOX 9003, GRAND FORKS, ND 58202
TEL: 701-777-2260 FAX: 701-777-2217
E-MAIL: HOFFMAN@LAW.UND.EDU • WEBSITE: WWW.LAW.UND.NODAK.EDU

Life

One student describes UND School of Law as "the greatest place on earth." The atmosphere is familial, and there's "a common understanding that different people are good at different things." The student body isn't "terribly competitive." Even the faculty participate in law school events, such as the "annual Malpractice Bowl" and "The Gong Show," a student organized talent show. Students do mention the "snow and freezing temperatures," which sometimes last for many months. One student describes the winter as "constant zero degree weather." Even still, "There are always parties of one kind or another going on." Additionally, there's an annual get-together thrown by the Student Association for those second years who have reached the midpoint of their studies. Alternately, UND is "quite accommodating for those who have kids, and students come to know one another's families." The school is also "very welcoming to different cultures and ethnicities," and there are "a surprising number of out-of-state attendees."

Getting In

The admissions committee equally weighs the following when considering candidates for admission: LSAT scores, undergraduate GPAs, personal essays, and letters of recommendation. It also considers oral and written communication skills. Admitted students in the 25th percentile had GPAs right at 3.0 and LSAT scores of almost 150. Admitted students in the 75th percentile had GPAs of almost 3.75 and LSAT scores in the low 150s.

ADMISSIONS

Selectivity Rating	80
# applications received	534
% applicants accepted	35
% acceptees attending	46
Average LSAT	152
LSAT Range	149–153
Average undergrad GPA	3.37
Application fee	$35
Regular application	Rolling, up to 7/31
Regular notification	Rolling
Early application program	No
Transfer students accepted	Yes
Evening division offered	No
Part-time accepted	No
CAS accepted	Yes

FINANCIAL FACTS

Annual tuition (in-state/out-of-state)	$6,595/ $17,610
Books and supplies	$1,000
Fees	$2,866
Room and board	$14,000
Financial aid application deadline	4/15
% first-year students receiving some sort of aid	84
% receiving some sort of aid	91
% of aid that is merit based	7
% receiving scholarships	30
Average grant	$1,434
Average loan	$17,102
Average total aid package	$18,536
Average debt	$59,271

EMPLOYMENT INFORMATION

Career Rating	79
Rate of placement (nine months out)	91
Average starting salary	$50,850
State for bar exam	ND, MN, WI, NV, MO
Pass rate for first-time bar	87

Employers Who Frequently Hire Grads
Judicial systems of ND & MN; Private firms in ND and MN

Prominent Alumni
Earl Pomeroy, Congressman–ND; H.F. Gierke, Chief Justice–U.S. Armed Forces Court of Appeals; Kermit Bye, Judge–8th Circuit Court of Appeals; Peter Pantaleo, DLA Piper, NY Managing Partner; Mary Maring, Justice–ND Supreme Court

Grads Employed by Field (%)
Business/industry (17)
Government (5)
Judicial clerkship (15)
Military (3)
Private practice (57)

University of Notre Dame
Law School

Academics

True to its Catholic heritage, the University of Notre Dame Law School boasts a "strong moral center" with "lots of emphasis on being a 'different kind of lawyer.'" Students are drawn here for the school's "academic rigor," "world-renowned faculty," "affordable tuition," "clinical opportunities," "national name," "small class sizes," and impressive "alumni network." Students say, "The Catholic character of our law school is one of our greatest strengths." Others concur, "Notre Dame's Catholic character only adds to the richness of the legal education. Schools that downplay morals, faith, and religion are only giving you half of the story." Many say that by and large the professors here "are exceptional teachers," as well as "respected academics who get published and make contributions to the field." Instructors also "incorporate ethical dilemmas and large questions of law rather than black letter law." As one 1L notes, "Fifty percent of my first year core curriculum was taught by professors who clerked for the U.S. Supreme Court."

The "family-like atmosphere of the students and the faculty" "makes a very great learning environment." Some say the faith-based nature of the school can lead to heated in-class discussions; "We have a few more conservative professors and students than many other schools, so when we have discussions we really hear a diversity of viewpoints." Others say the school can be a bit "homogeneous and conservative for a university of its stature. Everyone's very nice and generally respectful, but being a diversity student here takes some thick skin." For those seeking alternate opportunities to traditional course work, the University of Notre Dame offers "the London Law Program, where students can spend their entire second year...exposed to the global legal community, and are taught by both English and American faculty." Notre Dame "also places a strong emphasis on public interest law careers, and offers students summer scholarships for those who work for public organizations who cannot afford to pay them."

Thanks to recent renovations, when it comes to classroom facilities, Notre Dame is "second-to-none!" The new Eck Hall of Law opened in January 2009 and it is" both architecturally impressive and technologically advanced." The law school's building was recently renovated, and now includes plentiful library and study space. The administration at Notre Dame has recently undergone some transition, and change is underfoot. After some revolving door action, the school's Career Services office is now at full staff, providing some stability for the students.

Life

Set on one of "the most beautiful campuses in America," Notre Dame boasts "a very strong sense of community." ND law students "like to balance work with play." There are "frequent social events sponsored by the Student Bar Association." "Relations among students are good—there are lots of law school social events and parties that people go to." Others note "a camaraderie that I believe is unrivaled by other law schools."

MELISSA FRUSCIONE, DIRECTOR OF ADMISSIONS AND FINANCIAL AID
NOTRE DAME LAW SCHOOL, P.O. BOX 780, NOTRE DAME, IN 46556
TEL: 574-631-6626 FAX: 574-631-5474
E-MAIL: LAWADMIT@ND.EDU • WEBSITE: LAW.ND.EDU

Located in South Bend, the surrounding town "is not the most cosmopolitan place, though it isn't as bad as some people make it out to be." Others say South Bend is "a fun college town." The cost of living is "really reasonable." However, due to the school's small size, "social life can be a little bit NDLSHS (Notre Dame Law School High School)." For those looking to get away for the weekend, "The proximity to Chicago is great." And if you like sports, "There is no better place to go!" ND is "one of the most active law schools in the country in terms of intramural sports." "Football games and tailgating really are fun, too." As one student jokes, "There is no better way to make immediate bonds with classmates than tailgating under the watchful eye of Touchdown Jesus."

Getting In

Applicants are encouraged to take the LSAT in June, September/October, or December in the year preceding enrollment, as doing so provides the advantage of receiving full consideration for scholarship assistance. The median undergraduate GPA for the fall 2009 entering class was 3.57 with an average LSAT of 167. It is NDLS policy to review the highest LSAT score when an applicant has taken the LSAT more than once within a five-year period.

Clinical program required	No
Legal writing course requirement	Yes
Legal methods course requirement	Yes
Legal research course requirement	Yes
Moot court requirement	Yes
Public interest law requirement	No

ADMISSIONS

Selectivity Rating	**95**
# applications received	4,014
% applicants accepted	16
% acceptees attending	26
LSAT Range	162–168
Application fee	$65
Regular application	Rolling, up to 2/15
Regular notification	Rolling
Early application program	Yes
Early application deadline	11/1
Early application notification	12/15
Transfer students accepted	Yes
Evening division offered	No
Part-time accepted	No
CAS accepted	Yes

International Students

TOEFL required of international students	

FINANCIAL FACTS

Annual tuition	$42,870
Books and supplies	$1,500
Fees	$465
Room and board	$8,850
Financial aid application deadline	2/28
% of aid that is merit based	95
Average debt	$92,310

EMPLOYMENT INFORMATION

Career Rating	**95**
Rate of placement (nine months out)	99
State for bar exam	IL, CA, NY, TX, IN
Pass rate for first-time bar	87

Employers Who Frequently Hire Grads
Major law firms in locations throughout the country and abroad: federal circuit and district judges; state judges at all levels, government agencies, corporations, not-for-profits and public interest organizations

UNIVERSITY OF OKLAHOMA
COLLEGE OF LAW

INSTITUTIONAL INFORMATION

Public/private	Public
Student/faculty ratio	14:1
% faculty part-time	29
% faculty female	27
% faculty minority	15
Total faculty	55

SURVEY SAYS...

Great research resources, Great library staff, Beautiful campus

STUDENTS

Enrollment of law school	537
% male/female	55/45
% from out-of-state	32
% full-time	100
% minority	21
# of countries represented	3
Average age of entering class	24

ACADEMICS

Academic Experience Rating	85
Profs interesting rating	82
Profs accessible rating	79
Hours of study per day	4.08

Academic Specialties

Civil Procedure, Commercial, Constitutional, Corporation Securities, Criminal, Environmental, International, Labor, Property, Taxation, Intellectual Property, Native American Law

Combined Degrees Offered

JD/MBA, JD/MPH, JD/generic dual degree, 4 years

Clinical program required	No
Legal writing course requirement	Yes
Legal methods course requirement	No
Legal research course requirement	Yes
Moot court requirement	Yes
Public interest law requirement	No

Academics

"An incredible, first-class facility" is one of the most appealing aspects of the University of Oklahoma College of Law. Chief new features of the remodeled law school building include "a new library and a new state-of-the-art courtroom, which has brought several appellate courts, including the *en banc* Tenth Circuit, to hold hearings at OU, video conferencing capabilities in the classrooms [that] make distance learning from specialized lawyers possible, in-house clinical facilities, and a designated lab for writing and research." The recent expansion and renovation is just the tip of the iceberg. According to one student, "The administration is committed to shaking down the alumni to continue to build up OU's facilities as well as its scholarship fund."

Posh surroundings might make the school a comfortable place to study, but its professors are what garner the most unequivocal student praise. These dedicated professionals are both knowledgeable and accessible: they're "always wandering the halls talking to students outside of class." It's worth noting that OU students describe their law professors in terms seldom (if ever) uttered about any law professor anywhere: Namely, "Our professors are so cool." One first-year student reports that his professors for constitutional law and torts "both play in bands"—one "actually invited our section to come and hear his jazz band play, and they were good." Savvy recruitment has something to do with the presence of such uncommon law professors. "As far as the professors go we have some hidden gems at our law school, which in large part is due to our dean, Andrew Coats. We have brought in some incredible professors, especially bright and engaging women," a contingent one student sees missing at other schools. The addition of these "new, young professors in the past few years has been an invaluable addition to the school, providing instruction from varied backgrounds from throughout the country." Students can easily get to know these brilliant young minds because "small sections provide very good access to faculty." The administration earns equally high marks: Administrators are "open to suggestions by students who wish to begin new programs or expand the curriculum in a new direction. Innovation, enthusiasm, and activism by the student body is both encouraged and appreciated."

As far as career planning goes, student opinion is divided. While some think that "our Career Services Office could be better funded in order to assist the students in finding the best career, not just a job," others contend that the "College of Law offers outstanding career opportunities within the Midwest and Southwest, but...is only slowly gaining the national prominence needed to place well outside of these regions."

The administration has responded to these student concerns by doubling the size of the placement staff, developing new support services, and changing the name to the office of Professional Career Development.

Life

While small size might be a boon to students in the classroom, it can be a bit of a problem outside of it. At OU, "The student body is so small and spends so much time around each other that we often morph into high school students, including the rumor mill." This clique-ishness "can be disappointing to see in aspiring professionals, but also teaches you to watch your step and remember that your colleagues are going to be observing your actions [when] forming their opinions of you." Unlike many law school student bodies, "OU's student community encourages us to work hard and excel, but doesn't have the issues with 'gunner' students who will do anything to succeed." Most students agree, "The student body on the whole possesses the proper balance between commitment to academic excellence and being a normal well-rounded person with a life outside of law school." Politically, "The student population is somewhat conservative," but "The classrooms are full of debate, and everyone is treated fairly."

There are "lots of clubs" at OU, and "Student organization participation is excellent." "There is never a shortage of social events hosted by someone affiliated with the law school," and the "Halloween party" and "Law School Prom" are popular events. Off-campus entertainment options are also plentiful, as the school is within easy reach of Oklahoma City.

Getting In

Admission to OU is "highly competitive," with just over a quarter of applicants accepted. The average GPA of accepted students last year was 3.51, and the average LSAT score was 157. Both GPA and LSAT score are large factors in admissions, but so are personal statements and letters of recommendation. The school's website states, "In addition to giving considerable weight to the LSAT and undergraduate grade point average, the Admissions Committee also examines the other more personal variables of motivation, character, and capability. Insight into these variables can be derived from a careful examination of your resume, personal statement, and other contents in the file."

ADMISSIONS

Selectivity Rating	88
# applications received	1,111
% applicants accepted	30
% acceptees attending	52
LSAT Range	157–161
Application fee	$50
Regular application	Rolling, up to 3/15
Regular notification	Rolling
Early application program	No
Transfer students accepted	Yes
Evening division offered	No
Part-time accepted	No
CAS accepted	Yes

International Students

TOEFL recommended of international students

FINANCIAL FACTS

Annual tuition (in-state/out-of-state)	$13,122/ $23,050
Books and supplies	$1,400
Fees	$4,984
Room and board (on/off campus)	$15,824/ $17,923
Financial aid application deadline	3/1
% first-year students receiving some sort of aid	88
% receiving some sort of aid	92
% of aid that is merit based	59
% receiving scholarships	76
Average grant	$4,000
Average loan	$25,028
Average total aid package	$20,500
Average debt	$78,644

EMPLOYMENT INFORMATION

Career Rating	79
Rate of placement (nine months out)	92
State for bar exam	OK, TX, CO, MO, KS
Pass rate for first-time bar	96

Employers Who Frequently Hire Grads
McAfee & Taft; Crowe & Dunlevy; Conner & Winters; Gable & Gotwals; Hall, Estill, Hardwick, Gable & Nelson; Phillips & Murrah; State of Oklahoma, Chesapeake Energy Corp.; Hartzog, Conger, Cason & Neville; Fellers, Snider, Blankenship, Baily & Tippens; Thompson & Knight; Devon Energy; Andrews, Davis; Haynes, Boone; Baker & Botts

Prominent Alumni
Frank Keating, Former Gov. of Oklahoma; David L. Boren, Pres. of OU (Former U.S. Senator); William T. Comfort, Pres. CitiCorp Venture Capital; Robert Henry, Judge, 10th Circuit Court of Appeals; Brad Henry, Gov. of Oklahoma

Grads Employed by Field (%)
Academic (3)
Business/industry (17)
Government (17)
Judicial clerkship (2)
Private practice (58)
Public interest (3)

UNIVERSITY OF OREGON
SCHOOL OF LAW

INSTITUTIONAL INFORMATION

Public/private	Public
Student/faculty ratio	9:1
% faculty part-time	36
% faculty female	49
% faculty minority	14
Total faculty	59

SURVEY SAYS...
Liberal students, Beautiful campus

STUDENTS

Enrollment of law school	526
% male/female	56/44
% from out-of-state	65
% full-time	100
% minority	17
% international	1
# of countries represented	4
Average age of entering class	26

ACADEMICS

Academic Experience Rating	**80**
Profs interesting rating	76
Profs accessible rating	85
Hours of study per day	5.44

Academic Specialties
Civil Procedure, Commercial, Constitutional, Corporation Securities, Criminal, Environmental, Government Services, Human Rights, International, Property, Taxation, Intellectual Property, Dispute Resolution, Estate Planning, Green Business Law, Public Interest and Public Service Law

Advanced Degrees Offered
Master's in Conflict and Dispute Resolution, 2 years; LLM in Environmental and Natural Resources Law

Combined Degrees Offered
The concurrent degree program enables a student to earn a JD/MBA Business & Law, JD/MA or JD/MS Environmental Studies, JD/MA International Studies, JD/MA, or JD/MS Conflict & Dispute Resolution in approximately four years.

Academics

The University of Oregon School of Law offers a "diverse" and "amazing" array of opportunities "to see what practice is like before getting out into the field." The school has "a strong pro bono and public interest program." It's also a "great school" for environmental and natural resources law. Students in the "fantastic" clinics get a chance to help to advance cutting-edge and previously untested legal theories. Every year, the Public Interest Environmental Law Conference, one of the biggest and longest-running events of its kind, is "an unbelievable mash-up of activists and public interest attorneys." The Center for Law and Entrepreneurship works to "integrate the Portland campus into business law study." A litany of other clinics is available as well. Despite the breadth of hands-on opportunities, students gripe that UO Law could "offer a few more practical courses" and "use a bit more diversity in the classes offered."

"The course work is challenging" but the "intelligent and often quirky" professors are "supportive and enthusiastic." "They have high expectations while demonstrating genuine interest in students," reports one student. "The business law professors are fantastic," although "A couple of professors are extremely confusing and hard to follow." Nearly all professors here are "excellent teachers." "Overall, I'd say B-plus," assesses a 3L. "Stimulating class discussions about a wide variety of topics" are the norm. Also, "the entire faculty" is "very approachable outside of class" and "willing to help." "Oregon is probably one of the most liberal schools" anywhere and some note that "the liberal bias in the faculty is rather extreme"—a good or bad thing depending on your perspective. The "friendly" and "helpful" administration is also "very approachable" and "singularly focused on making law school the smoothest experience possible for the students."

UO grads face a highly competitive local job market. Some students find that "it is harder to find a job in Oregon than elsewhere." Portland is a very "desirable place to live" and boasts the state's largest legal job market. The city attracts the majority of UO graduates—and unfortunately, competition from lawyers from other states. Also, "A lot of students come here thinking they will return to their home state, but end up wanting to stay." "Opportunities for jobs and externships are particularly limited" in the surrounding college town of Eugene. "Our removed location makes it more difficult to network in other areas of Oregon," advises a 3L. "Many students need to relocate during the summers or commute during the school year for the better jobs."

The "new" building here is "gorgeous" and "very well-designed," "allow[ing] for lots of light." "Students enjoy spending time at the school and the common area acts as a social meeting place," says one student. The facility is "super wired" and generally "a great place to have classes." "State-of-the-art" classrooms provide "the ability to do multimedia presentations." A student explains, "Many faculty members have added multimedia aspects to class to enhance lessons, aid understanding, and even entertain. (One professor shows clips of *The Simpsons* and *Saturday Night Live* to illustrate the rules of evidence.)"

Life

UO Law is "small," and students appreciate the "congenial atmosphere." "The school has the feel of a small community within the larger UO campus," notes one student. The student body is "fun but serious, and many are committed to making positive social change through the law." There are "lots of very active minority student groups," and "Lots of students are California transplants." "There certainly is a competitive environment but in a good way" due to the "strong feeling of getting through this together

LAWRENCE SENO, JR., ASSISTANT DEAN OF ADMISSIONS
1221 UNIVERSITY OF OREGON, EUGENE, OR 97403-1221
TEL: 541-346-3846 FAX: 541-346-3984
E-MAIL: ADMISSIONS@LAW.UOREGON.EDU • WEBSITE: WWW.LAW.UOREGON.EDU

rather than competing against one another." What's more is that "even the most alpha and turbo students can't help but be calmed by the surrounding community's hippie culture." "The cooperative spirit among the students is pretty amazing," says an awed 2L. "When you need to miss class, students are very happy to provide notes or to pass along outlines or answer questions."

"Student groups are very active on campus," but life "behind the Granola Curtain" in "very small" Eugene, Oregon is "laid-back." There are "cultural activities" and "big-name music performances throughout the year," but "Eugene is not a glamorous town." "Don't come here if you are looking for a cosmopolitan experience," says one student. However, "The great thing about Oregon is there are several ways to disconnect yourself from the inherent stress" of law school. Students here "are very outgoing, and there's always something you could do on any night of the week." Whether it's a casual study group or a night on the town, "UO students are serious about fitting in time for social gatherings." Also, the "geographically breathtaking location" affords "biking trails, hills to climb, [and] outdoor activities galore."

Getting In

When applying to a strong law program located in a gorgeous setting, expect some competition. Oregon's admitted students at the 25th percentile have LSAT scores of 157 and GPAs of 3.12. Admitted students at the 75th percentile have LSAT scores of 161 and GPAs of 3.56.

Clinical program required	No
Legal writing course requirement	Yes
Legal methods course requirement	No
Legal research course requirement	Yes
Moot court requirement	No
Public interest law requirement	No

ADMISSIONS

Selectivity Rating	**82**
# applications received	2,285
% applicants accepted	39
% acceptees attending	20
Average LSAT	159
LSAT Range	157–161
Average undergrad GPA	3.43
Application fee	$50
Regular application	Rolling, up to 3/1
Regular notification	Rolling
Early application program	No
Transfer students accepted	Yes
Evening division offered	No
Part-time accepted	No
CAS accepted	Yes

International Students

TOEFL required of international students	

FINANCIAL FACTS

Annual tuition (in-state/out-of-state)	$22,770/ $28,692
Books and supplies	$1,600
Fees	$1,261
Room and board	$10,854
Financial aid application deadline	3/1
% first-year students receiving some sort of aid	94
% receiving some sort of aid	94
% receiving scholarships	56
Average grant	$5,868
Average loan	$31,386
Average total aid package	$33,189
Average debt	$68,618

EMPLOYMENT INFORMATION

Career Rating	**76**
Rate of placement (nine months out)	78
Average starting salary	$54,945
State for bar exam	OR, CA, WA, NV, NY
Pass rate for first-time bar	87

Employers Who Frequently Hire Grads
Law firms from Portland, Eugene (OR) Seattle, California; federal courts; Oregon appellate courts, Lane County and Portland area state and trial courts; Oregon Department of Justice; Washington Attorney General's office

Prominent Alumni
Ron Wyden, U.S. Senator; Alfred T. Goodwin, Former Chief Judge, U.S. Ct. of Appeals, Ninth Cir.; Jim Carter, VP & General Counsel, Nike; Matthew McKeown, Acting Asst. Atty Gen., Envir. & Nat. Res., USDOJ; Katherine Gurun, Former VP & General Counsel, Bechtel Corporation

UNIVERSITY OF THE PACIFIC
MCGEORGE SCHOOL OF LAW

INSTITUTIONAL INFORMATION

Public/private	Private
Student/faculty ratio	13:1
% faculty part-time	57
% faculty female	38
% faculty minority	16
Total faculty	112

SURVEY SAYS...

Diverse opinions accepted in classrooms, Beautiful campus

STUDENTS

Enrollment of law school	1,037
% male/female	50/50
% from out-of-state	23
% full-time	64
% minority	13
% international	1
# of countries represented	20
Average age of entering class	23

ACADEMICS

Academic Experience Rating	75
Profs interesting rating	90
Profs accessible rating	85
Hours of study per day	5.33

Academic Specialties

Criminal, Environmental, Government Services, International, Property, Taxation, Intellectual Property, Advocacy and Dispute Resolution

Advanced Degrees Offered

JD, 3–4 years; JSD International Water Law, LLM Transnational Business Practice, LLM International Law, LLM Public Law & Policy, LLM Experiential Law Teaching, 1 year

Combined Degrees Offered

JD/MBA, JD/MPPA, JD/MA, or MS upon approval, planned for 4 years

Academics

Students agree that one of the best things about Pacific McGeorge School of Law is that it's a stand-alone law school. Although Pacific McGeorge is part of the University of the Pacific in Stockton, California, the law school is self-contained in Sacramento, where it "isn't overshadowed by undergrads and other programs." For a relatively new school, it boasts a strong reputation in a few select areas, but it still has many that are in their infancy. "The downside of potential is that McGeorge doesn't now have the reputation it eventually will," surmises a student. This "student-centered environment" stresses academics, but not stress, as the administration "wants the students to do well and be happy." "It's a communal learning experience, which is just what I was hoping for," says a 1L. In addition to theoretical courses, McGeorge promotes a strong commitment to practical skills (including legal research and writing and appellate advocacy), and the clinic and internship/externship possibilities provide "practical, hands-on experience to what would otherwise be a very expensive bar prep course." The unique combination of the full-time day and part-time evening programs "complement each other well," providing a level of flexibility and diversity not available at other law schools. The year-long core classes during the first year make the learning experience much more in-depth, and the school also requires students to take a class in every subject tested on the California Bar. "Because of the requirements, I've taken several classes that I wouldn't have otherwise and discovered that I enjoyed some of those classes very much," says one student. If you're motivated, research opportunities abound, including "working with professors on their research, designing independent study to do your own research, and research related to newly enacted laws coming out of the state capitol."

The school has a great "desire to obtain constructive feedback from students," and the administration even voluntarily rescheduled a huge summer construction project around bar review lectures in response to such feedback. The "efficiency, promptness, accuracy, and student focus," with which the administration runs the school makes law school more enjoyable for all that go here. Most of the "extremely brilliant and passionate" professors "are very active in the McGeorge community" and will do whatever they can to ensure that their students succeed. "Most even give out their phone numbers, allowing them to be reached at any time," and they're "eager to help you get the most out of your time in law school." "I cannot imagine going through this traumatic experience anywhere else with less supportive teachers," says a 1L. Furthermore, the professors find interesting and unique ways to help students learn and retain the information needed. "Videos, props, and costumes are just a few examples." Students also like that there's a good mix of "teaching to the exam," teaching what is needed for the California Bar, and "learning the overall picture, including public policy concerns and where the law should change."

The school has an excellent writing curriculum and a two-year "Global Lawyering Skills" program comprehensively linking legal writing to other aspects of the core law curriculum. Faculty members prepare their graduates to be practice ready, and "The employers in the area know it," though many wish this reputation traveled outside of the region. "The employers in Sacramento and northern California know that McGeorge grads are going to have far more practical experience, with better research and writing skills." The campus is small, but "clean and friendly," and the facilities are excellent. The library, which is undergoing renovations, "has every source imaginable (and some that aren't imaginable)."

ADAM W. BARRETT, DEAN OF ADMISSIONS
3200 FIFTH AVENUE, SACRAMENTO, CA 95817
TEL: 916-739-7105 FAX: 916-739-7301
E-MAIL: ADMISSIONSMCGEORGE@PACIFIC.EDU • WEBSITE: WWW.MCGEORGE.EDU

Life

Although there's some competition, overall the student body is "like a big, stressed out family," and second- and third-year students are "always willing to help and give advice to the first-year students." Students are "highly intelligent and competitive, yet social and very cooperative/helpful," and there's "amazing" support for all students—including those with children, full-time jobs, or disabilities—to "participate fully in the academic and extracurricular life of the school." The school "encourages students to seek out activities that balance the rigors and stress of school life with real life." The school and a "rich set of student-run organizations" sponsor several popular social events each year (including "Raft Race, Barrister's Ball, Women's Caucus Wine Tasting, Public Legal Services Society Live and Silent Auction, Oktoberfest, and Halfway There Party"), along with "barbecues, speakers, community service opportunities, training, and networking opportunities." But it's the first-year classes that are probably the biggest bonding mechanism: "If you're going to spend three years at a law school stressing out, why not do it with people you can also hang out with?" Although the school is located in a "blighted," "questionable neighborhood," the campus itself is extremely safe and "especially beautiful' on sunny days when "students mill around the quad and chat at tables outside the Student Center."

Getting In

The most important factors in admissions decisions are a student's previous academic record, LSAT scores, graduate school or post-college career experience, and community service or extracurricular activities. For last year's entering class, LSAT scores at the 25th percentile were 155, and GPAs were 3.07; for the 75th percentile, LSATs were 160, and GPAs were 3.55. Although the admissions office has access to all LSAT scores (for applicants who take the test multiple times), the highest score is used for purposes of admission.

Clinical program required	No
Legal writing course requirement	Yes
Legal methods course requirement	No
Legal research course requirement	Yes
Moot court requirement	Yes
Public interest law requirement	No

ADMISSIONS

Selectivity Rating	81
# applications received	2,659
% applicants accepted	43
% acceptees attending	21
Average LSAT	158
LSAT Range	155–160
Average undergrad GPA	3.41
Application fee	$50
Regular application	Rolling, up to 6/9
Regular notification	Rolling
Early application program	No
Transfer students accepted	Yes
Evening division offered	Yes
Part-time accepted	Yes
CAS accepted	Yes

International Students

TOEFL required of international students	

FINANCIAL FACTS

Annual tuition	$38,556
Books and supplies	$1,600
Fees	$73
Room and board	$9,738
% first-year students receiving some sort of aid	97
% receiving some sort of aid	97
% of aid that is merit based	65
% receiving scholarships	57
Average grant	$11,787
Average loan	$43,937
Average total aid package	$47,474
Average debt	$124,488

EMPLOYMENT INFORMATION

Career Rating		82
Rate of placement (nine months out)		87
Average starting salary		$72,490
State for bar exam		CA, NV, HI, OR, D.C.
Pass rate for first-time bar		81

Employers Who Frequently Hire Grads
National and California law firms, Federal and California State Agencies, Sacramento County DA and PD

Prominent Alumni
Scott Boras, Sports Agent/Baseball; Bill Lockyer, Attorney General/CA Gvt; Steve Martini, Novelist; Johnnie Rawlinson, U.S. 9th Circuit Court of Appeals; Consuelo M. Callahan, U.S. 9th Circuit Court of Appeals

Grads Employed by Field (%)
Academic (2)
Business/industry (11)
Government (21)
Judicial clerkship (4)
Military (1)
Private practice (49)
Public interest (12)

University of Pennsylvania

Law School

INSTITUTIONAL INFORMATION

Public/private	Private
% faculty part-time	39
% faculty female	30
% faculty minority	13
Total faculty	99

SURVEY SAYS...

Great research resources,
Great library staff

STUDENTS

Enrollment of law school	802
% male/female	52/48
% from out-of-state	89
% full-time	100
% minority	30
% international	2
# of countries represented	20
Average age of entering class	24

ACADEMICS

Academic Experience Rating	96
Profs interesting rating	86
Profs accessible rating	78
Hours of study per day	3.84

Academic Specialties

Business, Civil Procedure, Commercial, Constitutional, Corporation Securities, Criminal, Environmental, Government Services, Health, Human Rights, International, Labor, Legal History, Legal Philosophy, Property Regulation, Taxation, Intellectual Property

Advanced Degrees Offered

JD, 3 years; LLM, LLCM, 1 year; SJD, at least 1 year

Combined Degrees Offered

JD/MBA, JD/MA or MS in Criminology, JD/MSEd in Educational Policy, JD/MSEd in Higher Education, JD/MES in Environmental Studies, JD/MPA in Government, JD/MA in International Studies, JD/MBE in Bioethics, JD/MS in Social Policy, JD/MSW (for students with a BSW), JD/LLM Hong Kong University, 3 years;

Academics

Life is good at Penn Law in Philadelphia, where the size of the law school is "ideal," there is no GPA or class rank, and the curve grades around a "sweet, sweet B," meaning "class sizes are small and minimally competitive." This Ivy League bunch creates a collegial atmosphere of "high-caliber" minds, all of which have a mutual respect for their classmates. "Law school can be extremely stressful, and having colleagues who are both brilliant and brave enough to share their angst makes all the difference in the world. You do not go it alone at Penn Law," says one.

One "unique feature" of Penn Law is its focus on cross-disciplinary studies, as it makes earning a master's in another field "pretty simple to do"; the school also allows a number of courses to be taken in other graduate schools, and has certificate programs with other schools at the university. "I have friends learning Portuguese and Dutch; pursuing their passion for English in grad-level classes, or obtaining a Business and Public Policy certificate from Wharton," says a 3L. To top it off, the "diversity of faculty interests" also provides research opportunities in other interest areas, as "most hire a few student research assistants each semester and summer."

The course load at Penn Law is anything but easy, as first semester 1Ls are loaded with more than seventeen hours of mandatory classes per week, causing "a lot of near-mental breakdowns because of the sudden amount of preparation required." Mandatory first semester classes include torts, contracts, civil procedure, property, and legal writing, and the Socratic Method is an everyday part of life. Luckily, second semester is "a bit less stressful," and "even the [professors] who are certified geniuses make an effort to have lunch with small groups of 1Ls." In fact, the professors do quite a bit to make students love their legal life from the start: "Every professor I've had clearly loves the field he/she is in, and their enthusiasm is infectious," says a student.

The "incredibly flexible" administration is "full of nothing but caring and cuddly individuals. Beware: They will suck you in with their personalized phone calls and attention," says a 3L. "I feel like I know who everyone is and exactly where to go to if there is a problem," says another. The dean of students in particular "is an incredibly thoughtful and compassionate person who can solve any sort of personal or academic problem that one can dream up." Many students do wish that Career Services was more supportive of students looking to go the public interest or judicial internship route, but other than that, there are no complaints. "[The administration] has a very clear vision for what they want Penn Law to be, from the learning environment, to the faculty expertise, to the student-run clubs and social activities."

Though the current law school building is far from pretty, massive renovations have recently commenced, so things are looking up. Research facilities are "top rate," to the point where "even the undergrads seem to prefer the law library—fortunately, the administration kicks them out during reading period and exams."

Life

People at Penn Law are "exceptionally talented and come from very high-achieving professional backgrounds," and most students will have no trouble "meeting like-minded, hardworking, friends." Students spend hours "hanging out" at the law school after classes, and the "opportunities are plentiful" to "[mingle] with non-law students," as "UPenn is replete with other graduate schools. Law students don't have to feel like the

RENEE POST, ASSOCIATE DEAN, ADMISSIONS AND FINANCIAL AID
3400 CHESTNUT STREET, PHILADELPHIA, PA 19104-6204
TEL: 215-898-7400 FAX: 215-898-9606
E-MAIL: ADMISSIONS@LAW.UPENN.EDU • WEBSITE: WWW.LAW.UPENN.EDU

oldest kids on campus." However, with only 250 people per class, students say an inevitable high school feeling abounds, and "gossip is rampant."

As for the perks, "Let it never be said that Penn Law is cheap!" There is "lots of free booze and food at events," which is good, since drinking is a popular form of social activity. Various student organizations also have dinners in Philadelphia with different professors, so students can "learn what they've done and what they're doing." The administration takes every effort to make the experience less stressful, from "hosting keg-in-the-courtyard parties to wearing tutus on exam days." The campus itself is three blocks away from a riverside park and bike trail, and is surrounded by numerous upscale restaurants, not to mention its close proximity to Philadelphia, "a great city" and a "really vibrant area for students."

Getting In

Last year, the University of Pennsylvania received more than 6,000 applications for an entering class of 250 students. The entering class had a mean LSAT score of 170 and a mean GPA of 3.85. Penn evaluates an applicant's entire academic history, including grade trends and rigor of undergraduate course work. The admissions committee also evaluates a candidate's writing ability, as well as leadership experience, personal background, and achievements.

JD/MCP in City & Regional Planning, JD/MPH in Public Health, JD/AM in Islamic Studies, JD/MSW, JD/MBA, JD/MA in Global Business Law, JD/MS in Historic Preservation, JD/MA in Philosophy, 4 years; JD/PhD in American Legal History, JD/PhD in Philosophy, JD/PhD in Communication, JD/EdD, JD/MD; JD/BA, JD/BS in the university, philosophy, JD/PhD American Legal History, 6 years

Clinical program required	No
Legal writing course requirement	Yes
Legal methods course requirement	Yes
Legal research course requirement	Yes
Moot court requirement	No
Public interest law requirement	Yes

ADMISSIONS

Selectivity Rating	98
# applications received	6,003
% applicants accepted	14
% acceptees attending	29
Average LSAT	170
LSAT Range	166–171
Average undergrad GPA	3.85
Application fee	$80
Regular application	Rolling
Regular notification	Rolling
Early application program	Yes
Early application deadline	12/1
Early application notification	12/31
Transfer students accepted	Yes
Evening division offered	No
Part-time accepted	No
CAS accepted	Yes

FINANCIAL FACTS

Annual tuition	$47,600
Books and supplies	$7,150
Fees	$3,118
Room and board	$13,392
Financial aid application deadline	3/1
% first-year students receiving some sort of aid	81
% receiving some sort of aid	78
% of aid that is merit based	26
% receiving scholarships	41
Average grant	$17,113
Average loan	$42,377
Average total aid package	$59,490
Average debt	$105,297

EMPLOYMENT INFORMATION

Career Rating	**98**	**Grads Employed by Field (%)**
Rate of placement (nine months out)	99	Business/industry (4)
Average starting salary	$137,500	Judicial clerkship (17)
State for bar exam	NY	Private practice (77)
Pass rate for first-time bar	98	Public interest (3)
Employers Who Frequently Hire Grads		
Variety of Major Corporate Law Firms Nationwide; Prestigious National Fellowship Organizations and Public interest Organizations; Federal and State Judges		

UNIVERSITY OF PITTSBURGH
SCHOOL OF LAW

INSTITUTIONAL INFORMATION

Public/private	Public
Student/faculty ratio	14:1
% faculty part-time	46
% faculty female	34
% faculty minority	7
Total faculty	150

SURVEY SAYS...

Great research resources,
Students love Pittsburgh, PA

STUDENTS

Enrollment of law school	771
% male/female	56/44
% from out-of-state	40
% full-time	99
% minority	16
% international	2
# of countries represented	5
Average age of entering class	24

ACADEMICS

Academic Experience Rating	**80**
Profs interesting rating	78
Profs accessible rating	81
Hours of study per day	4.70

Academic Specialties
Civil Procedure, Environmental, International, Taxation, Intellectual Property, Health Law and Innovation Practice Institute

Advanced Degrees Offered
Master of Laws LLM for foreign-trained attorneys, a two-semester program that allows foreign-trained lawyers to study common law in a U.S. context.

Combined Degrees Offered
JD/MPA, Law and Urban and Public Administration, JD/MPIA, Law and International Affairs, JD/MS, Law and Public Management (in conjunction with Carnegie Mellon University), JD/MBA (in conjunction with Tepper School Carnegie Mellon University, JD/MSW with the School of Social Work, 4 years; JD/MBA, Law and Business Administration,

Academics

The "underrated" University of Pittsburgh School of Law has "a very good position in the Pittsburgh community" and features a "very strong" faculty. "Legal theory" is here, of course, and so is "real-world application." But there is also "a great deal of emphasis on practical skills such as legal writing, oral arguments, and externships." "Many strong clinical programs" include a tax clinic and a civil practice clinic that focuses on both health law and elder law. A host of "fantastic" certificate programs includes civil litigation and intellectual property. Students interested in international law will find "a strong and effective emphasis" on this area through study abroad opportunities, internships, and classes." There's also Jurist, a very comprehensive legal news and research online service run exclusively by faculty and staff. Pitt Law's new program in Law & Entrepreneurship will provide a range of opportunities for students interested in counselling entrepreneurs or in thinking entrepreneurially about their own careers.

Pitt has "a number of highly energetic, brilliant, [and] helpful" professors. "Some members of the faculty are absolutely astounding," and several adjunct professors "are really impressive." "Many of our professors are active practitioners in the fields that they teach, giving students opportunities to participate in ongoing cases and to hear about the issues that are most pressing in the field at that moment," adds a 2L. However, "There are some truly awful professors here too." One student notes that the "younger ones tend to be better." Ultimately though, "almost all" of the professors are "very friendly" and "exceedingly accessible" outside of class.

Many students say that "aesthetically, Pitt could use an upgrade." The Law School building "sits right in the middle" of Pitt's "urban" campus. While the building "certainly isn't beautiful," one student says, "it isn't as bad as everyone likes to pretend;" indeed, construction was just completed on a brand new Student Lounge that includes seating, a Starbucks, lockers, and group and solo study spaces. A 1L offers, "The building as a whole reminds me of a 1970s fort." Classrooms are "laptop friendly" but "can be quite uncomfortable and acoustically flawed."

Many students tell us that "the administration is incredibly frustrating" and "often seems adrift." They say there is too much "needless bureaucracy." Other students have had a very different experience. They contend that the administration is "open and responsive to student concerns." "The school is small enough that you can get to know someone in the Registrar's Office, Career Services, and the Dean's Office," claims a satisfied 3L. Speaking of Career Services, it "still gets mixed reviews," but students report that "they are working hard at reaching out." Students also say that Pitt is "strong" regionally. If you want to practice law in Pennsylvania or in Washington, D.C., "good job opportunities" are abundant, and the alumni network is solid. Students in their second or third year can also receive a semster's worth of academic credit for working as an extern or government agency or non profit in D.C.

Life

Students confide that Western Pennsylvania is "not the most diverse school in the world"; however, the campus has a "clear liberal bent" politically. Many here say that Pitt is "a warm, friendly place to learn." "Even during the first year," one student says, "Students at the school are generally pretty laid-back, friendly, and non-competitive."

CHARMAINE C. McCALL, ASSISTANT DEAN FOR ADMISSIONS AND FINANCIAL AID
3900 FORBES AVENUE, PITTSBURGH, PA 15260
TEL: 412-648-1413 FAX: 412-648-1318
E-MAIL: ADMITLAW@PITT.EDU • WEBSITE: WWW.LAW.PITT.EDU

On the other hand, some find that "people are normal on the outside and freaking out on the inside." "I was really, really surprised at how friendly other students are," gushes a 1L. "If I miss a class I never have a problem getting notes from someone, and students tend to help each other out with research questions."

Outside of class, "There is a great social scene," and "Making friends is fairly easy." The Student Bar Association sponsors "a lot of social events." The 'Burgh is "a cheap city with lots of cultural activities" and it is perennially rated among the best cities in the United States in which to live and work. "Pittsburgh is far more beautiful than people who have never been here would imagine," promises a 1L. There are good bars "right across the street from the law school." "There is tons of cheap…housing within walking distance," and "nicer housing" is only "a bus ride away." With your Pitt ID you can ride the buses for free. (If you drive, though, students warn that "parking is a nightmare.") "You absolutely need a car" because many places you'll have to go "are all fifteen miles away from each other." But for those that are still unsure, one student suggests: "Drive up Mt. Washington and look down on the Pittsburgh skyline and the rivers, and you'll be convinced."

Getting In

Admitted students at the 25th percentile have LSAT scores of roughly 158 and GPAs of 3.1. Admitted students at the 75th percentile have LSAT scores of about 161 and GPAs of just over 3.6. Pitt's administration says that it will consider your highest score if you take the LSAT multiple times. Decisions are based on many factors, and the admissions committee prefers online applications through LSAC starting September 1 through March 1. Applications are considered for only the current year for the full semester.

JD/MPH, Law and Public Health,
JD/MA, Law and Medical Ethics,
3.5 years

Clinical program required	No
Legal writing course requirement	Yes
Legal methods course requirement	No
Legal research course requirement	Yes
Moot court requirement	No
Public interest law requirement	No

ADMISSIONS

Selectivity Rating	85
# applications received	2,756
% applicants accepted	35
% acceptees attending	27
LSAT Range	158–161
Application fee	$55
Regular application	Rolling, up to 3/1
Regular notification	Rolling
Early application program	Yes
Early application deadline	12/1
Early application notification	12/31
Transfer students accepted	Yes
Evening division offered	No
Part-time accepted	No
CAS accepted	Yes

International Students

TOEFL required of
international students

FINANCIAL FACTS

Annual tuition (in-state/out-of-state)	$25,708/ $33,334
Books and supplies	$1,530
Fees	$842
Room and board	$15,430
Financial aid application deadline	3/1
% first-year students receiving some sort of aid	87
% receiving some sort of aid	87
% of aid that is merit based	60
% receiving scholarships	55
Average grant	$10,000
Average loan	$22,800
Average total aid package	$40,000
Average debt	$84,772

EMPLOYMENT INFORMATION

Career Rating	83
Rate of placement (nine months out)	87
Average starting salary	$80,205
State for bar exam	PA, VA, MD, NY, CA
Pass rate for first-time bar	87

Employers Who Frequently Hire Grads
Buchanan Ingersoll & Rooney; K&L Gates; Reed Smith,; Morgan, Lewis & Bockius; Jones Day; Pepper Hamilton; Dechert; Fox Rothschild; Cadwalader Wickersham & Taft; Milbank Tweed; Davis Polk & Wardwell; McGuireWoods; Duane Morris; Dechert; Hogan & Hartson; Blank Rome; Ballard Spahr

Prominent Alumni
Richard Thornburg, Former U.S. Attorney General; Orrin Hatch, Senator,Utah; Joseph Weis, Senior Judge for the Third Circut; Ruggerio Aldisert, Senior Judge for the Third Circuit; Ralph J. Cappy, Former Chief Justice of Pennsylvania

Grads Employed by Field (%)
Business/industry (18)
Government (11)
Private practice (57)

UNIVERSITY OF RICHMOND
SCHOOL OF LAW

INSTITUTIONAL INFORMATION

Public/private	Private
Student/faculty ratio	14:1
% faculty part-time	63
% faculty female	40
% faculty minority	5
Total faculty	122

SURVEY SAYS...

Diverse opinions accepted in classrooms, Great research resources, Great library staff, Beautiful campus, Students love Richmond, VA

STUDENTS

Enrollment of law school	455
% male/female	55/45
% from out-of-state	45
% full-time	100
% minority	18
% international	2
# of countries represented	3
Average age of entering class	24

ACADEMICS

Academic Experience Rating	**90**
Profs interesting rating	88
Profs accessible rating	95
Hours of study per day	4.54

Academic Specialties
Civil Procedure, Commercial, Constitutional, Corporations Securities, Criminal, Environmental, International, Labor, Legal History, Property, Taxation, Intellectual Property, Family

Advanced Degrees Offered
JD, 3 years

Combined Degrees Offered
JD/MBA, JD/Master's in Urban and Regional Planning, JD/MHA, JD/MSW, JD/MPA, each 4 years

Academics

Those looking to receive a first-rate law education while enjoying "Southern hospitality at its finest" would be wise to look into University of Richmond School of Law, where students say "The open dialogue among students and between students and professors is truly special." By all accounts, a "very friendly," "almost family-like" atmosphere prevails at this small school. "It amazes me that I'm able to walk down the hallway and have even professors whose classes I have not taken greet me by name," a satisfied 3L writes. The "well-educated, well-published" faculty members here are "dedicated to bettering their students and compassionate to their needs as individuals." The majority of professors "offer their home numbers and cell phone numbers so that we can call whenever we need help, or even just a little advice."

Professorial love is of the tough variety in the classroom, where students say "the use of the Socratic Method" "can be a bit intimidating," particularly for first-year students, though "It makes class entertaining and ensures that you are prepared," a 1L offers. All students here go through "an outstanding lawyering skills program. During these courses, our legal writing and actual courtroom skills are emphasized in very precise, methodical ways," a 2L writes. If students run into academic difficulties, they can take advantage of Richmond's Academic Success Program, which provides a full-time faculty member to assist students with their course work. The downside to the school's small size is "limited course selection," and "only one section" of most upper-level classes each semester. To expand its offerings, the School of Law partners with other schools within the University of Richmond—for example, the Robins School of Business and the Jepson School of Leadership Studies—to offer students a "diversity of dual degrees" which allows students "to really focus on particular fields of interest."

Richmond enjoys "a tremendous reputation in the Commonwealth of Virginia" and students believe that "the fact that there are so many opportunities for legal experience in Richmond," the state capital, "is a great strength" of the school. "We have access to county, state, and district courts and often have lectures and course[s] taught by Virginia Supreme Court Justices," a sanguine student writes. Many clerkships and externships are made possible through a "highly involved alumni community" in the area and help students to figure out what type of practice they would like to enter when they graduate. Because many students "fall in love with the city," the school's Career Services Office (CSO) has historically taken a somewhat provincial approach. However, it "recently hired a new dean and two new staff members," and students are beginning to feel that the CSO "has the resources to help any student find a job anywhere in the world."

Administrators are described as "doting," and all maintain an "open-door policy." While there are a few reports of disorganization, the vast majority here believe the "personal approach" and lack of red tape transcend the minor difficulties. The "entire campus has wireless Internet access," which allows students to "study anywhere." In addition, "You are provided your own personal study carrel in the library, which functions as a locker and, most importantly, a nice quiet place to study." If students require more incentive to head to the library, "ample" staffing ensures that all customers "find what they are looking for." The student body's biggest complaint is that Richmond is "very underappreciated." "I have friends at Georgetown, UNC, Wake Forest, Duke, NYU, and UVA law schools, and none of them are as happy as I am at Richmond," a 2L boasts.

MICHELLE RAHMAN, ASSOCIATE DEAN FOR ADMISSIONS
LAW SCHOOL ADMISSIONS OFFICE, 28 WESTHAMPTON WAY, UNIVERSITY OF RICHMOND, VA 23173
TEL: 804-289-8189 FAX: 804-287-6516
E-MAIL: LAWADMISSIONS@RICHMOND.EDU • WEBSITE: LAW.RICHMOND.EDU

Life

Not only is the University of Richmond campus "one of the most beautiful in the country," it is "surrounded by a safe and pristine neighborhood that is also easily affordable." Adding to the pleasant environment, "Competition among students is healthy and not overwhelming." "I almost enjoy the daily grind of law school when I can so easily relate to my fellow students," a 2L reports. "Little things, like taking lunch breaks at the dining hall or going through flashcards together during exams, [have] helped me find a comfortable niche here." Richmond is "a very social school," and "numerous events and groups meetings" are held "every week." In addition, "The school sponsors monthly happy hours in order to encourage students and faculty/staff to interact," and "There is always the opportunity for free food." The student body can be cliquey, however, "especially if you don't fit in with the pretty and party-oriented mid-twenties crowd." Fortunately, "There's plenty to do in Richmond. I went to the opera with one of my friends and his wife," a 2L writes. Bars in the Fan district, "in the heart of Richmond," are very popular with students of all ages.

In recent years, "the school has significantly improved its minority enrollment," and "they are well integrated (I am one of them) and treated exactly as any individual regardless of race or gender by students, faculty and staff alike." A former bastion of conservatism, Richmond is "middle of the road these days, and there is a definite liberal presence on campus."

Getting In

Students frequently mention "the Admissions Office ladies" as a major resource of Richmond. "Literally, if you need a hug, they are there," a 2L reports. Their "personal acceptance phone call" initiates students to an environment in which "Every student is given plenty of attention." The advice the associate dean provides on the law school's website is another way in which the staff here goes above and beyond the call of duty.

Clinical program required	No
Legal writing course requirement	Yes
Legal methods course requirement	Yes
Legal research course requirement	Yes
Moot court requirement	No
Public interest law requirement	No

ADMISSIONS

Selectivity Rating	88
# applications received	2,105
% applicants accepted	27
% acceptees attending	26
Average LSAT	162
LSAT Range	159–163
Average undergrad GPA	3.47
Application fee	$35
Regular application	Rolling, up to 7/15
Regular notification	3/31
Early application program	Yes
Early application deadline	12/15
Early application notification	12/24
Transfer students accepted	Yes
Evening division offered	No
Part-time accepted	No
CAS accepted	Yes

International Students

TOEFL required of international students	

FINANCIAL FACTS

Annual tuition	$35,430
Books and supplies	$4,980
Room and board (on/off campus)	$9,350/ $10,800
Financial aid application deadline	2/25
% first-year students receiving some sort of aid	94
% receiving some sort of aid	91
% of aid that is merit based	19
% receiving scholarships	63
Average grant	$11,319
Average loan	$36,971
Average total aid package	$41,520
Average debt	$94,223

EMPLOYMENT INFORMATION

Career Rating	85
Rate of placement (nine months out)	94
Average starting salary	$77,352
State for bar exam	NC, NY, FL, VA, D.C.
Pass rate for first-time bar	88

Employers Who Frequently Hire Grads

Baker Botts, McGuire Woods, Troutman Sanders, Hunton & Williams, Christian & Barton, Hirschler Fleischer, Hogan & Hartson, Jackson Kelly, Kaufman & Canoles, Kennedy Covington, LeClair Ryan, Odin Feldman, Reed Smith, Thompson McMullan, Venable, Wilcox & Savage, Williams Mullen, Woods Rogers

Prominent Alumni

Lawrence L. Koontz, Justice, VA Supreme Court; Harvey E. Schlesinger, U.S. District Court Judge, Middle Dist. of FL; Frederick P. Stamp, Jr., U.S. District Court Judge, Northern District of WV; Robert P. Merhige, Jr., U.S. District Court Judge, Eastern District of VA; Anthony F. Troy, Former Attorney General of Virginia

Grads Employed by Field (%)

Business/industry (21)
Government (12)
Judicial clerkship (21)
Military (2)
Private practice (38)
Public interest (4)

University of San Diego
School of Law

INSTITUTIONAL INFORMATION

Public/private	Private
Affiliation	Roman Catholic
Student/faculty ratio	14:1
% faculty part-time	37
% faculty female	36
% faculty minority	16
Total faculty	93

SURVEY SAYS...

Diverse opinions accepted in classrooms, Beautiful campus, Students love San Diego, CA

STUDENTS

Enrollment of law school	1,109
% male/female	54/46
% from out-of-state	29
% full-time	80
% minority	26
Average age of entering class	24

ACADEMICS

Academic Experience Rating	86
Profs interesting rating	89
Profs accessible rating	73
Hours of study per day	4.06

Academic Specialties

Commercial, Constitutional, Criminal, Environmental, International, Taxation, Intellectual Property, Public Interest Law, Children's Advocacy

Advanced Degrees Offered

JD, 3 years full-time, 4 years part-time; Master of Law, General with Concentrations, Taxation, Business and Corporate, International, Comparative Law for Foreign Attorneys, approximately 1 year; Master of Science in Legal Studies

Combined Degrees Offered

JD/MBA, JD/Master of Arts in International Relations, JD/International Master in Business Administration, 4–4.5 years

Academics

A stalwart Southern California institution, the University of San Diego draws rave reviews for its fine faculty, practical programs, and, of course, weather. A large and diverse program, "USD attracts some of the finest professors from across the country, specializing in criminal law, corporate, international law and IP [Intellectual Property]." A current student enthuses, "Each professor is unique in their approach to teaching, and because most of them are the brightest minds in their field, they are able to give you the tools you will need to succeed as a practicing attorney." Academically, the "Socratic Method isn't so big at USD" and, on the whole, the curriculum is "conscious of the practical aspects of lawyering, and doesn't obsess over theory." Even so, course work is challenging, and faculty is "helpful and welcoming, yet not afraid to be blunt and mean business." When considering USD, students remind us of the school's Catholic affiliation, telling us that the professors are "rather conservative in their approach to teaching and the law in general." A current student shares, "It's no secret that the legal profession is a liberal one, so USD Law is a refreshing haven for more moderate and right-thinking students."

Despite the practical emphasis, many feel that USD could offer more courses that directly prepare you for the legal profession. For example, "USD offers no classes whatsoever in drafting or licensing, and what courses are offered in interviewing and negotiations are typically oversubscribed two to one [or] three to one." However, those looking for practical experience will find "a multitude of opportunities outside of the classroom that simultaneously offer course credit." For example, the school operates a "competitive mock trial team, which provides very rigorous and thorough training and preparation for future trial practice." Students may also participate in one of "thirteen clinics in diverse areas that offer hands-on legal experience with a classroom component." A 3L shares, "I never got law school burnout because I was able to work for credit for a nonprofit, a government agency, and a court, which all kept me focused on my future career as a lawyer instead of the daily grind of a law student."

Students point out that the "USD campus is beautiful." Though in the past students have noted "the law school is outdated and needs a massive face-lift," the school has recently major renovations to offices and classrooms. "The library resources are also unparalleled. There are literally floors of books, journals, microfiches, and other legal resources."

Maybe it's the school's hefty tuition that has USD students dreaming of dollar signs; whatever the reason, "Most students that come to USD seem to be far more focused on fields that make money more than anything else, and the culture is very conservative." Lucky for them, "USD Law is considered the preeminent local law school, so networking and job opportunities abound." In fact, students insist, "This is a very 'hometown' area, and is not welcoming to outsiders. To employers here, USD really is a better school than Harvard."

Life

Beachside living and law school aren't necessarily a natural pair. A student bemoans, "There's nothing like spending three years living next to the beach yet never having time to actually go to the beach." However, students unanimously agree that the mellow San Diego atmosphere really reduces the stresses of law school. "Being able to spend a

Saturday at the beach or riding your bike or doing something outdoors on a regular basis makes a huge difference in how positive you feel about your life during law school," confesses a current student.

You'll bump into quite a few beemers in the USD parking lot, and students admit the school "has the SoCal rich-kid culture one would expect from a conservative, wealthy, private school with a student body drawn primarily from upper-class kids in and around the LA, OC, and San Diego regions." On the whole, however, "Most people are pleasant and friendly, help each other, and have interests beyond studying." If you want to connect with your classmates, "There are more than enough social opportunities including the famed Bar Review every week. There are also more alumni/networking events than anyone could every find time to attend." Around town, "San Diego is full of young people around my age, and there is always something to do whether it is hanging at the beach, going to the bars, or taking in a Chargers or Padres game." When it's time to blow off steam, "San Diego has a great bar scene, and finals aside you'll never be lacking an excuse to go grab a beer."

Getting In

While there are no pre-legal courses required for entry to the USD law program, all applicants must have a bachelor's degree from an accredited college. LSAT scores and GPA are important to an admissions decision, as are the personal qualities and skills demonstrated by your personal statement and letters of recommendation. The 2010–2011 entering class had a median LSAT score of 161 and a median GPA of 3.49.

Clinical program required	No
Legal writing course requirement	Yes
Legal methods course requirement	No
Legal research course requirement	Yes
Moot court requirement	Yes
Public interest law requirement	No

ADMISSIONS

Selectivity Rating	**87**
# applications received	5,179
% applicants accepted	31
% acceptees attending	20
Average LSAT	161
LSAT Range	159–163
Average undergrad GPA	3.49
Application fee	$50
Regular application	Rolling, up to 6/15
Regular notification	Rolling
Early application program	Yes
Early application deadline	12/1
Early application notification	12/31
Transfer students accepted	Yes
Evening division offered	Yes
Part-time accepted	Yes
CAS accepted	Yes

International Students

TOEFL required of international students

FINANCIAL FACTS

Annual tuition	$41,200
Books and supplies	$1,299
Fees	$214
Room and board	$21,686
Financial aid application deadline	3/1
% first-year students receiving some sort of aid	87
% receiving some sort of aid	84
% of aid that is merit based	60
% receiving scholarships	44
Average grant	$21,000
Average loan	$40,511
Average total aid package	$54,000
Average debt	$119,331

EMPLOYMENT INFORMATION

Career Rating	**89**
Rate of placement (nine months out)	94
Average starting salary	$96,414
State for bar exam	CA, NV, AZ
Pass rate for first-time bar	81

Employers Who Frequently Hire Grads
Gibson Dunn & Crutcher; Latham & Watkins; Fish & Richardson; Cooley; DLA Piper; Wilson Sonsini; Orrick; Department of Justice; Jones Day; Foley Lardner; Ernst & Young; PricewaterhouseCoopers

Prominent Alumni
Shelley Berkley, Congresswoman from Nevada; Frances Townsend, Former Homeland Security Advisor; Hon. Thomas Whelan, U.S. District Court, So. California; Steve Altman, President Qualcomm; Leonard Armato, Chief Marketing Officer & Pres. Fitness Group Skechers USA, Inc.

Grads Employed by Field (%)
Academic (9)
Business/industry (13)
Government (9)
Judicial clerkship (3)
Private practice (60)
Public interest (6)

UNIVERSITY OF SAN FRANCISCO
SCHOOL OF LAW

INSTITUTIONAL INFORMATION

Public/private	Private
Affiliation	Roman Catholic
Student/faculty ratio	16:1
% faculty part-time	67
% faculty female	32
% faculty minority	27
Total faculty	101

SURVEY SAYS...

Great research resources,
Beautiful campus

STUDENTS

% full-time	100
Average age of entering class	25

ACADEMICS

Academic Experience Rating	92
Profs interesting rating	90
Profs accessible rating	81
Hours of study per day	4.80

Academic Specialties

International, Intellectual Property, Business Law, Public Interest

Advanced Degrees Offered

LLM in International Transactions and Comparative Law and Intellectual Property, 1 year

Combined Degrees Offered

JD/MBA, 4 years

Clinical program required	No
Legal writing course requirement	Yes
Legal methods course requirement	No
Legal research course requirement	Yes
Moot court requirement	Yes
Public interest law requirement	No

Academics

A "sincere focus on public interest work" sets the Jesuit-affiliated University of San Francisco School of Law apart. "We also walk the walk when it comes to working toward social justice," proclaims a 2L. USF's Public Interest Law Foundation "offers grants to students working in the public interest over the summer, and there is a loan forgiveness program for graduates pursuing public interest careers." A strong, practical focus is another perk. "USF is very good at developing lawyers who can actually practice when they graduate," asserts a 3L. Eight clinical programs cover a wide range of legal areas. "I worked in the predatory lending clinic, which was life-changing for me," reflects a 3L. "It helped me get perspective on the practice of law and what it means to work with low-income clients." A notable international focus is yet another point of pride here. "Many students enjoy studying overseas through summers abroad" in Ireland and the Czech Republic. There are also summer internships in several developing nations including Cambodia, India, and Argentina. Academic complaints are limited, but they include the range of courses. "The class selection is interesting, but not very broad," says a 2L. Also, while some students call the legal research and writing program "extremely thorough and practical," others grumble that it's "not up to par at all." Several students also note that tuition is "high."

The school's alluring Bay Area location means that "USF attracts and retains many truly excellent professors." Not every professor gets top marks in the classroom, but generally speaking, there's "a palpable sense of energy in class." "Professors don't play 'hide the ball,' and prefer to offer the black-letter law outright," reports a 1L, "allowing for in-depth discussions on larger, more interesting issues, such as policy implications and general jurisprudence." Accessibility isn't a problem. Professors "make ample time to meet with students" and "take a personal stake" in their students' success. The administration is "transparent" and "approachable" enough but "frighteningly resistant to change," and "There is a lot of red tape" and some operations glitches in the administrative departments.

Students are quick to point out that USF has "a great alumni network that helps students" find jobs. "Alumni connections at public-interest law firms, governmental agencies, and nonprofits" are particularly outstanding. Also, USF students are "very well-positioned to get summer jobs with the district attorney, public defender, or other criminal law employers" after first year. Nevertheless, the immediate market "in which the school is located is a fierce one," and the reputation of USF is "very California-based." Students aren't particularly enthusiastic about the Office of Career Planning. There are lots of great resources, but the staff "is not very aggressive about actual job placement."

The larger campus of the University of San Francisco is a "lovely" urban oasis, and the law school facilities are "wonderful, clean, and modern." "The rooms are all up-to-date with the highest tech equipment." "The amazing library is full of big, plush chairs." "There are nice views," too. "The school is bursting at the seams in terms of space," however, and "The campus is, to some degree, stranded." You can't just walk out of the library and immediately get whatever you need.

ALAN GUERRERO, DIRECTOR OF ADMISSIONS
2130 FULTON STREET, SAN FRANCISCO, CA 94117
TEL: 415-422-6586 FAX: 415-422-6433
E-MAIL: LAWADMISSIONS@USFCA.EDU • WEBSITE: WWW.LAW.USFCA.EDU

Life

USF School of Law is home to a "really ethnically and culturally diverse student body." "There is diversity in terms of age, work experience, country of origin, ambitions, sense of humor, and facial hair," reports a 3L. "There is diversity in political opinion, too: liberal to very liberal." Students describe themselves as "courageous, inspiring, and intelligent." They're "friendly and happy." There's a "low level of misery in the student body," as well. "There are no jerks here." It's also "a very tightly knit community." "This compact campus doesn't afford many opportunities for anonymity," explains a 3L. "You can't help but see your classmates and professors regularly."

Life outside the classroom is vigorous. "Extracurricular activities are plentiful." The school brings "many reputable speakers to campus," and "There are lots of free lunches and events that make school less stressful." "Weekly Thursday night bar nights" are also well-attended. The City by the Bay is "one of the best cities in the world." You can watch the sunset over the Golden Gate Bridge while reading case law, and "You've got every-thing that San Francisco and the Bay Area have to offer" to take up your free time. "Public transportation is really accessible," and restaurants, nightlife, and culture are world class. The privilege will cost you, though. The "cost of living in San Francisco can be pretty steep."

Getting In

Admitted students at the 25th percentile have LSAT scores of approximately 155, and undergraduate GPAs just higher than 3.0. At the 75th percentile, LSAT scores are a little higher than 160, and GPAs are about 3.6.

ADMISSIONS

Selectivity Rating	83
# applications received	3,391
% applicants accepted	37
% acceptees attending	18
Average LSAT	158
LSAT Range	155–160
Average undergrad GPA	3.41
Application fee	$60
Regular application	Rolling, up to 2/1
Regular notification	Rolling
Early application program	No
Transfer students accepted	Yes
Evening division offered	Yes
Part-time accepted	Yes
CAS accepted	Yes

International Students

TOEFL required of international students	

FINANCIAL FACTS

Annual tuition	$37,230
Books and supplies	$1,500
Fees	$80
Room and board (on/off campus)	$14,500/ $13,500
Financial aid application deadline	2/15
% first-year students receiving some sort of aid	92
% receiving some sort of aid	90
% of aid that is merit based	15
% receiving scholarships	30
Average grant	$10,950
Average loan	$30,216
Average total aid package	$24,000
Average debt	$92,500

EMPLOYMENT INFORMATION

Career Rating	85
Rate of placement (nine months out)	90
Average starting salary	$85,945
State for bar exam	CA, FL, NY, TX,
Pass rate for first-time bar	81

Employers Who Frequently Hire Grads

Bingham & McCutcheon; Morgan, Lewis & Brockius; Reed Smith; Wilson, Sonsini, Goodrich & Rosati; Legislative Counsel; San Francisco Superior Court; Alameda County District Attorney and Public Defender Offices; San Francisco County District Attorney and Public Defender Offices; Townsend & Townsend & Crew LLP; Gordon & Rees; Hanson Bridgett Marcus Vlahos & Rudy; Folger, Levin & Kahn; Nixon Peabody

Prominent Alumni

Justice Ming Chin, CA Supreme Court; Judge Martin Jenkins, U.S. District Court Northern California; Judge Saundra B. Armstrong, U.S. District Court Northern California; John Burton, Retired President Pro Tem, California State Senate; Marjorie Scardino, CEO Pearson PLC

Grads Employed by Field (%)

Academic (16)
Business/industry (16)
Government (6)
Judicial clerkship (3)
Military (1)
Private practice (55)
Public interest (4)

University of South Carolina

School of Law

INSTITUTIONAL INFORMATION

Public/private	Public
Student/faculty ratio	15:1
% faculty female	45
% faculty minority	9
Total faculty	45

SURVEY SAYS...

Diverse opinions accepted in classrooms, Great library staff

STUDENTS

Enrollment of law school	706
% male/female	58/42
% from out-of-state	23
% full-time	100
% minority	10
% international	1
# of countries represented	6
Average age of entering class	25

ACADEMICS

Academic Experience Rating	**74**
Profs interesting rating	76
Profs accessible rating	74
Hours of study per day	4.44

Advanced Degrees Offered

JD, 3 years

Combined Degrees Offered

Master of Accountancy, Master of Criminology and Criminal Justice, Master of Earth and Environmental Resource Management, Master of Economics, Master of Studies in Environmental Law and Policy (with Vermont Law School), Master of Health Services Policy & Management, Master of Human Resources, International Master of Business Administration, Master of Mass Communication, MPA, MSW, 4 years

Academics

In terms of location, the University of South Carolina School of Law features something of a trifecta. It's situated on the campus of the state's flagship university, in the state's largest city, and in the state capital "near the state house and all of the courts." Academic highlights here include a "plethora of journals and extracurricular activities," a smorgasbord of joint-degree options, and an extensive pro bono program that provides "a great way to make contacts." Five clinics cover criminal practice, consumer bankruptcy, federal litigation, nonprofit organizations, and veterans' rights. Children's law externships allow students to represent litigants in family court and work on various child welfare and juvenile matters. There's also a very cool study abroad program in London that takes place for three weeks in May, as well as a separate foreign practice externship that allows students to work for three weeks at a law firm in London.

Students at USC generally rave about their "all-star faculty." A few older professors are just "going through the motions" at this point, but most faculty members are "enthusiastic about teaching and very knowledgeable about the course material." They are "excellent teachers who take their teaching duties very seriously." "The school's faculty is its biggest asset," beams a 3L. "Professors truly care for students," and they are "willing to move mountains for you." Student views concerning the administration clash pretty dramatically. According to one faction of students, management is "horrible." There's "a lack of communication," they say. Registration can be "an absolute madhouse." They could go on and on. Others tell us that the deans are "accommodating" and the staff is "very approachable and eager to assist students." The attitude of the administration is very hands off," explains a 2L, "which I mean as a compliment. The students are treated like professionals and expected to take care of themselves."

Without question, the facilities are the biggest source of dissatisfaction among students at USC Law. Technology really isn't that bad and the "very respectable" library houses one of the largest collections of legal information in the Southeast. However, virtually everything else is reportedly "old and deteriorating." The school "keeps saying it's going to get a new building" but nothing has materialized to supplant the "dark, windowless, ugly place" where students currently must spend their semesters. Classrooms "were modernized in the 1970s." "There are gaping holes in the ceiling." "The building is absolutely disgusting," assesses a 2L. "At this very moment, I am sitting below a ceiling tile that is covered in mold and dripping."

Career-wise, "USC is the law school in South Carolina." If you want to practice in the Palmetto State, there's really no better place to be. "Ties with alumni" and firms of all sizes around the state are strong. At the same time, this school is not necessarily the place to be if you want to practice somewhere else. "Almost everything taught—or provided via Career Services—is exclusive for South Carolina," counsels a 3L. Upon graduation, about two-thirds of the students here take jobs in the private sector. Also, a very large chunk takes the judicial clerkship route.

LEWIS L. HUTCHISON, JR., ASSISTANT DEAN FOR ADMISSIONS
701 SOUTH MAIN STREET, COLUMBIA, SC 29208
TEL: 803-777-6605 FAX: 803-777-7751
E-MAIL: USCLAW@LAW.SC.EDU • WEBSITE: WWW.LAW.SC.EDU

Life

Students are "very driven to do well and work very hard." Most of them hail from South Carolina. Most out-of-state students are from nearby Southern states. Ethnic minorities make up about twelve percent of the population. "While generally the students are conservative, there is enough diversity of political beliefs and backgrounds for almost anyone to find their niche," promises a 1L. "There are lots of liberals in the student body" and Columbia is, "almost without question, the most liberal place in South Carolina (for whatever that's worth)."

Students "get along very well" and "camaraderie is great." The academic atmosphere is "collegial." "The students treat each other with kindness and respect no matter where they stand on the law school hierarchy." "We all help each other out and share notes," adds a 1L. The "stellar" social environment "can be characterized as open-armed Southern hospitality in an academic setting." "The students are, without a doubt, the best thing about this law school," proclaims a 3L. "I was afraid when I came to law school I would run into some ultra-competitive, private-school-since-first-grade, never-been-to-a-real-party group of students but that has not been my experience at all," agrees a relieved 1L. "We go out on the weekends, go to sporting events, study together-things that I was terrified wouldn't happen." Beyond the law school orbit, hometown Columbia is temperate and very affordable. It's also very much a college town with a "big university feel" and "a number of bars."

Getting In

Getting into USC Law isn't easy. Admitted students at the 25th percentile have LSAT scores around 156 and undergraduate grade point averages a little over 3.0. At the 75th percentile, LSAT scores are right at 161 and GPAs are approximately 3.6.

Clinical program required	No
Legal writing course requirement	Yes
Legal methods course requirement	No
Legal research course requirement	Yes
Moot court requirement	No
Public interest law requirement	No

ADMISSIONS

Selectivity Rating	86
# applications received	2,185
% applicants accepted	34
% acceptees attending	32
LSAT Range	156–161
Application fee	$60
Regular application	Rolling, up to 4/1
Regular notification	Rolling
Early application program	No
Transfer students accepted	Yes
Evening division offered	No
Part-time accepted	No
CAS accepted	Yes

International Students

TOEFL required of international students

FINANCIAL FACTS

Annual tuition (in-state/out-of-state)	$19,836/ $40,094
Books and supplies	$936
Fees	$400
Room and board	$11,661
Financial aid application deadline	4/1
% receiving scholarships	53
Average grant	$12,198
Average debt	$75,718

EMPLOYMENT INFORMATION

Career Rating	77
Rate of placement (nine months out)	88
Average starting salary	$55,000
State for bar exam	SC, NC, GA, FL
Pass rate for first-time bar	82

Employers Who Frequently Hire Grads
Nelson Mullins Riley & Scarborough; Alston & Bird; Haynsworth Sinkler Boyd; Nexsen Pruet; Womble Carlyle Sandridge & Rice

Prominent Alumni
Richard W. Riley, Former U.S. Secretary of Education; Lindsey Graham, U.S. Senate; Karen J. Williams, 4th Circuit Court of Appeals; Joe Wilson, U.S. Congress; Jean Hoefer Toal, Chief Justice of South Carolina Supreme Court

Grads Employed by Field (%)
Academic (2)
Business/industry (9)
Government (13)
Judicial clerkship (21)
Military (5)
Private practice (35)
Public interest (3)

THE UNIVERSITY OF SOUTH DAKOTA
SCHOOL OF LAW

INSTITUTIONAL INFORMATION

Public/private	Public
Student/faculty ratio	13:1
% faculty female	31
% faculty minority	1
Total faculty	13

SURVEY SAYS...

Diverse opinions accepted in classrooms, Great library staff

STUDENTS

Enrollment of law school	205
% male/female	54/46
% full-time	99
% minority	7
Average age of entering class	27

ACADEMICS

Academic Experience Rating	71
Profs interesting rating	80
Profs accessible rating	73
Hours of study per day	4.65

Academic Specialties

Environmental, Indian Law

Combined Degrees Offered

JD/MBA, JD/MPA(Professional Accountancy, JD/M Education Administration, JD/M English, JD/M History, JD/M Pol Sci, JD/M Public Administration), JD/M Psychology, JD/M Administrative Studies

Clinical program required	No
Legal writing course requirement	Yes
Legal methods course requirement	Yes
Legal research course requirement	Yes
Moot court requirement	No
Public interest law requirement	No

Academics

The University of South Dakota School of Law is a tiny place that provides "a great education at a great value." In addition to a decent number of joint-degree programs available, there's a host of curricular tracks, as well as specializations in Indian law and natural resources and environmental law. Students can also get involved in a handful of interesting public interest centers and projects. Otherwise, the curriculum doesn't boast a lot of bells and whistles, and "The frequency with which some of the more obscure electives are offered" is low. The setting is intimate, though, and "There are numerous opportunities to gain hands-on experience even in the first year."

At USD, "You know everyone and your professors know you." Few upper-level courses enroll more than twenty-five students. "With the number of people in each year only around seventy-five," notes a 1L, "it's hard to have more than that many people in the biggest lecture." Professors are "very well-versed in the area of law they teach" and receive generally excellent reviews. "A few are terrible," but most are "friendly" and "invested in their students." It's "very easy to get one-on-one attention" outside of class, and professors are "very much involved with the student population, including social activities outside of school." The "accessible" administration is "great to work with" as well. "If you haven't chatted with the deans over a meal by the end of the first week," notes a 1L, "you must be pretty evasive." "The greatest strength of our law school is that it is a small-town atmosphere," beams a wistful 3L. "The teachers know the students and are always inquiring about their lives. They want to be there to help in whatever manner they can possibly serve."

The bar passage rate is very high here, and USD's position as the only school in the state that offers a law degree is certainly beneficial. "The school has a good rapport with local attorneys and judges," so there are "a lot of opportunities to meet important people." "South Dakota Supreme Court justices pop in now and again." At least once a year, it's on official business, as the school hosts the court's March term each year. Oral arguments are presented right in the USD's courtroom. Many students are positive about their employment prospects after graduation. Others aren't as confident, however, and wish for "better Career Services."

On the whole, the facilities here are a little depressing. "They went a touch heavy on concrete during construction," appraises a 2L. The building was "built with form and function much higher on the priority list than aesthetics," and it "just isn't as pretty as the other buildings on campus." Inside, the classrooms are serviceable, but "outdated." However, "There are outlets and internet hook-ups at every seat making laptop use very easy." "The research facilities are adequate," but "The library cannot compete with larger schools," and there could be more study carrels. On the plus side, law students can access the library twenty-four hours a day.

Life

Attending law school at USD is a little bit like existing in a fishbowl, but students tell us that the advantages definitely outweigh the hardships. "There is definitely the feel that you are being evaluated and sized up against one another," but students are generally "helpful," and the nice and cozy atmosphere "is invaluable for the 1L experience." The environment is very communal and fraternal. "The nice thing is everyone knows everybody, and the bad thing is everybody knows everybody," explains a 2L. "Everyone finds their niche, though, whether it is with a co-curricular or a social group, so really it's not that different from the real world."

JEAN HENRIQUES, ADMISSION OFFICER/REGISTRAR
414 EAST CLARK STREET, VERMILLION, SD 57069-2390
TEL: 605-677-5444 FAX: 605-677-5417
E-MAIL: LAW.@USD.EDU • WEBSITE: WWW.USD.EDU/LAW

The surrounding town of Vermillion is "located in the far southeast corner of the state." It's pretty rural, and the weather in the winter can be brutal. Vermillion is also home to the larger University of South Dakota, which provides some energy and cultural flair. Overall, though, you won't find a slew of distractions around here, which isn't necessarily ideal for a rich social life but is very ideal when you want to focus on reading case law.

Getting In

Admission to USD is moderately competitive. The grades of incoming students are much more impressive that the LSAT scores. Admitted students at the 25th percentile have LSAT scores around 150 and undergraduate GPAs close to 3.2. At the 75th percentile, LSAT scores are about 156, and GPAs are just higher than 3.7. The Law Screening Program offers applicants an opportunity to prove themselves.

ADMISSIONS

Selectivity Rating	69
# applications received	449
% applicants accepted	49
% acceptees attending	34
Average LSAT	151
LSAT Range	149–154
Average undergrad GPA	3.37
Application fee	$35
Regular application	Rolling, up to 5/1
Regular notification	Rolling
Early application program	No
Transfer students accepted	Yes
Evening division offered	No
Part-time accepted	Yes
CAS accepted	Yes

International Students

TOEFL required of international students

FINANCIAL FACTS

Annual tuition (in-state/out-of-state)	$5,664/ $16,416
Books and supplies	$1,400
Fees	$5,544
Room and board (on/off campus)	$5,438/ $7,262
% first-year students receiving some sort of aid	87
% receiving some sort of aid	90
% of aid that is merit based	90
% receiving scholarships	26
Average grant	$3,013
Average loan	$22,580
Average total aid package	$22,345
Average debt	$71,730

EMPLOYMENT INFORMATION

Career Rating	63
Rate of placement (nine months out)	86
Average starting salary	$44,343
State for bar exam	SD, IA, NE, CO
Pass rate for first-time bar	97

Employers Who Frequently Hire Grads

U.S. Eighth Circuit Court of Appeals; U.S. District Court; South Dakota Supreme Court; South Dakota Circuit Court; Minnehaha Public Defender, Firms, Minnesota State District Courts, Iowa State District Courts, Higher Education Administration, Investment Banking Institution, Technology/E-Commerce Company, Accounting Firm, Federal Agencies, Tribal Government, Public Interest Legal Services

Prominent Alumni

Tim Johnson, U.S. Senator; David Gilbertson, Chief Justice, SD Supreme Ct; Judith Meierhenry, Justice, SD Supreme Court; Thomas J. Erickson, Past Commissioner, U.S. Commodity Futures Trading Commis; Roger Wollman, U.S. Court of Appeals for the 8th Circuit

Grads Employed by Field (%)

Academic (5)
Business/industry (14)
Government (7)
Judicial clerkship (25)
Private practice (36)
Public interest (5)

UNIVERSITY OF SOUTHERN CALIFORNIA
GOULD SCHOOL OF LAW

Academics

Many students come to USC's Gould School of Law for "the weather," but all end up "staying for the professors" and "friendly student body." The faculty here is highly praised as being "very approachable" as well as "brilliant and engaging." "[They're] some of the brightest professors I've ever had," says a 2L. "They strike the right balance between learning the material and making sure we stay interested and involved throughout the course." This enthusiasm extends even to those unhappy with their studies. "I hate law school, but I adore USC," says a 3L. "USC has made what could have been an absolutely nightmarish three years into a tolerable and occasionally even fun experience. Our students are brilliant, funny, and strange. Our professors are either unapologetically academic or real, live working attorneys with loads of hilarious horror stories and practical advice...When you join USC, you join it forever. And that's a good thing. Everyone is miserable in law school, but at least here, you can be miserable together." Students admit that while "there may be the typical 'red tape'" when dealing with the administration, the school "wants everyone to succeed" and offers "many resources to help students along." "The administration is very impressive and accessible," says a 1L. "They are supportive of students making the transition to law school." Some find that while being "very organized," the administration can "often treat students like they're children," but overall, if students are willing to "ask for help," the "school administration takes [their] concerns very seriously."

Most professors are "very influenced by the Law and Economics movement," meaning that "there aren't many alternative theoretical perspectives presented convincingly, but they are very good at what they do." Some students would like to see "more emphasis on teaching practical skills in the practical skills courses," as well as "higher-quality professors for some of the big, basic bar classes." Others wouldn't mind more "criminal law" courses. "There is currently only one trial advocacy course and no mock trial opportunities," says a 2L. "Also, there is too much focus on firm practice, with much less attention given to students who aren't interested in working for a large firm." The issue of Big Firm versus Public Interest careers is a contentious one at USC Law—many feel that the school "puts too much of a focus on entering the big firm marketplace," while another majority feels that the school "encourages students to go into public interest." "I know more people who are going into public interest and governmental positions than working in big law firms," says a 3L.

It's no secret that jobs can be scarce in the current economic climate; however, students find that "the location and reputation of the school are an invaluable asset" when job hunting. That said, many students aren't so impressed with the Career Services department. As one 2L explains, "I'm not 100 percent sold on the effectiveness of the Career Center—it feels like our awesome alumni connections makes them complacent." On the upside, the office "keeps a constant supply of coffee and hot chocolate," and at least one student says the "career service people played an essential role in my employment."

Despite being located on a "beautiful campus," the law building is "outdated" and "unimpressive." "Most of the classrooms are less than aesthetically inspiring, and are, at times, technologically awkward (as in, plugging in your laptop into the sockets under the tops of desks can bring you dangerously close to violating your neighbor's very personal space)," explains a 1L. Fortunately, students can find a more pleasant atmosphere and some nice places to eat at the brand new Tutor Campus Center, located just a stone's throw from the law school. Plus, "Plans for a new building [are] in the works." "Meetings have already been held with students regarding elements they want to see, and plenty of windows and a 'less sucky' wireless Internet have been promised," says a 2L. And there's more good news: USC is "getting a metro stop!"

Life

USC Law doesn't just boast a "competitive, yet modest and cooperative student body," but a "community" otherwise known as "the Trojan Family." "A lot of emphasis is placed on a sense of camaraderie and that we are all in this together," says a 2L. "My experience at USC could not be further from those law school horror stories regarding competition…Students routinely share each others' notes and outlines without a second thought." The "great" student population is "on the younger side," but "an amazing social life" is the result. Students are also "very diverse," and "every student has an interesting background and a different view because of it."

Thanks to its "tight-knit, family-like atmosphere," social opportunities "abound for more outgoing students," but "less socially active students still have a place as well." By all accounts, the bar reviews, often held at "top Hollywood hotspots," are "extremely well-attended," which, according to some, can lead to "lots of intermingling among the law students." However, it's estimated that "outside of the weekly bar reviews," a "good eighty percent of the people at the law school never really see Los Angeles." "It's like pulling teeth trying to get people at the law school to do anything that doesn't involve the chance for alcohol or food (preferably both), which is actually pretty sad, considering the amazing things that Los Angeles has to offer," says a 2L. Though being in Los Angeles is "great," the "area around USC is a bit sketch." But, "once you get over the traffic" and seek out the "diverse, large, and exciting city" of Los Angeles, "You'll never find yourself at a lack of things to do."

Getting In

Recently admitted students at USC Law at the 25th percentile have LSAT scores of 166 and GPAs in the 3.47 range. Admitted students at the 75th percentile have LSAT scores of 169 and GPAs of roughly 3.73.

Political Science, 4 years; JD/Master of Real Estate Development, 3.5 years; JD/PhD in Economics, JD/PHD California Institute of Technology, JD/PHD in Political Science, 5 years

Clinical program required	No
Legal writing course requirement	Yes
Legal methods course requirement	No
Legal research course requirement	Yes
Moot court requirement	No
Public interest law requirement	No

ADMISSIONS

Selectivity Rating	**94**
# applications received	6,587
% applicants accepted	22
% acceptees attending	15
Average LSAT	167
LSAT Range	165–169
Average undergrad GPA	3.64
Application fee	$75
Regular notification	Rolling
Early application program	No
Transfer students accepted	Yes
Evening division offered	No
Part-time accepted	No
CAS accepted	Yes

International Students

TOEFL recommended of international students

FINANCIAL FACTS

Annual tuition	$48,434
Books and supplies	$1,990
Fees	$1,362
Room and board (on/off campus)	$15,700/ $12,214
Financial aid application deadline	3/2
% first-year students receiving some sort of aid	84
% receiving some sort of aid	88
% of aid that is merit based	25
% receiving scholarships	60
Average grant	$14,000
Average loan	$39,000
Average total aid package	$70,000
Average debt	$118,000

EMPLOYMENT INFORMATION

Career Rating   **96**
Rate of placement (nine months out)   98
Average starting salary $125,000
State for bar exam   CA, NY, D.C., WA, TX
Pass rate for first-time bar   90

Employers Who Frequently Hire Grads
Private firms, corporations, federal judges, government and public interest nonprofits

Prominent Alumni
Justice Joyce Kennard, California Supreme Court; Amy Trask, General Manager, Oakland Raiders; Judge Dorothy Nelson, Ninth U.S. Circuit Court of Appeals; Walter Zifkin, CEO of William Morris Agency; Carlos Moorehead, U.S. Congressman

Grads Employed by Field (%)
Academic (3)
Business/industry (7)
Government (6)
Judicial clerkship (8)
Private practice (72)
Public interest (3)

University of St. Thomas
School of Law

INSTITUTIONAL INFORMATION

Public/private	Private
Affiliation	Roman Catholic
Student/faculty ratio	15:1
% faculty part-time	68
% faculty female	32
% faculty minority	13
Total faculty	82

SURVEY SAYS...

Beautiful campus, Students love Minneapolis, MN

STUDENTS

Enrollment of law school	475
% male/female	56/44
% from out-of-state	44
% full-time	100
% minority	12
Average age of entering class	25

ACADEMICS

Academic Experience Rating	**75**
Profs interesting rating	94
Profs accessible rating	92
Hours of study per day	4.65

Combined Degrees Offered

Five joint-degree programs with College of Business (JD/MBA), Catholic Studies (JD/MA); Public Policy (JD/MA); Professional Psychology (JD/MA); Social Work (JD/MSW), all about 4 years

Clinical program required	No
Legal writing course requirement	Yes
Legal methods course requirement	No
Legal research course requirement	Yes
Moot court requirement	No
Public interest law requirement	Yes

Academics

The University of St. Thomas School of Law is a "small," "relatively new," and steadfastly Catholic bastion of legal education in downtown Minneapolis with an "intense" legal writing program and a "strong focus on doing the right thing over the profitable thing." A Catholic mass is held every weekday in UST Law's chapel, and the trappings of faith are very visible. At the same time, students are quick to call attention to the fact that "the curriculum is not permeated with dogma." "You can't go to St. Thomas and completely miss the fact that it's a Catholic law school," relates a 1L, "but, after the first week, it's fairly easy not to notice it anymore." You probably will notice the "commitment to public interest law" and the "emphasis on public service," though, because students here are required to perform at least fifty hours of community service work before graduation. The biggest complaint among students at UST Law is that "the diversity of available classes leaves something to be desired relative to larger schools." "Quite literally, there are some upper-level classes that you might only get one shot at taking while in law school because they are offered so infrequently," though the school does participate in a consortium with three other nearby law schools, which allows for students to cross-register for classes not offered at their own school.

In addition to the required service hours, there's a "unique," innovative, and mandatory mentor externship program that "allows for networking from the outset." Students pair up an attorney or judge in the area "to shadow intermittently throughout the year." Employment prospects are solid. Students say that "the school has developed a great reputation in the Minneapolis–St. Paul area in a short amount of time." The budding alumni community is "extremely supportive." However, "There is not a strong alumni network" because the school hasn't been around that long. "It still needs to build its reputation for job placement." "I feel like right now we are a well-kept secret," laments a 2L, "a great, new law school that no one knows about." Most students seem more optimistic, though. "I think our credibility in the community is growing," says a 3L. "More and more of our graduates are landing top clerkships and jobs."

The administration here is full of "exceptionally responsive" and "effective managers and organizers." The "eccentric and eclectic" faculty is full of "engaging," "kind," and "extremely personable" professors who "come from diverse geographic and legal backgrounds, yet share a common passion for teaching." "They are remarkable educators and interesting and down-to-earth people." Professors are "visible, available, and approachable" outside of class as well. "Their office doors line the hallways," and e-mails are answered promptly.

The "bright and welcoming" facilities at St. Thomas are "impressive architecturally and comfortable for late night studying." "There's natural light through the whole building, which is therapeutic during long Minnesota winters." "The technology in the classroom is top-of-the-line." The library is also excellent. "It's big enough never to be overcrowded, but yet small enough to not get lost in." The school is also "blocks away" from a bevy of Minneapolis firms, and it "provides skyway access most everywhere," "which is especially great to avoid the cold weather." "Taking study breaks and getting to the coffee shop is a breeze."

CARI HAALAND, ASSISTANT DEAN FOR ADMISSIONS
1000 LASALLE AV, MSL 124, MINNEAPOLIS, MN 55403
TEL: (651) 962-4895 FAX: (651) 962-4876
E-MAIL: LAWSCHOOL@STTHOMAS.EDU • WEBSITE: WWW.STTHOMAS.EDU/LAW

Life

UST Law could "be a lot more diverse" ethnically and otherwise. Nevertheless, "There is an incredible sense of community" among the students here as well as a "sense of building something great." The academic atmosphere includes "a healthy level of competition." "There are a few gunners who'd probably throw you under the bus," admits a 2L, "but they are outnumbered by the nice, fun, and not-super-high-strung students." Mostly, "People are extremely cooperative in class, often sharing notes and ideas with people who need them before they are requested." "The culture is so inclusive and congenial that I wouldn't want to be anywhere else," gushes a 1L. "You always have someone to go to," adds a 3L, "whether it is a fellow student, professor, or administrative personnel."

"Discussions about morality, particularly morality in the law, happen in and out of classrooms," and there's a reasonably thriving social scene. "A weekend does not go by where I am not made aware of three or four separate events that the students have organized to hang out with each other," observes a 1L. Students also tell us, "It is tough to beat the location in the heart of downtown Minneapolis," "within walking distance of" virtually anything you need. "A downtown atmosphere without the big-city feel is the perfect atmosphere for a law school," enthuses a 3L.

Getting In

Admitted students at the 25th percentile have LSAT scores in the mid 150s and undergraduate GPAs close to 3.0. At the 75th percentile, LSAT scores are just higher than 160, and GPAs are about 3.5.

ADMISSIONS

Selectivity Rating	76
# applications received	1,801
% applicants accepted	51
% acceptees attending	18
Average LSAT	157
LSAT Range	154–161
Average undergrad GPA	3.21
Application fee	$0
Regular application	Rolling, up to 8/15
Regular notification	Rolling
Early application program	No
Transfer students accepted	Yes
Evening division offered	No
Part-time accepted	No
CAS accepted	Yes

International Students

TOEFL required of international students

FINANCIAL FACTS

Annual tuition	$36,022
Books and supplies	$1,600
Fees	$290
Room and board	$16,695
Financial aid application deadline	7/1
% first-year students receiving some sort of aid	94
% receiving some sort of aid	93
% of aid that is merit based	100
% receiving scholarships	58
Average grant	$21,405
Average loan	$35,952
Average total aid package	$44,779
Average debt	$97,327

EMPLOYMENT INFORMATION

Career Rating	80
Rate of placement (nine months out)	86
Average starting salary	$54,600
State for bar exam	MN, WI, CA, CO, AZ
Pass rate for first-time bar	91

Employers Who Frequently Hire Grads

Faegre & Benson Robins, Kaplan, Miller & Ciresi Dorsey & Whitney LLP Southern Minnesota Regional Legal Services Target Corporation State of Minnesota Hennepin County

Prominent Alumni

Jake Schunk, Trial Attorney, United States Department of Justice; Erin Collins, Law Clerk, The Honorable Diana E. Murphy, U.S. Court of Appeals for the Eighth Circuit; Joel Schroeder, Associate, Faegre & Benson, LLP; Marie K. O'Leary, Associate at the International Criminal Tribunal for the former Yugoslavia; Katie Tinucci, Press Secretary, Minnesota Governor Mark Dayton

Grads Employed by Field (%)

Academic (4)
Business/industry (22)
Government (8)
Judicial clerkship (10)
Military (2)
Private practice (31)
Public interest (7)

THE UNIVERSITY OF TENNESSEE
COLLEGE OF LAW

INSTITUTIONAL INFORMATION

Public/private	Public
Student/faculty ratio	13:1
% faculty part-time	58
% faculty female	39
% faculty minority	4
Total faculty	105

SURVEY SAYS...
Great research resources,
Beautiful campus

STUDENTS

Enrollment of law school	482
% male/female	57/43
% from out-of-state	16
% full-time	100
% minority	25
% international	1
# of countries represented	5
Average age of entering class	25

ACADEMICS

Academic Experience Rating	87
Profs interesting rating	84
Profs accessible rating	87
Hours of study per day	5.05

Academic Specialties
Business Transactions, Advocacy and Dispute Resolutions

Advanced Degrees Offered
JD, 3 years (6 semesters)

Combined Degrees Offered
JD/MBA, 4 years; JD/MPA, 4 years

Clinical program required	No
Legal writing	
course requirement	Yes
Legal methods	
course requirement	Yes
Legal research	
course requirement	Yes
Moot court requirement	No
Public interest	
law requirement	No

Academics

Affordable, practical, and blessed with a touch of Southern charm, the University of Tennessee is a friendly place to study the law and to learn to be a lawyer. Across the board, UT students praise their school's unequivocal "emphasis on practical and 'real' lawyering instead of just philosophical theory." The school's fleet of faculty is equipped with impressive real-world credentials, and "Several classrooms are laid out exactly like courtrooms" to help students hone their litigation skills. In addition to the tenured staff, the "Adjunct professors for skills-based classes are a wonderful resource." UT students can further augment course work through the school's ample and long-standing clinical programs, which teach lawyering skills through real-world experience, including a pro bono clinic for indigent clients. They can also pursue a specialization in advocacy through the Center for Advocacy and Dispute Resolution. While the practical offerings are outstanding, many students mention that they would like to see more diverse academic specializations. A student clarifies, "Classes in a wide number of specialties are available, but it wouldn't hurt to hire a few more professors to have more options available in a given semester. It would seem the school has taken a "quality-over-quantity" approach in this regard."

Although University of Tennessee is a stalwart Southern institution, "There are numerous professors that cater to a wide range of philosophical beliefs and legal theories ...from the far-left stereotypical 'academics' all the way to the right side with Instapundit.com creator Glenn Reynolds." A stimulating academic atmosphere, "The class discussions that ensue between such a faculty and the geographically and academically diverse student body are most rewarding." The notorious Socratic method remains a classroom favorite; however, it's never used to torture or embarrass. Rather, it "is a tool to encourage learning, and professors and students are seen as partners in that endeavor, as opposed to adversaries." Outside the classroom, "Teachers are willing to meet you after class and help you in anyway possible," and students reassure us, "There isn't a faculty member I would feel intimidated approaching." A satisfied student sums it up: "The laid-back attitude juxtaposed with expert instruction and the feeling that the UT College of Law, while already well-ranked, is one of the most underrated schools and is by all means a rising star among law schools nationwide."

When transitioning to the real world, UT grads are prepared to hit the ground running. A 3L shares: "I worked at a big New York firm last summer with several Ivy Leaguers. Everyone was very smart, but many of them were just as lost when it came to advocacy skills (namely trial practice and negotiation). What I learned at Tennessee gave me an opportunity to shine in these areas." Another 3L chimes in, "I have a great job in Atlanta after graduation. When I was clerking down there this summer, I really enjoyed surprising people with how well-prepared I am to practice." On that note, career placement is no problem for UT grads—especially those looking to work in the South; however, generally speaking, "The Career Services Center is geared toward students who want to practice in Tennessee or in big law firms elsewhere. Other career options are usually up to the students to pursue."

Life

The UT campus is a pleasant place for work and play, and students admit, "The beautiful classrooms and library make coming to school a lot easier." In and out of the classroom, "The majority of students are very friendly and cooperative," and most strike a good balance between recreation and study. To burn some calories and blow off steam,

Dr. Karen R. Britton, Director of Admissions and Financial Aid
Director, The Betty B. Lewis Career Center
1505 West Cumberland Avenue, Suite 161, Knoxville, TN 37996-1810
Tel: 865-974-4131 Fax: 865-974-1572
E-Mail: lawadmit@utk.edu • Website: www.law.utk.edu

there are "law school teams in several of the intramural sports leagues on campus." When its time for a study break, there is a social event for almost every night of the week in Knoxville, a first-rate college town, boasting "a good music scene, an independent film theater, and lots of local festivals." Law students get together for "mixers every Thursday, bowling every Monday in the spring semester, and tailgates every Saturday in the fall." In addition to the weekly gatherings at local watering holes, the school sponsors many special events including "the yearly Halloween party called Chilla" and the enticing (or so students assure us) Learned Hand Bowling League. Within this tight-knit community, "Even if you don't go out every night you still develop good friendships with your peers."

Despite the social vibe, a student admits, "We have had some racial tension. We are trying to work on it and have less social segregation." Another student adds this perspective: "There are different social circles, but it is natural that people with common interests will be drawn to one another. On the whole, I feel that we have active and amiable community here."

Getting In

UT received more than 1,400 applications for an entering class of about 150 students. Undergraduate GPA and LSAT scores are important to an admissions decision; however, the school also considers qualitative factors including strength of undergraduate institution, extracurricular activities, and professional experience. The school has no minimum LSAT requirement; however, seventy-five percent of the entering class had an LSAT score 161 or lower, and twenty-five percent had an LSAT score of 157 or lower. Tennessee residents made up more than seventy percent of entering students.

ADMISSIONS

Selectivity Rating	89
# applications received	1,508
% applicants accepted	27
% acceptees attending	41
Average LSAT	159
LSAT Range	156–162
Average undergrad GPA	3.58
Application fee	$15
Regular application	Rolling
Regular notification	Rolling
Early application program	No
Transfer students accepted	Yes
Evening division offered	No
Part-time accepted	No
CAS accepted	Yes

International Students

TOEFL required of international students

FINANCIAL FACTS

Annual tuition	
(in-state/out-of-state)	$12,540/ $30,984
Books and supplies	$1,792
Fees	
(in-state/out-of-state)	$1,922/ $2,222
Room and board	$10,550
Financial aid application deadline	3/1
Average grant	$5,774
Average loan	$24,831
Average total aid package	$35,458
Average debt	$65,082

EMPLOYMENT INFORMATION

Career Rating	82
Rate of placement (nine months out)	90
Average starting salary	$65,300
State for bar exam	TN
Pass rate for first-time bar	88

Employers Who Frequently Hire Grads

Legal employers, law firms, judges, government agencies, corporations, public interest organizations, and academic institutions–nationwide

Prominent Alumni

The Honorable Howard H. Baker, Jr., Former U.S. Ambassador to Japan and former U.S. Senator, Tennessee; The Honorable Saxby Chambliss, U.S. Senator, Georgia; James L. Clayton, Chairman, Clayton Bank and Trust; Founder and Former CEO, Clayton Homes and Vanderbilt Mortgage and Finance; Wendy H. Goggin, Chief Counsel, U.S. Drug Enforcement Agency; Joel A. Katz, Founding Shareholder; Chair, Global Media and Entertainment Practice, Greenberg Traurig LLC, Atlanta; Lowry F. Kline, Chairman and CEO (Retired), Coca-Cola Enterprises; The Honorable Sharon Lee, Justice, Tennessee Supreme Court; The Honorable Gary Wade, Justice, Tennessee Supreme Court; Robert Alderson, CEO, Kirkland's, Inc.; James F. Hall, Former Chair, National Transportation Safety Board

Grads Employed by Field (%)

Academic (4)
Business/industry (12)
Government (13)
Judicial clerkship (11)
Military (3)
Private practice (53)
Public interest (4)

THE UNIVERSITY OF TEXAS AT AUSTIN
SCHOOL OF LAW

INSTITUTIONAL INFORMATION

Public/private	Public
Student/faculty ratio	11:1
% faculty part-time	46
% faculty female	37
% faculty minority	2
Total faculty	205

SURVEY SAYS...

Great library staff, Abundant externship/internship/clerkship opportunities, Students love Austin, TX

STUDENTS

Enrollment of law school	1,133
% male/female	53/47
% from out-of-state	24
% full-time	100
% minority	27
% international	1
# of countries represented	18
Average age of entering class	24

ACADEMICS

Academic Experience Rating	**88**
Profs interesting rating	86
Profs accessible rating	80
Hours of study per day	3.17

Academic Specialties

Commercial, Constitutional, Corporation Securities, Criminal, Environmental, International, Labor, Legal Philosophy, Property, Taxation, Intellectual Property

Advanced Degrees Offered

LLM, 1 year; LLM in Global Energy, International Arbitration and Environmental Law; LLM Latin American and International Law

Combined Degrees Offered

JD/MBA; JD/MPA; JD/MA in Latin American Studies; JD/MS in Community and Regional Planning; JD/MA in Russian, East European, European Studies; JD/MA in Middle Eastern Studies; JD/MSW; JD/Master of Global Policy Studies; JD/

Academics

Students at the University of Texas at Austin School of Law receive "the most bang for the buck in Texas" and a "great overall education." UT boasts a "huge network of alumni," a "focus on high-level analytical thinking," and a "diverse student body and faculty." Tuition is "relatively low," and graduates rack up very little debt. "I couldn't imagine a better law school as far as the quality of the professors," says one student. Another writes, "What I particularly appreciate is how they encourage us to try new areas of law. They show such enthusiasm and knowledge in the courses they teach that even the most boring or difficult course can be interesting and not so difficult after all." Another student brags, "In my first semester, I had the leading expert in admiralty law teach torts by singing songs on guitar, a contracts professor who could have been the stunt-double-professor in *The Paper Chase*, and a criminal law professor who clerked for Thurgood Marshall." Students praise the "writing program," "constitutional law instruction," and "great clinics" that include a mental health clinic, a capital punishment clinic, and an actual innocence clinic, in which students screen and investigate claims of innocence from prison inmates. "The legal research and writing program is undervalued and under-funded," reports one student. Others would like to see "bar preparation improved." "Public interest law" could use more "interest" too. Students note smaller classes "would be nice." On the plus side, though, "going to such a large law school [guarantees a] wide range of courses."

When the time comes to get a real job, "The academic reputation enjoyed by Texas is unsurpassed in this part of the country." Thanks to this, students have "many great opportunities for jobs, internships, and clerkships." Being "right in the middle of one of the nation's biggest legal markets," UT maintains a "strong presence in the business and law communit[es]," effectively providing "ample employment opportunities." If you want to get out of the Lone Star State, no problem: More than sixty percent of the employers who interview on campus are from other states. There are differing views on Career Services, with some students seeing them as focusing "too much on students that want to go into a big-firm environment," while others find them "open, helpful, [and] a valuable resource."

"The facilities are generally nice" at UT, though they "could use some updating." "The law school occupies an oddly cobbled together set of interconnected buildings representing a number of architectural styles," says one student. Unfortunately, "The older buildings were not built to accommodate the number of students that attend this law school—it can get quite crowded at times." The "pretty" and "wonderfully comprehensive" law library is one of the "largest in the country," thanks to the "generous donations of alumni." Students are pleased that "the school is complete with wireless Internet throughout."

Life

Is UT competitive? It depends on whom you ask. According to one school of thought, "A lot of kids are really tough, [and] competition among 1Ls can be fierce." Others tell us that UT doesn't have "competitive tension running throughout the student body" and that the school "does a good job of making it seem more like a family and a support network."

"Many political [and] social viewpoints are represented here," but lots of those viewpoints come from Texas. Most agree that the majority of students here were "born and raised in Texas." A student explains, "The saying that Texas is its own country and culture

Monica Ingram, Assistant Dean for Admissions and Financial Aid
727 East Dean Keeton Street, Austin, TX 78705-3299
Tel: 512-232-1200 Fax: 512-471-2765
E-Mail: admissions@law.utexas.edu • Website: www.utexas.edu/law

seems to be pretty accurate, [Yet despite] these negative impressions, I am falling in love with the charm of the area and may even stay here upon graduation." Students do add that the school "could improve by having more students with life and work experience."

Because the school's law student population "is so large, there's not a real feeling of camaraderie." Nevertheless, "The campus is very social" and "There's always something fun to do." "There are a wide variety of student organizations, from political or ethnic groups, to journals or practice-oriented organizations, to a hugely successful variety show written, produced, and performed by law students," a student explains. Students can take advantage of "tons of opportunities to do extracurricular things off campus" as well.

If there's one thing people agree on, it's that "Austin is a truly fascinating city with a bundle of outdoor activities, social life, and dining experiences."

Getting In

Admitted students at the 25th percentile have an LSAT score of 164 and a GPA of 3.57. Admitted students at the 75th percentile have an LSAT score of 169 and a GPA of 3.84. If you take the LSAT more than once, the school will consider all scores—not just the average of them. Note also that nonresident matriculation can only constitute thirty-five percent of the student body.

MIS; informal combined programs leading to JD/PhD in Government, History, or Philosophy

Clinical program required	No
Legal writing course requirement	Yes
Legal methods course requirement	No
Legal research course requirement	Yes
Moot court requirement	Yes
Public interest law requirement	No

ADMISSIONS

Selectivity Rating	95
# applications received	5,815
% applicants accepted	23
% acceptees attending	30
Average LSAT	167
LSAT Range	164–169
Average undergrad GPA	3.71
Application fee	$70
Regular notification	4/1
Early application program	Yes
Early application deadline	11/1
Early application notification	1/31
Transfer students accepted	Yes
Evening division offered	No
Part-time accepted	No
CAS accepted	Yes

FINANCIAL FACTS

Annual tuition (in-state/out-of-state)	$29,640/ $45,720
Books and supplies	$1,130
Room and board (on/off campus)	$10,112/ $10,250
Financial aid application deadline	3/15
% first-year students receiving some sort of aid	73
% receiving some sort of aid	76
% of aid that is merit based	65
% receiving scholarships	60
Average grant	$14,400
Average loan	$30,770
Average total aid package	$45,170
Average debt	$78,408

EMPLOYMENT INFORMATION

Career Rating	93
Rate of placement (nine months out)	95
Average starting salary	$104,528
State for bar exam	TX, NY, CA
Pass rate for first-time bar	92

Employers Who Frequently Hire Grads

Baker Botts LLP.; Vinson & Elkins LLP; Akin Gump Strauss Hauer & Feld LLP; Fulbright & Jaworski LLP; Bracewell & Giuliani LLP; Locke Lord Bissell & Liddell LLP; Latham & Watkins LLP; Jones Day; Haynes & Boone LLP; Skadden, Arps, Slate, Meagher & Flom LLP; U.S. Court of Appeals for the Fifth Circuit; Thompson & Knight LLP; Office of Texas State Attorney General

Prominent Alumni

Joseph D. Jamail, Jr., Jamail & Kolius Law Firm; Kay Bailey Hutchison, United States Senator; Frederico Pena, Former Secretary of Transportation; Ron Kirk, United States Trade Representative; Diane Wood, United States Court of Appeals, 7th Circuit

Grads Employed by Field (%)

Academic	(1)
Business/industry	(10)
Government	(13)
Judicial clerkship	(14)
Military	(1)
Private practice	(49)
Public interest	(7)

UNIVERSITY OF TOLEDO
COLLEGE OF LAW

INSTITUTIONAL INFORMATION

Public/private	Public
Student/faculty ratio	14:1
% faculty part-time	43
% faculty female	34
% faculty minority	1
Total faculty	53

SURVEY SAYS...

Diverse opinions accepted in classrooms, Great research resources, Abundant externship/internship/clerkship opportunities

STUDENTS

Enrollment of law school	464
% male/female	63/37
% from out-of-state	27
% full-time	79
% minority	11
% international	3
# of countries represented	5
Average age of entering class	25

ACADEMICS

Academic Experience Rating	81
Profs interesting rating	73
Profs accessible rating	87
Hours of study per day	3.87

Academic Specialties

Criminal, Environmental, International, Labor, Intellectual Property, Employment

Combined Degrees Offered

JD/MBA, JD/MSE, JD/MPA, JD/Masters in Criminal Justice, JD/Masters in Political Science, 3–3.5 years

Clinical program required	No
Legal writing course requirement	Yes
Legal methods course requirement	No
Legal research course requirement	Yes

Academics

The University of Toledo College of Law offers an affordable and welcoming, yet structured atmosphere designed to "accommodate, relax, and train students." The school has climbed in stature the last couple of years, yet retains its rather "humble, calm nature," partially due to its "intelligent, caring, involved, and self-regulating" students and decidedly non-arrogant professors who "are truly incredible individuals." "Every aspect of the school strikes the perfect balance between professionalism and personal attention," says a 2L. Students speak overwhelmingly of the school's obvious care and concern for their future, and the faculty's "willingness to sit and chat with students about class at any time, while connecting what we learn to real-life use." Thanks to the smaller number of students, "Everyone is able to develop personal relationships with faculty and staff." In an effort to keep anxiety levels down, a lot of the professors stay away from the old version of the Socratic Method, which too often "puts you on edge." If you do want to discuss flagging grades or class issues, all professors "go out of their way to make themselves available to students." "It is not uncommon for professors to 'hang out' in the forum chatting with students," says one. "I feel I can approach them with everything: my fears, thoughts, and course questions," says another. The "relatively new" administration "takes a personal and vested interest in seeing us succeed," and "Everything and everyone is very easily and readily accessible." Students do wish for a "more formalized joint degree program" and a "broader variety of courses," as well as a less rigid attendance policy.

The research and writing program is "very thorough and puts an emphasis on real-world concerns," and the school furthers each student's practical background through almost-weekly opportunities to attend speeches or lectures, like one given by U.S. Supreme Court Justice Antonin Scalia. Law Career Services "has put a great deal of effort" into the school's Public Service Externship programs to ensure that students have the opportunity to network while still in school. There's a "very big involvement of [the] Toledo Bar Association and Federal Bar Association in the school's life." The office "[does] it's best to help us in this tough economy," although the employment rate after graduation leaves something to be desired. However, students complain that much of this is due to the "oversaturated" Toledo and Midwest market, and the school's lack of reputation means that more help is needed in other regions.

Aside from the somewhat archaic building and library, which are "more appropriate to an era of bellbottoms and platform shoes," the law school's facilities are up-to-date (though definitely "not glamorous"), with wireless Internet access available in "every corner of the building" and Smart Boards in every classroom.

Life

Racial diversity isn't exactly at United Colors of Benetton levels here, but it "is quite good for this area of the country," and the faculty is very sensitive to both racial and gender issues. The political views also "follow a Midwestern range," ranging from liberal to conservative. The student body remains uncompetitive and "gets along great," even though many students (especially 1Ls) have GPA-based scholarships, and there's a great camaraderie among classes. The student mentor program receives raves, and to further this sense of interconnectedness, intramural sports are big. "There are many organizations to get involved with," and the Student Bar Association does "a very good job at bringing students together through social events (including weekly bar reviews) and volunteer opportunities."

JESSICA MEHL, ASSISTANT DEAN FOR ADMISSIONS
2801 WEST BANCROFT, TOLEDO, OH 43606
TEL: 419-530-4131 FAX: 419-530-4345
E-MAIL: LAW.ADMISSIONS@UTOLEDO.EDU • WEBSITE: WWW.UTLAW.EDU

"Toledo isn't exactly a party town," and it's "not the most enjoyable place to be," so there aren't too many distractions from school, but for those looking to blow off steam, "There are amazing metro parks, art, music, a zoo, and baseball and hockey games to attend." As one might expect of a small school in a small city, "The sense of community that Toledo strives for is amazing and then stems into the larger Toledo legal community." UT Law is also located within an hour of Detroit and Sandusky, within two hours of Dayton and Cleveland, and within five hours of Chicago, Indianapolis, Columbus, and Cincinnati. Still, when students are on campus, "It's difficult to get any kind of food after 11:00 P.M.," and the law school doesn't have any food options that can accommodate for the late hours students normally spend here.

Getting In

The college enrolls about 100 full-time students in each entering class, for which the college receives approximately 1,000 applications (including two required letters of recommendation) annually. Part-time programs have slightly less competitive admissions requirements. Currently, the top quartile of the 1L class has an LSAT of 156 with a GPA of 3.5, while the median has an LSAT of 153 and a GPA of 3.22.

Moot court requirement	No
Public interest law requirement	No

ADMISSIONS

Selectivity Rating	76
# applications received	879
% applicants accepted	58
% acceptees attending	24
Average LSAT	154
LSAT Range	151–156
Average undergrad GPA	3.19
Application fee	$0
Regular application	Rolling, up to 8/1
Regular notification	Rolling
Early application program	No
Transfer students accepted	Yes
Evening division offered	Yes
Part-time accepted	Yes
CAS accepted	Yes

FINANCIAL FACTS

Annual tuition (in-state/out-of-state)	$18,208/ $28,988
Books and supplies	$3,066
Fees	$1,486
Room and board (on/off campus)	$9,354/ $10,384
Financial aid application deadline	8/1
% first-year students receiving some sort of aid	88
% receiving some sort of aid	88
% of aid that is merit based	13
% receiving scholarships	40
Average grant	$15,500
Average loan	$29,913
Average total aid package	$34,859
Average debt	$76,898

EMPLOYMENT INFORMATION

Career Rating	80
Rate of placement (nine months out)	88
Average starting salary	$58,918
State for bar exam	OH, MI
Pass rate for first-time bar	88

Employers Who Frequently Hire Grads
Air Force/Army JAG, Cooper & Walinski, Eastman & Smith, Legal Aid of Western Ohio, Lexis Nexis, Lucas County Prosecutors Office, Marshall & Melhorn, Ohio Attorney General, Reminger & Reminger, Robison Curphey & O'Connell, Shumaker, Loop & Kendrick, Spengler Nathanson, Janik LLP

Prominent Alumni
Honorable Judith Lanzinger, Justice, Ohio Supreme Court; Robert E. Latta, Ohio Fifth Congressional District; Honorable Joseph Farnan, U.S. District Court, Wilmington, DE; James D. Thomas, Partner, Squire, Sanders & Dempsey, Miami, Florida; Honorable Deborah Agosti, former Chief Justice, Nevada Supreme Court

Grads Employed by Field (%)
Academic (5)
Business/industry (22)
Government (13)
Judicial clerkship (6)
Military (2)
Private practice (43)
Public interest (9)

THE UNIVERSITY OF TULSA
COLLEGE OF LAW

INSTITUTIONAL INFORMATION

Public/private	Private
Affiliation	Presbyterian
Student/faculty ratio	12:1
% faculty part-time	13
% faculty female	45
% faculty minority	13
Total faculty	31

SURVEY SAYS...
Diverse opinions accepted in classrooms, Great research resources, Great library staff

STUDENTS

Enrollment of law school	146
% male/female	60/40
% from out-of-state	51
% full-time	100
% minority	32
% international	1
# of countries represented	2
Average age of entering class	25

ACADEMICS

Academic Experience Rating	75
Profs interesting rating	77
Profs accessible rating	78
Hours of study per day	4.13

Academic Specialties
Environmental, International, Sustainable Energy & Resources Law, Native American Law, Comparative & International Law, Health Law, Public Policy, Entrepreneurial Law

Advanced Degrees Offered
LLM in American Indian and Indigenous Law Available in an academic or research track, minimum of 24 units over 1–3 years; LLM in American Law for foreign graduates, minimum of 24 units over 1–2 years

Combined Degrees Offered
JD/MA in Anthropology, Clinical Psychology, Computer Science, English, History, Industrial Organization Psychology, JD/MS in Biological Sciences, Finance,

Academics

Students at the University of Tulsa College of Law call their law school "amazing." "If you want a practical legal education in a happy environment," advises a 2L, "TU is certainly your best option." "Some essential courses are rarely offered," but you'll find "a broad range of opportunities to engage in practical, professional development activities" here. There are quite a few joint-degree programs available. "Both journals are excellent." Areas of concentration include a "highly regarded energy law program" and a "strong," in-depth certificate program in Native American law. There are programs in health law and international law as well. Also, the "top-notch" immigration rights clinic, which provides representation to non-citizens in immigration matters, "does great things and gives students practical experience."

Tulsa Law is on the smaller side, and "small class sizes" are the norm. "Lousy professors" do exist, but "Most of the professors are really good at conveying the black-letter law, policy considerations, as well as practical info." "Professors are willing to engage personally with students" as well. The faculty is "firm but fair," "dedicated to student success and achievement," and "willing to help you at the drop of the hat." "They are easy to talk with, accessible, friendly, and genuinely concerned with students' academic and professional success," declares a 2L. Reviews of management are more mixed. "The administration is dedicated first and foremost to serving the students," decrees a 3L. Some students find staffers "difficult to talk to," though. "The administration tends to spring mandatory meetings on us as well," adds a 2L.

The consensus here seems to be that "the school needs to do a better job placing students outside of Oklahoma." Students with professional destinations, "such as Dallas, Kansas City, and Denver," must be prepared to sell themselves. Otherwise, though, employment prospects are respectable, and most students are satisfied. Tulsa Law has a "reputation within and throughout the state of Oklahoma" and "strong ties" locally. "The integration of the Tulsa legal community with the law school is incredible," boasts a 2L. "On a daily basis, you will see attorneys, judges, scholars, and other alumni walking around." "The Professional Development Office is also very helpful in offering mock interviews, assisting with resumes and cover letters, offering workshops in guiding students to meet their full potential, and offering a multitude of networking opportunities."

The campus at the University of Tulsa is beautiful, but the law school building itself "needs a makeover." "Renovation of classrooms is in the works." Until then, though, "It's like the 1970s in here." "The Internet is temperamental at times," but technology is generally "state-of-the-art," and the research facilities are "wonderful." The "huge" and "exceptionally clean" library is "pretty fantastic," which "makes for a positive studying experience." The librarians are "invaluable," and "There are plenty of study areas and meeting rooms."

Life

Tulsa Law "attracts students from many states," and more than half the students hail from outside of Oklahoma. This school is highly regional, though. "Most of the students who aren't from Oklahoma are from one of the surrounding states." The academic atmosphere generally ranges from "close-knit" to "cooperative to a fault." "With the exception of a few bad apples, the students are extremely supportive of one another," says a 2L. "Competition seems to be something reserved for the mock trial teams." "There seems to be a collective understanding that the student body will cooperate and help one other, and we'll just leave the academic curve up to the professors," relates a 1L.

Tulsa Law's ideal size enhances life outside the classroom. "Gossip is rampant," but students tell us, "The social life at the school is fantastic." "At TU, you really get a chance to meet and grow closer to a small group of students," reflects a 3L. The Student Bar Association is very active, and "Student organizations put on many different events," such as a talent shows, pub crawls, and various auctions. The law school is located on the campus of the larger university "in a mixed residential and business neighborhood" about "a five-minute drive from downtown." The surrounding city of Tulsa has devotees as well as detractors. Aficionados point out that it's a fairly large metropolis that's home to a decent number of large corporations. "Getting around Tulsa is usually easy and stress free." It's the perfect size for anyone who doesn't want to live in crowded cities, but who also doesn't want to be stuck in the middle of nowhere. Critics disagree. They say Tulsa itself is "very boring"

Getting In

Reasonable grades and test scores will do the trick in most cases here. Admitted students at the 25th percentile have LSAT scores in the lower 150s and undergraduate GPAs right about 3.0. At the 75th percentile, LSAT scores are a little lower than 160, and GPAs are a little higher than 3.6.

Geosciences, JD/MBA, JD/Master's of Taxation, approximately 4 years

Clinical program required	No
Legal writing course requirement	Yes
Legal methods course requirement	Yes
Legal research course requirement	No
Moot court requirement	No
Public interest law requirement	No

ADMISSIONS

Selectivity Rating	74
# applications received	1,373
% applicants accepted	43
% acceptees attending	25
Average LSAT	155
LSAT Range	152–158
Average undergrad GPA	3.27
Application fee	$30
Regular application	Rolling, up to 7/30
Regular notification	Rolling
Early application program	No
Transfer students accepted	Yes
Evening division offered	No
Part-time accepted	Yes
CAS accepted	Yes

International Students

TOEFL required of international students	

FINANCIAL FACTS

Annual tuition	$30,320
Books and supplies	$1,500
Fees	$174
Room and board (on/off campus)	$9,118/ $12,642
% first-year students receiving some sort of aid	90
% receiving some sort of aid	92
% of aid that is merit based	23
% receiving scholarships	56
Average grant	$16,387
Average loan	$34,003
Average total aid package	$40,049
Average debt	$95,703

EMPLOYMENT INFORMATION

Career Rating		80
Rate of placement (nine months out)		94
Average starting salary		$54,071
State for bar exam	OK, TX, NY, CO, MO	

Employers Who Frequently Hire Grads
Law Firms; Energy Companies; State and Federal Government

Prominent Alumni
Layn R. Phillips, Member, Irell & Manella; former U.S. District Judge, Western District of OK; Hon. Elizabeth Crewson Paris, U.S. Tax Court Judge; Toni D. Hennike, Exxon Mobil Corp Coord. Int'l Investments & Arbitration; William Chistopher Carmody, Partner, Susman Godfrey, voted as a Super Lawyer in Texas and New York; Chadwick Smith, Principal Chief, The Cherokee Nation

UNIVERSITY OF UTAH
S. J. QUINNEY COLLEGE OF LAW

Academics

Students at the S.J. Quinney College of Law at the University of Utah are quite confident that they are receiving the "best law education available in the country for the price." The "extremely approachable" and "very student-oriented" professors "make every effort to meet with students and make sure they understand the material." "I went to an expensive liberal arts school for undergrad that advertised itself as offering available and motivated professors," relates a 3L. "My undergrad experience pales in comparison to the individual attention and encouragement I have received at this state school." "Professors here actually try to minimize stress rather than build it up," agrees a 1L. The standard Socratic Method is not en vogue. Some students tell us that professors' more easygoing approach allows "for a more comfortable environment in which to learn." Other students say it's "just too easy to doze off." "I know this sounds crazy," admits a 1L, "but I wish more of the professors would use the Socratic Method or, at least, engage the students in class more."

The administration at Utah "is always looking for new, creative ways to improve the school." "The new dean has brought a new vision of Dream Big," and administrators "demonstrate a great interest in not only hearing the students' voices, but in improving student experience, academic quality, and transition to real-world practice." "All the deans keep themselves highly available." "Nobody's got an attitude," and "no one is too busy to answer a question."

Students here are "right in the middle of Salt Lake City, surrounded by large and prestigious law firms." The College of Law has "a great relationship with practitioners and judges in the community" and "There are plenty of opportunities to gain practical experience." "It is fairly easy to do judicial clinics and other legal internships." "Terrific outreach programs afford students opportunities to work pro bono with public interest organizations." The "excellent first-year legal writing program" is "rigorous and well thought out." "You'll walk out of here writing better than most lawyers who have been practicing for years," claims a 2L. If you want to specialize, "There are plenty of courses, especially in natural resources law." The Professional Development Office is "friendly and helpful," but "A lot of students get jobs from other sources."

"A new [law school] building is in the works," but in the meantime, the current "aging" and "undersized" building is "from the late 60s and reflects that boring architecture." "Our building sucks, in a word," laments a 2L. "The campus seems designed to drive students off campus as soon as classes are over." The computer network is "spotty in some places," and the library gets average reviews.

Life

"People at this school actually seem happy," and "There is a sense of community and connectedness" on campus. "We're small," explains one student. "You'll know most of the school and faculty by the time you're a 2L." "The U fosters a great environment, where everyone helps everyone else." "Individual personalities flourish and the interaction of personalities is like that among family members who have known each other their entire lives." "People here see the whole person. It's a very collaborative environment."

Students report that their peers are "equal parts brilliant, collegial, encouraging, competitive, and just flat-out a joy." It's "probably an older and more mature crowd than at the average law school." Many students "are married with children." "I don't regret for a moment choosing to come here as a thirty-something, second-career mom," says a 2L.

SUSAN BACA, OPERATIONS MANAGER FOR ADMISSIONS & FINANCIAL AID
ADMISSIONS, 332 SOUTH 1400 EAST, ROOM 101, SALT LAKE CITY, UT 84112-0730
TEL: 801-581-7479 FAX: 801-581-6897
E-MAIL: ADMISSIONS@LAW.UTAH.EDU • WEBSITE: WWW.LAW.UTAH.EDU

"I fit in." "The nontraditional demographic allows for an interesting mix and a few extra designated drivers." The Church of Latter-day Saints is, of course, prevalent everywhere in Utah. "Don't think that because this isn't BYU there won't be plenty of Mormons." Politically, "The school is fairly evenly split between liberals and conservatives." "The divide can be fierce at times," but "Overall there is great acceptance of different viewpoints and lifestyles."

"The social life is not great" here. "Salt Lake culture is fairly conservative," and "The Mormon influence is felt both in the city and in the law school." Though wild parties are few, Utah sponsors "many social events which are geared toward building relationships between the school and the local bar." "Throughout the week there are plenty of opportunities to hang out with students in many different social settings and activities." Off campus, "Salt Lake City is a gorgeous place to live" "The city is clean; the crime rate is low." And It's surrounded by "one of the most scenic and beautiful areas in the country." "Outdoor life is great." "We are six hours away from red-rock desert and half an hour's drive from the greatest snow on earth," declares a 1L. "You can spend all that tuition money you're saving on ski passes and road trips."

Getting In

Recently admitted students at the 25th percentile have LSAT scores of 157 and GPAs of nearly 3.4. Admitted students at the 75th percentile have LSAT scores of 164 and GPAs of about 3.8. If you take the LSAT more than once, Utah will presume to use the highest score.

| Moot court requirement | No |
| Public interest law requirement | No |

ADMISSIONS

Selectivity Rating	89
# applications received	1,365
% applicants accepted	29
% acceptees attending	31
Average LSAT	161
LSAT Range	157–164
Average undergrad GPA	3.63
Application fee	$60
Regular application	Rolling, up to 7/31
Regular notification	Rolling
Early application program	No
Transfer students accepted	Yes
Evening division offered	No
Part-time accepted	No
CAS accepted	Yes

International Students

| TOEFL required of international students | |

FINANCIAL FACTS

Annual tuition (in-state/out-of-state)	$18,784/ $36,409
Books and supplies	$1,916
Fees	$853
Room and board	$9,126
Financial aid application deadline	4/1
% first-year students receiving some sort of aid	94
% receiving some sort of aid	87
% of aid that is merit based	29
% receiving scholarships	51
Average grant	$6,386
Average loan	$26,581
Average total aid package	$32,967
Average debt	$61,665

EMPLOYMENT INFORMATION

Career Rating	75
Rate of placement (nine months out)	94
Average starting salary	$74,643
State for bar exam	UT, CA, NV, AZ, ID

Employers Who Frequently Hire Grads
Alverson Taylor Mortensen & Sanders (Las Vegas); Parsons, Behle & Latimer (SLC, UT); Ray Quinney & Nebeker (SLC, UT); Stoel Rives (SLC, UT); Snell & Wilmer (SLC, UT)

Prominent Alumni
Kelli L. Sager, Chair, Media Practice, Davis, Wright, Tremaine; Hon. Stephen Anderson, 10th Circuit Court of Appeals; Gary Kennedy, General Counsel & Vice President for American Airlines; Kate Kendell, Director, National Center for Lesbian Rights; Hon. Nancy Rice, Colorado

Supreme Court; Christopher B. Nelson, President, St. John's College; Larry Echo Hawk, Assistant Secretary, Indian Affairs, U.S. Department of the Interior

Grads Employed by Field (%)
Academic (2)
Business/industry (10)
Government (9)
Judicial clerkship (8)
Military (4)
Private practice (60)
Public interest (3)

UNIVERSITY OF VIRGINIA
SCHOOL OF LAW

INSTITUTIONAL INFORMATION

Public/private	Public
Student/faculty ratio	12:1
% faculty part-time	50
% faculty female	23
% faculty minority	9
Total faculty	170

SURVEY SAYS...

Great research resources, Great library staff, Good social life

STUDENTS

Enrollment of law school	1,106
% male/female	55/45
% from out-of-state	64
% full-time	100
% minority	23
% international	1
# of countries represented	16
Average age of entering class	24

ACADEMICS

Academic Experience Rating	99
Profs interesting rating	97
Profs accessible rating	97
Hours of study per day	4.29

Academic Specialties

Civil Procedure, Commercial, Constitutional, Corporation Securities, Criminal, Environmental, Government Services, Human Rights, International, Labor, Legal History, Legal Philosophy, Taxation, Intellectual Property, Communications and Media Law, Family Law, Health Law, Race and Law

Advanced Degrees Offered

LLM, 1 year; SJD, 2–5 years

Combined Degrees Offered

JD/MA in English, Government, Foreign Affairs, History, Philosophy, 3–4 years; JD/MS in Accounting, JD/MPH, 3.5 years; JD/MBA, JD/Masters in Urban and Environmental Planning, JD/MPA, JD/MA in Law and Diplomacy, JD/MPP JD/MA in International Relations, 4 years

Academics

It's all about a work-life harmony at the University of Virginia School of Law in Charlottesville, Virginia. Students talk nonstop about the school's "high level of academic focus mixed with the importance [it places on] having an enjoyable three years," which is "a combination that's really tough to find in a top law school." When the "demanding course work" required is through, the "play hard" part of the equation begins, and the school is great about "combining out-of-class social activities with in-class work." "It is amazing how much individual attention each student receives...considering the size of the school" says a student.

Most professors here are "truly wonderful, [care] deeply about students, and [are] terrific in the classroom," though many admit that "there are a couple of duds here," whose primary focus is on "their research." They're also all "extraordinarily accessible": "I eat lunch with my professors on a regular basis," says a student. UVA is great about hiring up-and-coming faculty members who are "young, funny, and soon-to-be stars in their fields." Though the professors may know their material "backwards and forwards," a few could stand to brush up on the technology the school provides them with for demonstration purposes. Opportunities for research assistantships are "numerous," and independent studies, directed research, and clinics are also "extremely popular." Small 1L sections (about thirty students) and a strong peer advisor program (which lasts informally beyond the first year) make for "a really supportive atmosphere."

There are a few kinks in the administrative process—"course registration and [the] grade system could be better"—but the school runs "very smoothly...for an institution this size." There's a good sense of appreciation for "the freedom with which we can select our courses." The loan assistance program has been redesigned, and "The Career Services Department has hired new staff." Indeed, many people commend the Career Services and Clerkship offices for their work in placing students at jobs during hard times, and one student even claims, "The national reputation of the school for turning out well-rounded students was noted in many of my interviews at firms and for clerkships."

Don't be fooled by outer appearances; though the law school buildings might not look it from the outside, the facilities within are "top notch," "classy, and modern," and the grounds are well-landscaped and "beautifully appointed." Students' satisfaction with their three years at UVA builds a strong and fondly reminiscent alumni network and a nationwide reputation that is "simply incredible." It's no surprise that people are nostalgic for the school before they've even left: "Not only am I being challenged academically, but I'm taking courses that interest me, I have solid job prospects, and, more importantly than some people admit, I love being here."

Life

"It is hard to imagine a group of people more laid-back" than UVA Law students and faculty. People here manage to be "smart, driven, and successful, and at the same time be down-to-earth, fun, and friendly." "Many schools boast a 'collegial' atmosphere, but I don't believe that any [other school] could top UVA," says a 3L. "The keg in the quad every Thursday afternoon really says it all," says a 2L. There's also the school's legendary "Feb Club," which is a month of themed (and well-attended) parties on every single day of the week. "People of all persuasions attend and it is truly remarkable," says a non-drinking

ANN RICHARD, SENIOR ASSISTANT DEAN
580 MASSIE ROAD, CHARLOTTESVILLE, VA 22903-1738
TEL: 434-924-7351 FAX: 434-982-2128
E-MAIL: LAWADMIT@VIRGINIA.EDU • WEBSITE: WWW.LAW.VIRGINIA.EDU

student. But don't let Feb Club fool you—"People here are smart and always find the time to get their work done."

Students are "fairly non-competitive with each other but tough on themselves." If you miss a class, you'll often have notes from several other students "before you even have a chance to ask." This "smart but well-rounded student body" is pretty diverse (the level has been increasing in recent years), but can "be a little fratty." Cliques only tend to develop "along section lines, not really along racial or gender lines." In fact, there are "tons" of social events organized through sections, including "section mixers, a tubing trip, Fall Foxfield [a horserace], softball, [and] potluck dinners." It's rare to find an unhappy student here, perhaps evidenced by the abundance of major social outlets and the "ubiquity of softball in the fall and spring seasons." "Softball games are much more competitive than grades," says a student. Charlottesville is a mid-Atlantic paradise for this happy crowd, who love the "beautiful, vibrant, small city" that boasts "wineries, hiking, golf, volunteering, [and] great bars and restaurants." "I have absolutely loved living here and will be sorry to go back to the real world in May!" says a 3L.

Getting In

Admitted students at the 25th percentile have LSAT scores of roughly 166 and GPAs of about 3.5. Admitted students at the 75th percentile have LSAT scores of about 171 and GPAs of just over 3.9. In the case of multiple LSAT scores, UVA gives the most weight to the highest submitted LSAT score; however, the school evaluates all information submitted as part of the application for admission, and encourages applicants with a significant difference in LSAT scores to include with their application any information that may be relevant to the interpretation of test results, such as illness or testing conditions.

Clinical program required	No
Legal writing course requirement	Yes
Legal methods course requirement	Yes
Legal research course requirement	Yes
Moot court requirement	No
Public interest law requirement	No

ADMISSIONS

Selectivity Rating	99
# applications received	8,560
% applicants accepted	11
% acceptees attending	40
Average LSAT	166
LSAT Range	166–171
Average undergrad GPA	3.51–3.92
Application fee	$80
Regular application	Rolling, up to 3/1
Regular notification	4/15
Early application program	Yes
Early application deadline	None
Early application notification	15 days
Transfer students accepted	Yes
Evening division offered	No
Part-time accepted	No
CAS accepted	Yes

FINANCIAL FACTS

Annual tuition (in-state/out-of-state)	$40,188/$44,516
Books and supplies	$5,050
Fees (in-state/out-of-state)	$2,312/$2,984
Room and board	$15,150
Financial aid application deadline	2/18
% first-year students receiving some sort of aid	90
% receiving some sort of aid	89
% receiving scholarships	48
Average grant	$19,652
Average loan	$43,939
Average total aid package	$49,411
Average debt	$92,207

EMPLOYMENT INFORMATION

		Grads Employed by Field (%)
Career Rating	96	
Rate of placement (nine months out)	99	Academic (2)
State for bar exam	NY	Business/industry (2)
Pass rate for first-time bar	96	Government (12)
Employers Who Frequently Hire Grads		Judicial clerkship (14)
Graduates are employed in every top 100		Military (2)
firm in the country.		Private practice (61)
		Public interest (6)

UNIVERSITY OF WASHINGTON
SCHOOL OF LAW

INSTITUTIONAL INFORMATION

Public/private	Public
Student/faculty ratio	10:1
% faculty part-time	29
% faculty female	43
% faculty minority	17
Total faculty	77

SURVEY SAYS...

Great research resources, Great library staff, Beautiful campus, Students love Seattle, WA

STUDENTS

Enrollment of law school	528
% male/female	41/59
% from out-of-state	40
% full-time	100
% minority	21
% international	2
# of countries represented	8
Average age of entering class	25

ACADEMICS

Academic Experience Rating	75
Profs interesting rating	62
Profs accessible rating	75

Academic Specialties

Civil Procedure, Commercial, Constitutional, Corporation Securities, Criminal, Environmental, Government Services, Human Rights, International, Labor, Legal History, Legal Philosophy, Property, Taxation, Intellectual Property, Dispute Resolution, Asian Law, International and Comparative Law, Health Law

Advanced Degrees Offered

LLM Asian Law, Law of Sustainable International Development, Taxation, Intellectual Property, 1-year full-time; Taxation/IP, evening, full- or part-time

Combined Degrees Offered

Can set up with 90 graduate programs

Academics

The University of Washington School of Law, one of three law schools in the country on the quarter system, offers great opportunities to control your own legal education and lots of opportunities for learning and experience outside class. The school is well known for its numerous student organizations, many of which have a big public interest/community volunteering aspect; there's also a public service requirement that has "spawned many interesting externship and clinic opportunities for students." Still, students say that despite the touting of public service law, most of the events and funding are driven almost solely by these groups, and the school "doesn't offer much formal curriculum in that area." The Contorts program here is especially "spectacular," as it "allows students to look at a legal problem from a variety of perspectives which you don't get by looking at torts and contracts individually." Small section sizes help make UW seem cozier, and while the forced curve and the newly introduced class rankings system does mean that it can be a competitive place, this competition is "mostly because people want to do well, not because they want others not to do well."

The collaborative atmosphere between the students and faculty is a great boon to the school and makes for a great working environment and a very collegiate atmosphere, so "gunners and ultra-competitive attitudes are frowned on here." Many of the professors are brilliant in their field, and they "bring their own expertise and practical real world experience in the field in ways that really animate and extend the subject matter." Their willingness to discuss almost anything outside of class is deeply appreciated by students, even if there are "a few professors that should never be allowed anywhere near 1Ls." The law building is new and built with a grant from Bill Gates, so classrooms and study areas are "clean and up-to-date," and the building itself is "light and spacious" and has incredible views out over the sound and downtown Seattle. Classes are recorded and podcast for those with parental responsibilities (an accommodation "especially invaluable to student-parents") and the law library is amazing and gorgeous, with librarians that "are among the best anywhere."

The administration is genuine in their care for students, and one of the deans even hired an on-call psychologist for students to use for free in the interest of helping them to maintain their mental health, but the two hands-down weakest areas are found in Financial Aid and Career Services. The single administrator who runs all of the Financial Aid accounts for the law school is "unable to answer routine questions" and "can tell you the ins and outs of computer solitaire, but wouldn't know where to find a grant or extra loan if it bit him on the butt," and the Career Services office is "great if you want to work in a private law firm" or stay in Washington to practice, but "if you want to work in international human rights/humanitarian law or domestic nonprofit law" the institutional resources aren't really there, and "job postings themselves are mostly centered in the Pacific Northwest." "They are more talk than action and somewhat out of touch with what employers are really looking for," says a student.

KATHY SWINEHART, ADMISSIONS SUPERVISOR
WILLIAM H. GATES HALL, BOX 353020, SEATTLE, WA 98195-3020
TEL: 206-543-4078 FAX: 206-543-5671
E-MAIL: LAWADM@U.WASHINGTON.EDU • WEBSITE: WWW.LAW.WASHINGTON.EDU

Life

Like any other law-school, UW has their share of type-A's, but the personality clashes are minimal. It's a small and tight-knit community, so naturally gossip can travel at the speed of light, but "it's all good natured and there is rarely, if ever, any rancor or backbiting." Competitiveness is kept to a minimum, and one student says that if he were to miss class, "several people would e-mail and offer to review the material with me." UW's rather long orientation really bonds folks, and many people report having made some of the best friends of their lives in their classes. Located in a neighborhood of Seattle that "is reasonably funky and fun, and not too far from the center of town," there are also a lot of student groups at the law school that are active, as well as intramural sports and school-organized weekly meet-ups at bars, so students can easily find something to match their interests. "There are not parties every weekend, but there are plenty of social events if you make the effort to find out about them and get involved," says a student. The left-leaning school is really committed to diversity and as a result, there's a wide range of age, experience, class, nationality, ethnicity, and disability; the sizeable older crowd "is great in the school environment, but socially nonexistent outside the school."

Getting In

It's tough getting admitted to the University of Washington, but the school follows your basic law school admissions policy: It puts heavy weight on applicants' undergraduate records and LSAT scores, also considering letters of recommendation, work and volunteer experience, and personal statements. The vast majority of enrollees (about seventy percent) are residents of Washington State; however, residency is not a major factor in an admissions decision.

Clinical program required	No
Legal writing course requirement	Yes
Legal methods course requirement	Yes
Legal research course requirement	Yes
Moot court requirement	No
Public interest law requirement	Yes

ADMISSIONS

Selectivity Rating	93
# applications received	2,585
% applicants accepted	23
% acceptees attending	31
Average LSAT	162
LSAT Range	159–165
Average undergrad GPA	3.65
Application fee	$50
Regular notification	4/1
Early application program	No
Transfer students accepted	Yes
Evening division offered	No
Part-time accepted	No
CAS accepted	Yes

FINANCIAL FACTS

Annual tuition (in-state/out-of-state)	$17,846/ $26,231
Books and supplies	$1,500
Room and board	$16,626
Financial aid application deadline	2/28
% first-year students receiving some sort of aid	85
% receiving some sort of aid	85
% of aid that is merit based	10
% receiving scholarships	43
Average grant	$7,500
Average loan	$22,500
Average total aid package	$30,000
Average debt	$65,507

EMPLOYMENT INFORMATION

Career Rating	83
Rate of placement (nine months out)	97
Average starting salary	$90,000
State for bar exam	WA
Pass rate for first-time bar	90

Employers Who Frequently Hire Grads

Preston Gates & Ellis; Davis Wright Tremaine; Perkins Coie; Stoel Rives; King County Prosecuting Attorney; Garvey Schubert & Barer; Columbia Legal Services; Northwest Justice Project; Washington State Attorney General; Washington Supreme Court. An increasing number of students accept judicial clerkships upon graduation.

Prominent Alumni

Tom Foley, Former Speaker, U.S. House of Representatives; Gerry Alexander, Chief Justice, Washington Supreme Court; Betty Fletcher, Judge, U.S. Court of Appeals (9th Circuit); William H. Gates, Attorney; Foundation Chair; Virginia B. Smith, President Emerita, Smith College; Mills College

Grads Employed by Field (%)

Academic (2)
Business/industry (7)
Government (14)
Judicial clerkship (16)
Private practice (54)
Public interest (6)

UNIVERSITY OF WISCONSIN—MADISON

LAW SCHOOL

INSTITUTIONAL INFORMATION

Public/private	Public
Student/faculty ratio	13:1
% faculty part-time	42
% faculty female	46
% faculty minority	19
Total faculty	117

SURVEY SAYS...

Students love Madison, WI

STUDENTS

Enrollment of law school	246
% male/female	53/47
% from out-of-state	38
% full-time	97
% minority	25
% international	2
# of countries represented	3
Average age of entering class	24

ACADEMICS

Academic Experience Rating	85
Profs interesting rating	81
Profs accessible rating	73
Hours of study per day	4.39

Academic Specialties

Civil Procedure, Commercial, Constitutional, Corporation Securities, Criminal, Environmental, Government Services, Human Rights, International, Labor, Legal History, Legal Philosophy, Property, Taxation, Intellectual Property, Biotechnology Law, Islamic Law, Estate Planning, Family Law, Health Law, Law Practice Skills

Advanced Degrees Offered

JD, 3 years; LLM, 1 year; SJD, 3 years

Combined Degrees Offered

Joint Degree with Environmental Studies, 4 years; Business, 4 years; Public Affairs, 4 years; Sociology, 8 years; Political Science, 5 years; Library Information Science, 4 years; Latin American Studies, 4 years; and Philosophy, 6 years

Academics

University of Wisconsin Law School is considered to be "the flagship law school in the state [of Wisconsin]," offering "a great legal education" and hosting some of "the best and brightest legal minds" on its illustrious faculty. Though students admit that professors can "vary in teaching styles" and "in their teaching abilities," nearly all agree that "it's clear that our professors are respected in Wisconsin and the nation." "It's exciting taking criminal law courses with professors who wrote the criminal code in Wisconsin and have an ongoing impact on criminal law in the state," says a 2L. "There are professors that are former Wisconsin Supreme Court Justices, former 'big law' partners, current appointees on national and international committees, and other well-respected scholars in their field." Professors teach "subjects that they enjoy and can shed real-life experience on, which really helps you to imagine using that law in practice." At the same time, "Many of the professors are old," and, as they retire, students would like the school to "bring in younger, top-notch professors." Along those lines, UW recently hired new faculty in tax, constitutional law, civil procedure, and other key areas. The administration can be "very accessible and accommodating of students," though some feel that it is "too disconnected" and a "little slow in getting out the class schedules."

Classes become "relatively small" after 1L (where "eighty [students in class] is the norm"), giving "everyone [the] opportunity to speak and learn in a smaller setting." But that's not to say there aren't small classes for 1Ls. "Keeping the 1L legal writing courses at only twelve students always increases interaction between each student and professor," says a 1L. Despite its intimacy, some students felt the "the legal writing program could be improved [as the school] does not put enough emphasis on writing or provide courses that teach students how to write the documents they are most likely to write as lawyers." In response, the UW hired a new Legal Writing Director, who is redesigned the program. On the upside, there are "significant opportunities" for "practical experience" through legal clinics and electives, but taking part in these relies on students being motivated to seek them out. "[UW Law] doesn't work to make sure that students are getting the practical 'Law in Action' experience they need in the classroom," says a 2L. "It's left to the students to get involved in a clinical. Yet, due to the realities of law school and the economy, this is not always a feasible option."

On the job front, the common consensus among students is that "Career Services needs to be revamped." "[It] does not actively create jobs but rather puts on workshops about how we should make sure that we repay our debt after graduation," says a 3L. A 2L adds, "I think that Career Services could be a little more creative, knowledgeable, and proactive." Luckily, the school's "proximity" to Chicago means that students have a large job market nearby in which they can "visit law firms" and "interview for jobs."

The law building is "located on Bascom Hill," considered to be "the focal point of the campus," however students aren't positive it deserves such a prominent view. "The older parts of the building are beyond outdated," says a 1L. A 2L concurs: "Although the building is in good condition and well-maintained, the furniture in the classrooms and library could be nicer." Classrooms have "wireless Internet, electric outlets, and projection screens," and while the building itself doesn't have the "elegant wood floors and paneling of some places," it's "more modern and functional than [other schools]." "Some of the technology in the classrooms is not as 'spiffy' as private schools, but the wonderful professors and overall supportive academic environment more than make up for these shortcomings," says a 1L.

REBECCA L. SCHELLER, INTERIM DEAN FOR ADMISSIONS AND FINANCIAL AID
975 BASCOM MALL, MADISON, WI 53706
TEL: 608-262-5914 FAX: 608-263-3190
E-MAIL: ADMISSIONS@LAW.WISC.EDU • WEBSITE: LAW.WISC.EDU

Life

Students at UW Law note the "strong sense of community" and "cooperation" that "permeates the student body" and allows them "to work at a higher level than if there was a more cutthroat environment." Though it can get "competitive during finals and tryouts for prestigious organizations," students "all help each other" and "no one is ripping pages out of books in the library." Diversity is "promoted heavily" and students "interact [both] within and outside of their ethnic/sexual orientation/political groups." "The school is accessible for all kinds of students [whether they're] right out of college or in their thirties married with kids," says a 1L. "Every group of students has their own active organization, putting [on] events and volunteering. Everyone can find someone to get along with here."

When students need a break from their studies, "Madison's nightlife being geared toward undergrads," students here "make do with what they have." Madison is a "great college town" and an "amazing place to go to law school." It "has all the resources of a city but feels like a town." With the law school "situated right on the Hill in the heart of campus" students are "close to everything," such as "restaurants, bars, and [other] things to do." And what might those other things be? According to these "word hard, play hard" types, "It's not uncommon to study until 9 P.M. and then go out to the bars."

Getting In

Recently admitted students at UW Law at the 25th percentile have LSAT scores of 158 and GPAs in the 3.29 range. Admitted students at the 75th percentile have LSAT scores of 164 and GPAs of roughly 3.76.

Clinical program required	No
Legal writing course requirement	Yes
Legal methods course requirement	Yes
Legal research course requirement	Yes
Moot court requirement	No
Public interest law requirement	No

ADMISSIONS

Selectivity Rating	89
# applications received	2,829
% applicants accepted	21
% acceptees attending	41
Average LSAT	161
LSAT Range	158–164
Average undergrad GPA	3.51
Application fee	$56
Regular application	Rolling, up to 3/1
Regular notification	Rolling
Early application program	No
Transfer students accepted	Yes
Evening division offered	No
Part-time accepted	Yes
CAS accepted	Yes

International Students

TOEFL required of international students

FINANCIAL FACTS

Annual tuition (in-state/out-of-state)	$18,099/ $37,586
Books and supplies	$2,300
Room and board	$9,250
Financial aid application deadline	3/1
% first-year students receiving some sort of aid	90
% receiving some sort of aid	90
% of aid that is merit based	20
% receiving scholarships	31
Average grant	$12,000
Average loan	$23,000
Average debt	$76,845

EMPLOYMENT INFORMATION

Career Rating	92
Rate of placement (nine months out)	93
Average starting salary	$102,732
State for bar exam	WI
Pass rate for first-time bar	100

Employers Who Frequently Hire Grads
Foley & Lardner; Quarles & Brady; Godfrey & Kahn; Reinhart Boerner; Michael Best & Friedrich; McDermott Will & Emery; Skadden Arps; Latham & Watkins; Sidley & Austin; Mayer Brown; Jenner & Block; Paul Hastings; Morgan Lewis & Bockius; Dorsey & Whitney; Jones Day

Prominent Alumni
Tommy Thompson '66, Fmr Sec. of Health & Human Srvc, former Gov of WI; Tammy Baldwin '89, U.S. House of Representatives, Madison, WI; David Ruder '57, dean of Northwestern U Law School, frm chair SEC; John Rowe, CEO of Exelon Corp. in Chicago; Francis Ulmer, Lt. Governor of Alaska, 1995–2003

Grads Employed by Field (%)
Academic (9)
Business/industry (10)
Government (13)
Judicial clerkship (4)
Military (3)
Private practice (52)
Public interest (9)

UNIVERSITY OF WYOMING
COLLEGE OF LAW

INSTITUTIONAL INFORMATION

Public/private	Public
Student/faculty ratio	10:1
% faculty part-time	19
% faculty female	42
% faculty minority	15
Total faculty	26

SURVEY SAYS...

Diverse opinions accepted in classrooms, Great research resources, Great library staff

STUDENTS

Enrollment of law school	219
% male/female	47/53
% from out-of-state	41
% full-time	100
% minority	11
% international	2
# of countries represented	3
Average age of entering class	27

ACADEMICS

Academic Experience Rating	73
Profs interesting rating	73
Profs accessible rating	88
Hours of study per day	4.32

Academic Specialties
Environmental, Natural Resources Law, Energy Law

Advanced Degrees Offered
JD, 3 years

Combined Degrees Offered
JD/MPA, JD/MBA, 3.5–4 years; JD/MA Environment & Natural Resources, 3.5–4 years

Clinical program required	No
Legal writing course requirement	Yes
Legal methods course requirement	Yes
Legal research course requirement	Yes
Moot court requirement	Yes
Public interest law requirement	No

Academics

Looking to get your JD in a place where everybody knows your name? Consider heading down to Laramie to get a degree from the University of Wyoming College of Law, where the "close-knit community of the law school is by far its greatest attribute." "You know everyone and everyone knows you" is how students sum up the faculty, staff, administration, and students of the school—and, as the only law school in the state, the same familiarity extends to the courtrooms. In a small school, in a small state, with a small legal community, "you can really get access to the people and issues that make a difference to you." The school regularly hosts the Wyoming Supreme Court and 10th Circuit proceedings in its law school building. "That kind of access is not available everywhere," says a student.

UW has an extremely low student-to-faculty ratio, and the professors "are extremely interested in each student's success and are willing to go out of their way to assist you in any way you need assistance." "I have never seen this level of wanting their students to succeed," says a 2L. They do an "amazing job of being accessible to the students" and "go above and beyond" what is asked of them. However, a few students point out that the school keeps on less-than-stellar professors "due to their unwavering adherence to the tenure system."

One student describes UW as being "like a blue-collar school," where faculty and staff "work hard every day to make the education for the students the best it can be." The school has "rightly focused on natural resources and energy law" in its environmental program, which is "getting bigger all the time," but there is a desire for more diverse programs in family and business law, and greater practical experience through "more skills-oriented classes" and clinics. Scheduling is a bit of a problem, too, as the school could stand to "offer more courses, or offer the most popular courses every semester as opposed to every other semester."

The school is "supremely respected within the state," with state supreme court justices routinely getting involved with the law students, but the Career Services Office "does very little outreach beyond this state," which compounds the problem of the school's limited reputation outside of Wyoming. There is a large population of Coloradoans attending school here, and one of them complains, "Colorado firms turn their nose up at our grads." However, one of the best parts of UW Law is the "access to externships." "I got a judicial externship effortlessly (a resume and no interview), whereas at most schools getting any sort of externship, let alone a judicial externship, is a competitive nightmare," says a pleased 2L. "My externship is one of the best things I've ever done for myself, to be honest."

The administration "is not particularly accommodating or flexible to individual needs, which is remarkable at a school of only 200 students," but it does a good job overall, and it does "ask for student and faculty input whenever making major decisions, such as new hires or curriculum changes." UW also just completed a massive renovation of the facilities, including "fantastic" new moot courtrooms.

Life

"If you want to be away from the distractions of an awesome nightlife, lots of shopping, and tons of cultural events so that you can focus on law school, Laramie may be the perfect place for you," says a second-year optimist. For other, glass-half-empty types, "Laramie is quite possibly the most boring place on the face of the earth." Still, this relative isolation

Coordinator of Admissions
Dept. 3035, 1000 E. University Ave., Laramie, WY 82071
Tel: 307-766-6416 Fax: 307-766-6417
E-Mail: lawadmis@uwyo.edu • Website: www.uwyo.edu/law

and small classes really fosters close relationships, and "many of these people are going to be lifelong friends." "My class is like a seventy-five-member family," says a 2L. Keep in mind that "it's a very small world here," which "can be a blessing or a curse." Granted, "there's a lot of drama," but "it's more like siblings fighting—we get [upset], and we're fine an hour later." The atmosphere "is not ultra-competitive, more of a cooperative environment. We cheer for the high-achievers and encourage those who aren't." This cohesive group "takes care of one another, and [is] quick to help each other in tough times."

For fun, students "participate in intramural sports" and other activities outside of the school; "Because it is a small town, it is easy to find classmates and law students out in the community almost all the time." Most of the student body is the expected just-out-of-college, mid-twenty-something, but there are a fair number of older students, which the school embraces by "inviting students' spouses, kids, dogs, and friends to school functions."

Getting In

The 25th percentile of admitted students has LSAT scores of 151 and GPAs of 3.23. Admitted students at the 75th percentile have LSAT scores of 157 and GPAs of about 3.7. A whopping seventy-eight percent of all the law students at UW receive scholarships or financial aid of some kind.

ADMISSIONS

Selectivity Rating	80
# applications received	583
% applicants accepted	34
% acceptees attending	42
Average LSAT	154
LSAT Range	150–157
Average undergrad GPA	3.50
Application fee	$50
Regular application	Rolling, up to 3/1
Regular notification	4/1
Early application program	Yes
Early application deadline	12/1
Early application notification	12/31
Transfer students accepted	Yes
Evening division offered	No
Part-time accepted	No
CAS accepted	Yes

International Students

TOEFL required of international students	

FINANCIAL FACTS

Annual tuition (in-state/out-of-state)	$13,095/ $25,425
Books and supplies	$1,200
Fees	$1,042
Room and board	$10,837
Financial aid application deadline	3/1
% first-year students receiving some sort of aid	70
% receiving some sort of aid	78
% of aid that is merit based	100
% receiving scholarships	58
Average grant	$2,500
Average loan	$17,438
Average total aid package	$19,680
Average debt	$50,000

EMPLOYMENT INFORMATION

Career Rating	78
Rate of placement (nine months out)	85
Average starting salary	$59,456
State for bar exam	WY, CO, UT, WA, TX, NM, CA, AZ, LA, SD, OK
Pass rate for first-time bar	87

Employers Who Frequently Hire Grads
Government (Attorney General, Federal and District courts, Supreme Court, Public Defender, County Attorney); General practice firms

Prominent Alumni
Mike Sullivan, former Ambassador to Ireland, governor, Wyoming; Gerry Spence, Trial Lawyer, author, TV personality; Alan K. Simpson, former U.S. Senator, Wyoming, political commentator; Dave Freudenthal, former governor, Wyoming; Matt Mead, current governor, Wyoming; Marilyn Kite, Chief Justice, Wyoming Supreme Court

Grads Employed by Field (%)
Business/industry (13)
Government (10)
Judicial clerkship (18)
Private practice (49)
Public interest (10)

VANDERBILT UNIVERSITY
LAW SCHOOL

INSTITUTIONAL INFORMATION

Public/private	Private
Student/faculty ratio	14:1
% faculty part-time	60
% faculty female	36
% faculty minority	8
Total faculty	118

SURVEY SAYS...

Diverse opinions accepted in classrooms, Beautiful campus, Students love Nashville, TN, Good social life

STUDENTS

Enrollment of law school	612
% male/female	53/47
% from out-of-state	88
% full-time	100
% minority	18
% international	8
# of countries represented	10
Average age of entering class	23

ACADEMICS

Academic Experience Rating	97
Profs interesting rating	96
Profs accessible rating	86
Hours of study per day	4.08

Academic Specialties

Civil Procedure, Commercial, Constitutional, Corporation Securities, Criminal, Environmental, Government Services, Human Rights, International, Labor, Legal History, Legal Philosophy, Property, Taxation, Intellectual Property. Students can also craft their own specializations.

Advanced Degrees Offered

LLM Program, 1 year; JD/PhD in Law and Economics, 6 years

Combined Degrees Offered

JD/MBA, JD/MTS, JD/MPP, 4 years; JD/MA, JD/MDiv, 5 years; JD/PhD, 7 years; JD/MD, 6 years; LLM/MA of Latin American Studies, 2 years; PhD in Law and Economics, 5–6 years

Academics

Motivated legal eagles tend to fall in love with Vanderbilt University Law School's "collegial, relaxed environment." This "collegiality sets it apart from most other law schools of similar academic reputation." "The people are incredible, the classes are interesting and challenging, the building is beautiful, and [hometown] Nashville is the best city in the world." Others add, "You get all the benefits of a top-five law school, both faculty-wise and job-wise, but in a comfortable and low-key environment."

Academically speaking, Vanderbilt offers an array of joint-degree, specialized, interdisciplinary and clinical offerings. Education here begins with "an orientation week 'boot-camp' course called Life of the Law," during which "all 1L's are brought up to speed. [The course] gives everyone a sense of what law school [will] be like." Though many tout the overall academic experience at Vanderbilt as "fantastic," with "great faculty" and "bright, sociable students," some students desire "more practical experiences. The only classes that really focus on skills are limited enrollment and/or clinical courses (our clinic is *awesome* by the way)."

The top brass has taken steps to implement classes that remain on "the cutting edge of legal education." Students who have felt the effect of these changes say, "There are numerous specialization programs you can choose from. The most well-known and demanding is probably the law and business program." Students in this specialization benefit from "the ability to...gain practical experience from actual practitioners." The legal writing program, however, continues to be "less than inspiring" and "somewhat weak, as compared to the rest of the curriculum."

Professors at Vanderbilt "are outstanding; they challenge you to find good arguments and are very fair with students. You can tell they want to teach, not just do research." In addition, there are "outstanding opportunities for practical experience (externships, clinics)." When it comes to outside help, "Professors are beyond accessible." They "invite us to their houses for dinner and go out of their way to find us jobs." Overall students say the administration "is super involved in student life." "You can easily find a Dean with whom you feel comfortable." "The administration goes above and beyond to look out for the well-being of the students, especially during the first year when students are adjusting to law school." Others have a more mixed view, pointing out that though the administration tries to be "helpful and responsive to student needs," "they don't listen to what we actually need versus what they think we need."

In the wake of recent renovations, classrooms at Vanderbilt are "comfortable and up-to-date on technology with remote-control everything. Many of the smaller classrooms are beautiful conference rooms with high-tech amenities. Even the hallways are littered with lounge furniture." When it comes to students' list of gripes, very few rumblings are heard save for a few complaints about the "tough job market." Some feel that Career Services "does not do enough to give us access to alumni or search out alternative career paths." Others cite a "strong alumni network" and applaud "a strong Career Services staff" that has "eased the stress of the floundering economy." As one student aptly appends, "law school opens doors, but the extent to which certain doors will always [be open] depends on the student."

G. Todd Morton, Assistant Dean for Admissions
131 21st Avenue South, Nashville, TN 37203
Tel: 615.322.6452 Fax: 615.322.1531
E-Mail: admissions@law.vanderbilt.edu • Website: www.law.vanderbilt.edu

Life

Students here "are without a doubt the most social group of law students in the top twenty and Vandy facilitates this." A mixture of book smart and social butterfly, students say the typical Vanderbilt law student tends to be "a little bit younger on average than some other law schools." The law school here "is extremely collegial" and there is never a lack of social activities; "Mondays are trivia night at the local bars. We all get together for bar review on Thursdays. Fridays are free dinner and drinks at the law school…People gather around the free drink station across from our mailboxes in the mornings, and there are talks by industry giants (with free lunch) nearly every day." These institutional opportunities for connecting with colleagues "serves [you] well when you need class notes, a study group, or just some stress relief." Overall, quality of life "is exceptional."

Hometown Nashville is "a fine city with a vibrant nightlife and excellent restaurants." Others add, it's "a fantastic town to go to law school in because it's chill, young, and fun." One lighthearted law student here jokes, "It is February nineteenth and it's sixty-one degrees, eat your heart out, Harvard." Known to foster a "balance of work and play," Vanderbilt "is big enough to be nationally competitive and to offer a huge variety of courses and activities, and small enough that you will know most of the people at the weekly Friday kegger. And yes, we really do have (free) weekly Friday keggers. It's awesome."

Getting In

A plethora of qualified candidates apply to Vanderbilt each year, and the school's rolling admission policy allows it to take the time it needs to consider each application carefully. The average undergraduate GPA for the fall 2010 entering class was 3.72 with a median LSAT of 169.

Clinical program required	No
Legal writing course requirement	Yes
Legal methods course requirement	No
Legal research course requirement	Yes
Moot court requirement	No
Public interest law requirement	No

ADMISSIONS

Selectivity Rating	92
# applications received	4,885
% applicants accepted	25
% acceptees attending	16
Average LSAT	169
LSAT Range	165–170
Average undergrad GPA	3.72
Application fee	$50
Regular application	Rolling, up to 3/15
Regular notification	5/1
Early application program	No
Transfer students accepted	Yes
Evening division offered	No
Part-time accepted	No
CAS accepted	Yes

International Students

TOEFL required of international students	

FINANCIAL FACTS

Annual tuition	$44,900
Books and supplies	$1,788
Fees	$386
Room and board	$12,900
Financial aid application deadline	2/15
% first-year students receiving some sort of aid	86
% receiving some sort of aid	80
% of aid that is merit based	83
% receiving scholarships	71
Average grant	$17,000
Average loan	$41,784
Average total aid package	$67,360
Average debt	$114,720

EMPLOYMENT INFORMATION

Career Rating	97
Rate of placement (nine months out)	97
Average starting salary	$128,875
State for bar exam	NY, TN, IL, TX, CA
Pass rate for first-time bar	93

Employers Who Frequently Hire Grads
King & Spalding LLP Alston & Bird LLP Bass, Berry, & Sims PLC Locke Lord Bissell & Liddell Bryan Cave, LLP Orrick Herrington & Sutcliff Paul, Hastings, Janofsky & Walker, LLP DLA Piper U.S. LLP

Prominent Alumni
Greg Abbott, Texas Attorney General; Fred Thompson, Senator; Counsel Watergate Committee, Actor; Martha Daughtrey, U.S. Circuit Court Judge; Paul Atkins, SEC Commissioner; Pauline Gore, Attorney, Mother of VP Al Gore

Grads Employed by Field (%)
Academic (1)
Business/industry (7)
Government (13)
Judicial clerkship (19)
Military (2)
Private practice (51)
Public interest (8)

VERMONT LAW SCHOOL

Academics

At Vermont Law School, the students, faculty and staff "are anything but 'typical.'" Students are drawn here for the school's "environmental focus, non-competitive atmosphere, great professors with a variety of legal experience, and the willingness of professors/students to help you." As one student notes, "The high moral and ethical fiber of the school's community cannot be overstated." Vermont Law provides an "educational environment [which] emphasizes community above competition and everyone is encouraged to use their legal degree to give back." In essence, "Vermont Law is the place to go if you want to feel like you're part of a community."

Many choose VLS for its "stellar reputation in environmental law"; however, others say they are "equally impressed by their international law program and their unbelievable foreign exchange and dual-degree opportunities." "At the end of my law school career, I hope to be eligible to take the bar in both France and the U.S., and to practice environmental law on an international scale," says one student. Administration and professors here "are all highly regarded in their respective fields and are completely available and willing to help students with intern/externships and employment opportunities." On the whole, instructors "are intelligent, kind, and accessible people." "It is easy to find a mentor you connect with because our faculty possess[es] a broad range of experience and specialties." Perhaps unsurprisingly, others note, "Much of the faculty is overly liberal. However, they are also extremely approachable and always willing to assist outside of class. If you are looking to study environmental law, there's no place on Earth like VLS. The number and depth of environmental classes is unbeatable." In addition, "The Academic Success Program is an excellent resource and utilizes student mentors to make asking for help a lot less frightening."

Classroom and research facilities on campus "are brand-new, state-of-the-art, and are comfortable." True to the school's sustainable roots, "Even the desks and podiums in the classrooms are made by local Vermont woodworkers with local materials." In addition, "The majority of the buildings that VLS students frequent (i.e., those that house all the classrooms, the cafeteria, the student center, the library, student mailboxes, the Environmental Law Center, and IT) are all interconnected—which is ideal during cold and snowy Vermont winters!" The library "is beautiful" with "a lot of sunlight on the top floor." Whatever it may be "lacking in books in-house," it is "helpful in acquiring through interlibrary loan." The IT department, however, "is a nightmare. E-mail tends to be slow, the Internet connection on campus is often slower than at home, and the servers use unsecured certificates."

When it comes to post-law school placement, some students feel "career development and alumni relations are very, very weak and need a huge revamping." However, "The administration is awesome. They always have their doors open to all students no matter what our issues may be. Especially Dean J, she's an amazing woman that inspires me to be a better person and motivates me to change the world around me."

Life

Attending Vermont Law School "is a lot like summer camp." "The location is unlike any other." Located in the Green Mountains with the White River running through campus "(complete with a nearby rope swing and kayak/tubing drop-in point)," the school's

Kathy Hartman, Associate Dean for Enrollment Management
Chelsea Street, South Royalton, VT 05068-0096
Tel: 888-277-5985 Fax: 802-831-1174
E-Mail: admiss@vermontlaw.edu • Website: www.vermontlaw.edu

facilities "even offer composting toilets, which give it an outhouse sort of feeling (don't worry, we have real toilets, too.)" Some say hometown South Royalton "is a perfect example of a small, New England village." "You're about thirty minutes from the nearest 'city.'" Others say, the "town is quaint but in the middle of nowhere and has no facilities. I mean none. One bar, [one] small grocery, one restaurant. [You] have to drive over twenty minutes for anything more." Basically," If you love doing outdoor activities every day, this place is for you. If you have any ambivalence about your feelings toward outdoor sports, seriously evaluate how happy you would be here."

Students are quick to add, "What we lack in access to shopping or amenities, we make up for in community." "Most of the events on campus (I'd estimate ninety percent or more) are student-organized and student-run. This includes educational dinners, speaking events, talent shows, costume contests, movie nights, outdoor adventures, competitions, festivals, and blood drives." The "summer camp feel" also translates "into a high level of camaraderie." "Everybody is always willing to lend a hand, a book, a ride, or a shovel." And shovel they do! "We are in the middle of nowhere and it is very cold and snowy during the winter. However, I like that everyone socializes together on the weekends. We go to parties hosted by our friends or the one pub in town. We are inspired to create our own social events."

The campus itself "is beautiful; it's in rural Vermont which affords wonderful opportunities to do activities outdoors: skiing, hiking, floating down the river, etc." Amenities-wise, students complain that the current gym is "embarrassingly unattractive and budget-looking."

Getting In

Undergraduate GPA for the fall 2010 entering class ranged from 3.13 (25th percentile) to 3.55 (75th percentile). LSAT scores in the same range were 153 (25th percentile) to 159 (75th percentile).

Clinical program required	No
Legal writing course requirement	Yes
Legal methods course requirement	Yes
Legal research course requirement	Yes
Moot court requirement	Yes
Public interest law requirement	No

ADMISSIONS

Selectivity Rating	**72**
# applications received	1,056
% applicants accepted	59
% acceptees attending	34
Average LSAT	156
LSAT Range	153–159
Average undergrad GPA	3.35
Application fee	$60
Regular notification	4/1
Early application program	No
Transfer students accepted	Yes
Evening division offered	No
Part-time accepted	No
CAS accepted	Yes

International Students

TOEFL required of international students	

FINANCIAL FACTS

Annual tuition	$42,220
Books and supplies	$1,500
Fees	$425
Room and board	$10,280
Financial aid application deadline	3/1
% first-year students receiving some sort of aid	93
% receiving some sort of aid	98
% of aid that is merit based	76
% receiving scholarships	67
Average grant	$14,550
Average loan	$42,745
Average total aid package	$56,235
Average debt	$127,914

EMPLOYMENT INFORMATION

Career Rating	**78**
Rate of placement (nine months out)	89
Average starting salary	$53,610
State for bar exam	NY, VT, MA, NH, NJ
Pass rate for first-time bar	80

Employers Who Frequently Hire Grads
Federal & State Judges in the Northeast (varies from year to year as to which particular judges & courts hire); Law firms throughout New England (again it varies from year to year as to which ones hire each year); Beveridge & Diamond in Washington, D.C.; Federal & State Agencies; and public interest organizations including legal aid, public defenders

Prominent Alumni
Glenn Berger, Partner, Skadden Arps; Charles diLeva, Lead Environmental Counsel World Bank; Linda Smiddy, Professor of Law, Vermont Law School; Cindy Burns, Sr Representative High UN Commission on Refugees; Steve Mashuda, Staff Attorney, Earth Justice

Grads Employed by Field (%)
Private practice (29)

VILLANOVA UNIVERSITY
SCHOOL OF LAW

INSTITUTIONAL INFORMATION

Public/private	Private
Affiliation	Roman Catholic
Student/faculty ratio	18:1
% faculty part-time	53
% faculty female	39
% faculty minority	17
Total faculty	119

SURVEY SAYS...

Great research resources, Great library staff, Beautiful campus

STUDENTS

Enrollment of law school	765
% male/female	57/43
% from out-of-state	49
% full-time	100
% minority	19
% international	1
# of countries represented	5
Average age of entering class	23

ACADEMICS

Academic Experience Rating	77
Profs interesting rating	77
Profs accessible rating	82
Hours of study per day	4.80

Advanced Degrees Offered

JD, 3 years; LLM-Taxation, 24 credits

Combined Degrees Offered

JD/MBA, 3–4 years; JD/LLM-Taxation, 3.5 years; JD/LLM in International Studies (third year abroad), 3 years

Clinical program required	No
Legal writing	
course requirement	Yes
Legal methods	
course requirement	No
Legal research	
course requirement	Yes
Moot court requirement	Yes
Public interest	
law requirement	No

Academics

At Villanova University School of Law, students find "a good balance in an interactive and educational atmosphere" through a blend of lecture, discussion, and serious hands-on experience. Students say the "absolutely wonderful" professors are the heart and soul of the program. "Instructors are all extremely intelligent and have a wealth of real-world experience, yet remain in touch with students," says a 1L. In fact, he tells us, "My law school professors are much more helpful and approachable than my undergrad professors were." Another student agrees that the "professors' knowledge and experience is fundamental to the Villanova experience." Many here happily report a lack of the "heavy competitive atmosphere that you hear about at other schools," noting, "We all encourage each other to do well."

Villanova takes a fairly traditional approach to introductory course work, and students say, "There is still a heavy reliance on the Socratic Method and many classes use a lecture format (especially in the first year)." In the next two years, students continue studying the basic principals of law, while adding elective courses to their schedule. Experiential learning is emphasized throughout the curriculum, and students dole out praise for the school's strong legal writing and research courses, simulation programs, clinics, and externships. The school has a "clear emphasis" on "solidifying students' legal writing skills." In addition, students take on real legal work thanks to the school's "strong commitment to community service and pro bono work."

For a Catholic institution, it should come as no surprise that a "Catholic identity" reigns supreme. However, some students wish opportunities for service were not restricted by the administration's commitment to Catholic values. ("No 'regular hours' in the forty-hour work week can be spent helping efforts to litigate for women's reproductive freedom, and the participating organization must be aware of the policy.") Ultimately, many wonder "how the administration will balance the school's Catholic mission with its mission as a legal institution."

Villanova's eagerly anticipated, state-of-the-art law school facility opened in August 2009 on a site adjacent to the university's suburban Philadelphia campus. Law students no longer have cause to bemoan the "severe lack of classrooms, computers, parking spots, hallways, lockers, and space in general" that they complained about in years prior as the new facility offers twice as much space as the old building and a new 500-car parking garage, to boot. While they may complain that the campus has a "high school atmosphere," students also say they leave Villanova well-prepared for their professional career in the adult world. Students insist that "opportunities for practical experience are abundant," and the "Career Services Department works really hard to help students find jobs in the private and public sectors." They note that the school has "strong professional contacts in Pennsylvania, New Jersey, and Delaware" and that "major firms routinely interview on campus and hire many Villanova graduates."

Noe Bernal, Assistant Dean for Admissions
299 North Spring Mill Road, Villanova, PA 19085
Tel: 610-519-7010 Fax: 610-519-6291
E-Mail: admissions@law.villanova.edu • Website: www.law.villanova.edu

Life

When they are not hitting the books, Villanova students live the high life at the many bars, clubs, and restaurants in Philadelphia, as well as at campus events. A student assures us, "The Student Bar Association spends a lot of time planning activities to students. There are many active students groups as well." According to another, "Students get along well and the ones that choose to socialize together have a great time."

Still, many students choose to maintain a life outside of school, living off-campus with their friends or spouses. Getting to campus is easy since "The train runs literally out the front door of the law school." One student advises, "There is a bar that students usually hang out at which can be fun, but sometimes after seeing these people all day and every day, it's good to do something away from the law school crowd." Luckily, that is easy to accomplish at Villanova thanks to the school's "amazing" location. One student enthuses, "It is twenty-five minutes from Philadelphia, as well as a short drive to New York City, Washington, D.C., Baltimore, the beaches, and skiing!"

Most students say that they get along with their classmates, though some say the student body is pretty "homogenous" and "not exactly diverse." However, "Villanova has openly stated that they feel that diversity is a compelling interest at the institution" and many believe that "in time, Villanova will be one of the more diverse legal institutions."

Getting In

For the admitted class, students in the 25th percentile had an average LSAT score of 160 and a 3.27 GPA. Admitted students in the 75th percentile had an average LSAT score of 163 and a 3.62 GPA. However, Villanova may consider students with a lower GPA if they offer other important qualities, such as commitment to service, volunteer work, or unique professional experience. The majority of students who enter do so within a year or two of college, and the average age of a Villanova student in their first year is twenty-five.

ADMISSIONS

Selectivity Rating	80
# applications received	3,739
% applicants accepted	44
% acceptees attending	15
LSAT Range	159–163
Application fee	$75
Regular application	Rolling, up to 4/1
Regular notification	Rolling
Early application program	No
Transfer students accepted	Yes
Evening division offered	No
Part-time accepted	No
CAS accepted	Yes

FINANCIAL FACTS

Annual tuition	$36,690
Books and supplies	$4,845
Fees	$390
Room and board	$15,975
Financial aid application deadline	4/1
% first-year students receiving some sort of aid	83
% receiving some sort of aid	83
% of aid that is merit based	6
% receiving scholarships	26
Average grant	$16,361
Average loan	$40,639
Average total aid package	$43,407
Average debt	$116,878

EMPLOYMENT INFORMATION

Career Rating	75
Rate of placement (nine months out)	86
State for bar exam	PA, NJ, NY, DE
Pass rate for first-time bar	91

Employers Who Frequently Hire Grads
Law firms in the mid-atlantic region, particularly in Philadelphia, New York, New Jersey, and Delaware; state and federal judges; and government agencies at all levels

Prominent Alumni
Hon. Edward G. Rendell, Governor, State of Pennsylvania; Hon. Marjorie O. Rendell, Judge, U.S. Court of Appeals for the Third Circuit; Jeffrey S. Moorad, General Partner, Arizona Diamondbacks; Richard L. Trumka, Secretary-Treasurer, AFL CIO; Kelly A. Ayotte, Attorney General, State of New Hampshire

Grads Employed by Field (%)
Academic (2)
Business/industry (12)
Government (5)
Judicial clerkship (14)
Military (1)
Private practice (44)
Public interest (4)

WAKE FOREST UNIVERSITY
SCHOOL OF LAW

Academics

Ideally sized, Wake Forest School of Law is "extremely generous with aid money" and "provides an intimate community while still being academically challenging." "There aren't very many specialized course offerings," but "the size is fantastic because you can really connect with the professors." "Sections are relatively small, but not annoyingly so," "and in a bevy of upper-level classes you get seminars with just a handful of students." Classrooms are "colorful, stimulating, and full of open discussion." "I can't imagine an atmosphere more conducive to building competent and ethical legal professionals," says a 3L. "The only students who don't enjoy it are the ones who want to sit in the back of a large class and blend into the rest of the numbers. That strategy has little success at Wake." The legal writing program is "extensive" and "practical training opportunities are excellent"—especially if you're interested in litigation. "I had the opportunity to try cases before graduation and take a deposition on my own," reports a 3L. "I feel like I could go into practice today and have some idea of what I am doing."

There are "a few crusty old battle-axes" on the faculty. On the whole, though, students at Wake revere their "diverse and brilliant," "amazing," and "entirely accessible" professors. Their "doors are always open and they genuinely care about their students, not only academically, but personally as well." Administratively, the school "does a lot visibly to try and work hard for their students." The top brass is "fantastic" and "ready to help students without hesitation." "When you have a concern, they are able to do something about it right away," says a 1L, "unlike at a large school where people can get lost in the shuffle." "Some of the midlevel administration is mediocre," though, and "not very organized."

"The facilities are relatively new compared to many other schools in the region." "They certainly aren't terrible." "There has been a big technology push, especially in the library." "Every carrel has plugs and lights." "The courtyard is always abuzz with students when the weather is nice." The larger undergraduate campus is "gorgeous." However, the consensus among students here is that Wake "desperately needs more space." "The law school is in the most horribly designed building on earth," gripes a 3L. "Getting from one class to the next requires training." Between classes, hallways are "crowded" with "mobs of law students." Group study space is "limited," too.

Students are confident about their job prospects. About seventy percent take the private practice route on graduation. The Carolinas and Georgia are the most frequent destinations but a law degree from Wake Forest travels pretty decently. It's not at all uncommon for grads to find work in New York, Texas, California, and a number of other states. We hear some grumbling that Career Services is "very much set in the old go-work-in-large-law-firm mentality." Also, internship and externship options are somewhat scarce. Career Services provides "tremendous amounts of resources," though, and the staff "actively facilitates students in finding a job that fits them and their individual preferences, personality, and long-term plans." "The school also does a great job of providing opportunities to meet lawyers and judges."

Life

"One of the best things about Wake is the diversity of backgrounds and hometowns," declares a 1L. "We get people from all over the country." Students come here "with a broad range of" experiences and "there is an excellent balance of political views" represented in each entering class. Some students say that the academic environment is "very

R. Jay Shirely, Assistant Dean of Admissions and Financial Aid
Box 7206, Winston-Salem, NC 27109
Tel: 336-758-5437 Fax: 336-758-3930
E-Mail: admissions@law.wfu.edu • Website: www.law.wfu.edu

competitive." Others say that "there are the occasional gunners" but it's a miniscule group. Still other students tell us that "there is a strong sense of cooperation and collegiality." "I have not felt an ounce of competition in this school," swears a 1L.

"Winston-Salem isn't New York" but it's "a very cute little city" with "warm Southern temperatures" throughout most of the year and there's affordable housing "within walking distance or a short drive" from campus. Socially, "there is not much else going on in students' lives aside from school." "There are definitely cliques." "Because of the small size, everyone knows everyone's business" and "the gossip mill runs completely amok." Nevertheless, most everyone is very happy. "This school is vibrant," promises a 2L. "There is always something going on. We have a broad spectrum of guest speakers on a regular basis." "Wake has a lot of lunch programs," adds a 1L, "and they usually feed us." "I got a ton of free food," notes a nostalgic, satiated 3L. "Football and basketball games are a big draw with most law students during the fall and winter." There are weekly bar reviews and "lots of" opportunities for weekend revelry. "I did not think I would ever be able to recapture the community atmosphere, social bonds, and personal experience that made my undergraduate experience at a small liberal arts college unique," beams a 1L. "However, Wake Law has done the impossible. "

Getting In

Enrolled students at the 25th percentile have LSAT scores of about 160 and GPAs around 3.25. At the 75th percentile, LSAT scores are roughly 164 and GPAs are just over 3.70.

Clinical program required	
Legal writing	
course requirement	Yes
Legal methods	
course requirement	No
Legal research	
course requirement	Yes
Moot court requirement	No
Public interest	
law requirement	No

ADMISSIONS

Selectivity Rating	88
# applications received	2,984
% applicants accepted	33
% acceptees attending	17
Average LSAT	163
LSAT Range	160–164
Average undergrad GPA	3.60
Application fee	$60
Regular application	Rolling
Regular notification	4/15
Early application program	No
Transfer students accepted	Yes
Evening division offered	No
Part-time accepted	No
CAS accepted	Yes

International Students

TOEFL of international students

FINANCIAL FACTS

Annual tuition	$36,514
Books and supplies	$1,000
Fees	$318
Room and board	$14,000
Financial aid application	
deadline	5/15
% first-year students	
receiving some sort of aid	78
% receiving some sort of aid	78
% of aid that is merit based	74
% receiving scholarships	42
Average grant	$21,911
Average loan	$45,000
Average debt	$93,223

EMPLOYMENT INFORMATION

Career Rating	**95**	**Grads Employed by Field (%)**
Rate of placement (nine months out)	96	Academic (3)
Average starting salary	$102,450	Business/industry (8)
State for bar exam	NC, VA, GA, NY, FL	Government (7)
Pass rate for first-time bar	95	Judicial clerkship (8)
Employers Who Frequently Hire Grads		Military (1)
For a representative list, see Career		Private practice (62)
Services website at www.law.wfu.edu.		Public interest (12)

WASHBURN UNIVERSITY
SCHOOL OF LAW

Academics

As a law school, Washburn University is "committed to all three stages of a law student's experience: getting you to go to their school, getting you through school, [and] getting you a job during and after school." It is the "quality of the professors and their commitment to students' educations" that "without a doubt" makes Washburn an "excellent choice for law school." "The school focuses on developing individual legal skills for the 'real-life' practice of law," says a 2L. "Washburn is outstanding for economic reasons as well. The tuition is very reasonable compared to [tuition at] other law schools, the scholarship program is very generous, and the cost of living in Topeka is low." The "outstanding" professors "want their students to succeed," as evidenced by the "personal attention that each professor gives each student." Similarly, the administration "strives to create a positive learning environment" for students by making "the transition into law school as simple as [possible]." "[The administration] called me when I was accepted, and when my wife and I visited they made us feel at home," says a 1L. A 2L adds, "I am satisfied with the administration. The career services, professors, and library staff are all great-[they're] very available and always willing and happy to assist you."

Washburn Law's curriculum places a "strong emphasis on legal research and writing," with its "required year-long course" that is "extremely beneficial" for those looking for "creating writing samples and real world experience." Students also appreciate the "natural resources certification program" and the "fantastic two-semester course in oil and gas law." However, some would like to see "more writing and bar prep opportunities in the classroom." "I've had too many classes that teach some law, but don't help the student much for passing the bar and providing practical writing experience," says a 2L. Others wouldn't mind more "opportunities for externships and internships outside of Topeka," as well as "improvement" in course offerings, such as "environmental law."

"Being located" in Topeka, the "state capital," goes a long way in offering "many oppor- tunities for those seeking" both traditional and "nontraditional legal careers." Despite this, many students feel uncertain about their career prospects in the current economic climate. "It's most unfortunate to spend all this money on a legal education, have stellar grades, great references, and still face unemployment due to terrible job markets," says a 3L. However, the Professional Development Office "makes every opportunity available to [students]" and takes "extra efforts to ensure career success."

From a research standpoint, Washburn Law's library is "outstanding" and has "an impressive number of legal resources available to its students." However, on an aesthetic level, the building is "not impressive." "The library has almost no windows," says a 1L. "It is like living in a basement. Humans need vitamin D! Vitamin D deficiencies make a hard year even more depressing." Indeed, despite "great" and "spacious" classrooms that feature "plenty of electrical outlets for laptops," students agree that "the school needs a cosmetic makeover." "The facilities are outdated and the law library needs more room to expand," says a 1L. "We simply cannot achieve our greatness with such a small footprint on this campus."

KARLA WHITAKER, DIRECTOR OF ADMISSIONS
1700 COLLEGE AVENUE, TOPEKA, KS 66621-1140
TEL: 785-670-1185 FAX: 785-670-1120
E-MAIL: ADMISSIONS@WASHBURNLAW.EDU • WEBSITE: WASHBURNLAW.EDU

Life

Washburn Law has a "diverse student body" thanks to a "larger population of non-traditional students than [at] most [other] schools." And though students are a "competitive" and "driven" group, the school lacks a "cutthroat attitude." "My classmates are the best," says a 2L. "Someone is always willing to pass along notes when I miss class [and] I've never even heard of someone hiding a book." A 1L agrees, "People are here to help you succeed. Competition exists, but it is more a desire to do well than hold your peers back." Because of this environment, there is "a significant amount of collaboration" between students on projects and "work opportunities." Interestingly, this collaboration "is not required," but rather, according to students, an "indication of personal values and the student body's overall support for one another."

Students are nearly unanimous in their praise of Washburn Law, but the good vibes don't extend to the school's location in Topeka, Kansas. As a 2L quips, "The law school is great; Topeka is really terrible." "Topeka is not a nice place to live, but deal with it, you should be studying anyway," says a 1L. Others have a more rose-tinted view. "Topeka is an ideal place for a law school," says a 1L. "There are plenty of outdoor activities available and plenty of places to hang out. Where else can you go to law school and not have to pay for parking and not have rush hour to worry about?!" Some even find that Topeka is "going through a renaissance in many respects," particularly in the "arts," since "young people" are "staying around" and "investing in their community."

Getting In

Washburn does not base its decisions solely on numerical scores but considers a variety of factors. Recently admitted students at Washburn Law at the 25th percentile have LSAT scores of 153 and GPAs in the 3.0 range. Admitted students at the 75th percentile have LSAT scores of 158 and GPAs of roughly 3.71.

MBA that unites business and legal perspectives. Students in this dual degree program may transfer 6 law credits to the MBA and 6 business credits to the JD.

Clinical program required	No
Legal writing course requirement	Yes
Legal methods course requirement	Yes
Legal research course requirement	Yes
Moot court requirement	No
Public interest law requirement	No

ADMISSIONS

Selectivity Rating	82
# applications received	1,102
% applicants accepted	39
% acceptees attending	39
Average LSAT	155
LSAT Range	153–158
Average undergrad GPA	3.22
Application fee	$40
Regular application	Rolling
Regular notification	6/1
Early application program	No
Transfer students accepted	Yes
Evening division offered	No
Part-time accepted	No
CAS accepted	Yes

International Students

TOEFL recommended of international students

FINANCIAL FACTS

Annual tuition (in-state/out-of-state)	$16,560/ $25,830
Books and supplies	$2,500
Fees	$70
Room and board	$9,074
Financial aid application deadline	7/1
% first-year students receiving some sort of aid	94
% receiving some sort of aid	91
% of aid that is merit based	18
% receiving scholarships	46
Average grant	$10,753
Average loan	$26,626
Average total aid package	$29,674
Average debt	$80,488

EMPLOYMENT INFORMATION

		Grads Employed by Field (%)
Career Rating	76	Academic (2)
Rate of placement (nine months out)	88	Business/industry (10)
Average starting salary	$54,680	Government (19)
State for bar exam	KS, MO	Judicial clerkship (6)
Pass rate for first-time bar	87	Military (3)
Prominent Alumni		Private practice (47)
Lillian A. Apodaca, Past President Hispanic		Public interest (11)
Bar Association; Robert J. Dole, Former		
U.S. Senator; Bill Kurtis, Journalist/		
American Justice; Delano E. Lewis, Former		
Ambassador to South Africa; Ron Richey,		
Chair of Exec. Comm. of Torchmark Corp.		

WASHINGTON UNIVERSITY
SCHOOL OF LAW

INSTITUTIONAL INFORMATION

Public/private	Private
Student/faculty ratio	13:1
% faculty part-time	66
% faculty female	31
% faculty minority	2
Total faculty	177

SURVEY SAYS...

Diverse opinions accepted in classrooms, Great research resources, Beautiful campus

STUDENTS

Enrollment of law school	952
% male/female	56/44
% full-time	100
% minority	21
% international	7
# of countries represented	5
Average age of entering class	23

ACADEMICS

Academic Experience Rating	82
Profs interesting rating	87
Profs accessible rating	84
Hours of study per day	3.50

Academic Specialties

Civil Procedure, Commercial, Constitutional, Corporation Securities, Criminal, Environmental, Government Services, Human Rights, International, Labor, Legal History, Legal Philosophy, Property, Taxation, Intellectual Property

Advanced Degrees Offered

JD, 3 years; JSD; LLM for Foreign Lawyers; LLM in Taxation; LLM in Intellectual Property and Technology Law

Combined Degrees Offered

JD/MBA, JD/MS in Economics, JD/MSW in Social Work, JD/MA in Jewish, Islamic & Near Eastern Studies, JD/MA in East Asian Studies, JD/PHD in Political Science

Academics

Washington University School of Law in St. Louis is a "student-centered institution" with "outstanding" clinical programs. One of the biggest draws here is that "all students are guaranteed the opportunity to participate in at least one clinic during law school." Those clinics are stellar. In the Congressional and Administrative Law Clinic, as one example, 3Ls get to spend their spring semester interning in Congress and federal agencies. Notable joint-degree programs include the traditional JD/MBA as well as a unique JD/MA in East Asian studies. "Excellent specializations" include international law, intellectual property, and business law.

WashU's "diverse" and "accomplished" faculty is "available virtually all the time to answer student questions." Many professors here are "great teachers and terrific human beings" who "have a passion for imparting their knowledge upon the students." "Several rank among the best instructors I've had in my educational career," gloats a 2L. However, there are "some mediocre" professors in the mix. Another 2L elaborates: While "a handful of my professors have exceeded my highest expectations as instructors, in a few other classes, I am certain I could teach more effectively than my professors given a month's notice." Administratively, "There is really almost no red tape." The "wonderful," "student-focused" administration "will do anything to help a student survive and flourish." "They do their best to make law school as touchy-feely an experience as possible," describes one student. "From Admissions to the Registrar's Office to various professors' assistants, everyone at WULaw is just great." "Financial aid is lightning fast too."

Students are irreconcilably split when it comes to Career Services. One faction maintains that the staff has a "willingness to get you where you want to go." In addition to St. Louis and other Midwestern metropolises, "Many grads go to D.C. and New York City." "I think that Career Services does a good job of getting people national exposure," agrees a 2L. "I had callbacks in D.C., Orlando, Chicago, Philadelphia, Minneapolis, and New York, and I didn't finish in the top twenty-five percent." Another faction contends that Career Services is "not very helpful" and "could do more to bring in employers." "The vast majority of students will tell you that CSO is worthless unless you are in the top fifteen percent or want to work in the public interest sector in St. Louis," asserts a 2L. "We have some of the best law students in the country, and some employers seem to not recognize this."

The "beautiful" facilities at WashU "seem brand new." Anheuser-Busch Hall "is an amazing place to go to school every day" and "what an undergraduate student dreams of when they think about law school." The law school building is "only a few years old and it has its own cafeteria," an indoor courtyard, and "impressive architectural details." Students do complain a lot about "wireless dead spots," though. Otherwise, the research facilities and technological resources are "nothing short of absolutely satisfactory" and "really enhance the law school experience." "The library is outstanding" and "has lots of study rooms," though it "can be a little congested at times." "The reading room is amazing."

Life

WashU is pretty small, so "You will definitely not be lost in the shuffle." There is a "unique group of talented, intelligent," and "well-rounded" students here and, if these students do say so themselves, they are "the friendliest and funniest people you will ever meet." It tends to be a younger crowd and, while "the paradigmatic law student wearing

JANET BOLIN, ASSOCIATE DEAN OF ADMISSIONS AND STUDENT SERVICES
1 BROOKINGS DRIVE, CAMPUS BOX 1120, ST. LOUIS, MO 63130-4899
TEL: 314-935-4525 FAX: 314-935-8778
E-MAIL: ADMISS@WULAW.WUSTL.EDU • WEBSITE: LAW.WUSTL.EDU

social blinders" is easily recognizable at WashU, the social scene is very much "a priority." "The students at the law school take its name"—Anheuser-Busch Hall—"very seriously." "We have fun, smart, competitive students who are generally as interested in having a social life as they are in ranking toward the top of our class," explains a 2L. "Every Friday," the school hosts a "well-attended" happy hour in the courtyard. "Students, professors, kegs, and, yes, beer pong," is how one student characterizes the event. "Plenty of organized school activities" also include an annual student-produced comedy called the "Barely Legal Law Revue."

Academically, a few students claim that WashU is "becoming more competitive," but most tell us that "competition is unspoken and left to dark corners of the library." "I have yet to sense any competitiveness among students, even when exams came around," observes a discerning transfer student. "The student population is very laid-back" and students "are always willing to help one another understand the material." Self-scheduled exams for 2Ls and 3Ls help ease some of the tension.

"The WashU campus is located in an upscale suburb of St. Louis with an air of subdued sophistication." The campus is "right by Forest Park, home to the largest free zoo in the country, as well as many other attractions" and not far from bars, restaurants, and things to do. It's a fine place to spend a few years as a student. "St. Louis is not as chic as a lot of cities in the country," admits a 1L, "but it is cheap."

Getting In

The 25th percentile of admitted students has LSAT scores of about 161 and GPAs of about 3.2. Admitted students at the 75th percentile have LSAT scores of roughly 167 and GPAs of about 3.7.

Clinical program required	No
Legal writing course requirement	Yes
Legal methods course requirement	No
Legal research course requirement	Yes
Moot court requirement	No
Public interest law requirement	No

ADMISSIONS

Selectivity Rating	72
# applications received	3,700
Average LSAT	167
LSAT Range	162–168
Average undergrad GPA	3.6
Application fee	$70
Regular notification	4/15
Early application program	No
Transfer students accepted	Yes
Evening division offered	No
Part-time accepted	No
CAS accepted	Yes

International Students

TOEFL recommended of international students	

FINANCIAL FACTS

Annual tuition	$39,700
Books and supplies	$2,000
Fees	$796
Room and board	$16,600
Financial aid application deadline	3/1
% first-year students receiving some sort of aid	85
% receiving some sort of aid	82
% of aid that is merit based	100
% receiving scholarships	60
Average grant	$15,000
Average loan	$40,200
Average total aid package	$57,000
Average debt	$102,000

EMPLOYMENT INFORMATION

Career Rating	72
State for bar exam	MO, IL, CA, NY

WAYNE STATE UNIVERSITY
LAW SCHOOL

Academics

Wayne State University Law School "in the heart of Detroit" is "a phenomenal value" for both residents of Michigan and out-of-staters. The "very high" bar-passage rate is consistently among the best in the state, and "The part-time evening program allows students to study the law while still maintaining families and other employment." Also, "There is no lack of opportunity to gain professional experience" here, and "Many of us leave law school with a good idea of how to actually practice law." Wayne offers easy access to a host of state and federal courts and "a plethora of resources." There are, for example, five joint-degree programs and six clinics that allow students to represent real clients.

Students here have nary a negative word to say about their "knowledgeable and caring" professors. "Wayne, by and through its professors, does a great job of helping students become acclimated to learning the law," says a 2L. Many (if not most) of them have practiced law before becoming professors, so they have "real-world" experience to bring to the classroom. "This helps students better prepare for what to expect in practice," says one. Professors are also "real people" who are "very accessible and easygoing" outside of class about anything "from job search information to current trends in legal theory." "My 1L torts professor and criminal law professor were even in a rock band together," says one student.

Many students at WSU believe that Career Services "needs to be improved," which the new dean has committed to do. "If you're in the top ten percent here, you can definitely get into a large firm" through on-campus interviews. As for the other ninety percent, the staff can be an "invaluable tool." "They are not going to look for jobs for you or do your work, but they are more than willing to offer you assistance in your job search, including advice about where to apply, how to find jobs, and look over resumes and cover letters, etc." Still, this school is "strictly regional." "The overwhelming majority of its grads become practicing attorneys in Michigan." Nevertheless, for those looking for this end, the school is "well-esteemed in the state," and students are pretty optimistic about their employment prospects. Wayne Law's location in metro Detroit is a major plus, as it's "the biggest legal market in the state, which allows practicing lawyers and judges to teach courses and gives students the opportunity to learn practical skills." WSU's "very active" alumni network dominates the Michigan legal community, and graduates "teach classes, attend events, and recruit at Wayne." Courts and small and mid-size firms all over southeastern Michigan "respect the school and are confident in hiring Wayne graduates." "It's not the University of Michigan, so employers aren't going to be just handing out jobs," cautions a 3L. "But if you work hard enough, you'll find employment."

Classrooms at Wayne State are old, but "kept up well," and there are "plugs at every seat and wireless Internet throughout." Other aspects of the facilities are much newer, and the library in particular is "amazing" and "has everything you could ever need."

Life

"The student body is interesting and diverse and friendly," reports a 2L. "You regularly find a mix of young and old, liberal and conservative, various ethnicities, and work experiences in Wayne State classrooms." This diversity of opinion and students "creates

ERICKA M. JACKSON, ASSISTANT DEAN OF ADMISSIONS
471 W. PALMER, DETROIT, MI 48202
TEL: 313-577-3937 FAX: 313-993-8129
E-MAIL: LAWINQUIRE@WAYNE.EDU • WEBSITE: WWW.LAW.WAYNE.EDU

an atmosphere where everyone feels welcome" and "enhances the exchange of ideas in class." According to the majority, "There is a lot of camaraderie, especially within the sections" and "competitiveness among students is generally low." "If you find that you need help with anything," promises a 1L, "other students are always willing to help you out."

Socially, Wayne Law "isn't a traditional campus environment." This campus is "located in the center of a community that has seen some rough times." Many students tell us, "There isn't as much of a sense of community as at other schools." "Most of the events end by 5:00 P.M.," they say, and a large segment of the student body "flees back to the suburbs and their respective lives" as soon as class ends; however, there's "a growing law student social scene within Detroit proper." "Those of us who live near the school tend to stick together, and there are a wide variety of activities and bars surrounding the Wayne State campus," says a 3L. There are also "intramural sports teams as well as competitions between schools within the university, like law versus med school, where the law students really bond together." "There are a lot of social outlets within Detroit and its suburbs that are frequented by the law students." "Royal Oak is a big area for law students to live," explains a 2L, "and generally, we tend to congregate in the downtown Royal Oak area to socialize."

Getting In

Admitted students at the 25th percentile tend to have LSAT scores in the low 150s and GPAs in the 3.2 range. Admitted students at the 75th percentile have LSAT scores approaching 160 and GPAs of about 3.7. Aside from LSAT scores and GPA, the admissions committee also considers relevant personal qualities and characteristics of significance such as socioeconomic and educational disadvantage, work experience, leadership qualities, commitment to volunteer and community service, and communication skills.

Moot court requirement	No
Public interest	
law requirement	No

ADMISSIONS

Selectivity Rating	**80**
# applications received	1,219
% applicants accepted	45
% acceptees attending	31
Average LSAT	155
LSAT Range	153–159
Average undergrad GPA	3.34
Application fee	$50
Regular application	Rolling, up to 3/15
Regular notification	Rolling
Early application program	No
Transfer students accepted	Yes
Evening division offered	Yes
Part-time accepted	Yes
CAS accepted	Yes

FINANCIAL FACTS

Annual tuition	
(in-state/out-of-state)	$23,424/ $25,740
Books and supplies	$1,240
Fees	$1,447
Room and board	
(on/off campus)	$7,660/ $12,350
Financial aid application	
deadline	6/30
% first-year students	
receiving some sort of aid	89
% receiving some sort of aid	91
% of aid that is merit based	18
% receiving scholarships	41
Average grant	$13,016
Average loan	$26,136
Average total aid package	$29,416
Average debt	$67,029

EMPLOYMENT INFORMATION

Career Rating	**82**
Rate of placement (nine months out)	86
Average starting salary	$72,471
State for bar exam	MI, NY, IL, CA, GA
Pass rate for first-time bar	90

Employers Who Frequently Hire Grads
Leading law firms in Michigan, in-house legal departments of Fortune 500 and other corporations and governmental agencies

Prominent Alumni
Eugene Driker, Business Law; Hon. Nancy G. Edmunds, Judge, U.S. District Court; Tyrone C. Fahner, Antitrust; Hon. Damon J. Keith, Civil rights; Judge, U.S. Court of Appeals for the Sixth Circuit; Marilyn Kelly, Justice, Michigan Supreme Court

Grads Employed by Field (%)
Academic (1)
Business/industry (17)
Government (9)
Judicial clerkship (5)
Private practice (63)
Public interest (5)

WEST VIRGINIA UNIVERSITY
COLLEGE OF LAW

Academics

West Virginia University's College of Law provides students with a "personal, yet professional, atmosphere," where the "emphasis [is] on being a functional lawyer." The dirt-cheap tuition (for in-state residents, who comprise the overwhelming majority of students here) and "passionate, intelligent, and helpful" people that make up the faculty, staff, and student body, all converge to offer a "great value" to the happy students that go here.

As one might expect from the only law school in the state, the school has "a great relationship with the state and state bar." This you-rub-my-back-and-I'll-rub yours relationship leads one second-year student to comment, "If you plan to practice law in West Virginia, the College of Law is a brilliant choice—who better to learn from than the justices and lobbyists who wrote the law?" Indeed, much of the curriculum is designed to groom students into local West Virginia lawyers, with many classes devoted to property law, especially coal, oil, gas, and mineral rights law. Most students do choose to practice within the state after graduation, which helps the school focus both its curriculum and its alumni network with stellar results. Career Services is "particularly strong" in placing students in jobs throughout West Virginia, attributable in part to "an active on-campus interview program and in part to WVU's intimate connection with the West Virginia legal community."

The College of Law enjoys faculty members who are a combination of "inspirational, well-published, and leading state authorities in their subjects." Professors "care about students as individuals" and "encourage...and help them to achieve whatever types of goals that individual has." All teachers "know material well and convey the information in an easy-to-understand way." People are torn as to the efficacy of the Legal Research and Writing Program, which has undergone a recent revamping, but the Academic Excellence Program is available to "provide an essential foundation for struggling students."

The administration at West Virginia University's College of Law is "very laid-back" and follows the same open-door policy as the faculty. Although there are around 450 students, the administration "seemingly knows everyone's names," and it's not unusual to see "both faculty and administrators lounging with students during lunch hours." Students share some grievances regarding the rather clunky and inflexible registration system, as courses for first-year students are pretty much set in stone, and "you get the classes at the times they pick, no exceptions." Fortunately, the diversity of classes expands in the second year of law school, but even then, the online registration process can feel like a "gladiatorial battle to get into the classes you like." Moral of the story: get there first. "I know many students who routinely have 'unusual' schedules made up of whatever was left over after twenty minutes of registration," says a 2L.

Though the law school building is "outdated," the recently renovated classrooms within are "fantastic," which is also how students describe WVU Law's staff—particularly the "very friendly and helpful" library staff, which includes" a librarian that will literally help you at any hour of the night (she'll even be your Facebook friend)."

Life

The camaraderie among WVU Law students lends to an atmosphere that is "like one big family." "West Virginia has a small bar and we will all be practicing together after graduation, so everyone treats each other with respect," says a 2L. Students "form study

JANET ARMISTEAD, ASSISTANT DEAN FOR ADMISSIONS
P.O. BOX 6130, MORGANTOWN, WV 26506-6103
TEL: 304-293-5304 FAX: 304-293-6891
E-MAIL: WVULAW.ADMISSIONS@MAIL.WVU.EDU • WEBSITE: WWW.WVU.EDU/~LAW

groups, help each other out, and much more." "We do not see one another as competition, but as colleagues," says a student. The student body (and the faculty) is "not very racially diverse," "not too competitive," and there are "excellent relations amongst students."

The school provides a good deal of social events for students to take part in. And take part they do: Students "work during the week, and cut loose on the weekends." WVU football is the fulcrum of many social activities, and there is a fair amount of alcohol involved in the ample tailgating and extracurricular activities on offer here. Luckily, Morgantown is a "social city," providing "ample opportunities to explore your social life to any extent to which you desire," though students note it does help to have a car.

Getting In

For a recently admitted class, accepted students at the 25th percentile had an average LSAT score of 153 and an average GPA of 3.42. Applicants are required to submit three letters of recommendation from people who have personal knowledge of their character, skills, and aptitude for law study and practice. At least one recommendation must be from a former professor.

ADMISSIONS

Selectivity Rating	77
# applications received	903
% applicants accepted	39
% acceptees attending	47
Average LSAT	152
LSAT Range	148–155
Average undergrad GPA	3.42
Application fee	$50
Regular application	Rolling, up to 2/1
Regular notification	Rolling
Early application program	No
Transfer students accepted	Yes
Evening division offered	No
Part-time accepted	Yes
CAS accepted	Yes

International Students
TOEFL required of international students

FINANCIAL FACTS

Annual tuition (in-state/out-of-state)	$4,926/ $14,278
Books and supplies	$1,125
Fees	$4,416
Room and board	$11,356
Financial aid application deadline	3/1
% first-year students receiving some sort of aid	36
% receiving some sort of aid	91
% of aid that is merit based	1
% receiving scholarships	32
Average grant	$1,822
Average loan	$15,800
Average total aid package	$19,150
Average debt	$54,881

EMPLOYMENT INFORMATION

Career Rating	77	
Rate of placement (nine months out)	92	
Average starting salary	$52,610	
State for bar exam	WV	
Pass rate for first-time bar	75	

Employers Who Frequently Hire Grads
Law Firms, State & Federal Judges/Courts, Business/Corporate, Government Agencies

Grads Employed by Field (%)
Business/industry (8)
Government (4)
Judicial clerkship (21)
Private practice (60)
Public interest (1)

WHITTIER COLLEGE
WHITTIER LAW SCHOOL

INSTITUTIONAL INFORMATION

Public/private	Private
Student/faculty ratio	17:1
% faculty part-time	47
% faculty female	48
% faculty minority	14
Total faculty	88

SURVEY SAYS...

Diverse opinions accepted in classrooms, Students love Costa Mesa, CA

STUDENTS

Enrollment of law school	303
% male/female	57/43
% from out-of-state	21
% full-time	82
% minority	36
% international	7
# of countries represented	15
Average age of entering class	25

ACADEMICS

Academic Experience Rating	81
Profs interesting rating	87
Profs accessible rating	71
Hours of study per day	4.81

Academic Specialties

Commercial, Criminal, International, Intellectual Property, Children's Rights, Health Law, Entertainment Law

Advanced Degrees Offered

JD, 3 years full-time, 4 years part-time; LLM, Foreign Legal Studies, 24 credits, 1 year

Clinical program required	No
Legal writing	
course requirement	Yes
Legal methods	
course requirement	Yes
Legal research	
course requirement	Yes
Moot court requirement	Yes
Public interest	
law requirement	No

Academics

Classes are small at Whittier Law School. "This is important because it personalizes the classroom experience," explains a 2L. "The quality of teaching is extremely high" as well. The "amazing" professors at Whittier are "dedicated, smart, funny," and they are "there to teach you the law, not to hide the ball or play games." Faculty members are accessible, too, even though many practice as real attorneys at least part time. "They are always available and attend many of our student events," beams a 2L. Students are split in their views concerning the administration. Enthusiasts note that "everyone who counts knows your name and says hello." They say that the "very responsive" top brass tries to accommodate all types of students. Critics charge that the indifferent management is "a dysfunctional nightmare." "They might find it good to start caring about their students," suggests a disgruntled 3L.

Academic bells and whistles here include a "ridiculously comprehensive legal writing program." There's a specialized certificate in intellectual property and additional concentrations in both business law and criminal law. There are five clinics. There are summer study abroad opportunities in China, France, Israel, Mexico, and Spain. Whittier is also "a school that is serious about helping with bar prep." "The grading system is particularly harsh," though. The "vicious" curve allows "A" grades for no more than ten percent of the students in any course. Some twenty percent of all the students in every 1L course will get a "D" or an "F." Students at the bottom of the heap end up getting kicked out after the first year.

Career Services offers a Career Law Day, as well as private externship placements, and Whittier also has more than 4,000 alumni. The immediate region is pretty rich with law firms. It also happens to be the tenth largest economy on the planet. "Career Services makes an effort for motivated students," relates a 2L. "If you don't make an effort, they will not see you out or help you. But if you are motivated, they will provide a strong support structure to help you get jobs."

Whittier Law School is located in "a very office building-heavy section" in the heart of suburban Orange County, "ten minutes from the Orange County and U.S. district courthouses." The library and research facilities are reportedly "excellent," but "The classrooms have no windows," observes a 2L. "There's nothing aesthetically pleasing about it at all."

Life

The student population at Whittier is pretty diverse. "Many ethic groups and nationalities" are represented. "There also seems to be socioeconomic diversity," notes a 1L. "There are many stereotypical Orange Countians filling the parking lot with cars that cost more than houses. However, there are also many students getting by on loans and part-time jobs." Students describe themselves as "extremely intelligent." Politics vary widely. "There's a decidedly conservative bent among students who've been out in the world," though, and, on the whole, it's probably safe to say that "the students are more conservative than the teachers."

Some students warn that the academic environment is really intense. "Sabotage" does happen, they claim. First-year students are "crazy competitive and not always nice to each other." Others tell us that a "friendly, familial atmosphere" and a great sense of camaraderie" pervade the campus. "We are silently competitive though against each other academically. In general, we are like a big law school family," says a 3L. "Most

Thomas McColl, Assistant Dean for Admissions and Financial Aid
3333 Harbor Boulevard, Costa Mesa, CA 92626
Tel: 714-444-4141 Fax: 714-444-0250
E-Mail: info@law.whittier.edu • Website: www.law.whittier.edu

students are very friendly and helpful." Either way, there seems to be some consensus that full-time day students are "more competitive" while the "older, working" nontraditional students who attend at night "are more willing to help each other."

The quality of life outside the classroom is pretty high. The cost of living is "reasonable," at least compared to the much higher rents and costs in nearby Los Angeles. Sunshine is constant, and the weather is nice pretty much all the time. Students enjoy "close proximity to Southern California beaches such as Huntington, Newport, and Laguna." "There is an active organization on campus for just about anything a student could think of." "Students who live near the campus are exceedingly social." "There are some cliques and an in crowd." "There are many groups of people who strike me as being very tight," observes a 2L.

Getting In

Whittier has a perennially generous acceptance rate. At the same time, the raw numbers for admitted applicants are pretty high. Admitted students at the 25th percentile have LSAT scores around 150 and GPAs in the B–/C+ range. Admitted students at the 75th percentile have LSAT scores of 155 or so, and their undergraduate GPA is a tad over 3.3.

ADMISSIONS

Selectivity Rating	**72**
# applications received	2,164
% applicants accepted	51
% acceptees attending	27
Average LSAT	151
LSAT Range	149–153
Average undergrad GPA	3.10
Application fee	$60
Regular application	Rolling, up to 8/1
Regular notification	Rolling
Early application program	No
Early application deadline	3/15
Transfer students accepted	Yes
Evening division offered	No
Part-time accepted	Yes
CAS accepted	Yes

International Students

TOEFL required of international students	

FINANCIAL FACTS

Annual tuition	$37,950
Books and supplies	$7,580
Fees	$40
Room and board	$14,130
Financial aid application deadline	5/1
% first-year students receiving some sort of aid	78
% receiving some sort of aid	63
% of aid that is merit based	12
% receiving scholarships	38
Average grant	$4,526
Average loan	$36,621
Average total aid package	$38,120

EMPLOYMENT INFORMATION

Career Rating	**84**
Rate of placement (nine months out)	95
Average starting salary	$70,000
State for bar exam	CA, NV, AZ, NY, TX
Pass rate for first-time bar	83

Employers Who Frequently Hire Grads
Small law firm practices (2–10 attorneys)

Prominent Alumni
Florence Marie Cooper, U.S. District Judge; Garo Mardirossian, Mardirossian and Associates, Personal Injury; Judith Ashmann-Gerst, California Court of Appeal; Mablean Ephraim, Presiding Judge, Divorce Ct. TV Program; Kathleen Strottman, Counsel to Senator Mary Landrieu

Grads Employed by Field (%)
Academic (3)
Business/industry (22)
Government (8)
Judicial clerkship (2)
Private practice (62)
Public interest (3)

WIDENER UNIVERSITY
SCHOOL OF LAW—DELAWARE CAMPUS

INSTITUTIONAL INFORMATION

Public/private	Private
Student/faculty ratio	15:1
% faculty part-time	17
% faculty female	47
% faculty minority	14
Total faculty	59

SURVEY SAYS...

Diverse opinions accepted in classrooms, Great research resources

STUDENTS

Enrollment of law school	1,028
% male/female	59/41
% from out-of-state	81
% full-time	64
% minority	17
# of countries represented	6
Average age of entering class	23

ACADEMICS

Academic Experience Rating	77
Profs interesting rating	80
Profs accessible rating	83
Hours of study per day	4.58

Academic Specialties

Civil Procedure, Commercial, Constitutional, Corporation Securities, Criminal, Environmental, International, Health Law, Trial Advocacy

Advanced Degrees Offered

LLM in Corporate Law and Finance, LLM in Health Law, 24 credits; MJ, 30 credits; SJD in Health Law, DL in Health Law, 8 credits

Combined Degrees Offered

JD/PsyD, 6 years; JD/MBA, JD/ Master of Marine Policy, JD/MPH, 4 years

Academics

Students are drawn to Widener University School of Law's Delaware Campus for the "availability of the part-time evening program for full-time working students, flexibility in scheduling, experienced faculty, prime location," and "the diversity of the student body." For those looking to pursue a legal degree while holding down a career, "Widener offers many people an opportunity to pursue a law school education that might not otherwise be available."

Academics at Widener place an "emphasis on practical lawyering skills and [fostering] a slightly more relaxed atmosphere among students." The program is known for its "great corporate law and health law focus." Students say the number of required classes is ample. "While some may dislike the fact that we simply don't have time to take a lot of electives, it's a lot easier preparing for the bar exam having taken those classes." Others wish the school would consider "adding more extensive elective courses."

As the only law school in the state of Delaware, "Widener students have tremendous access to clinical and externship opportunities that are difficult to come by elsewhere, including opportunities with State Supreme Court Justices, the Delaware Attorney General's Office...as well as opportunities throughout the region, with both top firms as well as government agencies." The clinic program here is "remarkable" and "headed by the most passionate professor I have ever had." In addition, "the research facilities/ resources are easily accessible." "While the library is not open twenty-four hours, it is open fifteen hours a day with extended hours during finals." Classrooms feature "the use of smart boards and video-interactive classrooms. In other words, many of the classrooms are equipped with TVs and webcams so that professors can teach via satellite in real time from either the Pennsylvania or Delaware campus for the smaller, more specialized classes."

When it comes to faculty, students say, "The majority of the tenured teachers are outstanding," but add a note of caution: "There are a portion of 'grandfathered' tenured professors and adjunct professors that seem to just be here to. . .meet operation requirements." Others say, "I have to admit that I was a little surprised by how strong an academic background the professors at Widener have. Every professor I have had thus far have not only graduated from the 'top ten' law schools, but they all have a vast amount of practical experience they are willing to share with students." When it comes to big name faculty, one student adds, the "current Vice President of the U.S., Joe Biden was an adjunct professor, as was Clinton CIA Director, Louis Freeh. Two of my former professors have sat on the Delaware Supreme Court." Students' biggest gripe academically is the grading curve. As one explains, "Some law schools have a lower curve for first-year students which is bumped up to a reasonable 3.0 for 2L and 3L years. Widener students remain on a 2.75 curve so our grades, even though they may be the same as Penn, Temple, Villanova, Rutgers, or Dickinson, look far worse. It has created problems for students who seek internships and post-graduation employment."

Facilities on campus need "to be upgraded." "Not all classrooms have the requisite number of power outlets to facilitate laptop use throughout. There [have] been some rumblings about barring laptop use in the classroom, but thankfully most professors are in tune with the times." Commuters lament, "Parking is atrocious. When the front lots are filled, students and faculty must park in a rear lot that is not well-lit [and is] surrounded by trees."

Barbara Ayars, Assistant Dean for Admissions
P.O. Box 7474, 4601 Concord Pike, Wilmington, DE 19803-0474
Tel: 302-477-2703 Fax: 302-477-2224
E-Mail: lawadmissions@mail.widener.edu • Website: law.widener.edu

Professionally, students note that "networks are rather geographically limited to Delaware and Philly despite being a short distance from both New York and D.C. However, if you want to do corporate law there is no better law school. Wilmington is at the center of the corporate law universe in the U.S. and Widener is at the forefront of developing exceptional talent."

Life

Though admittedly the evening and day students at Widener are "two different animals," each group tends to find its own nexus, and "There is a really strong sense of community [at] the school." It helps that due to Widener's small size, "everyone knows each other."

The campus is "functional" (partly as a function of being "situated near Philadelphia and [within] an easy train ride to New York"). While some say, "They are improving the campus environment, but too slowly," others praise the "beautiful," "clean" grounds and newly renovated buildings. The most critical say, "The dorms and attached building are quite hideous."

On the whole, Widener students "are usually very friendly." "There is a definite sense of community and [a] willingness to help one another amongst the students at Widener." In addition, the school hosts "a very active Student Bar Association which pushes the student organizations to host many events throughout the school year."

Getting In

While the admissions committee at Widener gives the most weight to undergraduate GPA and LSAT scores, they also consider work experience, other graduate study, extracurricular activities, and community involvement. Applications are accepted on a rolling basis though candidates are encouraged to apply early. Applicants may apply to both the Harrisburg and Delaware campuses. However, in doing so, candidates may waive their right to choose which campus they will attend.

Clinical program required	No
Legal writing course requirement	Yes
Legal methods course requirement	Yes
Legal research course requirement	Yes
Moot court requirement	No
Public interest law requirement	No

ADMISSIONS

Selectivity Rating	**69**
# applications received	1,869
% applicants accepted	59
% acceptees attending	24
Average LSAT	153
LSAT Range	151–154
Average undergrad GPA	3.15
Application fee	$60
Regular application	Rolling, up to 5/15
Regular notification	Rolling
Early application program	No
Transfer students accepted	Yes
Evening division offered	Yes
Part-time accepted	Yes
CAS accepted	Yes

International Students
TOEFL recommended of international students

FINANCIAL FACTS

Annual tuition	$34,800
Books and supplies	$1,200
Fees	$90
Room and board	$10,260
Financial aid application deadline	4/1
% first-year students receiving some sort of aid	92
% receiving some sort of aid	94
% of aid that is merit based	10
% receiving scholarships	29
Average grant	$10,223
Average loan	$37,082
Average total aid package	$38,168
Average debt	$108,394

EMPLOYMENT INFORMATION

Career Rating	**82**
Rate of placement (nine months out)	93
Average starting salary	$62,934
State for bar exam	PA, NJ, DE, MD
Pass rate for first-time bar	85

Employers Who Frequently Hire Grads
Law firms, judges, corporations, and other government employers

Prominent Alumni
Risa Vetri Ferman, Class of '92, Montgomery County District Attorney; Cynthia Rhoades Ryan, Class of '79, Chief Counsel, Natl Geospatial Intell Agency; Hon. Susan Del Pesco, Class of '75, Director, Delaware Division of Long-Term Care Residents Protection; Lee A. Solomon, Class of '78, President, Board of Public Utilities (NJ); Alan B. Levin, Class of '80, Director, DE Economic Development Office

Grads Employed by Field (%)
Academic (2)
Business/industry (23)
Government (9)
Judicial clerkship (16)
Military (1)
Private practice (45)
Public interest (4)

WIDENER UNIVERSITY
SCHOOL OF LAW—HARRISBURG CAMPUS

INSTITUTIONAL INFORMATION

Public/private	Private
Student/faculty ratio	15:1
% faculty part-time	13
% faculty female	51
% faculty minority	20

SURVEY SAYS...

Diverse opinions accepted in classrooms, Great research resources, Great library staff

STUDENTS

Enrollment of law school	454
% male/female	57/43
% from out-of-state	33
% full-time	77
% minority	12
# of countries represented	1
Average age of entering class	23

ACADEMICS

Academic Experience Rating	**77**
Profs interesting rating	85
Profs accessible rating	80
Hours of study per day	5.06

Academic Specialties

Constitutional, Corporation Securities, Environmental, Government Services, International, Health Law

Combined Degrees Offered

JD/MSLS (in conjunction with Clarion University of PA), 4 years

Clinical program required	No
Legal writing course requirement	Yes
Legal methods course requirement	Yes
Legal research course requirement	Yes
Moot court requirement	No
Public interest law requirement	No

Academics

Tucked away in Harrisburg, Pennsylvania, Widener University Law School is truly a "hidden gem." While perhaps "not [yet] a household name," one content first-year student nonetheless asserts that "There's a distinct charm about our university." She goes on to say that, "From the moment that I began, it was clear that the faculty was here to help me make the transition from undergraduate to the professional level." This sentiment can easily be attributed to the school's "small size" which really helps to foster a "tight-knit community." Indeed, Widener is truly a place where one is "able to develop relationships with professors and the student body [alike]."

Students here are practically unanimous in their effusive praise for their professors. As a second-year student boldly proclaims, "The professors here are top-notch. They bring both practical and theoretical information to every class and are all overly willing to talk outside the classroom about future plans and anything else we may want to talk about." Impressively, "Every one of them is willing to go out of their way to make sure that you understand the concepts being taught." They frequently encourage students to take full advantage of their "open-door policies." As a satisfied 3L sums up, "It was clear that they wanted all of us to succeed if we were willing to put in the time and effort."

Importantly, the "school places a large emphasis on...writing skills which are essential to practicing in any area of law." Indeed, there's a focus on "practical skills that will set you apart from other young lawyers in the profession. Specifically, the legal methods/writing program is intensive but creates confidence that one will be proficient once a summer internship at a firm rolls around." Students also speak glowingly about the "fantastic" clinical program, which is "run by a group of dedicated staff attorneys who [really] teach you the practice of law." However, many warn of the school's "stringent grading curve." The curve results in "most students [having] an overall GPA between 2.3 and 2.75." Fortunately, many at Widener view their peers as "friendly and genuine" and assure us that no one is "cutthroat" or overly "competitive."

While the "facilities are not the largest," students assure us, "The classrooms have the latest technology and [the] research resources [are] more than enough to find any information [you need]." Additionally, the "administrative staff is very nice and accessible," and "They do a great job making everyone feel welcome and are always willing to help a student out."

One area that does need improvement is the career services department. While the office does "offer a lot of information, it does not seem to provide enough opportunities." As one frustrated first year shares, "The Career Development Office tends to take a laid-back approach, where you need to ask for them to do work. Otherwise, you are on your own." Fortunately, there are "strong alumni connections" along with a "strong [local] reputation." Additionally, the proximity to "Harrisburg provides the students with many opportunities for legal experience." Students frequently turn to professors "who take an extremely active interest in our...future success."

Life

Widener provides students with a "very cordial and cooperative atmosphere." The small size allows for an intimate environment that often feels like a "big family." There is a "strong sense of community," and students "are all very social." They also appreciate the fact that everyone "seems to know each other." However, there is a downside, as "sometimes this can cause people to know too much of other [people's] business."

Barbara Ayars, Assistant Dean of Admissions
3800 Vartan Way, P.O. Box 69381, Harrisburg, PA 17106-9381
Tel: 717-541-3903 Fax: 717-541-3999
E-Mail: lawadmissions@widener.edu • Website: law.widener.edu

While some students might describe themselves as "competitive," a first-year student stresses, "We are also extremely supportive of one another." A 2L continues, "In class, you do not see students 'gunning' to show off to professors. Instead, you see students working hard to understand the legal concepts and make arguments. You see students trying to help each other outside of class, by studying together and teaching each other the law."

When students do want to unwind, they take advantage of "nightlife in Harrisburg, i.e., bars, restaurants, bowling alleys. For local sports, there is a minor league hockey team…and minor league baseball team." "Most students go dancing at bars on [the] weekends, but during the week they hit the books hard."

Getting In

While the admissions committee at Widener gives the most weight to undergraduate GPA and LSAT scores, they also consider work experience, other graduate study, extra-curricular activities and community involvement. Applications are accepted on a rolling basis though candidates are encouraged to apply early. Applicants may apply to both the Harrisburg and Delaware campuses. However, in doing so, candidates may waive their right to choose which campus they will attend.

ADMISSIONS

Selectivity Rating	65
# applications received	1,231
% applicants accepted	57
% acceptees attending	20
Average LSAT	151
LSAT Range	149–153
Average undergrad GPA	3.10
Application fee	$60
Regular application	Rolling, up to 5/15
Regular notification	Rolling
Early application program	No
Transfer students accepted	Yes
Evening division offered	Yes
Part-time accepted	Yes
CAS accepted	Yes

International Students
TOEFL recommended of international students

FINANCIAL FACTS

Annual tuition	$34,800
Books and supplies	$1,200
Fees	$90
Room and board	$10,260
Financial aid application deadline	4/1
% first-year students receiving some sort of aid	92
% receiving some sort of aid	94
% of aid that is merit based	8
% receiving scholarships	33
Average grant	$8,180
Average loan	$39,457
Average total aid package	$43,393
Average debt	$119,191

EMPLOYMENT INFORMATION

Career Rating	80
Rate of placement (nine months out)	94
Average starting salary	$50,237
State for bar exam	PA, NJ
Pass rate for first-time bar	89

Employers Who Frequently Hire Grads
Law firms, judges, corporations, and other government employers

Prominent Alumni
William N. Nettles, Class of '92, United States Attorney, District of South Carolina; Michael J. Aiello, Class of '94, Partner, Weil, Gotshal & Manges; Annmarie Kaiser, Class of '93, Secretary for Legislative Affairs (PA); Rory G. Ritrievi, Class of '98, President and CEO of Mid Penn Bank; Michael F. Consedine, Class of '94, Pennsylvania Insurance Commissioner

Grads Employed by Field (%)
Academic (2)
Business/industry (16)
Government (13)
Judicial clerkship (20)
Private practice (40)
Public interest (8)

WILLAMETTE UNIVERSITY
COLLEGE OF LAW

INSTITUTIONAL INFORMATION

Public/private	Private
Affiliation	Methodist
Student/faculty ratio	15:1
% faculty part-time	35
% faculty female	30
% faculty minority	14
Total faculty	57

SURVEY SAYS...

Great research resources,
Great library staff

STUDENTS

Enrollment of law school	431
% male/female	55/45
% from out-of-state	57
% full-time	100
% minority	18
% international	<1
Average age of entering class	26

ACADEMICS

Academic Experience Rating	80
Profs interesting rating	84
Profs accessible rating	79
Hours of study per day	4.76

Academic Specialties

Government Services, Dispute Resolution, Law and Business, International and Comparative Law, Sustainability Law

Advanced Degrees Offered

LLM in Transnational Law, 1 year

Combined Degrees Offered

JD/MBA with Willamette University Atkinson Graduate School of Management, 4 years

Clinical program required	No
Legal writing course requirement	Yes
Legal methods course requirement	No
Legal research course requirement	Yes
Moot court requirement	Yes
Public interest law requirement	No

Academics

Willamette University College of Law is "a smaller school in the Pacific Northwest," "in the state capital city" of Salem, Oregon. Highlights here include an exemplary legal research and writing program. A JD/MBA program allows students to earn both degrees in four years. There are three journals, six specialized clinics, and a broad externship program. Certificates are available in dispute resolution, business law, international and comparative law (reportedly "wonderful"), law and government, and sustainability law. Study abroad programs in Hamburg, Germany; Quito, Ecuador; and Shanghai, China are another big hit. Students also laud their surroundings. "The facilities at Willamette are, by far, among the best," they say. The "beautiful building" is located on the peaceful and collegiate-looking campus of the larger university. Classrooms are recently renovated and modern. "You have access to the library 24/7," too, which can be an invaluable perk when finals roll around each semester.

Classes are definitely on the smaller side, and they're generally "entertaining." "The greatest strength of Willamette Law has to be the faculty," relates a 2L. "The faculty is knowledgeable, accessible, and seems to generally enjoy teaching students—an extremely valuable trifecta." The "very helpful" top brass gets a lot of love as well. "The school's administration works as effectively as possible," says a 3L. "They are very focused on getting us to pass the bar," agrees a happy 1L, "and very focused on getting us a job post graduation."

Course scheduling is probably the biggest single source of frustration among students. After the first year, it can be hard to get into the classes you want (and occasionally need). The fairly strict grading curve comes in for some grief as well. "Grade deflation" is alive and well, and a handful of 1Ls at the bottom of the class at Willamette are inevitably asked to leave each year. On one hand, it's an intimidating situation. On the other hand, it "will really help motivate." Computing issues can also be a pain. Willamette has wireless, but the connection can be spotty sometimes. "Perhaps they will employ technology that is commensurate with the decade we are currently in," suggests one student.

When the time comes to get a job as an actual attorney, there's good news and bad news for newly minted Willamette alums. On the minus side, the generally mild climate and the culture of Oregon are both professionally appealing for many people. Competition for jobs (especially in Portland) is fierce because the legal market is not huge and a lot of transplant lawyers want to work in the state. On the plus side, the law school here is "down the street from" the Capitol building and various courts. Consequently, students have "fantastic access" to state legislative bodies, state courts, and state agencies. "Great networking opportunities" and prospects for practical experience outside of school abound. Students can "cooperate with the judicial process" in ways that students at the other two law schools in the state cannot.

Life

Students tell us that ethnic diversity is "increasing" at Willamette. More than twenty percent of the population here represents some minority group. "No longer can you count the number of minority students on one hand." Diversity shows itself in other ways, too. There's a decent-sized contingent of older students who are looking to transition into another, more lucrative career, for example. Also, just more than half the students come from a state other than Oregon. Some students are "very competitive" when it comes to grades. At the same time, "Willamette is a tight-knit community."

CAROLYN DENNIS, DIRECTOR OF ADMISSION
245 WINTER STREET SE, SALEM, OR 97301-3922
TEL: 503-370-6282 FAX: 503-370-6087
E-MAIL: LAW-ADMISSION@WILLAMETTE.EDU • WEBSITE: WWW.WILLAMETTE.EDU/WUCL

"People generally hang out with the same group of friends they made in their first year of law school, but everyone still remains friendly to others."

Views about life outside the classroom vary. Some students consider the "small" surrounding burg of Salem "an inexpensive and livable town in a pleasant state." They call the immediate location "great for serious students." They point out that "Salem is less than an hour's drive from Portland and is in the heart of wine country." They also note that temperatures are mild all year, and the surrounding area is a paradise for lovers of the outdoors. Opportunities for hiking, skiing, and frolicking at the beach are all within relatively easy reach. Closer to home, students also have access to a fabulous campus recreation center, although a few complain about the "gloomy Oregon weather."

Getting In

The acceptance rate is high, but Willamette is a small school and the candidates competing for spots tend to have solid credentials. Admitted students at the 25th percentile have LSAT scores that hover in the low 150s and GPAs around 3.0. Admitted students at the 75th percentile have LSAT scores of 158 or so; their GPAs are about 3.5.

ADMISSIONS

Selectivity Rating	78
# applications received	1,432
% applicants accepted	37
% acceptees attending	30
Average LSAT	156
LSAT Range	154–159
Average undergrad GPA	3.30
Application fee	$50
Regular application	Rolling, up to 7/1
Regular notification	Rolling
Early application program	No
Transfer students accepted	Yes
Evening division offered	No
Part-time accepted	No
CAS accepted	Yes

International Students

TOEFL required of international students	

FINANCIAL FACTS

Annual tuition	$32,460
Books and supplies	$1,460
Fees	$80
Room and board	$14,510
Financial aid application deadline	3/1
% first-year students receiving some sort of aid	98
% receiving some sort of aid	99
% of aid that is merit based	18
% receiving scholarships	61
Average grant	$12,277
Average loan	$38,099
Average total aid package	$43,912
Average debt	$108,002

EMPLOYMENT INFORMATION

Career Rating	82	**Grads Employed by Field (%)**
Rate of placement (nine months out)	99	Academic (2)
Average starting salary	$53,435	Business/industry (16)
State for bar exam	OR, WA, CA, ID, UT	Government (8)
Pass rate for first-time bar	76	Judicial clerkship (4)

Employers Who Frequently Hire Grads
Stoel Rives, Schwabe Williamson Wyatt, Washington State Attorney General, Lane County Circuit Court, Lane Powell LLP, Oregon Department of Justice, Miller Nash, Oregon Legislature, Davis Wright Tremaine, Dunn Carney

Prominent Alumni
Lisa Murkowski, U.S. Senator from Alaska; Paul De Muniz, Chief Justice Oregon Supreme Court; Lindsay D. Stewart, former Vice President, Law and Corporate Affairs, Nike; Mark Prater, Chief Tax Counsel, U.S. Senate Committee on Finance; Stanton Anderson, Chief Legal Officer, U.S. Chamber of Commerce

Grads Employed by Field (%):
Private practice (66)
Public interest (4)

WILLIAM MITCHELL COLLEGE OF LAW

INSTITUTIONAL INFORMATION

Public/private	Private
Student/faculty ratio	20:1
% faculty part-time	84
% faculty female	41
% faculty minority	24
Total faculty	252

SURVEY SAYS...
Great research resources, Great library staff, Students love St. Paul, MN

STUDENTS

Enrollment of law school	1,013
% male/female	50/50
% from out-of-state	30
% full-time	66
% minority	12
% international	1
# of countries represented	22
Average age of entering class	26

ACADEMICS

Academic Experience Rating	**73**
Profs interesting rating	77
Profs accessible rating	71
Hours of study per day	4.46

Academic Specialties
ADR, Business, Civil Litigation, Commercial, Criminal, Elder, Estates, Family, Government Services, Indian, Intellectual Property, International, National Security, Public Interest, Real Estate, Taxation, Torts

Advanced Degrees Offered
JD, 3 years full-time, 4 years part-time

Combined Degrees Offered
Dual Degree in conjunction w/ Minnesota State University, Mankato. JD-MA in Public Administration and JD-MS in Community Health. If classes are taken concurrently can be accomplished in 4 years, however must be completed within 6 years

Academics

"Unlike some of the other top law schools, William Mitchell College of Law prepares its students to actually practice law upon graduation and not five years down the road." At William Mitchell, a private institution in St. Paul, most students acknowledge this as fact; they feel competent and ready. The legal writing, research, moot courts, and other competitions prepare students for the real world, as well as bolster confidence. One student had an externship "with a judge and worked fifteen-plus hours a week as a law clerk." The school places "a huge emphasis on getting involved in clinics, becoming research assistants, and networking with other lawyers and judges." This is all made possible by the "Mitchell Mafia," an alumni network comprising more than 11,000 graduates, which is "one of the greatest strengths of William Mitchell." "The alumni are constantly working to ensure that students have the best opportunities available to them." "If you want practical experience to set your resume apart, such as clinics, externships, internships, moot court, journal, volunteer work, etc., you will get it, if you apply." William Mitchell also offers courses in which students practice law in a simulated environment, such as Legal Practicum and Advanced Advocacy. Don't worry—there's theory thrown in as well, but it all seems to work together to instill a confidence in the graduating class that's seen in few other law schools.

Most adjunct faculty members maintain a practice outside of academia. Students say this enhances the classroom experience. "They have pushed me to think outside the box analytically and to view the assigned readings with a critical eye." The professors "care deeply about sharing their knowledge." "They are teachers at heart first, academics second." In addition to full-time professors, there are "a plethora of wonderful adjunct faculty, who are willing to teach specialized courses." For one student who was called to duty and another studying abroad, the professors remained accessible through prompt e-mails and lecture podcasts. "These are people who love to teach." Also, "There is a good balance in age and experience of faculty members, and new adjunct faculty are constantly being recruited." They're "some of the best professors I have experienced in any educational setting." "The intellectual property courses and faculty were amazing and have prepared me for a successful career in entertainment law."

"William Mitchell seems to go out of its way to assist students." Both part- and full-time students think the administration is "helpful, friendly, and accessible." They're "willing to bend over backwards to make things happen." They "learn the students' names and often engage them in casual conversation." The "library is beautiful," "definitely one of the best in the country." The technology, accessibility, materials, and study space are much better than at other schools. Classrooms are aesthetically pleasing, as well as "very modern, and equipped with the newest technology." "The reference librarians are very accommodating and patient." "I cannot emphasize how smoothly things are done."

Life

"The environment fostered here is incredibly welcoming and supportive, yet challenging at the same time." "I don't think we are a competitive school at all. We support each other; no one wants others to do poorly, so they can do better." One student mentions feeling "comfortable here from day one." Students are on the fence about the degree of diversity at William Mitchell, but one student says, "I happened to be incredibly intrigued by the diversity within the institution. It is not every day that I have an opportunity to argue the pros and cons of affirmative action with an African American

KENDRA DANE, ASST. DEAN & DIRECTOR OF ADMISSIONS
875 SUMMIT AVENUE, ST. PAUL, MN 55105
TEL: 651-290-6476 FAX: 651-290-6414
E-MAIL: ADMISSIONS@WMITCHELL.EDU • WEBSITE: WWW.WMITCHELL.EDU

biochemist from Illinois and a former Soviet refugee from the Ukraine." More than a few described the school's desire for students to maintain "life balance" while in law school. "Many have made long-lasting friendships" and "found a great social culture at Mitchell," regardless of whether they're part- or full-time students. "The school does a nice job of catering to working professionals." "Late-night happy hours after class are routine." However, if you don't drink, you'll "still find a great social culture at Mitchell."

Students like that William Mitchell "is only a law school." Administratively and otherwise, there are no undergraduates and no other professionals working toward degrees. The "beautiful" campus is in a "perfect" location, "one block over from St. Paul's popular Grand Avenue." There are "plenty of bars and restaurants along with an eclectic mix of retail stores." It's "one of the most beautiful neighborhoods in any major American city." Although some admit the campus is slightly remote, "There are two bus lines within blocks of the school that run to downtown St. Paul and Minneapolis, and from there you can go anywhere."

Getting In

William Mitchell has a high acceptance rate. LSAT scores, undergraduate GPAs, a personal essay, and letters of recommendation are all considered important by the admissions committee. Admitted students in the 25th percentile have GPAs close to 3.15 and LSAT scores of 152. Admitted students in the 75th percentile have LSAT scores close to 159 and GPAs of 3.6.

Clinical program required	No
Legal writing course requirement	Yes
Legal methods course requirement	Yes
Legal research course requirement	Yes
Moot court requirement	No
Public interest law requirement	No

ADMISSIONS

Selectivity Rating	78
# applications received	1,448
% applicants accepted	55
% acceptees attending	44
Average LSAT	156
LSAT Range	152–159
Average undergrad GPA	3.37
Application fee	$50
Regular application	Rolling, up to 5/1
Regular notification	Rolling
Early application program	No
Transfer students accepted	Yes
Evening division offered	Yes
Part-time accepted	Yes
CAS accepted	Yes

International Students

TOEFL required of international students

FINANCIAL FACTS

Annual tuition	$35,660
Books and supplies	$1,550
Fees	$50
Room and board	$16,574
Financial aid application deadline	3/15
% first-year students receiving some sort of aid	94
% receiving some sort of aid	96
% of aid that is merit based	100
% receiving scholarships	50
Average grant	$7,634
Average loan	$30,425
Average total aid package	$38,922
Average debt	$81,532

EMPLOYMENT INFORMATION

Career Rating	84
Rate of placement (nine months out)	91
Average starting salary	$63,336
State for bar exam	MN, WI
Pass rate for first-time bar	86

Employers Who Frequently Hire Grads
Briggs & Morgan; Faegre & Benson; Gray Plant Mooty; Robins Kaplan Miller & Ciresi; Leonard Street & Deinard; 3M; Merchant and Gould; Fredrickson and Byron; Thomson-Reuters; Oppenheimer; Target; State of Minnesota

Prominent Alumni
Warren E. Burger, Chief Justice of U.S. Supreme Court; Rosalie Wahl, Justice Minnesota Supreme Court (retired); Douglas Amdahl, Chief Justice Minnesota Supreme Court (retired); Sam Hanson, Justice, Minnesota Supreme Court; Kathleen Flynn Peterson, former President, American Association for Justice; Eric Magnuson, former Chief Justice, Minnesota Supreme Court

Grads Employed by Field (%)
Academic (1)
Business/industry (28)
Government (11)
Judicial clerkship (10)
Military (1)
Private practice (44)
Public interest (5)

YALE UNIVERSITY
LAW SCHOOL

INSTITUTIONAL INFORMATION

Public/private	Private
Student/faculty ratio	7:1
Total faculty	65

SURVEY SAYS...

Great research resources, Great library staff, Abundant externship/internship/clerkship opportunities, Beautiful campus

STUDENTS

Enrollment of law school	669
% male/female	51/49
% full-time	100
% minority	28
Average age of entering class	25

ACADEMICS

Academic Experience Rating	83
Profs interesting rating	65
Profs accessible rating	62

Advanced Degrees Offered

JD, 3 years; LLM, 1 year; MSL, 1 year; JSD, up to 5 years

Combined Degrees Offered

JD/PhD History, JD/PhD Political Science, JD/MS Forestry, JD/MS Sociology, JD/MS Statistics, JD/MBA and JD/PhD (w/ Yale School of Management) and others

Clinical program required	No
Legal writing course requirement	Yes
Legal methods course requirement	No
Legal research course requirement	No
Moot court requirement	No
Public interest law requirement	No

Academics

It's hard to beat Yale Law School, where the atmosphere is "highly intellectual" and classes are mostly "small" (first-year classes vary in size from fifteen to ninety students). One of the many uniquely cool things about Yale is that "there aren't very many required courses." All 1Ls must complete course work in constitutional law, contracts, procedure, and torts. There's also a small, seminar-style legal research and writing course, and that's pretty much it. Best of all, there are "no grades." First semester classes are graded pass/fail. After first semester, there is some semblance of grades but, since Yale doesn't keep track of class rank, it's not a big deal.

Academically, "This is the best place in the world." "It's easy to learn about whatever you're interested in, from medieval European law to helping immigrants in the modern-day United States," says one student. Yale is home to cutting-edge centers and programs galore. Clinical opportunities are vast and available "in your first year," which is a rarity. You can represent family members in juvenile neglect cases, provide legal services for nonprofit organizations, or participate in complicated federal civil rights cases. It's also "easy" to obtain joint-degrees or simply "cross-register for other classes" at Yale. A particularly unique program allows students to get a joint-degree at the Woodrow Wilson School of Public and International Affairs at Princeton.

Student report that the administration is "generally friendly." Word on the faculty is mixed. "I love all my professors," beams a 2L. "They will help me with anything." Nearly all agree that "most professors are delighted to help you." When jobs and clerkships are on the line, it's not uncommon for professors to personally make calls on behalf of students "to high-profile firms or government officials." Other students, however, tell us the faculty isn't all it's cracked up to be. "Quality teaching is not valued enough," gripes a critic. "Professors are hired based on their scholarship rather than their ability to teach or their interest in interacting with students."

Employment prospects are simply awesome. A degree from Yale virtually guarantees "an easy time finding a good job" and a lifetime of financial security. There is "very solid career support" (including "lots of free wine" at recruiting events). But did you know that Yale prolifically produces public interest attorneys? It's true. Every one of Yale's graduates could immediately take the big firm route but, each year, hordes of them don't. Yale "encourages diverse career paths" and "nontraditional routes" ("especially in academia and public interest") and annually awards dozens of public interest fellowships to current students and newly minted grads. There's a "great" loan forgiveness program too.

Facilities are phenomenal. Yale boasts wireless Internet access throughout the Law School, wireless common areas, and perhaps the greatest law library in the history of humanity. "The research facilities are spectacular." Aesthetically, "Everything is beautiful," especially if you are into "wood paneling, stained glass windows, and hand-carved moldings." "If you care about architecture and Ivy League ambiance, come to Yale."

Life

Though the student population "is a bit Ivy heavy," it doesn't necessarily follow that everyone is wealthy. Approximately eighty percent of the lucky souls here receive financial assistance of some kind. It does follow, however, that students are pretty conceited about their intelligence and their privileged educational status. "If egos were light, an

ASHA RANGAPPA, ASSOCIATE DEAN
P.O. BOX 208215, NEW HAVEN, CT 06520-8215
TEL: 203-432-4995
E-MAIL: ADMISSIONS.LAW@YALE.EDU • WEBSITE: WWW.LAW.YALE.EDU

astronaut on the moon would have to shade his eyes from the glare of New Haven," analogizes one student. "I'm not sure there's a cure for that, but it might not be wise to tell us in the first week of torts that many of us will wind up on the federal bench."

"There are parties," swears a 1L. However, for many students, the social scene at Yale is simply an extension of academic life. Lectures and cultural events of all kinds are, of course, never-ending. The surrounding city of New Haven is lively in its own way and New York City and Boston are both easily accessible by train. On campus, Yale offers an "encouraging environment" and a "wonderful community." "Because of the small size of each class and the enormous number of activities, it is incredibly easy to get involved with journals (even the *Journal*) and any other student group you might want to try." "Students are very engaged and motivated, but not generally in a way that stresses everyone else out," explains one student. "The no-grades policy for first semester completely eliminates the competition I expect exists at other schools." "People ask me what law school is like, and I can honestly say, 'I work pretty hard, but it's fun,'" says a satisfied student. "Then those people stare at me oddly, and maybe they're right that 'fun' isn't exactly the right word. But I've found it enriching and enjoyable and the people I've met here have been great."

Getting In

Let's not sugarcoat the situation: It's ridiculously hard to get into Yale Law School. With a stellar grade point average of 3.75 and a near-perfect LSAT score of, say, 176, you have about a forty percent chance of getting accepted. With a perfectly good GPA of 3.4 and a perfectly good LSAT score of 168, your shot at getting into Yale is a little more than one percent. The folks in admissions at Yale say that they don't use any kind of formula or index. They consider many factors including grades; LSAT scores (including multiple LSAT scores), extracurricular activities, ethnic and socioeconomic diversity, and letters of recommendation.

ADMISSIONS

Selectivity Rating	**99**
# applications received	3,797
% applicants accepted	7
% acceptees attending	80
Average LSAT	173
LSAT Range	171–176
Average undergrad GPA	3.88
Application fee	$75
Regular application	Rolling, up to 2/15
Regular notification	Rolling
Early application program	No
Transfer students accepted	Yes
Evening division offered	No
Part-time accepted	No
CAS accepted	Yes

FINANCIAL FACTS

Annual tuition	$48,500
Books and supplies	$1,100
Fees	$2,250
Room and board	$16,770
Financial aid application deadline	3/15
% first-year students receiving some sort of aid	77
% receiving some sort of aid	77
% receiving scholarships	59
Average grant	$21,992
Average loan	$38,882
Average total aid package	$60,874
Average debt	$110,267

EMPLOYMENT INFORMATION

Career Rating	92	Grads Employed by Field (%)
Rate of placement (nine months out)	96	Academic (3)
State for bar exam	NY, CA	Business/industry (4)
Pass rate for first-time bar	96	Government (10)
		Judicial clerkship (36)
		Military (1)
		Private practice (36)
		Public interest (11)

YESHIVA UNIVERSITY
BENJAMIN N. CARDOZO SCHOOL OF LAW

INSTITUTIONAL INFORMATION

Public/private	Private
Affiliation	Jewish
Student/faculty ratio	15:1
% faculty part-time	61
% faculty female	33
% faculty minority	13
Total faculty	151

SURVEY SAYS...

Diverse opinions accepted in classrooms, Students love New York, NY

STUDENTS

Enrollment of law school	1,228
% male/female	48/52
% from out-of-state	50
% full-time	91
% minority	24
% international	5
# of countries represented	15
Average age of entering class	24

ACADEMICS

Academic Experience Rating	93
Profs interesting rating	82
Profs accessible rating	75
Hours of study per day	3.50

Academic Specialties

Commercial, Constitutional, Corporation Securities, Criminal, International, Legal Philosophy, Property, Taxation, Intellectual Property, Dispute Resolution, Family Law, Litigation

Advanced Degrees Offered

JD, 2.5–3 years; LLM in Intellectual Property Law, Comparative Legal Thought, Dispute Resolution and Advocacy or General Studies, 1 year full-time, up to 3 years part-time

Combined Degrees Offered

JD/LLM in Dispute Resolution and Advocacy, and Intellectual Property Law, 7 semesters; JD/MSW, 4 years

Academics

Despite having been around only about thirty years, Benjamin N. Cardozo School of Law "has accomplished much" in that time and offers "a top-notch legal education" to its students. Academic life at the "underrated, under-known" law school in New York City is pretty exciting. There are "weekly debates featuring legal experts from around the country." Plus, there are lunches or roundtables "every single day with public officials like the New York City Police Commissioner."

Offering "a strong balance of theory and practice," Cardozo provides "superb" opportunities for practical experience. Students also love the "envied" clinical opportunities available. "I've spent a full semester in the New York DA's office, tried a civil case from pleadings to judgment, and this week will argue an appeal at the New York's Appellate Division First Department," says one student. Likewise, a participant in Cardozo's Innocence Project tells us, "Spending eight straight hours in the library doesn't seem so bad after you meet a guy who spent eighteen years in jail for a crime he didn't commit." Cardozo also boasts a strong intellectual property program, a unique Public Service Scholars program, several "great journals," and study abroad programs.

Student are "continually impressed" by the "high caliber" of Cardozo's professors. "The faculty is composed of nationally recognized scholars who care deeply about their specialized fields of law and their students' progress within it," says one student. They "really care about how you are progressing." Not only are they "smart," but they also make "fantastic teachers, which don't always go hand in hand." However, "Some teachers are clearly experts in their field but are unable to convey their knowledge as effective instructors," claims one student. Another remarks, "Cardozo's faculty is a mix of brilliant young stars who have clerked in high places and old-school Socratic Method actors straight out of *The Paper Chase*. My experiences vary so widely from those of 1Ls in other sections that it's as though we go to different schools."

Students find that "some areas of the administration are very strong and certain administrators are particularly sensitive to the needs of the students." Most students are satisfied with their career prospects. "The school's reputation is growing by leaps and bounds," however, Cardozo graduates "unfortunately have to compete with intense competition from Columbia, NYU, and Fordham grads for jobs."

Students applaud the "great facility face-lift in the last few years" and "amazing" location. One student reports that "it's a pretty aesthetically pleasing place to be these days." Many find the moot court room "impressive" but say that "technology across the board" (especially the "website, online course reviews, e-mail system, [and] online research resources") could be improved. Also, technology is not cutting-edge. Cardozo's library has "great reading rooms," but many students complain because it is "closed every Friday night and Saturday." (Cardozo is a Jewish-affiliated law school.)

Life

Besides the fact that the library is closed on Saturdays, "Cardozo does not feel like a religious law school." There are "exceptionally hardworking and dedicated" students of every "religion, ethnicity, and background." Another student adds, "Law school is not about religion, unless one wishes to specialize in religious law." One student explains, "We feel that the school is consistently underrated." This feeling gives students "a strong bond and sense of community." However, the school is "shedding its underdog character every year" as its profile rises and successful alumni base expands. Students are divided when it

DAVID G. MARTINIDEZ, DEAN OF ADMISSIONS
55 FIFTH AVENUE, NEW YORK, NY 10003
TEL: 212-790-0274 FAX: 212-790-0482
E-MAIL: LAWINFO@YU.EDU • WEBSITE: WWW.CARDOZO.YU.EDU

comes to the level of competition at Cardozo. Some perceive a "very competitive" atmosphere. Others "would like nothing better then to give you their notes." "The students are more competitive with themselves than with other students," writes a student in the latter camp. "There is generally a very supportive and friendly environment among students."

Cardozo's location in "the heart of New York City is its best asset." Certainly, getting a legal education in the world's capital of business and finance has its perks. If urban life is what you are after, you would be hard-pressed to do better. However, it can be somewhat of a "commuter school," and the location "drives students into the city, not into school to socialize." Also, housing comes at a hefty premium in New York City. Some students find housing in Greenwich Village, Tribeca, SoHo, and other nearby neighborhoods. Others aren't so lucky. The law school also has a residence hall, (but space is limited and priority is given to out-of-towners), although it has been possible to accommodate all students in recent years.

Getting In

Admitted students at the 25th percentile have an LSAT score of 161 and a GPA of 3.47. Admitted students at the 75th percentile have an LSAT score of 166 and a GPA of 3.74. If you take the LSAT more than once, Cardozo will review all scores and may give consideration to the highest LSAT score. If you score significantly better on one LSAT, write an explanatory letter to the Admissions Committee—it can do wonders. Finally, note that you can enter Cardozo in January and May as well as in September.

Clinical program required	No
Legal writing course requirement	Yes
Legal methods course requirement	Yes
Legal research course requirement	Yes
Moot court requirement	Yes
Public interest law requirement	No

ADMISSIONS

Selectivity Rating	89
# applications received	5,091
% applicants accepted	24
% acceptees attending	23
Average LSAT	164
LSAT Range	161–166
Average undergrad GPA	3.62
Application fee	$75
Regular application	Rolling, up to 4/1
Regular notification	Rolling
Early application program	No
Transfer students accepted	Yes
Evening division offered	No
Part-time accepted	Yes
CAS accepted	Yes

FINANCIAL FACTS

Annual tuition	$46,224
Books and supplies	$5,854
Fees	$570
Room and board	$18,600
Financial aid application deadline	3/1
% first-year students receiving some sort of aid	81
% receiving some sort of aid	83
% of aid that is merit based	28
% receiving scholarships	56
Average grant	$25,017
Average loan	$43,089
Average total aid package	$53,840
Average debt	$118,939

EMPLOYMENT INFORMATION

Career Rating		92
Rate of placement (nine months out)		93
Average starting salary		$87,904
State for bar exam		NY
Pass rate for first-time bar		86

Employers Who Frequently Hire Grads

International and national law firms of all sizes; corporations; federal and state judges nationwide; district attorney's offices and other state and federal government entities; public interest organizations. See the Cardozo website at www.cardozo.yu.edu/RecentEmployers.

Prominent Alumni

Randi Weingarten '83, President, American Federation of Teachers; Hon. Sandra J. Feuerstein '79, Federal Judge, U.S. District Court, Eastern District of NY; David Samson '93, President, Florida Marlins; Jeff Marx '96, Composer/lyricist, *Avenue Q* (Tony-winner); Steven Spira '79, President, Worldwide Business Affairs, Warner Bros

Grads Employed by Field (%)

Academic (1)
Business/industry (19)
Government (14)
Judicial clerkship (6)
Military (1)
Private practice (49)
Public interest (12)

LAW SCHOOL DATA LISTINGS

In this section you will find data listings of the ABA-approved schools not appearing in the "Law School Descriptive Profiles" section of the book. Here you will also find listings of the California Bar Accredited, but not ABA-approved law schools, as well as listings of Canadian law schools. Explanations of what each field of data signifies in the listings may be found in the "How to Use This Book" section.

ATLANTA'S JOHN MARSHALL LAW SCHOOL

1422 W. Peachtree St. NW, Atlanta, GA 30309
Admissions Phone: 404-872-3593 • Admissions Fax: 404-873-3802
Admissions E-Mail: admissions@johnmarshall.edu
Website: www.johnmarshall.edu

INSTITUTIONAL INFORMATION
Public/private: Private
faculty part-time: 20
faculty female: 48
faculty minority: 23
Total faculty: 55

STUDENTS
Enrollment of law school: 168
male/female: 51/49
from out-of-state: 20
part-time: 33
minority: 23
# of countries represented: 1
Average age of entering class: 26

ACADEMICS
Advanced Degrees Offered: Juris Doctor, 88 credit hour program, full-time, 3 years, part-time, 4 years
Clinical program required: No
Legal writing course requirement: Yes
Legal methods course requirement: No
Legal research course requirement: Yes
Moot court requirement: Yes
Public interest law requirement: No

ADMISSIONS
Selectivity Rating 69
applications received: 1,252
% applicants accepted: 38
% acceptees attending: 24
Average LSAT: 151
LSAT Range: 149–153
Average undergrad GPA: 2.97
Application fee: $50
Regular application: Rolling, up to 8/15
Regular notification: Rolling
Transfer students accepted: Yes
Evening division offered: Yes
Part-time accepted: Yes
CAS accepted: Yes

INTERNATIONAL STUDENTS
TOEFL required of international students?: Required

FINANCIAL FACTS
Annual tuition: $29,280
Books and supplies: $2,360
Fees: $150
Room and board: $17,100
Financial aid application deadline: 6/9
% first-year students receiving some sort of aid: 86
% receiving some sort of aid: 90
% of aid that is merit based: 1
% receiving scholarships: 5
Average loan: $48,740
Average total aid package: $48,740
Average debt: $60,688

EMPLOYMENT INFORMATION
Rate of placement (nine months out): 94
Average starting salary: $60,069
State for bar exam: GA, TN, FL, VA, WA
Pass rate for first-time bar: 79
Employers Who Frequently Hire Grads: Georgia Public Interest Organizations, Georgia District Attorney's, Georgia Public Defender's, Georgia Solicitor General's, small and medium firms. Many John Marshall Grads start their own practice or business.
Prominent Alumni: Honorable Alan Blackburn, Presiding Judge, Court of Appeals; Honorable Alvin T. Wong, Judge, State Court of DeKalb County; Honorable James Bodiford, Chief Judge, Cobb Superior Court; Joan Boilen Sasine, Partner, Powell Goldstein, Adam Malone, Attorney, Malone Law Office
Grads Employed by Field (%)
Academic: (2)
Business/industry: (15)
Government: (10)
Judicial clerkship: (5)
Private practice: (64)
Public interest: (4)

BARRY UNIVERSITY
School of Law

6441 E. Colonial Drive, Orlando, FL 32807
Admissions Phone: 321-206-5600 • Admissions Fax: 321-206-5620
Admissions E-Mail: lawinfo@mail.barry.edu • Website: www.barry.edu/law

INSTITUTIONAL INFORMATION
Public/private: Private
Student/faculty ratio: 19:1
% faculty part-time: 16
% faculty female: 43
% faculty minority: 17
Total faculty: 37

STUDENTS

Enrollment of law school: 262
% male/female: 48/52
% from out-of-state: 74
% part-time: 11
% minority: 18
% international: 16
# of countries represented: 2
Average age of entering class: 25

ACADEMICS

Clinical program required: No
Legal writing course requirement: Yes
Legal methods course requirement: Yes
Legal research course requirement: Yes
Moot court requirement: No
Public interest law requirement: Yes

ADMISSIONS

Selectivity Rating 62
applications received: 2,238
% applicants accepted: 56
% acceptees attending: 21
LSAT Range: 149–153
Application fee: $60
Regular application: Rolling, up to 5/1
Regular notification: Rolling
Transfer students accepted: Yes
Evening division offered: Yes
Part-time accepted: Yes
CAS accepted: Yes

FINANCIAL FACTS

Annual tuition: $26,000
Books and supplies: $1,400
Room and board: $10,400
Financial aid application deadline: 6/30
% first-year students receiving some sort of aid: 90
% receiving some sort of aid: 94
% of aid that is merit based: 16
% receiving scholarships: 67
Average grant: $6,779
Average loan: $28,400
Average total aid package: $32,598
Average debt: $70,780

EMPLOYMENT INFORMATION

Average starting salary: $57,275
State for bar exam: FL
Pass rate for first-time bar: 58
Grads Employed by Field (%)
Academic: (6)
Business/industry: (26)
Government: (23)
Military: (2)
Private practice: (41)
Public interest: (2)

CALIFORNIA WESTERN
School of Law

225 Cedar Street, San Diego, CA 92101
Admissions Phone: 619-525-1401 • *Admissions Fax:* 619-615-1401
Admissions E-Mail: admissions@cwsl.edu
Website: www.californiawestern.edu

INSTITUTIONAL INFORMATION

Public/private: Private
Student/faculty ratio: 17:1
% faculty part-time: 22
% faculty female: 35
% faculty minority: 11
Total faculty: 118

STUDENTS

Enrollment of law school: 905
% male/female: 47/53
% from out-of-state: 45
% part-time: 10
% minority: 34
% international: 1
# of countries represented: 15
Average age of entering class: 25

ACADEMICS

Academic Specialties: Constitutional, Criminal, Human Rights, International, Labor, Taxation, Intellectual Property, Health Law, Family Law, Biotech Law, Telecomm Law, Creative Problem Solving
Advanced Degrees Offered: JD, 2–3 years; MCL/LLM (Master of Comparative Law, Master of Laws on Comparative Law), 9 months; LLM-Trial Advocacy, 1 year
Combined Degrees Offered: JD/MSW Juris Doctor/Master of Social Work, 4 years; JD/MBA Juris Doctor/Master of Business Administration, 4 years; JD/PhD Juris Doctor/Doctor of Philosophy in Political Science or History, 5 years. Master's in Health Law
Clinical program required: No
Legal writing course requirement: Yes
Legal methods course requirement: Yes
Legal research course requirement: Yes
Moot court requirement: No
Public interest law requirement: No

ADMISSIONS

Selectivity Rating 60*
applications received: 2,433
% applicants accepted: 54
% acceptees attending: 26
Average LSAT: 153
LSAT Range: 150–155
Average undergrad GPA: 3.25
Application fee: $55
Regular application: Rolling, up to 4/1
Regular notification: Rolling
Transfer students accepted: Yes
Evening division offered: No
Part-time accepted: Yes
CAS accepted: Yes

INTERNATIONAL STUDENTS
TOEFL required of international students?: Required

FINANCIAL FACTS
Annual tuition: $38,400
Books and supplies: $1,300
Fees: $100
Room and board: $11,600
Financial aid application deadline: 4/1
% first-year students receiving some sort of aid: 87
% receiving some sort of aid: 87
% receiving scholarships: 29
Average grant: $20,918
Average loan: $51,750
Average total aid package: $59,612
Average debt: $96,502

EMPLOYMENT INFORMATION
Rate of placement (nine months out): 86
Average starting salary: $73,999
State for bar exam: CA, NV, AZ, NY
Pass rate for first-time bar: 86
Employers Who Frequently Hire Grads: Multiple private, public, and nonprofit employers of all sizes from many regions nationally
Prominent Alumni: Lisa Haile, Partner at DLA Piper, Rudnick, Gray, Cary; Garland Burrell, U.S. District Court Judge; Duane Layton, Partner at Mayer, Brown, Rowe and Maw; David Roger, D.A., Clark County, Nevada, James Lorenz, U.S. District Court Judge
Grads Employed by Field (%)
Academic: (1)
Business/industry: (13)
Government: (12)
Judicial clerkship: (5)
Military: (2)
Private practice: (60)
Public interest: (7)

DUQUESNE UNIVERSITY
School of Law

900 Locust Street, Pittsburgh, PA 15282
Admissions Phone: *412-396-6296* • **Admissions Fax:** *412-396-1073*
Admissions E-Mail: *campion@duq.edu* • **Website:** *www.law.duq.edu*

INSTITUTIONAL INFORMATION
Public/private: Private
Student/faculty ratio: 23:1
% faculty female: 21
% faculty minority: 16
Total faculty: 26

STUDENTS
Enrollment of law school: 630
% male/female: 50/50
% from out-of-state: 38
% part-time: 35
% minority: 7
Average age of entering class: 23

ACADEMICS
Combined Degrees Offered: JD/MBA, 4 years; JD/MDiv, 5 years; JD/MA Environmental Science and Management, 4 years; JD/MS Taxation, 4 years
Clinical program required: No
Legal writing course requirement: Yes
Legal methods course requirement: Yes
Legal research course requirement: Yes
Moot court requirement: No
Public interest law requirement: No

ADMISSIONS
Selectivity Rating 60*
Average LSAT: 154
Average undergrad GPA: 3.40
Application fee: $50
Regular notification: Rolling
Transfer students accepted: Yes
Evening division offered: Yes
Part-time accepted: Yes
CAS accepted: Yes

INTERNATIONAL STUDENTS
TOEFL required of international students?: Required

FINANCIAL FACTS
Annual tuition: $19,394
Books and supplies: $1,000
Fees: $660
Room and board: $8,000
% first-year students receiving some sort of aid: 40
% receiving some sort of aid: 35
% of aid that is merit based: 50
Average grant: $4,500
Average loan: $12,000
Average total aid package: $11,000
Average debt: $35,000

EMPLOYMENT INFORMATION
Average starting salary: $59,693
State for bar exam: PA
Pass rate for first-time bar: 71
Employers Who Frequently Hire Grads: Reed Smith, Kirkpatrick & Lockhart, Buchanon Ingersoll, Eckert, Seamans
Grads Employed by Field (%)
Academic: (1)
Business/industry: (25)
Government: (4)
Judicial clerkship: (6)
Private practice: (61)
Public interest: (3)

ELON UNIVERSITY*

Elon University School of Law

201 N. Greene Street, Greensboro, NC 27401
Admissions Phone: 336-279-9200 • **Admissions Fax:** 336-279-8199
Admissions E-Mail: law@elon.edu • **Website:** law.elon.edu

INSTITUTIONAL INFORMATION
Public/private: Private
% faculty part-time: 53
% faculty female: 28
% faculty minority: 17
Total faculty: 60

STUDENTS
Enrollment of law school: 342
% male/female: 54/46
% minority: 13
Average age of entering class: 23

ACADEMICS
Academic Specialties: Business, Litigation, Public Interest, General Practice
Advanced Degrees Offered: JD, 3-year full-time program
Clinical program required: No
Legal writing course requirement: Yes
Legal methods course requirement: Yes
Legal research course requirement: Yes
Moot court requirement: No
Public interest law requirement: Yes

ADMISSIONS
Selectivity Rating 60*
applications received: 885
% applicants accepted: 41
% acceptees attending: 37
LSAT Range: 153–159
Application fee: $50
Regular application: Rolling, up to 6/30
Regular notification: Rolling
Transfer students accepted: Yes
Evening division offered: No
Part-time accepted: No
CAS accepted: Yes

INTERNATIONAL STUDENTS
TOEFL required of international students?: Required

FINANCIAL FACTS
Annual tuition: $32,600
Books and supplies: $1,600
Room and board: $22,200
Financial aid application deadline: 7/1
% first-year students receiving some sort of aid: 95
% receiving some sort of aid: 96
% of aid that is merit based: 23
% receiving scholarships: 82

*Provisionally approved by the ABA

Average grant: $7,500
Average loan: $37,453
Average total aid package: $43,611
Average debt: $103,059

EMPLOYMENT INFORMATION
Rate of placement (nine months out): 84
State for bar exam: NC
Pass rate for first-time bar: 80
Grads Employed by Field (%)
Academic: (1)
Business/industry: (20)
Government: (8)
Judicial clerkship: (6)
Private practice: (62)
Public interest: (3)

FLORIDA A&M UNIVERSITY

College of Law

P.O. Box 3113, Orlando, FL 32802
Admissions Phone: 407-254-3268 • **Admissions Fax:** 407-254-3213
Admissions E-Mail: famulaw.admissions@famu.edu
Website: www.famu.edu/law

INSTITUTIONAL INFORMATION
Public/private: Public
Student/faculty ratio: 13:1
Total faculty: 40

STUDENTS
Enrollment of law school: 293
% male/female: 40/60
% part-time: 31
% minority: 53
Average age of entering class: 33

ACADEMICS
Advanced Degrees Offered: JD, 3 year full-time; 4 year part-time
Clinical program required: Yes
Legal writing course requirement: No
Legal methods course requirement: Yes
Legal research course requirement: No
Moot court requirement: No
Public interest law requirement: Yes

ADMISSIONS
Selectivity Rating 69
applications received: 540
% applicants accepted: 36
% acceptees attending: 62
Average LSAT: 148
LSAT Range: 143–150
Average undergrad GPA: 3.10
Application fee: $20

Regular application: Rolling, up to 5/1
Regular notification: Rolling
Transfer students accepted: No
Evening division offered: Yes
Part-time accepted: Yes
CAS accepted: Yes

FINANCIAL FACTS
Annual tuition (in-state/out-of-state): $7,140/$26,580
Books and supplies: $13,591
Financial aid application deadline: 4/1
% first-year students receiving some sort of aid: 88
% receiving some sort of aid: 92
% receiving scholarships: 16
Average grant: $1,800
Average loan: $18,500

FLORIDA COASTAL SCHOOL OF LAW

8787 Baypine Road, Jacksonville, FL 32256
Admissions Phone: 904-680-7710 • Admissions Fax: 904-680-7692
Admissions E-Mail: admissions@fcsl.edu • Website: www.fcsl.edu

INSTITUTIONAL INFORMATION
Public/private: Private
% faculty part-time: 31
% faculty female: 49
% faculty minority: 13
Total faculty: 137

STUDENTS
Enrollment of law school: 1,308
% male/female: 54/46
% from out-of-state: 60
% part-time: 11
% minority: 24
% international: 1
# of countries represented: 8
Average age of entering class: 25

ACADEMICS
Academic Specialties: Commercial, Constitutional, Criminal, Environmental, International, Labor, Property, Taxation, Sports Law, Advaned Legal Research & Writing
Advanced Degrees Offered: JD, 2.5–3 years full-time, 3.5–4 years part-time
Combined Degrees Offered: JD/MBA The Davis College of Business at Jacksonville University (JU) and Florida Coastal School of Law (Coastal Law) have created a joint degree program through which qualified individuals may enroll in the Coastal Law JD and the Davis MBA programs simultaneously.
Clinical program required: Yes
Legal writing course requirement: Yes
Legal methods course requirement: Yes
Legal research course requirement: Yes
Moot court requirement: No
Public interest law requirement: No

ADMISSIONS
Selectivity Rating 61
applications received: 6,331
% applicants accepted: 62
% acceptees attending: 16
Average LSAT: 150
LSAT Range: 147–153
Average undergrad GPA: 3.21
Application fee: $0
Regular application: Rolling, up to 7/31
Regular notification: Rolling
Transfer students accepted: Yes
Evening division offered: No
Part-time accepted: Yes
CAS accepted: Yes

INTERNATIONAL STUDENTS
TOEFL required of international students?: Recommended

FINANCIAL FACTS
Annual tuition: $31,124
Books and supplies: $1,200
Fees: $1,468
Room and board: $19,570
Financial aid application deadline: 8/1
% first-year students receiving some sort of aid: 85
% receiving some sort of aid: 85
% of aid that is merit based: 10
% receiving scholarships: 25
Average grant: $6,200
Average loan: $18,500
Average total aid package: $23,000
Average debt: $60,000

EMPLOYMENT INFORMATION
Rate of placement (nine months out): 97
Average starting salary: $48,525
State for bar exam: FL, GA, SC, NC
Pass rate for first-time bar: 85
Employers Who Frequently Hire Grads: Small to mid-sized Florida firms, Florida prosecutors' and public defenders' offices

GOLDEN GATE UNIVERSITY
School of Law

536 Mission Street, Law Admissions Office San Francisco, CA 94105
Admissions Phone: 415-442-6630 • Admissions Fax: 415-442-6631
Admissions E-Mail: lawadmit@ggu.edu • Website: www.ggu.edu/law

INSTITUTIONAL INFORMATION
Public/private: Private
Student/faculty ratio: 19:1
% faculty part-time: 62
% faculty female: 43
% faculty minority: 17
Total faculty: 108

STUDENTS
Enrollment of law school: 655
% male/female: 43/57
% from out-of-state: 28
% part-time: 21
% minority: 25
% international: 2
# of countries represented: 28
Average age of entering class: 27

ACADEMICS
Academic Specialties: Criminal, Environmental, International, Labor, Property, Taxation, Intellectual Property, Business Law, Litigation, Public Interest Law
Advanced Degrees Offered: JD, 3 years full-time; JD 4 years part-time; LLM, 1 year; SJD, 1 year; JD/LLM in Taxation, 3.5 years
Combined Degrees Offered: JD/MBA, 4 years; JD/PhD, 7 years
Clinical program required: No
Legal writing course requirement: Yes
Legal methods course requirement: No
Legal research course requirement: Yes
Moot court requirement: Yes
Public interest law requirement: No

ADMISSIONS
Selectivity Rating 68
applications received: 2,410
% applicants accepted: 52
% acceptees attending: 17
Average LSAT: 153
LSAT Range: 151–155
Average undergrad GPA: 3.13
Application fee: $60
Regular application: Rolling, up to 4/1
Regular notification: Rolling
Transfer students accepted: Yes
Evening division offered: Yes
Part-time accepted: Yes
CAS accepted: Yes

INTERNATIONAL STUDENTS
TOEFL required of international students?: Required

FINANCIAL FACTS
Annual tuition: $32,700
Books and supplies: $1,200

Fees: $255
Room and board: $13,500
% first-year students receiving some sort of aid: 92
% receiving some sort of aid: 95
% of aid that is merit based: 90
% receiving scholarships: 40
Average grant: $8,000
Average loan: $30,000
Average total aid package: $49,360
Average debt: $112,477

EMPLOYMENT INFORMATION
Rate of placement (nine months out): 80
Average starting salary: $86,166
State for bar exam: CA
Pass rate for first-time bar: 68
Employers Who Frequently Hire Grads: Small, medium, and large firms, government agencies, public interest organizations, and businesses and corporations
Prominent Alumni: Justice Jesse Carter (deceased), California Supreme Court Justice; Patrick Coughlin, Partner, Coughlin, Stoia, Steller, Rudman, & Robbins, LLP; Karen Hawkins, Director of Professional Responsibility, IRS; Mark S. Anderson, Vice President and General Counsel, Dolby Labs., Marjorie Randolph, Senior VP for HR and Admin., Walt Disney Studios
Grads Employed by Field (%)
Academic: (6)
Business/industry: (19)
Judicial clerkship: (2)
Public interest: (17)

HOWARD UNIVERSITY
School of Law

2900 Van Ness Street, NW, Suite 219 Washington, DC 20008
Admissions Phone: 202-806-8008 • Admissions Fax: 202-806-8162
Admissions E-Mail: admissions@law.howard.edu
Website: www.law.howard.edu

INSTITUTIONAL INFORMATION
Public/private: Private
Student/faculty ratio: 13:1
% faculty part-time: 45
% faculty female: 40
% faculty minority: 78
Total faculty: 67

STUDENTS
Enrollment of law school: 402
% male/female: 40/60
% minority: 94

ACADEMICS
Academic Specialties: Commercial, Constitutional, Corporation Securities, Criminal, Environmental, Human Rights, International, Labor, Property, Taxation, Intellectual Property
Advanced Degrees Offered: LLM (foreign lawyers only), 1–2 years
Combined Degrees Offered: JD/MBA, 4 years
Clinical program required: No

Legal writing course requirement: Yes
Legal methods course requirement: Yes
Legal research course requirement: No
Moot court requirement: No
Public interest law requirement: No

ADMISSIONS
Selectivity Rating 76
applications received: 2,550
% applicants accepted: 17
% acceptees attending: 37
Average LSAT: 153
LSAT Range: 148–158
Average undergrad GPA: 2.50
Application fee: $60
Regular application: Rolling, up to 3/31
Regular notification: Rolling
Transfer students accepted: Yes
Evening division offered: No
Part-time accepted: No
CAS accepted: Yes

INTERNATIONAL STUDENTS
TOEFL required of international students?: Required

FINANCIAL FACTS
Annual tuition: $15,990
Books and supplies: $1,103
Fees: $655
Room and board: $10,169
Financial aid application deadline: 3/1
% first-year students receiving some sort of aid: 90
% receiving some sort of aid: 95
% of aid that is merit based:58
Average grant: $13,000
Average loan: $18,500
Average total aid package: $29,000
Average debt: $60,000

EMPLOYMENT INFORMATION
Rate of placement (nine months out): 96
Average starting salary: $72,465
Employers Who Frequently Hire Grads: Law Firms; Judicial clerkships; Government
Grads Employed by Field (%)
Academic: (3)
Business/industry: (13)
Government: (18)
Judicial clerkship: (15)
Military: (1)
Private practice: (43)
Public interest: (7)

LIBERTY UNIVERSITY
School of Law

1971 University Blvd., Lynchburg, VA 24502
Admissions Phone: (434) 592-5300 • Admissions Fax: (434) 592-5400
Admissions E-Mail: law@liberty.edu • Website: law.liberty.edu

INSTITUTIONAL INFORMATION
Public/private: Private
% faculty part-time: 6
% faculty female: 31
% faculty minority: 6
Total faculty: 16

STUDENTS
Enrollment of law school: 223
% male/female: 61/39
% from out-of-state: 75
% minority: 14
% international: 2
# of countries represented: 2
Average age of entering class: 25

ACADEMICS
Academic Specialties: Civil Procedure, Commercial, Constitutional, Criminal, Government Services, International, Legal History, Legal Philosophy
Advanced Degrees Offered: JD, 3 years
Clinical program required: No
Legal writing course requirement: Yes
Legal methods course requirement: Yes
Legal research course requirement: Yes
Moot court requirement: Yes
Public interest law requirement: No

ADMISSIONS
Selectivity Rating 71
applications received: 491
% applicants accepted: 38
% acceptees attending: 58
Average LSAT: 150
LSAT Range: 148–153
Average undergrad GPA: 3.15
Application fee: $50
Regular application: Rolling, up to 6/1
Regular notification: Rolling
Transfer students accepted: Yes
Evening division offered: No
Part-time accepted: No
CAS accepted: Yes

INTERNATIONAL STUDENTS
TOEFL required of international students?: Required

FINANCIAL FACTS
Annual tuition: $25,369
Books and supplies: $3,062
Fees: $1,140
Room and board: $9,993
Financial aid application deadline: 6/1
% first-year students receiving some sort of aid: 100

% receiving some sort of aid: 100
% of aid that is merit based: 40
% receiving scholarships: 100
Average grant: $13,995
Average loan: $22,805
Average total aid package: $34,781
Average debt: $60,663

EMPLOYMENT INFORMATION

Rate of placement (nine months out): 72
State for bar exam: VA, FL, AR, CA, GA
Pass rate for first-time bar: 91
Prominent Alumni: Jeff Johnson, U.S. Federal Court of Appeals, 6th Circuit; Sarah Seitz, Legislative Assistant, Congressional Prayer Caucus; Sarah Smith, IRS Legislative Affairs, Legislation and Reports Branch; Kevin Qualls, Assistant Professor, Dept. of Journalism and and Mass Communication, Murray State University, Mark Pemberton, Kutak Rock, Kansas
Grads Employed by Field (%)
Academic: (5)
Business/industry: (19)
Government: (11)
Judicial clerkship: (5)
Private practice: (27)
Public interest: (5)

NORTHERN KENTUCKY UNIVERSITY

Salmon P. Chase College of Law

Nunn Hall, Room 101, Highland Heights, KY 41099
Admissions Phone: 859-572-5490 • Admissions Fax: 859-572-6081
Admissions E-Mail: chaselaw.nku.edu/admissions
Website: chaselaw.nku.edu

INSTITUTIONAL INFORMATION

Public/private: Public
% faculty part-time: 46
% faculty female: 38
% faculty minority: 10
Total faculty: 52

STUDENTS

Enrollment of law school: 614
% male/female: 58/42
% from out-of-state: 64
% part-time: 39
% minority: 6
# of countries represented: 2
Average age of entering class: 27

ACADEMICS

Academic Specialties: Labor, Taxation, Advocacy, Transactional Law
Combined Degrees Offered: JD/MBA, 4 years full-time
Clinical program required: No
Legal writing course requirement: Yes
Legal methods course requirement: Yes
Legal research course requirement: Yes
Moot court requirement: No
Public interest law requirement: Yes

ADMISSIONS

Selectivity Rating 74
applications received: 1,145
% applicants accepted: 48
% acceptees attending: 37
Average LSAT: 155
LSAT Range: 152–157
Average undergrad GPA: 3.28
Application fee: $40
Regular application: Rolling, up to 6/1
Regular notification: Rolling
Transfer students accepted: Yes
Evening division offered: Yes
Part-time accepted: Yes
CAS accepted: Yes

INTERNATIONAL STUDENTS

TOEFL required of international students?: Recommended

FINANCIAL FACTS

Annual tuition (in-state/out-of-state): $15,054/$32,812
Books and supplies: $1,000
Fees: $70
Room and board: $9,674
Financial aid application deadline: 3/1
% first-year students receiving some sort of aid: 90
% receiving some sort of aid: 90
% of aid that is merit based: 21
% receiving scholarships: 44
Average grant: $12,949
Average loan: $26,028
Average total aid package: $29,836

EMPLOYMENT INFORMATION

State for bar exam: KY, OH
Pass rate for first-time bar: 83
Employers Who Frequently Hire Grads: Procter & Gamble; Dinsmore & Shohl; U.S. Department of Labor; Kentucky Department of Public Advocacy; Taft, Stettinius & Hollister; Freund, Freeze & Arnold; Adams, Stepner, Woltermann & Dusing; Keating Muething & Klekamp; Frost Brown Todd; Kentucky Office of Commonwealth's Attorney; Deters, Benzinger & LaVelle; and Fidelity Investments
Prominent Alumni: Steve J. Chabot, United States Congressman; Patricia L. Herbold, Former United States Ambassador to Singapore; Dustin E. McCoy, Chair & CEO, Brunswick Corp.; Robert P. Ruwe, Judge, U.S. Tax Court, Washington, D.C., Katie Kratz Stine, Senator & President Pro Tempore, KY State Senate

OHIO NORTHERN UNIVERSITY

Pettit College of Law

Ohio Northern University, Pettit College, Ada, OH 45810-1599
Admissions Phone: 877-452-9668 • Admissions Fax: 419-772-3042
Admissions E-Mail: law-admissions@onu.edu • Website: www.law.onu.edu

INSTITUTIONAL INFORMATION
Public/private: Private
Student/faculty ratio: 12:1
% faculty part-time: 25
% faculty female: 30
% faculty minority: 3
Total faculty: 30

STUDENTS
Enrollment of law school: 320
% male/female: 51/49
% from out-of-state: 65
% minority: 15
% international: 1
# of countries represented: 8
Average age of entering class: 25

ACADEMICS
Academic Specialties: Civil Procedure, Commercial, Constitutional, Corporation Securities, Criminal, Environmental, Human Rights, International, Labor, Legal History, Legal Philosophy, Property, Taxation, Intellectual Property, Capital Punishment
Advanced Degrees Offered: JD, 3 years
Clinical program required: No
Legal writing course requirement: Yes
Legal methods course requirement: Yes
Legal research course requirement: Yes
Moot court requirement: No
Public interest law requirement: No

ADMISSIONS
Selectivity Rating 72
applications received: 1,424
% applicants accepted: 35
% acceptees attending: 24
Average LSAT: 152
LSAT Range: 150–155
Average undergrad GPA: 3.35
Application fee: $40
Regular notification: Rolling
Transfer students accepted: Yes
Evening division offered: No
Part-time accepted: No
CAS accepted: Yes

INTERNATIONAL STUDENTS
TOEFL required of international students?: Required

FINANCIAL FACTS
Annual tuition: $24,840
Books and supplies: $900
Fees: $270
Room and board (on/off campus): $11,237/$12,137
Financial aid application deadline: 4/6
% first-year students receiving some sort of aid: 97
% receiving some sort of aid: 97
% of aid that is merit based: 23
% receiving scholarships: 51
Average grant: $16,390
Average loan: $25,140
Average total aid package: $31,023
Average debt: $74,380

EMPLOYMENT INFORMATION
Rate of placement (nine months out): 95
Average starting salary: $50,000
State for bar exam: OH, FL, PA, NC, MD
Pass rate for first-time bar: 78
Prominent Alumni: Michael DeWine, U.S. Senator; Gregory Frost, U.S. District Judge Southern Ohio; Benjamin Brafman, Senior Partner at Brafman & Ross, New York City; Greg Miller, U.S. Attorney for Northwest Florida
Grads Employed by Field (%)
Academic: (3)
Business/industry: (11)
Government: (13)
Judicial clerkship: (2)
Military: (12)
Private practice: (54)
Public interest: (4)

THE PENNSYLVANIA STATE UNIVERSITY

The Dickinson School of Law

Lewis Katz Building, University Park, PA 16802
Admissions Phone: 814-867-1251 • Admissions Fax: 814-863-7274
Admissions E-Mail: admissions@law.psu.edu • Website: www.law.psu.edu

INSTITUTIONAL INFORMATION
Public/private: Public
% faculty part-time: 21
% faculty female: 43
% faculty minority: 13
Total faculty: 89

STUDENTS
Enrollment of law school: 617
% male/female: 58/42
% minority: 14
% international: 2
Average age of entering class: 24

ACADEMICS

Academic Specialties: Civil Procedure, Commercial, Constitutional, Corporation Securities, Criminal, Environmental, Government Services, Human Rights, International, Labor, Legal History, Legal Philosophy, Property, Taxation, Intellectual Property, Arbitration, Sports Law, Mergers and Acquisitions

Advanced Degrees Offered: JD, 3 years; LLM in Comparative Law, 1 year

Combined Degrees Offered: JD/MIA; JD/MBA; JD/MPA; JD/MEPC; JD/MS Information Systems; JD/MS or PhD Forest Resources; JD/ MA or PhD Educational Theory & Policy; JD/ MEd, MS, DEd, or Ph.D Educational Leadership; JD/ MEd, DEd, or PhD, Higher Education; JD/MS in Human Resources & Employment Relations

Clinical program required: No

Legal writing course requirement: Yes

Legal methods course requirement: Yes

Legal research course requirement: Yes

Moot court requirement: No

Public interest law requirement: No

ADMISSIONS

Selectivity Rating 77

 # applications received: 5,326

% applicants accepted: 29

% acceptees attending: 15

LSAT Range: 151–172

Application fee: $60

Regular application: Rolling, up to 3/1

Regular notification: Rolling

Transfer students accepted: Yes

Evening division offered: No

Part-time accepted: No

CAS accepted: Yes

INTERNATIONAL STUDENTS

TOEFL required of international students?: Required

FINANCIAL FACTS

Annual tuition: $35,928

Books and supplies: $1,456

Fees: $888

Room and board: $22,300

Financial aid application deadline: 3/1

% first-year students receiving some sort of aid: 95

% receiving some sort of aid: 92

% of aid that is merit based: 83

% receiving scholarships: 60

Average grant: $12,172

Average loan: $38,987

Average total aid package: $45,672

Average debt: $117,988

EMPLOYMENT INFORMATION

Rate of placement (nine months out): 78

State for bar exam: PA

Pass rate for first-time bar: 89

Employers Who Frequently Hire Grads: Dickinson graduates are hired by a variety of employers each year including national law firms, small firms, federal and state judges, government agencies, public interest organizations, and other entities.

Prominent Alumni: Hon. Thomas Ridge, Secretary of Homeland Security and PA Governor; Hon. Pedro Cortes, PA Secretary of the Commonwealth; Hon. D. Brooks Smith, Third Circuit Court of Appeals; Hon. Thomas Vanaskie, Third Circuit Court of Appeals, Hon. J. Michael Eakin, PA Supreme Court

Grads Employed by Field (%)

Academic: (4)

Business/industry: (23)

Government: (14)

Judicial clerkship: (19)

Military: (1)

Private practice: (31)

Public interest: (3)

SAINT LOUIS UNIVERSITY
School of Law

3700 Lindell Boulevard, Morrissey Hall, Suite #120 St. Louis, MO 63108

Admissions Phone: *314-977-2800 •* ***Admissions Fax:*** *314-977-1464*

Admissions E-Mail: *admissions@law.slu.edu •* ***Website:*** *law.slu.edu*

INSTITUTIONAL INFORMATION

Public/private: Private

% faculty female: 57

% faculty minority: 4

Total faculty: 67

STUDENTS

Enrollment of law school: 334

% male/female: 51/49

% from out-of-state: 50

% part-time: 11

% minority: 11

# of countries represented: 3

Average age of entering class: 23

ACADEMICS

Academic Specialties: Civil Procedure, Commercial, Constitutional, Corporation Securities, Criminal, Environmental, Government Services, Human Rights, International, Labor, Legal History, Legal Philosophy, Property, Taxation, Intellectual Property, Public Law, Urban Planning & Development, Health Law

Advanced Degrees Offered: LLM Health Law, 1 year full-time, 2 years part-time; LLM for Foreign Lawyers, 1 year full-time

Combined Degrees Offered: JD/MBA, JD/MA in Public Administration, JD/MHA JD/MPH, JD/MA in Urban Affairs, JD/MSW, JD/MA in Sociology in Criminal Justice, JD/MA in Public Health–Health Policy, 4 years; JD/PhD in Health Care Ethics, 4–6 years

Clinical program required: No

Legal writing course requirement: Yes

Legal methods course requirement: Yes

Legal research course requirement: Yes

Moot court requirement: No

Public interest law requirement: No

ADMISSIONS

Selectivity Rating 76
 # applications received: 2,157
% applicants accepted: 50
% acceptees attending: 28
Average LSAT: 156
LSAT Range: 153–159
Average undergrad GPA: 3.44
Application fee: $55
Regular application: Rolling, up to 7/1
Regular notification: Rolling
Transfer students accepted: Yes
Evening division offered: Yes
Part-time accepted: Yes
CAS accepted: Yes

INTERNATIONAL STUDENTS

TOEFL required of international students?: Required

FINANCIAL FACTS

Annual tuition: $35,030
Books and supplies: $1,660
Fees: $446
Room and board: $12,350
% first-year students receiving some sort of aid: 89
% receiving some sort of aid: 89
% of aid that is merit based: 31
% receiving scholarships: 40
Average grant: $17,617
Average loan: $38,648
Average total aid package: $25,741
Average debt: $102,829

EMPLOYMENT INFORMATION

Rate of placement (nine months out): 93
Average starting salary: $59,000
State for bar exam: MO, IL
Pass rate for first-time bar: 95
Employers Who Frequently Hire Grads: Bryan Cave, LLP; Husch & Eppenberger; Lewis, Rice & Fingersh; Armstrong Teasdale, LLP; Sonnenschein, Nath & Rosenthal; Greensfelder, Hemker & Gale; Blackwell, Sanders, Peper, Martin; Missouri State Public Defender; Evans & Dixon; Brown & James; King & Spalding; ProsKruer Rose; Thompson Coburn; Shook, Hardy & Bacon; U.S. Postal Service; Missouri Attorney General ·
Grads Employed by Field (%)
Academic: (6)
Business/industry: (19)
Government: (11)
Judicial clerkship: (2)
Military: (1)
Private practice: (56)
Public interest: (3)

St. Mary's University School of Law

One Camino Santa Maria, San Antonio, TX 78228-8601
Admissions Phone: 866-639-5831 • **Admissions Fax:** 210-431-4202
Admissions E-Mail: lawadmissions@stmarytx.edu
Website: law.stmarytx.edu

INSTITUTIONAL INFORMATION

Public/private: Private
Student/faculty ratio: 22:1
% faculty part-time: 63
% faculty female: 39
% faculty minority: 15
Total faculty: 82

STUDENTS

Enrollment of law school: 887
% male/female: 54/46
% from out-of-state: 10
% part-time: 24
% minority: 32
Average age of entering class: 25

ACADEMICS

Academic Specialties: Constitutional, Criminal, Human Rights, International, Advocacy
Advanced Degrees Offered: LLM in International and Comparative Law for U.S. educated graduates, LLM in American Legal Studies for foreign educated graduates, (Each 1 year)
Combined Degrees Offered: JD/MA International Relations; JD/MPA Public Administration; JD/MA English Language and Literature; JD/MA Theology; JD/MS Computer Science; JD/MS Engineering; JD/MBA Business Administration; JD/MA Communication Studies (all 3.5–4 years total)
Clinical program required: No
Legal writing course requirement: Yes
Legal methods course requirement: Yes
Legal research course requirement: Yes
Moot court requirement: Yes
Public interest law requirement: No

ADMISSIONS

Selectivity Rating 72
 # applications received: 1,965
% applicants accepted: 43
% acceptees attending: 35
LSAT Range: 151–156
Application fee: $55
Regular application: Rolling, up to 3/1
Regular notification: Rolling
Transfer students accepted: Yes
Evening division offered: Yes
Part-time accepted: Yes
CAS accepted: Yes

INTERNATIONAL STUDENTS

TOEFL required of international students?: Recommended

FINANCIAL FACTS

Annual tuition: $26,520
Books and supplies: $1,300
Fees: $500
Room and board: $8,072
Financial aid application deadline: 3/31
% first-year students receiving some sort of aid: 85
% receiving some sort of aid: 85
% of aid that is merit based: 6
% receiving scholarships: 28
Average grant: $4,270
Average loan: $29,303
Average total aid package: $32,047
Average debt: $91,841

EMPLOYMENT INFORMATION

Rate of placement (nine months out): 86
Average starting salary: $53,607
State for bar exam: TX, FL, MO, OK, NM
Pass rate for first-time bar: 83
Employers Who Frequently Hire Grads: Bexar County District Attorney's Office; Fourth Court of Appeals; Cox Smith Matthew LLP; Texas Office of the Attorney General
Prominent Alumni: John Cornyn, United States Senator from Texas; Charles Gonzalez, Congressman; Alma L. Lopez, Former Chief Justice of the Texas Court of Appeals; Thomas Mummert, U.S. Magistrate Judge, Nelson Wolff, Former Mayor of San Antonio
Grads Employed by Field (%)
Business/industry: (11)
Government: (15)
Judicial clerkship: (4)
Private practice: (63)
Public interest: (5)

ACADEMICS

Academic Specialties: Commercial, Corporation Securities
Clinical program required: No

ADMISSIONS

Selectivity Rating 61
applications received: 1,460
% applicants accepted: 37
% acceptees attending: 49
Average LSAT: 141
LSAT Range: 138–144
Average undergrad GPA: 2.80
Application fee: $50
Regular notification: Rolling
Transfer students accepted: Yes
Evening division offered: No
Part-time accepted: No
CAS accepted: No

FINANCIAL FACTS

Annual tuition (in-state/out-of-state): $4,466/$7,562
Books and supplies: $700
Room and board: $6,000

EMPLOYMENT INFORMATION

State for bar exam: TX
Pass rate for first-time bar: 68
Grads Employed by Field (%)
Government: (2)
Judicial clerkship: (4)
Private practice: (87)
Public interest: (5)

TEXAS SOUTHERN UNIVERSITY

Thurgood Marshall School of Law

3100 Cleburne Avenue, Houston, TX 77004
Admissions Phone: 713-313-7114 • Admissions Fax:
Admissions E-Mail: lawadmit@tsulaw.edu • Website: www.tsulaw.edu

INSTITUTIONAL INFORMATION

Public/private: Public
Student/faculty ratio: 17:1
% faculty female: 20
% faculty minority: 83
Total faculty: 35

STUDENTS

Enrollment of law school: 541
% male/female: 57/43
% minority: 77

TEXAS WESLEYAN UNIVERSITY

Texas Wesleyan School of Law

1515 Commerce Street, Office of Admissions Fort Worth, TX 76102
Admissions Phone: 817-212-4040 • Admissions Fax: 817-212-4141
Admissions E-Mail: lawadmissions@law.txwes.edu • Website: law.txwes.edu

INSTITUTIONAL INFORMATION

Public/private: Private
% faculty part-time: 59
% faculty female: 38
% faculty minority: 9
Total faculty: 64

STUDENTS

Enrollment of law school: 253
% male/female: 50/50
% from out-of-state: 17
% part-time: 32
% minority: 18
% international: 1
# of countries represented: 10
Average age of entering class: 28

ACADEMICS

Advanced Degrees Offered: JD, 3 years full-time, 4 years part-time
Clinical program required: No
Legal writing course requirement: Yes
Legal methods course requirement: Yes
Legal research course requirement: Yes
Moot court requirement: Yes
Public interest law requirement: Yes

ADMISSIONS

Selectivity Rating 70
 # applications received: 1,746
% applicants accepted: 40
% acceptees attending: 24
Average LSAT: 153
LSAT Range: 151–156
Average undergrad GPA: 3.23
Application fee: $55
Regular application: Rolling, up to 3/31
Regular notification: Rolling
Transfer students accepted: Yes
Evening division offered: Yes
Part-time accepted: Yes
CAS accepted: Yes

INTERNATIONAL STUDENTS

TOEFL required of international students?: Required

FINANCIAL FACTS

Annual tuition: $26,650
Books and supplies: $1,800
Fees: $790
Room and board: $10,845
Financial aid application deadline: 8/1
% receiving some sort of aid: 88
% receiving scholarships: 47
Average grant: $8,976
Average loan: $28,444
Average total aid package: $37,420
Average debt: $88,062

EMPLOYMENT INFORMATION

Rate of placement (nine months out): 85
Average starting salary: $73,058
State for bar exam: TX, OK, NY, NV, NM
Pass rate for first-time bar: 80
Employers Who Frequently Hire Grads: Mid-sized to small private practice firms, District Attorney's Offices, Government Agencies, various corporations and businesses
Prominent Alumni: Craig Watkins, Dallas County District Attorney; Carlos Cortez, Judge, 44th District of Dallas County; Susan Hawk, Judge, 291st Criminal District Court; Nancy Berger, Judge, 322nd District Family Court of Tarrant County, Phil King, State Representative, 61st District
Grads Employed by Field (%)
Academic: (3)
Business/industry: (26)
Government: (9)
Judicial clerkship: (2)
Private practice: (58)
Public interest: (2)

THOMAS JEFFERSON SCHOOL OF LAW

2121 San Diego Avenue, San Diego, CA 92110
Admissions Phone: *619-297-9700* • **Admissions Fax:** *619-294-4713*
Admissions E-Mail: *admissions@tjsl.edu* • **Website:** *www.tjsl.edu*

INSTITUTIONAL INFORMATION

Public/private: Private
Student/faculty ratio: 21:1
% faculty part-time: 40
% faculty female: 50
% faculty minority: 6
Total faculty: 61

STUDENTS

Enrollment of law school: 439
% male/female: 52/48
% from out-of-state: 33
% part-time: 25
% minority: 36
% international: 2
# of countries represented: 5
Average age of entering class: 27

ACADEMICS

Academic Specialties: Civil Procedure, Commercial, Constitutional, Corporation Securities, Criminal, Environmental, Government Services, Human Rights, International, Labor, Property, Taxation, Intellectual Property, Sports and Entertainment Law, Family Law, Health Law, Litigation & Dispute Resolution
Advanced Degrees Offered: JD, 3 years full-time; JD, 4 years part-time
Clinical program required: No
Legal writing course requirement: Yes
Legal methods course requirement: No
Legal research course requirement: No
Moot court requirement: No
Public interest law requirement: No

ADMISSIONS

Selectivity Rating 68
 # applications received: 2,979
% applicants accepted: 51
% acceptees attending: 26
Average LSAT: 151
LSAT Range: 148–153
Average undergrad GPA: 2.96
Application fee: $50
Regular notification: Rolling
Transfer students accepted: Yes
Evening division offered: Yes
Part-time accepted: Yes
CAS accepted: Yes

INTERNATIONAL STUDENTS

TOEFL required of international students?: Required

FINANCIAL FACTS

Annual tuition: $36,300
Books and supplies: $3,228
Fees: $150
Room and board (on/off campus): $11,500/$11,100
Financial aid application deadline: 4/25
% first-year students receiving some sort of aid: 94
% receiving some sort of aid: 92
% of aid that is merit based: 15
% receiving scholarships: 40
Average grant: $10,394
Average loan: $27,607
Average total aid package: $30,078
Average debt: $99,000

EMPLOYMENT INFORMATION

Rate of placement (nine months out): 84
Average starting salary: $59,251
State for bar exam: CA, NV, AZ, CO, FL
Pass rate for first-time bar: 67
Employers Who Frequently Hire Grads: Various private law firms throughout California, Nevada, Arizona, Florida and Illinois; government agencies, such as Attorney General, District Attorney, City Attorney and Public Defender, national and international corporations
Prominent Alumni: Bonnie Dumanis, San Diego District Attorney; Duncan Hunter, Member of U.S. Congress; Roger Benitez, U.S. District Court, Southern District, CA; Mattias Luukkonen, Baker & McKenzie, Dan Vrechek, Qualcomm
Grads Employed by Field (%)
Business/industry: (25)
Government: (13)
Judicial clerkship: (4)
Military: (1)
Private practice: (47)
Public interest: (10)

UNIVERSITY OF BALTIMORE
School of Law

1420 North Charles Street, Baltimore, MD 21201
Admissions Phone: *410-837-4459* • **Admissions Fax:** *410-837-4450*
Admissions E-Mail: *lwadmiss@ubmail.ubalt.edu* • **Website:** *law.ubalt.edu*

INSTITUTIONAL INFORMATION

Public/private: Public
Student/faculty ratio: 18:1
% faculty part-time: 58
% faculty female: 34
% faculty minority: 14
Total faculty: 146

STUDENTS

Enrollment of law school: 1,077
% male/female: 48/52
% from out-of-state: 15
% part-time: 41

% minority: 12
% international: 1
Average age of entering class: 26

ACADEMICS

Academic Specialties: Criminal, Government Services, International, Property, Intellectual Property, Business Law, Estate Planning, Litigation and Advocacy, Family Law
Advanced Degrees Offered: LLM in Taxation LLM in Law of the United States
Combined Degrees Offered: JD/MBA, JD/MS in Criminal Justice, JD/MPA, JD/PhD in Policy Science in conjuction with the Univ. of Maryland at Baltimore, JD/LLM in taxation, JD/MS in Negotiation and conflict Management. Most Combined degrees add 1 year of study.
Clinical program required: No
Legal writing course requirement: Yes
Legal methods course requirement: Yes
Legal research course requirement: Yes
Moot court requirement: No
Public interest law requirement: No

ADMISSIONS

Selectivity Rating 80
applications received: 1,781
% applicants accepted: 32
% acceptees attending: 27
Average LSAT: 156
LSAT Range: 153–159
Average undergrad GPA: 3.52
Application fee: $60
Regular application: Rolling, up to 7/30
Regular notification: Rolling
Transfer students accepted: Yes
Evening division offered: Yes
Part-time accepted: Yes
CAS accepted: Yes

INTERNATIONAL STUDENTS

TOEFL required of international students?: Recommended

FINANCIAL FACTS

Annual tuition (in-state/out-of-state): $20,591/$33,137
Books and supplies: $1,000
Fees: $1,736
Room and board: $10,000
Financial aid application deadline: 4/1
% first-year students receiving some sort of aid: 88
% receiving some sort of aid: 86
% receiving scholarships: 36
Average grant: $7,330
Average loan: $19,552
Average total aid package: $28,113
Average debt: $42,961

EMPLOYMENT INFORMATION

Rate of placement (nine months out): 95
Average starting salary: $62,672
State for bar exam: MD
Pass rate for first-time bar: 87
Employers Who Frequently Hire Grads: Law Firms, Judges, Government Agencies, Corporations, Nonprofit Organizations; DLA Piper, Venable LLP, Miles & Stockbridge, Ober Kaler, Gordon Feinblatt, Ballard Spahr, Whiteford Taylor, Saul Ewing, Office of the Public Defender, Office of the State's Attorney, Department of Justice, McGuire Woods, Public Interest Organizations

Prominent Alumni: William Donald Schaefer, Former Governor of Maryland; Nancy Forster, Public Defender of Maryland; C.A. Dutch Ruppersberger, US Congress, House of Representatives; Joseph Curran, Former Attorney General of Maryland, Peter Angelos, Owner, Baltimore Orioles

Grads Employed by Field (%)
Academic: (3)
Business/industry: (18)
Government: (19)
Judicial clerkship: (21)
Military: (1)
Private practice: (31)
Public interest: (7)

UNIVERSITY OF DETROIT MERCY
School of Law

651 East Jefferson Avenue, Detroit, MI 48226
Admissions Phone: 313-596-0264 • Admissions Fax: 313-596-0280
Admissions E-Mail: udmlawao@udmercy.edu
Website: www.law.udmercy.edu

INSTITUTIONAL INFORMATION
Public/private: Private
Student/faculty ratio: 16:1
% faculty part-time: 45
% faculty female: 31
% faculty minority: 6
Total faculty: 67

STUDENTS
Enrollment of law school: 751
% male/female: 57/43
% part-time: 21
% minority: 10
% international: 19
Average age of entering class: 25

ACADEMICS
Academic Specialties: Comprehensive legal education with courses in all areas
Advanced Degrees Offered: JD, 3 years full-time; JD/MBA, 4 years full-time; JD/LLB, 3 years full-time
Combined Degrees Offered: JD/MBA, 4 years full-time; JD/LLB, 3 years full-time; JD/LED, 4–5 years full-time
Clinical program required: Yes
Legal writing course requirement: Yes
Legal methods course requirement: Yes
Legal research course requirement: Yes
Moot court requirement: Yes
Public interest law requirement: Yes

ADMISSIONS
Selectivity Rating 63
applications received: 1,714
% applicants accepted: 47
% acceptees attending: 27
Average LSAT: 149
LSAT Range: 146–153
Average undergrad GPA: 3.14
Application fee: $50
Regular application: Rolling, up to 4/15
Regular notification: Rolling
Transfer students accepted: Yes
Evening division offered: Yes
Part-time accepted: Yes
CAS accepted: Yes

INTERNATIONAL STUDENTS
TOEFL required of international students?: Required

FINANCIAL FACTS
Annual tuition: $28,500
Books and supplies: $7,390
Fees: $80
Room and board (on/off campus): $11,406/$11,166
Financial aid application deadline: 4/1
% first-year students receiving some sort of aid: 74
% receiving some sort of aid: 81
% receiving scholarships: 18
Average grant: $6,646
Average loan: $32,898
Average total aid package: $44,236
Average debt: $86,431

EMPLOYMENT INFORMATION
Rate of placement (nine months out): 92
Average starting salary: $71,980
State for bar exam: MI
Pass rate for first-time bar: 81
Employers Who Frequently Hire Grads: Private sector employers, including local firms (Dykema Gossett PLLC; Butze Long, Plinkett Cooney PC) and national firms (Shearman & Stearling LLP and Paul, Hastings, Hanofsky & Walker LLP in NY); Public sector employers, including state and deferal judges and county prosecutors' offices

Grads Employed by Field (%)
Academic: (2)
Business/industry: (14)
Government: (7)
Judicial clerkship: (1)
Private practice: (70)
Public interest: (5)

University of
La Verne*

College of Law

320 East D Street, Ontario, CA 91764
Admissions Phone: (877) 858-4529 • Admissions Fax: (909) 460-2082
Admissions E-Mail: lawadm@laverne.edu • Website: http://law.laverne.edu

INSTITUTIONAL INFORMATION

Public/private: Private
Student-faculty ratio: 16:1
% faculty part-time: 46
% faculty female: 39
% faculty minority: 46
Total faculty: 41

STUDENTS

Enrollment of law school: 425
% male/female: 55/45
% part-time: 27
% minority: 40
% international: 3
Average age of entering class: 27

ACADEMICS

Advanced Degrees Offered: JD, 3 years full-time, 4 years part-time
Combined Degrees Offered: JD/MBA, JD/MPA, 4 years
Clinical program required: No
Legal writing course requirement: Yes
Legal methods course requirement: Yes
Legal research course requirement: Yes
Moot court requirement: No
Public interest law requirement: No

ADMISSIONS

Selectivity Rating 60*
applications received: 1,231
% applicants accepted: 45
% acceptees attending: 24
Average LSAT: 153
LSAT Range: 150–155
Average undergrad GPA: 3.06
Application fee: $50
Regular application: Rolling, up to 7/1
Regular notification: Rolling
Transfer students accepted: Yes
Evening division offered: Yes
Part-time accepted: Yes
CAS accepted: Yes

INTERNATIONAL STUDENTS

TOEFL required of international students?: Recommended

FINANCIAL FACTS

Annual tuition: $39,900
Books and supplies: $1,656
Fees: $862
Room and Board: $18,225
Financial aid application deadline: 3/2

EMPLOYMENT INFORMATION

Rate of placement (nine months out): 60
Average starting salary: $61,002
State for bar exam: CA, TX, AZ, UT, MT
Pass rate for first-time bar: 53
Employers Who Frequently Hire Grads: Private law firms, business, govern-
ment, public interest organizations
Grads Employed by Field (%)
Academic: (3)
Business/industry: (26)
Government: (7)
Judicial clerkship: (2)
Private practice: (62)

University of Louisville

Louis D. Brandeis School of Law

University of Louisville, Wyatt Hall - Room 107 Louisville, KY 40292
Admissions Phone: 502-852-6364 • Admissions Fax: 502-852-8971
Admissions E-Mail: lawadmissions@louisville.edu
Website: www.law.louisville.edu

INSTITUTIONAL INFORMATION

Public/private: Public
Student/faculty ratio: 14:1
% faculty part-time: 17
% faculty female: 34
% faculty minority: 10
Total faculty: 35

STUDENTS

Enrollment of law school: 417
% male/female: 58/42
% from out-of-state: 23
% part-time: 24
% minority: 5
# of countries represented: 1
Average age of entering class: 24

ACADEMICS

Academic Specialties: Civil Procedure, Commercial, Constitutional,
Corporation Securities, Criminal, Environmental, International, Labor, Legal
Philosophy, Property, Taxation, Intellectual Property
Advanced Degrees Offered: JD, 3 years full-time, 4–5 years part-time
Combined Degrees Offered: Dual-Degree Programs: JD/MBA, JD/MSSW, JD/M
Div, JD/MA in Humanities, JD/MA in Poli Sci, and a JD/MA in Urban Planning;
JD/MA Bioethics (4–5 years)

*Provisionally approved by the ABA

Clinical program required: Yes
Legal writing course requirement: Yes
Legal methods course requirement: Yes
Legal research course requirement: Yes
Moot court requirement: Yes
Public interest law requirement: Yes

ADMISSIONS
Selectivity Rating 81
applications received: 1,065
% applicants accepted: 33
% acceptees attending: 29
Average LSAT: 157
LSAT Range: 157–159
Average undergrad GPA: 3.48
Application fee: $50
Regular application: Rolling, up to 4/1
Regular notification: Rolling
Transfer students accepted: Yes
Evening division offered: No
Part-time accepted: Yes
CAS accepted: Yes

INTERNATIONAL STUDENTS
TOEFL required of international students?: Recommended

FINANCIAL FACTS
Annual tuition (in-state/out-of-state): $14,440/$28,980
Books and supplies: $1,000
Room and board: $8,484
Financial aid application deadline: 4/15
% first-year students receiving some sort of aid: 85
% receiving some sort of aid: 85
% of aid that is merit based: 100
% receiving scholarships: 60
Average grant: $7,000
Average loan: $20,687
Average total aid package: $27,687

EMPLOYMENT INFORMATION
Rate of placement (nine months out): 98
Average starting salary: $63,000
State for bar exam: KY, IN, TN, OH
Pass rate for first-time bar: 89
Employers Who Frequently Hire Grads: Frost, Brown & Todd ; Dinsmore & Shohl; Greenebaum, Doll & McDonald; Wyatt, Tarrant & Combs; Stites & Harbison
Prominent Alumni: Chris Dodd, US Senator; Ron Mazzoli, Former US Congressman; Joseph Lambert, Chief Justice of Kentucky; Stanley Chauvin, Former ABA President, Ernie Allen, Director, National Center for Missing & Exploited
Grads Employed by Field (%)
Public interest: (7)

UNIVERSITY OF MONTANA
School of Law

Admissions Office, Missoula, MT 59812
Admissions Phone: 406-243-2698 • Admissions Fax: 406-243-2576
Admissions E-Mail: heidi.fanslow@umontana.edu
Website: www.umt.edu/law

INSTITUTIONAL INFORMATION
Public/private: Public
Student/faculty ratio: 19:1
% faculty part-time: 18
% faculty female: 32
% faculty minority: 5
Total faculty: 22

STUDENTS
Enrollment of law school: 241
% male/female: 56/44
% from out-of-state: 29
% minority: 3
Average age of entering class: 28

ACADEMICS
Academic Specialties: Environmental, Taxation, Indian Law and Trial Advocacy
Advanced Degrees Offered: JD, 3 years
Combined Degrees Offered: JD/MPA, 3 years; JD/MBA, 3 years JD/MS-EVST, 4 years
Clinical program required: Yes
Legal writing course requirement: Yes
Legal methods course requirement: Yes
Legal research course requirement: Yes
Moot court requirement: No
Public interest law requirement: Yes

ADMISSIONS
Selectivity Rating 80
applications received: 550
% applicants accepted: 32
% acceptees attending: 44
Average LSAT: 155
LSAT Range: 152–157
Average undergrad GPA: 3.40
Application fee: $60
Regular application: Rolling, up to 3/1
Regular notification: Rolling
Transfer students accepted: Yes
Evening division offered: No
Part-time accepted: No
CAS accepted: Yes

INTERNATIONAL STUDENTS
TOEFL required of international students?: Required

FINANCIAL FACTS

Annual tuition (in-state/out-of-state): $8,710/$17,475
Books and supplies: $1,010
Room and board: $9,300
Financial aid application deadline: 3/1
% first-year students receiving some sort of aid: 85
% receiving some sort of aid: 88
% of aid that is merit based: 3
% receiving scholarships: 40
Average grant: $1,457
Average loan: $14,350
Average total aid package: $14,619
Average debt: $48,504

EMPLOYMENT INFORMATION

Average starting salary: $41,063
State for bar exam: MT, WA
Pass rate for first-time bar: 80
Employers Who Frequently Hire Grads: Church, Harris, Johnson, & Williams; Moulton, Bellingham, Longo, & Mather; Crowley, Haughy, Hanson, Toole, & Dietrich; Towe, Ball Enright, MacKey, & Summerfeld; Smith, Walsh, Clark, & Gregoire; Jardine, Stephenson, Blewett, & Weaver; Montan Supreme Court; Montana District Courts; Montana Federal District Courts

Grads Employed by Field (%)
Academic: (11)
Business/industry: (6)
Government: (12)
Judicial clerkship: (23)
Private practice: (35)
Public interest: (1)

UNIVERSITY OF NEW HAMPSHIRE
School of Law

Two White Street, Concord, NH 03301
Admissions Phone: *603-228-9217* • **Admissions Fax:** *603-228-1074*
Admissions E-Mail: *admissions@piercelaw.edu*
Website: *www.piercelaw.edu*

INSTITUTIONAL INFORMATION

Public/private: Private
Student/faculty ratio: 13:1
% faculty part-time: 46
% faculty female: 36
% faculty minority: 5
Total faculty: 58

STUDENTS

Enrollment of law school: 427
% male/female: 62/38
% from out-of-state: 87
% part-time: 1
% minority: 17
% international: 4
# of countries represented: 15
Average age of entering class: 27

ACADEMICS

Academic Specialties: Commercial, Criminal, Human Rights, Intellectual Property, International Criminal Law and Justice
Advanced Degrees Offered: LLM, 1 year Master of Intellectual Property; Commerce & Technology (MIPCT), 1 year
Combined Degrees Offered: JD/MIPCT, 3 years
Clinical program required: No
Legal writing course requirement: Yes
Legal methods course requirement: Yes
Legal research course requirement: Yes
Moot court requirement: Yes
Public interest law requirement: No

ADMISSIONS

Selectivity Rating 71
 # applications received: 1,447
% applicants accepted: 49
% acceptees attending: 22
Average LSAT: 154
LSAT Range: 150–156
Average undergrad GPA: 3.20
Application fee: $55
Regular application: Rolling, up to 4/1
Regular notification: Rolling
Transfer students accepted: Yes
Evening division offered: No
Part-time accepted: No
CAS accepted: Yes

INTERNATIONAL STUDENTS

TOEFL required of international students?: Required

FINANCIAL FACTS

Annual tuition: $29,000
Books and supplies: $1,000
Fees: $50
Room and board: $9,220
% first-year students receiving some sort of aid: 92
% receiving some sort of aid: 97
% of aid that is merit based: 63
% receiving scholarships: 72
Average grant: $8,600
Average loan: $32,440
Average total aid package: $37,274
Average debt: $93,476

EMPLOYMENT INFORMATION

Rate of placement (nine months out): 92
Average starting salary: $85,000
State for bar exam: MA, NH, NY, DC, CA
Pass rate for first-time bar: 84
Employers Who Frequently Hire Grads: Connecticut Superior Court Fenwick & West, Palo Alto, Calif. Fitzpatrick, Cella Harper & Cinto, New York Kirkpatrick Gates, Boston New Hampshire Superior Court Paul Hastings, San Diego
Prominent Alumni: Hon. Samuel Der-Yeghiayan, U.S. District Court for Northern Illinois; Hon. Timothy Ryan, U.S. House of Representatives; Douglas Wood, Esq., Partner, Reed Smith; Dawn Evonocore, Calvin Klein, Trademark Counsel
Grads Employed by Field (%)
Academic: (8)
Business/industry: (23)
Government: (9)
Judicial clerkship: (6)
Private practice: (49)
Public interest: (4)

VALPARAISO UNIVERSITY SCHOOL OF LAW

Wesemann Hall, Valparaiso, IN 46383
Admissions Phone: 888-825-7652 • Admissions Fax: 219-465-7808
Admissions E-Mail: valpolaw@valpo.edu • Website: www.valpo.edu/law/

INSTITUTIONAL INFORMATION
Public/private: Private
Student/faculty ratio: 17:1
% faculty part-time: 50
% faculty female: 42
% faculty minority: 6
Total faculty: 50

STUDENTS
Enrollment of law school: 523
% male/female: 55/45
% from out-of-state: 68
% part-time: 8
% minority: 12
% international: 2
# of countries represented: 4
Average age of entering class: 24

ACADEMICS
Academic Specialties: Civil Procedure, Commercial, Constitutional, Corporation Securities, Criminal, Environmental, Government Services, Human Rights, International, Labor, Legal History, Legal Philosophy, Property, Intellectual Property
Advanced Degrees Offered: JD, 3 years full-time, 5 years part-time; LLM, 1 year full-time
Combined Degrees Offered: All dual-degree programs take 4 years JD/MBA JD/CMHC JD/PSY JD/MA International Commerce and Policy JD/MA Sports Administration JD/MALS—Create your own program
Clinical program required: No
Legal writing course requirement: Yes
Legal methods course requirement: Yes
Legal research course requirement: Yes
Moot court requirement: No
Public interest law requirement: Yes

ADMISSIONS
Selectivity Rating 72
applications received: 2,589
% applicants accepted: 30
% acceptees attending: 22
Average LSAT: 151
LSAT Range: 144–162
Average undergrad GPA: 3.31
Application fee: $60
Regular notification: Rolling
Transfer students accepted: Yes
Evening division offered: No
Part-time accepted: Yes
CAS accepted: Yes

INTERNATIONAL STUDENTS
TOEFL required of international students?: Required

FINANCIAL FACTS
Annual tuition: $28,250
Books and supplies: $2,000
Fees: $612
Room and board: $7,300
Financial aid application deadline: 4/1
% first-year students receiving some sort of aid: 90
% receiving some sort of aid: 95
% of aid that is merit based: 35
% receiving scholarships: 34
Average grant: $15,214
Average loan: $18,500
Average total aid package: $39,850
Average debt: $56,000

EMPLOYMENT INFORMATION
Average starting salary: $56,000
State for bar exam: IN, IL, MI, WI, GA
Pass rate for first-time bar: 84
Employers Who Frequently Hire Grads: These statistics may be reviewed on our website www.valpo.edu/law or you may contact our Career Planning Office at 219-465-7814.
Prominent Alumni: Stephan Todd, VP Law & Environment US Steel Corporation; Cornell Boggs, VP & General Counsel, Tyco Plastics & Adhesives; Honorable Nancy Vaidik, Justice, Indiana Court of Appeals; Koreen Ryan, Senior Council, South Asia McDonald's Corporation, Honorable Robert Rucker, Justice, Supreme Court of Indiana
Grads Employed by Field (%)
Academic: (1)
Business/industry: (16)
Government: (12)
Judicial clerkship: (4)
Military: (1)
Private practice: (63)
Public interest: (2)

WASHINGTON AND LEE UNIVERSITY
School of Law

Admissions Phone: 540-458-8503 • Admissions Fax: 540-458-8586
Admissions E-Mail: lawadm@wlu.edu • Website: www.law.wlu.edu

INSTITUTIONAL INFORMATION
Public/private: Private
Student/faculty ratio: 10:1
% faculty part-time: 42
% faculty female: 15
% faculty minority: 5
Total faculty: 60

STUDENTS
Enrollment of law school: 144
% male/female: 63/37
% from out-of-state: 81
% minority: 15

...ered: Master of Laws (LLM) in United States Law
...grees Offered: JD/MHA, 6 years
...ical program required: No
Legal writing course requirement: Yes
Legal methods course requirement: No
Legal research course requirement: Yes
Moot court requirement: No
Public interest law requirement: No

ADMISSIONS
Selectivity Rating 60*
applications received: 4,582
% applicants accepted: 22
% acceptees attending: 14
LSAT Range: 161–167
Average undergrad GPA: 3.44
Regular application: 3/1
Regular notification: 4/6
Transfer students accepted: Yes
Evening division offered: No
Part-time accepted: No
CAS accepted: Yes

INTERNATIONAL STUDENTS
TOEFL required of international students?: Required

FINANCIAL FACTS
Annual tuition: $38,875
Books and supplies: $2,200
Room and board: $17,673
Financial aid application deadline: 2/1
% first-year students receiving some sort of aid: 94
% receiving some sort of aid: 93
% of aid that is merit based: 27
% receiving scholarships: 66
Average grant: $18,696
Average loan: $35,942
Average total aid package: $48,293
Average debt: $109,214

EMPLOYMENT INFORMATION
Rate of placement (nine months out): 90
Average starting salary: $73,113
Grads Employed by Field (%)
Academic: (8)
Business/industry: (7)
Government: (18)
Judicial clerkship: (18)
Military: (2)
Private practice: (29)
Public interest: (8)

WESTERN NEW ENGLAND COLLEGE SCHOOL OF LAW

1215 Wilbraham Road, Springfield, MA 01119
Admissions Phone: 413-782-1406 • Admissions Fax: 413-796-2067
Admissions E-Mail: admissions@law.wnec.edu
Website: www.law.wnec.edu

INSTITUTIONAL INFORMATION
Public/private: Private
Student/faculty ratio: 13:1
% faculty part-time: 42
% faculty female: 32
% faculty minority: 6
Total faculty: 52

STUDENTS
Enrollment of law school: 525
% male/female: 48/52
% from out-of-state: 70
% part-time: 26
% minority: 12
% international: 3
# of countries represented: 2
Average age of entering class: 24

ACADEMICS
Academic Specialties: Criminal, International, Estate Planning, Business Law, Public Interest Law, Real Estate, Gender and Sexuality Studies
Advanced Degrees Offered: Western New England College School of Law offers classes toward an LLM in Estate Planning and Elder Law. The program can be completed over two or three years. This program is offered entirely online.
Combined Degrees Offered: JD/Master of Regional Planning with University of Masssachusetts, 4 years total; JD/Masters of Social Work with Springfield College, 4 years total; JD/Masters of Business Administration with Western New England College, as short as 3 years or as long as 4 years; JD/Masters of Accounting with Western New England College, 4 years total
Clinical program required: No
Legal writing course requirement: Yes
Legal methods course requirement: No
Legal research course requirement: Yes
Moot court requirement: Yes
Public interest law requirement: No

ADMISSIONS
Selectivity Rating 67
applications received: 1,318
% applicants accepted: 53
% acceptees attending: 19
Average LSAT: 153
LSAT Range: 151–155
Average undergrad GPA: 3.17
Application fee: $50
Regular application: Rolling, up to 6/1
Regular notification: Rolling
Transfer students accepted: Yes
Evening division offered: Yes
Part-time accepted: Yes
CAS accepted: Yes

INTERNATIONAL STUDENTS
TOEFL required of international students?: Required

FINANCIAL FACTS
Annual tuition: $35,582
Books and supplies: $1,528
Fees: $1,272
Room and board: $13,400
% first-year students receiving some sort of aid: 99
% receiving some sort of aid: 97
% receiving scholarships: 71
Average grant: $15,978
Average loan: $36,880
Average total aid package: $49,034
Average debt: $99,946

EMPLOYMENT INFORMATION
Rate of placement (nine months out): 76
Average starting salary: $49,132
State for bar exam: CT, MA, NY, NJ, MD
Pass rate for first-time bar: 76
Employers Who Frequently Hire Grads: Law firms (e.g., Robinson & Cole; Halloran & Sage; Murtha Cullina; Shipman & Goodwin) accounting firms and government agencies
Prominent Alumni: Lois Lerner, Director, IRS; Timothy Murray, Lt. Governor, Massachusetts
Grads Employed by Field (%)
Academic: (3)
Business/industry: (25)
Government: (16)
Judicial clerkship: (7)
Private practice: (41)
Public interest: (7)

WESTERN STATE UNIVERSITY COLLEGE OF LAW

1111 North State College Boulevard, Fullerton, CA 92831
Admissions Phone: 714-459-1101 • Admissions Fax: 714-441-1748
Admissions E-Mail: adm@wsulaw.edu • Website: www.wsulaw.edu

INSTITUTIONAL INFORMATION
Public/private: Private
% faculty part-time: 40
% faculty female: 38
% faculty minority: 21
Total faculty: 47

STUDENTS
Enrollment of law school: 215
% male/female: 64/36
% from out-of-state: 23
% part-time: 17
% minority: 35
% international: 2
Average age of entering class: 26

ACADEMICS
Academic Specialties: Criminal, Business Law
Advanced Degrees Offered: Juris Doctor, 4 years part-time, 3 years full-time
Clinical program required: No
Legal writing course requirement: Yes
Legal methods course requirement: No
Legal research course requirement: Yes
Moot court requirement: Yes
Public interest law requirement: No

ADMISSIONS
Selectivity Rating 60*
applications received: 1,895
% applicants accepted: 56
% acceptees attending: 20
Average LSAT: 150
LSAT Range: 148–153
Average undergrad GPA: 3.08
Application fee: $50
Regular notification: Rolling
Transfer students accepted: Yes
Evening division offered: Yes
Part-time accepted: Yes
CAS accepted: Yes

INTERNATIONAL STUDENTS
TOEFL required of international students?: Required

FINANCIAL FACTS
Annual tuition: $34,900
Books and supplies: $2,400
Fees: $290
Room and board: $10,669
Financial aid application deadline: 3/15
% first-year students receiving some sort of aid: 93
% receiving some sort of aid: 92
% of aid that is merit based: 18
% receiving scholarships: 45
Average grant: $15,757
Average loan: $37,584
Average total aid package: $43,035
Average debt: $89,151

EMPLOYMENT INFORMATION
Rate of placement (nine months out): 74
State for bar exam: CA, NV, PA, VA, WA
Pass rate for first-time bar: 86
Employers Who Frequently Hire Grads: Medium-sized law firms, district attorneys, public defenders, corporations, state governments, federal governments
Prominent Alumni: Lucetta Dunn, CEO, Orange County Business Council; George Gascon, District Attorney of San Francisco; Lien Ski Harrison, Managing Partner, Rutan & Tucker; Carolyn Kirkwood, Presiding Judge, Orange County Superior Court, Juvenile Panel, John Montevideo, President, Consumer Attorneys of California
Grads Employed by Field (%)
Academic: (4)
Business/industry: (5)
Government: (5)
Private practice: (82)
Public interest: (2)

CAL NORTHERN SCHOOL OF LAW

1395 Ridgewood Drive, Suite 100, Chico, CA 95973
Admissions Phone: *530-891-6900* • **Admissions Fax:** *530-891-3429*
Admissions E-Mail: *info@calnorthern.edu* • **Website:** *www.calnorthern.edu*

INSTITUTIONAL INFORMATION
Public/private: Private
Student/faculty ratio: 4:1
% faculty part-time: 100
% faculty female: 28
Total faculty: 18

STUDENTS
Enrollment of law school: 60
% part-time: 100
Average age of entering class: 32

ACADEMICS
Advanced Degrees Offered: JD only, 4 year program
Clinical program required: No
Legal writing course requirement: Yes
Legal methods course requirement: Yes
Legal research course requirement: Yes
Moot court requirement: Yes
Public interest law requirement: No

ADMISSIONS
Selectivity Rating 61
applications received: 29
% applicants accepted: 72
% acceptees attending: 100
Average LSAT: 145
Average undergrad GPA: 3.03
Application fee: $50
Regular notification: Rolling
Transfer students accepted: Yes
Evening division offered: Yes
Part-time accepted: Yes
CAS accepted: No

INTERNATIONAL STUDENTS
TOEFL required of international students?: Recommended

FINANCIAL FACTS
Annual tuition: $7,920
Books and supplies: $800
Fees: $115
Average grant: $250
Average loan: $8,000

EMPLOYMENT INFORMATION
Rate of placement (nine months out): 100
State for bar exam: CA
Pass rate for first-time bar: 67
Employers Who Frequently Hire Grads:
Prominent Alumni: Rick Keene, California State Assemblyman

CALIFORNIA PACIFIC SCHOOL OF LAW

1600 Truxton Avenue, Suite 100, Bakersfield, CA 93301
Admissions Phone: *805-322-5297* • **Admissions Fax:** *805-322-3409*
Admissions E-Mail: *inquiry@calpaclaw.edu* • **Website:** *www.calpaclaw.edu*

INSTITUTIONAL INFORMATION
Public/private: Private
% faculty part-time: 100
% faculty female: 25
% faculty minority: 5
Total faculty: 40

STUDENTS
Enrollment of law school: 32
% part-time: 100
Average age of entering class: 31

ACADEMICS
Clinical program required: No
Legal writing course requirement: No
Legal methods course requirement: Yes
Legal research course requirement: No
Moot court requirement: No
Public interest law requirement: No

ADMISSIONS
Selectivity Rating 60*
Average LSAT: 140
LSAT Range: 134–150
Average undergrad GPA: 2.80
Application fee: $75
Regular notification: Rolling
Transfer students accepted: Yes
Evening division offered: Yes
Part-time accepted: Yes
CAS accepted: No

INTERNATIONAL STUDENTS
TOEFL required of international students?: Required

FINANCIAL FACTS
Annual tuition: $8,580
Books and supplies: $400
Fees: $40
% first-year students receiving some sort of aid: 30
% receiving some sort of aid: 30

EMPLOYMENT INFORMATION
Average starting salary: $40,000
State for bar exam: CA
Pass rate for first-time bar: 100

EMPIRE COLLEGE
School of Law

3035 Cleveland Avenue, Santa Rosa, CA 95403
Admissions Phone: 707-546-4000 • **Admissions Fax:** 707-284-2814
Admissions E-Mail: spatel@empirecollege.com • **Website:** www.empcol.edu

INSTITUTIONAL INFORMATION
Public/private: Private
Student/faculty ratio: 3:1
% faculty part-time: 100
% faculty female: 22
Total faculty: 59

STUDENTS
Enrollment of law school: 128
% part-time: 100
Average age of entering class: 38

ACADEMICS
Academic Specialties: Civil Procedure, Constitutional, Criminal,
    Environmental, Legal History, Property, Intellectual Property
Clinical program required: No
Legal writing course requirement: Yes
Legal methods course requirement: No
Legal research course requirement: Yes
Moot court requirement: Yes
Public interest law requirement: No

ADMISSIONS
Selectivity Rating 60*
applications received: 79
Average LSAT: 25
LSAT Range: 20–96
Average undergrad GPA: 2.95
Application fee: $50
Regular notification: Rolling
Transfer students accepted: Yes
Evening division offered: Yes
Part-time accepted: Yes
CAS accepted: No

FINANCIAL FACTS
Annual tuition: $12,255
Books and supplies: $400
Fees: $223

EMPLOYMENT INFORMATION
State for bar exam: CA
Pass rate for first-time bar: 44
Employers Who Frequently Hire Grads: Office of the District Attorney, Public
    Defender's office, Private, Business
Prominent Alumni: Jeanne Buckley, Superior Court Commissioner (ret.); Raima
    Ballinger, Judge, Sonoma Co. Superior Court; Francisca Tisher, Judge, Napa
    Co. Superior Court; Lawrence E. Ornell, Juvenile Superior Court Commis-
    sioner, Ron Brown, Judge, Mendocino Co. Superior Court
Grads Employed by Field (%)
Business/industry: (12)
Government: (22)
Private practice: (58)

GLENDALE UNIVERSITY
College of Law

220 North Glendale Avenue, Glendale, CA 91206
Admissions Phone: 818-247-0770 • **Admissions Fax:** 818-247-0872
Admissions E-Mail: admissions@glendalelaw.edu
Website: www.glendalelaw.edu

INSTITUTIONAL INFORMATION
Public/private: Private
Student/faculty ratio: 25:1

STUDENTS
Enrollment of law school: 130
% part-time: 100
Average age of entering class: 32

ACADEMICS
Advanced Degrees Offered: Juris Doctor, 4 years
Clinical program required: No
Legal writing course requirement: Yes
Legal methods course requirement: Yes
Legal research course requirement: Yes
Moot court requirement: Yes
Public interest law requirement: No

ADMISSIONS
Selectivity Rating 62
applications received: 140
% applicants accepted: 49
% acceptees attending: 71
Average LSAT: 145
Average undergrad GPA: 3.00
Application fee: $65
Regular notification: Rolling
Transfer students accepted: Yes
Evening division offered: Yes
Part-time accepted: Yes
CAS accepted: Yes

EMPLOYMENT INFORMATION
State for bar exam: CA
Pass rate for first-time bar: 50

HUMPHREYS COLLEGE
School of Law

6650 Inglewood Avenue, Stockton, CA 95207
Admissions Phone: 209-478-0800 • **Admissions Fax:** 209-478-8721
Admissions E-Mail: selopez@humphreys.edu
Website: www.humphreys.edu/law/

INSTITUTIONAL INFORMATION
Public/private: Private
Student/faculty ratio: 6:1
% faculty part-time: 83
% faculty female: 17
Total faculty: 12

STUDENTS
Enrollment of law school: 60
% part-time: 100
Average age of entering class: 33

ACADEMICS
Clinical program required: No
Legal writing course requirement: No
Legal methods course requirement: Yes
Legal research course requirement: No

ADMISSIONS
Selectivity Rating 61
applications received: 52
% applicants accepted: 62
% acceptees attending: 59
Average LSAT: 149
Average undergrad GPA: 2.80
Application fee: $20
Regular notification: Rolling
Transfer students accepted: Yes
Evening division offered: Yes
Part-time accepted: Yes
CAS accepted: No

INTERNATIONAL STUDENTS
TOEFL required of international students?: Required

FINANCIAL FACTS
Annual tuition: $7,062
Books and supplies: $650
% first-year students receiving some sort of aid: 21
% receiving some sort of aid: 66
% of aid that is merit based:
Average loan: $14,658
Average total aid package: $14,658
Average debt: $48,000

EMPLOYMENT INFORMATION
State for bar exam: CA
Pass rate for first-time bar: 54
Employers Who Frequently Hire Grads: D.A. offices; Police Departments
Grads Employed by Field (%)
Academic: (5)
Business/industry: (5)
Government: (30)
Private practice: (60)

JOHN F. KENNEDY UNIVERSITY
School of Law

100 Ellinwood Way, Pleasant Hill, CA 94523
Admissions Phone: 925-969-3330 • **Admissions Fax:** 925-969-3331
Admissions E-Mail: law@jfku.edu • **Website:** www.jfku.edu/law

INSTITUTIONAL INFORMATION
Public/private: Private
Student/faculty ratio: 30:1
% faculty part-time: 94
% faculty female: 54
Total faculty: 54

STUDENTS
Enrollment of law school: 154
% male/female: 43/57
% part-time: 6
# of countries represented: 1
Average age of entering class: 37

ACADEMICS
Clinical program required: No
Legal writing course requirement: Yes
Legal methods course requirement: Yes
Legal research course requirement: Yes
Moot court requirement: No
Public interest law requirement: No

ADMISSIONS
Selectivity Rating 64
applications received: 122
% applicants accepted: 43
% acceptees attending: 43
Average LSAT: 148
Average undergrad GPA: 3.03
Application fee: $75
Regular notification: Rolling
Transfer students accepted: Yes
Evening division offered: Yes
Part-time accepted: Yes
CAS accepted: Yes

INTERNATIONAL STUDENTS

TOEFL required of international students?: Required

FINANCIAL FACTS

Annual tuition: $9,920
Books and supplies: $1,540
Fees: $198
% first-year students receiving some sort of aid: 70
% receiving some sort of aid: 70
% of aid that is merit based: 1
Average loan: $18,500
Average total aid package: $18,500
Average debt: $70,000

EMPLOYMENT INFORMATION

State for bar exam: CA
Pass rate for first-time bar: 45

LINCOLN LAW SCHOOL OF SACRAMENTO

3140 J Street, Sacramento, CA 95816
Admissions Phone: *916-446-1275* • **Admissions Fax:** *916-446-5641*
Admissions E-Mail: *info@lincolnlaw.edu* • **Website:** *www.lincolnlaw.edu*

INSTITUTIONAL INFORMATION

Public/private: Private
Student/faculty ratio: 40:1
% faculty part-time: 100
% faculty female: 20
% faculty minority: 10
Total faculty: 25

STUDENTS

Enrollment of law school: 275
% part-time: 100
Average age of entering class: 35

ACADEMICS

Academic Specialties: Civil Procedure, Commercial, Constitutional, Corporation Securities, Criminal, Environmental, Government Services, Labor, Legal History, Legal Philosophy, Property, Taxation, Intellectual Property, Family Law, Applied Legal Reasoning
Advanced Degrees Offered: Juris Doctor, 4 years
Clinical program required: No
Legal writing course requirement: Yes
Legal methods course requirement: Yes
Legal research course requirement: Yes
Moot court requirement: Yes
Public interest law requirement: No

ADMISSIONS

Selectivity Rating 61
applications received: 150
% applicants accepted: 70
% acceptees attending: 90
Average LSAT: 145
LSAT Range: 8–86
Average undergrad GPA: 2.80
Application fee: $30
Regular application: Rolling, up to 6/15
Regular notification: Rolling
Transfer students accepted: Yes
Evening division offered: Yes
Part-time accepted: Yes
CAS accepted: Yes

INTERNATIONAL STUDENTS

TOEFL required of international students?: Recommended

FINANCIAL FACTS

Annual tuition: $7,000
Books and supplies: $500
Room and board: $6,000
Financial aid application deadline: 6/1
% first-year students receiving some sort of aid: 10
% receiving some sort of aid: 20
% of aid that is merit based: 2
% receiving scholarships: 20
Average grant: $500
Average loan: $10,000
Average total aid package: $7,000
Average debt: $10,500

EMPLOYMENT INFORMATION

Average starting salary: $40,000
State for bar exam: CA, OR, NV, AZ, CO
Pass rate for first-time bar: 60
Employers Who Frequently Hire Grads: District Attorney's Office; Attorney Generals Office; Public Defender's Office; local private firms
Prominent Alumni: Jan Scully, Sacramento County District Attorney; Brad Fenocchio, Placer County District Attorney; Robert Holzapfel, Glenn County District Attorney; Hon. Gerald Bakarich, Sacramento County Superior Court Judge, Hon. Sue Harlan, Amador County Superior Court Judge
Grads Employed by Field (%)
Business/industry: (10)
Government: (30)
Judicial clerkship: (5)
Private practice: (50)
Public interest: (5)

LINCOLN LAW SCHOOL OF SAN JOSE

One North First Street, San Jose, CA 95113
Admissions Phone: 408-977-7227 • **Admissions Fax:** 408-977-7228
Admissions E-Mail: admissions@lincolnlawsj.edu
Website: www.lincolnlawsj.edu

INSTITUTIONAL INFORMATION
Public/private: Private

ACADEMICS
Clinical program required: No

ADMISSIONS
Selectivity Rating 60*
Application fee: $45
Regular notification: Rolling
Transfer students accepted: Yes
Evening division offered: Yes
Part-time accepted: Yes
CAS accepted: Yes

INTERNATIONAL STUDENTS
TOEFL required of international students?: Recommended

FINANCIAL FACTS
Fees: $130

MONTEREY COLLEGE OF LAW

100 Col. Durham St., Seaside, CA 93955
Admissions Phone: 831-582-4000 • **Admissions Fax:** 831-582-4095
Admissions E-Mail: wlariviere@montereylaw.edu
Website: www.montereylaw.edu

INSTITUTIONAL INFORMATION
Public/private: Private
Student/faculty ratio: 25:1
% faculty part-time: 100
% faculty female: 23
% faculty minority: 2
Total faculty: 44

STUDENTS
Enrollment of law school: 100
% part-time: 100
# of countries represented: 3
Average age of entering class: 30

ACADEMICS
Academic Specialties: Civil Procedure, Commercial, Constitutional, Corporation Securities, Criminal, Environmental, Government Services, Human Rights, International, Labor, Property, Taxation, Intellectual Property
Advanced Degrees Offered: JD, 4-year evening program; Master of Legal Studies, 2-year evening program
Clinical program required: Yes
Legal writing course requirement: Yes
Legal methods course requirement: Yes
Legal research course requirement: Yes
Moot court requirement: Yes
Public interest law requirement: No

ADMISSIONS
Selectivity Rating 74
 # applications received: 120
% applicants accepted: 44
% acceptees attending: 102
Average LSAT: 153
LSAT Range: 141–169
Average undergrad GPA: 3.17
Application fee: $75
Regular application: Rolling, up to 5/1
Regular notification: Rolling
Transfer students accepted: Yes
Evening division offered: Yes
Part-time accepted: Yes
CAS accepted: No

INTERNATIONAL STUDENTS
TOEFL required of international students?: Recommended

FINANCIAL FACTS
Books and supplies: $1,000
% first-year students receiving some sort of aid: 26
% receiving some sort of aid: 55
% of aid that is merit based: 30
% receiving scholarships: 25
Average grant: $750
Average loan: $5,000

EMPLOYMENT INFORMATION
Rate of placement (nine months out): 90
Average starting salary: $35,000
State for bar exam: CA
Pass rate for first-time bar: 40
Employers Who Frequently Hire Grads: Governmental Offices, Public Agencies, Private Law Firms, Public Defender's Office, District Attorney's Office
Prominent Alumni: Hon. John Salazar, Judge; Hon. Kim Baskett, Judicial Commissioner; Hon. Denine Guy, Judge; Hon. Russel Scott, Judge, Hon. Sam Lavarato, Jr., Judge
Grads Employed by Field (%)
Business/industry: (35)
Government: (5)
Private practice: (40)
Public interest: (20)

NEW COLLEGE OF CALIFORNIA

School of Law

50 Fell Street, San Francisco, CA 94102
Admissions Phone: 415-241-1374 • **Admissions Fax:** 415-241-9525
Admissions E-Mail: Lawadmissions@newcollege.edu
Website: www.newcollege.edu

INSTITUTIONAL INFORMATION
Public/private: Private
Student/faculty ratio: 15:1
% faculty female: 50
% faculty minority: 50
Total faculty: 36

STUDENTS
Enrollment of law school: 200
% male/female: 35/65
% from out-of-state: 10
% part-time: 25
% minority: 35
% international: 10
Average age of entering class: 35

ACADEMICS
Academic Specialties: Constitutional, Environmental, Government Services, Human Rights, Labor, Property
Advanced Degrees Offered: JD, 3 year, full-time, 4 year, part-time
Clinical program required: No
Legal writing course requirement: Yes
Legal methods course requirement: Yes
Legal research course requirement: Yes
Moot court requirement: No
Public interest law requirement: Yes

ADMISSIONS
Selectivity Rating 64
applications received: 250
% applicants accepted: 44
% acceptees attending: 59
Average LSAT: 147
Average undergrad GPA: 3.00
Application fee: $55
Regular notification: Rolling
Transfer students accepted: Yes
Evening division offered: No
Part-time accepted: Yes
CAS accepted: Yes

FINANCIAL FACTS
Annual tuition: $15,214
Books and supplies: $400
Fees: $100
Financial aid application deadline: 8/7
% first-year students receiving some sort of aid: 90
Average grant: $500
Average loan: $18,500
Average total aid package: $22,000

EMPLOYMENT INFORMATION
Rate of placement (nine months out): 65
State for bar exam: CA
Pass rate for first-time bar: 25
Employers Who Frequently Hire Grads: All nonprofit agencies and small/solo law firms
Grads Employed by Field (%)
Government: (10)
Private practice: (30)
Public interest: (60)

SAN FRANCISCO LAW SCHOOL

20 Haight Street, San Francisco, CA 94102
Admissions Phone: 415-626-5550 • **Admissions Fax:** 415-626-5584
Admissions E-Mail: admin@sfls.edu • **Website:** www.sfls.edu

NFORMATION
Public/private: Private
Student/faculty ratio: 25:1
% faculty part-time: 100
% faculty female: 13
% faculty minority: 1
Total faculty: 32

STUDENTS
Enrollment of law school: 115
% part-time: 100
Average age of entering class: 38

ACADEMICS
Advanced Degrees Offered: JD, 4-year program beginning in August, 4.5-year program beginning in January
Clinical program required: No
Legal writing course requirement: Yes
Legal methods course requirement: No
Legal research course requirement: Yes
Moot court requirement: Yes
Public interest law requirement: No

ADMISSIONS
Selectivity Rating 60*
applications received: 150
% applicants accepted: 58
Average LSAT: 1
Average undergrad GPA: 2.80
Application fee: $50
Regular application: Rolling, up to 6/15
Regular notification: Rolling
Transfer students accepted: Yes
Evening division offered: Yes
Part-time accepted: Yes
CAS accepted: No

FINANCIAL FACTS
Annual tuition: $6,700
Books and supplies: $350
Fees: $170
Room and board: $25,000
% of aid that is merit based: 40

EMPLOYMENT INFORMATION
State for bar exam: CA
Pass rate for first-time bar: 30
Employers Who Frequently Hire Grads: SF Public Defender, SFDA, Private Sector
Prominent Alumni: Edmund G. Brown (late), Governor of California; Milton Marks, Jr. (late), California State Senator; Leo T. McCarthy, Lt. Governor of California; Hon. Lynn O'Malley Taylor, Judge of the Superior Court, Hon. Henry Needham, Judge of the Superior Court
Grads Employed by Field (%)
Academic: (5)
Business/industry: (5)
Government: (20)
Judicial clerkship: (5)
Private practice: (60)
Public interest: (5)

SAN JOAQUIN COLLEGE OF LAW

901 Fifth Street, Clovis, CA 93612-1312
Admissions Phone: 559-323-2100 • Admissions Fax: 559-323-5566
Admissions E-Mail: jcanalin@sjcl.org • Website: www.sjcl.edu

INSTITUTIONAL INFORMATION
Public/private: Private
Student/faculty ratio: 16:1
% faculty part-time: 83
% faculty female: 45
% faculty minority: 14
Total faculty: 36

STUDENTS
Enrollment of law school: 185
% male/female: 54/46
% part-time: 87
% minority: 26
Average age of entering class: 33

ACADEMICS
Academic Specialties: Commercial, Corporation Securities, Criminal, Environmental, International, Labor, Taxation
Advanced Degrees Offered: JD, 3–5 year program; MS Taxation, 2 years
Clinical program required: Yes
Legal writing course requirement: No
Legal methods course requirement: Yes
Legal research course requirement: No

ADMISSIONS
Selectivity Rating 61
applications received: 135
% applicants accepted: 80
% acceptees attending: 84
Average LSAT: 148
LSAT Range: 139–174
Average undergrad GPA: 2.90
Application fee: $40
Regular notification: Rolling
Transfer students accepted: Yes
Evening division offered: Yes
Part-time accepted: Yes
CAS accepted: No

FINANCIAL FACTS
Annual tuition: $10,212
Books and supplies: $550
Fees: $125
% first-year students receiving some sort of aid: 75
% receiving some sort of aid: 75
% of aid that is merit based: 12
% receiving scholarships: 14
Average grant: $1,600
Average loan: $14,500
Average total aid package: $18,500
Average debt: $62,500

EMPLOYMENT INFORMATION
State for bar exam: CA
Pass rate for first-time bar: 56
Employers Who Frequently Hire Grads: Local DA and DD; various small firms
Grads Employed by Field (%)
Government: (23)
Private practice: (70)
Public interest: (5)

SANTA BARBARA AND VENTURA COLLEGES OF LAW

Santa Barbara College of Law

20 East Victoria Street, Santa Barbara, CA 93101
Admissions Phone: 805-966-0010 • Admissions Fax: 805-966-7181
Admissions E-Mail: admit@venturalaw.edu
Website: www.santabarbaralaw.edu

INSTITUTIONAL INFORMATION
Public/private: Private
Student/faculty ratio: 11:1
% faculty part-time: 100
% faculty female: 26
% faculty minority: 5
Total faculty: 19

STUDENTS

Enrollment of law school: 917
% male/female: 51/49

ACADEMICS

Clinical program required: Yes
Legal writing course requirement: Yes
Legal methods course requirement: No
Legal research course requirement: Yes
Moot court requirement: No
Public interest law requirement: No

ADMISSIONS

Selectivity Rating 73
applications received: 2,528
% applicants accepted: 50
% acceptees attending: 23
Average LSAT: 156
LSAT Range: 153–158
Average undergrad GPA: 3.20
Application fee: $40
Regular notification: Rolling
Transfer students accepted: No
Evening division offered: Yes
Part-time accepted: Yes
CAS accepted: No

FINANCIAL FACTS

Annual tuition: $22,000
Books and supplies: $903
Room and board: $9,787
% first-year students receiving some sort of aid: 77
% receiving some sort of aid: 85
% of aid that is merit based: 7
% receiving scholarships: 31
Average grant: $8,071
Average debt: $60,379

EMPLOYMENT INFORMATION

Average starting salary: $58,000
State for bar exam: CA
Pass rate for first-time bar: 71
Grads Employed by Field (%)
Academic: (2)
Business/industry: (24)
Government: (8)
Judicial clerkship: (4)
Military: (1)
Private practice: (58)
Public interest: (3)

SANTA BARBARA AND VENTURA COLLEGES OF LAW

Ventura College of Law

4475 Market Street, Ventura, CA 93003
Admissions Phone: *805-658-0511* • **Admissions Fax:** *805-658-0529*
Admissions E-Mail: *bdoyle@CollegesOfLaw.org*
Website: *www.CollegesOfLaw.org*

INSTITUTIONAL INFORMATION

Public/private: Private
% faculty part-time: 100
% faculty female: 22
% faculty minority: 6
Total faculty: 18

STUDENTS

Enrollment of law school: 119
% part-time: 100
Average age of entering class: 35

ACADEMICS

Academic Specialties: Commercial, Criminal, Family Law, Estate Planning
Advanced Degrees Offered: JD, 4-year part-time evening program
Combined Degrees Offered: None
Clinical program required: Yes
Legal writing course requirement: Yes
Legal methods course requirement: Yes
Legal research course requirement: Yes
Moot court requirement: No
Public interest law requirement: Yes

ADMISSIONS

Selectivity Rating 60*
applications received: 111
Average LSAT: 148
LSAT Range: 137–160
Average undergrad GPA: 3.15
Application fee: $50
Regular application: Rolling, up to 7/15
Regular notification: Rolling
Transfer students accepted: Yes
Evening division offered: Yes
Part-time accepted: Yes
CAS accepted: Yes

EMPLOYMENT INFORMATION

Rate of placement (nine months out): 100
State for bar exam: CA
Pass rate for first-time bar: 34

SOUTHERN CALIFORNIA INSTITUTE OF LAW
College of Law

877 South Victoria Avenue, Ventura, CA 93003
Admissions Phone: *805-644-2327* • **Admissions Fax:** *805-644-2367*
Admissions E-Mail: *1973 scil@msn.com* • **Website:** *www.lawdegree.com*

INSTITUTIONAL INFORMATION
Public/private: Private
Student/faculty ratio: 5:1
% faculty part-time: 75
% faculty female: 50
% faculty minority: 10

STUDENTS
Enrollment of law school: 50
% male/female: 60/40
% part-time: 100
% minority: 15
Average age of entering class: 32

ACADEMICS
Legal writing course requirement: No
Legal methods course requirement: Yes
Legal research course requirement: No

ADMISSIONS
Selectivity Rating 60*
applications received: 50
Transfer students accepted: No
Evening division offered: No
Part-time accepted: No
CAS accepted: No

INTERNATIONAL STUDENTS
TOEFL required of international students?: Required

FINANCIAL FACTS
Annual tuition: $6,480
Books and supplies: $500
% of aid that is merit based: 100

EMPLOYMENT INFORMATION
Average starting salary: $30,000
State for bar exam: CA
Pass rate for first-time bar: 50
Employers Who Frequently Hire Grads: Local Law Firms, Government and State Agencies

UNIVERSITY OF WEST LOS ANGELES
School of Law

9920 S. La Cienega Blvd. #404, Inglewood, CA 90301
Admissions Phone: *310-342-5210* • **Admissions Fax:** *310-342-5295*
Admissions E-Mail: *tsmith@uwla.edu* • **Website:** *www.uwla.edu*

INSTITUTIONAL INFORMATION
Public/private: Private
Student/faculty ratio: 30:1
% faculty part-time: 81
% faculty female: 19
% faculty minority: 17
Total faculty: 36

STUDENTS
Enrollment of law school: 262
% male/female: 45/55
% part-time: 87
% minority: 24

ACADEMICS
Advanced Degrees Offered: JD, 3 years full-time, 4 years part-time
Clinical program required: No
Legal writing course requirement: Yes
Legal methods course requirement: Yes
Legal research course requirement: Yes
Moot court requirement: No
Public interest law requirement: No

ADMISSIONS
Selectivity Rating 65
applications received: 59
% applicants accepted: 47
% acceptees attending: 61
Average LSAT: 148
Average undergrad GPA: 3.10
Application fee: $55
Regular notification: Rolling
Transfer students accepted: Yes
Evening division offered: Yes
Part-time accepted: Yes
CAS accepted: Yes

INTERNATIONAL STUDENTS
TOEFL required of international students?: Recommended

FINANCIAL FACTS
Annual tuition: $19,488
Books and supplies: $900
Fees: $1,600
% receiving scholarships: 5

EMPLOYMENT INFORMATION
State for bar exam: CA
Pass rate for first-time bar: 35
Prominent Alumni: Paula Zinneman, California Real Estate Commissioner; Gail Margolis, Director, Mental Health Services, State of CA; Hon. Ron Skyers, LA Superior Court Judge; Lael Rubin, District Attorney's Office

DALHOUSIE
Dalhousie Law School

Dalhousie Law School, 6061 University Avenue Halifax, NS B3H 4H9
Admissions Phone: *902-494-2068* • **Admissions Fax:** *902-494-1316*
Admissions E-Mail: *law.admissions@dal.ca* • **Website:** *www.dal.ca/law/*

INSTITUTIONAL INFORMATION
Public/private: Public
Student/faculty ratio: 13:1
% faculty female: 45
% faculty minority: 6
Total faculty: 35

STUDENTS
Average age of entering class: 25

ACADEMICS
Academic Specialties: Commercial, Corporation Securities, Environmental, International
Advanced Degrees Offered: LLM, JSD
Combined Degrees Offered: LLB/MBA, LLB/MLIS, LLB/MPA, LLB/MHSA, 4 years
Clinical program required: No
Legal writing course requirement: Yes
Legal methods course requirement: No
Legal research course requirement: Yes
Moot court requirement: Yes
Public interest law requirement: No

ADMISSIONS
Selectivity Rating 85
applications received: 1,285
% applicants accepted: 30
% acceptees attending: 42
Average LSAT: 161
Application fee: $70
Regular application: Rolling, up to 2/28
Regular notification: Rolling
Transfer students accepted: Yes
Evening division offered: No
Part-time accepted: Yes
CAS accepted: No

FINANCIAL FACTS
Annual tuition: $12,475
Books and supplies: $1,200
Room and board: $3,500
Financial aid application deadline: 10/31
% of aid that is merit based: 43
Average grant: $4,212
Average loan: $8,000
Average total aid package: $2,500

EMPLOYMENT INFORMATION
Employers Who Frequently Hire Grads: Law firms, government, courts
Grads Employed by Field (%)
Business/industry: (1)
Government: (1)
Judicial clerkship: (1)
Private practice: (97)

MCGILL UNIVERSITY
McGill Faculty of Law

3644 Peel Street, Room #406, Montreal, QC H3A 1W9
Admissions Phone: *(514) 398-6646* • **Admissions Fax:** *(514) 398-8453*
Admissions E-Mail: *gradadmissions.law@mcgill.ca*
Website: *www.law.mcgill.ca/graduate/*

INSTITUTIONAL INFORMATION
Public/private: Public

STUDENTS
Average age of entering class: 35

ADMISSIONS
Selectivity Rating 60*
applications received: 248
% applicants accepted: 49
% acceptees attending: 25
Average undergrad GPA: 3.00
Application fee: $80
Regular application: Rolling, up to 2/1
Regular notification: Rolling
Transfer students accepted: No
Evening division offered: No
Part-time accepted: No
CAS accepted: No

INTERNATIONAL STUDENTS
TOEFL required of international students?: Required

FINANCIAL FACTS
Annual tuition (in-state/out-of-state): $9,876/$19,698
Books and supplies: $800
Fees (in-state/out-of-state): $3,211/$11,919
Room and board: $9,600

QUEEN'S UNIVERSITY
Faculty of Law

Macdonald Hall, Rm 200, 128 Union St., Queen's University Kingston, ON K7L 3N6
Admissions Phone: 613-533-2220 • **Admissions Fax:** 613-533-6611
Admissions E-Mail: jd@queensu.ca • **Website:** law.queensu.ca

INSTITUTIONAL INFORMATION
Public/private: Public
Student/faculty ratio: 16:1
% faculty part-time: 62
% faculty female: 38
% faculty minority:
Total faculty: 85

STUDENTS
Enrollment of law school: 470
% male/female: 50/50
% part-time: 2
Average age of entering class: 23

ACADEMICS
Academic Specialties: Civil Procedure, Commercial, Constitutional, Corporation Securities, Criminal, Environmental, Government Services, Human Rights, International, Labor, Legal History, Legal Philosophy, Property, Taxation, Intellectual Property

Advanced Degrees Offered: The Master of Laws (LLM) Program, administered jointly by the Faculty of Law and the School of Graduate Studies and Research, is designed to enable students of high academic merit to pursue advanced study independent research and coursework. Faculty and library resources enable the Faculty of Law to provide intensive supervision for about twelve full-time resident graduate students each year. Students enrolled in the LLM program are required to be in full-time residence in Kingston for two academic terms, normally from September to August, and are expected to complete all requirements for the degree during that period. However, the School of Graduate Studies allows up to five years for the completion of the thesis. For information about the PhD program, please see 'http://law.queensu.ca/graduateStudies/phdProgram.html. Application for admission to the PhD and LLM programs must be made online at http://www.queensu.ca/sgsr/. The e-mail address is lawgrad@queensu.ca.

Combined Degrees Offered: (1) JD/MA (Economics), 3 years. Queen's University's Faculty of Law and Department of Economics have partnered to offer a combined program that allows students to obtain a JD/MA in three years. The program provides highly focused interdisciplinary training for students interested in the many areas in which law and economic analysis intersect, such as international trade law and policy, corporate law and policy, competition law and policy, environmental and resource management, and tax law and policy. JD/MA students will receive excellent training and gain a strong comparative advantage to pursue careers in specialized legal work that requires knowledge of economic theory and social science methods, high-level policy work, and academia. Separate simultaneous applications to both the Faculty of Law (through OLSAS by November 1) and Graduate Studies (by January 15) are required. Applicants should indicate that they wish to be considered for the combined program in their MA application. Late applications may still be considered, but early applications are encouraged. See http://law.queensu.ca/prospective Students/combined/JDMAEcon.html. (2) JD/MBA, 4 years, 3.5-year early completion options. This combined program capitalizes on the internationally acclaimed, intensive 12-month MBA offered by Queen's School of Business and the rich program in business law offered by Queen's Faculty of Law. Students admitted to the combined program have the on-campus option and an option of completing the International Business Law Module at the Bader International Study Centre at Herstmonceux Castle in Sussex, England, and using a limited number of credits earned in the MBA by cross-crediting to complete the degree in 3.5 years. For further information about the program, visit http://business.queensu.ca/mba_programs/mba/JD_MBA.php. Application to the combined program will require separate, concurrent applications to OLSAS by November 1 for admission to the JD program in the following academic year. Application must also be made to the School of Business. (3) JD/MPA, 3.5 years, 3-year early completion option. The JD/MPA merges graduate studies in policy analysis with the substantive knowledge needed for successful policy interpretation and implementation. The School of Policy Studies has a strong reputation for policy development in respect to health policy, defense management studies, global governance, social policy, and public policy in the voluntary sector of nonprofit, community-based, nongovernmental organizations. Students register as graduate students in the first year, taking prescribed law electives in that year. The combined degree program can be completed in 3.5 years, but there is an option to complete both degrees in 3 years if a BISC global law program is completed in the spring term of the graduate registration year. See http://www.queensu.ca/calendars/law/Combined_Degree_Programs__M_I_R__J_D__and_M_P_A__J_D_.html. See also http://law.queensu.ca/international/globalLawProgramsAtTheBISC.html. Students in the combined program complete the articling requirement of the lawyer licensing process after graduation. Separate concurrent applications must be made to the JD program through OLSAS and the School of Policy Studies. The candidate must be accepted by both schools before being considered for the combined program. Further information about application to the MPA program is available at http://www.queensu.ca/sps/future_students/MPA/mpa_jd.php. Enquiries should be directed to the School of Policy Studies by e-mail at MPA.admissions@queensu.ca or by telephone at (613)533-6000 ext. 75144. (4) JD/MIR, 3.5 years, 3-year early completion option. The JD/MIR provides a foundation in human resources/industrial relations policy and practice to develop specialists in labor and employment law. Students have an early completion option to complete both degrees in 3 years if a global International Public Law program is completed at the BISC. See http://law.queensu.ca/international/globalLawProgramsAtTheBISC.html in the spring term of the first year. Students in the combined program article after graduation. Separate applications must be made to both OLSAS and the School of Graduate Studies, and the candidate must be accepted into both programs. Further information about application to the MIR Program is available at http://www.queensu.ca/sps/future_students/. Enquiries should be directed to the MIR Program Coordinator by e-mail at deej@queensu.ca or by telephone at (613)533-6000 ext. 77322. (5) Civil Law–Common Law Program, 1 year. Queen's Faculty of Law has partnered with the University of Sherbrooke of Quebec to permit civil law graduates to complete a further year of studies to earn the Common Law JD at Queen's. If there is sufficient space, civil law graduates from other Quebec law schools will be considered for admission. See http://www.queensu.ca/calendars/law/Civil_Law_Common_Law_Joint_Degree_Program.html.

Clinical program required: No
Legal writing course requirement: Yes
Legal methods course requirement: Yes
Legal research course requirement: Yes
Moot court requirement: Yes
Public interest law requirement: Yes

ADMISSIONS
Selectivity Rating 88
 # applications received: 2,632
% applicants accepted: 21
% acceptees attending: 30
Average LSAT: 162
LSAT Range: 157–177

Average undergrad GPA: 3.80
Application fee: $185
Regular notification: Rolling
Transfer students accepted: Yes
Evening division offered: No
Part-time accepted: Yes
CAS accepted: No

INTERNATIONAL STUDENTS
TOEFL required of international students?: Required

FINANCIAL FACTS
Annual tuition (in-state/out-of-state): $13,170/$24,895
Books and supplies: $2,580
Fees: $978
Room and board: $11,484
Financial aid application deadline: 10/31
% first-year students receiving some sort of aid: 68
% receiving some sort of aid: 83
% of aid that is merit based: 30
% receiving scholarships: 25
Average grant: $2,045
Average loan: $9,400
Average total aid package: $11,835

EMPLOYMENT INFORMATION
Rate of placement (nine months out): 98
Average starting salary: $60,000
State for bar exam: NY, MA
Pass rate for first-time bar: 100
Prominent Alumni: David R. Allgood (Artsci '70), Law '74, Executive Vice President & General Counsel, Royal Bank of Canada; Hon. Annemarie Bonkalo (Artsci '71), Law '76, Chief Justice, Ontario Court of Justice; Hon. Thomas A. Cromwell (Mus '73), Law '76, Justice, Supreme Court of Canada; Right Hon. David Johnston Law '66, LLD '91, Governor General of Canada; Hon. David Stratas, Law '84, Justice, Federal Court of Appeal
Grads Employed by Field (%)
Government: (10)
Judicial clerkship: (7)
Private practice: (83)

UNIVERSITE DE MONTREAL
Faculte de Droit

P.O. Box 6128, Stn. Centre-Ville, Monteal, Quebec Canada,
Montreal, Qc H3C 3J7
Admissions Phone: *514-343-6125* • **Admissions Fax:** *514-343-2030*
Admissions E-Mail: *monique.bourbonnais@umontreal.ca*
Website: *www.droit.umontreal.ca*

INSTITUTIONAL INFORMATION
Public/private: Public
Student/faculty ratio: 16:1
% faculty female: 28
% faculty minority: 2
Total faculty: 60

STUDENTS
Enrollment of law school: 68
% male/female: 99/1
% international: 7

ACADEMICS
Academic Specialties: Civil Procedure, Commercial, Constitutional, Corporation Securities, Criminal, Environmental, Government Services, Human Rights, International, Labor, Legal History, Legal Philosophy, Property, Taxation, Intellectual Property
Advanced Degrees Offered: LLD, 3 years; General LLM, 1–2 years; Specialized LLM or Graduate Studies Degree (DESS), 1 year, in Notarial Law, Tax Law, Business Law, Information Technologies, International and Transational Law, North American Common Law and ecommerce
Clinical program required: No
Legal writing course requirement: Yes
Legal methods course requirement: No
Legal research course requirement: No
Moot court requirement: No
Public interest law requirement: No

ADMISSIONS
Selectivity Rating 60*
applications received: 2,072
% applicants accepted: 21
% acceptees attending: 78
Average undergrad GPA: 3.00
Application fee: $40
Regular notification: Rolling
Transfer students accepted: Yes
Evening division offered: No
Part-time accepted: No
CAS accepted: No

FINANCIAL FACTS
Annual tuition (in-state/out-of-state): $1,400/$4,200
Books and supplies: $600
Average loan: $3,456

EMPLOYMENT INFORMATION
State for bar exam: QC, NY
Pass rate for first-time bar: 79
Prominent Alumni: Hon Michel Bastarache, Justice of the Supreme Court of Canada; Hon. Marie Deschamps, Justice of the Supreme Court of Canada; Louise Arbour, UN High Commissioner for Refugees, ex-JSCC; Philippe Kirsch, President, International Criminal Court, Morris Rosenberg, Deputy Minister, Health Canada

UNIVERSITY OF ALBERTA
Faculty of Law

University of Alberta, Law Centre Edmonton, AB T6G 2H5
Admissions Phone: (780) 492-3115 • **Admissions Fax:** (780) 492-4924
Admissions E-Mail: sgarskey@law.ualberta.ca
Website: www.law.ualberta.ca/

INSTITUTIONAL INFORMATION
Public/private: Public
% faculty part-time: 62
% faculty female: 33
Total faculty: 42

STUDENTS
Enrollment of law school: 518
% male/female: 47/53
% from out-of-state: 27
% minority: 3
# of countries represented: 2
Average age of entering class: 25

ACADEMICS
Academic Specialties: Civil Procedure, Commercial, Constitutional, Corporation Securities, Criminal, Environmental, Government Services, Human Rights, International, Labor, Legal History, Legal Philosophy, Property, Taxation, Intellectual Property
Advanced Degrees Offered: LLM can be completed in one year, some will take longer; PhD program newly approved in 2007
Combined Degrees Offered: LLB/MBA program, 4 years
Clinical program required: No
Legal writing course requirement: Yes
Legal methods course requirement: No
Legal research course requirement: Yes
Moot court requirement: Yes
Public interest law requirement: No

ADMISSIONS
Selectivity Rating 89
applications received: 1,232
% applicants accepted: 30
% acceptees attending: 48
Average LSAT: 161
LSAT Range: 149–178
Average undergrad GPA: 3.70
Application fee: $100
Regular notification: Rolling
Transfer students accepted: Yes
Evening division offered: No
Part-time accepted: Yes
CAS accepted: No

INTERNATIONAL STUDENTS
TOEFL required of international students?: Required

FINANCIAL FACTS
Annual tuition: $4,686
Books and supplies: $1,500
Fees: $4,773
Room and board (on/off campus): $6,500/$10,000
Financial aid application deadline: 6/1

% first-year students receiving some sort of aid: 44
% receiving some sort of aid: 42
% of aid that is merit based: 30
% receiving scholarships: 23
Average grant: $5,000
Average total aid package: $3,159

EMPLOYMENT INFORMATION
Prominent Alumni: Hon. Beverley McLachlin, Chief Justice Supreme Court of Canada; Hon. E. Peter Lougheed, Former Premier of the Province of Alberta; Frank MacInnis, CEO/President of EMCOR; David McLean, Chairman of CN Railway, Clarence Campbell, Former National Hockey League Pres/Rhodes Scholar
Grads Employed by Field (%)
Government: (6)
Judicial clerkship: (7)
Private practice: (85)
Public interest: (2)

UNIVERSITY OF BRITISH COLUMBIA
Faculty of Law

1822 East Mall, Vancouver, BC V6T 1Z1
Admissions Phone: 604-822-6303 • **Admissions Fax:** 604-822-9486
Admissions E-Mail: admissions@law.ubc.ca • **Website:** www.law.ubc.ca

INSTITUTIONAL INFORMATION
Public/private: Public
Student/faculty ratio: 14:1
% faculty part-time: 64
% faculty female: 33
% faculty minority: 11
Total faculty: 132

STUDENTS
Enrollment of law school: 582
% male/female: 48/52
% from out-of-state: 29
% part-time: 2
% minority: 5
% international: 1
# of countries represented: 10
Average age of entering class: 25

ACADEMICS
Academic Specialties: Corporation Securities, Criminal, Environmental, Human Rights, International, Legal History, Taxation, Business Law Concentration, Asian Legal Studies, Law and Social Justice Specialization, Environmental and Natural Resource Law Specialization, First Nations Legal Studies, Negotiation and Dispute Resolution, Feminist Legal Studies
Advanced Degrees Offered: JD, 3 years full-time; LLM, 12 months; LLM (Common Law), 1 year; PhD, 2–4 years
Combined Degrees Offered: The combined JD/MBA Program is 4 years in length and is administered jointly by the Faculty of Commerce and the Faculty of Law. Students are required to complete 86 credits in law and 45 credits in the MBA program. The combined JD/MA (MAPPS) permits students to

obtain the degrees of JD and MA in Asia Pacific Policy Studies (MAPPS) through combined enrollment in the Faculty of Law and the Institute of Asian Research. The program is 3 years in length and requires students to take 86 Law credits (excluding IAR 500) and 30 MAPPS credits. The University of British Columbia (UBC) Faculty of Law and the University of Hawai'i (UH) at Manoa William S. Richardson School of Law Joint Legal Education Program allows students who complete the 4 year program to receive a JD degree from UBC and a JD degree from UH. The University of British Columbia (UBC) and the University of Hong Kong (HKU) Joint Legal Education Program allows students who complete the 4 year program to receive a JD degree from UBC and a Postgraduate Certificate in Laws (PCLL program) from HKU.

Clinical program required: No
Legal writing course requirement: Yes
Legal methods course requirement: No
Legal research course requirement: Yes
Moot court requirement: Yes
Public interest law requirement: No

ADMISSIONS
Selectivity Rating 94
 # applications received: 2,074
% applicants accepted: 18
% acceptees attending: 48
Average LSAT: 166
LSAT Range: 156–178
Average undergrad GPA: 3.88
Application fee: $80
Regular application: Rolling, up to 2/1
Regular notification: Rolling
Transfer students accepted: Yes
Evening division offered: No
Part-time accepted: Yes
CAS accepted: No

FINANCIAL FACTS
Annual tuition: $10,135
Books and supplies: $2,293
Fees: $877
Room and board (on/off campus): $9,200/$10,400
% first-year students receiving some sort of aid: 61
% receiving some sort of aid: 64
% of aid that is merit based: 7
% receiving scholarships: 56
Average grant: $2,332
Average loan: $9,016
Average total aid package: $12,127
Average debt: $27,925

EMPLOYMENT INFORMATION
Rate of placement (nine months out): 99
Average starting salary: $40,000
State for bar exam: BC, AB, ON, NY
Pass rate for first-time bar: 99
Employers Who Frequently Hire Grads: British Columbia Law Firms and Government Agencies (including Lower Mainland, Vancouver Island and Interior); Ontario Law Firms and Government Agencies; Alberta Law Firms and Government Agencies; Yukon/Northwest Territories Law Firms; New York Law Firms; Canadian Public Interest Organizations; Canadian Courts (both Federal and Provincial); Corporate Legal Departments; Canadian Crown Corporations
Prominent Alumni: Frank Iacobucci, Former Justice Supreme Court of Canada; Lance Finch, Chief Justice of British Columbia; Kim Campbell, Former Prime Minister of Canada; Don Brenner, Chief Justice of British Columbia Supreme Court, Ujjal Dosanjh, Former Premier of British Columbia & Attorney General

Grads Employed by Field (%)
Academic: (1)
Government: (5)
Judicial clerkship: (9)
Private practice: (83)
Public interest: (2)

UNIVERSITY OF CALGARY
Faculty of Law

Murray Fraser Hall, 2500 University Drive NW, Calgary, AB T2N 1N4
Admissions Phone: 403-220-4155 • Admissions Fax: 403-210-9662
Admissions E-Mail: law@ucalgary.ca • Website: www.law.ucalgary.ca/

INSTITUTIONAL INFORMATION
Public/private: Public
Student/faculty ratio: 12:1
% faculty female: 50
Total faculty: 21

STUDENTS
Enrollment of law school: 304
% male/female: 42/58
% from out-of-state: 39
# of countries represented: 4
Average age of entering class: 25

ACADEMICS
Academic Specialties: Environmental, Natural Resource, Law Legal Skills Program
Advanced Degrees Offered: LLB, 3 years; LLM, 15–18 months
Combined Degrees Offered: LLB/MBA, 4 years Law and Masters of Business Administration; LLB/MEDes Law and Masters of Environmental Design
Clinical program required: No
Legal writing course requirement: Yes
Legal methods course requirement: Yes
Legal research course requirement: Yes
Moot court requirement: Yes

ADMISSIONS
Selectivity Rating 96
 # applications received: 907
% applicants accepted: 11
% acceptees attending: 100
Average LSAT: 158
LSAT Range: 32–98
Average undergrad GPA: 3.50
Application fee: $100
Regular notification: Rolling
Transfer students accepted: Yes
Evening division offered: No
Part-time accepted: Yes
CAS accepted: No

INTERNATIONAL STUDENTS
TOEFL required of international students?: Required

FINANCIAL FACTS
Annual tuition: $12,500
Books and supplies: $1,800
Fees: $581
Room and board (on/off campus): $8,000/$12,000

EMPLOYMENT INFORMATION
Average starting salary: State for bar exam: AB

University of Manitoba
Faculty of Law

424 University Centre, Enrolment Services/Admissions, University of
Manitoba Winnipeg, MB R3T 2N2
Admissions Phone: (204) 474-8825 • **Admissions Fax:** (204) 474-7554
Admissions E-Mail: lawadmissions@umanitoba.ca
Website: www.umanitoba.ca/law

INSTITUTIONAL INFORMATION
Public/private: Public
Student/faculty ratio: 15:1
% faculty part-time: 43
% faculty female: 30
% faculty minority:
Total faculty: 23

STUDENTS
Enrollment of law school: 315
% male/female: 49/51
% from out-of-state: 50
% part-time: 5
% minority: 10
% international: 1
Average age of entering class: 24

ACADEMICS
Academic Specialties: Civil Procedure, Commercial, Constitutional,
Corporation Securities, Criminal, Environmental, Government Services,
Human Rights, International, Labor, Legal History, Legal Philosophy, Property,
Taxation, Intellectual Property
Advanced Degrees Offered: LLM, 1 year
Clinical program required: No
Legal writing course requirement: Yes
Legal methods course requirement: Yes
Legal research course requirement: Yes
Moot court requirement: Yes
Public interest law requirement: No

ADMISSIONS
Selectivity Rating 84
applications received: 951
% applicants accepted: 32
% acceptees attending: 35
Average LSAT: 162
LSAT Range: 153–164
Average undergrad GPA: 3.50
Application fee: $125

Regular notification: Rolling
Transfer students accepted: Yes
Evening division offered: No
Part-time accepted: Yes
CAS accepted: No

INTERNATIONAL STUDENTS
TOEFL required of international students?: Required

FINANCIAL FACTS
Annual tuition: $5,300
Books and supplies: $3,000
Fees: $4,200
Room and board (on/off campus): $5,520/$11,420
Financial aid application deadline: 10/1
Average loan: $11,900
Average debt: $20,000

EMPLOYMENT INFORMATION
Rate of placement (nine months out): 97
Average starting salary: $45,000

University of New Brunswick
Faculty of Law

Law Admissions Office, Faculty of Law, P.O. Box 44271, University of New
Brunswick Fredericton, NB E3B 6C2
Admissions Phone: (506) 453-4693 • **Admissions Fax:** (506) 458-7722
Admissions E-Mail: lawadmit@unb.ca • **Website:** law.unb.ca

INSTITUTIONAL INFORMATION
Public/private: Public
Student/faculty ratio: 13:1
% faculty part-time: 9
% faculty female: 33
% faculty minority:
Total faculty: 20

STUDENTS
Average age of entering class: 26

ACADEMICS
Academic Specialties: Civil Procedure, Commercial, Constitutional, Criminal,
Environmental, Human Rights, International, Labor, Legal History, Legal
Philosophy, Taxation, Intellectual Property
Advanced Degrees Offered: LLB (Bachelor of Law), 3 year degree program
Combined Degrees Offered: LLB/MBA, 4 year degree program
Clinical program required: No
Legal writing course requirement: Yes
Legal methods course requirement: Yes
Legal research course requirement: No
Moot court requirement: Yes
Public interest law requirement: No

ADMISSIONS

Selectivity Rating 60*
applications received: 992
% applicants accepted: 22
% acceptees attending: 39
Average LSAT: 159
LSAT Range: 151–173
Average undergrad GPA: 3.80
Application fee: $50
Regular application: Rolling, up to 3/1
Regular notification: Rolling
Transfer students accepted: Yes
Evening division offered: No
Part-time accepted: No
CAS accepted: No

INTERNATIONAL STUDENTS

TOEFL required of international students?: Recommended

FINANCIAL FACTS

Annual tuition: $9,032
Books and supplies: $1,500
Fees: $663
Room and board: $6,000
Financial aid application deadline: 11/15
% first-year students receiving some sort of aid: 51
% of aid that is merit based: 82
% receiving scholarships: 44
Average total aid package: $1,000

EMPLOYMENT INFORMATION

Rate of placement (nine months out): 80
State for bar exam: NB, NS, NL, PE, ON
Grads Employed by Field (%)
Government: (6)
Private practice: (72)

UNIVERSITY OF OTTAWA
Faculty of Law

P.O. Box 450, Stn. A, 57 Louis Pasteur St. Ottawa, ON K1N 6N5
Admissions Phone: 613-562-5800 • **Admissions Fax:** 613-562-5124
Admissions E-Mail: comlaw@uottawa.ca
Website: www.commonlaw.uottawa.ca

INSTITUTIONAL INFORMATION

Public/private: Public
Student/faculty ratio: 17:1
% faculty part-time: 100
% faculty female: 51
% faculty minority: 15
Total faculty: 53

STUDENTS

Enrollment of law school: 219
% male/female: 42/58
% from out-of-state:
% part-time: 6
Average age of entering class: 26

ACADEMICS

Academic Specialties: Environmental, Human Rights, International, Intellectual Property
Combined Degrees Offered: LLB/JD, 4 years; LLB/MBA, 4 years; LLB/MA, 4 years; LLB/LLL, 4 years
Clinical program required: No
Moot court requirement: Yes
Public interest law requirement: Yes

ADMISSIONS

Selectivity Rating 87
applications received: 3,391
% applicants accepted: 18
% acceptees attending: 35
Average undergrad GPA: 3.53
Application fee: $75
Regular notification: Rolling
Transfer students accepted: Yes
Evening division offered: No
CAS accepted: No

FINANCIAL FACTS

Annual tuition: $9,180
Books and supplies: $1,100
Fees: $439
Room and board: $10,000
Financial aid application deadline: 3/15
% first-year students receiving some sort of aid: 65
% receiving some sort of aid: 65
% of aid that is merit based: 67
% receiving scholarships: 16
Average grant: $1,815
Average loan: $1,159
Average total aid package: $10,440

EMPLOYMENT INFORMATION

Rate of placement (nine months out): 60
State for bar exam: NY, MA
Pass rate for first-time bar: 95
Grads Employed by Field (%)
Private practice: (57)
Public interest: (1)

UNIVERSITY OF SASKATCHEWAN
College of Law

College of Law University of Saskatchewan, 15 Campus Drive Saskatoon, SK S7N 5A6
Admissions Phone: 306-966-5045 • **Admissions Fax:** 306-966-5900
Admissions E-Mail: law_admissions@usask.ca • **Website:** www.usask.ca/law/

INSTITUTIONAL INFORMATION

Public/private: Public
% faculty part-time: 10
% faculty female: 12
Total faculty: 34

STUDENTS

Average age of entering class: 25

ACADEMICS

Legal writing course requirement: Yes
Legal methods course requirement: No
Legal research course requirement: Yes

ADMISSIONS

Selectivity Rating 89
applications received: 963
% applicants accepted: 30
% acceptees attending: 43
Average LSAT: 158
LSAT Range: 148–168
Average undergrad GPA: 3.60
Application fee: $100
Regular application: Rolling, up to 2/1
Regular notification: Rolling
Transfer students accepted: Yes
Evening division offered: No
Part-time accepted: Yes
CAS accepted: No

FINANCIAL FACTS

Annual tuition: $7,353
Books and supplies: $2,200
Fees: $689

UNIVERSITY OF TORONTO

Faculty of Law

78 Queens Park, Toronto, ON M5S 2C5
Admissions Phone: *416-978-3716 •* **Admissions Fax:** *416-978-0790*
Admissions E-Mail: *law.admissions@utoronto.ca*
Website: *www.law.utoronto.ca*

INSTITUTIONAL INFORMATION

Public/private: Public
Student/faculty ratio: 10:1
Total faculty: 64

STUDENTS

Enrollment of law school: 621
% male/female: 50/50
% minority: 29
Average age of entering class: 24

ACADEMICS

Advanced Degrees Offered: Master of Laws (LLM), 1 year; Doctor of Juridical
Science (SJD), 1 year plus thesis; Master of Studies in Law (MSL), 1 year;
Global Professional LLM (GPLLM), 1 year
Combined Degrees Offered: JD/MBA, 4 years; JD/MSW, 4 years; JD/MA
(Criminology), 3 years; JD/MA (Economics), 3 years; JD/MA (English),
3 years; JD/Master of Global Affairs, 4 years; JD/MA (European, Russian
and Eurasian Studies), 4 years; JD/MISt (Master of Information Studies),
4 years; JD/Certificate in Environmental Studies, 3 years; JD/PhD (Econom-
ics), 4 years plus dissertation; JD/PhD (Philosophy), 4 years plus dissertation;
JD/PhD (Political Science), 4 years plus dissertation

Clinical program required: No
Legal writing course requirement: Yes
Legal methods course requirement: Yes
Legal research course requirement: Yes
Moot court requirement: Yes
Public interest law requirement: No

ADMISSIONS

Selectivity Rating 99
applications received: 2,229
% applicants accepted: 13
% acceptees attending: 68
LSAT Range: 154–180
Average undergrad GPA: 3.90
Application fee: $90
Regular application: Rolling, up to 11/1
Regular notification: Rolling
Transfer students accepted: Yes
Evening division offered: No
Part-time accepted: Yes
CAS accepted: No

FINANCIAL FACTS

Annual tuition (in-state/out-of-state): $23,508/$32,635
Books and supplies: $1,100
Fees: $1,116
Room and board (on/off campus): $14,855/$9,800
Financial aid application deadline: 7/15
% first-year students receiving some sort of aid: 44
% receiving some sort of aid: 43
% of aid that is merit based: 4
% receiving scholarships: 42

EMPLOYMENT INFORMATION

State for bar exam: NY, MA, CA
Employers Who Frequently Hire Grads: All major Toronto law firms, all pro-
vincial and federal government departments, a few New York and Boston law
firms, large and mid-size Vancouver, Halifax and Calgary law firms
Prominent Alumni: Justice Frank Iacobucci, Former Justice Supreme Court of
Canada; Justice Rosalie Abella, Supreme Court of Canada; Bob Rae & David
Peterson, Former Premiers of Ontario; The Hon. Paul Martin, Former Prime
Minister of Canada, Justice Ian Binnie, Supreme Court of Canada
Grads Employed by Field (%)
Judicial clerkship: (7)
Private practice: (74)
Public interest: (3)

UNIVERSITY OF VICTORIA

Faculty of Law

P.O. Box 2400, STN CSC, Victoria, BC V8W 3H7
Admissions Phone: 250-721-8151 • Admissions Fax: 250-721-6390
Admissions E-Mail: lawadmss@uvic.ca • Website: www.law.uvic.ca

INSTITUTIONAL INFORMATION
Public/private: Public
Student/faculty ratio: 7:1
% faculty part-time: 43
% faculty female: 30
% faculty minority: 9
Total faculty: 60

STUDENTS
Enrollment of law school: 360
% male/female: 40/60
% part-time: 2
% minority: 25
# of countries represented: 6
Average age of entering class: 26

ACADEMICS
Academic Specialties: Environmental, International, Intellectual Property, Alternative Dispute Resolution; Indigenous Law; International Law
Advanced Degrees Offered: LLM, 1 year; and PhD, 3 years
Combined Degrees Offered: Bachelor of Laws/Master's of Public Administration (LLB/MPA), 4 years; Bachelor of Laws/Master's of Business Administration (LLB/MBA), 4 years; Bachelor of Common Law/Bachelor of Civil Law (LLB/BCL), 4.5 years
Clinical program required: No
Legal writing course requirement: Yes
Legal methods course requirement: Yes
Legal research course requirement: Yes
Moot court requirement: Yes
Public interest law requirement: No

ADMISSIONS
Selectivity Rating 89
applications received: 1,018
% applicants accepted: 30
% acceptees attending: 35
Average LSAT: 162
LSAT Range: 157–172
Average undergrad GPA: 3.84
Application fee: $75
Regular application: Rolling, up to 2/1
Regular notification: Rolling
Transfer students accepted: Yes
Evening division offered: No
Part-time accepted: Yes
CAS accepted: No

INTERNATIONAL STUDENTS
TOEFL required of international students?: Required

FINANCIAL FACTS
Annual tuition (in-state/out-of-state): $8,178/$21,748
Books and supplies: $2,000
Fees: $1,009
Room and board (on/off campus): $7,000/$10,000
Financial aid application deadline: 6/1
% of aid that is merit based: 35
Average loan: $12,000
Average debt: $30,000

EMPLOYMENT INFORMATION
Rate of placement (nine months out): 95
Employers Who Frequently Hire Grads: Local, provincial and national law firms; federal and provincial government; judicial clerkships; and nonprofit organizations
Prominent Alumni: Laura Lynch (1988), International Correspondent, Canadian Broadcasting Corporation; Thomas Crabtree (1983), Chief Judge, BC Provincial Court; Gary Lunn (1995), Federal Minister of State for Sport; Carla Qualtrough (1997), President, Canadian Paralymipic Committee, Allan Seckel (1983), Deputy Minister to the Premier of British Columbia and Head of the BC Public Service
Grads Employed by Field (%)
Academic: (3)
Government: (10)
Judicial clerkship: (11)
Private practice: (55)
Public interest: (2)

THE UNIVERSITY OF WESTERN ONTARIO

Faculty of Law

Administrative Wing, Faculty of Law London, ON N5X 3T5
Admissions Phone: (519) 661-3347 • Admissions Fax: (519) 661-2063
Admissions E-Mail: lawapp@uwo.ca • Website: www.law.uwo.ca

INSTITUTIONAL INFORMATION
Public/private: Public
Student/faculty ratio: 7:1
% faculty part-time: 33
% faculty female: 27
Total faculty: 33

STUDENTS
Enrollment of law school: 161
% male/female: 52/48
% from out-of-state: 15
% part-time: 2
# of countries represented: 5
Average age of entering class: 25

ACADEMICS

Academic Specialties: Criminal, Taxation, Intellectual Property, Business Law
Advanced Degrees Offered: LLB, 3 years; LLM, 1 year–research based
Combined Degrees Offered: HBA/LLB BESc/LLB (4 degree programs in Engineering) BSc (Computer Science)/LLB Honors BA (History)/LLB BA (Kin)/LLB Honors BA (MIT)/LLB Honors BA (Political Science)/LLB LLB/MBA PhD Philosophy
Clinical program required: No
Legal writing course requirement: Yes
Legal methods course requirement: Yes
Legal research course requirement: Yes
Moot court requirement: Yes
Public interest law requirement: No

ADMISSIONS

Selectivity Rating 89
 # applications received: 2,374
% applicants accepted: 21
% acceptees attending: 32
Average LSAT: 160
LSAT Range: 155–173
Average undergrad GPA: 3.72
Application fee: $75
Regular application: Rolling, up to 11/1
Regular notification: Rolling
Transfer students accepted: Yes
Evening division offered: No
Part-time accepted: Yes
CAS accepted: No

INTERNATIONAL STUDENTS

TOEFL required of international students?: Required

FINANCIAL FACTS

Annual tuition: $11,372
Books and supplies: $1,400
Fees: $890
Room and board: $8,000
Financial aid application deadline: 10/7
% first-year students receiving some sort of aid: 60
% receiving some sort of aid: 50
% of aid that is merit based: 80
% receiving scholarships: 50
Average grant: $5,000
Average total aid package: $3,000

EMPLOYMENT INFORMATION

Rate of placement (nine months out): 99
Average starting salary: $50,000
State for bar exam: NY
Pass rate for first-time bar: 100
Employers Who Frequently Hire Grads: Toronto Canada, largest employers
Grads Employed by Field (%)
Business/industry: (2)
Government: (3)
Judicial clerkship: (3)
Private practice: (91)

UNIVERSITY OF WINDSOR
Faculty of Law

Faculty of Law, 401 Sunset Avenue, Windsor, ON N9B 3P4
Admissions Phone: *519-253-3000* • ***Admissions Fax:*** *519-973-7064*
Admissions E-Mail: *lawadmit@uwindsor.ca* • ***Website:*** *www.uwindsor.ca/law*

INSTITUTIONAL INFORMATION

Public/private: Public
% faculty part-time: 58

STUDENTS

Enrollment of law school: 217
% male/female: 50/51
% from out-of-state: 11
% international: 1
# of countries represented: 2
Average age of entering class: 24

ACADEMICS

Academic Specialties: Civil Procedure, Commercial, Constitutional, Corporation Securities, Criminal, Environmental, Human Rights, International, Labor, Legal History, Legal Philosophy, Property, Taxation, Intellectual Property
Advanced Degrees Offered: None
Combined Degrees Offered: MBA/JD, 3–4 years; Canadian & American Dual JD Program, 3 years; MSW/JD, 3–4 years
Clinical program required: No
Legal writing course requirement: Yes
Legal methods course requirement: Yes
Legal research course requirement: Yes
Moot court requirement: Yes
Public interest law requirement: No

ADMISSIONS

Selectivity Rating 60*
 # applications received: 2,524
% applicants accepted: 20
% acceptees attending: 42
Application fee: $185
Regular application: Rolling, up to 1/11
Regular notification: Rolling
Transfer students accepted: Yes
Evening division offered: No
Part-time accepted: Yes
CAS accepted: No

INTERNATIONAL STUDENTS

TOEFL required of international students?: Recommended

FINANCIAL FACTS

Annual tuition (in-state/out-of-state): $13,410/$22,711
Books and supplies: $2,000
Room and board: $9,225
% of aid that is merit based: 25
Average grant: $3,909
Average loan: $12,900

EMPLOYMENT INFORMATION

State for bar exam: ON, AB, BC, NS, NF
Pass rate for first-time bar: 99
Employers Who Frequently Hire Grads: Law Firms
Grads Employed by Field (%)
Government: (8)
Judicial clerkship: (4)
Private practice: (76)
Public interest: (2)

YORK UNIVERSITY
Osgoode Hall Law School

4700 Keele Street, Toronto, ON M3J 1P3
Admissions Phone: *416-736-5712 •* **Admissions Fax:** *416-736-5618*
Admissions E-Mail: *admissions@osgoode.yorku.ca*
Website: *www.osgoode.yorku.ca*

INSTITUTIONAL INFORMATION

Public/private: Public
Student/faculty ratio: 6:1
% faculty part-time: 66
% faculty female: 72
Total faculty: 159

STUDENTS

Enrollment of law school: 885

ACADEMICS

Academic Specialties: International, Taxation, Litigation
Advanced Degrees Offered: LLM; D JUR
Combined Degrees Offered: JD/LLM (NYU), 3.5 years; JD/MBA, 4 years; JD/MES, 4 years
Clinical program required: Yes
Legal writing course requirement: Yes
Legal methods course requirement: No
Legal research course requirement: Yes
Moot court requirement: Yes
Public interest law requirement: Yes

ADMISSIONS

Selectivity Rating 90
applications received: 3,086
% applicants accepted: 19
% acceptees attending: 53
Application fee: $75
Regular notification: Rolling
Transfer students accepted: Yes
Evening division offered: No
Part-time accepted: No
CAS accepted: No

INTERNATIONAL STUDENTS

TOEFL required of international students?: Required

FINANCIAL FACTS

Annual tuition: $17,631
Books and supplies: $1,100
Fees: $850
Room and board: $10,000
Financial aid application deadline: 9/7

EMPLOYMENT INFORMATION

State for bar exam: ON
Pass rate for first-time bar: 98
Employers Who Frequently Hire Grads: Aird & Berlis LLP; Baker & McKenzie; Bennet Jones LLP; Bereskin & Parr; Blake Cassels & Graydon LLP; Borden Ladner Gervais LLP; Cassels Brock & Blackwell LLP; Davies, Ward, Phillips & Vineberg LLP; Davis & Company; Department of Justice; Ontario Regional Office; Dimock Stratton Clarizio LLP; Fasken Martineau DuMoulin LLP; Fogler Rubinoff LLP; Fraser Milner Casgrain LLP; Gilbert's LLP; Goodman and Carr LLP; Goodmans LLP; Gowling Lafleur Henderson LLP; Heenan Blaikie LLP; Hicks Morley Hamilton Stewart Storie LLP; Hodgson Tough Shields Desbrisay O'Donnell LLP; Keyser Mason Ball LLP; Lang Michener Lenczner Slaght Royce Smith; Griffin Lerners LLP; Matthews Dinsdale & Clark LLP; McCarthy LLP; McMillan Binch LLP; Miller Thomson LLP; Ogilvy Renault Osler Hoskin & Harcourt LLP; Paliare Roland Rosenberg Rothstein LLP; Ridout Maybee LLP; Shearman & Sterling LLP; Toronto Skadden; Arps, Slate, Meagher & Flom LLP; Smart & Biggar Stikeman Elliott LLP; Torkin Manes Cohen & Arbus LLP; Torys LLP; Various Provincial Government Ministries; Blake, Cassels & Graydon; Borden Ladner Gervais Davis & Company; Farris, Vaughan, Wills & Murphy; Fasken Martineau DuMoulin Lawson Lundell Sangra Moller Smart & Biggar; Stikeman Elliott; Cadwalader, Wichersham & Taft; Clifford Chance Davies Ward Phillips & Vineberg; Davis Polk & Wardwell; Milbank, Tweed, Hadley & McCloy; Paul, Weiss, Rifkind, Wharton & Garrison; Shearman & Sterling LLP; New York Sidley Austin Skadden; Arps, Slate, Meagher & Flom; Sullivan & Cromwell; Weil, Gotshal & Manges; White & Case

SCHOOL SAYS

In this section, you'll find schools with extended listings describing admissions, curriculum, internships, and much more. This is your chance to get in-depth information on programs that interest you. The Princeton Review charges each school a small fee to be listed, and the editorial responsibility is solely that of the university.

CHAPMAN UNIVERSITY
School of Law

AT A GLANCE

Chapman University School of Law offers a collaborative, rigorous, and personalized legal education. Graduates develop the skills to provide passionate, ethical and accurate service to their clients and to society. With one of the best faculty/student ratios among American law schools, Chapman offers smaller class sizes and greater access to faculty both in and out of the classroom. Chapman provides practical training through a variety of clinical programs and externships, as well opportunities for students to participate on legal journals and award-winning competition teams. Chapman has a dedicated staff to help its graduating students obtain positions of responsibility in the legal workforce. Chapman is ABA accredited and a member of the Association of American Law Schools.

Chapman University School of Law offers a collaborative, rigorous, and personalized legal education. Graduates develop the skills to provide passionate, ethical and accurate service to their clients and to society.

CAMPUS AND LOCATION

The School of Law is located on the beautiful 42-acre Chapman University campus, in the heart of Historic Old Towne in Orange, California. The site was once part of the fabled Rancho Santiago de Santa Ana, a huge tract granted by the Spanish crown in 1810. The Plaza in downtown Orange has been featured in a number of movie productions because of its quaint array of restaurants and shops. The campus setting presents many opportunities to develop interdisciplinary courses and degree programs with other schools of the university, including popular joint programs with the business and film schools. Chapman University was founded in 1861 and the law school was established in 1995. The university is located 35 miles southeast of Los Angeles and 90 miles north of San Diego and Mexico.

For visitor information, see http://www.chapman.edu/law/about/community.asp.

DEGREES OFFERED

Chapman offers a traditional Juris Doctor and joint JD/MBA and JD/MFA in Film & Television Producing. LLM programs are offered in Business and Economics, Entertainment and Media Law, International & Comparative Law, Taxation and Trial Advocacy.

PROGRAMS AND CURRICULUM

The School of Law requires 88 academic credits for graduation. First-year courses are required and cover traditional subjects: Contracts, Torts, Civil Procedure, Property, Criminal Law, and Legal Research and Writing. Upper-level courses are also required in the following areas: Constitutional Law, Corporations, Evidence, Federal Income Taxation and Professional Responsibility. Law students may choose an emphasis in Advocacy and Dispute Resolution, Entertainment Law, Environmental, Land Use, and Real Estate (ENLURE), International Law or Tax Law.

FACILITIES

The four-story Kennedy Hall law school building offers an efficient and pleasant learning environment for law students. Classrooms and seminar rooms are equipped with state-of-the-art technology for enhanced teaching and learning, and are capable of accommodating future changes in electronic, visual and on-site learning. The library occupies one wing of the building. Two courtrooms, one designed for trials and the other for appellate hearings, provide fully equipped facilities for trial advocacy exercises, mock trial and moot court competitions, and formal hearings by visiting courts. Student lounges and facilities for student organizations and publications ensure that the law school experience at Chapman will be both productive and pleasant.

EXPENSES AND FINANCIAL AID

Chapman offers a generous scholarship program, awarding over 6.7 million dollars for 2010–2011. Most scholarships are merit-based (LSAT and GPA), with some need-based funds available as well. In addition, Chapman participates in all Federal Loan programs so that most students can meet all expenses while completing their JD or LLM degree. Tuition and fees for 2011–2012 are $44,303 for full time JD. There is no additional charge for out-of-state students. The total cost of living expense budget for an off campus student for 2011–2012 is $26,656.

FACULTY

Chapman law professors include four former U.S. Supreme Court Clerks, a former member of the United States Congress, a Nobel laureate and a host of distinguished scholars as well as distinguished visiting professors from other prestigious law schools. Students have easy access to the faculty and frequent opportunities to engage them in both formal and informal settings. Faculty papers have been published in prestigious law journals at Harvard, Stanford, U.C. Berkeley, and numerous other highly regarded law schools.

STUDENTS

Chapman provides a comfortable environment for the rigorous study of law. Students are collegial and collaborative and enjoy significant opportunities to work closely with faculty, administrators and staff. Chapman has more than 40 student law organizations, which provide valuable networking opportunities and guest speakers in a variety of legal specializations. Each spring, many students attend the Barrister's Ball, a popular dinner and dance party put on by the Student Bar Association. The School of Law is ranked in the top 10 of the nation's best law schools for "Best Classroom Experience" in The Princeton Review's *The Best 172 Law Schools* (2011).

ADMISSIONS

The School of Law at Chapman University has a rolling admissions policy. The admissions process is highly competitive, with over 2,800 applications for approximately 160–190 students in the entering class. Applicants are required to submit a formal application, personal statement, resume, two letters of recommendation, a non-refundable application fee of $75.00, and the CAS report from the Law School Admission Council (LSAC). The CAS report generally includes your LSAT score(s), official transcript(s), and letters of recommendation. Applicants should be advised that the law school averages LSAT scores and does not accept LSAT scores before February 2007 for the 2012 entering class. The application deadline is April 15 of each year.

SPECIAL PROGRAMS

Chapman University School of Law has a thriving clinical program. Clinics provide pro bono services to individuals in a diverse range of legal subject areas, including tax, entertainment, military justice, elder law, immigration, domestic violence, constitutional law and mediation. Each clinical program is directed by a faculty member with significant clinical experience. Students participate in classroom and hands-on field work that may include client contact, research projects, document preparation, brief writing, and court appearances. Chapman also offers a Supplemental Bar Preparation Program designed to provide intensive bar exam practice in addition to existing bar-tested curriculum. The program allows students to maximize their preparation for all three tested elements of the bar examination during their second and third years of law study.

CAREER SERVICES AND PLACEMENT

The Career Services Office at the School of Law offers comprehensive career services to aid students and alumni in selecting their career paths and achieve their employment goals. The attorney counselors help to match students' education, skill sets, and interests with both traditional and non-traditional employment opportunities. In keeping with Chapman's mission of personalized education, the CSO staff meet personally and often with individual students and alumni to review resumes and cover letters, to aid in self-assessment and goal orientation, to discuss specific opportunities unique to the student's needs, to provide training and support, to give encouragement in exploring career options, and to assist in building professional networks.

FAULKER UNIVERSITY
School of Law

AT A GLANCE

Faulkner University's Thomas Goode Jones School of Law is committed to the education of outstanding lawyers. In keeping with its distinctive Christian mission, the school embraces academic excellence and emphasizes a strong commitment to integrity within a caring Christian environment that sustains and nurtures faith. Students are encouraged to dedicate their lives to the service of others.

CAMPUS AND LOCATION

The School of Law is located in the capital of Alabama. Montgomery is known as the birthplace of the Confederacy and the civil rights movement. In 2011, Faulkner Law opened the newly built Allen Law Center. The Allen Law Center features over 17,000 additional square feet of library space, study space, classroom space, clinical space, and a state of the art additional Moot Courtroom.

The campus is located just a few miles from the Alabama State Capitol Building; the Alabama Judicial Building which houses the Alabama Supreme Court, the State Law Library, the Court of Civil Appeals and the Court of Criminal Appeals; and the Frank M. Johnson United States Courthouse Complex.

DEGREES OFFERED

The School of Law offers the Juris Doctor degree through a full-time program of study.

ACADEMIC PROGRAMS GENERAL

The School of Law's curriculum is comprised of fundamental courses such as Civil Procedure, Constitutional Law, Contracts Law, Criminal Law, Evidence, Professional Responsibility, Property Law, and Torts Law. In addition to these courses, all students take Foundations of Law in their first semester. This course is designed to provide students with the analytical framework to understand and critique the patterns of our legal heritage and the emerging trends in American law. The school also offers an extensive Legal Research & Writing program and a broad elective curriculum with courses in every area of law. Each student is appointed a faculty advisor who assists with course selection, particularly if a student wishes to pursue a certain area in special depth.

The school offers three clinical programs: the Mediation Clinic, the Family Violence Clinic and the Elder Law Clinic. The Mediation Clinic allows students to mediate cases set for trial at the Montgomery County District Court. The Family Violence Clinic provides pro bono services for clients unable to pay for representation and works in conjunction with Legal Services Corporation of Alabama and the Family Sunshine Center. The Elder Law Clinic allows students to represent low-income, elderly citizens in area counties. It works in cooperation with Legal Services Corporation of Alabama and the Alabama Department of Senior Services.

The School of Law's Advocacy Program is a vibrant program that provides students with the opportunity to hone their courtroom skills. Students can participate in national competitions in appellate advocacy, trial advocacy, and mediation. Students have had the opportunity to compete in New York, Washington, DC, Miami, St. Louis, Atlanta, Memphis, Cincinnati, Buffalo, and San Antonio (just to name a few). Also, the school hosts the Greg Allen Intra-School Mock Trial Competition, the 1L Moot Court Competition, and an intramural Closing Argument competition each year.

FACILITIES

The School of Law is housed in a beautiful, neo-federal-style building that accommodates the George H. Jones Jr. Law Library, the Judge Walter B. Jones Moot Court Room, and the Institute for Dispute Resolution. It includes state-of-the-art research and lecture facilities with seven classrooms and two large conference rooms. All classrooms are outfitted for laptop computers and wireless Internet is available throughout the building and library.

EXPENSES AND FINANCIAL AID

Tuition for the academic year of 2011–12 is $32,000 ($16,000 in the fall, $16,000 in the spring) for a full-time student.

Students can seek educational loans through the Federal Stafford Loan program and the Graduate PLUS loan program. The School of Law offers merit-based scholarships to qualified entering students. Admitted applicants are automatically under scholarship consideration. Scholarships are limited in number therefore prospective students are encouraged to apply early in the admissions cycle.

FACULTY

The School of Law's curriculum is taught by a dynamic group of faculty. Professors challenge students, welcome ideas and encourage debate. With a low student-to-faculty ratio and an emphasis on small class sizes and personalized instruction, the school provides a more intimate atmosphere that enhances a student's educational experience. The student-to-faculty to ratio is 12 to 1.

STUDENT BODY

The School of Law hosts fifteen student organizations. Those are: American Constitution Society, American Association for Justice, Animal Law Society, Black Law Students Association, Board of Advocates, Christian Legal Society, Delta Theta Phi, Federalist Society, Honor Court, Jones Public Interest Law Foundation, Jones Law Republicans, Jones Law Review, Phi Alpha Delta, Student Bar Association, and Women Students Association.

ADMISSIONS

The School of Law seeks to enroll a highly qualified and diverse student body. The two primary criteria used to make admissions decisions are an applicant's LSAT score and cumulative undergraduate grade point average. Other factors considered are the applicant's personal statement, undergraduate school, undergraduate and/or graduate courses of study, grade trends, community service/involvement and professional employment history. Letters of recommendation are welcome but not required.

SPECIAL PROGRAMS

The Alternative Dispute Resolution (ADR) Program enables law students to integrate their knowledge of conflict management principles and dispute resolution processes with professional skills. This program allows students to receive training normally available only through on-the-job experience after graduation.

Students can earn a certificate in ADR which is not a supplemental degree but an opportunity for Juris Doctor candidates to enrich their skills training while still in law school. The certificate in ADR requires completion of the following courses: Arbitration, Dispute Resolution Processes, Interviewing/Counseling & Negotiation, Mediation Clinic, and an elective skills course. All of the certificate courses contain both an academic component and a skills component.

As part of a Christian university, the School of Law seeks not only to provide legal knowledge and practical skills necessary to produce competent and ethical members of the legal community, but also to instill in students an attitude of service. This commitment to serve those who otherwise could not afford such assistance complements the legal profession's rich tradition of service.

The Public Interest Program provides opportunities for students to begin their career of service while utilizing the practical skills obtained in their legal education. This program is voluntary and provides students with opportunities to work for nonprofit organizations, government agencies, and private attorneys or firms conducting pro bono legal work. Students are challenged to perform at least 50 hours of voluntary service during their law school career.

CAREER SERVICES AND PLACEMENT

The School of Law's Career Services Office provides a full range of services to support students and alumni in their job search process. It actively develops relationships with employers, alumni, and professional organizations to assist students in developing a network of professional contacts. The school boasts a placement rate for its graduates in excess of 85%.

MISSISSIPPI COLLEGE
School of Law

AT A GLANCE

MC Law began educating future attorneys in 1930 as the Jackson School of Law, a night school for working professionals who wished to become attorneys.

Its location in Jackson, Mississippi's legal and governmental center, has been an advantage ever since the law school's earliest days; the original faculty members were practicing attorneys who pursued justice in the courtrooms of the capital city by day and encouraged the next generation of legal leaders in the evenings. Over the years, the law school grew from a night school into a fulltime institution, earning a reputation for outstanding instruction and the professional success of its graduates.

In 1975, the law school became a part of Mississippi College, the oldest university in the state. Combining a practical legal education with Christian principles, the law school has since become a premier legal center for the South.

MC Law is accredited by the American Bar Association, is a member of the American Association of Law Schools, charter member of the International Association of Law Schools and a member of the American Society of Comparative Law.

AT MC Law, students receive the superior education, uncommon support, and real world experience they need to become real world lawyers.

CAMPUS AND LOCATION

MC Law is located in downtown Jackson, Mississippi's capital city and the heart of the state's legal community. The State Capitol, Mississippi Supreme Court, federal courts, and many of Mississippi's most respected law firms are within walking distance of the campus.

The law school's strategic location puts students in the right place to interact with lawyers, judges, and other legal experts, many of whom visit the campus as speakers or teach classes as adjunct professors.

DEGREES OFFERED

MC Law's rigorous academic program combines a strong foundation in the law with opportunities to explore areas of personal interest and engage in hands-on legal work. First year students take foundational courses that teach them to think, speak, and write like lawyers. A legal research and writing program that includes small group and personal instruction is a key part of the first year curriculum. During the second and third year, students choose from a wide range of electives geared toward their areas of legal interest and complete and in-depth writing project.

PROGRAMS AND CURRICULUM

MC Law's six law centers offer students the opportunity for in-depth study and in some cases, practice, of a particular area of law. Each law center offers a stimulating mix of class offerings, writing and research opportunities, outside speakers, external moot court competitions focused on the subject area, and externships for practical experience. The International Law Center offers study abroad opportunities in Korea, Mexico, and Germany, as well as assistance coordinating individual study abroad programs.

FACILITIES

The MC Law campus is a showplace in the center of downtown Jackson and a legal center for all of Mississippi. MC Law recently completed a multi-million dollar construction and renovation project that included the latest advancements in classroom and courtroom technology. The campus's provides comfortable, high-tech classrooms with "clicker" technology and a range of audio-visual capabilities. All classrooms offer wireless connection to the internet and pop-up electrical outlets for laptop computers. The law library is the largest in the state and offers a range of research services.

EXPENSES AND FINANCIAL AID

Success includes making wise investments in your future. MC Law ranks among the most affordable private law schools in the country, offering an exceptional legal education at a reasonable cost. MC Law offers a locked tuition rate that makes budgeting for your legal education easier and surprise-free. Your tuition per hour is guaranteed to remain the same for the three years you are a student.

FACULTY

MC Law's faculty members are leaders in their fields of study and are regularly cited in courts, scholarly journals, and the media. But while their scholarship is outstanding, MC law professors are first and foremost teachers. At MC Law, professors are given the time and encouragement necessary to serve not only as instructors, but also as mentors. Professors are approachable, enjoying personal relationships with their students that extend beyond law school and continue throughout the course of their former students' careers.

STUDENTS

MC Law students come from a variety of geographic locations and cultural backgrounds, resulting in a diverse student body with a wide array of talents, personalities, and interests. The law school offers many opportunities for students to enhance their legal educations, expand their social circles, and form connections that extend beyond the classroom.

ADMISSIONS

MC Law encourages on-line applications through the LSAC process (application fee waived). Applications are considered on a rolling basis with a deadline of June 1.

As at any law school, your undergraduate grade point average and LSAT score are important elements of the evaluation. MC Law, however, also gives significant weight to your personal statement, recommendations, employment history, military service, graduate work, activities, community service, and personal circumstances..

SPECIAL PROGRAMS

MC Law offers a Louisiana Civil Law Certificate program for students who wish to practice in neighboring Louisiana.

ADDITIONAL INFORMATION

Jackson, Mississippi offers much more than access to the legal community. Home to 400,000 residents, the capital city combines the amenities of a large city with the warmth and welcome of a small town.

CAREER SERVICES AND PLACEMENT

The MC Law Career Services office is active and engaged in assisting students with job placement. This process begins in the first year and continues with classes and instructional programs on subjects ranging from interview techniques to dining and dress etiquette. The law school administers a viable on-campus recruiting program.

PACE UNIVERSITY
School of Law

AT A GLANCE

Pace University School of Law, founded in 1976, has over 7,000 alumni throughout the country and the world, and is consistently ranked among the nation's top four programs in environmental law. The school is recognized for excellence in several other areas, including its international, criminal justice, public interest law and clinical training and skills programs. Pace Law School offers full-time and part-time day J.D. programs, as well as a January accelerated program. Also offered are the Master of Laws degree in Environmental Law, including the nation's first graduate-level programs in Climate Change and Land Use and Sustainable Development, and Comparative Legal Studies, and a Doctor of Laws in Environmental Law. The Law School is part of Pace University, a comprehensive, independent and diversified university with campuses in New York City and Westchester County.

CAMPUS AND LOCATION

The Law School's White Plains campus houses its academic facilities, student activities center, and residence hall. Just 20 miles from Manhattan, the campus provides a suburban feel in an urban setting. With convenient access to New York City, Connecticut, and New Jersey, White Plains hosts the headquarters of some of the nation's largest corporations, a large legal community and local, county, state and federal courts. This concentration of resources enables Pace Law School to attract dynamic professors and speakers, and offer excellent opportunities for internships and post graduation employment.

DEGREES OFFERED

Pace Law School offers: J.D., LL.M. in Comparative Legal Studies, J.D./LL.M. and S.J.D. in Environmental Law, J.D./M.B.A. and J.D./M.P.A. with Pace University, J.D./M.E.M. with Yale University School of Forestry, J.D./M.S. with Bard College, Center for Environmental Policy, J.D./M.A. with Sarah Lawrence College in Women's Studies.

PROGRAMS AND CURRICULUM

Students can explore a range of subject areas or pursue a concentrated curriculum. The academic program prepares students to practice in any jurisdiction in the United States. Pace's accomplished faculty – comprised of dedicated scholars, researchers and practitioners – bring extensive experience and innovative teaching techniques to the classroom. Most classes have fewer than 25 students, facilitating close faculty-student relationships. Beyond the rich curricular programs, students have access to many extracurricular activities such as student-run organizations and law reviews, prominent on-campus lecture series, and research in highly regarded Centers.

FACILITIES

The library is an airy, modern facility with wireless access, two computer labs, and six public terminals. Housing over 403,000 volumes, the library also provides access through interlibrary loan to materials held in libraries throughout the United States. It is a member of several library consortia, through which students can use academic libraries located in the New York metropolitan region. The library subscribes to many online databases, including Lexis, Westlaw, HeinOnline, and BNA.

EXPENSES AND FINANCIAL AID

Tuition for the 2010–2011 year is $39,546/academic year for full-time students and $29,662/academic year for part-time students. The on-campus residence hall houses 100 full-time students and features single rooms with internet access, telephones, voice mail, and cable television. The Admissions Office also assists students in securing off campus housing.

A comprehensive aid program includes scholarships, need-based grants, employment loans, and a loan forgiveness program for graduates who choose a public interest career. In 2010, the average scholarship award totaled $17,500/year. Criteria for funds may include financial need, academic merit, education costs, or credit considerations.

FACULTY

The Law School includes 46 full-time and 125 adjunct professors. Faculty scholarship covers diverse areas of law such as Civil Litigation, Civil Procedure, Constitutional Law, Contracts, Evidence, Family Law, Federalism and Separation of Powers, Federal Jurisdiction, Federal Law and Procedure, Property, Torts, Animal Law, Gender Law, Prisoner's Rights, Feminist Legal Theory, Americans with Disabilities Act, Children's Legal Representation, Sexual Orientation and Gender Identity, Environmental, International Commercial Law, Land Use, and Prosecutorial and Judicial Ethics. Many faculty members author widely circulated influential legal publications and have drafted ground-breaking legislation.

STUDENTS

The diverse 2010 entering class represented 24 states, several countries, and over 125 undergraduate schools. The average age is 24 for full-time students and 30 for part-time students. The minority population is 17 percent. The new January-entering class, now in its second year, has 28 students representing six states and 23 undergraduate schools. Nearly one-quarter have masters degrees. The average age is 26, and students of diversity represent 18% of the class.

SPECIAL PROGRAMS

Pace Law School offers many clinics, simulation courses, and externships through on-campus centers, institutes and lawyering skills programs. Students represent clients through the Pace Women's Justice Center's Family Court Externship, preserve individual liberties through the John Jay Legal Services Immigration Justice Clinic, and prepare and prosecute criminal cases with Assistant District Attorneys through a prosecution externship. Environmental students work on conservation and development through the Land Use Law Center and accelerate the transition to clean, efficient and renewable energy alternatives through the Pace Energy and Climate Center.

The international programs allow students to spend a summer abroad at a United Nations War Crimes Tribunal, or intern with law firms and corporate legal departments handling international trade matters. Through judicial externship programs, students hone legal writing skills in the chambers of a state or federal judge. The Pace London Law semester program, in affiliation with University College Faculty of Laws, University of London, provides coursework and an internship with London barristers or solicitors, an international trade firm, a member of Parliament, or an international human rights or environmental organization.

ADDITIONAL INFORMATION

78 North Broadway, White Plains, NY 10603 Admissions Phone: 914-422-4210; Admissions E-mail: admissions@law.pace.edu; Web Address: www.law.pace.edu.

CAREER SERVICES AND PLACEMENT

Through a variety of outreach activities, the Pace Law School Center for Career Development and Public Interest Law Center actively work to foster and maintain relationships with the legal community. The Centers maintain a website for job postings and recruitment programs and host an annual career fair. In addition, the Centers arrange panels, networking events, and presentations to enable students to learn about legal fields and meet members of the bench and bar. The Public Interest Law Center sponsors a Pro Bono Justice Program, and facilitates funding for students working in public interest summer internships. The 2009 graduating class survey reported 88.1 percent employment and 6.1 percent pursuing an advanced degree within nine months following graduation. The majority of the class stayed in New York (78%), most (42%) went into private practice (median salary $62,500) and the median starting salary across all industries (private law firms, academics, business, public sector) was $55,000.

SEATTLE UNIVERSITY
School of Law

AT A GLANCE

Seattle University School of Law, the most diverse law school in the Pacific Northwest, is home to the country's top Legal Writing Program, the Ronald A. Peterson Law Clinic, distinguished centers, and a superb faculty, all of which support our mission to educate outstanding lawyers to be leaders for a just and humane world. The law school is recognized nationally for its welcoming environment and is the only Washington law school with a part-time program.

Seattle University School of Law, the most diverse law school in the Pacific Northwest, is dedicated to the twin goals of academic excellence and education for justice.

CAMPUS AND LOCATION

Located in the heart of Seattle, the law school is a vital part of the community. It is located on the beautiful urban campus of Seattle University just steps from downtown. The area offers a mix of exciting, professional, cultural and recreational opportunities. Seattle is a legal, business, technological and cultural hub that provides law students access to summer and school-year employment with major players in the economy, multinational law firms and public agencies.

DEGREES OFFERED

In addition to a J.D., the law school offers joint degrees in business, public administration, sports administration and leadership, criminal justice or transformational leadership.

PROGRAMS AND CURRICULUM

Through our broad and practical curriculum, we prepare students for the skilled and ethical practice of law in a global and highly complex society. We pay close attention to the rapidly changing profession and constantly revise our curriculum to ensure that our students graduate with both a concern for justice and the capacity to promote it.

A leader in global legal education, the law school has an International and Comparative Law Program, a Center for Global Justice and study abroad opportunities in South Africa, Ireland and Guatemala, as well as international externships throughout the world.

FACILITIES

Sullivan Hall is an award-winning, state-of-the-art facility with the latest technology throughout its impressive library, classrooms, courtroom and study and activity areas. The recently completed School of Law Annex less than a block from Sullivan Hall was built to accommodate the growing law school.

EXPENSES AND FINANCIAL AID

Tuition for the 2010-2011 academic year is $38,502 for 31 credits. Other non-tuition costs (books, room and board, transportation, and other living expenses) average about $17,500 per nine-month academic year.

The law school's Scholarship Program is among the most ambitious in the region, awarding more than $3 million per year to approximately 350 students. Its objectives are twofold: to offer to all students – regardless of economic or social background – the advantages of a private legal education, and to recognize and reward – regardless of financial need – the achievements and outstanding potential of the most highly qualified students in the applicant pool.

FACULTY

Seattle University School of Law is home to an outstanding faculty of committed teacher-scholars. Our professors do not choose between scholarship and teaching, but rather are experts in their fields who are drawn to share their knowledge with students.

A primary mission that drives the academic program is the faculty's desire to prepare students to practice the law with competence, honor and commitment to public service. Our talented faculty members teach students to analyze problems and construct policy arguments, as well as train them to write and speak with clarity and precision. The teaching is both demanding and humane. It blends legal theory, doctrinal analysis and comprehensive practical-skills training.

STUDENTS

The school enrolls more than 1,000 students representing more than 250 undergraduate schools and drawn from the top third of the national law school applicant pool. We serve an impressive body of students whose diversity encompasses age, life experience, and cultural heritage.

ADMISSIONS

In admission decisions, the law school places equal emphasis on three factors: (1) LSAT performance; (2) the undergraduate academic record; and (3) personal achievements, especially talents or factors that contribute to our law school community in special and significant ways. We admit a limited group of applicants through our Access Admission Program, which addresses applicants who don't meet traditional admission criteria but show great promise.

SPECIAL PROGRAMS

Our Access to Justice Institute inspires all law students toward a lifelong commitment to social justice. ATJI connects students to public interest opportunities that fulfill unmet legal needs, facilitates advocacy and legal skills training, hosts social justice events, counsels students in public interest career exploration, and collaborates with local, state, and national efforts to promote equal justice.

The Fred T. Korematsu Center for Law and Equality aims to advance social justice by fostering critical thinking about discrimination in U.S. society and through targeted advocacy to promote equality and freedom.

CAREER SERVICES AND PLACEMENT

Our Legal Writing program, clinical courses in 13 practice areas, internship and externship experiences at more than 200 agencies, courts and firms prepare our students to hit the ground running. Our Center for Professional Development staff equips students with the tools to prepare for life after law school. One-on-one coaching guides students in the career development process, which leads to them landing competitive positions, and building a network of relationships to guarantee long-term career success and fulfillment.

Our alumni are successful in every area of the law. They include a college president, a governor, and a state Supreme Court Justice. Our graduates work as top prosecutors, defense attorneys and judges. They are corporate lawyers and public interest attorneys, lawmakers and business leaders.

Some followed career paths into government jobs at agencies including the Environmental Protection Agency, the Securities and Exchange Commission, the Department of Justice and the House Committee on Homeland Security.

Others are employed by corporations including Microsoft, Boeing, REI, Costco, VeriSign and Nordstrom. Still more work with abused children, mentally ill offenders, immigrants and other underserved communities. Alumni work in places from Alaska and Seattle to New York and Washington, D.C., and abroad.

ST. THOMAS UNIVERSITY
School of Law

AT A GLANCE

St. Thomas University School of Law is a highly-regarded student-centered law school where diversity is cherished, a commitment to human rights and international law flourishes, and the Catholic heritage of social justice enhances the education of all faiths.

One of the greatest strengths of our law school is the profound sense of community shared by students, faculty, and administration. St. Thomas Law is a leader in diversity, boasting one of the most culturally diverse student bodies in the country. This global diversity, within such a close-knit community, facilitates a cosmopolitan learning environment where intellectual discovery thrives.

A hallmark of St. Thomas Law is our emphasis on practical training, student engagement, social justice, and ethical behavior. Our students and alumni have a deep sense of justice and charity, and fully utilize their education and experience to lead the way in making our legal system one that truly champions the rights of the powerless.

CAMPUS AND LOCATION

St. Thomas University School of Law's location in Miami, Florida, provides an ideal setting for the study of law. Miami is a vibrant, thriving international community. As a hub of domestic and international trade, an innovative center for fine arts and one of the world's most popular vacation spots, Miami is a dynamic place to live and study. Miami enjoys a rapidly expanding multinational legal community and is home to federal and state trial and appellate courts.

DEGREES OFFERED

St. Thomas University School of Law offers the traditional J.D. degree, several joint degrees, an LL.M. and J.S.D. degree and an LL.M in Environmental Sustainability. Our joint degree program includes:

J.D./M.B.A. or M.S. in Sports Administration;
J.D./M.B.A. in International Business;
J.D./M.B.A. in Accounting; and,
J.D./M.S. in Marriage and Family Counseling.

St. Thomas University School of Law also offers advanced degrees: the LL.M. and the J.S.D. in Intercultural Human Rights and the LL.M. in Environmental Sustainability.

J.D. students are able to enroll in the classes offered through the LL.M. programs and can earn Certificates in Human Rights and Environmental Sustainability.

SPECIAL PROGRAMS

St. Thomas University School of Law is committed to student success both in law school and beyond. Using an interactive and cooperative approach to learning, the Academic Support and Legal Research and Writing Programs emphasize the practical skills required for the successful practice of law.

Additionally, St. Thomas Law has a national reputation for its Appellate and Trial Advocacy Programs.

FACILITIES

The law school is designed to provide our students with an outstanding environment for learning the law. Computers and printers are in abundant supply throughout the law library. The law library offers Internet access to online databases and has been a leader in applying technology to legal education. Our wireless network allows students to conduct Internet-based research from anywhere on the law school's campus. Our classrooms and Moot Court Room have all been recently renovated.

EXPENSES AND FINANCIAL AID

Tuition and fees for the JD degree for 2011–2012 are $34,618 per year.

St. Thomas University School of Law offers merit-based scholarships to qualified students. St. Thomas also offers financial assistance apart from scholarships to eligible students in the form of loans. Many St. Thomas Law students receive some form of financial assistance. In addition St. Thomas Law covers the expense for a national BAR prep course for all graduates.

FACULTY

The faculty at St. Thomas is committed to teaching, research and service. Our exceptional faculty members have earned law degrees from some of the nation's most prestigious institutions, including Harvard, Yale, Columbia, Michigan, Pennsylvania, Georgetown, and New York University and many hold advance degrees. They are leaders in their fields with impressive records of publication in top law reviews and extensive practical experience.

A hallmark of the St. Thomas experience is the genuinely close relationship between faculty and students. Because of this relationship St. Thomas Law ranked 4th in the country for "Best Quality of Life" in the 2011 Princeton Reviews' *Best 172 Law Schools* (2011 edition).

STUDENT LIFE

St. Thomas University School of Law offers a rich student life. With more than twenty student organizations to choose from, students easily find activities that appeal to their interests. Students also enjoy the wealth of activities, cultural and sporting events, and nightlife offered in Miami and Fort Lauderdale.

ADMISSIONS

The Law School Admissions Committee evaluates each applicant's potential for excellence in the study of law. The Law School Admission Test (LSAT) score and undergraduate grade point average are factors; the committee also considers course of study, graduate degrees, work experience, community service, and so forth.

St. Thomas also offers an alternative process for admission for a select group of candidates through our Summer Conditional Admit Program. The Program targets candidates who demonstrate excellent qualitative credentials but lack certain quantitative measurements. Successful candidates are offered admission to the law school for that year's fall entering class.

CAREER SERVICES AND PLACEMENT

St. Thomas Law provides first-rate career services that result in successful and rewarding employment for our graduates, whether their goals are to enter into private law practice, government, business and industry, or public interest areas of law. St. Thomas Law graduates are partners in major national law firms.

STETSON UNIVERSITY
College of Law

AT A GLANCE
Stetson University College of Law, Florida's first law school, offers full- and part-time JD and LLM programs in Tampa Bay. Stetson is nationally ranked first for advocacy and third for legal writing.

CAMPUS AND LOCATION
Stetson's main law campus is located in Gulfport, a suburb of St. Petersburg. A satellite campus in downtown Tampa hosts some classes, conferences, and the Tampa branch of Florida's Second District Court of Appeal.

DEGREES OFFERED
In addition to the Juris Doctor degree, Stetson offers dual-degree programs for the J.D./M.B.A., J.D./Grado (Spain), J.D./M.D. and J.D./M.P.H. Stetson also offers an on-campus LL.M. in International Law and an online LL.M. in Elder Law.

PROGRAMS AND CURRICULUM
Stetson's curriculum combines a strong foundation of legal doctrine and theory with a nationally ranked program in the practical advocacy, legal research and writing skills required to become a successful attorney.

Stetson allows students the opportunity to specialize their legal education through a variety of programs. J.D. students may earn certificates of concentration in advocacy, elder law or international law, and J.D./M.B.A. students may pursue a certificate in eco-asset management. High-achieving students may be invited to participate in Stetson's Honors Program. Students interested in intellectual property law may participate in Stetson's semester exchange program with the University of New Hampshire School of Law.

Stetson's extensive international offerings include a fall semester in London, exchange programs with law schools in France, Mexico and Spain, summer programs in Argentina, China, the Netherlands, Spain and Switzerland, as well as a winter break course in the Cayman Islands.

Stetson also has centers for excellence and institutes that advance legal and policy issues in the fields of advocacy, biodiversity, the Caribbean, elder issues, higher education and international law. Stetson is home to the National Clearinghouse for Science, Technology and the Law, *Stetson Law Review*, *Journal for International Aging Law and Policy*, and the *Journal for International Wildlife Law and Policy*.

FACILITIES
Stetson's main law campus features technologically advanced classrooms, five courtrooms, library and recreational facilities, culminating in an idyllic environment for the study of law. The Tampa Law Center includes two courtroom spaces, fully equipped classrooms and seminar rooms, study rooms, and a satellite law library. The law libraries contain more than 419,000 volumes, 750,000 titles and 48 group study rooms. There is a laptop requirement for all admitted students, and high-speed wireless access is available on both campuses.

EXPENSES AND FINANCIAL AID
2011–2012 full-time tuition (fall/spring): $35,146
2011–2012 part-time tuition (summer/fall/spring): $30,192

Merit and diversity scholarships are offered on a competitive basis, and need and merit scholarships are offered for continuing students. There is no financial aid deadline, and a completed FAFSA is the only required form.

FACULTY
Stetson's full-time regular faculty of 52 professors engage in projects that bring them regional, national, and international prominence, but make teaching and working with students their top priority. Approximately 64 practicing attorneys and judges serve as adjunct professors.

STUDENTS
Stetson offers cultural programs, experiential education trips, community service opportunities, leadership workshops, and more than 45 active student organizations. The ABA Law Student Division has recognized Stetson with numerous regional and national awards, and Stetson's Student Leadership Development Program was awarded the ABA's prestigious E. Smythe Gambrell Award for excellence in professionalism. Stetson students donate more than 16,000 hours of pro bono service annually to more than 150 organizations.

ADMISSIONS
Stetson University College of Law admits full-time and part-time students each fall. As a prerequisite to enrollment, applicants are required to have earned a baccalaureate degree from a college or university that is accredited by an accrediting agency recognized by the U.S. Department of Education. A final, official transcript evidencing the conferral of the degree must be submitted before enrollment. All applicants are required to take the LSAT and register with the LSDAS. One letter of recommendation is required, and a maximum of three letters will be accepted. The personal statement is also required. More details are available at www.law.stetson.edu/admissions. An equal opportunity education institution, Stetson is fully accredited by the American Bar Association and has been an Association of American Law Schools member since 1931.

SPECIAL PROGRAMS
Recognized by *U.S. News* as No. 1 for advocacy and No. 3 for legal writing, Stetson routinely wins international, national, regional and state competitions for alternative dispute resolution, mock trials and moot court.

Stetson offers upper-level students a wide variety of opportunities to work closely with attorneys and judges, and, in some cases, actually represent clients and try cases. Hundreds of students are placed annually into more than 30 different clinical, internship and externship programs, including competitive opportunities to intern with the Florida and Georgia Supreme Courts, the U.S. Court of Appeals for Veterans Claims, and summer law and policy internships in Washington, D.C.

CAREER SERVICES AND PLACEMENT
Stetson's commitment to helping students achieve their goals is reflected in its strong career development program. The Office of Career Development assists students and alumni in securing all types of legal and law-related employment and provides group seminars and individual counseling on subjects ranging from interviewing techniques to résumé writing. More than 93 percent of the 2009 graduating class reported that they found employment within nine months of graduation. Stetson Law alumni reside in 48 states and 22 countries, and approximately 90 percent of recent graduates practice in Florida.

TOURO LAW CENTER

AT A GLANCE

Touro Law Center is committed to providing the best in legal education. Touro Law students are encouraged to examine the moral goals of the law while promoting social justice and community service. Touro Law, accredited by the American Bar Association (ABA) and a member of the Association of American Law Schools (AALS), offers students full-time and part-time J.D. programs as well as dual degree and LL.M. programs.

Touro Law Center is committed to providing the best in legal education. Touro Law students are encouraged to examine the moral goals of the law while promoting social justice and community service.

CAMPUS AND LOCATION

Touro Law occupies a 185,000 sq. ft state-of-the-art building in Central Islip on the south shore of Long Island, New York. Touro Law is at the center of what is arguably the nation's first integrated "law campus," comprised of a U.S. courthouse and New York State court center. More than mere physical proximity, students interact with legal professionals daily through classroom instruction, court visits, clinics, externships and other academic and social forums.

DEGREES OFFERED

Touro Law offers full-time and part-time (4 year part-time day, 4 year part-time evening and 5 year part-time evening) Juris Doctor programs as well as J.D./M.B.A., J.D./M.P.A. and J.D./M.S.W. dual degrees. Touro also offers an LL.M. degree in General Studies to graduates of U.S. law schools and an LL.M. degree in U.S. Legal Studies for foreign law graduates.

PROGRAMS AND CURRICULUM

The cornerstone of Touro Law's curriculum is the Collaborative Court Program —a new, integrative three-year curricular option for students. This comprehensive learning method has been designed to prepare students for the successful practice of law. The Program is comprised of three separate components: Court Observation, Court Integration and Court Specialization. Touro Law also offers several clinics: Civil Rights Litigation, Elder Law, Family Law, Mortgage Foreclosure and Bankruptcy, Not-for-Profit Corporation Law and Veterans' and Servicemembers' Rights.

Touro students also have the opportunity to participate in a variety of externships including Business, Law & Technology Externship, Civil Practice Externship, Criminal Law Externship, Judicial Clerkship, and the US Attorney's Office Externship. In addition, Touro Law also offers vibrant study abroad opportunities in Croatia, India, Germany, Israel and Vietnam as well as summer internships in law firms, courts, and government offices in Europe and Israel.

FACILITIES

Touro Law Center's facility was designed to be a student-centered learning center. The building houses a clinical wing, a state-of-the-art auditorium, a public advocacy center, mock trial classrooms, computer labs, meeting spaces, cafeteria, bookstore, the Gould Law Library and more. The infrastructure is high-tech, supporting wireless access, smart classrooms and new technology.

EXPENSES AND FINANCIAL AID

Generous institutional scholarship aid is available to entering and continuing students. Awards include dean's fellowships, merit scholarship, and incentive awards. Touro Law also offers stipends for Public Interest Law Fellowships, judicial clerkships, and summer federal work-study placements. Touro provides access to federal loans and work study, New York State loan and assistance programs, and need-based Touro Grants. Most students receive some form of financial aid, and 60 percent of entering students receive scholarships.

FACULTY

Touro Law's faculty is comprised of 50 full-time faculty members. Every entering student is assigned a faculty advisor, matched by background or interest area, for discussions on any aspect of the law school experience including study strategy, course selection, career goals, etc. With an open-door policy and a student faculty ratio of 16:1, Touro Law students benefit from a personal and dynamic educational experience.

STUDENTS

The Law Center's students, coming from diverse backgrounds and experiences, represent over 112 undergraduate institutions and a broad mix of majors. Women comprise approximately 45 percent of the total enrollment; minorities, 25 percent.

ADMISSIONS

Touro Law Center seeks to identify applicants who show an ability to pursue the study of law successfully and to make an important contribution to the Law Center's educational program, to the legal profession and to society. While significant weight is attached to a student's undergraduate cumulative grade point average and Law School Admission Test (LSAT) score(s), the selection process is not strictly mathematical and includes an evaluation of several other factors including professional experiences and achievement, writing ability, rigor of undergraduate institution, letters of recommendation, and more.

SPECIAL PROGRAMS

Touro Law Center is home to the William Randolph Hearst Public Advocacy Center, the first of its kind in the nation. Touro Law provides furnished offices at no cost to 15 non-profit legal advocacy agencies while providing hands-on working opportunities for students.

ADDITIONAL INFORMATION

Touro Law Center provides a unique program of outside-the-classroom assistance. Teaching assistants (TAs) review material covered in class and conduct small-group sessions on effective study methods and test-taking techniques. The Writing Resources Center offers workshops and tutorials to assist students in producing a professional work product. The Legal Education Access Program (LEAP) enhances the experience of students of color through a four-week summer program for new students with additional mentoring during the academic year. The Honors Program, beginning in the second year, allows outstanding opportunities for students who receive additional scholarship assistance and access to academic enrichment initiatives.

CAREER SERVICES AND PLACEMENT

The Career Services staff assists students and graduates in securing part-time, full-time and summer employment. In addition to placing students with national, regional and local law firms, there are opportunities in federal, state, and local courts and government agencies, and in the legal departments of corporations and municipalities.

THE UNIVERSITY OF THE DISTRICT OF COLUMBIA
David A. Clarke School of Law

AT A GLANCE

The University of the District of Columbia David A. Clarke School of Law (UDC-DCSL) is the only public law school in the Nation's Capital. The School of Law is unique among law schools, with a mission of recruiting and enrolling students from underrepresented communities, and one of the most diverse student bodies in the country, coupled with the most extensive clinical requirements of any law school in a top ranked clinical program.

CAMPUS AND LOCATION

UDC-DCSL is located on the campus of the University of the District of Columbia, the country's only urban public Land Grant Historically Black University. The University and School of Law are located in the upper Northwest section of the District on one of the city's major tree-lined avenues. The Van Ness/UDC Metro station is located directly in front of the University, making the campus easily accessible. The campus is surrounded by a quiet residential community, Rock Creek Park, the National Zoo, embassies and small businesses.

DEGREES OFFERED

The School of Law offers the Juris Doctor (J.D.) degree and full-time day and part-time evening divisions, and the LL.M. degree in Clinical Legal Education, Social Justice and Systems Change.

PROGRAMS AND CURRICULUM

The School of Law offers the best of both worlds for the study of law—a traditional legal education supplemented by hands-on clinical training. Students are required to complete 90 credits to graduate, 14 of which are earned in two semesters of clinical work. Clinics include Legislation, Housing & Consumer Law, Juvenile & Special Education, Community Development, Low-Income Tax, HIV/AIDS, Immigration & Human Rights, and the Government Accountability Project. Students are also required to complete 40 hours of community service, and they may participate in a 10- or 4-credit internship elective.

FACILITIES

The School of Law is located on the campus of the University, which sits on several acres of land on Connecticut Avenue, NW.

The School of Law will move into a newly renovated green facility in Building 52. The $1.6 million recently-renovated Mason Law Library is located in Building 39, Level B. Every seat in the library is wired and WIFI access is available everywhere in the library. The larger classrooms are wired and the large lecture classroom is wired and high-tech.

EXPENSES AND FINANCIAL AID

The School of Law offers its students an affordable legal education and a comprehensive financial aid program. Tuition for District of Columbia resident students is $8,850 per year (2010–11). Tuition for non-DC resident students is $17,700 per year (2010–11). Non-DC resident students may be eligible for resident tuition after residing in the District for one year. Students may be eligible as well for the following financial assistance: Federal loans, merit scholarships, need-based grants, work-study, Dean's Fellowships, Continuing Student Scholarships, and the full-tuition three-year Advocate for Justice Scholarship. For more information on the law school's financial aid program, you may visit www.law.udc.edu.

ADMISSION

The School of Law considers the entire applicant profile when rendering an admission decision. While the candidate's LSAT and grades play an important role in the admission process, other factors are also considered before a decision is made, e.g., the applicant's range of life experiences, the content and mechanics of the applicant's writing, community involvement, family background, and recommendations.

The average and median LSAT for the 2010 entering class is 153.

The Committee on Admission requests TOEFL on a case-by-case basis.

SPECIAL PROGRAMS

Other programs for students include the Summer Public Interest Fellowship Program for which all 1Ls are eligible to receive $4,000 grants for full-time, lawyer-supervised, law-related work at a non-profit, government agency, or judge's chambers anywhere in the world, the for-credit internship program, and federal work-study opportunities.

ADDITIONAL INFORMATION

Students enjoy a 12-to-1 student-faculty ratio and individualized attention from and access to faculty and administration. The small school also affords students a spirited, committed and collegial setting and community in which to study law.

CAREER SERVICES AND PLACEMENT

For more information on career services and placement, you may visit the school website at www.law.udc.edu or contact Career Services Director Dena Bauman at dbauman@udc.edu. The School of Law has over 3,000 alumni, the majority of whom are connected to the School of Law via email. Alumni provide invaluable resources to both students and other alumni. For information, contact Alumni Director Joe Libertelli at jfl@udc.edu.

WESTERN NEW ENGLAND COLLEGE
School of Law

AT A GLANCE

2010 Full-time Entering Class
LSAT median   153
  (25th percentile: 151; 75th percentile: 155)
GPA median   3.23
Average age   25
Age range   20–42
States represented   20
Total student enrollment: 551
Total students of color: 11.2%

CAMPUS AND LOCATION

Founded in 1919, the School of Law was originally part of Northeastern University and merged with Western New England College which itself was founded in 1951. Western New England College School of Law is located in Springfield, Massachusetts. Springfield is the third largest city in the Commonwealth, with 152,000 residents, and is home to a lively cultural scene. In the heart of the Pioneer Valley, Springfield is conveniently located near Boston, New York City, and Hartford, Connecticut.

DEGREES OFFERED

Western New England College School of Law offers many ways to earn a law degree. In addition to our three-year, full-time program, the School of Law also offers four-year, part-time evening and part-time day programs. Students may earn an advanced law degree in Estate Planning and Elder Law. The school of law also offers 3 joint degree options: JD/MBA, JD/MRP, and JD/MSW.

ACADEMIC PROGRAMS GENERAL

Western New England College School of Law offers students the opportunity to combine our law degree with three other programs. These programs include the JD/MBA (Master of Business Administration) with Western New England College, the JD/MSA (Master of Accounting) with Western New England College, the JD/MRP (Master of Regional Planning) with the University of Massachusetts, and the JD/MSW (Master of Social Work) with Springfield College.

To assist students in preparing for their careers, and selecting among electives, WNEC School of Law currently offers seven areas of concentration: Business Law, Criminal Law, Estate Planning, International and Comparative Law, Public Interest Law, Real Estate, and Gender and Sexuality studies.

WNEC School of Law affords students the opportunity to merge theory with practice. Students take advantage of clinical course work, internships and externships, a wide variety of simulation courses, and participate in a number of moot court teams in order to hone their lawyering skills. For more information on clinical opportunities, externships, and simulation courses visit our website at www.law.wnec.edu.

At WNEC School of Law, we keep our class size small to promote a collegial learning environment in which students are challenged to actively participate in their legal education.

EXPENSES AND FINANCIAL AID

In 2010, tuition for fulltime students is $35,582; part-time students pay $26,686 which includes both the academic year and five credit hours of summer study. Institutional scholarships are typically awarded to approximately 60% of each incoming class. Partial Scholarships may range from $5,000 to $30,000 a year and may be renewed provided requirements are met. Scholarships are also given based on background and life experiences.

Western New England College School of Law's support for Public Interest Lawyering includes the establishment of its Public Interest Scholars Program. Public Interest Scholars receive three-year tuition scholarships in values ranging from $16,000 up to the cost of full tuition. In addition to their tuition scholarships, Public Interest Scholars are awarded a one-time public interest stipend of $3,500 for approved public interest work in the summer months after the first or second year of law school. For more information on scholarship and loan opportunities, visit our website at www.law.wnec.edu.

The Oliver Wendell Holmes, Jr. Scholar's Program is designed for students who have demonstrated academic excellence. Recipients of the Holmes Scholarship receive a full-tuition scholarship, a $3,500 stipend to work as a research assistant for a member of our faculty or for the law library, and invitations to special events.

FACULTY

Our 31 full time faculty members have been educated at the nation's most prestigious law schools. All have practiced law before joining our faculty and several hold additional graduate degrees in other disciplines. The School of Law places a strong emphasis on collaborative learning and student-professor interaction. Faculty members foster an open and collegial interaction with the students that provides a positive legal education in a comfortable atmosphere. The School of Law also has more than 21 adjunct faculty members, including practicing attorneys and judges, who bring their current legal practices into the classroom setting.

STUDENT BODY

The Student Bar Association (SBA) is the student government of the School of Law. The SBA plays a significant role in the administration of the School of Law with representation at the Faculty Meetings and on the Faculty/Student Committees.

Total enrollment of the law school: 525
% Female/Male: 52% F/48% M
% fulltime enrolled   74%
Student/Faculty ratio   12.7: 1

ADMISSIONS

Each year, the Admissions Committee assembles a talented, interesting, and diverse class of students. We enroll a class whose members come from various races and ethnicities, ages, academic and professional backgrounds, and geographic areas.

Each completed application is read in its entirety and carefully reviewed to determine whether the applicant possesses the academic preparation and motivation necessary to complete the demanding workload of law school. Committee members attempt to gauge each applicant's prior academic performance, expected academic performance, and writing skills. While LSAT scores and undergraduate GPA are important to the Admissions Committee, they form just one part of the picture. We recognize that the ability to succeed in law school and contribute to our law school community and the legal profession is also demonstrated through the personal statement, letters of recommendation, and supplemental essays provided by the applicant. We therefore review these materials closely.

We encourage you to submit your application early since admissions decisions are made on a rolling basis. The Admissions Committee begins admitting applicants in January and completes the majority of its work by April. It is strongly recommended that applications for full-time enrollment be completed by March 15. Applications for part-time enrollment should be submitted by June 1.

Please visit our website at www.law.wnec.edu to view more details on admissions.

DEAN INTERVIEWS

FAULKNER UNIVERSITY

Q. What type of student thrives at your school? What are the student characteristics or interests that "fit" well with your school culture and community?

Dean Nelson

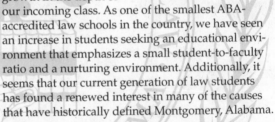

A. At Faulkner Law, we educate leaders. The students that join our incoming classes are well rounded, interesting, and unique students dedicated to studying the law in a place that emphasizes Christian character and academic excellence. They have excelled through their undergraduate programs by becoming influencers among their peers through their leadership positions in student organizations, civic involvement, and the pursuit of academic excellence. Last year's incoming class boasted students from sixty-nine different undergraduate institutions, twenty-three states and the District of Columbia, and forty-six different undergraduate majors.

Q. Can you describe the history of your school—its founding and core mission?

A. Montgomery County Circuit Judge Walter B. Jones founded the Law School in 1928. Judge Jones named the school in honor of his father, Thomas Goode Jones (1844–1914) Judge Jones owned and operated the School of Law until his death in 1963. He served as president, dean, and faculty member.

The University of Alabama acquired the School of Law from Judge Jones' heir in 1972 and transferred the School of Law's assets to Jones Law Institute, a nonprofit corporation. In August of 1983, Alabama Christian College (now Faulkner) purchased the School of Law from the University of Alabama and moved the School of Law to the Faulkner campus.

As part of the Faulkner University community, the School of Law shares Faulkner University's mission to glorify God by embracing academic excellence and emphasizing a strong commitment to integrity within a caring Christian environment.

Q. What type of admissions trends have your school experienced recently—over the past three to five years?

A. Recently we have seen a tremendous growth in the depth of our incoming class. As one of the smallest ABA-accredited law schools in the country, we have seen an increase in students seeking an educational environment that emphasizes a small student-to-faculty ratio and a nurturing environment. Additionally, it seems that our current generation of law students has found a renewed interest in many of the causes that have historically defined Montgomery, Alabama.

Q. What factors are most important in your admissions process? How important are non-academic factors such as extracurricular activities or volunteer work?

A. Our Office of Admissions and Admissions Committee take very seriously the process of deliberating upon each applicant that applies to Faulkner Law. The two primary criteria used to make admissions decisions are an applicant's LSAT score and cumulative undergraduate grade point average. Other factors considered are the applicant's personal statement, undergraduate school, undergraduate and/or graduate courses of study, grade trends, community service/involvement and professional employment history. Letters of recommendation are welcome but not required.

We also place a significant amount of influence on an individual applicant's character development, work ethic, volunteer activities, extracurricular activities, and organizational leadership.

When our graduates begin their careers, they do not merely practice law. Our graduates are positioned to be community leaders and civic influencers. They practice law while working with nonprofit organizations, being active leaders in their churches and religious organizations, and partner with countless charitable organizations meeting the needs of marginalized people. Our Admissions process is designed to identify people who are capable of serving in these roles and then to provide them the legal education necessary for accomplishing each of them.

Q. Describe the faculty at your school. What level of interaction do professors have with their students?

A. The School of Law's faculty is a dynamic group of attorneys tasked with teaching our rigorous curriculum in a way that is immediately translatable to the practice life of an attorney. Professors challenge students, welcome ideas and encourage debate. With a low student-to-faculty ratio and an emphasis on small class sizes and personalized instruction, the school provides a more intimate atmosphere that enhances a student's educational experience. Our faculty come from many of the most prominent educational institutions in the world and are dedicated to inspiring students in a proud tradition of challenging, demanding classroom excellence.

Our students have the real opportunity to work closely with our faculty in their roles as student organization sponsors, advocacy team coaches, clinical instructors, and legal mentors.

Q. Does Faulkner offer specializations?

A. We offer a variety of special instructional programming not available on most law school campuses. Perhaps our most prolific is our Alternative Dispute Resolution (ADR) Program. Our ADR program enables law students to integrate their knowledge of conflict management principles and dispute resolution processes with professional skills. Students can earn a certificate in ADR, which requires completion of courses such as Arbitration, Dispute Resolution Processes, Interviewing/Counseling and Negotiation, Mediation Clinic, and elective skills courses.

In addition to this specialization, we are also proud to offer highly innovative clinical experiences through our Mediation Clinic, Family Violence Clinic, and Elder Law Clinic. Beyond clinical experiences, our externship program includes a classroom component that covers topics relating to the legal system, judicial process and professionalism. Students develop their lawyering skills and gain real-world experience in the legal community, as they work side-by-side with judges and practicing lawyers.

Finally, our voluntary Public Interest Program provides opportunities for students to begin their career of service by working at least fifty hours for nonprofit organizations, government agencies, and private attorneys or firms conducting pro bono legal work.

Q. Can you describe the facilities and campus?

A. Faulkner University is located just a few miles from the Alabama State Capitol Building in Montgomery, Alabama, the birthplace of both the Confederacy and the Civil Rights movement.

The School of Law is housed in a beautiful, neo-federal-style building that accommodates the George H. Jones Jr. Law Library, the Judge Walter B. Jones Moot Court Room, and the Institute for Dispute Resolution. It includes state-of-the-art research and lecture facilities with seven classrooms and two large conference rooms. All classrooms are outfitted for laptop computers and wireless Internet is available throughout the building and library.

Faulkner Law held the groundbreaking ceremony for the Allen Law Center on October 15, 2010. The new $2.5 million facility will add approximately 17,000 square feet to the existing Law School building and will include additional study space in the law library, a classroom, faculty office space, and an additional courtroom. The Allen Law Center will house additional space for the Law School's renowned Elder Law, Family Violence and Mediation clinics, which provide low-income clients with student representation for legal situations.

Career Services

The School of Law's Career Services Office provides a full range of services to support students and alumni in their job search process. Beginning with first year students as early as November of each year to build a foundation, students can take full advantage of regular career service seminars on resume building, networking, and successfully identifying job placement opportunities, one-on-one resume review and job placement planning, and monthly mentor luncheons. Whether through traditional means such as each semester's on-campus interview (OCI) periods or through one-on-one training and mentoring, our Career Services office is dedicated to removing the barriers that law school graduates often face in the path to achieving their ideal career.

Q. What student organizations are available to Faulkner Law students?

A. Our student organizations provide invaluable opportunities for students to further enhance the law school experience. Co-curricular student organizations such as our Board of Advocates and Law Review offer students the opportunity to work intimately with faculty members in an academic context that hones the skills that students will use throughout their practice. Our Board of Advocates has produced two national titles, three national finalist finishes, five national semi-finalist finishes, twelve regional championships, and twenty-six individual advocacy awards since 2007.

The Faulkner Law Review strives to develop the legal writing skills of its members, improve their ability to engage in high level legal analysis, and assist in the fulfillment of the School of Law's overall mission to produce lawyers with the highest professional and ethical standards. The Faulkner Law Review achieves this by publishing a varied body of legal scholarship with the purpose of advancing legal discussion of timely theoretical and practical legal issues among the professional and academic communities.

In addition to these co-curricular organizations, the School of Law currently hosts fifteen extra-curricular student organizations, such as the American Constitution Society, Black Law Students Association, Christian Legal Society, Honor Court, and Women Students Association.

Q. How can a prospective student get more information about your school?

A. We encourage you to visit us in person. By visiting a class and speaking to faculty and students, you can experience firsthand what our law school has to offer. Our Admission Department is available to work with each applicant to answer any questions and provide any counseling needed throughout an applicant's law school decision making process. Our Admissions Department can be easily reached via email at law@faulkner.edu or by phone at 800.879.9816 ext. 7210 or at 334.386.7210.

MC Law

Q. *What type of student thrives at your school? What are the student characteristics or interests that "fit" well with your school culture and community?*

A. Our most successful students are those who are willing to devote the time and energy to prepare for class every day, who understand how facts relate to the law, and who have an appreciation of the forces of life and the role people play in our society. Certain categories of students seem to do especially well here—varsity athletes, those with business experience, military personnel, and those who held leadership positions in college. There is a place at MC Law for the confident, outgoing student as well as the reserved, introspective student. We respect individuals for what each brings to our student body.

Q. *Can you describe the history of your school—its founding, core mission, and how that has changed over time? What are the core mission and values of the school today?*

A. Our school is thirty-five years old and was founded when a group of judges, attorneys, and business leaders determined that Jackson—our capital city—should have a law school. Our core mission has not changed—to produce skilled lawyers with a heart for service who serve their clients and communities in accordance with the high standards of the profession.

Q. *What are the most important accolades and national/international recognition your school has received over the past three to five years?*

A. A strength of MC Law is its advocacy program. We have enjoyed success at the national level in appellate advocacy and trial competitions. In the last three years we won the Duberstein Bankruptcy Competition, won our region and placed second in the country in the National Moot Court competition, and won the Moot Court National Championship

Dean Nelson

(and Best Brief) in an invitational competition for the sixteen best moot court programs in the United States.

Q. *What factors are most important in your admissions process? How important are non-academic factors such as an interview, work experience, extracurricular activities, or volunteer work?*

A. We use a whole person concept in evaluating our applications—this strikes a responsive chord with those applicants who have leadership, service, and business experiences that add to the breadth and depth of our student body.

LSAT score, grades, and intangibles are the three key aspects of our application process. The first two factors are reported to us by LSAC. The third factor is presented to us through the personal statement of the applicant along with other documents such as letters of recommendation, descriptions of work or service experiences, or explanations of challenges overcome. We especially value applicants who demonstrated leadership in student government, organizations, or the military. We also value post graduate academic work. We have found that varsity athletes have time management skills that assist them in being successful in law school.

Q. *Describe the international population at your school (size and country diversity). Can you speak to any specific admissions differences relevant for international students?*

A. We have students who were born in countries other than the United States and applicants who have extensive overseas travel for study, business, or adventure. We have approved an LLM program for international students who will be immersed in the same courses taken by our JD students thereby providing an opportunity for interaction. We also have summer study programs in Mexico, Korea, and Berlin.

Q. How many application rounds are there for your school? Are there any advantages of applying at a certain stage?

A. We evaluate applications on a rolling basis. The applicants we accept in the later stages of the process possess very strong credentials as we fill the limited seats remaining in the entering class. It is always better to apply early. Our early action program gives a rapid admissions decision to those with outstanding credentials along with an automatic scholarship award. We have no application fee for those who apply on line.

Q. Describe the faculty at your school. What areas of academics/research have become the "hallmarks" of your faculty? What level of interaction do professors have with their students?

A. Our faculty are experts in their field, have superb academic credentials, and are devoted to their teaching. Our school size permits a collegial approach to student interaction. Our faculty serve as advisors to our student groups, coach moot court teams, assist with the admissions and placement processes, and interact with our students through all aspects of student life. They are approachable in the classroom or in their offices and make themselves available for student advising and discussion. Two of our faculty are native Germans and bring a comparative law focus to their work. Another professor is from Malaysia with an expertise in Intellectual Property.

One third of our faculty hold PhD degrees. Our faculty are active in their communities and actively interact with our Federal and State judges and attorneys. Several of our faculty chair code revision committees for the State and are active in professional legal organizations. They actively publish materials to include books, treatises, encyclopedias, law review, and journal articles.

Q. Does your school offer specializations? How/why were these developed?

A. Our specialties are based on the centers we maintain. These include our Litigation and Dispute Resolution Center, Bioethics and Health Law Center, International and Comparative Law Center, Business and Tax Law Center, Family and Children Law Center, and our Public Service Law Center. We also offer the only Civil Law program outside the State of Louisiana for those students who plan to take the bar and practice in Louisiana or who want a comparative law background. For our centers we normally have a moot court competition team, speakers, curricular offerings in that grouping, and student organizations.

Q. Please describe extracurricular academic programs at your school (for example, Clinics, Study Abroad, Journals).

A. We offer the Mississippi College Law Review and the MC Law Moot Court Board. Summer study programs are offered in Seoul, Korea (with a side trip to China); Merida, Mexico (Yucatan): and Berlin, Germany.

Q. Describe the typical internships among your students, and the full-time career placement mix (in terms of types of employers and jobs). What is the geographic diversity of your graduates (across states and countries)?

A. Our graduates are spread throughout the United States but tend to be concentrated in the mid-south from Texas to Washington, D.C. Some sixty percent of our students take an internship as part of their studies. These internships can be performed throughout the United States or in the vicinity of MC Law. Our location in the State Capital provides a host of internship opportunities that includes positions with the governor, legislature, judges, district attorneys, public defenders, and charitable organizations. Our Mission First Legal Aid Office offers a wonderful opportunity to gain client interviewing skills as well as the chance to work with attorneys to resolve legal issues. The distinct majority of our graduates go into private practice but a goodly segment serves in public service government positions, the military, or judicial clerks.

Q. Describe the need and merit-based aid offered by your school and the percentage of students who receive financial aid and scholarships.

A. All applicants are automatically considered for merit-based academic scholarships. Additional scholarships are awarded for leadership and mock trial achievement. We offer full-tuition scholarships to top applicants from eight feeder schools that send robust numbers of students to our school. Additional scholarships are awarded to students at the end of their first and second year based on academic achievement without regard to application statistics. Approximately thirty percent of students have scholarships that range from full tuition awards plus a stipend to partial tuition scholarships. Approximately eighty of our students receive financial aid. A number of our students go into public service where their student loan payments are adjusted to an income-based amount with any remaining balance forgiven at the end of ten years.

Q. Describe your highest achieving alumni.

A. MC Law graduates serve in the United States Congress and in our State Legislature, hold Federal and State judicial positions at the trial and appellate level, and are some of the most respected private practitioners and government attorneys. We are proud of all of our graduates who are active in their communities, churches, and local organizations and who commit to the welfare of their families. We have great respect for our graduates who serve their country in the military services and recently had four of our recent graduates serving in Iraq together. We do not limit the measure of our graduates' achievement to money or status.

Q. Speaking to the qualified students comparing your school to your top peer schools, what are the key advantages of your school?

A. The size and location of MC Law offers a student an opportunity to get a superb classroom education complemented by practical skills training in a supportive, collegial setting. For those students who seek to gain experience and confidence, our Advocacy program is one of the very best in the country as evidenced by our success in national advocacy competitions. We encourage our students to maintain a balance in their lives and not simply have a single dimension to their law school experience. Our student government association promotes the development of relationships that last for the rest of one's professional life. Our broad range of student organizations and athletic programs provide an extracurricular opportunity regardless of the area of interest.

Q. Are there any other key points you would like to share about your school that we haven't discussed?

A. MC Law is sensitive to the cost of a legal education. We are one of the most reasonably priced private law schools. We offer a fixed tuition rate that locks in tuition for all three years at the rate an entering student pays. Because of our location in downtown Jackson there are many part time work opportunities for our students during law school which arms them with practical skills and promotes their networking. We have a modern, hi-tech campus in a safe downtown location with ample surface parking adjacent to the law school. The downtown area offers a variety of dining, entertainment, and cultural activities. The air is clean, the highways are not crowded, and the quality of life is excellent. We embrace our students and commit to offering them a first-class legal education that will prepare them for the practice of law.

NOVA SOUTHEASTERN UNIVERSITY

Shepard Broad Law Center

Dean Interview

Q. Can you describe the history of your school?

A. Nova Southeastern University (NSU), as it is now known, is the product of the 1994 merger of two educational institutions in South Florida, the Nova University of Advanced Technology, chartered as a graduate institution in the physical and social sciences in 1964, and Southeastern University of Health Sciences, founded in 1981 and offering medical training in the colleges of Osteopathic Medicine. Today, NSU offers sixteen graduate programs, is classified by the Carnegie Foundation for the Advancement of Teaching as a research university, and was most recently awarded Carnegie's Community Engagement Classification for NSU's significant commitment to and demonstration of community engagement. NSU is one of only thirty-seven universities nationwide to have earned both Carnegie recognitions.

The Shepard Broad Law Center was formed in 1974. The Law Center is fully accredited by the American Bar Association and is a member of the American Association of Law Schools. The Law Center offers students an opportunity to earn a law degree in a full-time day or part-time evening program.

Q. Describe the faculty at your school.

A. Students looking to study in a diverse community will find that diversity in the faculty and student body. Of the fifty-seven full-time faculty members at the Law Center, twenty-six are women, nine are African American, five are Hispanic American, and two are Asian American. Nine faculty members openly identify themselves as gay or lesbian. Law Center faculty members have earned their JD degrees at thirty-three American and two

Dean Athornia Steele

foreign country institutions—thirteen faculty members have Master of Laws (LLM) degrees and three have Doctor of Juridical Science (SJD) degrees.

Q. What type of student thrives at your school? What are the student characteristics or interests that "fit" well with your school culture and community?

A. The student body is similarly diverse. Each year, the Law Center receives more than 2,500 applications for 350 seats in the entering class. The students come from twenty-eight states and represent 125 undergraduate institutions. Over the last three years, the average enrollment has been six percent African Americans, five percent Asian American/Pacific Islanders, and eighteen percent Hispanic Americans.

Q. Describe the international population at your school (size and country diversity). Can you speak to any specific admissions differences relevant for international students?

A. The Law Center proudly enrolls approximately eight percent foreign lawyers, primarily from the Caribbean. Through our international program, ten to fifteen international students from Italy, Spain and the Czech Republic study at the Law Center each year. As with the faculty there is also religious, social and political diversity, which creates an ideal setting for those seeking a broad legal education.

Q. *What are the core mission and values of the school?*

A. In the Law Center's most recent strategic plan, the faculty reaffirmed its historic mission of providing access and opportunity for students to study law and to become members of the legal profession.

Our Mission

To ensure that students develop the knowledge, skills, and values that are at the heart of becoming trusted, highly adept, professional lawyers who are respected for serving their clients, their communities, and justice.

Our Values

We believe in and model:
Respect for the law and the importance of lawyers in a free society
Equitable access to education
Diversity of background and viewpoint
Excellence in teaching that serves the students and their learning needs
High standards of ethics and professionalism
Evolution of the competencies lawyers need in an ever changing world
Support of successful entry and advancement in the bar and other professions
Assumption of leadership roles and service to the community

The mission statement has four important focal points—the student, the development of knowledge and skills, service to clients, communities and justice, and trust and respect earned through the demonstration of competencies and values. The faculty believes that the mission focal points and the core values represent what students want from their legal education and what the public seeks from the profession.

Q. *Describe your school's curriculum, and highlight other features of your program.*

A. Since its formation, the faculty of the Shephard Broad Law Center has made the preparation of "practice ready" lawyers, with a strong focus on skills development throughout the three or four years of a student's education, the center piece of the curriculum. Employers of our students recognize this strength in our graduates. Highlighted in our skills-based curriculum are the following:

Lawyering Skills and Values introduces first-year students to professional responsibility, client interviewing and counseling, and mediation in addition to providing instruction in traditional legal research and writing.

Critical Skills Program, a multiyear program, provides every first-year student with instruction in the American legal system and the skills necessary to be successful during the first-year of law school. The program continues through the second-year further stressing skills development necessary to excelling in law school and becoming a successful lawyer.

Advanced Lawyering Skills and Values provides a menu of upper-class courses centered on litigation, transactional and/or general practice. Advanced Lawyering Skills helps the student focus his or her learning based upon the student's aspirations and career objectives.

Clinical/Externship opportunities permit learning outside of the classroom for both part-time and full-time students. Clinic/externship opportunities include Children and Families and Mediation, Business Practice, Criminal Justice, Environmental, and International Practice. Several clinical/externship experiences are full-time providing for complete emersion into the practice of law.

Certificates of study in international and health law.

Intra- and Inter-Collegiate Competitions offer students an opportunity to develop advocacy and trial skills in a competitive atmosphere.

Q. *Are there any joint degree or international programs?*

A. As a doctoral university with sixteen graduates programs, the Law Center has created several joint degree programs including a JD/MBA in Business or Public Administration, JD/MS in Computer and Information Sciences, JD/MS or PhD in Conflict Analysis and Resolution and JD/MURP in Urban and Regional Planning. Exploration is underway to create a JD/DOM with the School of Osteopathic Medicine. The Law Center is also exploring more interdisciplinary study options that will allow students to use selected course work from other graduate programs to enhance their legal education and provide more value to employers.

Recognizing the global community we live in, students may want to take advantage of the international programs offered at NSU including the dual degree programs with the University of Roma Tre (Rome, Italy) and the University of Barcelona (Barcelona, Spain), and a developing JD/LLM program with Charles University in Prague (Czech Republic). Each of these programs permit students to study law in Rome (Italian required), Spain (Spanish required) and Prague in a semester abroad program. The student may later choose to earn the full foreign degree by transferring credits to the foreign law school, and seek admission to the bar of those countries.

Within the context of a traditional curriculum, the Shepard Broad Law Center has created an atmosphere where students can excel through the guidance of a competent and caring faculty and staff and with programs designed to help the student achieve his or her professional goals.

SEATTLE UNIVERSITY
SCHOOL OF LAW

Q. *Please tell us about Seattle University School of Law.*

A. Mark Niles: I'm so pleased to introduce you to this special place, Seattle University School of Law. We have a wonderful community of people dedicated to academic excellence, whose mission is to educate outstanding lawyers to be leaders for a just and humane world. I am so proud of our superb faculty, our leading academic programs, including the country's top-ranked Legal Writing Program and the Ronald A. Peterson Law Clinic, as well as distinguished centers and institutes.

The school enrolls just over 1,000 students representing more than 250 undergraduate schools and drawn from the top third of the national law school applicant pool. We are the only Washington law school with a part-time program geared to meet the needs of working professionals.

Q. *What type of student thrives at your school? What are the student characteristics or interests that "fit" well with your school culture and community?*

A. One of the greatest things about Seattle University School of Law is the diversity of our student body and our rich and supportive atmosphere, which helps all students thrive here. Many of our students are drawn to our focus on social justice, but others want to concentrate on corporate or business law, and we make sure all of them get the guidance they need.

We have an active student body, whose members are always planning educational and social events, such as serving as a Student Bar Association officer to volunteering with the Student Disaster Relief Network.

Dean Mark Niles

Students can find others who share their interests and views—and be exposed to many with divergent ideas. We also have exciting co-curricular opportunities with Moot Court and Dispute Resolution boards as well as three journals, Seattle University Law Review, the Seattle Journal for Social Justice and the Seattle Journal of Environmental Law. Students earn credit for these competitive co-curricular activities.

Q. *What are the core mission and values of the school?*

A. Very few law schools have such a strong and institutional defining mission as ours. The values of equal justice—of reaching out to underserved communities, ensuring access to the legal system and protecting society's most vulnerable—permeate the fabric of the law school. Even those who don't want to pursue public interest work as a career find value and meaning in this mission, and the law school inspires all students toward that goal, no matter where the profession takes them.

We highly value diversity, and Seattle University School of Law is ranked as one of the most diverse law schools in the nation. Almost thirty percent of the students are non-Caucasian, and faculty and staff represent a broad spectrum of backgrounds.

Q. What types of support does the law school provide for students who want to pursue social justice careers?

A. Throughout law school, you will have a chance to see how the law can truly effect change in people's lives. The Public Interest Law Foundation provides summer grants for students to work in public interest law with agencies ranging from the Northwest Justice Project in Seattle to the United Nations Inter-Agency on Human Trafficking in Bangkok, Thailand. Also, the student-run Seattle Journal for Social Justice provides students with the opportunity to produce articles on themes of justice.

We offer a loan repayment assistance program for graduates who work in the public interest, and we are the only law school in the state to offer two post-graduate fellowships for alumni to work on a specific social justice project.

Q. What programs set you apart from other law schools?

A. There are many programs that make me very proud to be dean of this law school—here are just a few:

Our top-ranked Legal Writing Program has set the standard for legal writing programs for more than twenty-five years and is a model for writing programs throughout the country.

Our international initiatives, including the International and Comparative Law Program, the Center for Global Justice, and Mexico/Latin American Initiatives, and summer study abroad opportunities in Guatemala and South Africa.

Our social justice programs, including the Access to Justice Institute, The Fred T. Korematsu Center for Law and Equality, and the exceptional Ronald A. Peterson Law Clinic, which helps students, supervised by faculty who are experts in their fields, represent juvenile offenders, aspiring entrepreneurs and victims of predatory lending.

The Adolf A. Berle, Jr. Center on Corporations, Law and Society, which facilitates the study of the constantly evolving American and global economic system, and the role of law in mediating and shaping the nature of our economic relations and institutions.

Q. Please tell us more about your curriculum.

A. The law school structures outstanding combinations of required courses in which students hone skills of legal analysis in civil procedure, contracts, criminal law, legal writing, property, and torts. We have recently revised our curriculum to offer first-year students the option of selecting elective courses in addition to the proscribed program.

One of our distinctive features is the Focus Area Curriculum, which allows students to select a primary area of interest and expand that interest by enrolling in courses that naturally build on one another. This is an integrated educational experience in which you can explore doctrine in-depth and learn lawyering skills in context and in logical order. Focus areas are not mandatory, you may choose one of the following focus areas: Civil Advocacy; Commercial Law; Criminal Law and Practice; Environmental, Natural Resource and Land Use; Estate Planning; Family and Juvenile Law; Health Law; Intellectual Property; International Law; Law and Social Inequality; Labor and Employment Law; Real Estate Law; or Taxation Law.

In addition to a JD, the law school offers joint degrees in business, public administration, sports administration and leadership, criminal justice, or transformational leadership.

Q. Please tell us about your admissions and financial aid process.

A. The law school places equal emphasis on three factors: an applicant's LSAT performance, undergraduate academic record and personal achievements, especially talents or factors that contribute to our law school community in special and significant ways. We have a rolling admissions program with a March 1 priority deadline. Students may choose to begin legal studies in the summer to reduce their fall course load or start in the fall.

We also admit a limited group of applicants annually through our life-changing Access Admission Program, which addresses those cases in which traditional admission criteria are inadequate predictors of success in law school and in the practice of law. Members of historically disadvantaged, underrepresented, or physically challenged groups are among those individuals considered for this program, which is limited to no more than ten percent of the entering class.

Upon admission, all entering students are automatically considered for scholarships. The School of Law administers a comprehensive financial assistance program through which $37 million dollars in scholarships, loans, and work-study funds are awarded annually to nearly ninety percent of our students.

The law school's Scholarship Program is among the most ambitious in the region, awarding more than $3 million per year to approximately 350 students. This program recognizes and rewards the achievements and outstanding potential of our most highly qualified applicants, regardless of financial need. We also award several full-tuition scholarships.

Q. Describe the faculty at your school.

A. A primary mission that drives the academic program is the faculty's desire to prepare students to practice the law with competence, honor, and commitment to public service. Our talented faculty members teach students to analyze problems and construct policy arguments, as well as train them to write and speak with clarity and precision.

The teaching is both demanding and humane. Reflecting the Jesuit tradition of open inquiry, social responsibility and concern for personal growth, the law school values freedom of conscience, thought, and speech.

Since 2000, faculty members have authored or coauthored more than 25 books, 18 book chapters, and more than 135 articles that have appeared in prestigious law reviews and specialized journals.

Q. Please discuss your career placement programs.

A. Our Center for Professional Development staff equips students with the tools to prepare for life after law school. One-on-one coaching guides students in the career development process, which leads to them landing competitive positions.

The Center for Professional Development has a counselor who specializes in helping students who want to explore and prepare for a career in the public interest sector, as well as a website with extensive information on public interest fields. CPD also sponsors the Northwest Public Service Career Fair and offers seminars on public interest careers and hosts a "Beyond the Traditional" Career Fair, which introduces students to a wide array of career possibilities in the public and private sector.

Q. What is your vision for the future of the law school?

A. I'm committed to raising the regional and national presence of the law school, so more prospective students and employers know about the extraordinary work being done here. We will also be working to increase the international opportunities available to students.

About Dean Mark C. Niles

Mark C. Niles became dean of Seattle University School of Law in July 2010. He has taught and specializes in civil procedure, administrative law, constitutional law, governmental liability, and law and literature. He has published numerous articles and essays on subjects including the Ninth Amendment, federal tort liability, airline security regulation and the depiction of law and justice in American popular culture. He is a graduate of Stanford Law School. He previously served as associate dean for academic affairs at American University, Washington College of Law. Earlier in his career, he served as a clerk for the Honorable Francis Murnaghan, Jr., of the U.S. Fourth Circuit Court of Appeals. He was an associate at the D.C. firm of Hogan and Hartson and an attorney on the civil appellate staff of the U.S. Department of Justice.

SOUTHERN ILLINOIS UNIVERSITY

Q. Are there particular strengths of your school associated with your parent university, such as key centers/institutes of research, facilities, joint-degree programs with other schools on campus, or other synergies?

A. Southern Illinois University Carbondale is a Carnegie-classified high research public university offering thirty-four doctoral and professional degree programs, seventy-three programs at the master's level, and more than eighty undergraduate fields of study. Being part of this system allows the law school the opportunity to work in collaboration with a wide variety of academic partners. Our longest standing and most developed partnership is with the School of Medicine. This partnership, which started in the early 1980s, allowed SIU to offer one of the first JD/MD programs in the nation. It also allows us to operate the Center for Health Law & Policy which gives students opportunities to attend annual programs such as a lecture series, Bioethicist-in-Residence, and Health Policy Institute, as well as experiential learning opportunities through the Elder Law Clinic, the Law & Health Project, and the Health Law & Policy Semester Away Program. We are also the host of the annual National Health Law Moot Court Competition which will hold its twentieth competition next fall.

Students who are interested in law and policy have the advantage of attending events and program put on by the Paul Simon Public Policy Institute whose guests, over the years, have included individuals such as Coretta Scott King, Ted Sorenson, Walter Cronkite, Maya Angelou, Morris Dees, and Barbara Bush.

An increasing number of our students are opting to distinguish themselves in the evolving legal employment market by earning a joint degree. Students can couple a JD with a PhD in Political Science, Masters of Accountancy, Masters of Business Administration, Masters of Science in Education, Masters of Public Administration, Masters of Social Work, or Masters of Electrical & Computer Engineering.

Dean Fountaine

Q. Describe the faculty at your school. What areas of academics/research have become the "hallmarks" of your faculty? What level of interaction do professors have with their students?

A. Our faculty members are drawn from distinguished practice and academic settings. They are known not only for their legal research and scholarship, but also for their ability and commitment to teaching, particularly in such fields as natural resources law, tax law, health law, criminal law, international law, and intellectual property. Our student/faculty ratio of twelve to one is one of the lowest in the country. With a total student body of less than 400 students, faculty are able to provide a highly personalized learning environment. Students can expect faculty to maintain an open-door policy, and serve as mentors throughout their time as students, and sometime throughout their careers as attorneys.

The nationally recognized Lawyering Skills Program and the ABA Gambrell Award–winning Professionalism Series bridge the gap between theory and practice and prepare graduates to function effectively as professionals. One component of the professionalism program is the Induction Ceremony during which first-year students recite the "Statement of Professional Commitment" that they draft as a class, with guidance from practicing attorneys and judges. Most years a member of the Illinois Supreme Court presides over the ceremony. SIU was the first law school in Illinois, and among the first in the country, to have a program like this for first-year students.

Q. *Please describe extracurricular academic programs at your school (for example, Clinics, Study Abroad, Journals).*

A. We have two, live-client Clinics that allow our students the opportunity for hands-on training, under the close supervision of expert attorneys. In the Civil Practice/Elder Law Clinic, students work under attorney supervision to provide civil legal representation to individuals who are sixty years or older and live in one of the thirteen southern most counties in Illinois. Students practice legal skills such as case management, legal drafting, client interviewing, presenting cases in court, etc. In the Domestic Violence Clinic, students work under the supervision of an attorney to represent victims of domestic violence. Students learn about the Illinois Domestic Violence Act and its enforcement, and practice legal skills such as client interviewing, court representation, legal drafting, etc.

Our Academic Success Program provides opportunities for first-year students to master the skills of legal analysis that they need to succeed in law school through small study groups led by an upper class student (Taylor Mattis Fellow). Each group leader helps 1Ls learn about law school classes, grading, exam protocol, etc., and also offers feedback on briefing, outlining and other skills. Students have the chance to join optional second semester study groups that focuses on reviewing material and preparing for exams. The Program also offers preparation for bar admission and the bar exam.

We offer three Semester Away Programs. The Law and Government Semester Away Program offers second- and third-year law students the opportunity to learn about State and Local Government while living and working in the capital, Springfield, Illinois. Residence in Springfield allows students to work in externship placements under the supervision of government or quasi-government lawyers, while still earning a full semester (fifteen credit hours) of academic credit. The Criminal Trial Practice Semester Away Program combines an externship at the Missouri Public Defender's Office in Jackson, Missouri, with criminal law courses. In the Health Law and Policy Semester Away Program students are able to spend a semester in Springfield, Illinois, where they earn academic credit working

at externship sites such as hospital and health care systems, health-related government agencies, and the SIU School of Medicine.

Qualifying students have the opportunity to write for the Southern Illinois University Law Journal or the Journal of Legal Medicine. The SIU Law Journal, published since 1976, is staffed and administered by students with the assistance of a faculty advisor. The Journal of Legal Medicine is the official quarterly publication of the American College of Legal Medicine. It is regarded as one of the prominent publications in the nation in the area of health law and each issue features a "Commentary" section with articles written by SIU law students.

We have an active and respected program for students interested in moot court. Early in the fall semester, second-year students may participate in the SIU Intramural Moot Court Competition. In teams of two, the students write a brief and argue a challenging problem of federal law. Most years, the Intramural Competition will use the problem written for the National Health Law Moot Court Competition, which SIU hosts in November. After the first year, students may compete for selection to the Appellate Advocacy Division of the Moot Court Board. Teams from the SIU School of Law have had much success in national competitions for more than twenty years. Students who are interested in trial rather than appellate argument may try out in their second year for membership in the Trial Advocacy Division of the Moot Court Board.

In partnership with the University of Missouri—Kansas City School of Law we offer an annual Ireland Summer Study Abroad Program at four different, premier institutions in Ireland. This program provides students both an opportunity to travel and earn between five and a half and seven hours of ABA-approved credit. The program is designed to provide students with an understanding of the legal structure, institutions, and social history of both Irish political entities and the laws applicable to the conduct of commerce by foreign (including U.S.) companies in Ireland and through Ireland to the European continent.

Q. Describe the typical internships among your students, and the full-time career placement mix (in terms of types of employers and jobs). What is the geographic diversity of your graduates (across states and countries)?

A. Through our Public Interest Extern Clinic, students work in publicly funded law offices, nonprofit agencies or corporations. Common placements include prosecutors' or defenders' offices, legal services offices, government offices with legal departments, etc. Although many of our placements are in Illinois (including Chicago and Springfield), we have approved sites all across the country. In addition to the states surrounding Illinois, students have also worked as far away as Alaska, New York, Washington State, and Canada. Because of our health law program, agency placements have included sites like the Centers for Disease Control and the National Institute of Health. Students who participate in the Law and Government Semester Away Program can choose from a long list of State and Local Government Externship sites in the state capital.

Students may also participate in the Judicial Extern Clinic where they can serve as student law clerks for judges in locations approved by the professor. Student clerks observe court proceedings, do research and writing and take part in all or most activities in Judge's chambers.

Our alumni enjoy success in many different areas, both in the public and private sectors. Alumni practice law in forty-nine of the fifty states and internationally in over ten countries. Seventy-seven alumni have or are currently filling federal and state judgeships.

Q. Speaking to the qualified students comparing your school to your top peer schools, what are the key advantages of your school?

A. Students considering the SIU School of Law should first understand that our academic program is truly excellent. I have taught at several law schools, and I can assure students that the education they receive here will be first-rate. Programs that provide practical skills training enhance our core curriculum, which prepare our students to compete well in the job market. As a relative newcomer to SIU myself, I would say that the twelve to one student/faculty ratio, small class sizes, faculty and staff that are accessible and truly committed to each student's success, and a strong sense of community, make SIU a very welcoming and supportive environment for someone who is embarking on the challenge of law school.

Finally, as one of only three law schools in Illinois that receive financial support from the state of Illinois, we are able to offer this level of quality for one of the lowest tuition rates in the country. This means that our graduates benefit from an average debt load below the national average, which gives them the freedom to consider a much wider range of career choices, including public interest work.

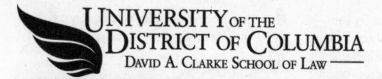

UNIVERSITY OF THE DISTRICT OF COLUMBIA
DAVID A. CLARKE SCHOOL OF LAW

Q. What type of student thrives at your school? What are the student characteristics or interests that "fit" well with your school culture and community?

A. The University of the District of Columbia David A. Clarke School of Law (UDC-DCSL) student body is among the most diverse in the nation, not only in terms of race and ethnicity, but also age and socioeconomic background. Commitment to public service is our common denominator; most anyone who is willing to roll up their sleeves and work for poor people in our mandatory clinical program will fit in superbly whether or not they intend to seek employment in the public interest world or in private practice.

Q. Can you describe the history of your school—its founding, core mission, and how that has changed over time? What are the core mission and values of the school today?

A. The roots of our law school can be traced directly to the Antioch School of Law, which was founded in 1972 by a pair of brilliant Yale law grads, Edgar S. and Jean Camper Cahn, an interracial couple.

The mission, carried on from that of Antioch, is to recruit and enroll students from groups underrepresented in the legal profession and to train them through the representation of low-income District of Columbia residents to the maximum extent feasible, through the School's legal clinics. Our goal is to become the top public interest, public service and public policy law school in America!

Q. What are the most important accolades and national/international recognition your school has received over the past three to five years?

Dean Katherine S. Broderick

A. US News ranked UDC-DCSL tenth in the nation in 2011 and eleventh in 2011 for our program of clinical legal education as well as among the top five law schools for diversity both years. The Princeton Review ranked us second on the list for Most Liberal Students, fourth for Most Diverse Faculty, and tenth for Best Environment for Minority Students.

Probably the most exciting recent recognition came in June 2010, when U.S. Attorney General Eric Holder hailed UDC-DCSL as a model program of legal education. He said, in part, "I agree…all publicly funded law schools should look to the Clarke School of Law for inspiration and consider a similar service requirement. That would be a profound and powerful change."

Another important form of recognition came this past May from the Crowell and Moring law firm, which committed to providing over $675,000 in funding to establish the Took Crowell Institute for At-Risk Youth, greatly expanding the capacity of our outstanding Juvenile and Special Education Clinic.

Q. What types of admissions trends have your school experienced recently?

A. Our applicant pool has risen to 1,750 applicants for 125 seats. Women continue to outnumber men and the percentage of white students has remained in the high forties with African American students in the thirties and Latinos in the teens. The average age of incoming students is twenty-eight.

Q. What factors are most important in your admissions process? How important are non-academic factors such as an interview, work experience, extracurricular activities, or volunteer work?

A. We pride ourselves for looking at the "whole person" and examine what applicants have done with their lives and what they stand for in addition to grades, LSATS, publications and the like. Work experience, extracurricular work and volunteering count for a lot because they give us an indication of a prospective students' values.

Q. How many application rounds are there for your school? Are there any advantages of applying at a certain stage?

A. Admission is rolling until the deadline (this year, April 30). Applicants should keep a sharp eye on the website! Applicants seeking merit scholarships are well-advised to apply early as some of those funds tend to be awarded before the deadline.

Q. Describe the faculty at your school. What areas of academics/research have become the "hallmarks" of your faculty? What level of interaction do professors have with their students?

A. All UDC-DCSL faculty members typically have a high level of interaction with students due both to the low twelve to one faculty/student ratio and our general emphasis on collaboration and collegiality. Many professors keep their doors open. ALL UDC-DCSL professors have extensive real-world practice experience, which they bring into the classroom as well as into supervision of students in clinic. The faculty is as diverse as the student body. Many have won awards for their legal advocacy and service.

The School of Law also boasts a fabulous cadre of adjunct professors drawn from the tens of thousands of legal practitioners in the nation's capital.

Q. Does your school offer specializations? How/why were these developed?

A. Our "specialty" is public interest law, which is reflected in our first year Community Service requirement, our paid summer public interest fellowship program, which is available to all 1L students, the mandatory 700-hour clinical requirement and the optional public interest internship program.

Q. Please describe extracurricular academic programs at your school (for example, Clinics, Study Abroad, Journals).

A. Our clinics are not "extracurricular" but an integral part of our program. Our eight clinics are Immigration/Human Rights; Whistleblower Protection (with the Government Accountability Project); HIV/AIDS, which works for both those infected and affected by the AIDS virus; Housing & Consumer; Community Development; Legislation; Juvenile and Special Education; and Low-Income Taxpayer. Participation in each clinic allows students to develop a specialty.

The UDC Law Review publishes public-interest related legal scholarship by students, faculty and attorneys and legal educators from around the nation.

Q. Describe the need and merit-based aid offered by your school, and the percentage of students who receive financial aid and scholarships.

A. Sixty-seven percent of our students receive merit scholarships including thirty-nine percent who win dean's fellowships based on their law school academic performance. Eighty-nine percent of our students receive financial aid or scholarship support of some kind.

We offer up to twenty full-tuition, three-year, scholarships annually through our Advocate for Justice scholarship program to applicants with both excellent academic track records and a demonstrated commitment to public service, activism, or justice in some form.

Q. Speaking to the qualified students comparing your school to your top peer schools, what are the key advantages of your school?

A. We're looking for students who want to use the law as a tool to help people and to effect much-needed change. Such students are often frustrated at the typical theory-heavy law school. At UDC, however, students begin engagement with the community immediately upon arrival, can do a paid summer fellowship anywhere in the world the summer after their first year, and begin to actually practice law, under faculty supervision, mid-way through their second year. Thus, activist law students need not put their values on the shelf for three years.

Also, if students are interested in becoming public interest lawyers, they have to be concerned about avoiding debt. Our low-tuition and generous scholarship support is absolutely critical in keeping debts low, thus allowing a lower-paying public service legal career to remain financially viable.

In addition, our location in the nation's capital allows students to work with and in support of an immense variety of cause-related organizations and government agencies while in law school. The educational and career-connections value of our location cannot be topped.

Q. What are your strategic goals for the school over the next three years?

A. The School of Law expects to move into new "green" facilities within the next year and that will allow us to expand to 650 students, 200 of whom will be in the part-time program.

We also plan to expand our new LLM program, launched this year, in Clinical Legal Education, Social Justice and Systems Change, and to add a growing number of electives in progressive areas of law.

WAKE FOREST
UNIVERSITY

SCHOOL *of* LAW

Dean Interview

Q. *What type of student thrives at your school? What are the student characteristics or interests that "fit" well with your school culture and community?*

A. As is shown by the high GPA and LSAT numbers, first and foremost we are looking for students with strong academic credentials. Wake Forest law school looks for a well-rounded student who is intellectually curious, has strong leadership skills, a willingness to serve the community, and an impeccable character. From among that group, students who have taken a break after college and have used that time to accomplish something that demonstrates their maturity and initiative certainly are appealing candidates for law school.

Q. *Can you describe the history of your school? What are the core mission and values of the school today?*

A. Wake Forest University was founded in 1834 outside the state capital of Raleigh, North Carolina. In 1941, the medical school moved to Winston-Salem, and the rest of the College followed in 1956. The School of Law was established in 1894, and in 1993 moved into its current facility, the Worrell Professional Center, which is also home to the Schools of Business.

Our central mission is the personal and professional development of our students through legal education on a human scale. Small by design, our programs produce astute and confident lawyers broadly educated in the skills, traditions, and ethics of practice. Since the mid-1980s, first-year law students at the Wake Forest University School of Law learn in sections with forty other peers under our 4-40 plan (four sections of forty students). There's

Dean Blake Morant

one exception—Legal Research and Writing, where students are in a class of only twenty. They also have access to the Academic Success Program, which helps new students study more effectively. Second- and third-year courses are mostly electives.

Q. *Are there particular strengths of your school associated with your parent university, such as key centers/institutes of research, facilities, joint-degree programs with other schools on campus, or other synergies?*

A. Wake Forest University law students have several options to complete dual degrees, including a JD/MA in Bioethics and a JD/MA in Religion, a JD/MBA with the WFU Schools of Business, and a JD/MDiv (Master of Divinity) through the School of Divinity.

In addition, students have the opportunity to participate in the Institute for Public Engagement. Building upon the educational philosophy of Wake Forest University and mindful of its motto, Pro

Humanitate, the Institute prepares students for civic leadership, action and reflection and supports innovative relationships among faculty, students, administration, staff, alumni, and the broader community. In addition, the university's Center for Bioethics, Health, and Society provides a collaborative intellectual environment for addressing ethical, social, and policy issues of importance for health care, biomedical research, and public health.

Q. *What are the most important accolades and national / international recognition your school has received over the past three to five years?*

A. Wake Forest University School of Law was named among the nation's best value in private law schools by National Jurist as well as being ranked consistently in the top forty law schools in the nation.

Dean Blake D. Morant was selected in October 2010 for the prestigious Equal Justice Works' John R. Kramer Outstanding Law School Dean Award. This award honors a law school dean who has successfully demonstrated leadership in building an institution that nurtures and fortifies a spirit of public service during his tenure at an Equal Justice Works participating member law school.

The National Jurist and preLaw magazines have named Wake Forest among the nation's best law schools for public interest. "Sometimes people look at public interest or pro bono work as an extracurricular activity," said Dean Blake Morant in the article. "We saw this as a very important part of the education of the student. Giving back is about being a true lawyer."

Q. *What types of admissions trends have your school experienced recently?*

A. Admittance to Wake Forest School of Law is extremely competitive. We received a significant increase in applications over the past two years. The law school consistently has close to 3,000 applicants and ultimately enrolls approximately 160 entering students per class. Those entering students have a median LSAT score of 163 and a median GPA of 3.6. Prospective students must take the LSAT to be considered for admission.

First-Year Class Profile (Class of 2013)
GPA 25th/75th percentile: 3.3/3.7
LSAT 25th/75th percentile: 160/164
# of states represented: 32 and 2 foreign countries
# of schools represented: 84
% women: 42% (up from 30% in 2008)
% minority: 20% (up from 18% in 2008)
Average age: 24

Q. *What factors are most important in your admissions process? Are there any advantages to applying early?*

A. In addition to the GPA and LSAT, we consider work experience, promise to the profession, recommendations, and personal attributes, such as community service, involvement with school activities, and the like. We use a rolling admissions process and applications are reviewed roughly in the order they are completed. So, the sooner one applies the better.

Q. *Describe the international population at your school (size and country diversity). Can you speak to any specific admissions differences relevant for international students?*

A. WFU School of Law has three international graduate programs: the Master of Laws (LLM) in American Law Program, the Visiting International Researcher Program, and the SJD program. Over 150 students have graduated in the past fifteen years from over thirty countries.

Q. *Please describe extracurricular academic programs at your school.*

A. The school is committed to helping students practice what they learn in the classroom. The school runs seven clinics that expose students to law practices including elder law, child advocacy, community law and business and litigation of civil and criminal law. Students can also get involved in more than thirty student organizations, as well as three legal journals: the Wake Forest Law Review, the Intellectual Property Law Journal, and the Journal of Law and Policy. For an experience outside of Winston-Salem, North Carolina, Wake Forest School of Law also offers a Metropolitan Externship semester in Washington, D.C., as well as resident study abroad programs in London, Venice, and Vienna.

Q. Describe the typical internships among your students, and the full-time career placement mix (in terms of types of employers, jobs, and states).

A. Students obtain summer internships in law firms, corporations, academia, and the federal and local government and judicial system. In our most recent graduating class, sixty-two percent of the recent graduates secured positions in private practice, twelve percent took jobs in public interest with prosecutors, public defenders and legal services. Seven percent of the graduates found employment in the federal and local government, and eight percent went into business. Another eight percent obtained a judicial clerkship, and three percent were employed in academia.

57.4 percent of our recent graduates took jobs outside of North Carolina in twenty-one different states across the country.

Q. What is the average starting salary of your graduates? How does that differ over time, and across different areas of employment?

A. The average starting salary in all practice areas for recent graduates of the class of 2009 was $103,169. This is an increase of nearly 4.2 percent from the class of 2008 where the average starting salary was $99,028.

The 2009 median private practice salary of $130,000 represents a ten percent increase from 2008, while the median public service salary rose by seven percent from $45,700 in 2008 to $49,100 in 2009.

Q. Describe the need and merit-based aid offered by your school, and the percentage of students who receive financial aid and scholarships.

A. Most scholarships are merit based but we do offer a few based on financial need. Last year approximately forty-two percent of the entering students received some sort of scholarship to attend Wake Forest Law.

Q. Describe your students' performance in passing the bar on the first try.

A. For the second time in two years, Wake Forest University School of Law graduates had the top bar passage rate among North Carolina universities for first timers taking the North Carolina bar exam. Ninety-two percent of Wake Forest graduates taking the state bar exam for the first time passed, according to the North Carolina Board of Law Examiners, compared with an eighty-five percent first-time bar-exam-passage rate for all North Carolina law schools.

Q. Speaking to the qualified students comparing your school to your top peer schools, what are the key advantages of your school?

A. Our small size is a huge advantage. We have a ten to one student/faculty ratio and our first-year classes are no larger than forty students. Small class size leads to a more intimate and engaged atmosphere of learning.

Q. What are your strategic goals for the school over the next three years?

A. The ideas in our long-range plan call for us to reach out, strengthening the connections between the law school and the legal community, our local community, the rest of the university, the broader scholarly community, and the world. Enhancement of the upper level curriculum should build upon the law school's strengths, which include small classes and a student-centered educational philosophy.

We plan to develop additional "capstone courses" for students in their third year, and semester-long externship programs in metropolitan areas in addition to the Washington, D.C., program. The primary objective of "capstone courses" is to provide students with an enriched, practice-like experience that exposes them to the complexities of law practice in certain fields. The "metropolitan externship" would provide some upper-level students with instruction in a classroom setting, combined with closely related work experience in a law firm, a nonprofit organization, or a government agency.

INDEX

ALPHABETICAL INDEX

INDEX BY LOCATION

INTERNATIONAL

INDEX BY COST

MORE THAN $30,000